The De Soto Chronicles

VOLUME II

The De

THE EXPEDITION OF HERNANDO

VOLUME II

Soto Chronicles

DE SOTO TO NORTH AMERICA IN 1539–1543

EDITED BY
LAWRENCE A. CLAYTON
VERNON JAMES KNIGHT, JR.
EDWARD C. MOORE

THE UNIVERSITY OF ALABAMA PRESS ❧ TUSCALOOSA

The University of Alabama Press
Tuscaloosa, Alabama 35487-0380
uapress.ua.edu

First Paperback Edition 1995

Illustrations on cover and title page from *The Conquistadores* by Terence Wise, © 1980, reprinted 1990; courtesy of Osprey Publishing, London
Cover and interior design: Paula C. Dennis

ISBN: 978-0-8173-6178-5 (paper)
ISBN: 978-0-8173-9563-6 (electronic)

Cataloging-in-Publication data is available from the Library of Congress.
ISBN: 978-0-8173-0593-2 (cloth)

Contents

Illustrations

Foreword

by Edward C. Moore

Of the four accounts of the De Soto expedition, *La Florida,* by Garcilaso de la Vega, is by far the longest and, with its commentary, occupies this entire volume. It is presented in a new translation, prepared originally by Charmion Shelby for the 1935 United States De Soto Expedition Commission but not published by them because of a lack of funds. It has been edited by David Bost, with notes by Vernon James Knight, Jr., and is introduced here by a biographical and critical essay, "Garcilaso de la Vega, the Inca" by Frances Crowley. We have added, as an appendix, the first English translation of the *Genealogy* of Garcilaso, which will be of much interest to Garcilaso scholars and to those interested in Hispanic-American genealogies.

Although *La Florida* is usually described as "Garcilaso's account," this is misleading. Garcilaso himself never saw North America. This account is Garcilaso's recording of what he was told—some forty to fifty years later—by a soldier who was on the expedition. Almost certainly his source was Captain Gonzalo Silvestre, who served with the expedition, who may or may not have had notes of his experiences on the expedition, and who undoubtedly told the account with the flourishes and embellishments of an old soldier reminiscing about an earlier period in his life. In Garcilaso's rendering of Silvestre's tale, literary liberties were often taken at the expense of historical accuracy.

However, W. H. Prescott, author of the great histories of the Spanish conquests in Peru and Mexico, once wrote about historiography: "Truth does not come from a single source." This is, indeed, the case with the four accounts of the De Soto expedition. But since the time of John Swanton's *Report* in 1939 it has been the custom to speak in a derogatory fashion about the account by Garcilaso. I think this is a mistake. Taken as adventure, the De Soto expedition can be compared to the experiences of Odysseus or El Cid, and to those described in the Song of Roland. What Garcilaso is describing here is a great exploration, not only of a continent, but also of the strengths of the human spirit in the face of tribulations of a magnitude that occur but rarely in human history.

Aristotle tells us that "science give us less truth but gives it more exactly; art gives us more truth but gives it less exactly." The account by Garcilaso is great art in that sense. It tells us more about what truly happened on the expedition than does any other account, even though it may tell it less exactly. The accuracy of Garcilaso's account has come under review primarily because he does not always agree with the other three accounts—but then they do not always agree with one another, either.

In Garcilaso, De Soto found his Homer. For readers who love a good, true adventure yarn, this account is one of the great literary classics—and, incidentally, our first American literary classic.

It has also been the custom to raise some questions about Garcilaso's motives in writing his account. Probably he had many motives. He was an author. To live, he had to write books that people would buy. Did he want to please his old friend, who told him the story, by describing his friend's leader, De Soto, in a favorable light? Possibly. Being a part Indian of Peru, did he want to vindicate the courage and resistance to the invader of the Indians of La Florida? Probably. Did he elaborate in telling some of the incidents or borrow them from stories about other expeditions? Perhaps. But did he give us the most fascinating of all looks at life on our continent before the white man came and changed it all? Certainly.

The De Soto Chronicles

VOLUME II

Garcilaso de la Vega, the Inca

by Frances G. Crowley

Garcilaso de la Vega, el Inca, was both a literary writer and a historical chronicler of the conquest of the Americas. It was his avowed primary goal to effectively represent the Inca cause before the Spanish Crown. This purpose is clearly stated in the prefaces and preambles of most of his works. As the presenter of the Indian cause, whether of the Indians in Peru or the Native Americans in the United States, he took positions on issues later challenged by historians; nonetheless he was and is among the first and foremost representatives of the mestizo viewpoint in the New World.

The author of *La Florida del Ynca,* who in Spain claimed his father's name, Garcilaso de la Vega, later adding "el Inca," was born in Cuzco, Peru, on April 12, 1539, and baptized Gómez Suárez de Figueroa, a name still extant on all documentation pertaining to his youth in Peru. His father was Captain Garcilaso de la Vega and his mother was the Inca noblewoman Chimpu Occlo. She was a *palla,* the granddaughter of the emperor Tupac Inca Yupanqui, niece of the legendary emperor Huayna Capac, and cousin of Atauhuallpa and Huascar. Thus, she represented the old Inca hierarchy, whereas Captain Garcilaso represented the Spanish conquistador. A member of the Spanish gentry, Captain Garcilaso de la Vega had left Spain and Badajoz for adventure in the New World. After a nine-year stay in Mexico and Guatemala, the captain followed Pedro de Alvarado to Peru. In his works Garcilaso stresses his father's leadership roles, his native ability to influence both peers and superiors, and the mixture of strictness and gentleness that endeared him as a father.

Garcilaso's education reflects Captain Garcilaso de la Vega's desire that his son be instructed in Spanish culture and the classics. He studied these subjects in Cuzco, under Father Juan del Cuellar, whose dream it was to send all his young mestizo students to the University of Salamanca. From his mother, Palla Chimpu Occlo, and his maternal relatives, especially his uncle, Garcilaso received instruction in the folklore and oral tradition of the

Inca people, including his family's hereditary role in the Inca hierarchy. Garcilaso's historical works and viewpoints reflect the dual and at times conflicting directions of such an education.

Although Captain Garcilaso was fond of his son and exerted throughout his life his paternal responsibility, he was not allowed, as an officer of the king, to regularize his relationship with Chimpu Occlo, or to adopt Garcilaso, lest mestizos gain proprietary rights on Spanish soil. Eventually he was forced to abandon Chimpu Occlo, for whom another marriage was arranged, and to marry Luisa Martel de los Ríos, his designated bride. Garcilaso moved quite freely from his mother's home to his father's. During the Francisco Hernández Girón uprising, while Captain Garcilaso was overseer of the city of Cuzco, his son formed part of the household. He refers to this period of his youth in his *Royal Commentaries* (Book 7, ch.9), where he gives a detailed description of people and events highlighting Cuzco's social and political life.

By 1557 Captain Garcilaso had decided to return to Spain. His departure was postponed because of a protracted illness from which he died. After his father's death in Peru on May 19, 1559, Gómez Suárez was informed that part of his father's estate was bequeathed to his legal wife, Doña Luisa Martel, and her two daughters (who died at an early age). As his natural son, Garcilaso inherited the coca fields of La Hauisca in Paucartambo and 4,000 pesos toward his education in Spain.

By 1560 his stepmother had remarried. This time she married Juan del Pedroche, by whom she had two daughters, Luisa de Herrera and Ana Ruiz. Garcilaso decided to try his fortune in Spain and embarked from Peru for Panama and from there for Lisbon, Portugal, on his way to Spain.

In his introductory letter to *La Florida,* dedicated to Theodosio of Portugal, Duke of Braganza, Garcilaso—who upon his arrival in Spain gradually assumed his father's name—wrote that he had always had a high esteem for Portugal. "This inclination was converted later into obligation, because the first land I saw when I came from my own, which is El Perú, was that of Portugal—the island of El Fayal and La Tercera, and the royal city of Lisbon, in which the royal ministers and the citizens, and those of the islands, being such religious and charitable people, gave me as warm a reception as if I had been a native son of one of them. In order not to weary your Excellency, I do not give you a full account of the gifts and favors they bestowed upon me, one of which was to save me from death." He offered his work as a gesture of gratitude for what he considered his obligation for the kindnesses he received there. Most biographers interpret these statements as flattery to the powerful, because they assume that he immediately traveled on to Spain. This seems unlikely in view of his statement that he was saved from death by either the duke or the Portuguese people.

He reiterated his offering of his book as an expression of his gratitude for this same favor, by which "I shall be able to repay and satisfy the obligation that I owe to the natives of this most Christian kingdom, for by means of Your Excellency's condescension and favor, I shall be one of them." These are strong words. It is not known when and how Garcilaso incurred an obligation so deep to either the Portuguese or the house of Braganza as to make him wish to be "one of them."

Not much is known about Garcilaso's activities during the year 1560, except for the fact that he went on to Spain, where he first visited Seville, and later Montilla, not far from Córdoba, where his paternal uncle, Captain Alonso de Vargas, resided and received him as a welcome relative.

By 1561 Garcilaso was headed for the Spanish court in Madrid to claim his father's inheritance. This Madrid trip is frequently mentioned in his *Royal Commentaries,* where Garcilaso referred to the hearings on his paternity accorded to him by Lope García de Castro, who blamed Garcilaso's father for lending the rebel Gonzalo Pizarro his horse when Pizarro's horse was killed in a battle. Since Captain Garcilaso and Pizarro had been enemies rather than friends, the allegation seems simply a lame excuse for denying Garcilaso his inheritance. By now he was the only living descendant on his father's side. Had he been legitimate, he could not have been denied his rights. Being Indian and illegitimate, any excuse would do, and one was found in Pizarro's horse (*A General History of Peru,* Book 5, ch. 23).

In 1563 Garcilaso was sufficiently upset by the ruling to decide that it was time to leave Spain and return to Peru. The royal decree permitting his departure was issued June 27, 1563, in Madrid, urging Seville officials to give safe conduct to Peru to "Gómez Suárez de Figueroa, son of Garcilaso de la Vega, who served in that country."[1]

Perhaps because Lope García de Castro, who as a judge denied him his request to be named his father's heir, was about to sail as viceroy of Peru on that very ship, Garcilaso decided to postpone his departure. This was a fortunate decision in light of subsequent events. Aware that his name of Gómez Suárez de Figueroa would not open the doors of Spanish social and political life, as he wished, he changed his name gradually, first to Gómez Suárez de

[1]Aurelio Miró Quesada, *Comentarios reales de los Incas* (Lima: Librería Internacional del Perú, 1959), xii.

la Vega, and on November 22, 1563, to Garcilaso de la Vega. These name changes appear in notarized documents that he signed.

On March 4, 1570, Garcilaso received orders signed by Philip II and issued in Córdoba, making him captain of three hundred men to serve under his relative, the Marquis de Priego. This was the first of a series of military duties he was to perform. While he was on his way to take up this assignment, his uncle, Captain Alonso de Vargas, died in Montilla. From him Garcilaso inherited the house in Montilla in which he would spend the next two decades. Although, because Captain Alonso's sister had inherited some of the money, the bequest left Garcilaso in only moderate financial circumstances, he was finally in a position to live off his writings and whatever opportunities for small assignments Montilla could offer. His mother, Princess Chimpu Occlo, who was his last direct link to his Peruvian family, had died in 1571. For reasons he did not disclose, he did not get this information until 1573.

These events may have persuaded Garcilaso to remain in Spain. Taken together they may have induced him to undertake to establish a literary career for himself by beginning a translation of the works written by the Portuguese neoplatonist Jehudah Abarbanel, or as he was generally known, León Hebreo. Hebreo's *Dialogues of Love,* originally written in Italian, had already appeared twice in Spanish, as well as in Latin and French editions. Garcilaso's version was elegant, and better conceived than its predecessors. He made a point of his Peruvian antecedents on the title page, where he described himself as "Garcilasso Inga de la Vega, native of Cuzco, head of the kingdoms and provinces of Peru."

After completing the manuscript on León Hebreo and while he tried to negotiate its publication, Garcilaso spent some time interviewing an old captain who had been a member of the Hernando de Soto expedition. The name of this captain, whom he did not identify as his source for *La Florida,* was Gonzalo Silvestre, the mysterious source about whom Garcilaso kept the reader guessing. Garcilaso often visited Silvestre in neighboring Las Posadas, taking notes from Silvestre's eyewitness account as one of Hernando de Soto's leading captains in the Florida expedition.

The question most often asked refers to the mystery of Silvestre's collaboration. He appears several times in *La Florida* as a participant in the expedition and is credited both favorably and adversely for his participation.

Apparently, Garcilaso's first draft of *La Florida* contained the Gonzalo Silvestre version, without mention of Silvestre's or Garcilaso's name, and included another literary effort by Garcilaso, his account of his own genealogy from the time of his ancestor Garcí Pérez de Vargas who fought for Córdoba and Seville during the reign of King Ferdinand the Saint. This was titled the *Genealogy or account of the Descendancy of the Famous Garcí Pérez de Vargas, with some historical selections worth remembering*. These two—the Silvestre version of the expedition and Garcilaso's *Genealogy*—formed the initial two chapters of what he now decided to call *La Florida*. He may have intended to include the *Genealogy* as the first chapter because it included some of the ancestors of Hernando de Soto.

On November 7, 1589, Garcilaso wrote the king concerning *La Florida*, which he considered almost finished. However, his estimate was considerably premature. It was not until 1596 that he separated *La Florida* from the *Genealogy* and made it a book in its own right. At that time he finished *La Florida*, that is, Silvestre's account of the De Soto expedition, to which he had now added the reports of Juan Coles and Alonso de Carmona, two other members of the expedition. No mention was made of the report by Rodrigo Rangel or of that by the Gentleman from Elvas. He now made a definitive copy of *La Florida*, which must be the one currently at the Biblioteca Nacional of Madrid.

In 1599 he tried to secure permission for publication in Madrid of *La Florida* through the scribe Juan Morales, doorkeeper of the King's Chamber. When it was rejected, the manuscripts of *La Florida* and of the now-completed first half of another book to be called the *Royal Commentaries* were forwarded to Lisbon, where they were almost immediately processed for publication by the house of Pedro Crasbeeck. Printing took more time, however, and it was not until 1605 that the first edition of *La Florida* appeared, and it was 1609 before the *Royal Commentaries* was published. According to the Peruvian scholar Aurelio Miró Quesada, Garcilaso sent the manuscripts to Lisbon, "where the expert printer Pedro Crasbeeck was working and where he hoped to find the support of the famous Portuguese House of Braganza."[2]

Without Crasbeeck, Garcilaso's main works might never have been published. There were some common characteristics between Garcilaso and Pedro Crasbeeck. Both were foreigners, Pedro from the Netherlands and Garcilaso from Peru. Both were trying to establish themselves, Pedro by creating one of the outstanding publishing houses in Lisbon, and Garcilaso by bringing the cultural heritage of Peru to the attention of Spain. Since Montilla, where Garcilaso lived, and Córdoba, where Crasbeeck lived, were

[2]Ibid., ch. 24.

very distant from Lisbon, where Crasbeeck had his publishing house, there arises the question as to how and when editor and author met.

Considering the cool reception of *La Florida* in Spain, the more rapid acceptance by the Portuguese might presuppose some previous contact with the Crasbeeck publishers. The fact that permission to publish the manuscript was speedily granted leads to the assumption that Crasbeeck had talked with Garcilaso and had prepared for the manuscript before its arrival.

Two Peruvian scholars, Aurelio Miró Quesada and Raúl Porras Barrenechea, tentatively placed Garcilaso in Montilla and Las Posadas during the 1580s, but there were many gaps in his activities there. One of these would have had to allow for a prolonged absence covering the time Garcilaso was to spend in Lisbon, in which city he might well have contacted leading publishing houses, including Crasbeeck.

Garcilaso spent this time in Lisbon because he was serving a tour of duty as captain of the ship *San Francisco* during the ill-fated expedition of the Invincible Armada of 1588. As I have reported in an article in *Hispania*, Garcilaso served in that campaign as captain and *tercio* (the commanding officer of a military force of several companies of infantry) on the ship *San Francisco* under Don Agostín Mexía. Garcilaso's name and title appear in the *Relación verdadera del Armada que el Rey nuestro Señor mandó juntar en el puerto de la Ciudad de Lisboa en el Reyno de Portugal en el año 1588.* Garcilaso likewise was mentioned as tercio of Don Agostín in Diego de Pimentel's *Declaración,* highlighting the brief history of the Armada. However, the most specific documentation relating to Garcilaso de la Vega's assignment can be found in the plans for the expedition, drawn by Marquis Alvaro Bazán de Santa Cruz.

These plans are contained under miscellanea in Codex 637 of the archives of the Lisbon National Library. In the "assento de Felipe II con o marqués de Santa Cruz," Garcilaso's name was listed on table 57 as captain of the *San Francisco,* which was also the "Almiranta de Garcilaso" (the flagship of the second in command, who guarded the rear of the convoy), and on table 71 under "tercios de Don Agostín Mexías." Santa Cruz further mentioned the fate of the ships of Agostín Mexías in a letter dated November 9, 1587, in which he stated that the vessels had been converted into hospital ships and that there were more than fourteen thousand patients in them. He suggested that, if after six months on board there was that much illness, it would be essential to clean the ships and try to contain the disease. The king replied that, instead, the fleet was to leave, and that the sailors who were ill were to be taken off their vessels prior to departure.

King Philip II, aware that the marquis de Santa Cruz was stalling him, began to listen to those who wanted to hasten the departure of the fleet. Upset by the course of events and by the apparent disfavor of the king, the marquis de Santa Cruz succumbed to a heart attack on February 9, 1588, at the age of sixty-three. During the nearly half year between the announcement of the departure and the time it actually took for some vessels to leave, the *San Francisco* remained in Lisbon, giving Garcilaso sufficient time not only to tend to his men, but to place his manuscript outlines with leading Lisbon publishers, including Pedro Crasbeeck.

Garcilaso was a friend of the marquis de Santa Cruz, who listed Garcilaso by his first name in his manifest. The marquis is described in Don Ramiro Blanco's *Elogio de Santa Cruz* as "well built, of brave and gentle presence, dark face and . . . well-shaped chestnut beard."[3]

Garcilaso and his former fellow officers from the Granada expedition must have been stunned by King Philip II's choice of Alfonso Pérez de Guzmán, duke of Medina Sidonia, as commander in chief of the Armada. The best that could be said about him was that he was honest enough to repeatedly turn down the assignment, admitting that he not only was not a seaman, but was prone to seasickness. However, the king was not to be put off. In spite of many problems, he requested that the fleet assemble at La Coruña and from there start the journey to England.

The details of the Spanish expedition appear, carefully assembled and annotated, in Cesáreo Fernández Duro's *La Armada invencible*,[4] a two-volume summary with tables of total ship deployment derived from documents then extant at Simancas. Tables on pages 30 and 80 list Garcilaso de la Vega as captain, among "the tertios [*sic*] of Don Agostín." On page 111 of *La Armada invencible*, the *San Francisco* is listed among the ships that arrived in the ports of Spain, with Garcilaso as *maestro de campo* of Don Pedro [de Valdés'] almiranta. Thus Garcilaso appears as second in command under orders from Don Pedro de Valdés and Agostín Mexía. In letter number 184 of the above-mentioned work, Duro relates on page 186 the king's explicit order that the fleet was to leave from La Coruña July 16, or the next Sunday at the latest, without waiting for the ships that were missing, "because it is preferable to begin this journey, than to take six ships more or less."

Garcilaso's ship appears on the list of vessels ready to leave La Coruña,

---

[3]Ramiro Blanco, *Elogio de Santa Cruz* (Madrid: Impreso de D. Pacheco Latorre, 1888).

[4]Cesáreo Fernández Duro, *La Armada invencible*, 2 vols. (Madrid: Est. tipográfico "Successores de Rivadeneyra," 1884–1885), vol. 1, pp. 30, 80, 101.

according to Duro, page 150. The ships missing after the projected departure were more than six. Letter number 156 on page 219 of Duro's collection reveals that during the storm that lashed the Spanish coast between July 12 and 20, forty Spanish ships of the squadron of Pedro Valdés were not accounted for. Although Valdés was confident he could assemble all the vessels, Admiral Martínez de Recalde reported problems with Don Agostín de Mexía's ships, of which Garcilaso commanded the almiranta—the title given the last ship of the convoy. Further delays are reported for vessels under Agostín Mexía, much of whose fleet, including the *San Francisco,* was to be found in Santander after the war. The scarce documentation pertaining to this aspect of the war is an inducement to further research.

In spite of Medina Sidonia's repeated warnings that captains of ships missing from the Armada during its military engagement would be severely punished, actually not much happened to them, because the storms were severe and the war came to an end so abruptly that damaged ships might not have been able to rejoin the fleet. According to Porras Barrenechea's *Garcilaso en Montilla, nuevos estudios sobre Garcilaso de la Vega,* page 34, "in 1588 there can be noticed prolonged absences during the second part of the year and he only appears incidentally in Montilla during August of 1589." During and after the war, many men were released from the Armada for age or infirmities. There is no evidence of what happened specifically to Garcilaso, nor does he ever refer to it. It was an Inca custom not to concentrate on the negative aspects of life and battles, but to simply move beyond them, which he did.

Garcilaso's life as a chaplain is detailed in *Garcilaso en Montilla.* Raúl Porras Barrenechea and the scholars who worked with him, among them Feliz Alvarez Brun, gathered all available legible letters, contracts, personal transactions, baptismal and wedding certificates, signed by Garcilaso during his chaplaincy. He inherited the chaplaincy, as well as property to maintain it in good condition, from his uncle Alonso de Vargas, who died in 1570. This arrangement allowed the Inca author to make a living from the interest, sales and rentals accruing to him as chaplain, and later, temporarily, provided a living for Diego de Vargas, his natural son by his housekeeper, Beatriz de Vega.

According to the documentation of *Garcilaso en Montilla,* the names appearing on documents vary from Gómez Suárez de Figueroa to Gómez de Figueroa, to Garcilaso de la Vega (page 203) to Garcí Inga de la Vega (page 204), to García Laso de la Vega (page 213) to Garcilaso de la Vega (page 214). As he gradually modified his name, he progressively changed his outlook.

After his captaincy in the Armada, he devoted himself to his chaplaincy. By helping the sick and comforting the dying, he demonstrated in his life a path from the sword he abandoned to the cross he embraced.

In 1596, at age fifty-nine, he had published the *Diálogos de amor* and had written *La Florida*. The documents found in Montilla reveal that his aunt, Doña Luisa Ponce de León, heiress of Don Alonso de Vargas's estate, had left her property to Garcilaso, who moved first to Las Posadas and later to Córdoba. Although the recipient of income from the marquis de Priego, he complained "about my lack of income" (*mi poca hacienda*). In 1591 he received funds for the house of Alonso de Vargas, sold in 1591. Between 1594 and 1597 he continued to own some real estate.

By 1592 Garcilaso had moved to Córdoba, where he was very active writing, entertaining friends both American and Spanish, collecting data and specimens of seeds and plants from the New World, and taking care of the sick. Between 1605 and 1608 Garcilaso was *mayordomo* at the hospital of the Immaculate Conception at the Cathedral of Córdoba. During free moments he spent his time revising manuscripts, arranging for their publication, helping his neighbors, and visiting the sick, until his death on April 23, 1616.

Garcilaso, who in his major works made an impassioned plea for the restitution of Inca rights and for peaceful relations between Incas and Spaniards, never lost the opportunity to mediate on behalf of Inca interests in Spain. To this effect, he even offered space in his tomb to those from both continents who wanted to join him. When, years later, his remains were finally brought to Cuzco, the Spaniards did not want them to leave Spain, nor could anyone tell for sure which they were, because they were fused with those of others. But the Spaniards were unable to prevent his removal, and the Inca, as he was and is still called, claimed his heritage—he went home to Cuzco. He had left Peru as Gómez Suárez de Figueroa; centuries later his remains returned to his country as Garcilaso de la Vega, el Inca, son of the conquistador.

Garcilaso's first claim to fame had consisted of his translation from Italian into Spanish of the three *Dialogues of Love* by León Hebreo (in Madrid, at the house of Pedro Madrigal, 1590). Garcilaso's translation of the *Dialogues* received an initial ten years' approval from the Crown. The Inquisition, however, finally refused to consider its further distribution in the vernacular, because, according to the Inquisitor, the work of an Inca was not needed, with so many Spaniards skilled in translation. Since there obviously was prejudice against his Inca origins, his translation remained dormant in Madrid catalogs.

To create greater interest in himself and his work, Garcilaso had earlier undertaken the compilation of the genealogy of his family in order to prove his Hispanic descendancy. The resulting material, called the *Genealogy*, was at first intended to form part of his narrative of the vicissitudes of the Florida expedition. How the two works were separated in 1596, and why *La Florida del Inca* appeared in Lisbon in 1605, is still difficult to determine, unless he had occasion to meet Pedro Crasbeeck in Portugal while with the Invincible Armada. If so, Crasbeeck might have urged the separation of the two works and offered to publish only *La Florida*.[5]

The Princeps edition in Spanish of *The Florida of the Inca* was published in 1605 by Crasbeeck. It was dedicated to the duke of Braganza with license of the Holy Inquisition. Garcilaso had less difficulty in obtaining the acceptance of the necessary permits in Portugal. The increasing importance of Pedro Crasbeeck's editorial fortunes in Lisbon may have been the cause of Garcilaso's success in getting a Spanish work published in the Portuguese capital. According to José Durand's bibliographical study, there are currently twenty-one copies of the Princeps editions available.[6] There were two Princeps editions, one dated and the other possibly undated.

The editor of the second edition of *La Florida del Inca,* which appeared in 1723, was the Spanish historian Andrés Gonzales de Barcía Carballido y Zuñiga under the pseudonym Daza de Cardenas. What was added at that time was a eulogy of Garcilaso and a chronology that disappeared in later works. *La Florida* was "directed to the Queen, our Lady." Errata were corrected and data up to 1722 were added. The printer was Nicolás Franco.

The errata dealt with the new Spanish emphasis. Garcilaso's importance as historian of the New World was de-emphasized, and preference was shown for tales that described him personally. Many current works are based on the second, or subsequent, editions, thus reflecting this bias. In these editions part of Garcilaso's introduction is often omitted. This was the case for all the editions by Doña Piñuela and Sons from 1829 on. However, cuts within the text of *La Florida* itself, not just the introduction, begin to appear in editions such as those by Jorge and Antonio Ulloa on which various German translations were based.

The reasons vary, but even before the rebellion of Tupac Amaru II (1779–

[5]Frances Crowley, "New Information on the Biography of Garcilaso de la Vega, Inca," *Hispania* 48 (September 1965): 481–83.

[6]José Durand, *La Florida del Inca, a Bibliographic Study* (Mexico City: Biblioteca Americana, Fondo Económico, 1956).

1785), which caused copies of Garcilaso's works to be labeled as incendiary by the Crown and to silently disappear from the stores, they became scarce. Hardly any of the copies were true to the original, and the cuts in the Ulloa versions, forming the basis of both the French and German translations, deleted important segments of the original. The resulting books gave European readers the impression that Garcilaso's work was less significant than it had appeared to be to his contemporaries.

At the same time the very foreshortened translations, especially the French ones, guaranteed his work its great popularity. In fact, if it were not for the popularity of the French translations, it is very possible that Garcilaso's works might be nearly impossible to find. The first French translator was Jean Baudoin, who in 1633 translated the "*Histoire de la conquête de la Floride*, à Paris, chez Courbe." There were various editions of *La Florida* in France and the Netherlands before the translation by Pierre Richelet, who joyfully tore into both Garcilaso and Baudoin. While he described the latter as a careless translator, on the prowl for easy money, he attacked the form and style of the author. He was positive that his translation, "Histoire de la Floride, oú relation de ce qui c'est passé dans la découverte de ce pays par Ferdinand de Soto . . . imprimé à Lille, Paris Y Nion, 1709," was better than Baudoin's. At least he recognized that *La Florida* concerned Hernando de Soto's Florida expedition and his problems in dealing with mostly hostile Indians. Richelet confirmed that for forty years copies of Garcilaso's works could be acquired only in auctions, at tremendous prices. He thought it was necessary to issue a new translation because, according to him, the Garcilaso text could not be recognized in the Baudoin edition. But first of all, Richelet felt that cuts were essential. Richelet resented the fact that Baudoin had the audacity to preserve parts of the text that he, Richelet, found boring, but Richelet himself had no such scruples. Thus, there were six abbreviated editions from 1780 on, containing Richelet's negative foreword. What made matters worse was the fact that the subsequent German translation by Konrad Böttger and the English translation by Bernard Shipp were based on Richelet's incomplete text!

The Richelet version was published in 1709 and 1711 by Nion in Paris. It was used as a basis for the translations in Leiden by Van der Aa, in 1737 at The Hague by J. Naulnes, and in the city of Amsterdam by J. F. Bernard. One of the earlier abbreviated Richelet versions was used as a basis for a German edition published in 1753, that, in turn, influenced Konrad Böttger's German version published in Nordhausen in 1785. Böttger's German version—by now, a severely edited version—was then used for the English translation by Bernard Shipp, *The History of Hernando de Soto and Florida*, Philadelphia, 1881.

If the Germans and the English were reading shortened versions of *La Florida*, and the French were influenced by biased introductions, the harm done to Garcilaso's image in Europe and later in America by these editors cannot be compared with what resulted from the even more radical changes occurring in *The Royal Commentaries of the Incas* from the Princeps edition to the twentieth century. Initially, few of the editors of the *Commentaries* and *The General History of Peru* realized Garcilaso's intent of actually using these works to promote a reinstatement of status for himself and some of the former Inca hierarchy. Having written the *Genealogy* and *La Florida* to showcase his relatives and to exalt his Spanish side, and having failed in this effort to achieve recognition for himself, he embarked on the bolder venture of using a historical buildup to bring the Incas, including himself, back to some degree of status in Peru. He did it so cleverly that the Spaniards who read the last chapters of both the *Commentaries* and *The General History of Peru* considered them reminiscences of past glory, rather than an exhortation for future action. It was not until the revolution of Tupac Amaru II that the Crown became aware of the real impact of Garcilaso's message. Copies of Garcilaso's works were then bought up by the Crown to remove them from the market throughout Latin America, but they survived in libraries and through translation to keep reappearing as symbols of both cultures, the Hispanic and the Inca.

Harold Livermore, in the introduction to his edition of *The Royal Commentaries of the Incas and General History of Peru*, describes the situation this way:

> The *Dialogues* and the *Florida* (or the greater part of it) were written before Garcilaso's departure from Montilla. His own material difficulties which followed his removal to Córdova inevitably sharpened his sympathy for the vicissitudes of his fellow Incas, and in the *Royal Commentaries* we find him gradually linking hands with them. If in Montilla he had identified himself with the great poet of his father's family, we now see him drawn steadily into the orbit of the Incas whose history he is rehearsing. Even while at Montilla he had kept in touch with the affairs of Peru, receiving not only letters and reports but also the visits of his former school fellows when they came to Spain. Shortly before he completed the manuscript of the first part [of the *Royal Commentaries*], moreover, the surviving Incas in Peru asked him to undertake a mission on their behalf. At a meeting held in Cuzco in March 1603 they had empowered him to seek relief [from taxes] from Philip III for the surviving mem-

bers of the imperial caste of Peru, and they supplied him with a genealogical tree "painted on a vara and a half of white China taffeta" with a list of 567 names of surviving Incas. Immersed in the *Royal Commentaries*, Garcilaso excused himself from this duty, though he expressed every sympathy with it—"I would willingly have devoted my life to this, for it could not have been better employed."[7]

But the existence of 567 petitioners steeled the Spanish government in its determination not to accept the royal origin of the Incas for purposes of tax exemption. Though Garcilaso seems to have come no nearer than this to engaging in political activities on their behalf, his reputation was to suffer. The final humiliation was having the proud title of *Royal Commentaries* suppressed by the Royal Council from his Part Two, which finally appeared seven months after his death under the innocuous guise of a *General History of Peru*.

Garcilaso's claim to be a loyal Spaniard is demonstrated also in the still extant manuscript of his *Genealogy*, which reveals that its early scope was aimed at bolstering his Spanish descent. And, indeed, in his family tree there were members of the Ponce de León and Hernando de Soto branches. Only later were the *Genealogy* and the *La Florida* separated; *La Florida* was to be the survivor of the split. *La Florida* keynotes the exploits of Hernando de Soto throughout his North American odyssey. The work is well planned. But, in fact, the chapter structure it contains is that of the *Genealogy*—which was originally supposed to be the first part of a larger book combining the two works.

The table of contents of *La Florida* graphically presents the steps of the conquest. Books I and II contain the preliminaries, from permission for the venture by Charles V, through the preparations at Havana, the description of Florida, as Garcilaso conceived it from reports, since he had not seen it, and the early battles faced by Hernando de Soto.

The third book narrates events after the departure from Apalache and contains tales of wealth, treachery, mutiny, and generosity on the part of the lady of Cofitachequi, the rebellion of Tascaluça, and the battle of Mauvila. The fourth book deals with the battle of Alibamo.

The fifth book is divided into two chapters, following the plan of the *Genealogy*. The first part contains the death of Hernando de Soto, and the

[7]Harold Livermore, *The Royal Commentaries of the Incas and General History of Peru* (Austin: University of Texas Press, 1966), xxv-vi.

second describes the return of the Spaniards down the Mississippi on their way to Mexico. The sixth book summarizes the reports of the expedition in Mexico and the attempts by Arias and Maldonado to obtain further news of De Soto.

In *La Florida,* the "Preface to the Reader" leaves many questions unanswered. First and foremost is the question of why as outstanding a firm as that of Pedro Crasbeeck accepted a manuscript in which the main source, who is today agreed to be Gonzalo Silvestre, was anonymous. Garcilaso admitted knowing Silvestre, working for him as a part-time secretary off and on at his home, and gave much information about him, but not his name. They discussed events of the expedition for years and finally decided to record them for posterity. Garcilaso's hesitancy in fully identifying his source may reflect a hesitancy on the part of his subject. Garcilaso did, however, introduce two other sources for minimal verification of his account, and he names them as Juan Coles and Alonso de Carmona. Perhaps their verification satisfied the publisher.

Juan Coles, an eyewitness to many of the events in *La Florida,* was a soldier on the expedition and came from Safra. He is supposed to have given his notes about the expedition to the Franciscan Fray Pedro Aguado, who collected them with others from the Windward Isles, Vera Cruz, Tierra Firme, and El Darien, only, according to Garcilaso, to forget them at a printer's in Córdoba, where Garcilaso found and used them. Alonso Priego de Carmona, another eyewitness, and a soldier on the expedition, forwarded his notes to Garcilaso for approval. According to Garcilaso, their notes were short, because they did not intend to print them under their own names. Indeed, since Juan Coles quoted verbal statements by participants, and since the report was written on legal paper, it might have been part of a legal deposition. Garcilaso claimed that Juan Coles's data agreed with the compilation of events gathered in Mexico for Don Antonio de Mendoza, whose papers would contribute greatly to future studies of *La Florida.*

In any evaluation of *La Florida* as a historical document, it is necessary to take notice of the author's first intent in combining the genealogy with *La Florida,* which was to reinforce the significance of his genealogy as a worthy subject of the king. Indeed, the conclusion of his message to the reader was an appeal on behalf of all Indians, criollos, and mestizos of Peru, as being worthy citizens who should be allowed to pursue higher endeavors.

As the *Genealogy* flowed into *La Florida,* so the *Royal Commentaries* were a sequel of that same attempt to promote the Inca cause. Whereas Pedro Crasbeeck published both *La Florida* and the first part of *The Royal*

Commentaries in Lisbon, on becoming court printer of Philip II, he did not print its second part, *The General History of Peru,* which was produced by the widow of Andrés Barrera at her own expense. Pedro Crasbeeck, as the shrewd founder of a growing enterprise, had probably detected what it took the Spanish government over a century to discover, that much of Garcilaso's work had a political emphasis directed toward restoring the status of the Inca royal family.

Critics have usually quoted Garcilaso's stated intent in the prefaces of his volumes and have criticized or praised him in direct relation to his stated intentions. Anthologies and censors have likewise followed his initial roadmarks and accepted his directions. Had the censors paid as much attention to the last chapter of *The Commentaries* and to the last chapter of his *General History of Peru* (see below), the manuscripts might at best have been edited and at worst not have been accepted. In order to observe how official approval was granted, it is necessary to follow the course of these works through channels.

As could be expected, first approval of *The Royal Commentaries* was granted shortly after submission in Lisbon, on November 6, 1604, by Father Luis Dos Anjos, who found the work very "curiously written and worthy of printing." By December 4, 1604, the book was referred to the Holy Office. At the same time the royal palace received the manuscript, which was approved by the Audiencia and by the House of Braganza as early as March 15, 1605. Although the work could not have met royal approval without church approbation, the latter was given officially only in September 1609.

In his introduction, addressed to Princess Catalina de Braganza, Garcilaso expressed his thanks for her official sponsorship of his work. In his "Preface to the Reader," he introduced the book as a faithful presentation of Inca customs and traditions. Claiming Spanish historians as sources, he professed to correct their statements through commentaries and glosses whenever he thought it necessary. The title page, printed in Spanish in Lisbon in 1609 by Pedro Crasbeeck, claimed that the work dealt with "Inca Kings of Peru, their idolatry, their laws, their government in peace and war, their lives and conquests and all that befell that empire and its republic until the Spanish occupation." No mention was made that Garcilaso also occasionally took the Spaniards to task for things they did, or failed to do.

The General History of Peru, which was to have been the second part of the *Commentaries,* did not get published until 1617, and it was not published by Pedro Crasbeeck. Questions pertaining to Garcilaso's relations with the firm of Pedro Crasbeeck are difficult to answer because the firm was burned with almost total destruction of documents not contained in libraries. What would be of interest is, why did Garcilaso change from a renowned publisher like Crasbeeck to a woman, and by whose initiative? All we know currently is that *The General History of Peru* appeared in 1617, printed by the widow Barrera.

The title change, from the second part of *The Royal Commentaries* to *The General History of Peru,* may have marked the recognition by his literary executors of a change in the role of the author, who no longer wrote as a commentator—one who comments on history, but instead assumed the role of historian—one who records history. The modification must have been gradual, as all permits and dedications were for the second part of *The Royal Commentaries.* These included the initial petition to print by the author in 1612, the request by Don Diego de Mardones, bishop of Córdoba, for the censor's approval, granted on January 6, 1613, the bishop's subsequent confirmation of the approbation, the approval of the Royal Council, issued in Madrid in 1614, and finally, the acceptance by the king himself. The title *The General History of Peru* is mentioned in none of these documents.

Behind the seemingly casual shift causing the title change, however, there may have been a well-thought-out plan that neither the Portuguese nor the Spanish hierarchy were aware of. The whole concept moved imperceptibly from the simple to the complex. Viewed simply, the *Commentaries* were what Garcilaso had presented them as being. On a more sophisticated level, however, they presented a peculiar double-pronged thrust: one prong was a plea for recognition of Garcilaso's own inheritance rights, which should have accrued to him as the only living son of a conquistador; a second prong was a claim of Inca succession rights involving not only himself, but all descendants of royal lineage. If only one part of the ploy worked, Garcilaso was sure to gain. If the Incas won their rights, his would be a leadership position. If neither possibility was realized, his would be the credit of writing a great work. To succeed, he needed the authority of being not just the author of commentaries, but an accredited historian. His goals must be so simple as to mislead possible political observers. The title page of *The History of Peru* is a masterpiece of understatement. His goals are disarming: "the discovery of Peru, the way the Spaniards won it, the civil wars between the Pizarros and the Almagros and the distribution of the land." Their simplistic nature makes them perfectly acceptable. The dedications were carefully prepared. For the bishop there was the repeated dedication to the Virgin, for the Incas there was praise of their native gifts, a sense of identification and pride and an equation of their prowess to the best that antiquity had to offer. For the king there was a reminder that Garcilaso's father had been a famous conquistador in the royal service and that Garcilaso's uncle had died for the Spanish cause.

It was common knowledge that Garcilaso had been told by his Spanish father—who had officially recognized Garcilaso as his son, although he had never married Inca Princess Chimpu Occlo—that he should come to Spain and claim his rights before the king. What was less obvious, especially to the Spanish reader of the day, was Garcilaso's thrust on behalf of Inca claims generally. That he favored the Inca cause could be seen in *The Royal Commentaries,* of which the seventh book resounds as a paean of Inca pride. In chapter eight Garcilaso professed to have undertaken the enormous task of recording all exploits of the Inca republic until its last days, as an act of historic preservation. Lest Cuzco be forgotten, he determined to describe it as its "natural son" must, the pun on words being that of *hijo natural* of his father and his city. As such, he saw in Cuzco not only a new Toledo, as some called it, but a new Rome. The only advantage Rome had over Cuzco was its literacy. Appropriately, he adds: "It is also a matter of doubt which of these famous men owe more to the others, whether the warriors to the writer, because by writing their exploits they committed them to eternity, or whether the men of letters owe more to the warriors for supplying them with daily accomplishments about which they may write the rest of their lives."

After examining the introductions and some significant passages of the texts, various conclusions as to the author's purposes can be drawn. As the Crasbeecks may have noticed, they are unusual. It may well be that Pedro Crasbeeck hesitated to continue publication because he saw some of these interpretations as real possibilities. He was originally of Jewish ancestry and he may have felt that during the Union of Spain and Portugal (1588–1640) he could not be involved with what he may have perceived as Garcilaso's commitment to Inca nationalism. For a commitment of some degree there was, as revealed in the fortieth chapter of the ninth book of the *Commentaries.* Originally the manuscript had thirty-nine chapters and was probably accepted and approved of with these. Then Garcilaso claimed to have received certain documents for safekeeping. As these reached him, he decided to incorporate their contents into the book and to add another chapter concerning the successors to Atahuallpa.

It is difficult in the absence of independent manuscript documentation to establish when exactly Garcilaso was contacted by the successors of Atahuallpa, but according to Garcilaso this was done at the end of 1603. The documents the Incas sent him, listing heirs to Inca realms and their corresponding claims, were forwarded by Garcilaso to Alonso de Mesa, son of his neighbor of Cuzco days, and to Melchior Carlos Inca. Both of these friends resided at the court in Valladolid. The documents were a full-fledged claim of royal descendancy, including a family tree with not only the names but the portraits of all Incas of royal descent entitled to succession status. The document followed both male and female lines of descendancy, was written partly in the Indian court language known to Garcilaso and partly in the vernacular, which he does not seem to remember well, and was signed by eleven Inca Indians, using both Indian and Christian names. Enclosed was a plea for tax exemption benefiting all royal descendants, including Garcilaso. By placing this information in the *Commentaries* with the list of all descendants of the Incas, as they still appear, Garcilaso entered a claim for himself and them for whatever benefits might accrue to them.

Initially, the plea seemed to have succeeded. As stated in the last paragraph of the *Commentaries,* Don Melchior Carlos Inca, son of Paullu Inca (godson of Garcilaso) and grandson of Manco Capac, was to be awarded 7,500 ducats of perpetual income, which was to be deposited by the king in Lima. He was to be granted a house in Spain and an official appointment in the Royal Palace. Indians who had come under his power were to pass to the Crown, nor was he to return to the Indies. He had negotiated these concessions since his arrival in Spain in 1602, but by the time the chapter was written in March 1604 none of the conditions had been fulfilled. Garcilaso promised to discuss the consequences of these transactions in the tenth book of the *Commentaries,* as he concluded the ninth book with this statement: "and with this we shall enter the tenth book, which will deal with the heroic incredible actions of the Spaniards who won that empire."

It is at this point that some drastic changes must have been made, for there is no tenth book in *The Royal Commentaries.* That change must not have been contemplated as early as the end of March 1604, nor as late as September 1609, when the Holy Office granted its license. It would be interesting to know when, exactly, the publishing plans were changed and how the title change came about. Perhaps the requests contained in the final chapter of Book 9 were enough to raise some eyebrows in Spain. The relevant portions of that final chapter are as follows:

> Many days after finishing this ninth book I received certain information from Peru, from which I have compiled the following chapter, for I thought that this matter belonged to my history and I have therefore added it here. The few Incas of the royal blood who survived the cruelties and tyrannies of Atahuallpa

and other later oppressions have more descendants than I had imagined, for at the end of the year 1603 they all wrote to Don Melchior Carlos Inca and to Don Alonso de Mesa, the son of Alonso de Mesa who was a *vecino* of Cuzco, and also to me, to ask us to beg His Majesty in the name of them all to have them exempted from the tribute they are paying and from other vexations that they undertook in common with the rest of the Indians. They sent the three of us powers to act together on their behalf with proofs of their descent, including details of which of them descended from which other king, down to the last of their line; and for clearer proof and demonstration they included a genealogical tree showing the royal line from Manco Cápac to Haina Cápac. . . . They write with great confidence, which we all entertain, that when His Catholic Majesty knows their plight he will relieve them and will confer many privileges on them, as befits the descendants of kings.[8]

Those who believe that the descendancy documents were casually inserted in the last book of *The General History of Peru* will find that, in the same last book, in the next to the last paragraph, Don Melchior Carlos Inca reappears. Fearful lest the long list of royal descendants should cause him to lose his privileges, he had not forwarded the documents to the court. This deprived him, as well as his relatives, including Garcilaso, of any benefits they might then have been able to claim. Garcilaso wanted his countrymen to know what happened lest they blame him for not representing them well. The relevant paragraph from the last chapter of the *General History of Peru* is:

With regard to the descendants of these kings not in the direct line, in the last chapter of the First Part of these *Commentaries* we mentioned how many descendants there were of each of the past kings. As I stated there, they themselves sent me a document in the name of all of them with power of attorney in favor of Don Melchior Carlos, Don Alonso de Mesa, and myself, so that any of the three of us could present it on their behalf of [to] His Catholic Majesty and the Supreme Royal Council of the Indies. This document requested that, as descendants of kings, they should be relieved of the vexations they suffered. I sent the petition and the accompanying papers (which were addressed to me) to the capital directed to the said Don Melchior Carlos and Don Alonso de Mesa, but the former, though his own claims were of the same nature and based on the same legal and natural arguments as those of the Incas, was unwilling to present the papers so as not to reveal how many persons there were of the royal blood, thinking that if he did reveal this, he would lose many of

[8]Ibid., pt. 1, p. 625.

the grants and honors he claimed and hoped to receive. He was therefore reluctant to raise his voice on his kinsmen's behalf; and he died, as has been said, without receiving anything for himself or his friends. I have mentioned this in order to clear myself and so that my relatives, wherever they may be, shall know what happened and not accuse me of neglect or ill-will in not having done what they bade and requested me. I would indeed have been glad to have devoted my life to the service of people who so greatly deserved it, but I have not been able to do more, as I have been engaged in writing this history, which I hope will have been as great a service to the Spaniards who won the empire as to the Incas who formerly possessed it.[9]

The fact that Garcilaso felt he must explain to his relatives and friends why the petition failed shows that he had accepted a commitment to represent the disenfranchised heirs of the Inca Empire. Without objection by the Royal Court, he had fought on two sides of the issue—the Spanish side of his father and the Inca side of his mother. Not until 1780 did the Spanish Crown become aware of the descendancy claims contained in the *Commentaries.* It was then that Charles III ordered local governors to purchase all available copies, lest the books, which he considered seditious, become instantly popular. There were, however, more books than he realized, because Garcilaso's claim still stands four centuries later as proof that history has often been produced to satisfy political ends. A key ingredient in the power game was the *Genealogy,* which he used before *La Florida* and throughout his later works, on both the Spanish and the Inca side of the spectrum, to pursue a respect and a status that, while never awarded him by the king, he received from future generations as a writer.

Appraisal of Garcilaso's *La Florida* among recent writers depends on whether the critics view the work as primarily literary or historical. Whereas the former do not concentrate on credibility, the latter see it as a prevailing issue. A literary critic, Arnold Toynbee, in his foreword to Harold Livermore's *Royal Commentaries* (p. xxiv), perceives the *Dialogues of Love,* the *Florida,* and the two parts of *The Royal Commentaries* as corresponding to successive stages of Garcilaso's development. Toynbee's view is that in *La Florida* Garcilaso leaves the world of philosophy and the speculations of León Hebreo to confront the problems of America and its conquest. His was the tale of a bold expedition among savage Indians, only lately removed from the rites of cannibalism, as this expedition was viewed by a Spanish

[9]Ibid., pt. 2, pp. 1486–87.

conquistador years after the fact. The ever-present contrast was that of conqueror and conquered, or of Hernando de Soto and his Spanish soldiers in their daily interaction with the native Indians. According to Toynbee, one striking aspect of Garcilaso's approach to the subject was his treatment of the two parties, European and Indian, as equals. Toynbee found in the work the romantic qualities of Ginés Pérez de Hita's *Civil Wars of Granada* in which a ruthless struggle between the peoples of two opposing religions is purged of its brutality to make for agreeable reading. It is the pleasant tempo of Garcilaso's narrative, the almost fictionlike alternation of battle and lush description of the hitherto unknown landscape, that endeared him to Europeans and kept them reissuing his editions across the centuries.

John Grier Varner, in his *El Inca,* praised Garcilaso's literary legacy: "To the world, he left the most picturesque of all accounts of a courageous journey through the vast regions of La Florida. Woven through it is the old cavalier's most splendid eulogy. He himself [the old cavalier] had dictated it to his Peruvian amanuensis [Garcilaso], who treated it with the warmth and sympathy it deserved."[10]

The very fact that the *Florida* was a eulogy weakened its historical accuracy. Garcilaso wanted his times to be remembered. He viewed history not unlike the ancient Greek historians, as the cumulative impact of men of action upon their times, their friends, and their foes. His was the song of the Indian, of the "natural man," whose cause Jean Jacques Rousseau espoused in his *Discours sur l'origine de l'inegalité* and in his *Contrat Social.* Rousseau's concept that the "natural man" was at the base of governance heightened French interest in Indian works during the French Revolution. It was Garcilaso's goal to show that the impact on the Americas of the Indian and Inca cultures was equal to the impact of Spain.

This perception of the greatness which was Inca America would inspire Simón Bolívar. According to John Grier Varner, "the famed Libertador in a moment of poetic ecstasy wrote to a friend of the unsurpassed wonders of the imperial city [Cuzco] and of the civilization, which it symbolized. Its history . . . was a tapestry of cruelty to the Indians, woven by Bartolomé de las Casas; its legend was to be found in the chronicles of the Inca, Garcilaso de la Vega."[11] The quotation is significant, because it brings to the fore Garcilaso's appeal to the liberators as a symbol for national unification. Part of a

[10]John Grier Varner, *El Inca* (Austin: University of Texas Press, 1968), 310.

[11]Ibid., 384.

letter written by Simón Bolívar to José Joaquín Olmedo, written from Cuzco on June 27, 1825, shows that the Garcilaso name itself had become a code word for unification.[12]

In an enlightening article, Hugo Rodríguez Vecchini draws attention to the fact that *La Florida* was published in the same year, 1605, as was Cervantes's *Don Quijote.*[13] Rodríguez Vecchini views *La Florida* as a work in the tradition of Ariosto and Boiardo, modeled equally on history and fiction. For him the majestic bearing of the lady of Cofachiqui is as reminiscent of Cleopatra, as the fierce Vitachuco is of the brave knights of Orlando, be he the Inammorato or the Furioso.

The accuracy of *La Florida* depends in large part, of course, on its original source. The original source of *La Florida,* Gonzalo Silvestre, was probably meant in the beginning to be the sole source. Perhaps, had Gonzalo lived longer, his story would have remained a family document, unpublished or privately printed. But, as John Grier Varner appropriately sums it up, Garcilaso took "occasional journeys back to Montilla and . . . down the dusty road of *Las Posadas* to recapture still what he could from the ailing Silvestre, whose days were ebbing fast. In 1592, after receiving an additional grant from the crown and after demanding that his body, when placed in the sepulcher, be resplendently armed, the gallant old adventurer expired."[14]

Silvestre left money to his nephew Alonso Diaz de Belcazar, to his friend Diego de Córdoba, and to Garcilaso, to whom he bequeathed his data and notes of obligation of 800 ducats. Garcilaso's new sponsor became Juan Fernández Franco, who would not match his friend's generosity, and Garcilaso dedicated the first manuscript to Pedro Fernández de Córdoba, marqués de Priego. It was no longer practical to start the book with a genealogy. Instead, *La Florida* was to be expanded to include the testimony by Coles and Carmona and to become a work of history in its own right.

As a source, Gonzalo Silvestre is vulnerable, since the events he describes were no longer recent. He admits to "presuming" to write the truth. Since both the conquistador and the writer are trustworthy men, *fide dignos,* their testimony, accompanied by that of Coles and Carmona, however admittedly inadequate as to the sequence of events, should be credited. (When Don Francisco de Toledo, who became viceroy of Peru in 1569, took the testi-

---

[12]*Cartas del Libertador,* vol. 5, pp. 6–8.

[13]H. Rodríguez Vecchini, "Don Quijote y la Florida del Inca," in *Historia y ficción en la narrativa hispanoamericana* (Coloquio de Yale; Caracas: Monte Avila Editores, 1984).

[14]Varner, *El Inca,* 310.

mony of Coles and Carmona at an inquiry he instituted in Cuzco into the nature and extent of the government of the Incas, their report before the viceroy and his son was so persuasive that the viceroy decided to recommend a continuance of the conquest and exploration of Florida.) But in *La Florida* as elsewhere, Garcilaso criticizes his sources, even as he makes common cause with them, so that at times his "I" as a historian becomes a consensus of "we."

In a way Garcilaso's genius for literary writing harmed him as a historian. His definite talent at storytelling, which made him so beloved especially to the French, caused him to be criticized by nineteenth- and twentieth-century authors. In her preface to *La Florida del Inca,* Silvia Lynn Hilton lists Ticknor, Tschundi, and Menendez Pelayo as detractors of Garcilaso, and reports that George Bancroft considered *La Florida del Inca* as nothing more than a novel.[15]

Similarly on the negative side were Manuel Gonzales de la Rosa, John Swanton in the *Final Report of the U.S. De Soto Expedition,* 1939, and Robert Levillier's refutation of many of Garcilaso's assumptions. Errors such as the wrong birthplace for De Soto caused critics, among them David Henige, to challenge "the context, content and credibility of La Florida del Ynca."[16] He questions whether Garcilaso ever heard of the gentleman of Elvas's *Relaçam,* or whether Garcilaso's work was to be an answer to it, extolling Silvestre. He also thinks it unlikely that he did not know about the Rangel and Biedma reports; Henige opts instead to assume that Garcilaso ignored them.

In tables that show that none of the sources agreed on any of the numbers of participants, he brings out that Garcilaso's numbers by far exceeded those of the others. The tables would seem more convincing if all other sources were unanimous, which they are not.

In spite of its acknowledged limitations, *La Florida* is defended as a valuable contribution to the literature and history of Hispanoamerica by José de la Riva Agüero, Aurelio Miró Quesada, José Durand, Silvia Lynn Hilton, and Donald G. Castanien.[17] In Castanien can be found one of the strongest defenders of the early Garcilaso. Castanien writes that "as a work of literary

[15]Silvia Lynn Hilton, *La Florida del Inca* (Madrid: Fundación Universitaria Española, 1982), 27.

[16]David Henige, "The Context, Content and Credibility of La Florida del Ynca," *The Americas* 43, no. 1 (July 1986).

[17]Donald G. Castanien, *El Inca Garcilaso de la Vega* (New York: Twayne, 1961).

art the *Florida* is by far the most satisfactory of Garcilaso's work, perhaps because it does have so many of the qualities of the novel."[18] In his opinion, and in that of most French authors reviewing *La Florida,* Garcilaso's borrowings from the conventions of romance enhanced the curiosity and the interest of readers.

The debates on the relative values of the writer and the historian have kept *La Florida* in print until the present, and as the debate goes on, Garcilaso will be a subject of further investigation. The work has been compared to the best of chivalric novels and even to the *Quijote,* yet it is unique in its kind as the product of a man of mixed allegiance. As fiction, it is well planned and written. Not many works of fiction have survived over three centuries with more or less continued publication. As a historical work, it poses problems, but so do all the other sources of the De Soto expedition. Anthropologists may have trouble with it, but then Garcilaso did not claim to be an anthropologist. As the debate continues, it will produce new outlooks pertaining to literary values versus historical accuracy. Whatever the outcome, Garcilaso's strength lies in his description of the people, the Indians, the Spaniards, Hernando de Soto, and their superhuman goals. In presenting the verdant scenery of Florida, in describing battles and conflicts, he undoubtedly excels.

[18]Ibid., 76.

La Florida

by the Inca

History of the Adelantado Hernando de Soto, Governor and Captain General of the Kingdom of La Florida, and of Other Heroic Gentlemen, Spaniards and Indians; Written by the Inca Garcilasso de la Vega, Captain of His Majesty, a Native of the Great City of El Cuzco, Capital of the Kingdoms and Provinces of El Perú

Translated by Charmion Shelby
Edited by David Bost
With Footnotes by Vernon James Knight, Jr.

La Florida

by the Inca

History of the Adelantado Hernando de Soto, Governor and Captain-General of the Kingdom of La Florida, and of Other Heroic Gentlemen, Spaniards and Indians; Written by the Inca Garcilasso de la Vega, Captain of His Majesty, a Native of the Great City of El Cuzco, Capital of the Kingdoms and Provinces of El Perú

Dedicated to the most serene Prince, the Duke of Braganza, etc.

---

with license of the holy Inquisition.

in Lisbon

Printed by Pedro Crasbeeck

---

with Royal privilege.

I examined these six books in one volume that treat of the discovery of La Florida, their author [being] the Inca Garcilaso de la Vega, and there is nothing in them contrary to our holy faith and good customs; rather, there is history worthy of being read, because they contain many curious things about various and unknown peoples and nations, very remarkable perils and events of war, and many other things that deserve to come to the attention of everyone. In Lisbon in San Francisco Denxobreguas, November 16, 1604.

FR. LUYS DOS ANJOS.

In consideration of the [above] approbation, this book entitled "Discovery of La Florida" may be printed, and after being printed let it be returned to this council to be compared with the original and to be given permission to circulate; without it, it may not circulate. In Lisbon, November 23, 1604.

MARCOS TEIXEIRA. RUY PIREZ DA VEIGA.

This book may be printed in consideration of the permission it has from the Holy Office. In Lisbon, February 21, 1605. This book may be seen at this tribunal.

DAMIÃO D'AGUIAR. SOUSA.

His Majesty concedes that no printer or bookseller may print or sell this book without permission from the author, for a period of ten years, under the penalties prescribed, as appear from the dispatch given in Lisbon on March 8, 1605, and from the enclosed patent, etc.

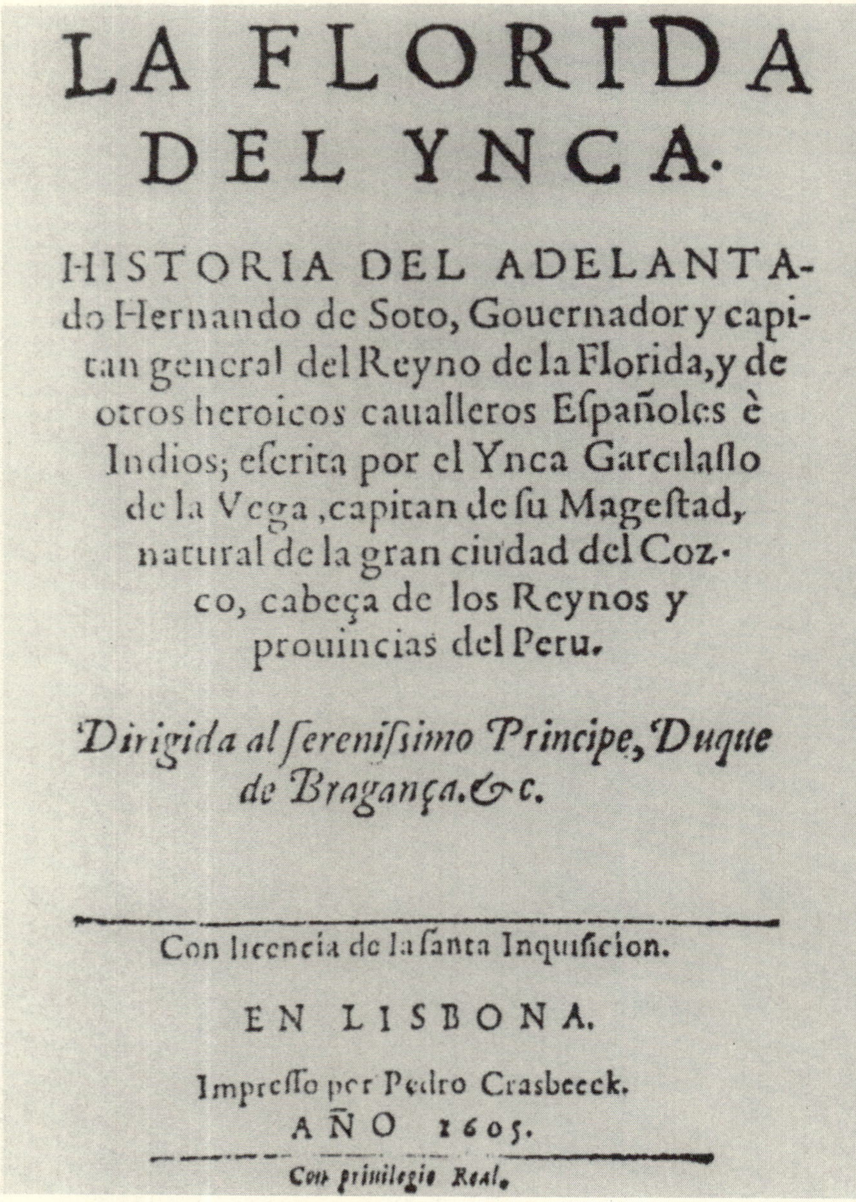

LA FLORIDA
DEL YNCA.

HISTORIA DEL ADELANTA-
do Hernando de Soto, Gouernador y capi-
tan general del Reyno de la Florida, y de
otros heroicos caualleros Eſpañoles è
Indios; eſcrita por el Ynca Garcilaſſo
de la Vega, capitan de ſu Mageſtad,
natural de la gran ciudad del Coz-
co, cabeça de los Reynos y
prouincias del Peru.

*Dirigida al ſereniſsimo Principe, Duque
de Bragança. &c.*

Con licencia de la ſanta Inquiſicion.

EN LISBONA.

Impreſſo por Pedro Crasbeeck.
AÑO 1605.

Con priuilegio Real.

Title Page of the 1605 Edition of La Florida, *by The Inca, Garcilaso de la Vega, Printed in Lisbon.*

Contents

FIRST PART OF THE SECOND BOOK OF THE *HISTORY OF LA FLORIDA* BY THE INCA, WHERE IT IS TOLD HOW THE GOVERNOR ARRIVED IN LA FLORIDA, AND FOUND TRACES OF PÁNPHILO DE NARVÁEZ, AND A CHRISTIAN CAPTIVE; THE TORTURES AND THE CRUEL LIFE THE INDIANS GAVE HIM; THE GENEROSITY OF AN INDIAN LORD OF VASSALS; THE PREPARATIONS THAT WERE MADE FOR THE DISCOVERY; THE EVENTS THAT TOOK PLACE IN THE FIRST EIGHT PROVINCES THEY DISCOVERED; AND THE WILD FEROCITY, IN WORDS AND DEEDS, OF AN OVERBOLD CACIQUE. IT CONTAINS THIRTY CHAPTERS, WHICH ARE THE FOLLOWING.

SECOND PART OF THE SECOND BOOK
OF THE *HISTORY OF LA FLORIDA* BY THE INCA, WHERE THERE WILL
BE SEEN THE MANY AND SEVERE COMBATS THAT INDIANS AND

SPANIARDS HAD IN DIFFICULT PASSES IN THE GREAT PROVINCE OF APALACHE; THE HARDSHIPS THROUGH WHICH THEY PASSED IN DISCOVERING THE SEA; THE EVENTS AND THE INCREDIBLE FATIGUES THAT THE THIRTY HORSEMEN WHO WENT BACK FOR PEDRO CALDERÓN EXPERIENCED IN GOING AND RETURNING; THE FEROCITY OF THE PEOPLE OF APALACHE; THE IMPRISONMENT OF THEIR CACIQUE; HIS STRANGE FLIGHT; AND THE FERTILITY OF THAT GREAT PROVINCE. IT CONTAINS TWENTY-FIVE CHAPTERS, WHICH ARE THE FOLLOWING.

THIRD BOOK

OF THE *HISTORY OF LA FLORIDA* BY THE INCA. IT TELLS OF THE DEPARTURE OF THE SPANIARDS FROM APALACHE; THE GOOD RECEPTION THEY GAVE THEM IN FOUR PROVINCES; THE HUNGER THEY SUFFERED IN SOME UNINHABITED REGIONS; THE INFINITE NUMBER OF PEARLS AND THE OTHER GRANDEUR AND RICHES THAT THEY FOUND IN A TEMPLE; THE GENEROSITY OF THE LADY OF COFACHIQUI AND OF OTHER CACIQUES, LORDS OF VASSALS; A VERY BLOODY BATTLE THE INDIANS GAVE THEM AFTER PROMISING FRIENDSHIP; A MUTINY CERTAIN CASTILIANS ATTEMPTED; THE LAWS OF THE INDIANS AGAINST ADULTERESSES; AND ANOTHER VERY FIERCE BATTLE THAT TOOK PLACE AT NIGHT. IT CONTAINS THIRTY-NINE CHAPTERS, WHICH ARE THE FOLLOWING.

FOURTH BOOK

OF THE *HISTORY OF LA FLORIDA* BY THE INCA. IT DEALS WITH THE COMBAT OF THE FORT OF ALIBAMO; THE DEATH OF MANY SPANIARDS FOR THE LACK OF SALT; HOW THEY COME TO CHISCA AND CROSS THE RÍO GRANDE; HOW INDIANS AND SPANIARDS FORM A SOLEMN PROCESSION TO ADORE THE CROSS, ASKING GOD FOR MERCIES; THE CRUEL WAR AND PILLAGE BETWEEN CAFA [CAPAHA] AND CASQUIN; HOW THE SPANIARDS DISCOVER A MEANS OF MAKING SALT; THE FEROCITY OF THE TULAS IN APPEARANCE AND WEAPONS; AN AGREEABLE WINTER THE CASTILIANS SPENT IN UTIANGUE. IT CONTAINS SIXTEEN CHAPTERS, WHICH ARE THE FOLLOWING.

FIRST PART OF THE FIFTH BOOK OF THE *HISTORY OF LA FLORIDA* BY THE INCA, WHERE AN ACCOUNT IS GIVEN OF A SPANIARD WHO REMAINED AMONG THE INDIANS; THE EFFORTS THAT WERE MADE TO RECOVER HIM; A LONG JOURNEY OF THE CASTILIANS, IN WHICH THEY TRAVERSED EIGHT PROVINCES; THE ENMITY AND CRUEL WAR BETWEEN GUACHOYAS AND ANILCOS; THE LAMENTABLE DEATH OF GOVERNOR HERNANDO DE SOTO, AND TWO BURIALS HIS MEN GAVE HIM. IT CONTAINS EIGHT CHAPTERS, WHICH ARE THE FOLLOWING.

SECOND PART OF THE FIFTH BOOK OF THE *HISTORY OF LA FLORIDA* BY THE INCA. IT TELLS HOW THE SPANIARDS DECIDED TO ABANDON LA FLORIDA; A LONG JOURNEY THAT THEY MADE IN ORDER TO GET OUT OF IT; THE INSUPPORTABLE HARDSHIPS THAT THEY ENDURED IN GOING AND RETURNING ON THAT JOURNEY, UNTIL THEY CAME BACK TO THE RÍO GRANDE; SEVEN BRIGANTINES THEY BUILT IN ORDER TO LEAVE BY WAY OF IT; THE LEAGUE OF TEN CACIQUES AGAINST THE CASTILIANS; THE SECRET NOTICE THAT THEY HAD OF IT; THE OFFERS OF GENERAL ANILCO AND HIS GOOD QUALITIES; A REMARKABLE FLOOD ON THE RÍO GRANDE; THE ACTIVITY IN BUILDING THE BRIGANTINES; A CHALLENGE FROM THE GENERAL ANILCO TO THE CACIQUE GUACHOYA AND THE REASON FOR IT; THE PUNISHMENT THAT WAS GIVEN TO THE AMBASSADORS OF THE LEAGUE. IT CONTAINS FIFTEEN CHAPTERS, WHICH ARE THE FOLLOWING.

SIXTH BOOK

OF THE *HISTORY OF LA FLORIDA* BY THE INCA. IT CONTAINS THE ELECTION OF THE CAPTAINS FOR THE VOYAGE; THE MULTITUDE OF CANOES THAT OPPOSED THE SPANIARDS; THE ORDER AND MANNER OF THEIR FIGHTING, WHICH LASTED ELEVEN DAYS WITHOUT CEASING; THE DEATH OF FORTY-EIGHT CASTILIANS BECAUSE OF THE RASHNESS OF ONE OF THEM; THE RETURN OF THE INDIANS TO THEIR HOMES; THE ARRIVAL OF THE SPANIARDS AT THE SEA; AN ENCOUNTER THEY HAD WITH THE PEOPLE OF THE COAST; THE EVENTS OF THEIR FIFTY-FIVE DAYS OF NAVIGATION UNTIL THEY REACHED PÁNUCO; THE MANY QUARRELS THAT THEY HAD THERE AMONG THEMSELVES, AND THE REASON FOR THEM; THE GOOD RECEPTION THAT THE IMPERIAL CITY OF MÉXICO GAVE THEM; AND HOW THEY WERE SCATTERED THROUGH VARIOUS PARTS OF THE WORLD; THE PEREGRINATION AND LABORS OF GÓMEZ ARIAS AND DIEGO MALDONADO WITH WHICH THE *HISTORY* ENDS. IT CONTAINS TWENTY-TWO CHAPTERS, WHICH ARE THE FOLLOWING.

To the Most Excellent Señor Don Theodosio of Portugal

Duke of Braganza and of Barcelos, etc.

Through having heard in my childhood, most serene Prince, from my father and from his relatives, of the heroic virtues and great exploits of the kings and princes of glorious memory, your Excellency's progenitors, and of the prowess in arms of the nobility of that famous kingdom of Portugal; and through having read of them here later in the course of my life—not only those they have performed in Spain, but also those in Africa and in the great oriental India—and of their extensive and admirable navigation, and of the toils and hardships the illustrious Lusitanians have experienced in its conquest and in preaching of the holy gospel, and of the noble things the kings and princes have ordered for the one and the other, I have always been much inclined toward the service of their Majesties and of all those of their kingdom. This inclination was converted later into obligation, because the first land I saw when I came from my own, which is El Perú, was that of Portugal—the island of El Fayal and La Tercera, and the royal city of Lisbon, in which the royal ministers and the citizens, and those of the islands, being such religious and charitable people, gave me as warm a reception as if I had been a native son of one of them. In order not to weary your Excellency, I do not give a full account of the gifts and favors they bestowed upon me, one of which was to save me from death. Seeing myself, therefore, on the one hand so obligated and on the other so inclined, I did not know how to repay my obligation or how I could show my affection, except by this bold act (too much so for an Indian) of offering and dedicating this *History* to your Excellency. I have been moved no little to do so by the exploits recounted therein of the gentlemen and hidalgos, natives of this kingdom, who went on the conquest of La Gran Florida. It is fitting that they should thus employ themselves worthily and appropriately, in order that they may live under your Excellency's protection and may be esteemed and favored as they deserve.

I beg your Excellency that, with the affability and generosity to which your royal blood obligates you, you will be pleased to accept and receive this small *servicio,* and the desire I have always had and now have to see myself included among the number of the subjects and servants of your Excellency's royal house. This favor being conferred, as I hope, I shall have many of my affectionate desires gratified, and with this same favor I shall be able to repay and satisfy the obligation that I owe to the natives of this most Christian kingdom, for by means of your Excellency's condescension and favor I shall be one of them. May our Lord preserve your Excellency for many happy years as a refuge and protection of the poor and needy. Amen.

THE INCA GARCILASSO DE LA VEGA

Preface to the Reader

Conversing many times and in various places with a gentleman, a great friend of mine, who was on this expedition, and hearing from him of the many and very great feats that Spaniards and Indians alike performed in the course of it, it seemed to me an unbecoming thing and a great pity that deeds as heroic as any that have taken place in the world should remain in perpetual oblivion. I myself, therefore, being obligated to both nations, because I am the son of a Spaniard and an Indian woman, importuned that gentleman many times that we write this history, I serving him as amanuensis. And although this end was desired by both of us, it was prevented by the times and occasions that arose, now of war, to which I went, now of long periods when we were apart, in the course of which more than twenty years passed. With time, however, my desire increased, and on the other hand the fear that if one of us should die our purpose would never be fulfilled, because, I being dead, he would have no one to encourage him and act as clerk; and he being lost to me, I would not know from whom to obtain the account that he could give me. I determined to make an end of the impediments and delays that existed by leaving the establishment and ease I had in a pueblo where I was living, and go to his. There we busied ourselves with care and diligence in writing down everything that took place on this expedition from its beginning to its end, for the honor and fame of the Spanish nation, which has done such great things in the New World, and no less for that of the Indians, who in this history show themselves and appear worthy of the same honor.

In this history, besides the exploits and hardships the Christians performed and passed through, singly and in common, and besides the notable things that were found among the Indians, an account is given of the many and very large provinces the governor and *adelantado* Hernando de Soto and many other gentlemen—Extremadurans, Portuguese, Andalusians, Çastilians, and those from all the other provinces of Spain—discovered in the great kingdom of La Florida, in order that henceforth (the bad name that

that country has of being sterile and swampy, which it is on the seacoast, being obliterated) Spain may be obliged to win and settle it, even though, aside from the principal motive, which is the increase of our holy Catholic faith, it is only to establish colonies where her sons can be sent to live, as the ancient Romans did when there was no room for them in their own country. It is a fertile land, abounding in everything necessary for human life, and it may be made much more productive †[than it is naturally at present, with crops and cattle that can be introduced there from Spain and other places, for which it is very well fitted, as will be seen in the course of this *History*.

The chief care that has been exercised was to write the things that are told herein as they are and as they happened, because my main purpose is for that land to be won, to which end, as has been said, I attempted to obtain from the one who gave me the account of everything that he saw, he being a nobleman and hidalgo and as such taking a pride in telling the exact truth in regard to everything. The royal Council of the Indies (as I know) has summoned him often, as a trustworthy man, to make statements before it concerning the things that took place on this expedition as well as on others in which he took part.

He was a very good soldier and often was a commander, and he participated in all the events of this discovery. Thus he was able to give the account of this *History* in a form as complete as it is. And if anyone should say what is often said in attempting to censure as cowards or liars those who give good accounts of the particular events that take place in the battles in which they participate—for they say that if they were fighting, how could they see all that happened in the course of the battle; and if they saw it, how could they fight, because two jobs together, such as watching and fighting, could not be done well—the answer to this is that it is a common custom among these soldiers, as it is in all wars throughout the world, to return to report to the general and the other officers the most notable dangers they have passed through in the battles. And often when what some captain or soldier reported was very extravagant and difficult to believe, those who heard him went to see and ascertain the facts for themselves. And in this manner he could have knowledge of everything that he told me in order that I might write it down. He was aided no little in recalling past events to memory by the many and repeated questions I would ask him concerning them and concerning the peculiarities and qualities of that country.

---

†*Translator's note*: This section set off by brackets (pp. 54–56) is missing from the photostatic copy of the 1605 edition, and has been supplied from the 1723 edition.

Besides the authority of my author, I have the confirmation of two other soldiers, eyewitnesses, who took part in the same expedition. One is named Alonso de Carmona, a native of the villa of Priego. Having traveled through La Florida during the six years of this discovery, and afterward spent many others in El Perú, and then having returned to his own country, because of the pleasure he received from the recollection of his past labors he wrote these two *Peregrinations* of his, and so named them. Not knowing that I was writing this *History*, he sent me both of them, so that I might see them. I was very pleased with them because his account of La Florida, although very brief, and without order either in time or in events, and without naming provinces, except a very few, jumping about from one place to another, recounts the most notable events of our *History*.

The other soldier is called Juan Coles, a native of the villa of Zafra. He wrote another disorganized and brief *Relation* of this same discovery and tells of the most notable events that occurred in it. He wrote them down at the request of a provincial of the province of Santa Fe in the Indies, named Fray Pedro Aguado, of the Order of seraphic father St. Francis. This religious, with the desire of serving the Catholic king, Don Felipe II, had collected many and varied accounts from trustworthy persons of the discoveries they had witnessed in the New World, particularly in this first one made in the Indies, including all the islands they call the Windward Islands, Vera Cruz, Tierra Firme, El Darién, and other provinces in those regions. These accounts he left in Córdoba in the power and custody of a printer, and busied himself with other matters in the interest of his Order, abandoning his accounts, which still were not in proper form for printing. I saw them and they were in very bad condition, half of them having been consumed by moths and mice. They covered more than a ream of paper, divided into sections just as each narrator had written them, and among them I found the one I mentioned of Juan Coles. This was a little after Alonso de Carmona had sent me his, and although it is true that I had finished writing this *History*, seeing these two eyewitnesses so in agreement with it, it seemed well to me (on going back to rewrite it) to name them in the proper places and to include in many passages a literal copy of their own words, in order to present two witnesses confirming my author, so that it might be seen that all three accounts agree.

It is true that in their proceedings they have no regard for chronology, unless it be at the beginning, nor for order in the events they recount, because they put some too soon and others too late, nor do they name provinces, except for a few scattered ones. They simply tell the most important things that they saw as they happen to remember them; but upon comparing the events they recount with those of our *History,* they are the same, and in some cases they report them with the addition of greater amplification and embellishment, as will be seen set down in their own words.

These inadvertences they had must have been due to the fact that they did not write with the intention of printing; at any rate Carmona did not, because he desired no more than that his relatives and neighbors read of the things that he had] seen in the New World, and thus he sent me the *Relations* as an acquaintance who had been born in the Indies, so that I also might see them. Nor did Juan Coles put his account in historical form, and the reason might have been that since the work was not to come out in his name he was under no obligation to take the trouble to put it in order, and told what he remembered more as an eyewitness than as the author of the work, understanding that the father provincial who asked for the *Relation* would put it in the proper form for printing. Thus the account is written in the manner of a legal process, appearing that another person set down what he said, because sometimes it says: "This witness states thus and so"; and again it says: "This declarant states that he saw such and such a thing." In other places he speaks as if he himself had written, saying, "We saw this and did that, etc." Both accounts are so short that that of Juan Coles contains no more than ten sheets of paper, written in a legal script with the letters linked together, and that of Alonso de Carmona has eight and a half sheets, though on the contrary it is in a very cramped handwriting.

Some noteworthy things they tell, such as Juan Coles saying that he, going on with other infantrymen (it must have been without the general's orders), found a temple with an idol decorated with many pearls and seed pearls, and that it had in its mouth a hyacinth [i.e., a precious stone, perhaps a sapphire] as long as the distance between the ends of the thumb and forefinger, and as thick as the thumb, which he took, without anyone seeing him, etc.—this and many other similar things I did not include in our *History* because of not knowing in what provinces they occurred, for in this matter of naming the lands through which they passed, as I have already said, both are very defective, especially Juan Coles. In short, I say that they did not write of any other incidents except those in which I mention them, which are the most important ones. And I take pleasure in referring to them in these places in order to be able to say that I write from the accounts of three authors who confirm one another. In addition to these I have in my support a great favor that one of his Catholic Majesty's chroniclers did me, in writing, saying among other things the following: "I have compared this

History with an account I have, which was the one drawn up in México for Don Antonio de Mendoza from the [literary] remains of this excellent Castilian who entered La Florida, and I find that it is truthful and in conformity with the said account, etc."

This is sufficient in order that it may be believed that we did not write fiction; it would not have been just for me to do so, having to present this account to the whole Spanish commonwealth, which would have reason for indignation against me if I had acted falsely and without good faith.

Nor would the Eternal Majesty (which is what we ought to fear most) fail to be gravely offended if I, in attempting to incite and persuade the Spaniards to win that land for the increase of our holy Catholic faith, should mislead with fables and fictions those who desired to employ their property and lives in such an enterprise. Certainly, stating the whole truth, I say that I was moved by no other purpose in laboring and having written this work than the desire that the Christian religion be extended over such a large and broad country; that I neither aspire to nor hope for temporal benefits from this long labor; that long ago I gave up pretensions and abandoned hopes because of the adversity of my fortune. Looking at the matter dispassionately, however, I ought to congratulate myself very heartily for its having treated me badly, for if it had conferred its benefits and favors generously upon me, perhaps I would have gone by other roads and paths than I have taken, to worse misfortunes, or it would have drowned me in the waves and tempests of this great sea, as it almost always drowns those whom it has most favored and raised to the grandeurs of this world. With its frowns and persecutions it has forced me, having experienced them, to flee from it and hide myself in the refuge and shelter of the disillusioned, which are the retreats of solitude and poverty where, consoled and satisfied with the scantiness of my few possessions, I pass a quiet and peaceful life, thanks to the King of Kings and Lord of Lords, more envied by the rich than envious of them. In this life (so as not to be idle, which is more wearying than labor) I have engaged in other efforts and hopes more satisfying and more diverting to the mind than those of wealth, such as translating the three *Diálogos de Amor* of León Hebreo; having published them, I employed myself in writing this *History.* With the same pleasure I am now constructing, forming, and giving the finishing touches to that of El Perú: the origin of the Inca kings, their antiquity, idolatry and conquests, their laws and the method of their government in peace and in war. Through Divine favor, I now see myself almost at the end of all this. Although they are labors, and not small ones, in order to attempt and attain another, better end I value them more than the favors my fortune might have conferred upon me in case it had been very prosperous and favorable; because I hope in God that these labors will do me more honor and bring me better fame than the possessions I might have acquired from the gifts of this lady. Because of all this I am rather her debtor than her creditor, and as such I give her many thanks, because at her insistence, impelled by the Divine clemency, I was allowed to offer and present this *History* to the whole world. It is written in six Books, corresponding to the six years that were spent on the expedition. The Second Book and the Fifth were each divided into two parts; the Second so that it might not be so long as to weary the eye, for since in that year there occurred more things to relate than in any one of the others, it seemed well to me to divide it into two parts, so that each part would be proportionate in size to the other Books and the events of one year would be included in a single Book.

The Fifth Book was divided so that the acts of the governor and adelantado Hernando de Soto might be a part to themselves and not joined to those of Luis de Moscoso de Alvarado, who was the one that succeeded him in the governorship. Thus in the first part of that Book the history of Hernando de Soto proceeds down to his death and the two burials they gave him. The second part deals with what his successor did and ordered until the end of the expedition, which was in the sixth year of this *History.* I beg that the latter may be received in the same spirit in which I offer it, and that I may be pardoned for the faults it contains, because I am an Indian. To such, because they are barbarians and not instructed in sciences or arts, it is permissible that they shall not be guided by the rigorous precepts of art or sciences in what they may say or do, because they have not learned them; but they should be accepted as they are.

Carrying this pious consideration further, it would be a noble finesse and a generous ingenuity to favor through me (though I do not deserve it) all the Indians, mestizos, and criollos of El Perú so that they, seeing the kindness and favor that the prudent and wise are conferring upon the beginner among them, may be encouraged to go further in such things, produced by their uncultivated faculties. I hope that the illustrious of understanding and the generous of spirit will confer this kindness and favor upon them and me with much liberality and applause, because my desire and good will in their service (as my poor labors, past, present, and to come, will show) have well deserved it. May our Lord, etc.

First Book of the History of La Florida, by the Inca

It includes the description of it; the customs of its natives; who was its first discoverer, and those who have gone there afterward; the people whom Hernando de Soto took there; the singular events of his navigation; that which he ordered and prepared in La Havana; and how he embarked for La Florida. It contains fifteen chapters.

I

HERNANDO DE SOTO ASKS OF THE EMPEROR CHARLES V THE CONQUEST OF LA FLORIDA. HIS MAJESTY GRANTS IT TO HIM

The adelantado Hernando de Soto, former governor and captain-general of the provinces and seigniories of the great kingdom of La Florida, whose history this is, together with that of many other Spanish gentlemen and Indians—which we are attempting to write for the glory and honor of the Most Holy Trinity, God, our Lord, and with the desire of advancing His holy Catholic faith and the Crown of Spain—was present at the first conquest of El Perú, and at the imprisonment of Atahuallpa, the tyrant king. This king, being a bastard son, usurped that kingdom from the legitimate heir and was the last of the Incas that monarchy had. Through his tyrannies and cruelties, which were even greater when exercised against those of his own flesh and blood, the empire was lost; or at least the discord and division that his rebellion and tyranny occasioned among the natives facilitated the Spaniards' winning it with the ease with which they did (as we shall tell elsewhere, with Divine aid). From this conquest, as is well known, came that ransom so superb, vast and rich that it exceeds all belief that can be given to human histories, according to the report of an accountant of his Majesty's hacienda in El Perú, who stated the value of the fifth of it. Calculating the whole from the fifth and reducing it to the usual coinage of Castilian ducats, each worth 375 *maravedís,* it is known that it was equivalent to 3,293,000 ducats and some *dineros,* not including what was squandered without being counted for the fifths, which was another large sum. From this quantity and from the advantages that fell to him as such an important captain, and with what the Indians presented to him in Cuzco when he and Pedro del Barco went alone to see that city, and with the gifts this same King Atahuallpa gave him (because he took a fancy to him, he being the first Spaniard whom he had seen and spoken to), this gentleman had as his share more than 100,000 ducats.

Hernando de Soto brought this sum of money when he, together with sixty other conquistadores, arrived in Spain with the shares and profits they had acquired in Cassamarca [Cajamarca]. Although with this quantity of treasure (which then, because so much had not yet come from the Indies as has been brought here since, was of more value than at present) he could have purchased in his own country, which was Villanueva de Barcarota, much more property than could be bought at present, because then possessions were not held in the esteem and value that they have today, he did not desire to buy it. Rather, his ideas and his spirit elevated by the things that he had experienced in El Perú, not content with what he had already done and acquired, but desiring to undertake other similar or greater exploits, if greater there could be, he went to Valladolid, where the Emperor Charles V, king of Spain, had his court. He petitioned that he be granted the favor of the conquest of the kingdom of La Florida (so called because of its coast having been discovered on Easter Day), which he desired to make at his own cost and risk, expending therein his property and life to serve his Majesty and advance the Crown of Spain.

This Hernando de Soto did, moved by generous envy and magnanimous jealousy of the deeds newly done in México by the marqués del Valle, Don Hernando Cortés, and in Perú by Marqués Don Francisco Pizarro and Adelantado Don Diego de Almagro, which he saw and helped to perform. However, since his free and generous spirit could not tolerate being subject or inferior to those just named in valor and energy for war, or in prudence and discretion for peace, he left behind those exploits, thought so great, and undertook these other, for him, greater ones, for in them he lost his life and the property that he had won in the others. Wherefore, because of all the principal conquests of the New World having been made in such a manner, some, not without the fault of malice and with excess of envy, have been moved to say that Spain has bought the dominion of all the New World at the expense of madmen, fools, and visionaries, without having expended any other, greater treasure. They do not consider that they are her children and that the greatest resource and treasure that she has always had, and now has, was in producing and rearing them such as they have been in order to win the New World and make her feared by the Old. In the course of this *History* we shall make use of the two terms, Spaniards and Castilians; note that we mean to signify by them the same thing.

II

DESCRIPTION OF LA FLORIDA, AND WHO WAS THE FIRST DISCOVERER OF IT, AND THE SECOND, AND THIRD

The description of the great land of La Florida will be a difficult thing to depict as completely as we should like to do, for, as it is so extensive and large in every direction, and is not won or even discovered in its entirety, its confines are unknown.

What is most certain and not unknown is that to the south lies the Ocean Sea and the great island of Cuba. To the north (although they claim Hernando de Soto went a thousand leagues inland, as we shall tell below) it is not known where it ends—whether it borders upon the sea or upon other lands.

To the east it terminates at the land they call Los Bacallaos, though a certain French cosmographer places another extremely large province between, which he calls New France, because of having simply the name there.

To the west it borders upon the provinces of the Seven Cities, so called by the discoverers of those lands. They, having left México by order of Viceroy Don Antonio de Mendoza, discovered them in the year 1539, taking as captain Juan Vázquez Coronado, vecino of the said city. By vecino is understood, in the Indies, he who has a *repartimiento* of Indians; this is the significance of the term *vecino,* because they were obliged to maintain a domicile [*vecindad*] where they had the Indians, and they could not come to Spain without the king's permission under penalty of loss of the repartimiento, after the elapse of two years during which they have not maintained a domicile.

Juan Vázquez Coronado, having discovered an extensive and very fine country, could not settle it because of the great difficulties that he encountered. He returned to México, much to the viceroy's regret, because the large and very good force of men and horses he had assembled for the conquest had been dissipated without any gain whatever. La Florida also borders to the west upon the province of the Chichimecas, a most courageous people who live along the limits of the lands of México.

The first Spaniard who discovered La Florida was Juan Ponce de León, a gentleman who was a native of León and a nobleman, having been governor of Puerto Rico. Inasmuch as the Spaniards of that time thought of nothing except the discovery of new lands, he fitted out two caravels and went in search of an island they called Bimini or, according to others, Buyoca. There, according to fabulous tales of the Indians, was a fountain that rejuvenated the aged. He traveled in search of it for many days, lost, and without finding it. At the end of this time he was driven by a storm on the coast to the north of the island of Cuba, which coast he named Florida because of the day on which he saw it being Easter. It was in the year 1513, and according to the reckoners, Easter was celebrated that year on March 27.

Juan Ponce de León was content simply with seeing that it was land, and without making any effort to ascertain whether it was the mainland or an island, he came to Spain to ask for the government and conquest of that country. The Catholic kings granted it to him, and he went thither with three ships in the year '15; others say that it was in '21. I agree with Francisco López de Gómara: Whether it was the one year or the other matters little. Having experienced some misfortunes on the voyage, he landed in La Florida. The Indians came out to meet him and fought with him bravely until they routed him and killed almost all the Spaniards who had come with him. No more than seven escaped, among them Juan Ponce de León; they went, wounded, to the island of Cuba, where all died of the wounds they bore. Such was the unhappy end of the journey of Juan Ponce de León, the first discoverer of La Florida, and it appears that he left his misfortune as a heritage to those who have followed him there on the same errand.

A few years thereafter a pilot named Miruelo, master of a caravel, while traveling about bartering with the Indians, was driven by a storm upon the coast of La Florida, or to some other land whose location is not known, where the Indians received him peaceably. In the course of his trade, called barter [*rescate*], they gave him some trifles of silver and a small quantity of gold, with which he returned very satisfied to the island of Santo Domingo, without having performed the office of a good pilot in marking out the land and taking the latitude, as he might well have done to avoid finding himself in the plight in which he was afterward by reason of this negligence.

At this same time seven wealthy men of Santo Domingo, among whom was one Lucas Vásquez de Ayllón, *oidor* of that *audiencia* and former appellate judge in the same island before the audiencia was founded, formed a company and fitted out two ships and sent them among those islands to seek and bring out Indians, which they must obtain in any way possible in order to set them to work in the gold mines the company owned. The ships set out on their worthy enterprise, and during a severe storm they came by accident upon the cape they named Santa Elena, because it was her day, and the river called Jordán, so named on sight by the mariner who first saw it. The Spaniards went ashore, and the Indians advanced with great fear to see the ships, as a strange thing they had never before seen, and they wondered at seeing bearded men who wore clothing. But with all this they treated with one another amicably, each displaying the things that they had. The Indians gave some fine marten-skins that gave off a very fragrant odor, some irregular pearls [*aljófar:* also, a seed pearl—DB], and a small amount of silver. The Spaniards also gave them their articles of trade, which being ended, and the ships having taken the stores they needed and the necessary wood and water, the Spaniards very affably invited the Indians to come aboard to see the ships and the things that they carried in them. Whereupon, trusting in the friendship and good treatment they had experienced, and in order to see things so new to them, more than 130 Indians came aboard. When they had them below decks, the Spaniards, seeing the good catch that they had made, raised anchor and set sail for Santo Domingo. But on the way one of the two ships was lost, and the Indians who remained in the other, though they reached Santo Domingo, allowed themselves to die of sadness and hunger, for they refused to eat from anger at the deception that had been practiced upon them under color of friendship.

III

CONCERNING OTHER DISCOVERERS WHO HAVE GONE TO LA FLORIDA

With the account that these Castilians gave in Santo Domingo of what they had seen, and with that of Miruelo, both of which came at almost the same time, the oidor Lucas Vázquez de Ayllón came to Spain to ask for the conquest and government of that province, which, among the many names that La Florida had, was called Chicoria. The emperor granted it, honoring him with the habit of the Order of Santiago. The oidor returned to Santo Domingo and in the year 1524 fitted out three large ships and, taking Miruelo as pilot, went with them in search of the land that Miruelo had discovered, for they said that it was richer than Chicoria. But Miruelo, as much as he tried, was never able to hit upon the place where his discovery had been made, as a result of which misfortune he fell into such melancholy that within a few days he lost his reason and his life.

The licentiate Ayllón passed on in search of his province of Chicoria, and in the Río Jordán he lost the flagship. With his two remaining ships he continued his voyage to the east and reached the coast of a pleasant and delightful country near Chicoria, where the Indians received him with much festivity and rejoicing. The oidor, believing that everything was now favorable to him, ordered that two hundred Spaniards disembark and go to see the pueblo of those Indians, which was three leagues inland. The Indians guided them, and after they had regaled them for three or four days and assured them of their friendship, they killed them one night and made a sudden assault at dawn upon the few Spaniards who had remained with the oidor on the coast to guard the ships. Having killed and wounded most of them, they forced them, broken and defeated, to embark and go back to Santo Domingo, thereby avenging the Indians of the previous expedition.

Among the few Spaniards who escaped with the oidor Lucas Vázquez de Ayllón was a gentleman named Hernando Mogollón, a native of the city of Badajoz, who later went to El Perú where he recounted at great length that which we have told briefly of this journey. I knew him there.

Following the oidor Lucas Vázquez de Ayllón, Pánphilo de Narváez went to La Florida, in the year 1557,† where he perished miserably, with all the Spaniards whom he took with him, as Alvar Núñez Cabeza de Vaca, who went with him as treasurer of the *real hacienda,* recounts in his *Naufragios.* This man escaped, with three other Spaniards and a Negro; and God, our Lord, granted them such favors that they were able to perform miracles in His name, with which they acquired such reputation and esteem among the Indians that they worshipped them as gods. However, these Spaniards did not wish to remain among them, but left the country as rapidly as they could and came to Spain to ask for new governments; and having received them, the course of events was such that they unhappily lost everything, as Alvar Núñez Cabeza de Vaca himself relates. He died in Valladolid, having come under arrest from the Río de la Plata, where he went as governor.

When Pánphilo de Narváez made his voyage to La Florida he took a pilot named Miruelo, a relative of the other and as unfortunate as he in his office, for he was never able to find the land his uncle had discovered, from whose account he had information concerning it, for which reason Pánphilo de Narváez had taken him with him.

Following this unfortunate captain, the adelantado Hernando de Soto

†*Translator's note:* The 1723 edition has 1527. Neither date is correct: Pánphilo de Narváez reached Florida on April 14, 1528. See Woodbury Lowery, *Spanish Settlements within the Present Limits of the United States, 1513–1561,* p. 177.

went to La Florida, entering it in the year '39. His history and that of the many other famous Spanish gentlemen and Indians we are attempting to write at length, together with an account of the many and large provinces he discovered up to the time of his end and death, and that which his captains and soldiers did afterward until they left the land and at length reached México.

IV

CONCERNING STILL OTHERS WHO HAVE MADE THE SAME JOURNEY TO LA FLORIDA, AND CONCERNING THE CUSTOMS AND USUAL ARMS OF ITS NATIVES

As soon as the death of Hernando de Soto was known in Spain many pretenders arose to ask for the government and conquest of La Florida. The emperor Charles V, refusing them all, in the year 1549 sent at his own expense a Dominican religious named Fray Luis Cáncer Balbastro as leader of his Order, which had offered to convert those Indians to the evangelical doctrine with their preaching. Having arrived in La Florida, these religious disembarked to preach, but the Indians, taught by their former experience with the Castilians, refusing to hear them, fell upon them and killed Fray Luis and two of his companions. The others took refuge on the ship and returned to Spain, affirming that such barbarous and inhuman people had no desire to hear sermons.

In the year 1562 a son of the oidor Lucas Vázquez de Ayllón asked for the same conquest and government, and they gave it to him. He died in La Española while preparing his expedition, and his illness and death were caused by melancholy and despair from the difficulties that arose from day to day that made the enterprise increasingly impossible. Subsequently others have gone there, among them the adelantado Pedro Meléndez de Valdés [Menéndez de Aviles]; I refrain from writing about them for I have not complete information concerning their acts.

This, though brief, is the most accurate account that it has been possible to give of the land of La Florida, and of those who have gone there to discover and conquer it. Before going on, it will be well to describe some of the customs the Indians of that great kingdom had in common, at least those the adelantado Hernando de Soto discovered. In almost all of the provinces he traversed those customs are the same, and if they differ in some places, we shall take care to note them in the course of our *History;* but in general they all follow almost the same manner of life.

These Indians are a heathen race, and idolaters; they worship the sun and the moon as chief deities but without ceremonies involving idols, or sacrifices, or prayers, or other superstitions such as other heathens practice. They had temples that served them as burial places rather than as houses of prayer where, for pomp and display, besides being sepulchers for their dead, they kept all the best and richest of their treasures. These tombs and temples were held in extreme veneration, and they placed at their doors trophies of the victories that they won over their enemies.

In general they married only one woman, and she was obliged to be most faithful to her husband under penalty imposed by the laws they had for the punishment of adultery, which in some provinces was a cruel death and in others very ignominious punishment, as we shall tell later in its place. Because of their privileged position, the rulers had the right to take as many wives as they wished, and this law or privilege of the rulers was observed throughout the Indies in the New World, but always it was with the distinction of the principal legitimate wife from the others, who were more concubines than wives. Thus they acted as servants, and the children whom they bore were neither legitimate nor equal in honor or inheritance to those of the principal wife.

Throughout El Perú the common people married only one woman, and he who took two incurred the death penalty. The Incas, who were those of royal blood, and the *curacas,* who were the overlords of vassals, had the privilege of having as many wives as they wished or could support, but with the distinction described above of the legitimate wife from the concubines. And like heathen, they said that this custom was permitted and provided among them because it was necessary that the nobles have many wives in order to have many children; in order to make war and govern the commonwealth and augment their empire they affirmed that they must have many nobles, because it was they who spent themselves in war and died in battle; to carry burdens, till the soil, and act as servants there were more than enough of the common people, who (because they were not a people who were employed in the dangerous pursuits in which the nobles engaged), however few of them might be born, still multiplied greatly. They were useless for government, nor was it legal for them to concern themselves with it, which would be an offense against the office itself, because governing and dispensing justice was the function of persons of noble birth, and not of plebians.

Returning to those of La Florida, their ordinary food is maize, in place of bread, and their viands are beans and calabashes of the variety they call here *romana,* and a great deal of fish because of the many rivers they possess. There is a scarcity of meat, for they have no species of domesticated cattle. They kill in the chase with their bows and arrows red deer, fallow deer, and roe deer, which are numerous and larger than those of Spain. They kill many kinds of birds, both in order to eat the flesh and to adorn their heads with the feathers, which they wear in showy, multicolored headdresses half a fathom tall; thereby they distinguish the nobles from the plebians in time of peace, and the soldiers from those who are not such in time of war. Their drink is clear water, just as nature gives it to them, without the admixture of anything else. The meat and the fish they eat must be very well dressed and cooked, and the fruit very ripe. They will never eat it green or half-ripe and laugh at the Castilians for eating green fruit.

Those who say that they eat human flesh attribute this to them falsely, at least to those of the provinces our governor discovered. On the contrary they abominate it, as Alvar Núñez Cabeza de Vaca notes in Chapters 14 and 17 of his *Naufragios,* where he says that certain Castilians who were lodged apart died of hunger, and that their remaining companions ate those who had died, except for the buttocks, which none of them would eat, whereupon, he says, the Indians were so scandalized that they were on the point of killing all those who were left in another lodging. It may be that they eat it [human flesh] at places where our people did not go; La Florida is so large and extensive that there is room for all [customs].

They go about naked except for some garments of chamois-skin of various colors almost like very short breeches, which cover them decently, as much as necessary, in front and behind. In the place of a cloak they wear mantles clasped at the throat, which reach half-way down the leg; they are of extremely fine marten-skins, which give off the odor of musk. They also make them of small skins of various animals, such as several kinds of cat, fallow deer, roe deer, red deer, bears, lions, and of skins of cattle [buffalo]. Those hides they dress to such extreme perfection that the skin of a cow or a bear, with the hair on it, they prepare in a manner that leaves it so pliant and soft that it can be worn as a cloak, and it serves them for bed-covering at night. Their hair grows long and they wear it gathered up into a large knot on top of their heads. For a headdress they wear a thick skein of thread in whatever color they desire, which they wind about their heads and tie the ends over the forehead in two half-knots, so that one end hangs down over either temple as far as the ears. The women dress in chamois-skin, having the whole body decently covered.

The arms these Indians carry are bows and arrows, and—although it is true that they are skillful in the use of the other weapons they have, such as pikes, lances, darts, halberds, the sling, club, broadsword and staff, and other similar ones, if there are others except the harquebus and crossbow which they do not possess—with all this they do not [ordinarily] use any other arms except the bow and arrow, because for those who carry them they are the greatest embellishment and ornament. The ancient heathen for the same reason depicted their most beloved gods, as Apollo, Diana and Cupid, with bows and arrows, for besides that which these arms signify in themselves, they are very beautiful and add to the grace and elegance of him who carries them. For all these reasons, and because of the effectiveness of these arms, which are superior to all others at both short and long range, in retreating or attacking, in fighting in battle or in the recreation of the hunt, these Indians carry them, and these arms are much used throughout the New World.

The bows are of the same height as he who carries them, and as these Indians of La Florida are generally of large stature, their bows are more than two *varas* in length and thick in proportion. They make them of oak and of various other hard and very heavy woods they have. They are so hard to bend that no Spaniard, however much he tried, was able to pull the cord back so that his hand touched his face, but the Indians through their long experience and skill drew back the cord with the greatest ease to a point behind the ear and made such valiant and wonderful shots as we shall see presently.

They make the cords of the bows from deerskin, taking a strip two finger-breadths in width from the hide, running from the tip of the tail to the head. After removing the hair they dampen and twist it tightly; one end they tie to the branch of a tree, and from the other they hang a weight of four or five *arrobas*, and they leave it thus until it becomes about the thickness of the larger strings of a bass viol. These cords are extremely strong. In order to shoot safely in such a manner that when the cord springs back it may not injure the left arm, they wear as a protection on the inner side a half-bracer, which covers them from the wrist to the part of the arm that is usually bled [*sangradura*]. It is made of thick feathers and attached to the arm with a deerskin cord, which they give seven or eight turns at the place where the cord springs back most strongly.

This, in short, is what can be said of the life and customs of the Indians of La Florida; and now we shall return to Hernando de Soto, who asked for the conquest and the government of that great kingdom, which has been so luckless and so costly to all who have gone to it.

V

THE PROVISIONS OF THE CONQUEST ARE PUBLISHED IN SPAIN, AND THE GREAT PREPARATIONS THAT ARE MADE FOR IT

The Imperial Majesty granted the conquest to Hernando de Soto with the title of adelantado and marqués of a state thirty leagues in length and fifteen in breadth, in whatever place he might choose from that which he could conquer at his own expense. He was also conceded, for the term of his life, the office of governor and captain-general of La Florida, as he was also of the island of Santiago de Cuba, in order that its vecinos and inhabitants should obey him as their governor and captain, and aid him more promptly in the things that he might command them, necessary for the conquest. Hernando de Soto very prudently requested the governorship of Cuba, because it is a matter of great importance to him who goes to discover, conquer, and settle La Florida.

These titles and honors were published throughout Spain, with much noise about the new enterprise that Hernando de Soto was undertaking, of going to subjugate and win great kingdoms and provinces for the Crown of Spain. And as it was said everywhere that the captain who was doing this had been a conquistador of El Perú, and that, not content with the 100,000 ducats that he had brought from there, he was spending them in this second conquest, everyone marveled at it and considered this much better and richer than the first. Therefore from all parts of Spain there gathered many gentlemen of very illustrious lineage, many hidalgos, many soldiers experienced in the military arts who served the Spanish Crown in various parts of the world, and many citizens and laborers. All [attracted by] such favorable reports of the new conquest, and in view of such quantities of silver and gold and precious stones as they had seen brought from the New World, leaving their lands, parents, relatives and friends, and selling their property, appeared and offered themselves personally and by letter to go on this conquest, with hopes that it would be as rich as, or richer than, the two previous ones of México and El Perú. With the same hopes, six or seven of the conquistadores who we said had returned from El Perú also were moved to go on this journey to La Florida, not considering that the land they were going in search of could not be better than that which they had left, nor yet satisfied with the riches they had brought from it; it appears rather that their desire for them increased in accordance with their nature, which is insatiable. We will name the conquistadores in the course of this *History,* as they appear.

As soon as the governor ordered his concessions to be made public, he busied himself in giving directions for the purchase of ships, arms, munitions, provisions, and the other things pertaining to such a vast enterprise as the one that he had undertaken. For these duties he chose persons, each of whom was capable in his office; he assembled soldiers and named captains and officers for the army, as we shall recount in the following chapter; in short, he prepared with all the magnificence and liberality of one who could command and who desired everything conducive to his task.

Since the general and the other captains and officials attended with such liberality to the expenditure and with such diligence to the affairs that each had in his charge, they were concluded and all of them assembled together in San Lúcar de Barrameda (where they were to embark) in a little more than the year his Majesty's concessions had provided. The ships being brought up, the appointed day having come for the arrival at this same port of the men enlisted, and all of them having assembled, they being most excellent; and the other preparations being completed, alike of ship-stores, and of much iron, steel, irons for saddlebows, spades, mattocks, panniers, ropes, and baskets—things very necessary for settlements—they embarked and began their voyage in the following manner.

VI

OF THE NUMBER OF MEN AND CAPTAINS WHO EMBARKED FOR LA FLORIDA

Nine hundred and fifty Spaniards of all classes met in San Lúcar de Barrameda to go for the conquest of La Florida; all young men, for there was scarcely one among them who had gray hairs (a very important thing for withstanding the labors and difficulties offered by new conquests). To many of them the governor gave aid in the form of money, sending it to each one in accordance with his quality and condition and the following and servants that he brought with him. Many received this assistance through necessity, and others (with respect and civility, seeing the vast enterprise that the general had on his shoulders) refused to receive it, it appearing to them more fitting to assist the governor, if they could, than to be assisted by him.

When the time of the spring tides came, they embarked in seven large ships and three small ones, which had been purchased in various Spanish ports. The adelantado, with all his household, his wife, and family, embarked in a ship called the *San Cristóbal,* of eight hundred tons, which went as flagship of the fleet; it was well equipped with fighting men, artillery and munitions, as befitted the flagship of such a great captain.

In another ship, no smaller, called *La Magdalena,* embarked Nuño Tovar, one of the sixty conquistadores, a native of Xerez de Badajoz. This gentleman went as lieutenant general, and he took with him another nobleman, Don Carlos Enríquez, a native of the same city, the second son of one of its great estates. Luis de Moscoso de Alvarado, son of the knight commander Diosdado de Alvarado, a gentleman who was a native of Badajoz and a vecino of Zafra, and one of the sixty conquistadores, chosen and appointed *maese de campo* of the army, went as captain of the galleon called *La Concepción,* which was of more than five hundred tons' burden.

In another galleon, equally as large, called *Buena Fortuna,* went Captain Andrés de Vasconcelos, a Portuguese *fidalgo* and gentleman, native of Yelves. He took a very fine and resplendent company of Portuguese fidalgos, some of whom had been soldiers on the African frontiers. Diego García, son of the alcalde of Villanueva de Barcarrota, went as captain of another large ship, called the *San Juan.* Arias Tinoco, named as captain of infantry, went as captain of another large ship, called *Santa Bárbara.*

Alonso Romo de Cardeñosa, a brother of Arias Tinoco who also was named captain of infantry, went as captain of a small galleon called *San Anton.* With this captain went another of his brothers, named Diego Arias Tinoco, chosen as *alférez general* of the army. These three brothers were relatives of the general. Pedro Calderón, a gentleman who was a native of Badajoz, went as captain of a very fine caravel, and with him went Captain Micer Espíndola, a Genoese gentleman, who was captain of sixty halberdiers of the governor's guard. Besides these eight ships, they took two brigantines for the service of the fleet, which, being lighter and more easily handled than the large ships, served as scouts to keep watch on the sea in every direction.

In these seven ships, the caravel and the brigantines, the 950 fighting men embarked, besides the sailors and the people needed for the management and service of each vessel. In addition to the people whom we have named, there went with the fleet twelve priests, eight clerics and four friars. The clerics whose names can be recalled are Rodrigo de Gallegos, a native of Sevilla and a relative of Baltasar de Gallegos; Diego de Bañuelos and Francisco del Pozo, natives of Córdoba; and Dionisio de París, a native of France, of the same city of París. The names of the other four clerics have been forgotten. The friars were named Fray Luis de Soto, a native of Villanueva de Barcarrota and a relative of Governor Hernando de Soto; Fray Juan de Gallegos, a native of Sevilla and brother of Captain Baltasar de Gallegos—both friars of the Order of St. Francis; and Fray Francisco de la Rocha, a native of Badajoz, of the advocation and insignia of the Most Holy Trinity. All were most exemplary and learned men.

With this fleet of La Florida went that of México, composed of twenty large ships, of which Hernando de Soto also was general as far as the place of the island of Santiago de Cuba, where it separated from the others to go to Vera Cruz. There was named as its general, from that point onward, a prominent nobleman called Gonzalo de Salazar, the first Christian born in Granada after the Moors left from there; wherefore, though he was already a nobleman and hidalgo, the Catholic kings of glorious memory who won that city gave him great privileges and granted him favors from which he founded an entailed estate for his descendants. This gentleman had been a conquistador of México, and was returning as factor of the imperial hacienda of the city of México.

In this order the thirty ships of the two fleets left for the bar of San Lúcar and set sail on April 6 of the year 1538, and they navigated that day and many others with all the good fortune and fair weather that could be desired. The fleet of La Florida was so well supplied with all kinds of ship-stores that all who went in it were given double rations, an unwise thing, because all of the large surplus was squandered; but the general's munificence was such, and so great was his satisfaction in taking with him such a brilliant and noble company, that he had little regard for anything except his desire to regale them.

VII

WHAT HAPPENED TO THE FLEET ON THE FIRST NIGHT OF ITS VOYAGE

On the first day of their navigation, a little before nightfall, the general called a soldier named Gonzalo Silvestre, a native of Herrera de Alcántara, one of the many whom he had chosen to take near his person, and said to him: "Take care to give orders tonight to the sentries as to the manner of sailing, and direct the constable, who is the chief of artillery, to have all his guns prepared and ready, and if any suspicious-looking ship appears have him fire across it, and observe in everything the order required by good navigation." All this was provided for, as the governor ordered.

The voyage proceeding, then, with very favorable weather, a little after midnight it happened that the mariners of the ship that was to be flagship of the fleet of México, on which was the factor, Gonzalo de Salazar—either to demonstrate its speed and lightness, or assuming that it also was a flagship like that of Hernando de Soto, or, more likely, because the pilot and the master were asleep as a result of the fair weather, and the sailor who steered the ship was ignorant of the rules and laws of navigation—allowed it to outstrip the whole fleet and continue in advance of it a cannon-shot to the windward of the flagship. For either of these two things that mariners may do the penalty is death.

Gonzalo Silvestre, who, in order to give a good account of that which had been entrusted to him, though he had posted his sentinels, was not sleeping (as befits all good soldiers and hidalgos, such as he was), awakened the constable and asked him whether that ship belonged to their fleet and company or was an enemy. He replied to him that it could not belong to the fleet, for if it did, it would not dare to go where it was going because the mariners who did such a thing would incur the death penalty. Therefore he affirmed that it belonged to an enemy. With this both of them determined to fire on it. With the first shot all the sails were pierced through the center, from stem to stern, and with the second shot the upper works of one side were carried away. They were preparing to fire again when they heard its people shouting loudly, asking for mercy, and saying not to fire upon them, that they were friends.

The governor got up at the noise, and the whole fleet was aroused and placed under arms facing the Mexican ship, which, as its speed slackened because of the damage done to the sails by the cannon-shots, was falling to the leeward upon the flagship, and the latter, which was going after it, soon overtook it. Here there was about to happen another and greater evil and misfortune than that which had already taken place, which was that—as some, in fear and confusion from their dereliction, were more intent upon exculpating themselves than in managing their ship, and the others, in their wrath and anger in thinking that the action was due to want of respect and not to carelessness, and desiring to punish or avenge it, were not watching how or where they were going—the two ships were about to meet and collide broadside. They were so close together that those within them, in order to save themselves from this danger, finding no better remedy, hastily grasped many pikes with which they pushed the two ships apart so that they might not strike. They broke more than three hundred pikes, after the manner of a very fine irregular conflict in a foot tournament, and they produced a good effect. But although the pikes and other sticks prevented a violent collision, they did not prevent the rigging, sails and lateen yards from crossing and striking, so that both were in imminent danger of being sunk, for all was abandoned when everyone attempted to save himself, and the mariners, disturbed with such evident and sudden peril, trusted to no remedy nor knew what to do that would help them. When someone attempted to do something, the clamor of the people, who saw death before their eyes, was so great that they could not hear him; nor would the darkness of the night, which increases terrors, allow them to see what ought to be done; nor could those who had some valor and energy give orders, for there was no one to obey them or to listen when all was wails, shouts, clamor, outcries and confusion.

Both generals and their two flagships were at this pass when God, our Lord, succored them; the *tajamares* [cutwater, which divides the water before it reaches the bow—DB] or knives the governor's ship carried on its lateen yards cut through all the lines, rigging and sails on the factor's ship that held the two together. These being cut, the general's ship, with the good wind that was blowing, was able to draw off from the other, both being free.

Hernando de Soto was so wrathful, as much because of having found himself in this danger just passed and also because of thinking that the act that had caused it had been committed maliciously through disrespect, that he was on the point of committing a great excess in ordering that the factor be beheaded immediately. But the latter exculpated himself with great humility, saying that he was not to blame in any way for what had happened, and everyone on his ship testified to the same effect. With this, and with the friendly mediators who were not lacking on the governor's ship, who excused and took the part of the factor, the general's ire was appeased, and he pardoned him and forgot all that had taken place. The factor Gonzalo de Salazar, however, after his arrival in México, whenever the events of that night were mentioned always said, with the air of a man somewhat offended by the affair, that it would please him to meet Hernando de Soto on equal terms, in order to charge and challenge him regarding the high words that he had said to him in an excess of anger concerning a matter in which he was not to blame. And it was true that he was not at fault, but neither had the general said anything to him from which he could take offense; but as the one suspected that the action had been malicious, so the other was angered, considering his words to have been offensive. Neither of them forgot the affair, for suspicion and anger have very great force and influence over men so important and powerful as were our two captains.

The mariners of the factor's ship having repaired the damage to the sails and rigging with their accustomed promptness, diligence and skill in such cases, they continued their voyage, giving thanks to Our Lord for having delivered them from such peril.

VIII

THE FLEET ARRIVES AT SANTIAGO DE CUBA, AND WHAT HAPPENED TO THE FLAGSHIP AT THE ENTRANCE OF THE PORT

Without any other event worth relating, the governor arrived on Easter Day, April 21, at La Gomera, one of the Canary Islands, where he found the count who was lord of the island, and who received him with great festivities and rejoicing.

Concerning this episode, Alonso de Carmona in his *Peregrination* says the following:

> We left the port of San Lúcar in the year '38, during Lent, and sailed by way of the islands of La Gomera, which is where all the fleets go to take water and replenish the ship-stores. We sighted La Gomera after fifteen days' voyage, and I shall tell two things that happened that day in my ship. One was that two soldiers who were engaged in a fistfight fell into the sea and went under, and

> no trace of them was ever seen. The other was that a hidalgo named Tapia, a native of Arévalo, who was going there, was taking a very fine and valuable greyhound, and about twelve leagues from the port it fell into the sea. As we had a fair wind it happened that we could not recover it, and we proceeded on our voyage and came into port. On the morning of the next day the master saw his greyhound on shore and, wondering at it, went to recover it, much pleased. He who had it protested and averred that while coming in a boat from one island to the other they had found it swimming in the sea and had put it in the boat, and he asserted that the greyhound had been swimming for five hours. We took on fresh provisions and other things and proceeded on our voyage. In sight of La Gomera the master of the greyhound came aboard, and the sail gave him a push that threw him into the sea; he sank as if he were lead and never appeared again, which caused much sorrow to the whole fleet, etc.

All these are words of Alonso de Carmona, copied literally and included here because the three events he recounts are notable and also so that it may be seen how his account conforms with ours, alike with regard to the year and to the first fifteen days of the voyage, and to the storm and the port they made, all of which corresponds with our *History*. In the same way and for the same reason I shall include many other passages of his and of Juan Coles, who is the other eyewitness. They were in this expedition, along with my author.

After the three days of Easter in which they took on the needed supplies, they continued their voyage. During those days the governor prevailed upon the count, with many requests and supplications, to give him a natural daughter of his, seventeen years of age, named Doña Leonor de Bobadilla, to take with him and marry off and make a great lady in his new conquest. The count acceded to the governor's demands, confiding in his generosity to perform much more than he promised him, and thus she was turned over to Doña Isabel de Bobadilla, the wife of the adelantado Hernando de Soto, so that receiving her as a daughter, she should take her in her company.

With this lady, whose beauty was remarkable, the governor left the island of La Gomera very well content, on April 24, and with the fair wind he always had he sighted the island of Santiago de Cuba at the end of May. The factor Gonzalo de Salazar had asked permission twelve days before to withdraw with the fleet of México and direct his voyage to Vera Cruz, which he desired very much to do in order to leave another's jurisdiction (for the human will would always prefer command to obedience), and the governor had granted it very readily, understanding the desire he had for it.

The adelantado and those of his fleet were coming into port with much rejoicing and festivity at seeing the end of that long voyage and their arrival at a place so much desired by them, to attend to and make ready near at hand the things pertaining to their expedition and conquest, when suddenly they saw a man coming whom the people of the city of Santiago had sent out on horseback, running toward the entrance of the port and shouting to the flagship, which was on the point of entering it, saying, "A-port, a-port" (which in the language of sailors, for those who do not understand it, means to the right-hand side of the ship), with the intention that the flagship and those following it should all be lost on some very dangerous shoals and rocks in that part of the harbor.

That pilot and the mariners, who were not as well acquainted with the entrance of that port as they might have been (wherefore is seen the importance of knowledge and experience in this office), turned the ship in the direction indicated by the man on horseback. The latter, who had recognized that the fleet was of friends and not of enemies, turned again and in a louder voice shouted the opposite, "To the starboard" (which is the left-hand side of the ship); that they would be lost. [Garcilaso, apparently unfamiliar with such terminology, reversed *a babor* (port) and *a estribor* (starboard). Shelby's translation is correct.—DB] To make himself better understood, he dismounted and ran to his right, making signs with his arms and his cape and saying, "Turn, turn to the other side; you will all be lost!" Those on the flagship, when they understood him, turned as rapidly as possible to the left, but as hard as they tried they could not prevent the ship from striking so hard against a rock that all on board thought that it was stove in and lost. Resorting to the pump, they brought out along with the water a great deal of wine, vinegar, oil, and honey, many of the casks containing these liquors, which they were bringing, having been broken by the blow of the ship against the rock, at the sight of which were verified the fears that they had felt that the ship was lost. The small boat was launched hastily and took to land the governor's wife and her ladies and maids, and hard after them came some young gentlemen, inexperienced in such dangers, who were in such haste to enter the boat that they lost the respect due to the ladies and did not hold back or allow them to enter first, they feeling that it was no time for courtesy. The general, like a good and experienced captain, was unwilling to leave the ship, though they importuned him to do so, before seeing how much damage it had received, and also in order to be at hand to aid it if this should be necessary, and by his own presence to prevent all the others leaving it. A number of sailors going below, therefore, they found that there had been no damage besides the breaking of the casks, and that the ship was whole and sound, as was shown when the pump brought up no more water. Whereupon everyone rejoiced, and those who had conducted themselves so badly and had been in such haste to go ashore were ashamed.

IX

NAVAL BATTLE BETWEEN TWO SHIPS WITHIN THE HARBOR OF SANTIAGO DE CUBA, WHICH LASTED FOUR DAYS

For the exoneration of the people of the city it will be just for us to tell the reason that impelled them to give this false notice that led to the events that have been described. Certainly a fair consideration of the incident that caused it, and the stubborn contest that took place there, will show that it was a notable and memorable case, which in some sort excuses those citizens, because the fear in the minds of the common people prevents and hinders good counsels. It must be known, then, that ten days before the governor arrived at the port there entered it a very fine ship belonging to one Diego Pérez, a native of Sevilla, who was traveling through those islands trading. Although he went in the guise of a merchant, he was a very good soldier by land and by sea, as we shall see. It is not known what his rank was, but his habitual dignity and the nobility he showed in his conversation, dealings and trading showed, they say, that he was by rights an hidalgo; for certainly his actions were noble. This trading captain [*capitán plático*] brought his ship very well supplied with men, arms, artillery and munitions in case it should be necessary to fight with the corsairs whom he might meet among those islands and seas, they being very common there. After Diego Pérez had been in the port for three days, it happened that another ship, no smaller than his, belonging to a French corsair who was pursuing his enterprise, entered it.

As soon as the two ships recognized one another as belonging to enemy nations, both attacked, and they fought grappled together all day, until night separated them. As soon as the fighting ceased the two captains exchanged visits by sending messengers to one another with very courteous messages and with gifts and presents of wine and conserves and dried and fresh fruits, which each of them had, as if they were two very fast friends. And they made agreements on their word of honor that thenceforth they would not attack or commit hostilities at night, but only in the daytime, nor would they fire with artillery, saying that hand-to-hand combat, with swords and lances, more befitted brave men than did missile weapons, because cross-bows and harquebuses gave evidence in themselves of having been inventions of cowardly or needy spirits; and that not attacking with artillery, in addition to fighting in a genteel manner and conquering by strength of arm and personal prowess, would have the further advantage to the victor of leaving the ship and the prize he might gain in good condition and not damaged. The truces were kept inviolably, but it cannot be known for certain what they may have had in mind in not attacking with artillery unless it was the fear that both would perish without advantage to either of them. Notwithstanding the agreement made, they kept watch and were cautious at night in order not to be taken by surprise, because a good soldier ought not to trust the enemy's word to the point of neglecting proper precautions for his welfare and life.

On the second day they returned obstinately to the fray and did not stop fighting until weariness and hunger parted them; then, having eaten and rested, they returned anew to the battle, which lasted until sunset. Then they withdrew and took up their positions, and visited and exchanged presents as on the previous day. Each asked after the other's health and offered such medicines as he had for the wounded.

On the following night Captain Diego Pérez sent a message to the city saying that they had seen clearly what he had done during those days to kill or subdue the enemy, and as he had been unable to do so because of finding him very obstinate, he begged them (for it was very important to the city to rid their seas and coasts of such a corsair as that one) to agree to promise him that if he should lose the battle, as seemed probable, they would restore to him or to his heirs the value of his ship, less a thousand pesos. He offered to fight with the adversary until he overcame him or died at his hands, and he asked this recompense because he was poor and had no property except this ship; if he were rich he would take pleasure in risking it freely in their service. If he should win, he would desire no reward from them. The city was unwilling to grant this favor to Diego Pérez; on the other hand they replied rudely, saying that he might do as he liked, that they did not wish to obligate themselves to anything. Seeing the unfavorable reply to his petition and so much ingratitude in return for his good will and intentions, he determined to fight for his honor, life and property without expecting reward from another, saying that he who was able to serve himself so does ill in serving another; that the rewards of men almost always are like this one.

As soon as the third day of the battle of these brave captains dawned, Diego Pérez was ready to fight, and he went against his enemy with the same spirit and gallantry as on the two days past, in order to let those of the city understand that he was not relying upon them in fighting, but upon God and his own good spirit and strength. The Frenchman came out to meet him with no less desire to triumph or to die on that day as on the others. It seems certain that obstinacy and having made it an affair of honor impelled them to fight more than the advantage that might come to one in despoiling the other, because when the ships were taken their contents could have been of little value. Grappled with one another, then, they fought throughout that day as they had on the two previous ones, separating only to eat and rest when absolutely necessary. After a rest they returned to the battle with as much spirit as if it were just beginning, and always with more anger and fury at not being able to conquer. Darkness separated them, with many wounded and some dead on either side. But immediately upon retiring, they visited and regaled one another as before with gifts and presents as if there had never been any difference between them. Thus they passed the night, the whole city wondering that two private persons who were going out to make their living, without any other necessity or obligation to impel them, should persist so obstinately in killing one another, there being no other reward than having killed the other, nor any hope of recompense from their kings, for they were not acting in their service or in their pay; but human passion is capable of all this and more when it begins to prevail.

X

THE NAVAL BATTLE CONTINUES ITS COURSE, UNTIL IT IS FINISHED

With the coming of the fourth day, the two ships having fired a salvo and given a verbal salute to one another, according to the custom of navigators, Spaniards and Frenchmen returned stubbornly to the battle, with the same spirit and determination as on the three days past, although with smaller forces, for they were now very tired and many of them were badly wounded. But the desire for honor, which so influences generous spirits, gave them energy and strength to suffer and sustain such labor. They fought throughout the day, as before, separating only to eat and rest and tend the wounded, and then they returned to the battle anew until night imposed peace upon them. Having withdrawn, they did not fail to visit one another with their offerings of gifts and fair words. The two such contrary extremes of enmity and friendliness that were in evidence between these captains on those four days certainly are notable; for it is true that their conflict was of mortal enemies anxious to take one another's lives and property, and in quitting it, all became brotherly friendliness, they desiring to make every demonstration possible to show that they were no less courteous and affable in peace than valiant and fierce in war, and that they were no less desirous of conquering in one manner than in the other.

Returning to those [events] of the battle, the Spaniard, who that day had felt some weakness in his enemy, sent to him along with his compliments and gifts to say that he desired extremely that that battle, which had lasted so long, should not cease until one of the two had gained the victory; he begged him to await him on the following day, promising him good rewards if he would do so. In order to obligate him under military rules not to leave that night, he challenged him anew for the battle on the following day, saying that he was confident he would not refuse, for in all the past action he had shown himself such an illustrious and valiant captain.

The Frenchman, making a great show of enthusiasm for the new challenge, replied that he accepted it and would await the next day and many others, if necessary, to accomplish his desire and conclude that battle, whose end he desired no less than his adversary; of this he might be certain and might rest at ease throughout the night, gaining vigor and strength for the following day; and he begged him that that challenge should not be feigned and given slyly and artfully to reassure him and put him off his guard, so that he [the Spaniard] might go to seek safety during the coming night. This he desired, in truth and in fact, in order to show in his person the valor of his nation.

But after all this bravado, when he [the Frenchman] found a propitious time he weighed anchor as silently as possible and set sail, having no compunction at breaking a promise given, to his own prejudice and hurt; and in fact its observance in such cases would be fatuous, for a change of counsel is the part of a wise man, particularly in war because of the instability of its events, not seen in time of peace, and also because its ultimate purpose is to gain victory.

The sentries of the Spanish ship, though they heard some noise from the Frenchman, did not make an outcry or give the alarm, thinking that they were making ready for the coming battle and not for flight. When daylight came they found that they had been hoaxed. Captain Diego Pérez much regretted that his enemies had gone, because from the weakness he had observed in them on the previous day he was very sure of victory for himself; and still desiring it, taking from the city what he needed for his men, he went in search of his adversaries.

XI

OF THE CELEBRATIONS THEY HELD FOR THE GOVERNOR IN SANTIAGO DE CUBA

As the result of an affair so notable and so strange the city of Santiago was left much disturbed and very fearful, and as it occurred such a short time before the governor reached the port, they feared that it was the recent corsair who, having joined others with him, was returning to sack and burn the city. Therefore they gave the false directions of which we have told so that they might be wrecked on the rocks and shoals that are at the entrance of the harbor.

The governor disembarked, and the whole city went out with much rejoicing and gladness to receive him and give felicitations for his happy arrival. In apology for having angered him with their ill-directed precautions, they recounted at more length and in detail all the events of the four-day battle of the Frenchman with the Spaniard and the visits and the presents that were exchanged, and they begged him to pardon them, for their great fear had given rise to this bad counsel. But they did not exonerate themselves of having been so cruel and ungrateful toward Diego Pérez, as the governor learned later in more detail, and he wondered at it no less than at the fight and the courteous exchanges between the two captains. Because it is certain that they informed him that, besides the ungrateful reply they had given to the protection that Diego Pérez had offered them, they had been so severe with him that during the whole four days that he had fought, the battle being in their service, and the whole city having come out to see it every day, they had never offered to aid him while he fought or to give him so much as a jar of water while he was resting; rather they had treated him as scornfully as if he had been of a nation and a religion inimical to theirs. Nor had they been willing to do anything against the Frenchman to their own advantage, for by sending twenty or thirty men on a bark or raft to make a feint of falling upon the enemy from the other side, without ever engaging him and simply by diverting him, they could have given the victory to their friend. Any assistance, however small, would have been enough to win it, for their forces were so nearly equal that they were able to fight four days without either's gaining an advantage. But the people of the city were unwilling to do this or anything else for themselves or for the Spaniard, as if they themselves were not Spaniards, fearing that if the Frenchman were victorious he would sack or burn it, bringing in others to help him, as they had suspected him of doing, and not remembering that an enemy by nation or by religion, being victorious, does not know how to have regard for the evils that were not committed against him or gratitude for favors received or compunction at breaking a word or a promise given, as is seen by many examples, both ancient and modern. Therefore in war (especially against infidels) let the enemy always be regarded as an enemy and suspected, and the friend as a friend and to be trusted; for the latter ought to be relied upon, and the former feared and his word never trusted; better to lose one's life than to rely on it, because as infidels they boast of breaking their word and hold it as an article of religion, especially against the faithful. Therefore the governor did not fail to blame those of the city of Santiago who had not aided Diego Pérez, because he was of their same religion and nation.

As we said, the general was received with much festivity and universal rejoicing throughout the city, for from the favorable reports of his prudence and affability his presence had been much desired. To this satisfaction was added another, no lesser one, which doubled the pleasure and gladness, in the person of the bishop of that church, Fray Hernando de Mesa, Dominican, who was a holy man, and had gone in the same fleet with the governor, and was the first prelate who had come there. He was almost drowned in disembarking from the ship, for at the moment when his lordship was leaving the ship and stepping into the boat, the latter moved outward in such a manner that he could not reach it (because of his long robes) and fell between the two vessels. As he came to the surface of the water his head struck the boat, and he was about to perish when the sailors, jumping into the water, brought him out. The city, finding itself with two such important personages for the government of both estates, ecclesiastical and secular, for many days did not cease to entertain them, sometimes with dances, balls and masquerades, which were held at night; sometimes with games in which they ran and speared bulls with cane spears. On other days they entertained themselves on horseback by riding at the rings, and those who excelled in this sport either in dexterity with arms and in horsemanship, or in ingenuity in letters, or in novelty of invention, or in elegance of attire, were given prizes of honor consisting of ornaments of gold and silver, silk and brocade, which were set aside for the victors. On the other hand, they also gave rewards of abuse to those who performed worst. There were no jousts or tournaments, on horseback or on foot, for lack of armor.

Many of the gentlemen who had come with the governor took part in these celebrations and entertainments, both to show their skill in all these things as well as to entertain the people of the city, for the satisfaction was mutual. For these celebrations and entertainments the many and excellent horses—alike in performance, size and color—that they have in the island were of much assistance (as they always are both in sport and in work); because in addition to the natural excellence of those of this country, they bred them at that time with great care and in large numbers. There were private persons who had in their stables twenty or thirty horses, and the wealthy [had] fifty or sixty, for profit, because for the new conquests that had been made and were being made in El Perú, México, and other places, they sold very well, and this was the most important and largest source of revenue the inhabitants of the island of Cuba and its environs had at that time.

XII

THE PROVISIONS THE GOVERNOR OBTAINED IN SANTIAGO DE CUBA, AND A NOTABLE CASE CONCERNING THE NATIVES OF THOSE ISLANDS

For almost three months the governor's people amused themselves with celebrations and entertainments, all being peace and harmony between them and the people of the city, for they treated one another with all friendliness and good hospitality. The governor, who was attending to more-weighty matters, visited during this time the pueblos that were in the island, appointed ministers of justice to remain in them as his lieutenants, and purchased many horses for the journey. His chief subordinates did the same, for which reason he aided many of them even more than he had done in San Lúcar, because in order to buy horses it was necessary to assist them more generously.

The people of the island presented many to him, for as we have said they raised them in large numbers, and that country was then prosperous and wealthy and very well populated with Indians, almost all of whom hanged themselves shortly thereafter. The reason was that, as that whole region is a very warm and humid country, the natives who were there were delicate and lazy and unsuited to labor; and because of the great fertility of the land and the many fruits it produced, there was no necessity for them to work very much in sowing and harvesting, for from the little maize that they sowed they gathered each year more than they needed for obtaining a simple living, and they desired no more. Inasmuch as they did not recognize gold as wealth or esteem it, they regarded taking it out of the streams and from the face of the land where they were bred as an evil, and they felt excessively the molestation the Spaniards occasioned them in the matter, however slight it might be. Also, as the devil incited them on his part and could do whatever he liked with a people so simple, vicious and idle, it came about that, so that they might not have to extract gold, which is abundant in this island and of good quality, they hanged themselves in such manner and so hastily that one day at dawn there were fifty adjoining houses of Indians who were hanged, together with their wives and children, in the same pueblo, there scarcely remaining one man alive in it. It was the most pitiful thing in the world to see them hanging from the trees like thrushes caught in a snare, and the restraints the Spaniards adopted and applied were not enough to prevent them. The natives of that island and its environs were consumed by this such abominable evil, and today there are almost none of them left. This fact gave rise later to the present high price of Negroes, to be taken to all parts of the Indies for labor in the mines.

Among other things that the governor provided for in Santiago de Cuba was to order that a captain named Mateo Azeituno, a gentleman who was a native of Talabera de la Reyna, go with some men by sea to rebuild the city of La Havana, because he had received news that a few days before French corsairs had sacked and burned it, not respecting the temple nor venerating the images that were in it, whereat the governor and all his people, as Catholics, were much distressed. In short, the general provided everything that seemed to him necessary for proceeding with the conquest, to which end that which we shall tell was of no little assistance. This was that in the Villa de la Trinidad, which is one of the pueblos of that island, there lived a very wealthy and prominent gentleman named Vasco Porcallo de Figueroa, a near relative of the most illustrious house of Feria. He visited the governor in the city of Santiago de Cuba, and as he was there for some days and saw the gallantry and display of so many gentlemen and such good soldiers as were going on this expedition, and the magnificent equipment that was provided for it, he could not restrain himself, now that warlike affairs were recalled to his mind, and his own desires for them were kindled anew. He thereupon offered himself voluntarily to the governor to go with him for the conquest of La Florida, so renowned. Neither his age, now more than fifty years, nor the many hardships that he had undergone, alike in the Indies, in Spain, and in Italy, where in his youth he had triumphed in two remarkable battles, nor his large property, many cattle, and acquisitions by arms, nor the natural desire that men usually have to enjoy them, could deter him. Putting it all aside, he desired to follow the adelantado, for which purpose he offered him his person, life and property.

The governor, seeing such heroic determination and that he was not moved by desire for wealth or honor, but by the natural generosity and warlike spirit this gentleman had always had, accepted his offer, and having thanked him in extravagant terms, which were justified as an expression of the honor such a great deed merited, he named him as lieutenant general of his whole fleet and army. Some days previously he had deposed Nuño Tovar from this position for having married clandestinely Doña Leonor de Bobadilla, the daughter of the count of La Gomera.

Vasco Porcallo de Figueroa y de la Cerda, as a generous and very wealthy man, gave magnificent assistance for the conquest of La Florida, for besides the many Spanish, Indian and Negro servants he took on this expedition, and besides the rest of the equipment and movables of his household, he took thirty-six horses for his personal use and more than fifty others that he presented to private gentlemen in the army.

He provided a large supply of salt beef, fish, maize, cassava, and other things the fleet needed. He was the cause of many of the Spaniards who lived in the island of Cuba being moved, in imitation of him, to go on this expedition. With all these things, in a short time there were made ready those things needed so that the fleet and military forces could leave and set out for La Havana.

XIII

THE GOVERNOR GOES TO LA HAVANA, AND THE PREPARATIONS HE MAKES THERE FOR HIS CONQUEST

Toward the end of August of the same year of 1538 the general left the city of Santiago de Cuba with fifty mounted men to go to La Havana, having left orders that the rest of the horses, three hundred in number, should come after him in troops of fifty, each group leaving eight days after the previous one so that they might be better accommodated and provided for. He ordered that the infantry and all his household and family should go by sea, sailing around the island, all of them meeting at La Havana. The governor, having arrived there and having seen the destruction that the corsairs had made in the town, assisted its vecinos and inhabitants from his own resources in order to help rebuild their houses; and he repaired as best he could the temple and the images destroyed by the heretics. As soon as they arrived in La Havana, he gave orders that a gentleman named Juan de Añasco, a native of Sevilla who was acting as accountant of his Majesty's imperial hacienda and was a great mariner, cosmographer and astrologer, should go with the most experienced seamen in the two brigantines to the coast and explore the shores of La Florida, to see and note the ports, creeks, or bays that might be there.

The accountant went, and traveled for two months up and down the coast. At the end of this time he returned with a report of what he had seen and brought with him two Indians whom he had seized. Seeing the good results that Juan de Añasco had obtained, the governor ordered that he go back again and make a very careful examination of the coast so that the fleet could go directly to a suitable anchorage without having to cruise along the coast. Juan de Añasco returned on this errand and traveled along the coast with all care and diligence for three months, at the end of which he came back with a more accurate report of what he had seen and discovered there, and where the ships ought to anchor and make land. From this voyage he brought two other Indians whom he had picked up by dint of industry and persuasion. From this the governor and all his people derived much satisfaction, in having the ports where they were to disembark known and examined. At this point Alonso de Carmona adds that (because of Captain Juan de Añasco and his companions having been lost for two months on an uninhabited island where they ate nothing except pelicans, which they killed with clubs, and sea snails, and because of the great risk they ran of being drowned when they returned to La Havana) upon disembarking, all who came in the ship went on their knees from the edge of the water to the church where a mass was said for them; and after having fulfilled their promise, he says, they were very well received by the governor and all his people, who had been made very uneasy by the fear that they had perished at sea, etc.

While the adelantado Hernando de Soto was in La Havana preparing and providing what was necessary for his journey, he learned that Don Antonio de Mendoza, then viceroy of México, was making ready forces to send to conquer La Florida. The general, not knowing to what port he was sending them and fearing that the two might encounter and hinder one another, and that trouble might arise between them as had happened in México between the marqués del Valle, Hernando Cortés and Pánphilo de Narváez, who had gone in the name of Governor Diego Velázquez to demand an accounting of the forces and the trust that he had given him, and as had occurred in El Perú between the adelantados Don Diego de Almagro and Don Pedro de Alvarado at the beginning of the conquest of that kingdom—for which reason, and in order to prevent the infamy of selling and buying the men, as they told of those captains, it seemed to Hernando de Soto that it would be well to advise the viceroy of the titles and authority that his Majesty had conceded to him, so that he might be informed of them, and also to request him not to recruit men or hinder his expedition, and if necessary to make requisition and protest with them [i.e., his titles and authority—CS]. He sent to México for this purpose a Galician soldier named San Jurge, an able man capable for any business. He returned within a short time with a reply from the viceroy, who said that the governor might safely make his *entrada* and conquest in the place that he had indicated, without fear that the two would meet, for he was sending the men whom he had recruited to another region far distant from where the governor was going; that the land of La Florida was so large and broad that there was room for all; and that not only would he not attempt to stop him, but on the other hand he was desirous and willing to help and assist him in case of need, and thus he offered his person and property and everything to which his office and administration gave him access. The governor was satisfied with this reply and very grateful for the viceroy's offer.

By this time, which was the middle of April, all the cavalry that had remained behind in Santiago de Cuba had arrived in La Havana, having traversed by very short stages the 250 leagues [actually about 450 miles—CS], more or less, that lay between the two cities.

The adelantado, seeing that all his forces, both cavalry and infantry, were now assembled in La Havana, and that the time when they would be able to sail was drawing near, named Doña Isabel de Bobadilla, his wife and the daughter of Governor Pedro Arias de Avila, a woman of much goodness and discretion, as governor of that great island, and as her lieutenant a noble and virtuous gentleman named Joan de Rojas. In the city of Santiago he left as lieutenant another of his gentlemen, named Francisco de Guzmán. These gentlemen were governing those two cities before the general arrived in the island, and because of the good reports he heard of them, he left them in the same positions that they had before. He bought a very fine ship called the *Santa Ana,* which happened to arrive at the port of La Havana at that time. This vessel had come as flagship for the conquest and discovery of the Río de la Plata with the governor and captain-general Don Pedro de Zuñiga y Mendoza, who was lost on the journey and, returning to Spain, died of sickness at sea. The ship arrived at Sevilla from that voyage and returned on another to México, whence it was coming back when Hernando de Soto purchased it; it was so large and fine that he took eighty horses to La Florida in it.

XIV

A SHIP ARRIVES AT LA HAVANA IN WHICH COMES HERNÁN PONCE, COMPANION OF THE GOVERNOR

The governor was now very nearly ready to embark to go on his conquest and was only awaiting favorable weather, when another ship entered the port, coming from Nombre de Dios. It appeared that it entered unwillingly, forced by the foul weather it had encountered, for during four or five days in which it contended with contrary winds they saw it come up to the entrance of the port three times and as often return to the open sea, as if avoiding that port, so as not to enter it. But it could not withstand the high seas caused by the storm, and though its principal passenger had offered great inducements to the mariners not to enter that port, they were forced to make it, however unwillingly, being unable to do anything else, for there is no resisting the fury of the sea. Wherefore it must be known that when Hernando de Soto left El Perú to come to Spain, as is told in the first chapter, he had made a compact and association with Hernán Ponce to the effect that both should share that which the two of them might gain or lose during their lives, alike in the repartimientos of Indians that his Majesty might grant them and in the other things of honor and profit they might have. For Hernando de Soto's intention, when he left that land, was to return to it to enjoy the reward he had deserved for the services rendered in its conquest, though later, as has been seen, his thoughts were directed elsewhere. This compact was made then and afterward among many other gentlemen and leading persons who took part in the conquest of El Perú; I even came to know some of them who observed it as if they were brothers, enjoying the repartimientos that had been granted them without dividing them.

Hernán Ponce (whose parentage and country I was unable to learn, except that I heard it said that he was from the kingdom of León), after the arrival of Hernando de Soto in Spain, received in El Perú a very rich repartimiento of Indians (a concession which the marqués, Don Francisco Pizarro, made him in his Majesty's name), which gave him much gold and silver and many precious stones. With these things and with what more he could collect as the value of jewels and household furniture, for then everything was sold in exchange for gold [*a peso de oro:* this could also mean "at a very high price"—DB], and with the collection of some debts that Hernando de Soto had left him, he was coming to Spain very well supplied with money. Since he had learned in Nombre de Dios or in Cartagena that Hernando de Soto was in La Havana with such a collection of men and ships to go to La Florida, he desired to pass by at a distance without touching there, in order not to make an accounting between them and share with him things that he was bringing. He even feared that he might take possession of all of it, as a man who was necessitated to do because of heavy expenditures. This was the reason why he had held out for avoiding that port if he could, but it was not possible because fortune and storms at sea have no respect for anyone, and slight or favor whomever they wish.

As soon as the vessel entered the harbor, and the governor learned that Hernán Ponce was aboard, he sent visitors to welcome him and offer him his lodgings and all the rest of his possessions, offices and honors, for as companion and brother he owned the half of what he had and could command. Following this greeting, he went in person to see him and bring him ashore.

Hernán Ponce did not desire so much courtesy and brotherliness, but after they had spoken together with the usual fair and polite words, dissimulating his anxiety, he excused himself as best he could from going ashore, saying that because of his great labor and little sleep during those four or five days of storm at sea they were not ready to disembark; that he requested his lordship to permit that he remain aboard the ship, for that night at least, and that in the morning, if he were better, he would come to kiss his hands and receive and enjoy all the courtesies that he offered him. The governor let him have his own way, to show him that he did not wish to oppose him in anything, but sensing his ill will, he ordered very secretly that guards be posted by sea and by land who should keep a careful watch during the ensuing night and see what Hernán Ponce himself was doing.

The latter, not trusting in his companion's courtesy, nor being able to understand that it could be so great as he later saw it to be, nor taking counsel of anything except avarice (whose counsels always are to the prejudice of him who takes them), prepared to place under cover and conceal on land a large part of the gold and precious stones he was carrying, not considering that in that whole region he could not find a safe place for it, either on sea or on land, where it would be better to trust to the good will of another than to his own care; but the timid and suspicious always chooses a remedy which is a greater evil and injury. Thus did this gentleman, who, leaving the silver in order to make a show with it, ordered all the gold, pearls, and precious stones he was bringing in two small coffers, all of which exceeded 40,000 pesos in value, to be taken from the ship at midnight and carried to the pueblo to the house of a friend, or to be buried on the shore [near the] ship, so as to come back and recover it after the quarrel he feared he would have with Hernando de Soto. But the opposite happened, because the guards and sentries who were watching, concealed in the woods, which are very luxuriant in that port and along the whole coast, seeing the small boat coming toward them, remained quiet until whomever it was carrying should disembark, and when they saw the people on land at a distance from the boat they accosted them. The latter, abandoning the treasure, fled to the boat; some reached it and others jumped into the water in order not to be killed or taken prisoner. Those on shore, gathering up the spoils, took all of it to the governor, which occasioned him sorrow, seeing that his companion had become so suspicious of his friendship and amity as was shown by that act. He ordered it to be kept concealed until he saw how Hernán Ponce would come out of the business.

XV

THE THINGS THAT PASSED BETWEEN HERNÁN PONCE DE LEÓN AND HERNANDO DE SOTO, AND HOW THE GOVERNOR EMBARKED FOR LA FLORIDA

When the next day came Hernán Ponce left his ship in such grief and affliction at having lost his treasure when he was thinking to put it in safety, but dissimulating his sorrow, he went to lodge at the governor's inn, and they talked together alone for a long time about things past and present. Coming to the incident of the night before, Hernando de Soto complained to him with much feeling about the lack of confidence that he had shown in his friendship and brotherliness, for not trusting to it, he had attempted to conceal his property, fearing that he would take it away from him, which he was as far from doing as his future actions would show. So saying, he ordered brought before him everything that had been taken on the night before from the people on the boat and gave it to Hernán Ponce, bidding him look to see if anything were missing, and if so he would have it restored. And so that he might see how different his intent had been in not breaking the association and bond he had formed, he made him to understand that everything that he had spent to make that conquest, and his having asked it of his Majesty, had been under this union, so that the honor and profit of the expedition might go to both; and he could confirm this from the witnesses who were there, in whose presence he had executed the instruments and declarations necessary for it. For his further satisfaction, if he [Hernán Ponce] desired to go on that conquest, or not to go, as he liked, he [De Soto] said that whatever he chose to do he would at once renounce in his favor whatever title or titles he might desire to have therein of those his Majesty had granted to him. He said furthermore that he would be much pleased if he would advise him of everything that would be conducive to his desires, honor, and advantage, so that he might accede to his wishes, much to the contrary of what he had feared.

Hernán Ponce was confused by the governor's great generosity and by his own too great suspicion, and omitting explanations, for he found none to excuse him, he replied that he begged his lordship to pardon his past error and to be good enough to continue and confirm the favors that he had done him in calling him companion and brother, in which he held himself to be very fortunate without pretending to any higher title, because for him there could be none. He desired only that the instruments of their association and friendship be renewed in order to acknowledge it more publicly, that his lordship be attended by very good fortune on the conquest, and that he allow him to go to Spain. God granting them life and health, they would again enjoy their companionship, and afterward, if they wished, they would divide what they had gained. As a sign that he accepted for himself half of that which might be conquered, he begged his lordship to permit that Doña Isabel de Bobadilla his wife receive 10,000 pesos in gold and silver to help defray the expenses of the expedition, for in accordance with the terms of the association there belonged to his lordship half of what he was bringing from El Perú, which was a larger amount. The governor took pleasure in doing what Hernán Ponce asked, and much to the satisfaction of both there were renewed the writings of their association and friendship, and they maintained it during the time they were in La Havana. The governor directed his people secretly and led them by example in public to treat Hernán Ponce as they would [the governor], and this was done; all addressed him as lordship and respected him as the adelantado himself.

The matters we have told being concluded, and it appearing to the governor that the time was now propitious for navigation, he ordered the supplies and other things that were to be taken to be embarked with all haste, and when all were loaded on the ships and ready to go, the horses were embarked. In the ship *Santa Ana* were eighty; in the ship *San Cristóbal,* sixty; in that called *Concepción,* forty; and in the other three smaller vessels, the *San Joan, Santa Bárbara,* and *San Antón,* they embarked seventy; in all they took 350 horses on this expedition. When the military forces were embarked, which with those of the island who desired to go on this conquest, not counting the sailors of the eight ships, the caravel, and the brigantines, [they] came to a thousand men, all excellent people, well trained in arms, with equipment for themselves and trappings for their horses, so that neither up to that time nor afterward has there been seen here such a good force of men and horses assembled at one place for any expedition made in the conquest of the Indians.

Concerning the whole matter of ships, men, horses and military equipment, Alonso de Carmona and Juan Coles are in accord in their accounts.

The governor and adelantado Hernando de Soto took this number of ships, horses, and fighting men, exclusive of mariners, from the port of La Havana when he set sail on May 12 of the year 1539 to make the entrada and conquest of La Florida. He took his fleet so well supplied with all kinds of provisions that one seemed to be rather in a very well-provisioned city than navigating on the sea. There we shall leave him to return to a new disturbance that Hernán Ponce caused in La Havana, where under pretext of obtaining fresh provisions and awaiting a better season for the voyage to Spain, he had remained until the governor's departure.

Thus it is that, eight days after the general sailed, Hernán Ponce presented a writing to Juan de Rojas, the lieutenant governor, saying that he had given Hernando de Soto 10,000 pesos in gold that he did not owe, impelled by the fear that he would take away from him, since he had the power, all of the property he was bringing from El Perú. Therefore he demanded that Doña Isabel de Bobadilla, Hernando de Soto's wife, who had received them, be required to return them; otherwise he protested that he would complain of it before the majesty of the emperor, our lord.

When Doña Isabel de Bobadilla knew of this demand she replied that there were between Hernán Ponce and Hernando de Soto her husband many accounts both old and new that must be settled, as would appear from the instruments of the company and association formed between them. From the same it was apparent that Hernán Ponce owed Hernando de Soto more than 50,000 ducats, which was half of the expenditure he had made for that conquest. She therefore ordered the justice to take Hernán Ponce into custody and keep him well guarded until the accounts might be adjusted, which she offered to do at once in her husband's name. Hernán Ponce learned of this reply before the justice performed his duty (for there are double spies wherever there is money), and in order not to get into more difficulties and dangers like the past ones, he set sail and came to Spain, without awaiting the settlement of accounts, in which he would have been found to owe a large sum of money. Very often the avarice of self-interest blinds men's judgment, though they be rich and noble, causing them to do things that serve only to display and publish the meanness and depravity of their spirits.

END OF THE FIRST BOOK OF LA FLORIDA
BY THE INCA

First Part
of the Second Book
of the
History of La Florida,
by the Inca

Where it is told how the Governor arrived in La Florida, and found traces of Pánphilo de Narváez, and a Christian captive; the tortures and the cruel life the Indians gave him; the generosity of an Indian lord of vassals; the preparations that were made for the discovery; the events that took place in the first eight provinces they discovered; and the wild ferocity, in words and deeds, of an overbold cacique. It contains thirty chapters.

I

THE GOVERNOR ARRIVES IN LA FLORIDA, AND FINDS TRACES OF PÁNPHILO DE NARVÁEZ

The governor Hernando de Soto, who as we said was sailing toward La Florida, sighted its shores on the last day of May, having spent nineteen days at sea because of encountering unfavorable weather. The vessels anchored in a deep and good bay, which they named El Espíritu Santo, and because it was late, no one disembarked that day. On the first of June the small boats went to the shore and returned laden with grass for the horses, and they brought also many green grapes from the vines they found growing wild in the woods. The Indians of all this great kingdom of La Florida do not cultivate this plant or regard it as highly as do other nations, though they eat its fruit when it is well ripened or made into raisins. Our people were much pleased with these good specimens they brought from the land, for they were similar to the grapes of Spain, and they had not found them in the lands of México nor in the whole of El Perú. On the second day of June the governor ordered that three hundred infantry go ashore for the act and ceremony of taking possession of the land for the Emperor Charles V, king of Spain. Following the ceremony, the men marched all day along the coast without seeing a single Indian, and they remained that night and slept on land. Toward dawn the Indians fell upon them with such impetuosity and boldness that they retreated to the water's edge, and as they sounded the alarm both infantry and cavalry came out from the ships to their assistance as rapidly as if they had been on land.

The lieutenant general Vasco de Porcallo was in command of the relief party, and he found the infantry who were on the shore as confused and perturbed as raw recruits, getting in one another's way in fighting, and some of them already wounded with arrows. Having brought up the relief and followed the enemy for some distance, they returned to their quarters and had scarcely reached them when the lieutenant general's horse fell dead from an arrow wound near the saddle, which they gave him during the skirmish; the arrow passed through the trappings, saddletree and pads, and penetrated the ribs more than a third [of its length], up to the notch. Vasco Porcallo was much gratified that the first horse employed in the conquest and the first lance thrown against the enemy should have been his.

On this day and the next they continued to disembark the horses, and all

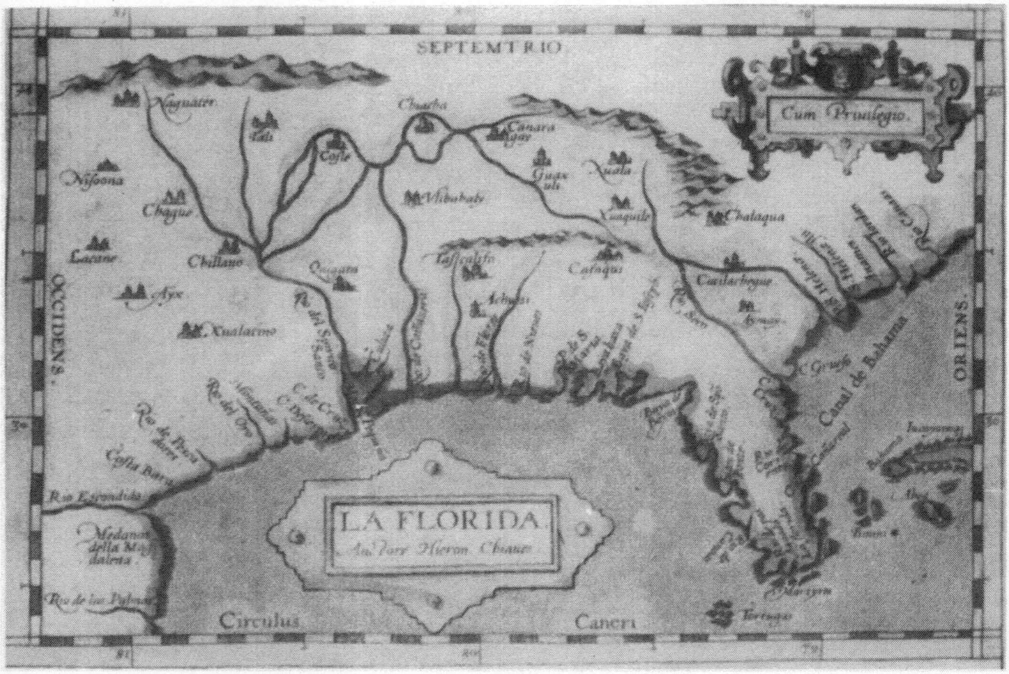

Gerónimo de Chavez's Map of La Florida. At the time of De Soto's North American expedition, all of the present Southeast was called "La Florida" by the Spaniards. This map, which appeared in 1584 in an atlas by Ortelius, was the first printed map to incorporate information about the De Soto expedition. (From a copy in The University of Alabama Library, Warner/Van Zele Collection)

the people went ashore. Having rested for eight or nine days and left orders with regard to the ships, they marched inland a little more than two leagues to the pueblo of a cacique named Hirrihigua [Rangel says that they were in the land of a chief named Oçita—DB], with whom Pánphilo de Narváez had fought when he went to conquer that province. Although afterward the Indian had been induced to become a friend, during that time, it is not known for what reason, Pánphilo de Narváez, angered, had committed certain offenses against him, which as they are so detestable are not recounted.

Because of these injustices and offenses the cacique Hirrihigua was left with such fear and hatred of the Spaniards that when he learned of the coming of Hernando de Soto to his country he went to the forest, abandoning his house and pueblo, and despite the friendly messages, gifts and promises the governor sent him by his Indian subjects whom he seized, he was never willing to come back peaceably nor to hear any of the messages he sent him. On the other hand he was incensed against those who brought them, saying that since they knew how offended and aggrieved he was with that nation they should have known better than to bring him their messages; that if it were their heads, he would receive them with pleasure, but their words and names he had no desire to hear. All this and more can infamy bring about, especially if it was done without blame on the part of the injured. So that the extent of this Indian's fury against the Spaniards may be better seen, it is fitting to tell here some of the cruelties and martyrdoms he imposed upon four Spaniards who must have been of Pánphilo de Narváez's party, which though it will prolong our *History* somewhat is not beside the point, but rather will be very useful for it.

Some days, then, after Pánphilo de Narváez left the country of this cacique, having done what we have told, there came to that bay one of his ships that had remained behind, in search of him. Inasmuch as the cacique suspected that it was one of Narváez's ships and that it was searching for him, he wished to capture all who were in it and burn them alive. In order to secure them, he feigned friendship for Pánphilo de Narváez and sent word to them saying that their captain had been there and had left orders as to what that ship was to do if it should make that port; and to persuade them to believe him, he showed from land two or three sheets of white paper and some old letters he had obtained from past friendship with the Spaniards or in some other manner, and had kept carefully.

In spite of all this, those on the ship were cautious and did not wish to go ashore. Then the cacique sent four of his principal Indians to the ship in a canoe, saying that since they did not trust him he was sending those four men, nobles and *caballeros* (this term *caballero* does not seem applicable to the Indians, because they had no horses, from which word the name is derived, but since in Spain they are regarded as nobles, and since among the Indians there are nobles of highest rank, they may also be called so), as hostages and security so that the Spaniards who desired word of their captain Pánphilo de Narváez might leave the ship, and if they still were not reassured, he offered to send them further pledges. Seeing this, four Spaniards came out and entered the canoe with the Indians who had brought the hostages. The cacique, who desired all of them, seeing that only four were coming, did not insist further upon asking for more Castilians, in order that these few who were going to him might not be alarmed and return to the ship.

As soon as the Spaniards set foot on the shore, the four Indians who had remained in the ship as hostages, seeing that the Christians were now in the power of their people, threw themselves into the water, and, diving deeply and swimming like fish, they went ashore, thus carrying out the order that their chief had given them. Those on the ship, seeing themselves victims of a hoax, left the bay before something worse should befall them, very sad at having lost their companions through such an indiscretion.

II

CONCERNING THE TORTURES THAT A CACIQUE INFLICTED UPON A SPANIARD, HIS SLAVE

The cacique Hirrihigua ordered the four Spaniards to be guarded securely so that on the occasion of their deaths he might hold a solemn festival, which according to his heathen custom he expected to celebrate within a few days. When the time came he ordered them to be brought forth naked to the plaza and to be shot with arrows one at a time like wild beasts, running them from one side to the other; and that too many arrows were not to be shot at the same time, in order that they should die more slowly, and their torment be greater, and the Indians' celebration and enjoyment longer and more festive. Thus they dealt with three of the Spaniards, the cacique deriving great satisfaction and pleasure from seeing them run in all directions, seeking help and nowhere finding succor, but only death. When they wished to bring out the fourth, who was a youth scarcely eighteen years of age, a native of Sevilla named Juan Ortiz, the cacique's wife came out accompanied by her three young daughters. Facing her husband, she said to him that she begged him to be content with the three Spaniards killed and pardon that youth, because neither he nor his companions had been to blame for the evil their predecessors had done, for they had not come with Pánphilo de Narváez; and that the boy especially deserved to be pardoned, for his youth absolved him of blame and called for mercy; and that it would be enough for him to remain as a slave and not be killed so cruelly without his having committed any crime.

In order to satisfy his wife and daughters, the cacique granted Juan Ortiz his life for the time, though afterward it was so sad and bitter that often he envied his three dead companions, because the continuous and unceasing labor of carrying wood and water was so great and his food and sleep so scanty, the daily cuffings, buffetings and lashes so cruel, besides the other torments that they inflicted upon him at the time of their special festivals, that often, if he had not been a Christian, he would have taken death by his own hands as a remedy. Thus it was that, aside from the daily torment, for his own pastime the cacique ordered on many festival days that Juan Ortiz run all day without stopping (from dawn to dark) in a large plaza that was in the pueblo, where they had shot his companions to death with arrows. The cacique himself would come out to see him run, and with him would come his nobles armed with their bows and arrows in order to shoot him if he ceased running. Juan Ortiz would begin his race at sunrise and would not pause on one side or the other of the plaza until sunset, which was the time that they set for him. And when the cacique would go to eat he would leave his nobles to watch him, so that, if he should cease running, they might kill him. At the end of the day he was left in the sad state that may be imagined, stretched on the ground, more dead than alive. The pity of the wife and daughters of the cacique succored him on these days, because they took him immediately, clothed him, and did him other kindnesses whereby they saved his life. It would have been better to take it away, in order to free him from those excessive hardships. Seeing that so many and such continuous tortures were not sufficient to kill Juan Ortiz, and the hatred that he bore him increasing hourly, the cacique, in order to put an end to him, commanded on one of his feast days that a great fire be built in the middle of the plaza, and when he saw a large bed of coals formed, he ordered it tended and a wooden framework [*barbacoa*] be placed over it in the form of a gridiron, one vara above the ground, and that they put Juan Ortiz upon it in order to roast him alive.

This was done, and here the poor Spaniard remained for some time stretched on one side, fastened to the frame. At the cries that the poor unfortunate gave in the midst of the fire, the wife and daughters of the cacique came, and begging the husband and even reproaching his cruelty, they took him from the fire, already half roasted, having blisters on that side as large as half-oranges, some of them broken and bleeding freely, so that it was pitiful to see him. The cacique allowed it because they were women for whom he cared so much, and perhaps he did it also in order to have someone upon whom to visit his wrath in the future and to show his desire for vengeance, because he would have someone to excite it, and though [this was] very little in proportion to his desires, still he could amuse himself with that little. Thus he said many times that he regretted having killed the three Spaniards so quickly. The women carried Juan Ortiz to their house, and moved by pity at seeing him in that state, they treated him with juices of herbs (the Indians, both men and women, since they have no physicians, are great herbalists). Time and again they repented having saved him from death on the first occasion, because of seeing how slowly and with what cruel tortures they were killing him day by day. After many days Juan Ortiz was cured, though large scars from the burns still remained.

In order not to see him thus, and to free himself from the bother that his wife and daughters gave him with their entreaties, and so that he [Juan Ortiz] might not become lazy, the cacique directed that he be exercised in another punishment, less severe than the past ones. This was that he guard day and night the dead bodies of the inhabitants of that pueblo, which were deposited in the country in a forest at a distance from the settlements, at a place set apart for them. They were placed above ground in wooden chests that served as sepulchers, without hinges or any other security for the cover than some boards placed over them, with stones or timbers on top. Because of the poor protection these chests afforded for the bodies of the dead, they were carried away by the lions [i.e., panthers], of which there are many in that country, much to the grief and anger of the Indians. The cacique ordered Juan Ortiz to guard this place carefully so that the lions should not carry off any body or part of it, protesting and vowing that, if they did so, he would infallibly be roasted to death. For guarding them he gave him four darts [*dardo:* dart or small lance thrown by hand—DB] to throw at the lions or at other wild beasts that might approach the chests. Juan Ortiz, giving thanks to God for having rid him of the continued presence of the cacique Hirrihigua, his master, went to guard the dead, hoping to have a better life with them than with the living. He guarded them with all care, chiefly at night, because then there was greater danger. It happened that, on one of the nights when he was thus watching, he fell asleep toward dawn, unable to resist his drowsiness, for at this hour it usually attacks most strongly those who are watching. Just at this time a lion came and, knocking off the covers of one of the chests, dragged out the body of a child, which had been thrown into it two days before, and carried it off. Juan Ortiz heard the noise that the covers made in falling, and as he hurried to the chest and failed to find the child's body therein, he considered himself lost; but with all his anxiety and dismay he did not cease hunting for the lion, so that, if he should find him, he might recover the body or die in the attempt. On the other hand he trusted to our Lord to give him strength to die on the following day, confessing and calling upon His name, for he knew that as soon as daylight came the Indians must visit the chests, and not finding the child's body, they would burn him alive. Walking through the forest from one side to another, in fear of death, he came to a wide path that passed through the center of it, and following it for a time with the intention of fleeing, though it was impossible to escape, he heard in the woods not far from where he was walking a noise as of a dog that is gnawing bones. Listening carefully, he made sure of it, and suspecting that it might be the lion that was eating the child, he felt his way very carefully through the underbrush, approaching the place where he heard the noise. By the light of the moon, which was shining, though not very brightly, he saw near him the lion, which was eating the child at its pleasure. Calling upon God and taking courage, Juan Ortiz threw a dart at it, and though he could not then see the shot that he had made, because of the underbrush, yet he felt that it had not been bad because his hand was left "salty," as the hunters say when they feel that they have made a good shot against wild beasts at night. With this very slender hope, and also because he had not heard the lion leave the place where he had shot at him, he waited for morning, commending himself to our Lord, that he might succor him in that necessity.

III

THE HARD LIFE OF THE CAPTIVE CHRISTIAN CONTINUES, AND HOW HE FLED FROM HIS MASTER

With the light of day Juan Ortiz verified the good shot that he had made by guess that night, for he saw the lion dead, the entrails and the center of the heart transfixed (as was found later when they opened it), a thing that he himself, though he saw it, could not believe. With a satisfaction and joy that may be better imagined than told, he dragged it by one foot, not pulling out the dart, so that his master might see it just as he had found it, having first gathered up and taken back to the chest the fragments of the child's body that he found uneaten. The cacique and all those in his pueblo wondered greatly at this deed, for in that land it is held generally to be a miraculous thing for a man to kill a lion, and thus they treat him who succeeds in killing one with great veneration and respect. And because this is such a fierce animal, he who kills it ought to be esteemed everywhere, especially if he does so without a shot from a crossbow or harquebus, as Juan Ortiz did. Although it is true that the lions of La Florida, México, and El Perú are not so large or so fierce as those of Africa, still they are lions, and the name is enough; and even if the popular proverb may say that they are not as fierce as they are painted, those who have been near them say that they are as much fiercer than their descriptions, as there is difference between the real and the imagined.

With this good fortune on the part of Juan Ortiz, the wife and daughters of the cacique took more spirit and courage to intercede for him, that he might be pardoned entirely and made use of in honorable employments worthy of his strength and valor. For a few days thereafter Hirrihigua treated his slave better, both in the esteem and favor he accorded him in his pueblo and house, and in referring to the heroic deed that they in their vain religion so esteem and honor that they regard it as sacred and more than human. However (and this was the injury that he could not pardon), every time he remembered that they [the Spaniards] had thrown his mother to the dogs and left her to be eaten by them, and when he went to blow his nose and could not find his nostrils, the devil possessed him to avenge himself on Juan Ortiz, as if he had cut them off; and inasmuch as he always carried the offense before his eyes, with the memory of it his ire, rancor, and desire to take vengeance increased from day to day. Though he restrained these passions for some time, being able to resist them no longer, he said one day to his wife and daughters that it was impossible for him to allow that Christian to remain alive because his life was very odious and abominable to him; that every time he saw him past injuries were revived and he was offended anew. Therefore he commanded them that they were in no manner to intercede for him further unless they desired to participate in the same rage and anger, and that in order to finish finally with that Spaniard he had determined that on a certain feast day (which was soon to be celebrated) he was to be shot to death with arrows as his companions had been, notwithstanding his bravery, for as an enemy he should be rather abhorred than esteemed. The wife and daughters of the cacique, because they saw him enraged and understood that no intercession would be effective, and also because it seemed to them that it was too much to importune and so displease the master for the sake of the slave, did not dare say a word in opposition to him. Rather with feminine astuteness they came to tell him that this would be a good thing to do because it was his pleasure. But the eldest of the daughters, in order to further her plan and make it succeed, a few days before the celebration secretly notified Juan Ortiz of her father's determination against him, and that neither she nor her sisters nor her mother would avail or could do anything with the father, he having imposed silence upon them and threatened them if they should break it.

Desiring to encourage the Spaniard, she added to this sad notice others contrary to it and said to him: "So that you may not distrust me, nor despair of your life, nor fear that I will not do all that I can to save it, if you are a man and have courage to flee, I will favor and help you so that you may escape and reach safety. Tonight at a certain hour and in a certain place you will find an Indian to whom I entrust your safety and my own. He will guide you to a bridge that is two leagues from here; upon reaching it, you will order him not to pass beyond but to return to the pueblo before dawn so that they may not miss him, and my own daring and his may not become known, so that evil may not befall him and me for having done you a good turn. Six leagues beyond the bridge is a pueblo whose lord wishes me well and desires to marry me; his name is Mucoço. Tell him on my behalf that I send you to him so that he may succor and favor you, as he ought to do. I know that he will do all he can for you, as you will see. Commend yourself to your God, for I can do no more for you." Juan Ortiz threw himself at her feet in acknowledgment of the mercy and favor that she was conferring and had always conferred upon him, and he at once made ready to travel on the following night. At the hour appointed, after the members of the cacique's household were asleep, he set out in search of the promised guide and left the pueblo with him without anyone hearing them. Upon reaching the bridge, he told the Indian to return at once very cautiously to his house, having first learned from him that there was no chance of his losing the road as far as the pueblo of Mucoço.

IV

OF THE MAGNANIMITY OF THE CURACA OR CACIQUE MUCOÇO, TO WHOM THE CAPTIVE COMMENDED HIMSELF

Juan Ortiz, as a man who was fleeing, reached the place before dawn but, for fear of causing a disturbance, did not dare enter it. When it was day he saw two Indians come out from the pueblo along the same road that he was taking. They attempted to shoot him with their bows and arrows, as they always go armed with these weapons. Juan Ortiz, who also had them, put an arrow in his bow to defend himself from them and also to attack them. How potent is a little favor, especially if it be from a lady! For we see that shortly before he did not know where to hide himself, being in fear of death; now he dared give it [death] to others with his own hand, simply because of having been favored by a pretty, discreet and generous girl, whose favor exceeds all other human gifts. With which, having recovered spirit and strength and even pride, he told them that he was not an enemy but that he was coming with a message from a lady for the lord of that place.

Hearing this, the Indians did not shoot him but returned with him to the pueblo and notified the cacique that the slave of Hirrihigua was there with a message for him. Mucoço or Mocoço—for it is the same—informed of this, went out to the plaza to receive the message Juan Ortiz was bringing to him. After having saluted him as best he could after the manner of the Indians themselves, Juan Ortiz told him briefly of the martyrdom his master had imposed upon him, as evidence of which he showed on his body the scars of the burns, blows and wounds they had given him, and how now finally his lord was determined to kill him in order to celebrate and solemnize with his death such and such a feast day, which he expected to hold soon. He told how the wife and daughters of the cacique, his master, though they had often saved his life, did not now dare to speak in his favor because of the lord's having forbidden it under penalty of his anger; and how the eldest daughter of his lord, desiring that he should not die, as the last and best remedy had ordered and encouraged him to flee and, giving him a guide, had set him on his way to his pueblo and house. In her name he presented himself before him, whom he supplicated by the love that he had for her to receive him under his protection, and as a thing commended by her to favor him, as he ought to do. Mucoço received him affably and heard him with pity at learning of the abuses and torments that he had experienced, which were plainly shown by the scars on his body, for, dressed after the manner of the Indians of the country, he wore only some trousers [*pañete:* thin cloth, perhaps loincloth; also trunks—DB].

Alonso de Carmona tells at this point, in addition to what we have said, that he embraced him and kissed him on the face as a sign of peace.

He [the cacique] replied that he was welcome and told him to try to forget the fears of his past life; that in his company and house he would have a very different and opposite existence; that for the sake of serving the person who had sent him, and for him who had come to his person and house for succor, he would do all he could, as he would see by future actions; and that he might be certain that while he lived no one would be allowed to molest him.

All that this good cacique said in favor of Juan Ortiz he performed, and indeed much more than he promised, for he immediately made him his steward and kept him constantly with him, day and night, doing him much honor, more particularly after he learned that he had killed the lion with the dart. In short, he treated him like a well-beloved brother (for there are brothers who love one another like water and fire), and although Hirrihigua, suspecting that he had gone to Mocoço for protection, asked for him many times, Mucoço always made an excuse for not giving him up, saying finally, among other things, that since he had come to his house to let him be, and that he was so odious that he [Hirrihigua] had lost very little in losing such a slave. He made the same reply to another cacique, his brother-in-law, named Urribarracuxi, through whom Hirrihigua made the request. Seeing that his messages were of no effect, he went personally to ask him, and in his presence Mocoço replied the same as in his absence, adding other angry words, and told him that since he was his brother-in-law it was unjust to order him to do a thing against his reputation and honor; that he would not be doing his duty if he should turn over to his own enemy an unfortunate who had come to him for refuge, so that the Hirrihigua might sacrifice and kill him like a wild beast for his own entertainment and pastime.

Mocoço defended Juan Ortiz from these two caciques, who asked for him so urgently and insistently, with such generosity that he was willing to forgo (as he did) the marriage he affectionately desired to make with the daughter of Hirrihigua, and the relationship and friendship of the father-in-law, rather than return the slave to him who asked for him in order to kill him. He kept the latter constantly with him, much esteemed and well treated, until Governor Hernando de Soto entered La Florida.

Juan Ortiz was among those Indians for ten years, one and a half in the power of Hirrihigua and the rest with the good Mocoço. Though a barbarian, he dealt with this Christian in quite another manner than those most famous men of the Triumvirate who at Layno, a place near Bologna, made that never sufficiently condemned proscription and agreement to give and exchange their relatives, friends, and defenders for enemies and adversaries. And he did much better than other Christian princes who later have committed here other acts as abominable and worse than that one, considering the innocence of those given up, the rank of some of them, and the faith that their betrayers should have had and kept with them; considering also that the former were heathen and the latter prided themselves on the Christian name and religion. These latter, breaking the laws and statutes [*fueros*] of their kingdoms and not respecting their own position and rank, they being kings and great princes, and disregarding their sworn and promised word (a thing unworthy of such names), simply for the purpose of avenging their own anger, delivered up those who had not offended them in order to obtain the offenders, exchanging the innocent for the guilty, as both ancient and modern historians will testify. But we shall leave them, so as not to offend powerful ears and distress the pious.

It suffices to describe the magnanimity of a heathen so that faithful princes may be forced to imitate and excel him if they can, not in his heathenism, as do some who are unworthy of that name [i.e., faithful], but in virtue and similar noble qualities, to which they are more obligated because of their higher estate. Certainly, considering well the circumstances of the courageous action of this Indian, and seeing by whom and against whom it was performed, and the amount that he was willing to put aside and lose, going even against his own affection and desires in refusing the succor and favor demanded and promised by him, it will be seen that it arose from a most generous and heroic mind, which did not deserve to have been born and to live amidst the barbarous heathendom of that country. But God and human nature often produce such spirits in such uncultivated and sterile deserts for the greater humiliation and shame of those who are born and reared in lands that are fertile and abound in all good doctrine, sciences, and the Christian religion.

V

THE GOVERNOR SENDS FOR JUAN ORTIZ

The governor heard this account, which we have given, of the life of Juan Ortiz, although in a confused form, in the pueblo of the cacique Hirrihigua, where we have left him at present; and he had heard it before, more briefly, in La Havana from one of the four Indians whom we said that the accountant, Juan de Añasco, had seized when he was sent to explore the coast of La Florida, and who happened to be a subject of this cacique. When this Indian mentioned Juan Ortiz in the account that he gave in La Havana, leaving off the name Juan, because he did not know it, he said Ortiz, and as to the poor speech of the Indian was added the worse understanding of the good interpreters who stated what he was trying to say, and as all the listeners had for their chief purpose going to seek gold, on hearing the Indian say "Orotiz," without waiting for further statements on his part they thought that he was plainly saying that in his country there was much gold [Spanish, *oro*—DB], and they congratulated themselves and rejoiced merely at hearing it mentioned, although with such a different significance and sense.

But when the governor ascertained that Juan Ortiz was in the power of the cacique Mucoço, he thought it would be well to send for him, alike in order to deliver him from the power of the Indians and because he was in need of a speaker and interpreter upon whom he could depend. He therefore chose a gentleman from Sevilla named Baltasar de Gallegos, who was serving as *alguacil mayor* of the fleet and the army—who because of his great virtue, strength and valor deserved to be general of a greater army than that one—and told him to take sixty lancers with him and go to Mucoço, and tell him on his behalf how gratified were he and all the Spaniards who accompanied him by the honor and favors he had shown to Juan Ortiz, and how much he desired that he might have an opportunity of requiting them. At present he begged that he give him [Juan Ortiz] to him [De Soto], for he needed him for very important matters, and he asked when it would be convenient for him to make him a visit, as it would give him great pleasure to know and have him for a friend. In accordance with the orders given him, Baltasar de Gallegos left the camp with the sixty lancers and an Indian guide.

The cacique Mucoço, on the other hand, having learned of the coming of the governor Hernando de Soto with such a force of men and horses, and that he had landed so near his own country, and fearing that he might do him some harm there, desired very prudently and advisedly to avert the evil that might come to him. In order to do so, he summoned Juan Ortiz and said to him: "You must know, brother, that in the pueblo of your good friend Hirrihigua there is a Spanish captain with a thousand fighting men and many horses, who are coming to conquer this country. You well know what I have done for you, and how in order to save your life and not deliver you to him who held you as a slave and desired to kill you, I chose rather to fall into disgrace with all my relatives and neighbors than to do what they asked me against you. Now a time and occasion has come in which you can repay me for the good reception, entertainment and friendship I have accorded you, though I never did it with the expectation of any reward, but since events have happened thus it will be wise not to lose what is offered us.

"Go to the Spanish general and on your behalf and my own beg him that, in return for the service that I have done him and his whole nation through you (since I would do the same for any of them), he be pleased not to do me harm in this small land that I have, and that he deign to receive me into his friendship and service; that from this time forth I offer him my person, house and estate to be placed under his guardianship and protection; and so that you may be escorted as becomes both you and me, I send with you fifty nobles of my household, and you will protect them and me as our friendship obligates you to do."

Juan Ortiz, rejoicing at the good news and inwardly giving thanks to God for it, replied to Mucoço that he was much pleased that a time and occasion had arisen in which to repay the kindness and benefits that he had done him, not only in saving his life, but also in the many favors, and the esteem and honor he had received from his great virtue and courtesy. He would give a very full account and report of all this to the Spanish captain and all his people, so that he might concede to and reward him with that which he asked of them now in his name, and in what might come up in the future. He was very confident that the general on his part would do what he asked, for the Spanish nation prided itself upon being a people grateful for favors received, and thus certainly he could confidently hope to obtain that which he sent to ask of the governor. The fifty Indians whom the cacique had ordered to prepare came at once, and with Juan Ortiz they took the public road that goes from one pueblo to the other; and they set out on the same day that Baltasar de Gallegos left the camp to find him [Ortiz].

It happened that, after the Spaniards had marched more than three leagues along the wide and straight highway that went to the pueblo of Muçoço, the Indian who guided them, thinking that it was not a good thing to behave so loyally toward people who were coming to subjugate them and take away their lands and freedom, and who long before had shown themselves to be declared enemies—though up to the present they had not received injuries of which they could complain from that army—changed his plan in guiding them and took the first footpath he saw that led into the highway. After following it a short distance, he left it, as it was not straight, and thus he led them most of the day without a road and lost, drawing them always in an arc toward the seacoast with the design of coming upon some swamp, creek, or bay in which to drown them, if possible. The Castilians did not discover the deception of the Indian, since they were not acquainted with the country, until one of them saw, through the trees of an open forest through which they were marching, the topsails of the ships they had left and saw that they were very near the coast, of which fact he advised Captain Baltasar de Gallegos. The latter, seeing the guide's iniquity, threatened him with death, making a gesture of throwing a lance at him. Fearing that they would kill him, the Indian indicated with signs and such words as he could that they should return to the highway, but that it was necessary to retrace all their route that lay off the road, and thus they returned by the same way to seek it.

VI

WHAT HAPPENED BETWEEN JUAN ORTIZ AND THE SPANIARDS WHO WERE COMING FOR HIM

Proceeding along the highway, Juan Ortiz came to the footpath by which the Indian led Baltasar de Gallegos and his Castilians off the road. Suspecting what had happened and fearing that the Castilians would go by another route and inflict some damage on the pueblo of Mucoço, he consulted with the Indians as to what they should do. They all agreed that it would be well to follow the trail of the horses as rapidly as possible until overtaking them, and that they would not take another road for fear of missing them.

Since the Indians followed the trail of the Spaniards, and the latter were returning by the same route that they had gone, they sighted one another on a large plain on a part of which was a dense growth of thick underbrush. The Indians, seeing the Castilians, said to Juan Ortiz that it would be prudent to safeguard their persons and lives by entering that thicket until the Christians should recognize them as friends, so that they should not fall upon them in the open field, believing them to be enemies. Juan Ortiz was unwilling to accept the good advice of the Indians, confiding in the fact that he was a Spaniard and that his people must recognize him as soon as they should see him, as if he were dressed in the Spanish fashion or were in any way different from the Indians, so that he might be known as a Spaniard. He, like the rest, wore only some trousers for clothing, carried a bow and arrows in his hands, and wore a plume half a fathom high upon his head for display and ornament.

The Castilians—being inexperienced and anxious to fight—on seeing the Indians, fell upon them violently, and as much as their captain shouted at them he could not stop them. Who can stop undisciplined troops when they get out of hand?

When they saw how boldly and recklessly the Castilians were coming at them, all the Indians threw themselves into the thicket, there remaining in the field only Juan Ortiz and an Indian who was not so quick as the others in placing himself in safety. He was wounded by a Spaniard from Sevilla who had been a soldier in Italy, named Francisco de Morales, by a lance-thrust in the loins, he overtaking him at the edge of the woods. Juan Ortiz was assailed by another Spaniard, named Alvaro Nieto, a native of the villa of Albuquerque, one of the stoutest and strongest Spaniards in the whole army, who, engaging Juan Ortiz, vigorously thrust a lance at him. Juan Ortiz had good luck and dexterity, so that, warding off the lance with his bow and jumping sideways, he avoided at the same time the blow of the lance and an encounter with the horse. Seeing that Alvaro Nieto was coming at him again, he shouted in a loud voice, saying "Xivilla, Xivilla" for "Sevilla, Sevilla."

Juan Coles adds at this point that Juan Ortiz, being unable to speak in Spanish, made the sign of the cross with his hand and the bow so that the Spaniard might see that he was a Christian. For with the little or no use that he had for the Spanish language among the Indians, he had even forgotten how to pronounce the name of his own country, as I can also say for myself. Because of not having had anyone in Spain with whom to speak my native and maternal tongue, which is the one generally spoken throughout El Perú (although the Incas have another special one that they speak among themselves, one to another), I have forgotten it to such an extent that—having once known how to speak it as well or better, and with more elegance, than the Indians themselves who are not Incas, because I am a son of palla and the nephew of Incas, who are the ones who speak it best and most correctly, because of its having been the language of the court of its princes and they having been the chief courtiers—now I am unable to put six or seven words together in a sentence in order to make clear what I wish to say, and, moreover, many terms have escaped my memory and I do not know what is the word for this or that thing in the Indian tongue. Although it is true that, if I should hear an Inca speak, I would understand all that he said, and, if I should hear the forgotten words, I could tell what they mean, I myself, however I try, cannot say what they are. This I have learned from experience in the use and neglect of languages, which foreigners learn by using them and natives forget in not using them.

Returning to Juan Ortiz, whom we left in great danger of being killed by those who most desired to see him alive, as Alvaro Nieto heard him say "Xivilla," he asked whether he were Juan Ortiz, and as he replied that he was, he grasped him by one arm and lifted him behind his horse as if he were a child, for this good soldier was stout and strong.

Much elated at having found the one he was seeking, and giving thanks to God for not having killed him, though it seemed to him that he was still in that danger, he took him to Captain Baltasar de Gallegos. The latter received Juan Ortiz with great joy and at once ordered them to recall the other horsemen who were scouring the woods, anxious to kill Indians, as if they were deer, so that all of them might assemble to enjoy the good fortune that had befallen them, and before they should do some injury to their friends because of not recognizing them. Juan Ortiz entered the woods to call the Indians, shouting to them to come out and not be afraid. Many of them did not stop until they reached their pueblo, to advise their cacique of what had happened. Others who had not gone so far returned in groups of three and four as they happened to be found, and together and singly they very angrily and bitterly reproached Juan Ortiz for his rashness and lack of caution. When they saw the Indian, their companion, wounded because of him they became so enraged that they scarcely could refrain from laying hands on him and would have done so had the Spaniards not been present. But they vented their wrath with a thousand insults they heaped upon him, calling him dolt, fool, meddler, and no Spaniard or soldier, and saying that he had learned little or nothing from his past sufferings and misadventures; that they had been inflicted upon him to no purpose, and he deserved much worse. In short, no Indian came out of the woods who was not quarreling with him;

all of them spoke almost the same words and he himself stated them to the other Spaniards, the more to reproach them. Juan Ortiz was well reprimanded for having been too confident, but it was worth it all provided he found himself among Christians. The latter treated the wounded Indian and, putting him on a horse, went with him and Juan Ortiz and the rest of the Indians to the camp, desirous of seeing the governor, in order to bring within so short a time such a good report of what he had ordered them to do. Before they left that place Juan Ortiz sent an Indian to Mucoço with the report of all that had happened, so that he would not be alarmed by what the Indians who fled might have told him.

All that we have said concerning Juan Ortiz, Juan Coles and Alonso de Carmona also tell in their accounts, and one of them says that he had worms in the sores made by the fire when they burned him. The other, who is Juan Coles, says that the governor gave him at once a black velvet suit, and that, because he was accustomed to go about unclothed, he could not tolerate it; that he wore only a shirt and linen trousers, a cap, and shoes, and that he went about thus for more than twenty days until, a little at a time, he was able to wear clothing. These two eyewitnesses say further that, among other benefits and favors that the cacique Mucoço conferred upon Juan Ortiz, one was to make him his captain-general on sea and land.

VII

THE CELEBRATION THAT THE WHOLE ARMY HELD FOR JUAN ORTIZ, AND HOW MUCOÇO CAME TO VISIT THE GOVERNOR

A good part of the night had passed when Baltasar de Gallegos and his companions entered the camp. The governor, who heard them, was alarmed, fearing that since they were returning so quickly, some accident had befallen them, because he had not expected them until the third day. But upon learning of the good report they brought, all his dismay was changed to rejoicing and pleasure. He thanked the captain and his soldiers, who had done so well, and received Juan Ortiz as his own son, with pity and grief at hearing of so many hardships and martyrdoms as he told of and as his own body showed that he had experienced—for the scars of the burns from the time that they had roasted him were so large that one whole side was nothing but a burn, or a scar of it—from which hardships he thanked God for having delivered him, and also from the peril of that day, which had not been the least of those through which he had passed. He treated kindly the Indians who came with him and ordered that the one who was wounded be treated with great care and attention. At the same hour he dispatched two Indians to the cacique Mucoço with acknowledgments for the kindnesses that he had done Juan Ortiz and for having sent him freely, and for the offer of his person and friendship, which he said he accepted in the name of the emperor and king of Spain, his lord, who was the chief and greatest of all Christendom, in the name of all those captains and gentlemen who were with him, and in his own, in order to acknowledge and repay what he had done for all of them in having rescued Juan Ortiz from death; he said also that all of them begged him to visit them, as they desired to see and know him.

The captains and officials, both of the army and of the real hacienda, and the gentlemen and all the other soldiers in general, entertained Juan Ortiz royally; they refused to accept as comrade anyone who did not come to embrace him and congratulate him on his arrival. So passed the night, in which they did not sleep for general rejoicing.

Then on the following day the general summoned Juan Ortiz so that he might inform him concerning what he knew about that country and might tell him in detail what had happened to him while he was in the power of those two caciques. He replied that he knew little or nothing about the country, although he had been there so long; because while he was in the power of Hirrihigua, his master, when he was not tormenting him with new martyrdoms, did not allow him to go a step beyond the ordinary service that he performed in carrying water and wood for all the households; and while he was in the hands of Mucoço, though he had freedom to go where he liked, he did not make use of it because the vassals of his master, seeing him apart from Mucoço, might kill him, as they had his order and command to do. For these reasons he could not give much information about the nature of the country, but he heard that it was good, and that the farther inland one went, the better and more fertile it became. The life he had led with the two caciques had been of the two extremes of good and evil that could be found in this world; because Mucoço had shown himself as compassionate and humane toward him as the other had been cruel and revengeful, without his being able to extol sufficiently the virtue of the one or the passion of the other, as his lordship had already been informed, as a proof of which he showed the scars on his body, uncovering those that could be seen and amplifying the account of his life, which we have given; and he related anew many other torments through which he had passed, which aroused the compassion of the listeners and which we shall omit, to avoid prolixity.

On the third day after the message had been sent to him by the Indians, the cacique Mucoço came with a large company of his people. He kissed the governor's hands with all veneration and respect and then spoke to the lieutenant general, the maese de campo, and the rest of the captains and gentlemen who were there, each according to his rank, first asking Juan Ortiz who was this, that and the other person, and although one of those who spoke with him told him that he was not a gentleman or a captain, but a private soldier, he treated him with great respect, but those who were nobles and officials of the army with much more, so that all the Spaniards noticed it. After he had spoken and given opportunity for those present to speak with him, Mucoço went again to salute the governor with new expressions of respect. The latter, having received him with much affability and courtesy, thanked him for what he had done for Juan Ortiz and for having sent him in such a friendly manner; he said that he and his army and the whole Spanish nation were so obligated to him that they would show their gratitude for all time. Mucoço replied that what he had done for Juan Ortiz had been done out of self-respect because—he having come to his person and household for refuge and succor, out of necessity—according to their law, he was obligated to do for him what he had done; and it seemed to him little enough because the virtue, strength and bravery of Juan Ortiz alone, without any other consideration whatever, deserved much more. His having sent him to his lordship was more for his own interest and benefit than to serve his lordship, for it had been in order that he might act as defender and advocate to obtain mercy and favor with his intercession and merits, so that he would not harm him in his country. Therefore his lordship was not obligated to reward or receive into his service either of them except as he might be pleased to do so; but he was gratified, however it might have come about, that he had happened to do a thing at which his lordship and those gentlemen and the whole Spanish nation, whose devoted servant he was, had been pleased and had shown their satisfaction. He begged that his lordship would receive him into his service with the same good will, and he placed his person, household, and estate under his protection and patronage, recognizing the emperor and king of Spain as his principal lord, and secondarily his lordship as his captain-general and governor of that kingdom. He would consider himself better rewarded by being granted this favor than his services rendered to Juan Ortiz deserved, or his having sent him freely, a thing that had so gratified his lordship, concerning which he said that he was more pleased and content at seeing him as he saw him that day, favored and honored by his lordship and by all those gentlemen, than at all the good that he had done throughout his life; and he protested that he would exert himself thenceforth to perform such actions in the service of the Spaniards, since those had brought him so much good.

This cacique expressed these and many other civilities with all the gracefulness and discretion that might be found in a practiced courtier, at which the governor and those who were with him marveled, no less than at the generosity he had shown to Juan Ortiz, which was borne out by his words.

Because of all this the adelantado Hernando de Soto and the lieutenant general Vasco Porcallo de Figueroa and other private gentlemen, attracted by the virtue and discretion of the cacique Mucoço, were moved to reciprocate on their own part, insofar as they could, in acknowledgment of such graciousness. Thus they gave many presents not only to him but also to the nobles who came with him, with which all of them were very well content.

VIII

THE MOTHER OF MUCOÇO ARRIVES, VERY ANXIOUS ABOUT HER SON

Two days after the events that we have related the mother of Mucoço arrived, very anxious and harassed because her son was in the power of the Castilians. Because of having been away, she did not know of her son's coming to see the governor, and would not have consented to it; thus the first words that she said to the general were that he give her the son before doing with him what Pánphilo de Narváez had done with Hirrihigua, and that if he intended doing such a thing that he set free her son, who was young, and do as he liked with her, who was old, so that she might bear the punishment for both.

The governor received her very kindly and replied that her son, because of his extreme goodness and discretion, did not deserve ill-treatment, but rather that everyone should serve him, and her as well, for being the mother of such a son; she might dismiss her fears because no harm would be done either to her or to her son or to anyone in his whole country, but on the contrary all the favors and kindnesses possible. The good old woman was somewhat reassured by these words and remained with the Spaniards three days, but was always so suspicious and fearful that, when eating at the governor's table, she asked Juan Ortiz if she dared eat what they gave her, saying that she feared and suspected that they might give her poison in order to kill her.

The governor and those with him laughed a great deal at this and told her that certainly she might eat, that they did not wish to kill her, but to entertain her; however, not trusting the words of strangers, though they gave her food from the same plate as the governor, she still would not eat or taste it until Juan Ortiz had first tried it. Whereupon a Spanish soldier asked her why she had recently offered her life for her son, since she was so afraid of dying. She replied that she did not abhor living, but loved it like other people, but that for her son she would give her life as often as might be necessary because she loved him more than living; therefore she begged the governor to give him to her, saying that she wished to go and take him with her and that she did not dare trust him to the Christians.

The general replied that she might go whenever she liked, that her son wished to remain for some days among those gentlemen who were young and soldiers and fighting men like himself, and that he would be safe with them; that whenever he desired he might go freely, and no one would molest him. With this promise the old woman left, although not content to have her son remain in the power of the Castilians. At parting she charged Juan Ortiz to free her son from that captain and his soldiers as her son had liberated him from Hirrihigua and his vassals, at which the governor and the other Spaniards laughed a great deal, and Mucoço himself joined in laughing at his mother's anxiety.

Following this time of pleasure and merriment, the good cacique remained with the army for eight days, during which he visited in their lodgings the lieutenant general, the maese de campo, the captains, the officials of the imperial hacienda, and many private gentlemen because they were nobles. He talked with all of them familiarly and with such readiness and courtesy that he seemed to have been brought up among them. He asked particular questions about the court of Castilla and the emperor, and the lords, ladies, and gentlemen in it, and said that he would like very much to see it if he could go there. At the end of the eight days he went to his house. He came later on other occasions to visit the governor, always bringing him presents of the things that were in his country. Mucoço was twenty-six or twenty-seven years old, a man of handsome body and face.

IX

OF THE PREPARATIONS THAT WERE MADE FOR THE DISCOVERY, AND HOW THE INDIANS CAPTURED A SPANIARD

The governor and adelantado Hernando de Soto was not idle while these things were taking place among his people; rather he was fulfilling his office of captain and commander with all care and diligence, because as soon as the provisions and munitions were disembarked and placed in the pueblo of the cacique Hirrihigua—since it was nearest the Bay of Espíritu Santo—so that they might be close to the sea, he ordered that the seven largest of the eleven ships that he had brought should return to La Havana so that his wife, Doña Isabel de Bobadilla, might dispose of them, and that the four smaller ones remain for use in such navigation as they might have occasion to make. The vessels that remained were the ship *San Antón* and the caravel and the two brigantines, of which Captain Pedro Calderón was put in command. He had among other excellent qualifications that of having served when very young under the command and government of the great captain Gonzalo Fernández de Córdoba. De Soto attempted with all diligence and care to win the cacique Hirrihigua to peace and friendliness, because it seemed to him that, according to the example set by this cacique, he might hope or fear what the other caciques of the region would do. He desired his friendship because he understood that with it he would gain that of all those of that kingdom, for he said that if that one, who had been so offended by the Castilians, should be reconciled and become their friend, would not the rest, who had not been offended, become so that much more quickly? Besides winning the friendship of the caciques, he hoped that his reputation and honor would be enhanced among Indians and Spaniards generally for having placated such a rabid enemy of his nation. Therefore whenever the Christians, in exploring the country, happened to take the vassals of Hirrihigua, he sent them with gifts and friendly messages, making amicable requests and enticing him with offers of satisfaction that he desired to give him for the injury done by Pánphilo de Narváez. The cacique not only refused to come out peaceably, but refused to accept the friendship of the Spaniards or even to reply a single word to any of the messages they sent him. He only said to the messengers that his injury did not admit of giving a favorable response, nor did the courtesy of that captain deserve that they give him an unfavorable one; and he never made any other reply to this proposal. But while the diligent efforts that the governor made to win the friendship of Hirrihigua did not suffice to gain the end and purpose that he desired, at least it served to mitigate to some extent the wrath and rancor this cacique felt against the Spaniards, as will be apparent in what we shall say presently.

The people in the service of the camp went out each day after grass for the horses, and there were accustomed to go continuously fifteen or twenty infantrymen and eight or ten cavalrymen to guard and defend them. It happened one day that the Indians who were following these Spaniards in ambush fell upon them so suddenly and with such shouts and cries that they terrified them simply by their clamor, without using their arms. The Spaniards, who were careless and disordered, were thrown into confusion, and before they collected themselves the Indians were able to get into their hands a soldier named Grajales, with whom they went away, very well satisfied with having taken him and not attempting to inflict any further injury on the other Christians.

The Castilians finally got themselves in order, and one of them hastened to the camp on horseback, giving the alarm and news of what had happened. At his story, twenty horsemen, well armed, left the camp with all haste, and finding the trail of the Indians who were going away with the Spaniard, they followed it. At the end of two leagues' travel they reached a large canebrake that the Indians had chosen as a secluded and hidden place where they had their women and children concealed. All of them, large and small, with much festivity and rejoicing at the fine prize they had taken, were eating very contentedly, failing to consider that the Castilians would make such haste to recover one lost Spaniard. They told Grajales to eat and not be uneasy, that they would not give him the wretched life they had given to Juan Ortiz.

The women and children said the same thing to him, each of them offering him the food they had for themselves, begging him to eat it and to console himself, and saying that they would deal with him as a friend and companion.

Hearing the Indians, the Spaniards entered the canebrake, making a noise as of more people than were actually coming, in order to alarm those within it with their clatter so that they would not defend themselves.

Hearing the trampling of the horses, the Indians fled along the lanes they had made in every direction through the canebrake in order to enter and leave it. In the middle of the canebrake they had cleared a large space as a dwelling-place for the women and children, who remained in the power of the Spaniards as slaves of him who shortly before had been theirs. So variable are the events of war and such is the inconstancy of its fortunes that there is recovered in a moment that which was held to be irretrievably lost, and in another is lost that which we believe to be safest.

Recognizing the voices of his people, Grajales went running out to receive them, giving thanks to God that they had delivered him so soon from his enemies. The Castilians scarcely knew him, because though the time of his imprisonment had been short the Indians had already stripped him and dressed him in no more than some trousers such as they wear. The Spaniards rejoiced with him, and gathering up all the people who were in the canebrake, who were women and children, went with them to the army where the governor received them with joy at their having recovered the Spaniard and, in freeing him, having captured so many of the enemy.

Grajales recounted immediately all that had happened to him and told how the Indians, when they came out of their ambuscade, had not desired to harm the Christians, because the arrows they had discharged had been more to intimidate them than to kill or wound them; that inasmuch as they had found them careless and off their guard, they could, if they liked, have killed most of them. And he said that as soon as they took him they were content and went without doing any other damage, leaving the rest of the Castilians; and that on the way and in the lodging in the canebrake they had treated him well, as had their women and children, speaking consoling words to him, and each of them offering him what they had to eat. The governor, learning of this, ordered brought before him the women, boys and children whom they had brought as prisoners and told them that he was much pleased at the good treatment they had accorded to the Spaniard, and at the friendly words that they had spoken to him, as a reward for which he was giving them their freedom so that they might go to their houses. And he charged them that thenceforth they should not flee from the Spaniards or stand in fear of them, but should communicate and deal with them as if they were all of the same nation; that he had not come there to mistreat the natives of the country, but to have them for friends and brothers; and that they were to tell this to their cacique and to their husbands, relatives and neighbors. Besides this cajolery, they gave them gifts and sent them away very contented with the kindness with which the general and all his people had treated them.

On two other occasions these same Indians later took two other Spaniards; one, named Hernando Vintimilla, was an expert seaman, and the other, Diego Muñoz, was a boy who was a page of Captain Pedro Calderón. They did not kill them or give them a miserable life as they had done with

Juan Ortiz, but allowed them to go about as freely as any Indian among them, so that later these two Christians, aided by their own cleverness, were able to escape from the power of the Indians in a ship that happened to be driven by a storm to that Bay of Espíritu Santo, as we shall tell below. In this way, with the fair words that the governor sent to say to the cacique Hirrihigua and with the good deeds that he did to his vassals, he forced him to mitigate and extinguish the fire of the anger and wrath against the Spaniards that he had in his heart. Kindness has such power that it even makes the fiercest of wild beasts change their original and natural savagery.

X

HOW THE DISCOVERY AND ENTRY OF THE SPANIARDS INTO THE INTERIOR COUNTRY IS BEGUN

Following these events, which took place in a little more than three weeks, the governor ordered Captain Baltasar de Gallegos to go with sixty lancers and as many more infantry, including harquebusiers, crossbowmen, and soldiers armed with shields [*rodeleros*], to explore the interior country, and they were to go as far as the chief pueblo of the cacique Urribarracuxi, which was the province nearest the two of Mucoço and Hirrihigua. The names of these provinces are not set down here because it is not known whether they were called by the name of the caciques or whether the caciques were called by the name of their lands, for we shall see below that in many parts of this great kingdom the lord and his province and its principal pueblo are called by the same name.

Captain Baltasar de Gallegos chose the same sixty lancers who had gone with him when he went in search of Juan Ortiz, and sixty more infantry. Juan Ortiz himself was among them, so that he might be their guide on the road and their interpreter among the Indians. Thus they went as far as the pueblo of Mucoço, who came out on the road to meet them, and he entertained and regaled them that night with much festivity and rejoicing at seeing them in his country. On the next day the captain asked him for an Indian to guide them to the pueblo of Urribarracuxi. Mucoço declined, saying that he begged him not to order him to do a thing against his own reputation and honor; that it would ill become him to furnish a guide to strangers against his own brother-in-law and brother. These would complain of him, with much reason, for having sent enemies to their land and house; now that he was a friend and servant of the Spaniards, he wished to be so without prejudice to another or to his honor. He said further that even if Urribarracuxi were not his brother-in-law, as he was, but an entire stranger, he would do the same thing for him; and certainly he would do so, since he was so nearly related by marriage and proximity. He also begged him very earnestly that they should not attribute that opposition to lack of love for and unwillingness to serve the Spaniards, for he certainly would not refuse except in order to avoid doing an unworthy thing by which he would become known as a traitor to his country, relatives, neighbors and friends; and that it would seem bad to the Castilians themselves if in that case or another like it he should do what they asked him, though it might be in their service, because, in short, it was ill done. Therefore he said that he would sooner choose death than to do a thing unbecoming to him.

Juan Ortiz replied by order of Captain Baltasar de Gallegos, and said that they had no need of a guide to show them the road, as it was well known that the one they had followed thus far was the public highway, which passed beyond to the pueblo of his brother-in-law. They requested the Indian for a messenger who would go ahead to notify the cacique Urribarracuxi of the coming of the Spaniards, so that he might not be alarmed, fearing that they had the intention of doing him evil and harm; and so that his brother-in-law might believe the messenger, who as a friend would not deceive him, they desired that he might be one of his vassals and not a stranger, so that he would be more readily believed. He was to say to Urribarracuxi on behalf of the governor that he and all his people desired not to offend anyone, and on behalf of Captain Baltasar de Gallegos, who was the one who was going to his country, he was to advise him that he carried orders and express commands from the general that, even if Urribarracuxi did not desire peace and friendship with him and his soldiers, they were to maintain it with the cacique, not out of respect for him, whom they did not know and to whom they owed nothing, but out of love for Mucoço, whom the Spaniards and their captain-general desired to please, and through him all his relatives, friends, and neighbors, as they had done in the case of Hirrihigua, who though he had been and was very rebellious, had not received nor would he receive any injury.

Much gratified, Mucoço replied that he kissed the hands of the governor, as a son of the Sun and Moon, and of all his captains and soldiers, his fellows, many times, for the grace and kindness he did him with those words, which obligated him anew to die for them; that now that he knew why they desired the guide he took great pleasure in giving one, and because it was fitting for both parties, he ordered that an Indian noble go who had been a great friend of Juan Ortiz in his past life. With him the Spaniards set out from the pueblo of Mucoço very happy and content, and still marveling to see that a barbarian should show such punctiliousness on all occasions.

In four days they went from the pueblo of Mucoço to that of his brother-in-law Urribarracuxi. From one pueblo to the other it was probably sixteen or seventeen leagues. They found it abandoned, for the cacique and all his vassals had gone to the forest in spite of the fact that the Indian friend of Juan Ortiz carried them the most affectionate message that it was possible to send them; and although after the Spaniards arrived in the pueblo he went back twice with the same message, the curaca neither wished to come out peaceably, nor to make war upon the Castilians, nor to give them an unfriendly reply. He excused himself with courteous words and with reasons that, though frivolous and vain, served his purpose.

This name *curaca* in the general language of the Indians of El Perú has the same meaning as cacique in the language of the island of Española and the neighboring ones, that is, lord of vassals. And while I am an Indian of El Perú and not of Santo Domingo or its environs, let me be permitted to introduce some words from my language in this, my work, so that it may be seen that I am a native of that land and of no other.

Throughout the twenty-five leagues that Baltasar de Gallegos and his companions marched from the pueblo of Hirrihigua to that of Urribarracuxi, they found many trees like those of Spain, there being wild grapevines, as we said above, walnuts, live oaks, mulberries, plums, pines and oaks. It was a pleasant and delightful country, which was divided between woodland and plain. There were some swamps, but they became fewer as one proceeded inland and left the seacoast.

Captain Baltasar de Gallegos sent four mounted men, among them being Gonzalo Silvestre, so that they might give this report of what they had seen to the governor, and state that there was food in that pueblo and its environs to sustain the army for some days. The four horsemen covered the twenty-five leagues that we mentioned in two days, without encountering anything worth recording on the journey. There we shall leave them in order to tell what happened in the camp meanwhile.

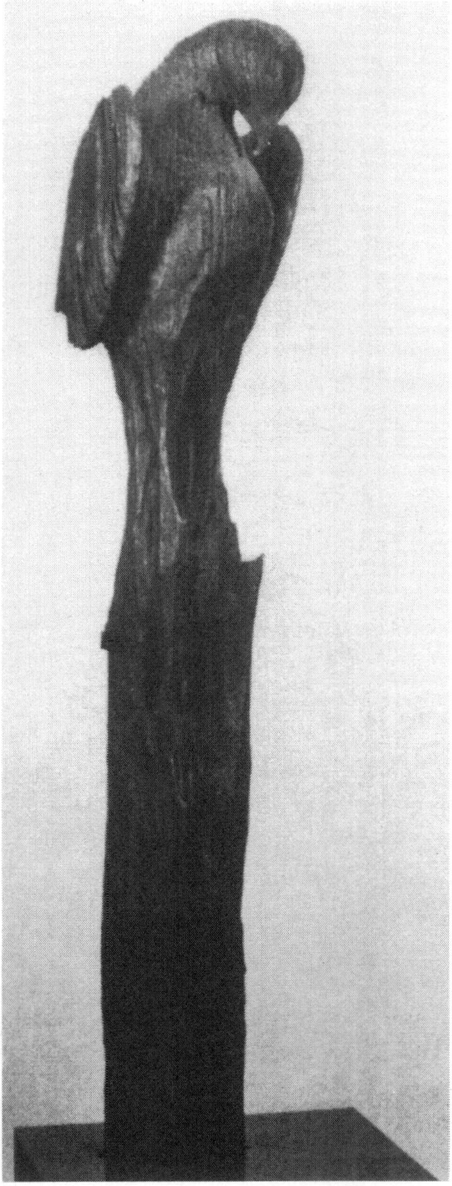

A Carved Wooden Bird on a Pedestal. Florida's wetlands preserve many kinds of native artifacts that are ordinarily lost to decay. This carving probably served in a religious context. Similar items would have been encountered by De Soto's men as they advanced from town to town after the landing. (From the Fort Center Site, Glades County, Florida, courtesy of the Florida State Museum)

XI

WHAT HAPPENED TO THE LIEUTENANT GENERAL ON GOING TO SEIZE A CURACA

One day while the governor was in the pueblo of Hirrihigua he received notice and certain information that the cacique had taken refuge in a forest not far from the army. The lieutenant general Vasco Porcallo de Figueroa, being a man so warlike and desirous of honor, wished to go for him in order to enjoy the glory of having brought him in, willingly or otherwise; and it was of no avail for the governor to attempt to prevent his journey, saying that he would send another captain. He desired to go himself, and thus he named the cavalry and infantry that he thought well to take with him and set out from the camp with great ostentation and greater hopes of bringing as a prisoner or making a friend of the curaca Hirrihigua. The latter, since he knew through his spies that the lieutenant general and many Castilians were coming to the place where he was, sent them a messenger saying that he begged them not to proceed farther, for he was in a secure place where they could not reach him however much they might try because of the many bad crossings of streams, swamps and forests that intervened. He therefore enjoined and begged them to return before some misfortune occur if they should enter some place from which they could not get out. He gave them this warning not out of fear that they would take him, but as a recompense and service for the kindness and favor they had done him in not having inflicted the harm and damage they could have done to his country and vassals.

The cacique Hirrihigua sent this message so many times that the messengers almost overtook one another, but the faster they came the more the lieutenant general desired to pass on, believing the contrary and persuaded that it was fear on the part of the curaca and not courtesy or any manner of friendship, and that he was so persistent with the messages because he could not escape him. These ideas hurried the march, serving as a spur to all who were with him, until they reached a large and dangerous swamp. Everyone raised difficulties about crossing it, yet Vasco Porcallo insisted that they enter it; and in order to inspire them by his example—for as an experienced soldier, which he was, he knew that there was no better way for a captain to be obeyed in difficulties than to go ahead of his soldiers (though this was rashness)—he spurred his horse and entered the swamp with a rush, and many others came in after him. But after the lieutenant general had taken a few steps, his horse fell with him, and both were about to drown, for those on foot could not swim out to reach him quickly and aid him because of the slime and mud, and they would have sunk in the mire if they had walked; and those on horseback could not come to his assistance for the same reason, for all were equally in danger, except that Vasco Porcallo's was much greater, he being weighted down with arms and enveloped in the mud with one leg pinned beneath his horse, and so he was drowning without being able to help himself.

Vasco Porcallo escaped from this danger more through Divine mercy than through human assistance, and seeing himself covered with mud, and with his hopes of taking the cacique gone, and that the Indian, without coming out to fight with him in an armed encounter, had overcome him simply with messages sent through friendship (being beaten and ashamed of himself and full of grief and melancholy), he ordered his men to return. Inasmuch as to his anger at this misfortune was added the memory of his large possessions and the ease and pleasure he had left behind in his house, and the fact that he was no longer young and the larger part of his life was now past, that all or most of the hardships of that conquest were yet to come, such as those of that day, or even worse, and that he was under no obligation to incur them of his own accord, for those that he had passed through were sufficient, he thought it well to return to his house and leave that expedition to the young men who were taking part in it.

These ideas went with him all the way; sometimes he spoke of them to himself and sometimes aloud, repeating the names of the two curacas Hirrihigua and Urribarracuxi continually, separating them into syllables and changing some of their letters so that what he wished to deduce from them would come out more clearly. He would say: "Hurri Harri, Hurri Higa. Burra coja [literally, a lame she-ass; an insult of some impact—DB], Hurri Harri; I consign to the devil the country where the first names that I heard in it, and all the rest, are so vile and infamous; I hereby aver ["Voto a tal," literally, "I swear to such"; a euphemism—DB] that from such princes there cannot be expected good middles or ends, nor from such omens favorable events. Let him work who must in order to live or to gain honor; I have more than enough property and honor for my lifetime and even after it."

With these words and other similar ones, repeated many times, he reached the army and at once asked the governor's permission to return to the island of Cuba. The governor granted it with the same liberality and graciousness with which he had received his offer for the conquest, and along with the permission he gave him the little galleon *San Antón,* in which he left.

Vasco Porcallo divided among the gentlemen and soldiers, as he saw fit, the arms and horses and other equipment and household service of very fine and excellent quality that he had brought, being such a wealthy and noble personage. He ordered left for the use of the army all the provisions and ship-stores he had brought from his house for himself and his family. He gave orders that a natural son of his, named Gómez Suárez de Figueroa, whom he had by an Indian woman in Cuba, should remain to accompany the governor on the expedition; he left him two horses and arms and the other things needed for the conquest. The latter conducted himself throughout as a very excellent gentleman and soldier, a worthy son of such a father, serving very readily on all the occasions that offered, and after the Indians killed his horses he always went on foot, not wishing to accept from the general or any other personage the loan or gift of a horse or any other present or favor, although he might be wounded and in great need. It seemed to him that all the gifts that they made and offered were not sufficient return for the services and benefits conferred by his father upon the whole army in general and upon individuals, whereupon the governor was distressed and desirous of pleasing and gratifying this gentleman, but his nature was so strange and distant that he was never willing to accept anything from anyone.

XII

THE REPORT THAT BALTASAR DE GALLEGOS SENT OF WHAT HE HAD DISCOVERED

The things that we have told being concluded in a very brief time, Vasco de Porcallo embarked and took with him all the Spaniards, Indians, and Negroes whom he had brought for his own service. The impression that he left with the whole army was not of cowardice, for it did not enter into his nature, but of his inconstancy, just as when he offered himself for the conquest in the island of Cuba he had left the impression of excessive ambition, through abandoning his house, property, and ease for new things, without any necessity for them. Always in serious matters, the decisions made imprudently and without consultation with friends are apt to give rise to desperate repentance, with evil and injury and much dishonor for him who acts so. If this gentleman had reflected before he left his house upon that which he reflected when he was returning to it, he would not have been censured as he was, nor he himself troubled by the belittling and loss of his reputation and waste of his property, which he could have employed in this expedition with more prudence and better counsel and with more credit and honor to himself. But who can subdue a wild beast or give counsel to the free and powerful, confident of themselves and persuaded that in proportion to worldly treasures they have those of the spirit, and that the same advantage that fortune gave them over other men in the property that the latter do not gain, it bestows upon them in discretion and wisdom, which they do not learn? Therefore they neither ask advice nor wish to receive it, nor can they heed those who are ready to give it.

On the day following the departure of Vasco Porcallo there arrived at the army the four horsemen whom Baltasar de Gallegos sent with a report of what he had seen and heard of the lands they had traversed. They reported very fully and much to the satisfaction of the Spaniards, because everything they said was favorable to their pretension and conquest, with one exception. They said that in front of the pueblo of Urribarracuxi there was an extremely large swamp, very difficult to pass. Everyone was joyful at the good news, and with regard to the swamp they replied that God had given man ingenuity and skill to overcome and pass through the difficulties that arose before him.

With this report the governor ordered a proclamation issued to the effect that preparations be made to march at the end of three days. He also ordered that Gonzalo Silvestre, with twenty more cavalry, return to advise Baltasar de Gallegos that the army would follow him on the fourth day.

Since the governor had to go away from the pueblo of Hirrihigua, it was necessary to leave a presidio and garrison to defend and guard the arms, provisions and munitions belonging to the army, for he had brought large quantities of all these things, and also in order that the caravel and the two brigantines that were in the bay should not be abandoned. He therefore named Captain Pedro Calderón to remain as land and sea commander, in charge of everything pertaining to both that remained. For their defense and protection, he left forty lancers and eighty infantrymen (exclusive of the sailors on the three vessels), with orders that they remain in that place, not moving to any other, until he should send them new orders, and that they should always endeavor to keep peace with the Indians of the vicinity and on no account to commit hostilities, even though they might suffer many affronts from them; and in particular they were to regale and maintain all friendly relations with Mucoço.

This order given, which Captain Pedro Calderón observed like a good captain and soldier, the governor left the Bay of Espíritu Santo and the pueblo of Hirrihigua and marched toward that of Mucoço, which he sighted on the morning of the third day of his march. Mucoço, who knew of his coming, went out to receive him with many tears and regrets at his departure, and begged him to remain that day in his pueblo. Not desiring to bother him with so many people, the governor told him that it was more convenient for him to go on, because he had each day's march set; he commended him to God and assigned to him as vassals the captain and soldiers who remained in the pueblo of Hirrihigua, thanking him anew for what he had done for him, his army, and Juan Ortiz. He embraced him with much tenderness and signs of great affection, which the goodness of this famous Indian merited. The latter kissed the governor's hands, with many tears, though he tried to keep them back, and among other expressions he used to show his grief at his absence he said that he could not tell which had been greater, his satisfaction at having known him and acknowledged him as lord, or his sorrow at seeing him leave without being able to follow his lordship, whom he begged, as a last favor, to remember him. Having taken leave of the general, he spoke to the rest of the captains and principal gentlemen and told them in fitting terms of the sorrow and solitude in which they were leaving him, and desired that the Sun direct and prosper them in all their actions. With this, the good Mucoço stopped, and the governor proceeded on his journey to the pueblo of Urribarracuxi without anything worthy of note occurring on the road.

From the Bay of Espíritu Santo to the pueblo of Urribarracuxi they traveled always to the northeast, that is, toward the north, bearing a little in the direction of the sunrise. With regard to this direction and all the rest that are stated in this *History*, it is to be noted that they are not to be taken as literally correct, in order that I may not be blamed if something else should prove to be true in the future when that country shall be won, God willing. Although I made every possible effort to set them down with certainty, I was unable to do so, because as the chief purpose of these Castilians was to conquer the land and seek gold and silver, they gave no attention to anything except gold and silver. Therefore they failed to do other things more important to them than marking out the confines of the land, and this is sufficient to excuse me for not having written with the certainty that I have wished and that was necessary.

XIII

THEY FAIL TWICE TO CROSS THE GREAT SWAMP, AND THE GOVERNOR GOES TO SEEK A PASSAGE, AND FINDS IT

Having arrived at the pueblo of Urribarracuxi, where Captain Baltasar de Gallegos was awaiting him, the governor sent messengers to the cacique, who was concealed in the woods, offering him friendship, but no effort was sufficient to make him come out peaceably. Seeing this, the governor left the Indian alone and busied himself in sending scouts in three directions, who went to find a passage through the swamp, which was three leagues from the pueblo and was large and very difficult to cross, for it was a league in breadth and contained a great deal of very deep mud (for which reason they call it a swamp), up to the very edge. Two-thirds of the swamp, on either side, were of mud, and the other third, in the center, was of water so deep that it could not be forded; but with all these difficulties the explorers found a crossing. They returned eight days after they had left, with news of having found it, and a very good one. With this report the governor and all his men set out from the pueblo and in two days reached the crossing of the swamp and passed over it easily, for the crossing was good; but because the swamp was so wide, they spent a whole day in passing through it. Half a league beyond the swamp they stationed themselves on a fine plain, and on the following day the same scouts, having gone out to see which way they must travel, returned saying that it was entirely impossible to go farther because of the many swamps along the streams that led out of the great swamp and inundated the flat country. This was the reason why the swamp was easily passed at the crossing of which we have told, because a great deal of water flowed out of the main body above the crossing, which facilitated the safe passage of the great swamp and made it very difficult to travel through the country. For this reason the governor wished to discover the road for himself, because if he himself could not find a way in the dangerous and difficult passes, he would not be satisfied with [sending] another. With this determination he again crossed to the other side of the swamp, and choosing a hundred cavalry and a hundred infantry to go with him, he left the rest of the army where it was with the maese de campo and marched three days up the swamp along one side of it, sending out scouts at intervals to see if some crossing could be found.

In all these three days there was no lack of Indians who, coming out of the woods along the edge of the swamp, assailed the Spaniards with arrows and then retreated to the woods; but some remained trapped, dead, or captured. In order to free themselves from the importunity and molestation of the Spaniards in questioning them about the road and crossing of the swamp, the prisoners offered to guide them, and as they were enemies, they led and put them into difficult passes and places where there were Indians in ambush, who came out to discharge arrows at the Christians. As soon as the Spanish perceived their malice they took four of them and threw them to the dogs, who killed them. Therefore one of the captured Indians, fearing death, offered to guide them faithfully, and taking them out of the bad passes through which they were traveling, he put them on a clear, plain and wide road, apart from the swamp. Having marched along it for four leagues, they turned back toward the swamp where they found a crossing that was free of mud at the entrance and exit, and the waters of which could be forded about breast-deep for the distance of a league except in the middle of the channel, which for a space of a hundred paces could not be forded because of its great depth. Here the Indians had made a poor sort of bridge of two large trees that had fallen into the water, and the space they did not cover was bridged over with large timbers fastened together and other smaller stakes laid athwart in the form of a balustrade. Pánphilo de Narváez had made this same crossing ten years before with his unhappy army.

Much pleased at having found this crossing, Governor Hernando de Soto summoned two soldiers, natives of the island of Cuba and mestizos, for thus throughout the West Indies they call us who are children of a Spaniard and an Indian woman or of an Indian and a Spanish woman. The children of a Negro and an Indian woman or of an Indian and a Negro woman they call *mulatos,* as in Spain. The Negroes give the name criollos to the children of Spanish men and women and to the children of Negro men and women who are born in the Indies, to signify that they are born there, as distinguished from those who go from here, Spain. The Spaniards have now introduced this word *criollo* into their language, giving it the same meaning as the Negroes. In the same way they call *cuarterón* or *cuatratuo* him who is one-fourth part Indian, as the son of a Spaniard and a mestiza or of a mestizo and a Spanish woman. The native of Guinea they call simply a Negro, and the Spaniard by what he is. They have all these names in the Indies to apply to the intrusive nations who are not natives.

As we were saying, the governor ordered the two islanders, whose names were Pedro Morón and Diego de Oliva, both very expert swimmers, to take axes and cut some branches to be placed crosswise on the bridge, and to do everything that they thought would contribute to the convenience of those who had to cross over it. The two soldiers carried out their orders with all promptness, and while they were most busily engaged therein they saw some canoes emerge with Indians who had been concealed among the many reeds and rushes that are along the margins of that swamp; they were coming at top speed to shoot arrows at them. The mestizos dived headlong from the bridge and stayed under water until they came up where their companions were, slightly wounded, for because they had been under water, the arrows had not penetrated very far. After making this assault, the Indians withdrew from the pass and went where they did not see them again. The Spaniards repaired the bridge without being troubled further, and three harquebus-shots above that crossing they found another very good one for the horses.

Having found the passes he desired for crossing the swamp, the governor thought it well to give information of them immediately to Luis de Moscoso, his maese de campo, so that he might march after him with the army, and also in order that as soon as he should receive the news he might send him a supply of biscuit and cheese, because the people whom he had with him were in need of food, as they had brought few provisions, not having intended going so far. The governor therefore called Gonzalo Silvestre and in the presence of everyone said to him: "There fell to your lot by chance the best horse in our whole army, and it means greater toil for you, because we have to entrust [to you] the most difficult tasks that present themselves to us. Therefore have patience and mark that our lives and our conquest require that you return tonight to the camp and tell Luis de Moscoso what you have seen, and how we have found a passage through the swamp. He is to march at once after us with all the men, and as soon as you arrive he is to send you back with two loads of biscuits and cheese upon which we can subsist until we find food, for we are feeling the need of it. And so that you may return more safely than you go, you are to order him to assign thirty lancers to guard you on the road. I will wait for you in this same place until tomorrow night, when you are to return here, and although the road may seem long and difficult to you, and the time short, I know to whom I am entrusting this affair. In order that you may not go alone, take anyone you choose for a companion and go immediately, as it will be well for you to arrive in the camp by dawn so that the Indians may not kill you if daylight should overtake you before you are through the swamp."

Gonzalo Silvestre, without replying a word, left the governor and mounted his horse. On the road as he went he met one Juan López Cacho from Sevilla, a page of the governor who had a good horse, and he said to him: "The general orders that you and I go with a message from him to the camp, by dawn; therefore follow me at once, for I am on my way." Juan López replied, saying: "By your life, take someone else! For I am tired and cannot go there." Gonzalo Silvestre answered: "The governor ordered me to choose a companion and I choose you; if you want to come, come and welcome, and if you want to stay, well and good. Our going together does not lessen the danger, nor does my going alone increase the hardship." So saying, he spurred his horse and continued on his way. Juan López, in spite of himself, mounted his horse and went after him. They left the place where the governor was at sunset, both youths, scarcely more than twenty years old.

XIV

WHAT THE TWO SPANIARDS EXPERIENCED ON THEIR JOURNEY UNTIL THEY ARRIVED AT THE CAMP

These two valiant and spirited Spaniards not only did not flee from hardship, though they found it quite excessive, nor fear danger, though it was so imminent, but with all readiness and promptness, as we have seen, they exposed themselves to both, and thus they traveled the first four or five leagues without any trouble whatever because the road was clear, without woods, swamps or streams, and in this distance they heard no Indians. But as soon as they had passed over it, they encountered the difficulties and bad passes they had found on going in, with deep miry places, woods, and streams that issued from the great swamp and turned to re-enter it. They could not avoid these difficult places because, as there was no open road and as they did not know the country, in order not to lose their way they were forced to return following the same trail that they had made three days before on their way in. They traveled only by the landmarks that they recognized as having seen and noted on going in.

The risk these two companions ran of being killed by the Indians was so evident that no effort they could make would have sufficed to save them from it if God in His mercy had not succored them, by means of the natural instincts of the horses. They, as if they had understanding, began at once to follow the trail they had taken on going in, putting their noses to ground like hounds or setters in order to find and follow the road; and although at first their masters pulled at the reins, not understanding the intention of the horses, they would not raise their heads, still seeking the trail. And when they lost it, in order to find it they gave some loud sniffs and snorts that greatly alarmed their masters, who feared that the Indians would hear them. Gonzalo Silvestre's horse was better at following the trail and at finding it when they lost it. But we should not wonder at this excellence nor at many others that this horse exhibited, because he was marked out naturally by signs and color as extremely good for both peace and war. He was dark chestnut, pitch-colored, with a white left foot and a matching mark on the forehead, signs that in horses of all colors promise more goodness and loyalty than any others, whether they be jades or hacks; and the chestnut, especially pitch-colored, is good above all others for work and sport, for mud and dust. Juan López Cacho's horse was a toast-colored bay, which they call *zorruno,* with black mane and tail, extremely good but not equal in excellence to the chestnut, who guided his master and his companion. Having recognized the intention and goodness of his horse when he lowered his head to find and follow the road, Gonzalo Silvestre gladly left him alone without opposing him in any way, for they got on better thus. With these difficulties and others that can be better imagined than written, these two brave Spaniards traveled without a road all night, perishing from hunger, since for two days past they had not eaten anything except stalks of maize that the Indians had planted. They were also overcome with sleep and fatigued with labor, as were the horses, they not having been unsaddled for three days and barely having had their bridles taken off so that they could eat a little. But seeing death before their eyes if they did not overcome these hardships gave them strength to go on. On either side as they traveled they left behind large bands of Indians, who by the light of the many fires they had built seemed to be dancing, leaping and singing, eating and drinking, with much joy and merriment and a great deal of talking and shouting among themselves, which kept up all night. Whether they were celebrating some of their heathen festivals or talking of the people newly arrived in their country is not known, but the cries and shouts the Indians gave in their rejoicing meant safety and life to the two Spaniards who were passing among them, because in the midst of their great confusion and hilarity they did not hear the horses pass nor pay attention to the loud barking of their dogs, which, hearing them go by, were raising a frantic hue and cry. All of which was a Divine providence, for if it had not been for this noise on the part of the Indians and the trailing of the horses, it would have been impossible to travel one league, much less twelve, among all those dangers without their being heard and killed.

Having traveled more than ten leagues with the difficulty that we have seen, Juan López said to his companion: "Either let me sleep awhile, or kill me with a lance-thrust on this road; I cannot go farther or stay on my horse, for I am dying for sleep." Gonzalo Silvestre, who had already twice refused him the same request, overcome by his importunity, said to him: "Get down and sleep if you like, but just because you cannot stay awake an hour longer you will have the Indians kill us. Considering the distance we have come, the crossing of the swamp cannot be far away, and it would be well for us to pass through it before daylight, for if day overtakes us here it will be impossible to escape death."

Without waiting for any more argument, Juan López Cacho fell on the ground like a dead man, and his companion took his lance and his horse's reins. At that hour a great darkness overspread everything, and with it came so much water from the sky that it seemed to be a deluge, but however much it rained on Juan López it did not wake him, for the power that sleep has over the human body is extremely great, and as such a necessary ailment it cannot be denied.

The rain ceased, the clouds passed away, and clear daylight appeared all in a moment, so much so that Gonzalo Silvestre blamed himself for not having seen the day dawn, but it might be that he had slept on horseback also, as did his comrade on the ground. I knew one gentleman (among others) who in traveling went three or four leagues while asleep, without waking or paying attention when they spoke to him, and at times he was thereby in great danger of being dragged on the ground by his pack animal. As soon as Gonzalo Silvestre saw the daylight so clearly, he hurriedly called Juan López, and because the hoarse, low, and quiet calls that he gave were not sufficient to awaken him, he made use of the butt-end of the lance and roused him with several good strokes, saying to him: "See what your sleepiness has caused us; look at the full daylight, which we feared, and which has caught us where we cannot escape death at the hands of our enemies."

Juan López mounted his horse, and they traveled with all haste at a faster gait than pacing, going at a canter, the horses being so good that they could stand both the past work and the present. By daylight the two horsemen could not avoid being seen by the Indians, and in a moment an alarm and outcry was raised, warning being sent from one side of the swamp to the other with such a buzz and clamor and resounding of conch shells, trumpets, drums, and other rude instruments that it seemed they wished to kill them with the noise alone.

At the same moment so many canoes appeared on the water, coming out from between the reeds and rushes, that these Spaniards, in imitation of the poetic fables, said that they looked like nothing so much as the leaves of the trees, which on falling into the water were converted into canoes. The Indians assembled so rapidly and swiftly at the crossing of the swamp that when the Christians reached it they were already waiting for them on the high ground.

The two companions, though they saw the imminent peril that after so much hardship undergone on land, was awaiting them in the water, considering that fear would make it greater and more certain than would daring, threw themselves at it with great force and boldness, without heeding anything except making haste to pass over that league that, as we have said, was the breadth of this bad swamp. It was God's will that, since the horses were covered with water and the riders well armed, all came out safely without wounds, which was no small miracle in view of the infinite number of arrows that they had shot at them. One of them, telling later of the mercy the Lord had shown them, particularly at this place, in that they had not killed or wounded them, said that, after coming out of the water, he had turned around to see what remained there and saw it as thickly covered with arrows as a street would be with rushes on some great and solemn festival day.

In the little that we have told about these two Spaniards, and in other similar cases we shall note later, may be seen the bravery of the Spanish nation, which, undergoing so many and such great hardships and others even more severe, which through their negligence have not been recorded, won the New World for their prince—a fortunate acquisition for both Indians and Spaniards, for the latter gained temporal wealth and the former spiritual.

The Spaniards who were with the army, hearing such a strange shouting and uproar among the Indians and suspecting what it might be, assembled with all haste, and more than thirty horsemen went out to the relief of the passage of the swamp.

Nuño Tovar was well in the lead of all of them, running full speed on a most handsome horse, a bright dappled gray, with such wildness and dash on the part of the horse and such an expression of intrepidity on the face of the rider that simply by the gallantry and nobility of his person, as such a fine figure of a horseman, he could reassure the two companions who were in such danger.

Although in disfavor with his captain-general, this good gentleman did not fail to show on all occasions his personal prowess and courageous spirit, always doing his duty in order to comply with the obligation and debt he owed to his own nobility. Disdain with all its power could never subdue him and make him do otherwise; generosity of spirit never permits depravity in those who truly possess it. To this the princes and the powerful who are tyrants, when, with or without reason, they become offended, rarely or never respond with the reconciliation and pardon such persons deserve. It seems rather that they become more and more offended as they dwell on their virtue; therefore he who finds himself in such a case, in my opinion and poor judgment, if he has nothing to eat should go beg it for the love of God rather than persist in their service, because whatever miracles he may perform in it will not suffice to restore him to their favor.

XV

THIRTY LANCERS GO OUT AFTER THE GOVERNOR WITH THE SUPPLY OF BISCUITS

Although they saw the two Spaniards come out of the water, the Indians did not cease pursuing them by land, shooting many arrows at them in the great anger they felt at their having traveled so many leagues without their people hearing them; but as soon as they saw Nuño Tovar and the rest of the horsemen who were coming to their aid, they left them and returned to the woods and the swamp in order not to be run down by the horses, as they could not sustain an engagement with them in the open field.

The two companions were received by their people with great pleasure and rejoicing, and much more so when they saw that they had not been wounded. The maese de campo Luis de Moscoso, learning of the general's order, prepared the thirty horsemen to return immediately with Gonzalo Silvestre, who scarcely took time to breakfast on two mouthfuls of half-matured maize cooked on the ear and a little cheese they gave him, as there was nothing else, for the whole camp was suffering from hunger. They took two pack mules laden with biscuits and cheese, a scanty enough provision for so many people if God had not provided another source, as we shall see later. Gonzalo Silvestre set out with these supplies and his thirty companions within an hour after he arrived at the camp. Juan López remained there, saying that the general had not ordered him either to return or to come.

The thirty mounted men crossed the swamp without opposition from the Indians, and although they brought men from the army to help them in the crossing, there was no necessity for it. They marched all that day without seeing the enemy, and notwithstanding the haste that they made they were unable to reach the place where the governor told them he would await them until two hours after dark. They found that the general had crossed the swamp and pressed forward, at which they were much disturbed, finding themselves thirty men alone in the midst of so many enemies as they feared were surrounding them. Because they did not know where the governor had gone, they did not follow him. They agreed to remain in the same camp that he had made on the previous night, adopting among themselves the plan that ten of them would make the rounds on horseback the first third of the night, another ten would stand watch with their horses saddled and bridled, with the reins in their hands in order to be able to go quickly wherever it might be necessary to fight, and the remaining ten would have their horses saddled but not bridled, and allow them to eat, so that in this manner, working and resting by turns, they could undergo their nocturnal toil. Thus the whole night passed, without any sign of the enemy.

As soon as daylight came, seeing the trail that the governor had left through the swamp, they passed on, experiencing good fortune in that the Indians had not occupied it in order to oppose their passage. It would have been a great hardship for them to have made it fighting in water breast-deep, without being able to attack or flee and having no missile weapons with which to keep the enemy at a distance; they, on the other hand, having great facility for going and coming in their canoes against our people and shooting arrows at them from a distance or at close range. Certainly on this occasion and on other similar ones the *History* will recount, one is moved to consider what might be the reason why the same Indians, in the same places and circumstances, on some days should fight with such eagerness and desire to kill the Castilians and on others pay no attention to them. I can give no other reason except that in fighting or not fighting they would be obliged to observe some of their heathen superstitions, as some nations did in the time of the great Julius Caesar, or that, seeing that the Spaniards were passing on and did not stop in their country, they let them alone. However it might be, the thirty horsemen accepted it as a piece of good luck and followed the governor's trail. Having marched six leagues, they found him encamped in some very beautiful valleys having large maize fields, so productive that each stalk had three or four ears, some of which they gathered while mounted on their horses, in order to appease their hunger. They ate them raw, giving thanks to

God, our Lord, for having succored them with such abundance, for to the needy anything seems a great deal.

The governor received them very well, and with generous words and much praise he commended the good work that Gonzalo Silvestre had done and the great danger and insupportable hardships that he had undergone. He said finally that he could not humanly have done more; he offered to reward such merit in the future, and on the other hand he asked his pardon for not having waited for him, as he had failed to do, saying by way of excuse that he had passed on, first, because the hunger they were experiencing could not be endured, and second, because he had little hope of his returning in view of the great risk that he ran, and that he had feared the Indians might have killed him.

This very fertile province where the thirty horsemen found the governor was called Acuera, and its lord had that same name.[1] The latter, learning of the arrival of the Castilians in his country, fled to the woods with all his people. From the province of Urribarracuxi to that of Acuera it is about twenty leagues, on a north-south line.

Having received the general's order, the maese de campo Luis de Moscoso immediately, on that same day, set the army in motion. They crossed the swamp easily, finding no opposition from the enemy, and continued their march. In three days they reached the other crossing of the same swamp, and as that ford was wider and carried more water than the other, they spent three days in crossing it, during which time, and in the twelve leagues they marched along the edge of the swamp, they did not see a single Indian. This was no small favor that they [the Indians] did them, for the crossings being so difficult in themselves, however little opposition they might have given them, it would have greatly increased their troubles.

While Luis de Moscoso was crossing the swamp, the governor, because his people were suffering from hunger, sent him a great deal of Indian corn

[1]In Rangel's account, Acuera was bypassed on the way to Ocale. Further, between Garcilaso's Acuera and Apalache it is difficult to reconcile the Inca's account with those of the other chroniclers. There is some disagreement on how best to correlate the conflicting itineraries. John R. Swanton believed that the Inca's misplaced Acuera equates with the Ocale (or Cale) of Rangel and Elvas, and that the Inca transplanted the name *Ocali* to the next province, Potano. John H. Hann, in contrast, prefers to stand by Garcilaso's Ocali as identical to the Ocale of the others. By Hann's reconstruction, the Potano province is altogether omitted in *La Florida*. John R. Swanton, *Final Report of the United States De Soto Expedition Commission* (Washington: U.S.G.P.O., 1939 [76th Cong., 1st sess., House. Doc. 71]), 144; John H. Hann, "De Soto, Dobyns, and Demography in Western Timucua," *The Florida Anthropologist* 43 (1990):3–4.

or maize, with which they satisfied themselves and arrived at the place where the governor was.

XVI

THE INSOLENT REPLY OF THE LORD OF THE PROVINCE OF ACUERA

The whole army having assembled in Acuera, while the men and horses were recovering from the hunger they had suffered in the days past, which was no small thing, the governor with his accustomed clemency sent messages to the cacique Acuera with some of his Indians whom he had captured, saying that he begged him to come out peaceably and to consent to have Spaniards for friends and brothers; that the latter were a warlike people and brave, who, if their friendship was not accepted, could do much harm and damage to his lands and vassals. At the same time he was to understand and be convinced that they did not have the intention of injuring anyone, as they had not done in the provinces they had left behind them, but on the contrary felt a strong friendship for those who had been willing to receive it. Their chief intention was to reduce through peace and friendship all the provinces and nations of that great kingdom to the obedience and service of the most powerful emperor and king of Castilla, their lord, whose servants they were; and the governor desired to see and speak with him in order to tell him these things more fully and to give him an account of the order that his king and lord had given him to deal and communicate with the lords of that land.

The cacique replied haughtily, saying that he had already had much information from other Castilians who had come to that country years before as to who they were, and he knew very well about their lives and customs, which consisted in occupying themselves like vagabonds in going from one land to another, living from robbing, pillaging, and murdering those who had not offended them in any way. He by no means desired friendship or peace with such people, but rather mortal and perpetual warfare, and even though they might be as brave as they boasted of being, he had no fear of them because he and his vassals considered themselves no less valiant, as proof of which he promised to wage war against them during all the time that they might see fit to remain in his province, not in the open nor in a pitched battle, although he could do so, but by waylaying and ambushes, taking them off guard. Therefore he warned and admonished them to watch and be on their guard against him and his people, whom he had ordered to bring him every week two heads of Christians, and no more; that this would satisfy him because by beheading two of them every eight days, he thought to put an end to all of them within a few years, for although they might settle and make establishments they could not perpetuate themselves because they brought no women to have children and carry the next generation onward. To what they said about giving obedience to the king of Spain, he replied that he himself was king in his own country and there was no necessity for becoming the vassal of another who had as many as he. Those who put themselves under a foreign yoke when they could live free he regarded as very mean-spirited and cowardly. He and all his people protested that they would die a thousand deaths to maintain their liberty and that of their country; and he gave that reply once and for all. With regard to their vassalage and their statement that they were servants of the emperor and king of Castilla, and that they were going about conquering new lands for his empire, he said that it was well and good that they were all of this; that now he held them in less esteem, since they admitted being servants of another and that they were laboring and gaining kingdoms so that others might rule them and enjoy the fruits of their labors. Inasmuch as they were undergoing hunger, fatigue, and other hardships in such an enterprise, and risking their lives, it would be better and more honorable and profitable for them to win and acquire these things for themselves and their descendants than for strangers; and since they were so mean-spirited that, being so far away, they did not abjure the name of servants, they need not hope for [his] friendship at any time, for he could not bestow it in such a mean way, nor did he wish to know the order of their king. He knew what he might do in his own country and the manner in which he must treat them; therefore they should leave as quickly as they could if they did not all wish to die at his hands.

On hearing the Indian's reply, the governor was amazed to see with what arrogance and pride of spirit a barbarian was able to say such things, for which reason from that time forward he attempted more insistently to win his friendship, sending him many messages couched in affectionate and courteous terms. But the curaca said to all the Indians who went to him that he had sent his reply the first time and that he intended to give no other response, nor did he.

The army was in this province twenty days, resting from the hardship and hunger of their past march and collecting the things necessary for passing on. During these days the governor was engaged in obtaining information and reports concerning the province. He sent runners in every direction to observe carefully and diligently and note the good parts of it, and they brought favorable news.

In those twenty days the Indians were not sleeping; on the other hand they did not fail to carry out the threats and menaces their curaca had made against the Castilians, and so that the latter might see that they had not been empty ones, they were so watchful and astute in their stratagems that no Spaniard wandered a hundred paces from the camp that they did not shoot him with arrows and immediately behead him, and as quickly as his people went to his assistance they found themselves without their heads, which the Indians carried off to present to their cacique, as he had ordered them to do.

The Christians interred the bodies of the dead where they found them. The Indians returned the following night, disinterred them, cut them in pieces, and hung them from the trees where the Spaniards could see them. By such acts they complied well with what their cacique had ordered them, namely, that they bring him two heads of Christians every week, for in two days they brought him four, two at a time, and fourteen during the whole space of time the Spaniards were in his country, not counting those whom they wounded, who were many more. They came out to make these assaults so safely and so near their haunts, which were the woods, that they could return to them very easily, having done as much damage as possible, without losing a single opportunity that was offered them. From this the Castilians came to verify the truth of the words that the Indians whom they found all along the road through the great swamp had shouted to them: "Go on, thieves, traitors; in Acuera and farther on in Apalache they will treat you as you deserve; they will cut you all in quarters and pieces and hang you from the highest trees along the road."

The Spaniards, however they might try, did not kill fifty Indians in that whole time, because they were very cautious and vigilant in their stratagems.

XVII

THE GOVERNOR ARRIVES IN THE PROVINCE OF OCALI, AND WHAT TOOK PLACE THERE

At the end of the twenty days the governor left the province of Acuera without doing any damage in the pueblos or the cultivated fields, so that they would not regard them [the Spaniards] as cruel and inhuman. He went in search of another province, called Ocali.[2] There are about twenty leagues from the one to the other. They directed their march toward the north, bearing a little to the northeast. They passed an uninhabited region ten or twelve leagues in extent, which lies between the two provinces, in which there were large forests of walnuts, pines, and other trees unknown in Spain. They all appeared to have been set out by hand, there being so much space from one to another that horses could even run between them. It was a very open and pleasant forest.

In this province there were no longer found so many swamps and difficult passes at miry places as were in the former ones, because, as it was farther removed from the coast, the salt marshes and bays that entered the others from the sea did not reach to them. In the former region the land is so low and flat that the sea extends into it in some places thirty leagues, in others forty, fifty or sixty, and in some more than a hundred, forming great swamps and morasses that make it difficult and even impossible to cross them. These Castilians found some so bad that upon placing the foot on them the earth trembled for twenty or thirty paces round about. On top it looked as if horses could pass over it, for the surface was dry, without a sign that there was water or mud underneath. On breaking through that surface the horses and the men as well sank and were drowned, unable to help themselves. They were put to much trouble in going around these places. They also found this province of Ocali more abundant in supplies than the others we have mentioned, both because there were more people in it who cultivated the soil and because it was more fertile in itself. The Spaniards noticed the same in all the provinces they traversed throughout this great kingdom, that is, the farther inland the country was and the more removed from the sea, the more populous it was and the more fertile and productive in itself.

In the four provinces referred to, and in the others we shall mention later, and generally throughout the land of La Florida that these Spaniards discovered, they experienced a great scarcity of provisions of meat, because they found none in all the region that they passed through, nor did the Indians have any domesticated cattle. There are many common deer and fallow deer throughout that country, which the Indians kill with their bows and arrows. The fallow deer are so large that they are little smaller than the red deer of Spain, and the red deer are like large bulls. There are also very large bears and panthers, as we said above.

---

[2]See note 1 concerning the identity of Garcilaso's Ocali in light of the other chronicles.

A Palmetto. From their landing site in Florida the expedition entered the flat, sandy, pine barrens of the southeastern coastal plain. Here they marched through seemingly endless forests of longleaf pine trees, broad swamps, and vast thickets of saw palmetto. The berries of the saw palmetto are edible, and the natives used the leaves to thatch their houses. (Courtesy of the University of Alabama Museum of Natural History)

Having passed over the twelve leagues of uninhabited country, they marched another seven through inhabited lands having a few homes scattered through the fields, not in the form of a pueblo. Throughout the seven leagues there was this form of habitation. At the end of them was the principal pueblo, called Ocali, like the province itself and its cacique. He and all his people, carrying what they had in their houses, fled to the woods.

The Spaniards entered the pueblo, which had six hundred houses. They lodged themselves in them, finding there much food in the form of maize and other grains, vegetables, and various fruits, such as plums, nuts, raisins, and acorns. The governor at once sent Indians to the chief curaca, offering him peace and the friendship of the Castilians. The Indian excused himself on that occasion with courteous words, saying that he could not come out so soon. After six days he came out peaceably, though still suspicious, because in all the time that he was with the Spaniards he never acted honestly. The governor and his people, having received him very affectionately, pretended not to see the ill will they perceived in him, so that he might not be more disturbed than he was already with his own evil plans, as we shall soon see.

Near the pueblo there was a large river, carrying much water, that even then, it being summer, could not be forded. There were precipices on either side as high as the length of two pikes and as perpendicular as walls. Throughout La Florida, because of the almost total absence of stone in the country, the rivers cut very deeply and have very steep banks. This river is described more fully than the others because further mention will be made of a notable feat that thirty Spaniards performed on it.

In order to cross this river it was necessary to construct a wooden bridge, and the governor having made an agreement with the curaca to have his Indians build it, they went out one day to see the site where it was to be placed. While they were walking about planning the bridge, more than five hundred Indian archers rushed out of some underbrush that was on the other side of the river and shouted loudly: "You want a bridge, do you, thieves, vagabonds, foreigners? Well, you will not see it made by our hands!" Whereupon they sent a shower of arrows toward the place where the cacique and the governor were. The latter asked, "How is it that you permit this impudence, when you have represented yourself as a friend?" The cacique replied that it was not in his power to remedy it because many of his vassals, seeing him inclined to the friendship and service of the Spaniards, had refused him obedience and lost respect for him, as was shown on that occasion, for which he was not to blame.

At the shout the Indians raised on shooting their arrows, a greyhound, which one of the governor's pages was leading by the collar, jumped and knocked down the page, dragging him on the ground. He gave a leap and threw himself into the water, and however much the Spaniards might call to him, he would not come back. Seeing the dog swimming, the Indians shot at him so skillfully that they placed more than fifty arrows in his head and shoulders, which were exposed. With all this the dog was able to come out on the bank, but on leaving the water he at once fell dead. This grieved the governor and all his people very much, because he was an extremely fine animal and much needed in the conquest, during which, in the short time that it had lasted, he had made forays that caused no little wonder against the Indian enemies, both by day and by night, only one of which we shall recount, in order to show his prowess.

XVIII

CONCERNING OTHER EVENTS THAT TOOK PLACE IN THE PROVINCE OF OCALI

During the six days that the cacique Ocali was in hiding in the woods, before he came out peaceably, the governor took care to send him three or four messengers every day with friendly messages, so that the Indian might see that they were not forgetting him. They returned with the reply that the curaca gave them. With one of these messengers there came four young Indian nobles with a great many plumes on their heads, which are the principal adornment that they wear. They came for no reason except to see the Spanish army and to note what kind of people the new arrivals were, how they looked, what kind of clothing and arms they wore, what sort of animals the horses were, with which they had so frightened them. In short, they came to confirm or undeceive themselves regarding the great things that they had heard said of the Spaniards.

Having received them affably, because he knew that they were nobles, and curious, and that they came only to see this army, the governor, having given them presents of things from Spain to make friends with them and through them with the cacique, ordered that they be taken to another part of his lodgings and served with food.

The Indians were eating very quietly when, at a moment when they felt that the Castilians were off their guard, all four jumped up together and ran at full speed toward the woods, so swiftly that the Christians were doubtful of being able to overtake them on foot, for they did not follow them, nor did they pursue them on their horses, as they did not have them at hand.

The greyhound, which happened to be nearby, hearing the shout the Indians gave and seeing them run, followed them. As if he had human understanding, he passed by the first whom he overtook and also the second and the third, until reaching the fourth, who was running ahead. Seizing him by the shoulder, he threw him down and held him on the ground. Meanwhile the Indian who was nearest came up; as the dog saw that he was passing by he loosed the first one and caught the one who was passing, and having thrown him down, he grasped the third, who was now passing by, and having done the same with him as with the first two, he went at the fourth, who now came up. Throwing him to the ground, he returned to the others and ran between them with such dexterity and skill, leaping at the one who was down and grasping and pulling down him who raised up, and threatening them with loud barks at the same time that he seized them, that he confused and held them until the Spaniards came up to their assistance. They took the four Indians and returned with them to the camp. Taking each one separately, they questioned them as to why they had fled, so without occasion, fearing that this might be a countersign for some treachery that they had plotted. All four replied as one person that they had done it for no reason at all except a vain fancy that seized them, it appearing to them that it would be a great exploit and proof of gallantry and agility if they should escape from the midst of the Castilians in that manner. They thought to boast of this brave exploit later among the Indians, because of its being in their opinion a great victory, of which they had been deprived by the hound Bruto, for so the dog was named.

At this point Juan Coles, having recounted some of the things that we have told, tells another particular exploit of the hound Bruto. He says that on another river, before coming to Ocali, some Indians and Spaniards being on its bank talking together peacefully, one daring Indian, there being many such, gave a Castilian a hard blow with his bow, for no reason whatever, and then jumped into the water, and all his people followed him. He says that the hound, which was nearby, seeing what happened, jumped in after them, and although he overtook other Indians, he says that he did not seize any of them until he came to the one who had struck the blow, and grasping him, he tore him to pieces in the water.

For these attacks and for others that Bruto had made upon them while guarding the army at night, so that no enemy Indian approached it whom he

Spanish Cavalier with War Dog, ca. 1500–1540. An armored horseman with shield and lance was a formidable foe to the Native American warriors of the Southeast. During the conquest the Spaniards used greyhounds trained as attack dogs to assist them. (Courtesy of Osprey Publishing, London)

did not immediately destroy, the Indians avenged themselves by killing him as has been told. Knowing about him from these stories, they shot him very willingly, at the same time showing their skill with their bows and arrows.

Greyhounds have performed wonderful feats in the conquests in the New World, as did Becerrillo on the island of San Juan de Puerto Rico, where the Spaniards gave to the dog from the profits that they made, or through him to his master, who was an harquebusier, the part and share of an harquebusier. To Leoncillo, as son of this hound, there fell 500 pesos in gold at one distribution of the riches won by the famous Vasco Núñez de Balboa, after having discovered the South Sea.

XIX

THE SPANIARDS BUILD A BRIDGE AND CROSS THE RÍO DE OCALI, AND ARRIVE AT OCHILE

The governor, seeing the little respect and less obedience that the Indians had for their cacique Ocali, and that keeping him with him would be of little or no use in the building of the bridge or for any other purpose, decided to release him so that he could return to his people, and so that the other lords of that region should not become alarmed, believing that they were detaining him against his will. Thus he called him one day and said that he had always given him his liberty and treated him as a friend, but that he did not desire that for the sake of this friendship he should lose the confidence of his vassals, nor that they, thinking that he was being held a prisoner, should become more rebellious than they were already. Therefore he begged that he go to them whenever he liked and return when he saw fit, or not, just as he pleased; that he gave him liberty to do anything.

The curaca gladly received it, saying that he wished to return to his vassals solely for the purpose of reducing them to obedience to the governor so that all of them might come to serve him, and if he could not win them over he would come alone, to show the love he had for his lordship's service. Along with this promise he made many others, but carried out none of them, nor did he return as he had promised; of the prisoners who have left prison under their own word of honor, few have done as did Atilius Regulus.

The cacique having gone, the Spaniards, through the efforts of a Genoese engineer named Maese Francisco, laid out the bridge by geometry and built it of large thick planks thrown out over the water and fastened together with heavy ropes (which had been brought along for such uses). The planks were joined and connected with large and thick stakes that were laid across the tops of them. As there was all the timber in that country that one could desire, they used as much as they liked, and with it the work on the bridge was finished in a few days. It came out so well that men and horses crossed on it at their pleasure.

Before crossing the river, the governor directed his men to set some ambushes in order to capture such Indians as they could to take along as guides, because the few who had come to serve the Castilians fled at the departure of the cacique. They captured thirty Indians, large and small, whom, with flattery, gifts, and promises, and on the other hand with many threats of cruel death if they refused, they induced to guide them to another province that is sixteen leagues from that of Ocali.[3] This distance, though uninhabited, was a pleasant country full of many forests and streams that flowed through it, and very level and fertile if it should be cultivated.

The army marched the first eight leagues in two days, and after covering half of the third day's march, the governor went ahead with a hundred cavalry and hundred infantry, and marching the rest of the day and all the following night he came at dawn to a pueblo called Ochile,[4] which was the first one of a large province named Vitachuco. This province was very extensive, and the route of the Spaniards lay through it for more than fifty leagues. Three brothers had divided it among them;[5] the eldest of them was named Vitachuco, as was the province itself and its chief pueblo, as we shall see below. He ruled over half of it as of five parts out of ten. The second, whose name is

---

[3]From this point Garcilaso's text diverges substantially from the other chroniclers, collapsing the itinerary by apparently deleting the province of Potano, and misidentifying the next several place-names. See the discussion in Hann, "De Soto, Dobyns, and Demography," 3–6.

[4]Both the names Ochile and Vitachuco are misplaced in Garcilaso's narrative. They properly belong in the Apalache province, but are here confused with places and events in Timucuan territory passed through before the army entered Apalache. Garcilaso's Ochile, equivalent in name to Rangel's Agile and Elvas's Axille, appears to be the same place as Aguacaleyquen or Caliquen of the other accounts. Similarly Vitachuco is here transposed and applied to the Napituca of Rangel and Elvas. Note that the Varners' translation of this passage erroneously has Ochile as "the principal village of Vitachuco." Swanton, *Final Report*, 145–46; Hann, "De Soto, Dobyns, and Demography," 5–6; John G. Varner and Jeanette J. Varner, trans. and eds., *The Florida of the Inca* (Austin: University of Texas Press, 1951), 129.

[5]The installation of brothers as district chiefs within a paramount or complex chiefdom was apparently a common political strategy among late Mississippian societies.

not given here because it has been forgotten, owned three of the other five parts, and the youngest, who was lord of this pueblo of Ochile, and of the same name, had the two [remaining] parts. For what reason or how such a division was made is not known, because in the rest of the provinces through which these Castilians traveled the firstborn inherited, in the manner in which entailed estates are inherited, without any part being given to the second sons. It might be that these parts had been joined through marriages that had been made with the provision that they would again be divided among the sons, or that relatives who had died without legal heirs had left them to the parents of these three brothers with the same condition that they be divided among their successors so that there might be some memory of them. The desire for immortality preserved in fame, since it is natural to men, is found in all nations, however barbarous they may be.

As we have said, then the adelantado arrived at dawn at the pueblo Ochile, which had fifty large and strong houses, because it was a frontier and defense against the neighboring province that he had left behind, which was an enemy, as almost all are in that kingdom to one another. He came upon the pueblo unawares and ordered the military musical instruments to be played, such as trumpets, fifes, and drums, so as to cause greater astonishment with their noise. They seized many Indians who, at the novelty of this clamor, came out of their houses terrified to see what was that thing they had never before heard. They assaulted the house of the curaca, which was a very fine one, consisting of a single chamber more than 120 paces in length and forty in width. It had four doors facing the four cardinal directions. Surrounding the principal chamber and joining it, on the outside, were many apartments that communicated with the interior of a large chamber, as its offices.[6]

In this house was the cacique with many warriors whom he was accustomed to keep with him constantly, as a man who had many enemies, and at the unexpected attack many more men came up from the pueblo. The curaca ordered the call to arms sounded and attempted to go out to fight with the Castilians, but for all the haste with which he and his Indians had taken up their arms to leave the house, the Christians already had gained the four doors and prevented their leaving, threatening to burn them alive if they did

[6]John H. Hann provides an alternative translation of this passage having potential ethnographic significance, thus: "Round about the great room, joined to it, there were many lodgings (*Aposentos*) on the outside, which opened into the inside of the room, like workshops of it . . . (*como oficinas de ella*)." Hann, "De Soto, Dobyns, and Demography," 4.

not surrender. On the other hand they offered them peace, friendship and all good treatment. But the curaca was unwilling to submit either as the result of threats or of rewards [promised] until, after the sun was up, they brought him many of his people whom they had taken. These Indians assured him that the Spaniards were very numerous and that they could not overcome them with arms, but that they could depend upon them and their friendship because they had treated none of the prisoners badly; that he would have to submit to the present necessity, for there was nothing else to do.

The cacique submitted to these persuasions; the governor received him kindly, ordered that the Spaniards treat the Indians in a very friendly manner, and keeping the curaca with him he caused all the rest of the Indians to be released, at which the lord and the vassals were very well pleased.

This victory being won, seeing that in a very beautiful valley on the other side of the pueblo there was a large settlement of houses scattered in groups of four or five, more or less, where there were many Indians, it seemed to the general that it would not be safe to pass the following night in that pueblo, because the Indians, joining together and seeing how few the Castilians were, might attempt to take the curaca away from them and instigate an uprising of all the lords of that district. Therefore he left the pueblo and went to the place where his men were, taking the curaca with him. He found his people camped three leagues from the pueblo; they had been anxious because of his absence, but rejoiced greatly at his coming and at the fine capture he had made. With the cacique went his servants and many other Indian warriors who wished voluntarily to go with him.

XX

THE BROTHER OF THE CURACA OCHILE COMES ON A FRIENDLY VISIT, AND THEY SEND AMBASSADORS TO VITACHUCO

On the following day the army entered Ochile in battle array, the infantry and cavalry formed in squadrons, sounding the trumpets, fifes, and drums, so that the Indians might see that they were not a people to be trifled with. The army being encamped, the governor agreed with the curaca Ochile to send messengers to his two brothers with overtures of peace and friendship, so that, the messages being from him, they would receive them better and give more credit to their statements. The cacique sent them to each of the two brothers separately with the most favorable words and arguments that he could form, telling them how those Spaniards had come to their country and that they had the desire and intention of having all the Indians for friends and brothers, and that they were traversing other provinces and did no damage where they passed, especially to those who came out to receive them peacefully; that they contented themselves simply with the necessary food; and that if they did not come out to serve them, they ravaged the pueblos, burned the wood of the houses in the place of firewood, so as not to go to the forest for it, consumed wastefully the provisions that they found, taking at discretion more than they needed, and acted otherwise as if they were in an enemy country. All of this was averted by receiving the peace they offered and showing themselves to be friends, if only for their own interests.

The second brother, who was nearest, and whose name we do not know, replied immediately, thanking his brother for the advice that he sent him and saying that he was much pleased at the arrival of the Castilians in his country, that he desired to see and know them, and that he did not come at once with the messengers because he was attending to the things necessary in order to serve them better and to receive them with the finest possible celebration and entertainment; that within three or four days he would go to kiss the governor's hands and give him obedience. Meanwhile he begged his brother to accept and confirm the peace and friendship with the Spaniards, as he regarded them as lords and friends from that time forth.

At the end of the three days Ochile's brother arrived, accompanied by many and very resplendent nobles. He kissed the governor's hands and talked with much familiarity to the captains, officials, and private gentlemen of the army, asking who each of them was, behaving as freely as if he had been brought up among them. The Spaniards made much of the cacique and all his attendants, for the general and his officers entertained with much care and attention the curacas and Indians who came out peacefully, nor did they harm those who were rebellious or damage their pueblos and lands, unless it were unavoidable in taking the necessary food.

The third brother, who was the eldest and the most powerful politically, was unwilling to reply to the message that his brother Ochile sent him; on the other hand he detained the messengers, not allowing them to return. Therefore the two brothers, persuaded and urged by the governor, again sent other messengers on the same errand, adding very favorable words in praise of the Spaniards, saying that he should not fail to accept the peace and friendship these Christians offered him, for they warned him that they were not people whom he could presume to conquer in war; that personally they were exceedingly brave and were regarded as invincible, and by their lineage, quality and nature they were children of the Sun and the Moon, their gods, and as such they had come from out there where the sun rises. They brought some animals they called horses, so swift, brave, and strong that it was impossible to escape them by flight, nor could they be resisted with arms and force.

Therefore, as brothers concerned for his life and safety, they begged him not to refuse to accept that which was conducive thereto, because to do otherwise would be simply to seek evil and harm for himself and his vassals and lands.

Vitachuco responded most extraordinarily, with a greatness of mind never before heard or imagined in an Indian, so that certainly, if the extravagant threats that he made and the arrogant words that he spoke could be written as the messengers reported them, none of the bravest gentlemen whom the divine Ariosto and the most illustrious and enamored Count Matheo María Boyardo, his predecessor, and other celebrated poets introduce in their works would equal those of this Indian. In the long interval that has passed meanwhile, many of them have been forgotten, and also the order in which they were spoken has been lost, but those who would remember them say explicitly that those words written in the following chapter indisputably and certainly are his, which he sent to say to his two brothers in reply to the embassy they sent to him.

XXI

CONCERNING THE ARROGANT AND PRESUMPTUOUS REPLY OF VITACHUCO, AND HOW HIS BROTHERS GO TO PERSUADE HIM TO PEACE

"It is very clear that you are young and lacking in judgment and experience to say what you do concerning these Spaniards; you praise them highly as virtuous men who do no harm or injury to anyone, and say that they are very brave and are children of the Sun, and deserve whatever service is done them. The confinement in which they have placed you, and the vile and cowardly spirit that has overcome you there in the short time since you have submitted to serve and become slaves, causes you to speak like women, praising what ought to be condemned and abhorred. Do you not see that these Christians cannot be better than the former ones who committed so many cruelties in this land, since they are of the same nation and laws? Are you not warned of their treachery and perfidy? If you were men of good judgment, you would see that their very lives and actions show them to be children of the devil and not of the Sun and Moon, our gods, because they go from one land to another, killing, robbing, and sacking whatever they find, taking the wives and daughters of others without bringing their own; and in order to settle and make establishments, they are not content with any country of all those that they see and traverse, for it delights them to go about like vagabonds, supporting themselves by the labor and sweat of others. If they were virtuous, as you say, they would not leave their own country, for they could make use of their virtue there, sowing, planting, and breeding in order to sustain life, without prejudice to others and infamy on their own part; but they go about as highwaymen, adulterers, and murderers, without shame before men or fear of any God.

"Tell them not to enter my territory; I promise them, however valiant they may be, that if they set foot in it they shall not leave, for I will consume and put an end to all of them; half of them will be roasted to death and the others boiled."

This was the first reply that the messengers brought from Vitachuco. Following it, he sent many other messages, so that two or three Indians came every day, always blowing a trumpet, and they uttered new threats and other menaces greater than the previous ones. Vitachuco thought to frighten them with various kinds of deaths he said he would visit upon the Castilians, imagined in his fierce mind. Sometimes he sent to say that when they should come to his province it would happen that the earth would open and swallow them all up; other times that he would order that wherever the Spaniards marched the hills that were there would close together and trap them in their midst, burying them alive; or that when the Spaniards should pass through a forest of pines and other very tall and thick trees that were along the road, he would order that such violent and furious winds should blow that they would throw the trees down upon them and crush all of them. At other times he said that he would order a great multitude of birds to pass over them with venom in their beaks that they would let fall upon the Spaniards, with which they would become putrid and corrupt, without any way of escaping it; or that he would poison the waters, grasses, trees, the fields, and even the air, in such manner that neither men nor horse among the Christians could escape with their lives, so that all of this may serve as a warning to those who might afterward have the boldness to go to his country against his will.

These wild messages and other similar ones Vitachuco sent to say to his brothers and the Spaniards together, with which he showed the ferocity of his spirit; and although at the time the Castilians laughed and joked about his words because they seemed to them absurd and foolish, as they were, because of what this Indian did afterward, as we shall see below, they understood that they had not been simply words, but most ardent desires of a heart as brave and arrogant as his was, and that they were not born of foolishness or simplemindedness, but of an excess of temerity and ferocity.

With these and other such messages that he sent the Spaniards anew every day, this curaca amused them during the eight days they spent in traveling through the states of the two brothers, who served and entertained the Castilians with all their resources and good will, giving them to understand that they desired to please them. On the other hand, they labored with all energy and solicitude to win the eldest brother to the general's obedience and service. Seeing that the messages and persuasions they sent to him availed little or nothing, they agreed to act as messengers themselves. Telling the governor of their decision, they asked permission to carry it out, which he granted, along with many gifts and offers of friendship for them to take to Vitachuco.

With the presence of his brothers and with all that they told him on the governor's behalf and on their own, and learning that the Spaniards were already within his territory and could do him harm if they liked, it seemed well to Vitachuco to put aside the ill will and hatred he felt toward the Castilians, saving it for a better time and occasion, which he expected to find in the carelessness and confidence the Spaniards would feel in his pretended friendship. Then, under guise of it, he would kill them all more easily and with less danger than in open war. With this sinister intention he changed the harsh words that he had used hitherto to others of much suavity and gentleness, saying to his brothers that he had not believed that the Castilians were people of such good parts and qualities as they told him; that now that he was convinced of it he would be very glad to have peace and friendship with them, but that first he wished to know how many days they would be in his country, what quantity of provisions he would have to give them when they went, and what other things they would need for their journey.

The two brothers sent a courier to the governor with this message, and he replied that they would not stay longer in his territory than Vitachuco desired to have them, nor did they want more supplies than he saw fit to give them, or need anything else except his friendship, with which they would have all that was necessary.

XXII

VITACHUCO COMES OUT PEACEFULLY, PLOTS TREASON AGAINST THE SPANIARDS, AND COMMUNICATES IT TO THE INTERPRETERS

Vitachuco indicated that he was satisfied with the affable reply the governor sent and, in order further to dissimulate his evil intentions, he let it be understood and said publicly that his inclination and desire to see the Spaniards in order to serve them increased from day to day, as they themselves would see. He ordered the nobles among his people to get ready to go out to receive the governor, and he ordered that there be on hand in the pueblo a large supply of water, wood, and food for the people, and grass for the horses, and that many provisions be brought from the other pueblos in his state, and all collected in that one where they were, so that there would be no lack of anything for the service and entertainment of the Castilians.

Juan Coles says in his *Relation* that the Indians affirmed that this province of the three brothers was two hundred leagues in length.

These things being provided for, Vitachuco went out from his pueblo accompanied by his two brothers and by five hundred Indian nobles handsomely adorned with plumes of various colors, with their bows in their hands and some of the finest and most elegant of the arrows they make for use on state occasions. After having marched two leagues, they found the governor encamped with his army in a beautiful valley. The general had marched there by very short stages because he knew that Vitachuco would wish to come out on the road to greet him, and so he did kiss his hands with a great show of peace and friendship. He begged the governor to pardon him for the disordered words that he had spoken concerning the Spaniards, through misunderstanding, saying that now since he was set right he would show by his actions how much he desired to serve his lordship and all his people, and by means of them he would make restitution for the offense committed against them by his words; and in order to do so with better right, he said that for himself and in the name of all his vassals he gave obedience to his lordship and acknowledged him as lord.

The governor received and embraced him with much punctiliousness and told him that he did not remember the past words because he had not heard them with the idea of keeping them in mind; that he derived much satisfaction from the present friendship and he would also be greatly pleased to learn his desires in order to comply with them and not go against his wishes.

The maese de campo and the other military officers, the ministers of his Majesty's hacienda, and all the Spaniards in general spoke to Vitachuco with signs of pleasure at his coming. He was about thirty-five years of age, of very good stature, as are all the Indians of La Florida generally; his aspect showed clearly the gallantry of his spirit.

On the following day the Spaniards entered in war formation into the principal pueblo of Vitachuco, called by the same name, which contained two hundred large and strong houses besides many other, small ones that were on their outskirts like suburbs. The Christians were lodged in the one and the other, and the governor and the men of his guard and in his service, and the three brother curacas were lodged in Vitachuco's house, which as it was large had room for all of them.

The Spaniards and the three caciques spent two days together with much celebration and rejoicing. On the third day the two younger curacas asked permission of the governor and of Vitachuco to return to their lands. Having received it and the gifts the general gave them, they went in peace, very well satisfied with the good treatment the Spaniards had accorded them.

For four days after his brothers had left, Vitachuco continued to make a great show of serving the Christians, so as to render them careless in order to be able to carry out his desires and plans against them more safely, because his purpose and intention was to kill all of them, without one escaping. This desire in him was so ardent and passionate that it blinded him, so that he did not weigh and consider the means he adopted to that end, or discuss them with his captains and servants, or obtain any counsel of relatives or friends who would tell him dispassionately what would be best. It seemed to him, on the other hand, that they would hinder rather than aid in his good work and that it was enough for him to desire it and plan it alone for everything to come out successfully. The counsel that he sought and took was from him who gave it in accordance with his own wishes and desires, without regard for obstacles, errors of judgment, or prudence, and he avoided those who could give sound advice—a condition peculiar to self-confident people, on whom their own actions inflict punishment for their imprudence, as happened to this cacique, poor of understanding and lacking in judgment.

Unable to endure longer the stimulus and fires of the passion and desire he had to kill the Castilians, on the fifth day after his brothers had gone Vitachuco secretly summoned four Indians whom the governor had brought as interpreters, for since the provinces had different languages, an interpreter was needed for almost every one of them, so that they could pass on from one to another what the first speaker had said. He told them about his fine plans, saying to them that he had determined to kill the Spaniards, who, through their great confidence in his friendship, it seemed to him, were now very much off their guard and trusted him and his vassals. He said that from the latter he had prepared more than ten thousand chosen warriors and had ordered them that, having hidden their arms in a forest that was nearby, they come in and out of the pueblo with water, firewood and grass, and the other things necessary for the service of the Christians, so that the latter, seeing them unarmed and in the guise of servants, would think nothing of it and trust them fully. After two or three more days had passed he would invite the governor to go out to the field to see his vassals, whom he wished to show him drawn up in war formation so that he could see his great power and the number of soldiers with whom he could serve him in the conquests that he might make in the future. To these arguments he added others, and said: "The governor, since we are friends, will go out unsuspectingly, and I shall order that a dozen strong and courageous Indians go near him. On approaching my squadron, they will carry him off by violence however he may come, on foot or mounted, and take him into the midst of the Indians, who will then assail the rest of the Spaniards, who will be off their guard and disturbed by the sudden seizure of their captain and so may be taken and killed very easily. Upon those who are captured I expect to visit all the forms of death I have sent to threaten them with, so that they may see that those were not follies and absurdities, as they thought when they ridiculed them as such, but real menaces." He said that he intended to roast some of them alive, boil others alive, and bury others alive with their heads outside; and that still others would be poisoned with poison from the yew tree so that they could see themselves become corrupt and rot away. Some would be suspended by the feet from the highest trees available, to become food for the birds. In short, there would be no manner of cruel death that he would not inflict upon them. He charged them [the interpreters] to give him their opinion and keep the secret; he promised them that when the affair was over, if they desired to remain in his country, he would give them honorable employments and offices, noble and beautiful women, and other privileges, honors and liberties that the highest nobles of his state enjoyed; and if they wished to return to their own country, he would send them well escorted and safeguarded along the roads they traveled, until they reached their houses. See how those Christians were taking them by force and making slaves of them, carrying them so far from their country that, although they might liberate them later, they could never return to it. Note, besides the particular injury to them, the general and universal hurt to all that great kingdom; the Castilians did not come to do them any good whatever, but to deprive them of their ancient liberty and make them their vassals and tributaries, and to take away their most beautiful wives and daughters and the finest of their lands and possessions, every day imposing on them new taxes and tributes. All this was not to be borne, but should be remedied in time, before they settled and established themselves among them. He begged and charged them, since the action was for the common good, to assist him with their efforts and counsel, to aid his attempt as just, his determination as courageous, and the scheme and plan as certain to succeed.

The four Indian interpreters replied to him that the enterprise and exploit were worthy of his spirit and valor, that all his plans seemed good to them, and that, in following such an excellent scheme, he could not fail to attain the end desired; that the whole kingdom was much indebted and obligated to him for having protected and defended the life, property, honor, and liberty of all its inhabitants; and that they would do what he ordered them, keep the secret, and supplicate the Sun and the Moon to promote and favor that project as he had planned and ordered it. They themselves could not serve him except in the will and spirit, but if they had the means in proportion to their desires, his lordship would need no other servants than themselves to execute that grand and notable project.

XXIII

VITACHUCO ORDERS HIS CAPTAINS TO CONSUMMATE THE TREASON, AND REQUESTS THE GOVERNOR TO COME OUT AND SEE HIS MEN

The arrogant Vitachuco and the four Indian interpreters separated after their consultation with great inward satisfaction, the latter expecting to see themselves soon free, enjoying important employments and offices and the possessors of noble and beautiful women, and the former already imagining himself successful in the project, which was poorly conceived and worse planned. It seemed to him already that he could see himself adored by the surrounding nations and by all that great kingdom for having freed them and preserved their lives and property; he imagined that he could already hear the praises and commendations the Indians must give him with great acclamation for such a notable deed. He heard in fancy the songs the women and children would sing in chorus, dancing before him, composed in praise and commemoration of his prowess, a thing very customary among those Indians.

Vitachuco became more arrogant hourly with these imaginings and others like them, which the imprudent and deranged are accustomed to conceive, to their greater harm and perdition. He summoned his captains and telling them of his vain thoughts and follies—not so that they might object, or advise what he ought to do, but so that they might obey unquestioningly and comply with his will—he said to them that they must make haste to carry out what he had ordered them so many days before for the purpose of killing those Christians, and not delay the honor and glory he would earn for that deed by means of their strength and valor, which glory he told them he was already enjoying in his imagination. He therefore charged them to release him from those cares that were oppressing him and fulfill the hopes he regarded as so certain.

The captains replied that they were ready and prepared to obey and serve him as a lord whom they loved so much, and said that they had the Indian warriors ready for the day they all looked forward to; that they were waiting only for the hour to be set to carry out their orders. Vitachuco was well satisfied with this reply and dismissed the captains, telling them that he would notify them in time of what they must do.

When the four interpreters again considered with better judgment what the cacique had said and communicated to them, the enterprise seemed to them difficult and its success impossible, alike because of the strength of the Spaniards who had shown themselves invincible, and because they had never considered them so unprepared and careless that they could be surprised by treason, nor were they so simple that they would allow themselves to be taken and carried off as Vitachuco had planned and ordered. Therefore, the immediate and certain fear overcoming the distant and doubtful hope—for it seemed to them that they would also have to die as parties to the treason if the Castilians learned of it before they revealed it—they decided to go over to the other side, and breaking their promise of secrecy, they told Juan Ortiz of the treason plotted, so that with a long account of everything that Vitachuco had communicated to them he could tell it to the governor.

When the adelantado learned of the curaca's wickedness and perfidy, and had consulted with his captains about it, it seemed to them advisable to dissemble to the Indian, allowing him to believe that they were ignorant of the affair. Thus they ordered the rest of the Spaniards to be on their guard and watchful, but to appear careless so that the Indians might not take alarm. They were also of the opinion that the best and surest method of capturing Vitachuco was the same one that he had planned for taking the governor, so that he might fall into his own trap. For this purpose they ordered a dozen very stout soldiers to prepare to go with the general so as to seize the cacique on the day on which he should invite the governor to go out to inspect his army. Having made these preparations secretly, the Castilians were on the watch to see what Vitachuco would do.

The latter, when the day he so desired had come, having prepared everything that seemed to him sufficient and necessary for carrying out his evil intentions, went early in the morning to the governor and with much humility and respect said to him that he begged his lordship to be pleased to do him and all his vassals the great kindness and favor of coming out to the field where they were awaiting him, so that he could see them drawn up in squadrons in battle array. Favored by his appearance and presence, all of them would feel obligated to serve him with greater spirit and readiness on the occasions that might arise in the future for his lordship's service, and he [Vitachuco] would be pleased to have him see them thus in battle array so that he might know the men and see the numbers with which he was able to serve him, and also in order to see whether the Indians of that country knew how to form squadrons like the other nations that he had heard were skilled in the military arts.

The governor, feigning ignorance and carelessness, replied that he would be very much pleased to see them as he said, and that in order to add to the display of the field and so that the Indians might also have something to see, he would order the Spanish cavalry and infantry to march out formed in squadrons, so that they could have friendly skirmishes with each other, exercising themselves in sport rather than in earnest.

The curaca did not desire so much ceremony and ostentation, but with the obstinate and blind determination he had in his mind to go on with that affair, he did not refuse the contest, believing that his own strength and bravery and that of his vassals would be enough to overcome and rout the Castilians, however well prepared they might be.

XXIV

HOW THEY TOOK VITACHUCO, AND THE OUTBREAK OF THE BATTLE THAT OCCURRED BETWEEN THE INDIANS AND THE SPANIARDS

The men of both sides having been ordered out, then, as has been said, the Spaniards advanced handsomely equipped, armed, and in battle array, formed in squadrons, the cavalry and the infantry separate. In order to pretend more convincingly that he did not know of the Indians' treason, the governor decided to go out on foot with the curaca.

Near the pueblo was a large plain. On one side was a high and dense forest that covered a large tract of land, and on the other were two lakes. The first was small, and would measure about a league in circumference; it was clear of growth and mud, but so deep that three or four steps from the shore one could not touch bottom. The second, which was farther away from the pueblo, was very large, more than half a league in breadth and so long that it looked like a large river, its extent being unknown. The Indians stationed their squadron between the forest and these two lakes, the lakes being on their right and the forest on their left. They would number almost ten thousand warriors, chosen men, brave and of fine appearance. On their heads were long plumes, their chief adornment, placed and arranged so that they extended up half a fathom high; with them the Indians appear taller than they really are.

They had their bows and arrows on the ground covered with grass, in order to make it appear that as friends they were unarmed. The squadron was drawn up with all military precision, not square but elongated, the files straight and somewhat open with two projecting wings at the sides, arranged in such good order that certainly it was a fine thing to see.[7] The Indians waited for Vitachuco, their lord, and Hernando de Soto to come out to see them. They came on foot, each accompanied by twelve of his men, both

[7]A cross-shaped military squadron formation, i.e., oblong and with "wings," was also described and illustrated by Jacques Le Moyne in the 1560s. A similar native formation is documented for the interior Mississippian chiefdom of Coosa. Stefan Lorant, *The New World: The First Pictures of America* (New York: Duell, Sloan & Pearce, 1946), 63; Charles Hudson, "A Spanish-Coosa Alliance in Sixteenth-Century North Georgia," *The Georgia Historical Quarterly* 72, no. 4 (1988):612–15.

with the same purpose and desire, one against the other. At the governor's right hand came the Spanish squadrons, the infantry adjoining the forest, and the cavalry in the middle of the plain.

The governor and the cacique having reached the spot where Vitachuco had said he would give the signal for the Indians to seize the general, the general gave it first, so that his adversary who was playing the same game should not win the first hand, by which he would gain this contest that was in progress between them. He had an harquebus fired, which was the signal for his men. Alonso de Carmona says that the signal was the sounding of a trumpet; it might have been both.

The twelve Spaniards who were near Vitachuco seized him, and though the Indians who came between them wished to defend him and attempted to do so, they could not release him from his captivity.

Hernando de Soto, who was secretly armed and had near him two horses led by the reins, mounted one of them, a dappled gray that they had named Azeituno because Mateo de Azeituno (who we said above had gone to rebuild La Havana and had remained there as alcalde of the fortress he was to found, the one that the city and port now has, which this gentleman founded, though not with its present grandeur and magnificence) had given it to him, and it was a most brave and handsome animal, worthy of having had such masters. The governor mounting, then, he charged the squadron of Indians and reached it ahead of all the other Castilians, both because he was nearer the squadron and because this brave captain in all the battles and encounters that occurred, by day or by night, in this conquest and in that of El Perú, always managed to be among the first. He was one of the four best lances that have passed to or are now in the West Indies, and although his captains often complained to him for exposing his person to too much danger and risk, because the safety of the whole army lay in the preservation of his life and health, as its head, and though he saw that they were right, he could not restrain his warlike spirit nor did he enjoy victories unless he were the first in winning them. Leaders ought not to be so bold.

The Indians, who now already had their arms in their hands, received the governor with the same spirit and gallantry he showed, and they did not allow him to break many of the files of the squadron, because on reaching the first ones, of the many arrows they shot at him eight reached the mark, all of them striking the horse. As we shall see in the course of this *History*, these Indians always attempted to kill the horses first, rather than the riders, because of the advantage they gave them. They pierced him with four arrows in the breast and four in the knees, two on each side, with such skill and savagery that without his moving a foot, as if they had shot him in the forehead with a piece of artillery, they struck him down dead.

Hearing the harquebus-shot, the Spaniards attacked the Indian squadron, following their captain-general. The horses came so near him that they were able to succor him before the enemy did him any further harm. One of his pages, one Viota, a native of Zamora and an hidalgo, dismounted from his horse and gave it to him, helping him to mount. The governor charged again against the Indians, who, unable to resist the impetus of three hundred horses together, as they had no pikes, turned and ran, without giving much proof of their strength and bravery, quite contrary to the opinion their cacique and they themselves had held shortly before, it appearing impossible to them that so few Spaniards could overcome so many and such brave Indians as they thought themselves to be.

Their squadron routed, the Indians fled to the nearest cover they could find. One large band of them entered the woods, thereby saving their lives. Many others threw themselves into the large lake where they escaped death. Others, who were the rear guard and were far from shelter, ran forward across the plain where more than three hundred were killed by lances, and some, though few, were taken prisoners.

Those in the vanguard, who were the best and as such always bear the brunt of battle, were more unfortunate because they received the first attack and the greatest impetus of the horses, and unable to reach the woods or the large lake, which were the best shelters, more than nine hundred of them threw themselves into the small lake. Such was the first outcome of Vitachuco's boasting. The encounter took place at nine or ten o'clock in the morning.

The Spaniards followed close after them in all directions until they entered the woods and the large lake, but seeing that however they tried they could not capture a single Indian, they all came back and gathered at the small lake where, as we said, more than nine hundred Indians had taken refuge. They fought them all day in order to induce them to surrender, more with threats and intimidation than with arms, shooting crossbows and harquebuses to frighten them but not to kill them, because, as people almost overcome and unable to flee, they did not wish to harm them.

Throughout the day the Indians did not stop shooting arrows at the Castilians, until they exhausted their supply, and to enable them to shoot from the water, as they could not get a foothold, one Indian would climb up on three or four others who would swim close together and support him until he used up the arrows of his whole party. In this manner they kept up all day, not one of them surrendering.

When night came the Spaniards surrounded the lake, stationing themselves at intervals in groups of two on horseback and of six infantry, near one another, so that the Indians would not escape in the darkness. Thus they continued to harass them, not allowing them to set foot on the bank, and when they heard them approach it they shot at them to force them back so that, tired of swimming, they would surrender more easily. On one hand they threatened them with death if they did not give themselves up, and on the other they promised pardon, peace and friendship to those who were willing to receive it.

XXV

OF THE SLOW SURRENDER OF THE CONQUERED INDIANS, AND THE CONSTANCY OF SEVEN OF THEM

As much as the Castilians persecuted the Indians who were in the lake, they could not prevent them from showing their spirit and strength. Although they recognized the difficulty and danger in which they were, without hope of assistance, they chose death as a lesser evil than showing weakness in that adversity.

They persisted in this obstinacy until midnight, not one of them being willing to give up, and they had passed fourteen hours in the water. From that time on, by means of the many persuasions of Juan Ortiz and of the four Indian interpreters who were with him, and by means of the promises and oaths they made them that their lives would be safe, the weakest ones began to come out and give themselves up, one by one, then two by two, so reluctantly that by daylight not fifty Indians had surrendered. At the persuasion of these latter, those in the water, seeing that they had not killed or otherwise harmed them but on the other hand, as they said, had treated them well, gave themselves up in larger numbers, though so slowly and unwillingly that many returned to the middle of the lake from near the banks, but the love of life drew them back again.

In this manner they continued to come out and surrender, distrustfully, until ten o'clock in the morning; then all who remained submitted at once, about two hundred men, having passed twenty-four hours' time swimming in the water. It was very distressing to see them half-drowned, swollen with the large amount of water they had swallowed, and afflicted by the hardship, hunger, fatigue, and lack of sleep that they had suffered.

Only seven Indians remained in the lake, so pertinacious and obstinate that neither the entreaties of the interpreters nor the promises of the governor nor the example of those who had surrendered were sufficient to make them do the same. It seemed instead that they had recovered the spirit that the others had lost, and wished to die rather than be conquered. Forced to do so, they replied to what was said to them, and said that they neither wanted their promises nor feared their threats, nor death.

They continued in this constancy and fortitude until three o'clock in the afternoon and were about to expire when, at that hour, it seeming to the governor inhuman to allow men of such fortitude and virtue—qualities that we admire even in enemies—to perish, he ordered twelve Spaniards who were expert swimmers to enter the lake carrying their swords in their mouths—in imitation of Julius Caesar at Alexandria in Egypt, and of the few Spaniards who, performing this same feat in the River Elbe, overcame the duke of Saxony and all his League—and bring out the seven valiant Indians who were in it. The swimmers entered the water and, seizing them by the leg, arm, or hair, as the case might be, pulled them out until they dragged them on shore, so nearly drowned that they were almost unconscious. They lay stretched out on the sand in a state that may well be imagined of men who for nearly thirty hours, without setting foot on the ground (as apparently they did not) or receiving any other relief, had been contending against the water. Certainly it was an incredible exploit, which I would not dare write down if it were not certified to me on the authority of so many gentlemen and great men, in speaking in the Indies and in Spain of this and of other [exploits] that they saw in the course of this discovery; and there is besides the authority and truthfulness of him who gave me the account of this *History*, which is trustworthy in all respects.

And since we have mentioned the River Elbe it gives occasion for not passing on without referring to a very Catholic saying that the maese de campo Alonso Vivas (a brother of the good Doctor Luis Vivas), who was charged with guarding the duke of Saxony, said after that defeat. It was that, talking one day in the presence of the most gross and fierce Saxon of the miracles the images of Our Lady have performed in various parts of the world, the duke (as a man tainted by the heresies of Martin Luther) spoke these words: "In one of my towns there was an image of Mary, and they said that it performed miracles; I had it thrown into the River Elbe but it did not work a single miracle." The maese de campo, offended by such evil words, came back very readily and said: "What greater miracle do you desire, Duke, than to have lost at this same river in the manner in which you did lose, so contrary to your hopes and to those of all your League?" The duke's head bowed until his beard rested on his chest and he did not raise it again all that day, nor did he come out of his lodgings for three days thereafter, from dismay and shame at that Catholic Spaniard's having convinced him of his infidelity and heresy by proving that that image of Our Lady had worked a miracle on his own person, which he had experienced to his own hurt. This story and many others of these times and of others still earlier, and later, were told to me by my uncle Don Alonso de Vargas, who was present and served throughout that expedition to Germany with the rank of *sargento mayor* in a Spanish regiment, calling himself Francisco de Plasencia, and afterward he was captain of cavalry.

The Spaniards, moved by pity and compassion for the hardships the seven Indians had suffered in the water, and admiring the fortitude and constancy of spirit they showed, took them to their lodgings and gave them every attention possible to bring them back to this life, with which, and with their good spirit, they were entirely restored by the following night, for all this time was needed to recover from their injuries.

When morning came the governor ordered them summoned and with a show of anger had them questioned as to the reason for their pertinacity and stubbornness; why, seeing themselves, as they were, without hope of succor, they had not been willing to surrender as the rest of their companions had done. Four of them were men about thirty-five years of age. They replied, first one and then another speaking, the last taking up the story where the other left it, being perturbed and not certain of how to go on. Again one of the silent ones would help with a word the speaker could not call to mind, which is the style of the Indians, who assist one another in discourses that they carry on with important persons before whom they are afraid of becoming confused.

Speaking after this fashion, then, the Indians replied to the governor, giving many and lengthy reasons, from which, in substance, it was understood that they had said the following: that they had seen very well the risk they ran of losing their lives and the little hope they had of being succored, but with all this it had seemed to them, and they regarded it as quite certain, that by surrendering they could in no way comply with the obligation of the offices and military rank they held; because, having been chosen in prosperity by their prince and lord, honored and distinguished with the name and insignia of captains, since he regarded them as men of fortitude, spirit, and constancy, it was just that in adversity they should fulfill the obligations of their offices and show that they had not been unworthy of them, and prove to their curaca and lord that he had not been mistaken in choosing them.

Besides complying with their military obligations and with what they owed to their lord, they wished also to leave an example to their sons and successors and to all soldiers and warriors of how they ought to behave in such cases, particularly to those stationed and appointed as captains and superiors of the others, whose deeds of spirit and fortitude or of weakness and cowardice were more noticed, to be honored or condemned, than those of the common people, the base, and the humble, who had no honor or charge to fulfill.

For all these reasons and because it had come about that their lives were saved, as his lordship had seen, they were not satisfied that they had done their duty or complied with their obligations as captain and commander; therefore it would be a greater mercy and honor to have allowed them to die in the lake than to have spared their lives. Thus, not overlooking the kindness that he had done them, they begged his lordship to order their lives taken, because they would live in the world in great shame and dishonor and would never dare to appear before their lord, Vitachuco, who had so honored and esteemed them, if they did not die for him.

XXVI

WHAT THE GOVERNOR DISCUSSED WITH THE THREE INDIAN LORDS OF VASSALS AND WITH THE CURACA VITACHUCO

The four Indian captains having made the reply that has been described in the last chapter, the governor, not without admiration at hearing their reasons, turned his eyes to the other three, who had been silent. They were youths, none of them being over eighteen years old, and were sons of lords of vassals of Vitachuco's district and vicinity, heirs to their fathers' estates. In order to hear what they would say, he asked them why they, not being captains and having the obligations of the other four, had persisted in the same obstinacy and pertinacity. With a fortitude strange in prisoners and with an aspect as composed as if they were free, assisting one another in their statements, the youths replied in their language the following words, which interpreted into Spanish run thus:

"The chief purpose that took us from the houses of our fathers, whose eldest sons we are, and future inheritors of their estates and seigniories, was not directly the desire for your death nor the destruction of your captains and army, although our intention could not be carried out without injury to you and to all of them. Neither were we impelled by the interest that those who engage in wars usually have in profiting from the sacking of pueblos and of conquered armies that generally takes place in the course of them, nor did we go out to serve our princes, so that gratified and obligated by our services they would afterward grant us favors in accordance with our merits. All these motives we lacked, for we needed none of these things.

"We left our homes with the desire to take part in the battle just passed solely through eagerness and ambition for honor and fame, because (as our fathers and teachers have taught us) that which is won in war is more valued and esteemed than anything else in this world. In this we were encouraged and incited by our neighbors and friends and for it we underwent the danger and fatigue in which you saw us yesterday, from which you rescued us through your clemency and pity. By the same token we are today your slaves.

"However, since fortune deprived us of the victory in which we thought to win the glory that we desired and gave it to you as one who better deserved it, and subjected us, on the contrary, to the misfortunes and hardships the conquered always suffer, it seems to us that we can gain from these same adversities, enduring them with the same spirit and strength that we felt in prosperity because, as our elders have told us, he who is loyal, though conquered, and who puts his life second to the honor of preserving the liberty of his country and his own, is no less deserving than the victorious conqueror who makes good use of his victory.

"We have been instructed by our fathers and relatives in all these things and many others. Therefore, though we hold no offices or military rank, it seemed to us that we were no less obligated than these four captains; rather we were more so, for fortune had chosen us for greater preeminence and rank, as we were to be lords of vassals. We wished to let the latter understand that we would endeavor to succeed to the estate of our fathers and predecessors by the same steps by which they arose to become lords, which were those of fortitude, constancy, and the other virtues that they possessed, with which they sustained their estates and seigniories. We also wished by our deaths to console our parents and relatives, dying in order to do our duty as their kinsmen and sons.

"These were the reasons, invincible captain, why we took part in this enterprise and also the causes of the obstinacy and pertinacity you say we have shown, if the desire for honor and fame and the fulfillment of our obligation and natural duty can be so called. The latter is greater in princes, lords, and gentlemen, in accordance with their higher quality and rank, than in the common people.

"If this is sufficient for our acquittal, pardon us, Child of the Sun, for our obstinacy did not arise from disrespect toward you, but from what you have heard. If we do not deserve pardon, here you see our throats; do what most pleases you with our lives, which are yours, and nothing is prohibited to the conqueror."

Many of the Spaniards present, on hearing the last words and seeing youths so noble and so young placed in such affliction and able to speak in that manner, could not refrain from showing their compassion and tenderness to the point of revealing it in their eyes. The governor, who likewise had a merciful disposition, was also moved, and raising them up as if they were his own sons, he embraced all three together and then each one separately, and among many other fond words he said to them that in the fortitude they had in war and in the discretion they had shown besides they proved very clearly what they were, and that such men deserved to be lords of great states. He was much gratified at having known them and saved their lives, and it also gave him great pleasure to set them at liberty at once, so that they might be comforted and freed of the depression caused by their misfortune.

The governor kept them with him two days after this conversation, entertaining and caressing them constantly and seating them at his own table to eat, in order to win their fathers to his friendship and devotion, which honor the youths esteemed very highly. At the end of two days he sent them to their homes with presents of linen, cloth, silk, mirrors, and other things from Spain that he gave them for their fathers and mothers, and accompanied by some Indians of theirs who were found among the prisoners. He ordered them to tell their fathers what a good friend of theirs he had been, and would be to them also if they desired his friendship.

The young men, after thanking the governor for having spared their lives and for the favors he was doing them at present, went to their countries well satisfied, having many favorable things to tell there. The governor ordered the four captains to be kept in confinement so as to reprimand them, together with their cacique. Thus on the day after the departure of the young men he had all five of them summoned, and he told them with serious words how ill they had done in having attempted to kill the Castilians under guise of peace and friendship, without the latter having harmed them in any way, for which they were deserving of an exemplary death that would be known throughout the world. But in order to show the natives of all that great kingdom that he did not wish to avenge himself for his injuries but to have peace and friendship with everyone, he would pardon them for their past crime so that they might be friends in the future, and since he on his part was showing himself to be such, he begged and charged them that, forgetting the past, they busy themselves with preserving their lives and property and not attempt to do anything else, for if they should make such an attempt it would succeed no better than the last one. He said many other things to the curaca privately in very friendly terms intended to mitigate the hatred and rancor that he felt toward the Christians, and he directed that he again eat at his table from which he had removed him hitherto as a punishment, ordering that he eat elsewhere.

But the arguments, caresses, presents, and many other things that the governor gave and said to Vitachuco not only did not have a good effect, such was the obstinacy and blindness of his passion, but they seemed rather to incite him to greater madness and wildness, for, dominated by fury and temerity, he was now incapable of all reasoning and of receiving advice, ungrateful and scornful of the pardon and the benefits conferred by the governor. Like a man doomed, governed by his passion, he did not stop short of his own destruction and death and that of his vassals, as we shall see presently.

XXVII

WHERE AN OBJECTION IS ANSWERED

Before going on with our *History*, it will be well to reply to an objection that could be made to us to the effect that in other histories of the West Indies there are not found actions and sayings of the Indians such as these we write here, for generally they are regarded as a simple people without reasoning power or understanding, and in peace and in war as little better than beasts; and accordingly it is thought that they could not say or do anything worthy of being remembered and praised, as some of them appear to have said hitherto and as will be told below, God willing. It might be supposed also that we do this in an attempt to extol or praise our nation, for although the regions and countries are so far apart, it seems that all are the Indies.

To this is replied first that the opinion held of the Indians is inaccurate and entirely contrary to that which ought to be believed, as is noted, argued, and proved very well by the very venerable Father Joseph de Acosta in the first chapter of Book 6 of the *Historia natural y moral del Nuevo Orbe,* which I submit, in confirmation of the present work, to all who may wish to see, where there will be found the admirable things written by this very noted master. And in what concerns particularly our Indians and the accuracy of our *History,* as I said at the beginning, I write from the account of another who saw and took part in these things personally. He endeavored to be so faithful in his account that he corrected it chapter by chapter, as it was written, taking away what was excessive or adding what was missing in that which he had said. He did not consent to a word that was not his own, so that I did nothing more than hold the pen as clerk. I thus can deny truthfully that any of it is an invention of my own, for all my life I have been an enemy of fiction (with the exception of good poetry), such as books of knight errantry and other similar ones. For this I am indebted to that illustrious gentleman, Pedro Mexía of Sevilla, because with a reproof he drew from the heroic work of the Caesars of those who employ themselves in reading and composing such books, he took away the love that I might have had for them as a boy and made me abhor them for all time.

To say, then, that I write with exaggeration in order to praise my own nation because I am an Indian certainly is a mistake, for I confess with shame to the truth, namely, that I found myself lacking in the necessary words to recount and set down in order the facts of history that presented themselves, rather than with an abundance of them to invent things that did not happen. This want was due to the unhappy circumstances of my childhood, when there was a lack of schools of learning and a superabundance of schools of arms for both foot soldiers and cavalry, particularly horsemanship. In this last, because of our country's having been won with the saddle, my fellow students and I drilled ourselves from a very early age, to such an extent that many or all of them became famous horsemen. Thus we learned little more than the rudiments, which today I regard as most unfortunate, though the fault was not ours nor our parents', but it was simply that fortune had then nothing more to offer us, because the country was so recently won and because of the civil wars that at once arose between the Pizarros and the Almagros, down to those of Francisco Hernández Girón. Under these circumstances teachers of the sciences were lacking, and of those of arms there were more than enough. Now in these days, through the mercy of God, the contrary is true, for the fathers of the holy Company of Jesus are founding so many schools of all the sciences that the universities of Spain are not needed.

Returning to our first purpose, which is to certify on the word of a Christian that in all the above we wrote the truth, and that with the aid of the Consummate Truth we shall write it in the future, I shall say that what took place was passed on to me by him who gave the account, and if I had not regarded him as an hidalgo and trustworthy, as he is, and as we shall tell afterward in other places with regard to his reputation, I would not presume to write all these truths as I do, certifying them to be such. I say, then, that coming to the reply that we have said the four Indian captains made to the governor, and then to that of the three young men, sons of lords of vassals, it appearing to me that the arguments (according to the common opinion that is held of the Indians) were too elaborate for barbarous Indians, I said to him: "According to the universal opinion concerning the Indians, it will not be believed that these arguments are theirs." He replied to me: "You know very well that the opinion is false and that it is not necessary to consider it; on the other hand it will be just to disprove it by telling the truth with regard to the matter, because as you yourself have seen and know there are Indians of very good understanding who in peace and in war and in times of adversity and of prosperity know how to speak as well as any other very cultivated nation.

"The Indians replied substantially what I have told you and used besides many other well-turned phrases that I do not recall—or, if I did, I could not remember how to say them as they themselves did—so that the governor and we who were with him wondered at their words and arguments more than at their feat of having continued swimming in the water for almost thirty hours. Many Spaniards, well read in history, said when they heard them that the captains appeared to have fought among the most famous ones of Rome when she dominated the world with her arms, and that the young lords of vassals seemed to have studied in Athens during her flourishing period of moral letters. Therefore as soon as they had made their replies and the governor had embraced them, there was no captain or soldier of note who did not embrace them most gladly, rejoicing at having heard them.

"For the same reason write what I have told you as fully as possible, and I promise you that however you may sharpen and consume your pen in praising the generosity and excellences of Muscoço, and the strength, constancy, and discretion of these seven Indian captains and lords of vassals, and however you may dwell upon the gallantry and ferocity of Vitachuco and of other chieftains whom we shall encounter later, you will not do justice to their nobility and exploits.

"Because of all this you may write without any scruples what I tell you, whether or not it may be believed; we comply with our obligation with having told the truth as to the things that took place, and doing otherwise would be to injure the parties concerned." All this passed between me and my author just as I have told it, and I include it here so that it may be understood and believed that we were attempting to write the truth rather with the lack of the elegance and rhetoric needful to place the events in their proper setting than with an excess of embellishment, because I was incapable of it. Since it will be necessary further on to reinforce our reputation and credit in other things as important, and more so, as we shall see, I shall say no more at present but shall return to our story.

XXVIII

CONCERNING THE RECKLESS ACTION THAT VITACHUCO ORDERED FOR THE PURPOSE OF KILLING THE SPANIARDS, AND THAT CAUSED HIS OWN DEATH

The Indians who came out of the small lake to surrender, more than nine hundred in number, had been kept prisoners by the governor's order and were distributed among the Castilians to act as their servants and to be held as such, as a penalty and punishment for the treason they had committed. This was done solely to intimidate and hold in check the Indians of the vicinity where the news of the recent action would circulate, so that they would not dare to make another such attempt. The intention, however, was to free and liberate them as soon as they [the Spaniards] should leave their province.

But since Vitachuco, who was held in his house as a prisoner, knew this—and since the poor unfortunate was blind in his passion and thought of nothing else, night and day, except how he could kill the Spaniards—already engulfed in his obstinacy and blindness, it seemed to him that since those nine hundred Indians (according to the story of four little pages who served him, and as was true) were among the noblest, bravest, and chosen men of all his people, they alone would be enough to do what all of them together had been unable to do, and that each one of them could kill a Castilian, as he himself thought to kill one, for the Indians and the Christians were about equal in numbers. He persuaded himself that at the time the act would be attempted the Indians would have an advantage over the Christians because it would be when all of them were eating and off their guard, and also because they would not be suspicious of men who had surrendered and become slaves, and were unarmed. And as he imagined this mad action, so he precipitated himself into it, without considering whether the Indians were prisoners or free, or whether they had arms or not, it appearing to him that as he himself had no lack of weapons, consisting of his own strong arms, so would all his men have them.

Vitachuco communicated this precipitate and mad determination through his four pages to the leaders among the nine hundred Indians, ordering that on the third day thereafter, precisely at noon, each one of them be ready to kill the Spaniard who had fallen to his lot as master; at the same hour he himself would kill the governor. They were to keep this a secret, passing the word from one to another, and as a signal to begin, at the moment he killed the general he would give a shout so loud that it would be heard throughout the pueblo. Vitachuco gave this command on the same day that the governor had reproved him and restored him to his friendship and favor, from which is seen the manner in which the ungrateful and unappreciative return benefits that are conferred upon them.

Although they saw the hopelessness of the thing their cacique sent them orders to do, the poor Indians obeyed and replied, saying that they would do what they were ordered with all their strength or die in the attempt.

The Indians of the New World have so much veneration, love and respect for their kings and lords that they obey and adore them not as men but as gods; if they so command, they throw themselves into the fire as readily as into the water, because they have no regard for life or death except in compliance with the precepts of their lord, in which their happiness consists. Because of this religion, for they regard it as such, they obeyed Vitachuco so implicitly that they did not reply a word.

Seven days after the recent skirmish and defeat, at the moment when the governor and the cacique had finished eating—for in order to win his friendship the general did him all the favors possible—Vitachuco rose from the chair in which he had been seated and, turning his body from one side to the other, he extended his arms to either side with the fists closed, and then brought them together until the fists were on the shoulders; from there he shook them once and twice with such force and violence that the bones and joints crackled like broken reeds. This he did to call up and summon his strength for what he intended to do, which is an ordinary thing and almost second nature to the Indians of La Florida when they wish to perform some feat of strength.

Having done this, then, Vitachuco got on his feet with all the bravado and fury that could be imagined and in an instant closed with the adelantado, at whose right hand he had been eating, and, grasping him by the collar with his left hand, he struck him such a hard blow with his right fist over the eyes, nose and mouth that he knocked him senseless on his back, overturning his chair, as if he had been a child. In order to finish killing him, he fell upon him with such a loud roar that it could be heard for a quarter of a league round about. The gentlemen and soldiers who happened to be at the general's table, seeing him so mistreated and his life in such danger through so strange and unexpected an action, grasped their swords and fell upon Vitachuco, and ten or twelve of them transfixed his body at the same moment, with which the Indian fell dead, blaspheming the heavens and the earth for not having succeeded in his evil purpose.

These gentlemen succored their captain in such good time and to such good effect that if they had not been present to defend him or had delayed a moment with their aid, allowing the Indian to strike him another blow, he would have succeeded in killing him, for the one that he did give was so severe that the governor did not regain consciousness for more than half an hour, and he was bleeding at the eyes, nose, mouth, gums, and upper and lower lips as if he had been struck with a large club. His teeth and jaws were so injured that the former were about to come out, and for more than twenty days he could not eat anything that had to be chewed, but only soft food. His face, especially the nose and lips, were so swollen that he had to apply plasters to them continuously during the twenty days. As we have said, Vitachuco showed himself so terrible and so strong in the manner of his death that it is clear that the strange threats and menaces he made from the beginning had arisen from this bravado and fierceness of spirit, which was so excessive that it did not admit the consideration, prudence, and counsel that great actions require.

Juan Coles adds, besides what we have said about the blow, that the governor lost two teeth on account of it.

XXIX

OF THE STRANGE BATTLE THE CAPTIVE INDIANS HAD WITH THEIR MASTERS

At the sound of the cacique's voice, which as we said he had given his vassals as the signal for the desperate act that caused his death, and theirs, there took place in the camp between the Indians and the Spaniards encounters no less cruel and horrible than laughable. Hearing the cacique's shout, each Indian fell upon his master to kill or wound him, carrying as weapons blazing sticks or other things that came to hand, for in the absence of those [arms] that they wished for, they converted into offensive arms whatever they found before them.

Many of them threw in their master's faces the pots containing their food, which, as they were boiling, burned some of them. Others fell upon them with plates, porringers, jugs and pitchers; others with benches, chairs and tables where they had them, and with anything else that came to hand, although it served only to show their desire to kill them, so that everyone can imagine what would happen under such circumstances.

They did more damage with the burning sticks than with other weapons, and it may be that they had prepared them for the purpose, because most of the Indians carried them. One Indian gave his master a blow on the head with a firebrand and laid him at his feet, and then knocked him senseless with two or three other blows. Many Spaniards had their eyebrows burned and their noses and arms injured by blows from firebrands; others received hard fist-cuffs and buffets and blows from rocks or sticks, according to what fell to their lot in such an unseemly brawl as they found confronting them unexpectedly in their own houses.

One Indian, after mistreating his master with blows from a stick and fist-cuffs in his face, on fleeing from the other Spaniards who came to his rescue, went up a ladder to an upper apartment, taking with him a lance he found leaning against the wall, and he defended the door with it so that no one could enter.

At this shout a gentleman, who was a relative of the governor, named Diego de Soto, came up carrying a crossbow ready to shoot and stationed himself in the patio to fire it. The Indian, who did not attempt to save his life but to sell it as dearly as possible, did not try to avoid the shot though he saw the Spaniard aim the crossbow at him. On the contrary, in order to make a good throw with his lance, he placed himself in front of the door and cast it at the moment that Diego de Soto fired the crossbow. The Indian did not hit him with the lance, but it passed so near his left shoulder that the haft gave him a hard blow, which knocked him to his knees on the ground and drove the lance into it half a fathom, where it remained trembling in the earth. Diego de Soto made a better shot than the Indian, whom he struck in the breast and killed.

Seeing the effrontery and boldness of the Indians and what bad condition the governor was in as a result of the blow given him, the Spaniards lost patience and began to kill and wreak vengeance upon them, especially those who had been hurt with sticks or affronted by blows; these latter in their anger killed the Indians who chanced to be in front of them.

Other Spaniards who had not been assaulted, thinking that it was a thing unworthy of their persons and quality to kill men who had surrendered and were held in the condition and name of slaves, took them to the plaza and turned them over to the halberdiers of the governor's guard who were there, to be executed; they killed them with their halberds and partisans. In order that the Indian interpreters and others who were serving the army, who had been taken from the provinces already left behind, should be hostages and become the enemies of the rest of the Indians of that country and not dare run away from the Spaniards in the future, they ordered that they shoot arrows at them [the other Indians] and help to kill them, which they did.

A Castilian named Francisco de Saldaña, of small stature and very neat in his person, so that he would not have to kill the Indian who had fallen to his lot when they gave them out as slaves, took him along behind him with a cord fastened around his neck to turn him over to the executioners. When he caught sight of the plaza and saw what was happening there, the Indian had such an excess of courage that he seized his master from behind as he was going along, by the collar with one hand and by the crotch with the other, and raising him up like a child, the Castilian being helpless, he threw him headlong on the ground with such force that he was stupefied, and then jumped on him with both feet in such anger and wrath that he would have torn him to pieces with kicks and blows.

The Spaniards who saw it ran to the rescue with their swords in their hands. The Indian, taking from his master the one [sword] that he was wearing, came out to meet them so fiercely and boldly that though there were more than fifty of them he held them off in a wide circle, using the sword with both hands with such agility of body and desperation of spirit that he showed well his desire and eagerness to kill someone before they should kill him. The Castilians drew away from him, not wishing to receive injury in killing a desperate man. Thus the Indian kept circling around in every direction attacking everyone, none of them being willing to attack him until they brought weapons with handles with which to kill him.

These and many other similar incidents occurred in this worse than irregular conflict, where four Spaniards were killed and many were badly wounded. And it was fortunate that most of the Indians were in chains and otherwise confined, for if they had been free they would have done still more damage, such was their bravery and spirit. But with all this, though prisoners, they tried to do as much as they could, and therefore they [the Spaniards] killed them all, not leaving one alive, which was a great pity.

Such was the result of the temerity and arrogance of Vitachuco, arising from his spirit that was more fierce than prudent, exceedingly presumptuous and disdainful of advice, which to no purpose whatever caused his own death and that of thirteen hundred of his vassals, the best and noblest in his state. All this was because he had not conferred with some of them as to what to do about the strangers, who, being such, later became his enemies.

He also caused the death of the four good captains who had escaped from the small lake, who were killed along with the other Indians, for the prudent who are subjected to and obliged to obey a madman and do what he orders are in an unfortunate situation, which is one of the greatest calamities that can be suffered in this life.

XXX

THE GOVERNOR GOES TO OSACHILE. AN ACCOUNT OF THE MANNER IN WHICH THE INDIANS OF LA FLORIDA ESTABLISH THEIR PUEBLOS

After the battle we have described, which was laughable, although bloody and cruel for the poor Indians, the governor remained four days in the pueblo of Vitachuco recovering from the injuries he and his men had received. On the fifth day they set out in search of another province, which was near that one, called Osachile.[8] On the first day they marched four leagues and

[8]In the other chronicles the chief of the province of Uçachile was paramount over the entire territory between Aguacaleyquen and Apalache, that is, over the Timucuan territory misnamed "Ochile" and "Vitachuco" by Garcilaso. Hann, "De Soto, Dobyns, and Demography," 6. See note 4.

camped on the bank of a large river that forms the boundary line of these two provinces. In order to cross it, it was necessary to build another bridge like that which was built on the Río de Ochile, because it could not be forded.

The Castilians having made the board platform to be put over the water, the Indians assembled on the opposite bank to oppose the work and the crossing. Stopping their work on the bridge, the Christians made six large rafts on which a hundred men crossed, including crossbowmen, harquebusiers, and fifty armed cavalrymen, who carried the saddles of their horses on the rafts.

When these had reached the opposite bank, the governor (who, though his face was bandaged, took part in everything) ordered fifty horses driven into the river, and they swam across.

The Spaniards who were on the other side, having received and saddled them, went out on the plain as quickly as possible. Seeing horses in a place clear of timber, the Indians abandoned their post and left the Christians free to build their bridge, which they put out on the water, and with their accustomed diligence they finished it in a day and a half.

The army crossed the river, marched two leagues through a country without timber, and at the end of the march found large fields of maize, beans, and calabashes of the kind called in Spain romana. With the fields began the settlement of scattered houses, separated from one another without the order of a pueblo, and these continued for a space of four leagues as far as the chief pueblo, called Osachile. It contained two hundred large and good houses and was the seat and court of the curaca and lord of that land, who had the same name of Osachile.

The Indians, who throughout the two leagues of open and level country had not dared to wait for the Spaniards, as soon as they saw them among the cultivated fields turned upon them, and from the cover of the maize fields they shot many arrows at them, attacking from all sides and losing no time, place, or occasion that presented itself where they could do them damage. They wounded many Castilians by this means, but neither did the Indians have reason for rejoicing, because the Christians, recognizing the bold and rabid courage the Indians showed for killing or wounding them and opposing their explorations, speared them without sparing anyone; they took very few prisoners. Thus this desperate game continued throughout the four leagues of the cultivated fields, with losses now on one side and now on the other, as always happens in war. From the pueblo of Vitachuco to that of Osachile there are six leagues of level and pleasant country.

The Spaniards found the pueblo of Osachile abandoned, for the curaca and his Indians had gone to the woods. The governor immediately sent messengers to him from among the few Indians they had captured in his country, offering him peace and friendship. But the curaca Osachile neither came out nor replied to the messages, nor did any of the Indians whom they had sent return. It might have been because of the short time that the Christians were in their pueblo, which was only two days. During this time, by placing themselves in ambush, the Spaniards captured many Indians to use as servants. After they gave themselves up they were domestic and gave good service, though with arms in their hands they had shown themselves to be fierce enough.

Because of the short time that the Spaniards were in this province and because it was small, though well populated with people and supplied with food, few things occurred worthy of recounting other than those already mentioned. Therefore it will be appropriate, in order not to leave it so soon, for us to describe the site, plan, and appearance of this pueblo Osachile so that from it may be seen the plan and form of the rest of the pueblos of this great kingdom called La Florida; because since the whole country is of almost the same plan and quality—flat, with many rivers flowing through it—so all its natives live, dress, eat, and drink in about the same way. Even in their heathenism, in their idolatries, rites, and ceremonies (of which they have few), and in their arms, condition, and ferocity, they differ little or none from one another. Thus having seen one pueblo we have seen almost all, and it will not be necessary to describe them separately unless one appears so different that it requires an account of its own.

Therefore it is to be noted that the Indians of La Florida always endeavor to live on a high point, at least in the case of the houses of the caciques and lords when the whole pueblo cannot do so. And because the whole country is very flat, and an elevated site is seldom found that has the other conveniences useful and necessary for a settlement, they make it by their own labor.[9] Amassing a very large quantity of earth, they pack it down by tread-

---

[9] This remarkable passage describing general Mississippian mound construction and the ideal village layout is not duplicated in the other De Soto narratives and is the earliest on record. Moreover, its essential accuracy, except for the apparently exaggerated number of buildings claimed for the mound's summit, is confirmed many times over in archaeological investigations throughout the Southeast. For an archaeological example conforming to this plan, see Richard R. Polhemus, *The Toqua Site: A Late Mississippian Dallas Phase Town*, Report of Investigations No. 41 (Knoxville: University of Tennessee, Department of Anthropology, 1987). For a defense of Garcilaso on this and other ethnographic particulars, see John R. Swanton, "Ethnological Value of the De Soto Narratives," *American Anthropologist* 34, no. 4 (1932):576–77.

ing on it, raising it up in the form of a hill two or three pike-lengths in height. On top they make a level space large enough for ten, twelve, fifteen, or twenty houses for the dwellings of the lord and his family and the people in his service, in accordance with his ability and the grandeur of his state. On the plain at the foot of the hill, natural or artificial, they make a square plaza corresponding to the size of the pueblo that is to be settled, surrounding which the nobles and chief men build their houses. Then the rest of the common people build theirs, endeavoring not to be too far from the hill where the lord's house is; they try rather to surround his with their own.

In order to go up to the curaca's house they make streets straight up the hill, two, three, or more as are needed, fifteen or twenty feet wide. For walls of these streets they drive thick logs into the ground, one after the other, which are sunk into the earth more than an *estado* deep. [An *estado* is a unit of measure about the height of an average man.—CS] For stairways they place other logs no less thick at right angles to those that form the walls, and join them together. These logs that form the stairs are planed on all four sides so that the ascent will be smoother. The risers are four, six, or eight feet from one another, according to the incline and steepness of the hill and its height. The horses could ascend and descend them easily because they were broad. All the rest of the hill, besides the stairs, they cut off in the form of a wall so that it is not possible to ascend it, and in this way the lord's house is better fortified. In this form and plan Osachile had his pueblo and house, which he abandoned because the forest seemed safer to him. There he remained without being willing to accept the friendship of the Spaniards or to reply to their messages.

Second Part of the Second Book of the History of La Florida, by the Inca

Where will be seen the many and severe combats that Indians and Spaniards had in difficult passes in the great Province of Apalache; the hardships through which they passed in discovering the Sea; the events and the incredible fatigues that the thirty horsemen who went back for Pedro Calderón experienced in going and returning; the ferocity of the people of Apalache; the imprisonment of their cacique; his strange flight, and the fertility of that great province. It contains twenty-five chapters.

I

THE SPANIARDS REACH THE FAMOUS PROVINCE OF APALACHE, AND THE RESISTANCE OF ITS INDIANS

The governor and his captains having learned in the pueblo of Osachile that the province of Apalache was nearby—concerning which they had heard so many amazing and great things, both as to the abundance and fertility of the land and the deeds of arms and bravery of the people, with whose ferocity and valor the Indians had threatened them so often along the road, saying that those of Apalache would surely attack them with arrows, and quarter, burn and destroy them—desiring now to see it and to winter in it if it were so fertile as they said, were unwilling to stop in Osachile more than two days. At the end of that time they left the pueblo, and in the next three days they marched without any opposition through twelve leagues of uninhabited country that lies between the two provinces. At noon on the fourth day they came to a swamp that was very large and difficult to cross, because the water alone, without the woods that were on either side, was half a league wide and as long as a river. At the edges of the swamp beyond the water was a forest with a great deal of thick and tall timber and much underbrush consisting of blackberry vines and other small growth, which, being interwoven with the large trees, so thickened and closed up the forest that it had the appearance of a stout wall. Therefore there was no passage for crossing the woods and the swamp except by a path the Indians had made, so narrow that two men abreast could scarcely go along it.

Before reaching the forest, the camp was made on a fine plain, and because it was early the governor ordered that a hundred infantry, including crossbowmen, harquebusiers, and men armed with shields [rodeleros], and thirty cavalry, with twelve swimmers appointed to find out the depth of the water, should go to reconnoiter the crossing of the swamp. They were to take special note of the difficult places they found in it so that they might be prepared for them on the following day.

These Spaniards set out, and a few steps after they entered the path through the woods they found Indians ready to oppose their passage, but, since the path was so narrow, neither the faithful nor the infidels were able to fight, with the exception of the two leaders of each party. Therefore, placing two of the best-armed Spaniards in the lead with their swords and shields, and two more crossbowmen and harquebusiers behind them, they drove the Indians before them all the way through the woods, until they came out on the water. There, since both parties could separate and scatter out, there was a lively combat with many and very good shots from one side to the other, and deaths and wounds on both sides.

Because of the strong resistance the Indians made in the water, the Christians were unable to ascertain just then how deep it was, and so reported to the general, who went in person to their assistance, taking with him the best infantry in the army. The enemy on their part also received reinforcements, making many more than they had formerly during the fight, with which they were strengthened, and the battle became more cruel and bloody. Both continued fighting in water halfway up their thighs, or waist-deep, moving with much difficulty because of the uneven ground caused by the undergrowth of blackberries and shrubs, and the fallen trees under the water. But with all these obstacles the Spaniards, knowing that they ought not to withdraw without having reconnoitered the crossing, made a great effort against the enemy and drove them to the other side of the water. They found that all of it could be forded waist- and thigh-deep except in midchannel, where for a distance of forty paces, because of the great depth, it was crossed by a bridge made of two fallen trees and other timbers fastened together. They saw also that under the water was a path just as there was through the woods, clear of the brush and vines that were on either side, off the path. Across the swamp on the other side, beyond the water, there was another forest as dense and thick as we have said was on this side, which also could not be traversed except along another narrow path or trail, made by hand. Each of these two forests and the swamp was half a league across, so that in all it was a league and a half.

Having examined the crossing well and considered the difficulties found in it, the governor returned with his men to his camp, to plan what must be done on the following day in accordance with what he had seen and learned. Having consulted with the captains regarding the inconvenience and dangers that the passage presented, he ordered a hundred cavalry made ready. These men being better armed than the infantry, they always suffered less injury from arrows. Taking shields and proceeding ahead on foot (because the horses were not needed), they protected a hundred more infantry, including crossbowmen and harquebusiers, who were to follow after them.

The governor also ordered that all of them be provided with axes, hatchets, and other tools with which to cut down a small tract of timber on the farther side of the swamp where the army could make camp, because the

Spaniards, having to cross one at a time, since the road was narrow, and having to dispute the pass with the enemy who had shown himself so fierce that day, it seemed to the governor impossible that his men could cross entirely in one day the two forests on the [sides of the] swamp. He therefore wished to prepare a camping place made thus laboriously in the second forest, for none was available otherwise.

II

THE SPANIARDS GAIN THE CROSSING OF THE SWAMP, AND THE MUCH AND BRAVE FIGHTING THAT TOOK PLACE THERE

With the preparations and orders that have been mentioned, each soldier carrying in his stomach the ration for that day, which was a little parched or boiled maize, and nothing else, two hundred Spaniards left the camp, from among the most chosen men there. Two hours before daylight they entered the path through the woods and proceeded along it as silently as possible until they came to the water where, finding the passage beneath it that was free of obstructions, they followed it to the bridge made of fallen trees and timbers fastened together, which was across the deepest part of the channel of the swamp. They crossed the bridge without a single Indian coming out to defend it, because they had thought the Spaniards would not dare enter at night into the thick woods and deep water with the undergrowth that was in it; therefore they had neglected to rise early in order to defend the crossing. But when daylight came and they perceived that the Christians had crossed the bridge, they gathered with furious shouts and clamor to defend the rest of the distance by water and swamp that was still to be passed, which was some quarter of a league. Angry at themselves for having been careless and slept so long, they charged upon the Castilians with great ferocity and violence. But the latter were well prepared, and being desirous that that fight should not last long, they pressed the Indians hard. Both were walking in water waist-deep. They drove them [the Indians] out of it, enclosing them in the passageway through the second forest, which was so close and thick that the Indians could not run through it in scattered formation, but only single file constrained by the narrow path. The Indians once enclosed in this path through the woods—since because of its narrowness few Spaniards were needed to defend it—they agreed that 150 of them busy themselves in clearing a site for establishing the camp, and the other fifty guard and defend the pass in case the Indians should attempt to come and stop the work; because, since there was no other way of reaching those who were clearing the timber except by way of the path or trail, the few Christians who were there were sufficient to defend it.

They continued thus all that day, the Indians shouting and clamoring in order to alarm their enemies with their noise, now that they could not do so with arms; and some of the Castilians laboring to defend the passage, others in cutting the trees, and still others in burning those [trees] already cut so that they would not obstruct the site. When night came each one of our men stayed where he was, without sleeping any part of it because of the sudden assaults and the shouting of the Indians.

At daylight the army began to cross over, and although they had no opposition from the enemy, they had it from the road itself, which was very narrow, and from the obstructions in the water that prevented their passing as they would have liked to do; therefore they were forced to go one by one. Because of this excessive delay the whole camp was barely able to reach the clearing on the other side in the course of the day. There, because of the clamor and the sudden attacks the enemy made upon them, they slept as little that night as they had the night before. Those who were defending the crossing were given food by passing it from hand to hand, until it reached the ones in front.

As soon as day came the Spaniards marched along the path through the woods, driving the Indians before them, who continued to shoot arrows at them, retiring a little at a time, unwilling to yield to them anything that they could not win by the sword.

Thus they traversed the half-league through that dense and thick forest. Coming out of the thicket, they entered another woodland, clearer and more open, in which the Indians could scatter and go and come through the undergrowth. They harried the Castilians greatly, attacking from both sides of the road and discharging many arrows. They observed some order and plan, however, so that when those on one side were attacking, the others did not do so until the first had withdrawn, so as not to wound one another with stray arrows. The arrows were so numerous that they looked like a rain falling from the skies.

The forest where the Indians and the Spaniards were now fighting, which we said was more open, was not enough so to permit the horses to run through it. For this reason the Indians were going in and out among the

Christians so boldly that they paid no attention to them, and though the crossbowmen and harquebusiers made a stand against them, it had no effect, for while a Spaniard was firing one shot and making ready for another, an Indian would shoot six or seven arrows. They are so skillful and ready that they scarcely have discharged one before they have another in the bow.

The spots of clear ground between the trees by which the horses could pass, the Indians had surrounded and obstructed with large logs fastened to trees at either end in order to protect themselves against the horses; and in the thick woods through which the Indians could not travel they had made clearings at intervals with entrances and exits by which they could attack the Christians without being harmed by them.

They made these preparations ahead of time, because they knew that inasmuch as the woods and the swamp were so dense they would not be able to attack the Castilians as they desired and could do if the forest were more open and clearer, as was that in which they now were. Seeing, then, the advantages they had over the Spaniards because of the site, they did not cease attempting and carrying out whatever action, stratagem, or deceit they could against the Christians, eager to wound or kill them.

In these woods the Castilians were engaged in defending themselves from the enemy rather than in attacking him, because they could not make use of their horses, because of the obstruction of the woods; thus they were fatigued by their own courage rather than by their adversaries' arms. Seeing that their enemies were thus burdened, the Indians pressed them more and more on all sides, eager and anxious to rout and destroy them. Some of them took new courage and strength from the memory and recollection of having defeated and destroyed Pánphilo de Narváez ten or twelve years before in this same swamp, though not at this pass. They recalled this exploit to the Spaniards and to their general, saying to them, among other taunts and insults, that they would do the same thing to them and to him.

With these difficulties from the road and injuries from the enemy, the Spaniards traveled through the two leagues of forest until they emerged on open and level ground. Reaching it and giving thanks to God for having brought them out of that prison, they gave rein to their horses and showed well the anger they felt against the Indians, because in the more than two leagues of open country that intervened before they came to the maize fields they did not meet a single Indian whom they failed to capture or kill, especially those who made a show of resistance, not one of whom escaped. Thus they killed many Indians and took few prisoners, and the mortality of that day was large. With this these Castilians avenged the offense and injury the

Apalaches did to Pánphilo de Narváez, and undeceived them regarding their opinion of themselves and their boast that they would kill and destroy these Castilians as they had the others.

III

OF THE CONTINUOUS FIGHTING THAT TOOK PLACE UNTIL THE ARRIVAL AT THE CHIEF PUEBLO OF APALACHE

It seemed to Governor Hernando de Soto that they had done enough for that day in having got out of the forest where they had encountered such difficulties, and in having partially punished the Indians. Thus he did not wish to go farther but encamped his army on that plain, it being a place clear of timber. The camp was pitched near a small pueblo where the settlements and cultivated fields of the province of Apalache began, so renowned and famous throughout that country.

The Indians were unwilling to repose on the following night, nor did they allow the Christians to rest from the bad days and nights that they had given them after their arrival at the swamp. Throughout the night they never ceased their shouts, alarms, and sudden attacks at all hours, shooting many arrows into the camp. The whole night passed with this uneasiness on both sides, without their coming to blows.

When daylight came the Spaniards marched through some large fields of maize, beans, calabashes, and other vegetables, the fields on both sides of the road extending across the plain out of sight, and it was two leagues through them. Among the fields were scattered a large number of separate houses at a distance from one another and not in the form of a pueblo.[10] The Indians came very hastily out of the houses and fields to shoot arrows at the Castilians, persisting in their desire and eagerness to kill or wound them. The latter, offended by such pertinacity and angered by the obstinacy and rancor they perceived in them, lost patience and speared them without mercy all through the maize fields, to see whether they could overcome or punish them by force of arms. But it was all in vain, because the anger and wrath

[10]Ordinary households among the early Apalache and many other Mississippian societies were dispersed across the landscape. These farmsteads, or household farming settlements, were tied to a nearby political center.

An Ear of Modern Corn. Corn was originally domesticated by the Native Americans, and it was the staple crop grown by the Mississippian cultures of the Southeast in De Soto's time. After landing in present Florida, De Soto's men did not see corn being grown until they reached the town of Paracoxi. Thereafter, when their food supplies brought from Cuba ran out, the Spaniards were forced to subsist mainly on corn taken from Indian stores. De Soto and Moscoso sought out well-populated places as they traveled, as much to ensure themselves of corn as to search for wealth. (Courtesy of the University of Alabama Museum of Natural History)

the Indians felt toward the Christians seemed to increase with the latter's desire for revenge.

Having passed over two leagues of cultivated fields, they came to a deep stream carrying much water and having thick timber on either side. It was a very difficult crossing, and the enemy had reconnoitered it well and prepared to attack the Castilians there. The latter seeing the obstacles and the defenses at the pass, the best-armed horsemen dismounted, and armed with swords and shields, and some with axes, they gained the pass and knocked down the palisades and barriers that had been built to prevent the horses from crossing, and their masters from attacking. The Indians charged here with greatest impetus and fury, placing their last hope of overcoming the Christians at this bad crossing because it was so difficult. Here the fighting was furious, and many Spaniards were wounded and some killed, because the enemy fought rashly, making the last stand of desperate men. But they could not succeed in their evil intent, for the Castilians won the victory through the spirit and strength that they showed and the great efforts that they made so that the injury might not be so great as they had feared to receive in such a dangerous place.

Leaving the stream, the Castilians marched two leagues more through a country without cultivated fields or settlements. The Indians did not oppose them there because in the field [*campo raso*] they could not stand against the horses. The Christians made camp in that place, which was clear of timber, so that the Indians with their fear of the horses, seeing them away from the woods, would allow them to sleep. After the past four days and three nights of watching and labor they were in need of rest. But that night they slept as little as before because the enemy, depending on the darkness, though in an open country, did not cease all night to give alarms and make sudden attacks on all sides of the camp. They disturbed the Castilians' rest so as not to lose the name and reputation the people of this province of Apalache had gained among all their neighbors and friends of being the bravest and most warlike.

On the next day, which was the fifth after they crossed the swamp, as soon as the army began to march the governor went ahead with two hundred cavalry and a hundred infantry, because he had learned from the Indian prisoners that two leagues from there was the pueblo of Apalache and in it its cacique with a large number of his bravest Indians, awaiting the Castilians to kill and quarter all of them. These words are precisely those that the prisoners said to the governor; although captives and in the power of their enemies they did not lose their bravado and their pride at being natives of Apalache.

The general and his men traveled the two leagues, spearing as many Indians as they met on either side of the road. They reached the pueblo and found that the curaca and his Indians had abandoned it. Knowing that they had not gone far, the Spaniards followed and traveled two leagues more on the other side of the pueblo, but though they killed and captured many Indians they could not come up with Capafi, for so the cacique was named. This is the first that we have found with a name different from his province. The adelantado returned to the pueblo, which consisted of 250 large and substantial houses, in which he found all his army lodged. He settled himself in those belonging to the cacique, which were on one side of the pueblo and, as the ruler's dwellings, were superior to all the others.

Besides this principal pueblo, there were many others throughout that district, half a league, one, one and a half, two, and three leagues away. Some had fifty or sixty houses, others a hundred or more, or less, not counting many other houses scattered about and not arranged in pueblos. The site of the whole province is pleasing, the soil fertile with a great abundance of food, and there are large quantities of fish, which the natives catch throughout the year for their subsistence and keep prepared for eating.

The governor and his captains and the officials of the real hacienda were all very pleased with what they saw of the good quality of that country and its fertility, and though all the provinces they had left behind them were good, this one had an advantage, inasmuch as its natives were indomitable and exceedingly bellicose, as has been seen and as we shall see later in some notable instances that occurred in this province between the Spaniards and Indians, individually and generally. To avoid prolixity, however, we shall not recount all of them, but from those that are told the ferocity of these Indians of Apalache will be seen clearly.

IV

THREE CAPTAINS GO TO DISCOVER THE BOUNDARIES OF APALACHE, AND THE REPORT THEY BRING

After the army had rested for several days and recovered somewhat from their recent great hardships, though during this time the constant alarms and sudden attacks of the enemy did not cease, night or day, the governor sent bands of men on foot and on horseback with specially selected captains to penetrate fifteen or twenty leagues into the interior, to see and discover what might be on the boundaries and in the environs of that province.

Two captains went by different routes toward the north, one of them being Arias Tinoco and the other Andrés de Vasconcelos, who returned without anything of importance having happened to them, one eight days and the other nine after leaving the camp. They reported almost in the same words that they had found many pueblos having many people, and that the land abounded in food and was free of swamps and dense forests. Captain Juan de Añasco, who went toward the south, reported on the contrary that he had found a very rough and difficult country, almost impassable because of the obstacles he had encountered in the form of woods and swamps, which became worse as he proceeded south. On noting this difference between the very good and very poor country, I do not wish to go on without mentioning that Alvar Núñez Cabeza de Vaca writes in his *Commentarios* concerning this province of Apalache. He describes it there as being rough, uneven, full of woods and swamps, with rivers and difficult passes, thinly populated and sterile, all of which is contrary to what we are writing. Therefore, with due regard for what that gentleman writes, for it is trustworthy, we understand that his journey was not so far into the interior as was that which Governor Hernando de Soto made, but was nearer the seacoast, and thus the land was found to be so rough and full of woods and bad swamps as he says. As we shall soon see, the same thing was found and discovered by Captain Juan de Añasco, who went from the chief pueblo of Apalache to find the sea, and he had great good luck in not losing himself time and again because of the bad country that he found. The pueblo that Cabeza de Vaca calls Apalache, to which he says Pánphilo de Narváez came, I believe was not this principal one that Hernando de Soto discovered, but another one of the many that are in this province that would be nearer the sea and, because of being in its jurisdiction, would be called Apalache like the province itself; for in the pueblo we have said was its capital there was found what we have seen. It is also to be noted that much of the account that Alvar Núñez wrote of that country is that which the Indians gave him, as he himself says. Those Castilians did not see it because, as they were few and most or all of them were captives, it was impossible for them to travel through it and see it with their own eyes, and even to seek food, and thus most of them were left to die of hunger. In the account that the Indians gave him it is to be believed that they would speak ill rather than well of their country, to discredit it so that the Spaniards would lose their desire to go there, and thus our *History* does not contradict the account of that gentleman.

V

OF THE HARDSHIPS THAT JUAN DE AÑASCO EXPERIENCED IN DISCOVERING THE SEACOAST

We said that one of the captains who went to explore the region of Apalache was Juan de Añasco. So that the hardships he experienced may be better known, then, it must be said that he took forty cavalry and fifty foot soldiers, and there was also with him a gentleman named Gómez Arias, who was a relative of the governor's wife, a great soldier and very useful wherever he was because along with his military skill, great industry, and good counsel, he was a very expert swimmer (a useful and necessary thing for conquests), and overcame difficulties that arose in the water and on land. He had been a slave in Barbary where he learned the Moorish language, and he spoke it so well that he came out from the interior many leagues away on a Christian frontier without the Moors whom he happened to meet discovering that he was a slave. This gentleman and the men whom we have mentioned went with Juan de Añasco to the south to discover the sea, as they had news that it was less than thirty leagues from Apalache. They took an Indian to guide them who offered to do so, making a great show of loyalty and friendship toward the Christians.

In two days' journey of six leagues each, which they traveled over a very good road, wide and smooth, they came to a pueblo called Aute; they found it without people but full of food. On this road they passed two small rivers, easy to cross.

From the pueblo of Aute they went on with their search, taking food for four days. On the second day that they traveled by this same wide and good road, the Indian who was guiding them began to deceive them, it appearing to him that it was a bad thing to be a faithful guide to his enemies. Thereupon he led them out of the wide and good road that they had followed up to that time and set them among some thick and dense woods, very hard to travel through, with many fallen trees and without a road or path. Some small plots of ground that they found, about the size of kitchen gardens, without timber, were themselves so miry that horses and foot soldiers sank into them. On top they were covered with grass and looked like solid ground on which one could walk safely. They found on this road—or in this forest, to speak correctly—a species of bramble with long and thick branches that extended over the ground and covered a large area. They had long straight thorns that hurt the horses and foot soldiers cruelly, and though they tried to guard against these vicious brambles, they could not, because there were a great many of them and they were spread between two layers of earth, covered with mud or sand, or with water. With these difficulties and others that can be imagined, these Castilians traveled off the road for five days, turning this way and that as the Indian wished to take them according to his whim, to deceive them or place them where they could not get out.

When the food that they took from the pueblo of Aute was exhausted, they decided to go back there to get more provisions and then continue their search. On turning back toward Aute, they suffered more hardships on the way than in going out, because they were forced to retrace their steps along the same route in order not to become lost; and, as they found the earth already trampled by their former passage, the horses and even the infantry sank in the mud more than when the trail was fresh.

In the midst of these fatigues and hardships the Castilians understood well enough that the Indian had lost the road purposely, because three times they found themselves in the midst of the woods so close to the sea that they could hear the surf. But as soon as he would hear it the Indian again would lead them into the interior, hoping to entrap them where they could not get out and would perish of hunger; and though he should die with them, he was satisfied if by so doing he could kill them. The Christians knew all this, but they did not dare confront him with it for fear of offending him more than he was already, and also because they had brought no other guide.

Having returned to Aute, where they arrived dying of hunger—as men who for four days had eaten nothing except herbs and roots—they took provisions for five or six days more, as there was a great abundance of them in the pueblo, and went back to their exploration, not by better roads than the past ones but by other, worse ones—if worse there could be, or if the diligence and malice of the guide could find them, as he desired to do.

One night when they were sleeping in the forest, the Indian, unable to put off longer the time of killing the Christians, seized a stick from the fire and struck and injured one of them in the face. The other soldiers wished to kill him for his shamelessness and boldness, but the captain prevented it, saying that they must tolerate him because he was the guide and they had no other. They went back to rest, and an hour later he did the same thing to another Castilian. Then they gave him many blows, kicks, and cuffs by way of punishment, but this did not prevent the Indian's beating still another soldier with another firebrand before morning.

The Spaniards now did not know what to do with him. For the time being they contented themselves with beating him and putting him in chains, by which he was attached to one of their number so that he could keep special watch over him.

As soon as morning came they resumed their march, suffering much from the hardships of their past route and the present one, and angered by the bad behavior of the guide. After they had traveled a short distance the latter, seeing himself in the power of his enemies and being unable to kill them or to escape from them, despairing of his life, attacked the soldier to whom he was chained and, grasping him from behind, raised him up and threw him full length on the ground; and before he could get up he jumped on him with both feet and kicked him. The Castilians and their captain, unable to endure such outrages any longer, stabbed and speared him until they left him for dead. A strange thing was noted, however, and this was that the swords and spearheads entered into and cut his body so little that he seemed to be enchanted; the many gashes he received wounded him no more than blows from a wand made of shoots from the quince or wild olive tree. Angered by this, Juan de Añasco raised himself in the stirrups and, grasping his spear with both hands, struck him with all his strength; and though he was a strong and robust man, the spearhead did not go halfway in. When the Spaniards saw this they wondered at it, and they loosed a greyhound to finish killing him by grasping and tearing him. So ended this treacherous and malicious Indian, as he deserved.

VI

CAPTAIN JUAN DE AÑASCO REACHES THE BAY OF AUTE, AND WHAT HE FOUND THERE

The Castilians had not gone fifty paces from the Indian, whom they believed to be dead and eaten by the dog, when they heard the hound giving great howls, clamoring as if they were killing him. Our men ran to see what it was and found that the Indian, with his little remaining strength, had placed his thumbs on either side of the dog's mouth and was tearing his jaws apart, the dog being unable to help himself. Seeing this, one of the Spaniards stabbed him repeatedly, finally killing him; and another cut off his hands with a hunter's cutlass that he carried, and after they were severed he could not loosen them from the dog's mouth, so desperately had he grasped it.

After this event the Spaniards resumed their march, marveling that a single Indian should have been the means of giving them so much trouble, but as they did not know in which direction to go, they were confused, uncertain what to do. In this dilemma they were helped by an Indian whom they had happened to take on their past route when they were returning to the pueblo of Aute, and they had kept him with them continuously. Though it is true that before the death of the Indian guide the Spaniards had questioned him many times as to whether he knew the route to the sea, he never answered a word, remaining silent because the other had threatened him with death if he talked. Seeing, then, that the obstacle was removed and that he was rid of his companion, and fearing that they might kill him as they had the other, he spoke and replied to what they were then asking him. By means of signs and a few words that he knew, he said that he would take them to the sea at the same place where Pánphilo de Narváez had built his boats and had embarked, but that it was necessary to go back to the pueblo of Aute because the direct route to the sea began there. Although the Spaniards told him that it must be nearby, because from where they were they could hear the sound of the waves and surf, he replied that they would never in their lives reach the sea by the way that they thought to go, and that the other Indian was taking them, because of the many swamps and the impassable woods that lay between; therefore they must return to the pueblo of Aute. Thereupon the Castilians returned to the pueblo, having spent five days on this second journey and ten on the first, at the cost of much personal hardship and with the loss of fifteen days, which was what they most regretted, because of the anxiety that the governor would feel at their delay.

Returning to the pueblo, then, Gómez Arias and Gonzalo Silvestre, who were going on ahead exploring the country, seized two Indians whom they found near the pueblo. Being questioned as to whether they knew how to guide them to the sea, they replied that they did and confirmed everything that the Indian whom they were bringing as a prisoner had told them. With these hopes the Spaniards rested that night somewhat more easily than on the fifteen nights past.

The next day the three Indians guided the Christians along a smooth, clear, and pleasant road between two large and good fields of stubble. Leaving them behind, the road became wider and more open, and they found no bad crossings throughout its length, except one narrow swamp that was easily passed, the horses sinking only to the pastern. Having marched a little more than two leagues, they reached a very wide and spacious bay, and, proceeding along its shore, they came to the site where Pánphilo de Narváez had camped. There they saw where he had the forge on which he made the nails for vessels; they found much charcoal around it. They saw also some thick beams hollowed like troughs, which had served as mangers for the horses.

The three Indians showed the Spaniards the site where the enemy had killed ten Christians of Narváez's party, as Alvar Núñez Cabeza de Vaca also tells in his history. They took them step by step all along the route followed by Pánphilo de Narváez, pointing out the spots where such and such things had occurred. Finally, they omitted none of the notable things that Pánphilo de Narváez did on that bay, recounting them by signs and with words well or ill understood, some spoken in Spanish, for the Indians of all that coast pride themselves greatly on knowing the Spanish language and try diligently to learn a few odd words, which they repeat over and over.

Captain Juan de Añasco and his soldiers went about very carefully looking to see whether they might have placed some letters in hollow trees or cut some words on the bark that would tell some of the things that these others had seen and noted—because it has been a very usual and customary thing for the first discoverers of new lands to leave such messages for their successors, and these messages often have been of great importance—but they could find nothing of the sort for which they were looking.

After doing this, they followed the shore of the bay to the sea, which was three leagues away, and at ebb tide ten or twelve swimmers embarked in some old abandoned canoes they found, and sounded the depth of the bay in midchannel.

They found it deep enough for large ships. Then they put signs on the highest trees thereabout so that those who came coasting by sea could recognize that site, which was the same one where Pánphilo de Narváez embarked in his five vessels, so unfortunate that none of them survived.

Having taken the precautions described and set them down in writing so that those who might come to it should not miss the place, they returned to the camp and reported to the governor everything that had happened and what they had done. The general was much relieved to see them because he had been concerned at their delay, and he was glad to know that there was a port for the ships.

VII

THIRTY LANCERS ARE MADE READY TO RETURN TO THE BAY OF ESPÍRITU SANTO

While the three exploring captains went out and returned with the reports of what each of them had seen and discovered, Governor Hernando de Soto did not rest or remain idle, but on the other hand, he was considering in his own mind and preparing with all care and vigilance the things most advantageous for his army. Therefore seeing that winter was approaching (it was then October), he thought it best not to continue his discoveries that year but to winter in that province of Apalache where there were plenty of provisions. He planned to send for Captain Pedro Calderón and the other Spaniards who had remained with him in the province of Hirrihigua to come and join him, because they were not doing anything of importance where they were.

To this end he ordered as many supplies collected as possible. He had many houses built besides those in the pueblo so that there would be comfortable lodgings for all his soldiers. He had a site fortified that seemed suitable, for the safety of his men. During this time he did not cease to send messengers to Capafi, the lord of that province, with gifts and friendly messages, begging him to come out peaceably and be his friend. The latter was unwilling to accept any of these terms but instead fortified himself in a very wild forest full of swamps and difficult passes, which he chose for the defense and protection of his person.

The things stated being arranged and provided for, the governor ordered the accountant Juan de Añasco to prepare to return to the province of Hirrihigua, because it seemed to him that this gentleman was the most successful captain and had had better fortune from the beginning of his expedition than any of his others, and that such a man who had also his other good qualities as a soldier was needed to surmount the dangers and difficulties he would encounter. In consideration of these things he ordered him to take twenty-nine other lancers who were ready, he himself making thirty, and return with them to the pueblo of Hirrihigua by the same road that the army had taken, so that Captain Pedro Calderón and the other soldiers who were with him might be advised of what the general ordered them to do.

The task was a very severe one because those [who went] would have to go back over almost 150 leagues of country inhabited by brave and cruel enemies, filled with large rivers, forests, swamps, and difficult passes, a crossing in which the whole army had been in great danger. This would be even greater now that only thirty lancers were going, and they would necessarily find the Indians better prepared than when the governor passed, and because of the injuries received, more angry and desirous of avenging them.

But all this did not suffice to make the thirty gentlemen now prepared refuse to go on the expedition; rather they obeyed readily and with all promptness. Because they were men of such spirit and courage, who went through so many hardships, dangers, and difficulties, as we shall see, it will be fitting to set down their names, and we are including those whose names are remembered. Those who are missing will forgive me and accept my respects, for I would like to have information not only of them but of all those who went to conquer and win the New World, and I wish also that I could attain the historical eloquence of the most illustrious Caesar in order to spend my life recounting and celebrating their great exploits. To the extent that these have been greater than those of the Greeks, the Romans, and other nations, so much more unfortunate have the Spaniards been in lacking someone to write of them, and it is no small misfortune to these gentlemen that [the story of] their deeds came into the hands of an Indian, whence they will emerge impaired and defaced rather than written as they deserve to be and as they occurred. In having done what I could, however, I have complied with this obligation, though I have a greater fund of good will to serve them than of power or ability.

The gentlemen chosen were the accountant and captain Juan de Añasco, a native of Sevilla; Gómez Arias, a native of Segovia; Juan Cordero and Alvaro Fernández, natives of Yelves; Antonio Garillo, a native of Yllescas (he was one of the thirteen who revolted in Cuzco with Francisco Hernández Girón in the year 1553); Francisco de Villalobos and Juan López Cacho, citizens of Sevilla; Gonzalo Silvestre, a native of Herrera de Alcántara; Juan de Espinosa, a native of Ubeda; Hernando Athanasio, a native of Badajoz; Juan de Abadía, a Biscayan; Antonio de la Cadena and Francisco Segredo, natives of Medellín; Bartolomé de Argote and Pedro Sánchez from Astorga; Juan García Pechudo, a native of Albuquerque; and Pedro Morón, mestizo, a native of the city of Bayamo in the island of Cuba. This soldier had a most unusual gift in that he scented and picked up a trail better than a pointer dog.

It often happened in the island of Cuba that when he and others went out to hunt for rebellious or runaway Indians he could follow their trails to the underbrush or hollow trees or eaves where they were hidden. He also could detect fire from the odor more than a league away, and many times in this exploration of La Florida, without flame or smoke having been seen, he said to his companions, "Look out, there is a fire near us," and they would find it half a league or a league away. He was a most expert swimmer, as we have said already. With him went his comrade and compatriot, Diego de Oliva, a mestizo and a native of the island of Cuba.

VIII

WHAT THE THIRTY HORSEMEN DID UNTIL THEIR ARRIVAL AT VITACHUCO, AND WHAT THEY FOUND THERE

These twenty [*sic*] horsemen and ten others whose names are lacking to make up the number of thirty, left the pueblo of Apalache on October 20 of the year 1539 to go to the province of Hirrihigua where Pedro de Calderón was. They carried orders that will be told later as to what they were to do on sea and on land.

All traveled very lightly, with only helmets and coats of mail over their clothing, their lances in their hands, and a pair of knapsacks on their saddles containing some horseshoes and nails and the food that they could put into them for horses and riders.

They left the camp a good while before daylight, and so that the news of their coming should not precede them and the Indians thus be warned to go out and take the passes, they traveled at a good speed, running where it was possible to do so. That day they speared two Indians whom they met on the road, killing them so that they might not give an alarm and warn those who were scattered about the country. They always traveled with this precaution against the news [of their coming] going ahead of them. Thus on that day they marched the eleven leagues between Apalache and the swamp, which they crossed without opposition from the enemy; no small advantage, because however few Indians might have come they would have been enough to shoot arrows at the horses in such a narrow road as that through the woods and the water.

The Spaniards slept on the plain entirely beyond the woods, having traveled and marched that day more than thirteen leagues. While resting they kept watch by thirds, in groups of ten, as we have told above.

They continued their march before daybreak and covered the twelve leagues of uninhabited country that lies between the swamp of Apalache and the pueblo of Osachile. They went with the fear that the Indians would know of their approach and would come out to oppose their passage, so they advanced slowly, waiting for nightfall, and about midnight they passed through the pueblo, going at a canter. A league beyond the pueblo they left the road and rested the remainder of the night, a third of them keeping watch, as we have said. That day they traveled more than thirteen leagues farther.

At dawn they continued their journey, going at a canter because there were people in the fields. They always did this when they were passing through inhabited country so that the news of their coming should not go ahead of them, which was what they most feared. Thus they traveled the five leagues from the place where they slept to the Río de Osachile at the expense of the horses, and they were so good that they endured everything. On approaching the river, Gonzalo Silvestre, who, because he had urged his horse more than the others, was riding ahead, went to look at it with much misgiving, fearing to find it higher than when the army had crossed it, but God willed that it now carried less water than before. In his satisfaction at seeing it thus he plunged into it and swam across and came out on the plain on the opposite side. When his companions saw him on the farther bank they were very pleased because all of them had had the same fear of finding the river swollen; they crossed without any mishaps and by way of celebration and rejoicing for having crossed the river they ate lunch. Then they traveled at a moderate pace the four leagues from this Río de Osachile to the pueblo of Vitachuco, the scene of the cacique Vitachuco's temerity.

The Castilians proceeded with the uneasy expectation of finding the pueblo of Vitachuco as they had left it, and they feared that they would have to fight with its inhabitants and gain passage by force, where it might happen that they [the Indians] would kill or wound some man or horse, a misfortune that would double the labors and difficulties of the road. They therefore agreed among themselves that none of them would remain to fight, but all would endeavor to pass on without stopping. With this determination they came to the pueblo, where they lost all their anxiety because they found it entirely burned and destroyed and the walls leveled to the ground; and the bodies of the Indians who died on the day of the battle and those whom they killed on the day that the cacique Vitachuco struck the governor were all heaped together in the fields, no one having desired to bury them. The Indians said later that they abandoned and destroyed the pueblo because it was founded on an unlucky and unfortunate site; and the dead Indians, as ill-fated men who had not carried out their pretensions, they left unburied as food for birds and wild beasts, for among them this was a very infamous punishment and was given to those who were unlucky and unfortunate in arms, as to people who were accursed and excommunicated, after their heathen custom. They so regarded this pueblo and those who died in it because it seemed to them that the disaster that happened there had been caused more by the unluckiness of the place and the ill-fortune of the dead than by the strength and bravery of the Spaniards, for their numbers were so small against so many and such brave Indians.

IX

THE JOURNEY OF THE THIRTY LANCERS CONTINUES, UNTIL REACHING THE RÍO DE OCHILE [OCALI]

Wondering at what they had seen, the Spaniards passed through the pueblo and had scarcely left it when they found two Indian nobles who, armed with their bows and arrows, were hunting, not expecting to see Christians that day; but when they saw them appear they took refuge under a very large walnut tree that was close by. One of them, not trusting much in the safety of his position, ran away from the tree and went to take shelter in the woods that were on one side of the road. Two of the Castilians, much against their captain's wishes, went to head him off, and before the Indian reached the woods they overtook him, a small enough accomplishment for two horsemen. The other Indian, who had more courage and waited under the tree, was luckier, because fortune favors the daring, as people who deserve it. Putting an arrow in his bow, he faced all the Spaniards—who came up at a canter, one after another—and made a gesture of shooting it if they should come nearer to him. Some of them, angered by the Indian's audacity and boldness, or envious at seeing a spirit and courage so unusual and strange, wished to dismount and attack him on foot with their lances in their hands. But Juan de Añasco would not consent to it, saying that it was not valor or prudence to kill a rash and desperate man with the risk that the Indian would kill or wound one of them or one of their horses at a time when they needed them so much, and where they were so ill prepared for treating the wounded.

Saying these words, as he was leading the rest, he made a wide circle, going away from the Indian and from the road that passed near the tree where he was so that the enemy might not shoot at them in passing and wound a horse, which was what he most feared. As the Spaniard went by, the Indian, with an arrow in his bow, pointed it at his face, threatening to shoot him. The first one having passed, and likewise the second and third and all the rest, as they went by in their order, the Indian remained in the same attitude until all had passed, and when he saw that they had not attacked him, but rather had left and fled from him, he began to shout insulting words at them, saying: "Cowards, bastards, cravens; thirty of you on horseback have not dared attack one on foot!" With these boasts he remained under his tree with more honor than all these famous [soldiers] had gained; so said the Castilians in their excessive envy of him, as they passed on shamed by the shouts that he sent after them. At this point they heard a great outcry and alarm that the Indians who were in the fields on either side gave, calling to one another to block their road.

The Spaniards escaped this danger and other similar ones by the swiftness of their horses, always hastening and leaving the enemy behind. On this day, which was the third of their march, well after dark, they reached a fine plain clear of timber where they rested, having traveled and marched seventeen leagues that day, the last eight through the province of Vitachuco.

On the fourth day they marched eighteen more leagues, all through the province of Vitachuco. Its natives being injured and offended from the past battle, and seeing them [the Spaniards] now marching through their country, and that they were few in number, wished to take revenge by killing them. Therefore they made up relays in order to pass the word on from one to another to give the news of the Spaniards' coming and assemble men to occupy some difficult pass and cut them off. Surmising the Indians' intention, our men followed them so closely that none who attempted to carry the message escaped them, and thus on that day they speared seven Indians. At nightfall they reached a plain having no timber, where they thought they might rest because they heard no sounds of Indians in the surrounding country.

A little after midnight they left their beds, and by sunrise they had marched five leagues, reaching the Río de Ocali where we said the Indians had shot the hound Bruto. The Castilians went with some hope of finding the river with less water than when they had crossed it [before], as they had found the Osachile, but the contrary was true, because for some time before they came to it they saw the banks, which as we said were two pike-lengths high, entirely covered with water that overflowed beyond them on the plain. The river ran so rapidly, turbidly and strongly, with so many whirlpools in every part of it, that simply looking at it inspired fear, much less having to swim across it. To this difficulty and danger was added another, greater one, which was the alarm and outcry that the Indians raised on both sides of the river when they saw the Christians appear, shouting to one another to kill them as they crossed.

The Spaniards, seeing that the safety of their lives lay in their good spirit, strength, and speed, immediately discussed what they ought to do in that danger, and as if by prearrangement—and as if all of them were captains—calling one another by their names, they ordered that twelve of them who were the best swimmers, wearing only their helmets and coats of mail over their shirts (without any other clothing, so as not to hinder the horses in swimming), and carrying lances in their hands, go into the river to gain the other bank before the Indians should reach it. As there were more of them on that side and as the whole pueblo could assemble there, it was more dangerous and it was necessary to keep it unobstructed and free, so that as the Spaniards swam across the Indians might not shoot arrows at them at their pleasure. The twelve men appointed, then, seeing the imminent danger in which they were, all said with one accord, reassuring one another, that whoever might get out or whoever might die it was impossible for them to do otherwise. They ordered also that fourteen of them cut as quickly as possible five or six thick timbers from the dead trees that had fallen on the riverbank and make a raft from them in which they could take over the saddles, clothing and knapsacks, and the Spaniards who did not know how to swim. The four remaining men were to endeavor to hold back the Indians who were coming at full speed from upstream and down on this side to prevent their crossing.

They had no sooner made this plan than they put it into operation. The twelve men named to cross the river, taking off their clothes, at once plunged into the water, and eleven of them succeeded in coming out on the opposite bank at a large gap in the bluff. The twelfth, who was Juan López Cacho, was unable to make the shore because his horse went a little downstream from the opening, and being unable to resist the velocity of the water to come out at this landing, he went on down the river to see if there were another opening by which he could come out. Although he attempted many times to ascend the bluff in order to land, he could not do so, for the bluff was as steep as a wall and the horse could not get a foothold. Therefore he had to go back to the other bank, and as the horse had been swimming for so long without resting, he was much fatigued. Juan López asked for help from his companions who were cutting the timber for the raft, and four of them who were expert swimmers, seeing his danger, jumped into the water and brought him and his horse safely to shore, which was no small feat because they were fatigued from their labors. Here we shall leave them to tell what the governor was doing meanwhile in Apalache.

X

THE GOVERNOR CAPTURES THE CURACA OF APALACHE

The adelantado Hernando de Soto was not idle while the accountant and captain Juan de Añasco and the thirty horsemen who went with him were making the expedition of which we have told. On the contrary, finding the Indians of the province of Apalache, where he was, with the eagerness and solicitude that we have seen to kill or wound the Spaniards, and that they were losing no occasion that presented itself to them on which they might do it, by day or by night, it seemed to him that, if he could get the cacique into his hands, the stratagems and treasonable acts of his Indians would cease at once. He secretly took great trouble to find out where the curaca was, and within a few days they brought him definite information that he was concealed in some high and very rough mountains where, though he was no more than eight leagues from the camp, the cacique believed himself to be safe, likewise because of the strength of his position and because of the many and good men whom he had with him for his defense.

With this certain news the general desired to make the journey himself, and taking the necessary cavalry and infantry and guided by the same spies, he set out for the place where the cacique was. Having traveled eight leagues in three days and experienced many hardships because of the difficulties of the road, he reached the place. The Indians had fortified it in the following manner. In the middle of a very large and dense forest they had cleared a space where the curaca and his Indians had their lodgings. As an entrance to this plaza they had opened through the same woods a narrow alley more than half a league in length. All along this alley at intervals of a hundred paces they had made strong palisades with thick logs, which commanded the passage. Men were designated for the defense of each palisade. They had not made an exit by which to escape at any other part of this fort because they believed that even though the Spaniards should reach it the site was so strong in itself and the men who were defending it were so numerous and so brave that it was impossible for them to gain it. Within it was the cacique Capafi, well supported by his people, all determined to die rather than see their lord in the power of his enemies.

Upon his arrival at the entrance of the alley, the governor found the men there well prepared to defend it. The Castilians fought bravely, but since the alley was narrow, only those in the lead could fight. With this labor, solely by dint of the sword, and receiving many arrow wounds, they gained the first palisade and the second, but inasmuch as it was necessary to cut the ropes made of willows and the other cords with which the Indians had fastened the cross-timbers, while they were cutting them they received much damage from the enemy. With all these difficulties, however, they gained the third palisade and all the rest up to the last one, though the Indians fought so obstinately that against their strong resistance the Spaniards gained the alley foot by foot, until they reached the clearing where the curaca was.

There the battle was hotly contested because the Indians, seeing their lord in danger of being killed or captured, fought like desperate men and thrust themselves among the swords and lances of the Spaniards in order to wound or kill them when they could not do so in any other way. On the other hand, the Christians, seeing so near the capture they desired to make, in order not to lose the result of their labor fought as hard as possible to prevent the cacique's escaping them. The struggle and combat between Indians and Spaniards continued for a long time, both showing their fortitude of spirit, though the Indians for lack of defensive weapons got the worst of it. The governor himself, desiring to have the cacique in his power and knowing him to be so near, fought like a very brave soldier, which he was, and like a good captain he encouraged his men, calling to them loudly by name. With this the Spaniards made a very great effort and fell upon the enemy with such ferocity and cruelty that they killed almost all of them.

Having done more than would have been thought possible for men not having defensive armor, these few Indians that remained, seeing that they could not now defend their cacique, laid down their arms and surrendered in order that the Spaniards might not kill him after killing them, and also because the curaca himself commanded them in a loud voice to do so. Falling on their knees before the governor, they all as one man begged him to spare their lord Capafi and to kill them instead. The general received the Indians mercifully and told them that he pardoned their lord and all of them for their past disobedience, and that in the future they would all be good friends.

The cacique arrived, carried in the arms of his Indians because he could not walk, and came to kiss the governor's hands; the latter received him very kindly, well satisfied to see him in his power. Capafi was a man with an extremely large body; so much so that because of being excessively fat and because of the indispositions and impediments that this always caused him, he was so helpless that he could not take a single step or stand on his feet. His Indians carried him on a litter, and wherever he wished to go in his house he went on all fours. This was the reason Capafi had not gone farther away from the Spaniards' camp than he did, believing that the place was sufficiently distant and strong enough and the road sufficiently rough to safeguard him from them, but his confidence was misplaced.

XI

THE CACIQUE OF APALACHE GOES BY THE GOVERNOR'S ORDER TO REDUCE HIS INDIANS

With the capture of the cacique, the general returned to the pueblo of Apalache very satisfied, for it seemed to him that with the imprisonment of the lord the impudences and boldnesses of the vassals would cease. These latter, after the Castilians had entered that pueblo, had not ceased day or night to make continuous attacks and sudden sallies and alarms, being so astute and diligent in their stratagems that they at once assaulted or wounded any Spaniard who strayed even a little distance from the camp. The general thought that all this would be ended by having the curaca in his power, but his hopes turned out to be in vain because the Indians, after the loss of their cacique, were more free and bold and molested the Christians more continuously, since as they had no lord in whose protection and service to occupy themselves, all turned more obstinately than before to molesting and injuring the Castilians. Angered by this, the adelantado talked one day with Capafi and told him of his displeasure at the great insolence and ingratitude his vassals showed at the good treatment he had accorded to their curaca and to them, in not having done the harm and damage that he might have done to their persons and property in punishment of their rebelliousness. On the contrary, he had treated them like friends, and unless it was provoked by themselves, they [the Spaniards] had not killed or wounded a single Indian nor moved to damage their pueblos or fields, when they were able to desolate and burn their whole province as lands and houses of enemies as perverse as they were. [He desired the cacique] to order them to cease their treasonable and shameless actions if he did not wish him to make war on them with fire and blood; he was to observe that he was in the power of the Spaniards, who were honoring and treating him with much respect and ceremony, and it could happen that the disrespect and excessive arrogance of his vassals would cause his death and the total destruction of his country.

The curaca replied with much humility and signs of great regret, saying that he was extremely grieved that his vassals did not comply with the obligation that the mercy his lordship had shown them had placed upon them, nor were serving as he himself desired and had attempted to [have them do] after he was in his [De Soto's] power, through the messengers that he had sent them, ordering them to cease angering and giving offense to the Castilians. But his messages had no effect because the Indians were unwilling to believe that they were from their cacique, but [thought they were] from strangers; nor could they bring themselves to believe in the clemency and respect his lordship had shown toward him, or that he was free. On the other hand they suspected that he had been very ill treated, kept in irons and in prison, and this was the reason they were now more persistent and obstinate in their stratagems than before. He therefore begged his lordship to order his captains and men that, taking him under strong guard, they go with him to a place five or six leagues from the camp to which he would guide them; there in a large forest were concealed the noblest and most important of his vassals. There, by day or night, he would shout to them in a loud voice, calling them by their names, and on hearing the voice of their lord they would all come at his summons. He having undeceived them of their evil suspicions, they would be appeased and would do what he ordered them, as the event would prove; and this was the most certain and quickest way to reduce the Indians to his service, because of the respect and veneration they naturally have for their curacas. Nothing would be gained by means of messengers nor could he negotiate through them, because they would reply that the messages were false and counterfeit, sent by the enemies themselves and not by their cacique.

With these words and a very chastened countenance, Capafi persuaded Hernando de Soto to send him where he asked, and thus it was ordered and carried out. Two companies went with him, one of cavalry and the other of infantry, and they went with strict orders to guard and watch the curaca closely lest he escape them. So cautioned, they left the camp before dawn, traveled six leagues toward the south, and arrived about nightfall at the place where the cacique said his people were in some woods nearby.

As soon as Capafi reached the appointed site, three or four of the Indians who had gone with him entered the woods, and in a short time ten or twelve others of those who had been in the woods came out. The curaca ordered them to notify that night all the principal Indians who were in the woods to assemble and appear before him on the following day; that he wished to tell them personally of things that were very important to the honor, safety and welfare of all of them. The Indians returned to the woods with this message, and the Castilians, having posted their sentries and a strong guard around the person of the cacique, rested that night well satisfied with what was arranged, it appearing to them that their business was so progressing that they would be able to return from their journey with honor and glory. They did not consider that the greatest hopes that men promise themselves often turn out most vain, as happened to these Spaniards.

XII

THE CACIQUE OF APALACHE, BEING CRIPPLED, ESCAPES FROM THE SPANIARDS ON ALL FOURS

Our Castilians, captains and soldiers, had retired to rest with great satisfaction and common rejoicing, believing that on the next day they would return to their captain-general with the victory and triumph of bringing him all the principal Indians of that province, reduced to his friendship and service, with which they all expected to be left in peace and quiet. But they found that their imaginings had deceived them, for as soon as daylight came they saw themselves without the cacique and without a single one of the few Indians who had come with him. Amazed by this, they asked one another what had happened, and all of them replied that it was impossible unless the Indians had conjured up demons who had carried them away through the air, because the sentries affirmed that there had not been any carelessness whatsoever through which the cacique might have made his escape.

But the truth of the matter was that the Castilians, both on account of their weariness from the long journey of the previous day and because of the confidence they felt in the friendliness and fair words of Capafi and the impediment and helplessness of his person, were careless and slept, the sentries as well as the rest. Seeing their sleep and the good opportunity, the curaca dared to escape from them, and did so by passing on all fours through the sentries. His Indians—who were not sleeping but were plotting to waylay the Spaniards—encountering him, had raised him on their shoulders, and it was a mercy God granted to the Christians that the heathen did not come back to cut their throats, because their own savagery and our men's drowsiness would have permitted them to do so entirely at their pleasure. But they contented themselves at seeing their lord out of the power of the Castilians, and so that he would not again fall into their hands they endeavored to put him in a more secure place than he had been formerly, and thus they took him where he was never seen again, then or later.

The two captains, whose names we omit to protect their reputation, and their good soldiers as well, made diligent search throughout these woods, hunting Capafi like a wild beast; but despite their efforts all through the day they found no trace of him, for the bird that escapes from the snare is seldom caught.

Having put the curaca in safety, the Indians came out to the Christians and uttered a thousand affronts and insults, ridiculing and mocking them, and without further provocation, since they did not want to fight with them, they left them to return to their camp. They arrived there much abashed and ashamed that an Indian, whom they had been so strictly charged to guard, had fled from them and escaped on all fours. They told the general and the other captains a thousand fabulous tales by way of excuse for their carelessness and to redeem their reputations, all affirming that they had heard very strange things that night, and that the thing was impossible unless he had been carried through the air by demons; they swore that in any other way it was not possible, in view of the strong guard that they had placed over him.

When he saw the poor precautions taken and that there was now no help for it, in order not to affront these captains and soldiers the governor pretended to believe what they said and helped them by stating that the Indians were such great sorcerers that they could do even more than that. He did not fail, however, to perceive their carelessness.

Returning to the thirty horsemen whom we left laboring to cross the swollen Río de Ocali, we said that those who were engaged in cutting logs in a short time had made the raft, because they had come prepared for such necessities with axes and ropes. They launched it on the water with two long ropes with which they drew it back and forth from one side of the river to the other, two good swimmers carrying one of the ropes to the opposite bank. The Spaniards had done all this when the Indians of Ocali approached the river with a great rush and clamor, with the desire and intention of killing the Christians.

The eleven horsemen who had gained the opposite bank of the river advanced to the encounter and engaged them with such determination and courage, spearing the first ones whom they met, that the Indians did not dare wait for them, because the land was free of both small and large timber and the horsemen were masters of the field. They therefore withdrew, retiring slowly and contenting themselves with shooting many arrows at them from a distance.

The four horsemen who were on this side of the river, where there were fewer enemies, divided in pairs, two going upstream and two down, for there were Indians coming from both directions, detaining them with their assaults so that they would not come to the place where the raft was. It made five voyages while the riders defended it on either side of the stream. On the first it carried the cloaks of the eleven horsemen who were on the other side of the river, who shouted to ask for them because a north wind had come up, striking them while they were damp and had no other clothing except their shirts with coats of mail over them, and they were chilled with the cold.

In four other voyages they took over the saddles, bridles, and knapsacks, and the men who did not know how to swim, who were few in number. Those who could, swam across in order not to lose time by making more voyages with the raft than were absolutely necessary. As they crossed they went out on the plain to assist those who were making a stand against the enemy there, whose numbers increased hourly. Finally, only two Spaniards remained to unload the raft and receive what was brought in it.

For the last voyage there remained on this side of the river only two men, one being Hernando Athanasio and the other Gonzalo Silvestre. The latter, while his companion drove his horse into the water and boarded the raft, went out to detain the enemy, and having driven them back with a good charge on horseback, he returned at full speed to get aboard the raft where his companion was awaiting him. Without removing the saddle or bridle from the horse, he drove him into the water and got on the raft, having unfastened the rope by which it was tied to the shore.

For all the speed with which the Indians came to discharge arrows at the Castilians, the latter were already in midstream, out of danger, because of the great diligence with which their companions on the other side had applied themselves to pulling the raft across. As the horses plunged into the water they crossed very willingly without anyone driving or guiding them, for they seemed to sense the harm that the enemy wished to do them, and, as if they were rational beings, they promptly obeyed what they told them to do, not refusing to enter and come out at the places their masters wished. For the Spaniards this was no small relief, and they even took an example from them for setting to work more promptly, seeing that the beasts did not refuse to do so.

XIII

THE EVENTS OF THE JOURNEY OF THE THIRTY HORSEMEN UNTIL THEY REACHED THE GREAT SWAMP

With the difficulties and hardships we have told, and many more that have been omitted because it is impossible to recount all of those that are experienced on such expeditions, the thirty brave and courageous horsemen crossed the Río de Ocali, God, our Lord, having favored them so mercifully that none of them or none of their horses were wounded. It was two o'clock in the afternoon when they finished crossing the river. They went to the pueblo because it was necessary to stop there, because Juan López Cacho, as a result of his struggle in the water and with the intense cold that came, had frozen and remained like a wooden statue, unable to move hand or foot.

Seeing the Spaniards coming to their pueblo, the Indians stationed themselves to oppose their passage in order to detain them while their women and children fled to the woods, and not to hinder their entrance and the stay they might wish to make in the pueblo. When they thought that their people would have reached safety they withdrew and abandoned the place. The Castilians entered it and camped in the middle of the plaza, not daring to go into the houses because the enemy, finding them divided, might surround them and take them while they were inside.

They built four large fires in the form of a square and put Juan López in the heat between them, well wrapped in all his companions' cloaks; one of them gave him a clean shirt that he was bringing for himself. It seemed to them a miracle that at such a time there should be found among them any shirts other than the ones they were wearing. It was the best present that could have been given him.

They remained in the pueblo all the rest of that day with great anxiety and fear about Juan López, wondering whether he would be able to travel that night or whether he would detain them so long that the Indians would send word to one another and join together to stop them and cut off the road. But whatever might happen, they determined to place the welfare of their companion above all the evils and dangers that could befall them. With this determination they gave the horses plenty of maize as preparation for their watch, fifteen of them eating while the others made the rounds; they dried the saddles and clothing that were wet, filled their saddlebags with food they found in the pueblo; and although there was an abundance of raisins, dried plums, and other fruits and vegetables, they did not attempt to carry anything except Indian corn because the first care that these Spaniards took was to see that they would not lack maize for the horses, and it also furnished subsistence for the riders.

When night came they stationed mounted sentries in pairs with orders to make the rounds on the outskirts of the pueblo, apart and at some distance from it, so that there would be time and opportunity to give warning if the enemy should come.

About midnight two of those who were thus making the rounds heard a murmuring as of people who were approaching. One of them went to warn their companions and the other remained to better identify and ascertain what it was. The night being clear, he saw a large and dark group of people who were coming toward the pueblo with a fierce and hoarse murmuring; looking again, he ascertained that it was an organized squadron of the enemy. He carried this news immediately to the other Spaniards, who, seeing Juan López somewhat improved, put him on his horse well wrapped up and tied him in the saddle, because he could not hold himself up. He was like the Cid Ruy Díaz when he went out of Valencia dead and won that famous battle.

One of his companions took the reins of his horse to guide him because Juan López was unable to do even this. In this manner, as secretly as possible, the thirty Spaniards left the pueblo of Ocali before the enemy reached it and marched at such a good pace that at daylight they found themselves six leagues from the pueblo.

They continued their journey always with this same swiftness, traveling with all speed through the inhabited country so that the news of their coming would not precede them; and they speared the Indians whom they encountered near the roads so that they might not give warning of them. Through the uninhabited country, where there were no Indians, they slowed their pace to allow the horses to rest and take breath in order to be ready to run where it might be necessary. Thus this day passed, which was the sixth of their journey, they having traveled and marched almost twenty leagues, part of them through the province of Acuera, a country inhabited by most warlike people.

On the seventh day after they had left the camp, one of the men, named Pedro de Atienza, became ill, and a few hours after he felt the illness, while they were on the march, he died on his horse. His companions buried him with much grief at such a death, for in order not to lose time on the road, they had not paid attention to the complaints that he made of his sudden illness. They made the grave with axes they carried for cutting firewood, which served even for this purpose. They passed on with regret that at such a time and from so small a number one should be missing.

At sunset they reached the crossing of the great swamp, having traveled and marched that day, as on the previous one, another twenty leagues. It is impossible for those who have not taken part in the conquest of the New World or in the civil wars of El Perú to believe that there are horses or men who can make such long daily journeys. But on the word of an hidalgo we affirm truthfully that in seven days these Castilians traveled the 107 leagues, more or less, of the route by which they went from the principal pueblo of Apalache to the great swamp. They found that it had become a sea of water with many branches that entered and flowed out of it, so rapid and swift that any one of them would be enough to impede their passage, much less all of them, and particularly the main stream. The reason the horses are able to withstand the excessive labor they have undergone and now undergo in the conquests in the New World, I believe—and I have the confirmation of all the Spaniards of the Indies whom I have heard speak about this matter—to be chiefly the good nourishment they have from the maize that they eat, because it has a great deal of substance and is much liked by them and by all animals. A proof of this is that the Indians of El Perú feed maize to the sheep [i.e., llamas] that serve them as beasts of burden, so that they can endure the excessive load that they ordinarily carry, which is equal to the weight of a man; the rest, although they carry burdens according to their ability, they sustain only by the pasturage that is found in the fields.

That night they slept, or rather they kept watch, on the borders of the swamp in the extreme cold that came with the rising north wind, which in all that region is most frigid. They built great fires and with their heat were able to endure the cold, though with the fear that the Indians would be attracted by the light of the fire; and if twenty of them should come, it would be enough to block their way and even to kill them all, because from their canoes in the water the Indians could attack the Spaniards entirely at their pleasure, and the latter could not make use of their horses to oppose the enemy, nor did they have harquebuses or crossbows with which to keep them at a distance. With this uneasiness and fear they kept watch and rested by thirds, preparing for the labors of the next day.

XIV

OF THE INSUPPORTABLE HARDSHIPS THE THIRTY HORSEMEN EXPERIENCED IN CROSSING THE GREAT SWAMP

Our Spaniards rested only a few hours when a sudden surprise occurred, though it was not caused by the enemy but by the excessive hardships they had suffered on the road. This was that about midnight, one of them, named Juan de Soto, who was a comrade of Pedro Atienza, whom we left behind in his grave, died almost as suddenly. One man in the party fled from them, running at full speed and shouting: "I swear that a pestilence has fallen upon us, because two Spaniards have died in such a short time and so suddenly." Gómez Arias, who was a sensible and prudent man, said to the one who was fleeing: "You are carrying enough pestilence in your flight, from which you cannot escape, however you may try. If you run from us, where do you think you will go? You are not on the sandy soil of Sevilla nor in its Ajarafe." Whereupon the fugitive came back and assisted in reciting the prayers that were said for the dead, but he did not dare attend the burial of the body, still insisting that he had died of the plague.

With such assistance in their hardships the night passed. When daylight came they made plans for crossing the swamp, which they saw had less water than on the previous day, no small relief in view of the labor that they expected to undergo. Eight Spaniards who did not know how to swim repaired the balustrade of the bridge across the deepest part of the swamp, which had been made of fallen trees, and carried over it the saddles of the horses and the clothing of all their companions. The other twenty Spaniards, naked as the day they were born, labored to get the horses into the water, but because the water was so cold the horses would not enter the deepest part where they had to swim. The Castilians fastened long ropes to the halters, and four or five of them would swim out to the middle of the current to pull the horses, and others would beat them with long rods to drive them in, but the horses planted their feet together and refused to move, and would allow themselves to be beaten almost to death rather than go into the water. Some of the horses thus driven and forced went in and swam for a little, but unable to endure the cold they fled back to land, dragging along the swimmers, who could not hold them; nor could those on the bank stop them, and though we said that they were on land, they were walking in water breast-deep.

Thus these twenty Spaniards continued to labor for more than three hours by the clock, and despite all their efforts they were unable to get a single horse to cross to the other side, though they changed them around, taking one and leaving the others, to see if any of them would go across.

At the end of three hours, as the result of many efforts two horses passed over, one belonging to Juan de Añasco and the other to Gonzalo Silvestre, and though these crossed, the others refused to do so because of their fear of the cold water. The masters who did not know how to swim saddled their horses and mounted them to be ready to do what they could if the enemy should appear.

Gómez Arias was the commander of the nineteen men who were swimming in the water, and it was he who labored hardest of all of them. These men, having been in the water for more than four hours enduring the cold the horses could not suffer, were numbed with the cold and their bodies were were so livid that they looked like Negroes. As they saw that all the efforts they were making and the hardships they were enduring (each one may imagine what they would be) were not gaining them anything in getting the horses to the other side, they were ready to give up their lives in despair. At this moment Juan de Añasco arrived, who as we said had his horse saddled, and he went through the part of the water that could be forded, up to the deep part of the channel. Vexed because no more horses had been taken across—not considering that this had not been due to lack of effort on the part of those who were working in the water, disregarding their sad condition, and urged on by a choler he possessed that occasioned a loss of the respect that should have been accorded this gentleman as commander—he said in a loud voice: "Gómez Arias, why don't you finish crossing those horses, confound you?" Seeing the state in which he and his companions were, who looked more like dead men than living, and already could not support the torment they felt, both of mind and body, and seeing that their captain rewarded so poorly the unendurable hardships that he and his companions were suffering—for certainly it would be impossible to exaggerate or tell fully what these twenty-eight companions passed through that day, especially those who were in the water; exasperated by the ingratitude Juan de Añasco showed for all his toil, Gómez Arias replied to him, saying: "Confound you and the evil bitch that gave birth to you! You are on your horse, fully dressed and wrapped in your coat, and you don't consider that we have been in the water for more than four hours, stiff with cold and doing all we can. Get down and come in, and we shall see if you can do better." To these words he added others no more polite, for wrath when it is ignited does not know when to stop.

Juan de Añasco made no answer because of what the others who came up to Gómez Arias told him, and also because he saw that he had been wrong in what he had said, and that his [Gómez Arias's] desperate condition had caused that outburst and its attendant disrespect for his person.

On many other occasions in this journey and in others that he made, the same thing happened, and because he did not consider first what he ought to say in such cases, he was often confused and his reputation suffered. Thus all men, and especially those who are appointed for commanders and superior officers in war, ought to note that at all times it is well for them to be gentle and affable toward their men, and that their orders to them in their work ought to be given rather by example than by words, and when they make use of the latter they should be good ones. It is difficult to say how much these gain and how much hard words lose, one being no more costly than the other.

XV

WHICH RECOUNTS THE JOURNEY OF THE THIRTY HORSEMEN UNTIL THEY ARRIVED WITHIN HALF A LEAGUE OF THE PUEBLO OF HIRRIHIGUA

As soon as the dispute was calmed the Spaniards went back to their work, and as it was now nearly noon, with the benefit of the sun's heat that tempered somewhat the coldness of the water, the horses began to cross over more easily than before, but not so rapidly as necessary, for it was more than three o'clock in the afternoon when they finished crossing.

It was a great shame and a pity to see how the Spaniards came out of the water, fatigued and exhausted by the long labor they performed, consumed by the cold they had suffered almost all day, and so broken and weary that they could scarcely stand. And with all this it is to be remembered that they had practically no comforts for restoring themselves in such an unfortunate situation; but they considered the time well spent in having crossed that bad swamp they so feared. They gave thanks to God that the enemy had not come up to oppose their passage; which was a particular Divine mercy, because if to the hardships we have said they endured there had been added the necessity of fighting and defending themselves from even fifty Indians, what would have happened to them? The reason the Indians did not come might have been because that swamp was some distance from the inhabited country and it was now winter, when, because they wore no clothing, the Indians were accustomed to leave their houses very little.

The Spaniards decided to spend the night on a large plain that was beyond the swamp, because they and their horses left it in such condition that they were unable to travel a step. They kindled great fires to warm themselves, consoled by the fact that from there on as far as Hirrihigua, where they were going, there were no bad crossings to pass over.

When night came they slept with the same precautions as formerly, and before dawn they were on their way. They speared five Indians whom they met so that they might not carry news of their coming ahead of them. The horses of the men who died traveled loose, saddled and bridled, following the others; often they went ahead, for they did not need their masters to guide them. That day they marched thirteen leagues. They halted on a fine plain where they slept that night in the usual way. At daylight they were traveling, and a little after sunrise they passed by the pueblo of Urribarracuxi, leaving it to one side, for they did not wish to enter it, in order not to have any quarrel with its inhabitants. On this day, which was the tenth of their journey, they marched fifteen leagues and stopped for the night three leagues before reaching the pueblo of Mucoço.

A little after midnight they left their beds, and having marched two leagues, they saw a fire in some woods near the road. The mestizo Pedro Morón had given warning of it more than a league back, saying, "Watch out, I can tell that there is a fire not far from where we are going." A league farther on he said again, "We are now very near the fire," and after they had gone a little distance they discovered it.

Wondering at such a strange thing, his companions went up to the fire and found many Indians with their wives and children, who were roasting skates for their breakfast. The Spaniards decided to capture as many as they could, although they might be vassals of Mucoço, until learning whether he had maintained peace with Pedro Calderón; because if he had not done so, they would try to send those that they took to La Havana, in order that they might be included among the other proofs and trophies of their victories. With this intention they advanced upon the fire. The young men among the Indians, terrified by the noise and trampling of the horses, fled into the woods beyond. Of the women and children they seized about eighteen or twenty persons whom they were able to stop, many others escaping because of the darkness of the night and the undergrowth in the woods. The prisoners clamored and wept in loud voices, calling the name of Ortiz and saying no other word except that, repeated many times, as if they were trying to recall to the Spaniards' memory the kindness their cacique and they themselves had done him. It did nothing toward freeing them from their captivity and restraint, for very few people remember to acknowledge favors already received. The Spaniards, still on horseback, breakfasted on the skates just as they were, and though the commotion of the Indians and the horses had filled them with sand they did not bother to get it off, for they said that it was like sugar and cinnamon to them because of their ravenous hunger.

They took an oblique route far from the pueblo of Mucoço, and having marched five leagues that morning, Juan López Cacho's horse gave out. We have forgotten him since they brought him out of the pueblo of Ocali bound [on his horse]; well, with the great excitement that they had that night from the coming of the enemy, and because of the vigor of his robust age, which was a little more than twenty years, he regained consciousness, became warm, and recovered from the illness that had overcome him because of that day's excessive cold and hardship, and all along the way thereafter he worked as well as any of his companions. As a result of laboring so hard to cross the Río de Ocali, his horse gave out so close to the pueblo where they were going to stop that they had only six more leagues to march. In spite of all their efforts it was impossible to get him to go farther, so they left him in a fine meadow with plenty of grass for him to eat, taking off the bridle and saddle and putting it in a tree so that any Indian who wished to use him could take him with all his equipment. They feared, however, and were grieved to think that as soon as they found him they would shoot him with arrows. Thus regretful, they marched nearly five leagues, until in the expectation of another, greater trouble they forgot that one. This was that as they came within a little more than a league of the pueblo of Hirrihigua where Captain Pedro Calderón had remained with the forty cavalry and eighty infantry, they examined the ground as they went, hoping to see some sign of the horses, for since they were so near the pueblo and the country was clear of timber, it seemed to them that it would be strange if they had not been riding and passing back and forth up to that point or even beyond. Inasmuch as they were unable to find footprints or any other signs of horses, they were much grieved and saddened, fearing lest the Indians had killed them [the other Spaniards] or they had left the country in the brigantines and the caravel that remained there, for they said that, if they were still there, it was impossible that there should be no signs of horses so near the pueblo.

With this suspicion and in their confusion as to what they would do if one thing or the other occurred, they decided on their future actions. They found themselves isolated in such a manner that in order to leave the country and go by sea they had no vessel nor any means for building one, and to return to where the governor had remained [at first] seemed to them impossible, in view of what they had experienced in coming from there. From these fears and misgivings, all of them came unanimously to the same opinion and decision, and said that, if they did not find their companions in Hirrihigua, they would go into some secret place in the woods that were close by where they would find grass for the horses, and while the latter were resting, they would kill the extra one and prepare dried meat from it for the journey. Having allowed the horses to rest for three or four days, they would attempt to go back to where the governor was; if they [the Indians] killed them on the road, they would have met death like good soldiers, performing the duty that their captain-general had entrusted to them; and if they came out safely, they would have done what he commanded them to do. All the twenty-eight Spaniards agreed to this as their final decision of what they would do in the future if they did not find Pedro Calderón in Hirrihigua.

XVI

THE THIRTY HORSEMEN REACH THE PLACE WHERE CAPTAIN PEDRO CALDERÓN IS, AND HOW THEY WERE RECEIVED

Having made this heroic decision, they continued their march, and the farther they went the more they were confirmed in the suspicion and fear that they felt, because they found no sign whatsoever of horses or any other indication by which they could ascertain that Spaniards had passed that way.

Thus they marched until they came to a small lake that was less than half a league from the pueblo of Hirrihigua, where they found fresh tracks of horses and signs that lye had been made and clothes washed there.

The Spaniards rejoiced greatly at these indications, and their horses, scenting the tracks of the others, were animated and took on new mettle in such manner that it seemed as if they were just going out of their stables after a twenty days' rest. With the satisfaction that can be imagined and with the new spirit of the horses, they traveled more rapidly. The horses went spurning the dust, with leaps and bounds their masters could not restrain; they were so good that, when it was thought they were too tired to stand, they could do this. They came in sight of the pueblo of Hirrihigua at sunset, having traveled that day, without hurrying, eleven leagues, and it was the shortest day's journey that they made on that whole trip. The mounted patrol was coming out from the pueblo two by two, with their lances and leather shields, to watch and guard their dwelling.

Juan de Añasco and his companions also formed in twos; and as if it were the opening of a tournament with reed spears, running their horses, with loud shouts and cries and much merriment and rejoicing, they came full speed toward the pueblo in such good order that when the first ones were coming to a stop the second were in the middle of the course and the third were leaving the post. Thus they all came in, making a fine show in the order they maintained; it was a glad and joyous festival, the end of a journey so laborious as we have seen.

At the shout given by the riders, Captain Pedro Calderón came out with all his men, and they were much pleased to see the fine entrance made by those who were arriving. They received them with many embraces and common rejoicing by all, and it was to be noted that in the first words spoken by those who were there—without having inquired after the welfare of the army or of the governor or of any particular friend—they asked almost with one voice, very anxious to know about it, whether there was much gold in that country. The hunger and craving for this metal often alienates and denies relatives and friends.

After passing through many more hardships and dangers than we have told, these twenty-eight horsemen ended their journey, though it did not see the end of their labors, for they were on the point of undertaking other, greater and more protracted toils, as we shall see below. They had spent eleven days on the road; one of these they spent in crossing the Río de Ocali, and the great swamp took another, so that in nine days they traveled 150 leagues or a little more, the distance from Apalache to the bay they call

Espirítu Santo and the pueblo of Hirrihigua. From the little that we have told of what they experienced on this brief journey, it may be understood and seen what the other Spaniards have passed through in conquering and winning the New World, so vast and forbidding in itself, without the ferocity of its inhabitants; and from the finger of the giant may be judged the magnitude of his body. In these days, however, those who have not seen this, as they enjoy with folded hands the fruits of the labors of those who won it, make sport of them, believing that the conquistadores gained it with the ease in which they now enjoy it.

As soon as he arrived at the pueblo of Hirrihigua, Captain Juan de Añasco asked Captain Pedro Calderón whether the Indians of that province and those of Mucoço had kept the peace and been friendly to him. Learning that they had, he ordered the immediate release of the Indian women and children whom he had brought as captives, and sent them to their own country with gifts, ordering them to tell their curaca Mucoço to come to see them [the Spaniards] and bring people to carry to their houses the ship's stores and many other things that the Spaniards intended to leave with them at their departure, and to say that he was turning over to him the horse that had been left in their country, tired out.

The women and children departed, very satisfied with such fine presents, and on the third day the good Mucoço came accompanied by his gentlemen and nobles. He brought the horse with him, and the Indians carried the saddle and bridle on their shoulders, not knowing how to put them on him. The cacique Mucoço embraced Captain Juan de Añasco and all those who came with him with much pleasure and affection, inquiring after the health of each one of them separately, and how they had left his lord the governor and the rest of the captains, gentlemen, and soldiers. After having informed himself about the army's health, he wished to know very particularly how they had fared on the road, going and coming; what battles, skirmishes, hunger, labor, and necessities they had experienced. At the end of his questions, the conversation having been very long and enjoyable, he said that it would give him great pleasure to be able to impose his own opinion and will upon all the curacas and lords of that great kingdom, so that they would all serve the governor and his Spaniards as they deserved and as he desired.

The accountant and captain Juan de Añasco, having noted how differently this curaca had received and spoken to them as compared with their own companions, who had asked about nothing but gold, thanked him in the name of all for the affection that he had for them, and on behalf of the general he praised him and all his people highly in acknowledgment of the peace and friendship they had maintained with Captain Pedro Calderón and his soldiers, and for the affection he had always shown for them. Besides these exchanges there were many other words of commendation and love on both sides, and the Spaniards wondered at those of the Indian, spoken so fittingly and aptly, for certainly he was endowed with all the good parts that a gentleman who had been brought up in the most polished court in the world could have. In addition to the corporal gifts of a well-formed body and handsome face, those of the spirit, such as virtue and discretion in deeds as well as in words, were such that our Spaniards had reason for marveling at him, seeing that he was born and bred in that wilderness. They were justified in loving him for his good understanding and many excellences, and thus it was a great pity that they did not invite him [to accept] the water of baptism, for in view of his good judgment few persuasions would have been needed to take him out of his heathenism and convert him to our Catholic faith, and it would have been an auspicious beginning for hoping that such seed would produce much grain and a bountiful harvest. But they are not to be blamed, because these Christians had decided to preach and administer the sacraments of our Law of Grace after having conquered and made an establishment in the land, and this delayed them, so that they would not administer them [the sacraments] immediately. This statement has been made here so that it may serve to exonerate and excuse these Castilians from having been guilty of the same carelessness in other similar instances we shall note below. Certainly they lost many very favorable opportunities for the gospel to be preached and received, and it is not surprising that they did so.

XVII

OF THE THINGS THAT CAPTAINS JUAN DE AÑASCO AND PEDRO CALDERÓN ARRANGED, IN ACCORDANCE WITH WHAT THE GENERAL HAD ORDERED THEM

The curaca Mucoço amused himself with Juan de Añasco and the other Spaniards for four days, during which, and in the rest of the time that our men were in the pueblo of Hirrihigua, his Indians, going and coming like ants, did not cease to carry to his country everything that the Spaniards had to leave in that pueblo because they were unable to take it with them. There were large quantities of these things, because of cassava alone, which is the bread of that island of Santo Domingo, of Cuba, and the surrounding ones, they had left more than five hundred quintels, besides large numbers of cloaks, coats, doublets, breeches, stockings, and footwear of all kinds—shoes, half boots, and sandals. Among the arms were many cuirasses, shields, pikes, lances, and steel helmets, of all of which the governor had brought a great abundance, as he was rich. There were also other things needed for the ships, such as sails, rigging, pitch, tow, tallow, ropes, baskets, crates, anchors, and cables; also much iron and steel. Although the governor had taken with him as many of these things as he could carry, a large quantity remained, and since Mucoço was a friend, the Spaniards were glad for them to take them, and his Indians did so and thereby became rich and very pleased.

Juan de Añasco had orders from the governor to go in the two brigantines that had remained at the Bay of Espíritu Santo, and coast along the shore to the west as far as the Bay of Aute, which Juan de Añasco himself had discovered with so much trouble, as we saw, and had left signs there so that it could be recognized when they should come along that coast by sea. In order to fulfill his commission he visited the brigantines that were near the pueblo, repaired them, provisioned them with food, and made the people ready who were to go with him; in doing this he spent seven days. He notified Captain Pedro Calderón of the order the governor sent him to set out on his march by land. Having taken leave of his other companions, he set sail for the Bay of Aute, where we shall leave him for the present.

That good gentleman, Gómez Arias, also had orders from the governor to go to La Havana in the caravel to visit Doña Isabel de Bobadilla and the city of La Havana and all the island of Santiago de Cuba, and to give them an account of everything that had happened to them up to that time and of the advantages and good qualities that they had seen and noted in La Florida. In addition he had to attend to other matters of importance of which no account is given because they do not belong to our *History*. Gómez Arias therefore sent to order the caravel to be careened and provided with men and supplies, and he set sail and in a few days reached La Havana safely. There he was well received by Doña Isabel and all the people of the island of Cuba, who celebrated with much festivity and rejoicing the news of the successful progress of the discovery and conquest of La Florida and the good health of the governor, whom all of them, individually and collectively, loved and wished all success, as if he were the father of each of them and had deserved it of them all.

Above in the First Book we mentioned that the Indians of this province of

Hirrihigua on two different occasions had captured two Spaniards, which was more the fault of the captured Spaniards themselves than from the desire of the Indians to harm them. Because these were things that happened during the time that Captain Pedro Calderón was in this province after the governor left it, though they are of little importance, and also because nothing else of more moment occurred, it will be well to recount them here. It is to be noted, then, that the Indians of that province had constructed on the Bay of Espíritu Santo large enclosures of rough stone in order to obtain skates and many other fish that came into them at high tide, and when it receded they were trapped there almost on dry land. The Indians killed a great many fish in this manner, and the Castilians who were with Captain Pedro Calderón also enjoyed them. It happened that one day two of these Spaniards, one named Pedro López and the other Antón Galván, natives of Valverde, decided to go and fish without the captain's order. They went in a small canoe and took with them a boy from Badajoz fourteen or fifteen years old, named Diego Muñoz, one of the captain's pages.

While the two Spaniards were fishing in one of the large enclosures twenty Indians came up in two canoes, besides many others who stayed on shore. They entered the enclosure with friendly words to the Spaniards, speaking half in Spanish and half in the Indian tongue, and said to them: "Friends, friends, we will all enjoy the fishing." Pedro López, who was an arrogant rustic, said: "Get out, you dogs; we don't want to be friends with dogs." So saying, he drew his sword and wounded an Indian who had approached him. The rest of them, seeing the Spaniards' injustice, surrounded them on all sides, and with arrows and blows from their bows and the canoe paddles they killed Pedro López, who had caused the dispute, and they left Galván for dead with his head opened up and his whole face battered from blows. They took Diego Muñoz prisoner, not harming him otherwise because he was so young.

The Castilians who were in the camp, on hearing the outcries, hastened in canoes to help their men, but they arrived too late, because they found the two companions dead and the other a captive in the hands of the Indians. They buried Pedro López and, seeing that Antón Galván was still breathing, they gave him treatment so that he was restored to this life, but his wounds were more than thirty days to heal, and for many months (although his body was cured) he remained like an idiot, his brain stupefied by the blows that they had given him. And he, [who] when in good health was not the most discreet of his countrymen, when he was telling what had happened that day always said, among other rustic words: "When the Indians killed me and my companion Pedro López, we did thus and so." His comrades, making sport of him, said: "They didn't kill you, but Pedro López; why do you say that they killed you when you are alive?" Antón Galván replied: "They killed me too, and if I am alive God restored me to life." To hear his rustic and clownish words they made him tell the story many times; and persisting in his polished language and always telling it in the same way, Galván entertained and amused his companions.

On another similar occasion the Indians of the province of Hirrihigua captured another Spaniard, named Hernando Vintimilla, an experienced sailor. He went out inadvertently one evening gathering shellfish and catching shrimp along the shore of the lower bay, at ebb tide, and thus carelessly he went on until he was out of sight behind some woods that were between the bay and the pueblo, in which some Indians were hidden. Seeing him alone, they came out to him and spoke in a friendly manner, asking that he divide his catch with them. Vintimilla replied haughtily, attempting to intimidate the Indians with words so that they would see that he was not afraid of them and would not dare do him any harm. The Indians, angry and offended that a single Spaniard should speak so arrogantly to ten or twelve of them, surrounded him and took him prisoner but did not do him any harm.

The Indians of this province kept these two Spaniards with them for ten years and allowed them to go about freely, as if they were one of themselves, until the year 1549, when there made port in this Bay of Espíritu Santo during a storm the ship of Father Fray Luis Cáncer de Balbestro, Dominican, who went to preach to the Indians of La Florida. The Indians had killed him and two of his companions, and those who remained on the ship took refuge on the open sea. As they were fleeing, they encountered a storm and were forced to enter that bay to save themselves from the fury of the sea. When the storm was over the Indians of Hirrihigua came out in many canoes to fight the ship, which, as it did not carry any fighting men, again went out to sea. The Indians still persisted in following it, and the two Spaniards, Diego Muñoz and Vintimilla, went with them by themselves in a discarded canoe, with the intention of escaping from the Indians and going to the ship if it would wait for them. As all of them were thus pursuing the ship a north wind came up. Fearing that the wind would increase in fury, as it is accustomed to do in that region, and blow them out to sea where they would be in great danger, the Indians thought it best to return to land. The two Spaniards very astutely stayed where they were, letting it be understood that the two of them alone could not row against the wind, and when they saw that the Indians were somewhat apart from them they turned the prow of their canoe toward the ship and rowed as hard as they could, as men who desired liberty, for which they put themselves in danger of losing their lives there, and shouted loudly to the others to wait for them. Seeing a single canoe coming toward them, those on the ship understood at once that they were people who needed them, and they lowered the sails and waited for the canoe. When it came up they received those two Spaniards in exchange for and in the place of those whom they had lost. In this manner Diego Muñoz and Vintimilla returned to the hands of Christians at the end of ten years they had spent in the power of the Indians of the province of Hirrihigua and the Bay of Espíritu Santo.

XVIII

PEDRO CALDERÓN LEAVES WITH HIS MEN, AND THE EVENTS OF HIS MARCH UNTIL REACHING THE GREAT SWAMP

As soon as Juan de Añasco and Gómez Arias set sail, one for the Bay of Aute and the other for the island of La Havana, Captain Pedro Calderón prepared the men who remained with him, who were seventy lancers and fifty infantry, because Juan de Añasco and Gómez Arias took the other thirty Spaniards in the brigantines and the caravel in order not to go with only the mariners. He set out from the pueblo of Hirrihigua, leaving the growing gardens the Castilians had planted for their use with much lettuce and with radishes and other garden stuff, having brought the seeds with them in case they should make a settlement.

On the second day of their march they reached the pueblo of the good Mucoço, who came out to receive them and that night offered them very good entertainment. On the next day he accompanied them to the borders of his territory and took leave of them with much affection and regret, saying: "Gentlemen, I now entirely lose the hope of ever seeing again my lord the governor, or any of his people; for hitherto, with having you in that presidio, I hoped to see his lordship, and I rejoiced, thinking to serve him as I have always desired, but now I shall mourn his absence all my life, without consolation. Therefore I pray that you give him this message and say that I beg him to receive it as it is sent." With these words and with many tears by which he showed his love for the Spaniards, he took leave of them and returned to his house.

Captain Pedro Calderón and his 120 companions made their daily marches until they came to the great swamp, without anything noteworthy happening to them, except that one night before they reached the swamp, when the Castilians had camped on a plain near some woods, many Indians came out to make sudden attacks and sallies against them at all hours, until they came into the camp itself and fought hand to hand. When the Spaniards pressed them they ran back to the woods, and then came out again to molest them. In one of those engagements one of the riders assailed an Indian who showed himself to be more daring than the others. He ran from the rider, but when he felt that he was overtaking him, he turned to receive him with an arrow in his bow, and he shot it at such short range that at the same moment the Indian loosed the arrow the Spaniard gave him a lance thrust from which he fell dead. But he did not avenge his death badly, because the arrow he shot entered the horse's breast, and though he was so close, the shot was so true that the horse fell dead at his feet, with all four legs outspread and without making another step or movement. Thus the Indian and the horse and its master all three fell at once, one on top of the other. This horse was the famous one belonging to Gonzalo Silvestre, and all his excellence was not enough to make the Indian respect him.

The Spaniards, wondering how an animal so spirited, fierce and brave as a horse could have died so suddenly from the wound of only one arrow, shot at such close range, as soon as it was light desired to see what kind of shot had been made. They opened the horse and found that the arrow had entered the breast and passed through the middle of the heart, stomach, and intestines, stopping finally in the latter; so bold, strong, and skillful in shooting arrows are the natives of this great kingdom of La Florida generally. But this is not to be wondered at if it is remembered that they exercise themselves continuously in this at all ages, for the boys of three years or less, as soon as they can walk alone, impelled by their natural inclination and by what they constantly see their fathers do, ask them for bows and arrows. If they are not given to them, they themselves make them from such small sticks as they can find, and proudly stalk the vermin in their houses. If they can catch sight of a mouse or lizard entering its hole, they will wait three, four, or six hours with an arrow in their bow, watching with the greatest attention that can be imagined for it to come out, in order to kill it, and they do not rest until they have accomplished their purpose. When they can find nothing else at which to shoot they go about killing the flies that are crawling on the walls and the floor. With such continual practice and the habit formed therein, they are thus skillful and cruel in discharging arrows, with which they make most wonderful shots, as we shall see and note in the course of this *History*. Because it fits in here it will be well to tell of an event that took place in Apalache, where the governor had remained, for when we come to that province we shall not lack things to tell about the bravery of its natives. Thus it was that in one of the first skirmishes the Spaniards had with the Indians of Apalache the maese de campo Luis de Moscoso received an arrow wound in the right side, which passed through a buckskin jacket and a coat of mail that he wore beneath it, which because it was so highly burnished had cost 150 ducats in Spain. The rich men had brought many of these, because they were so highly regarded. The arrow also passed through a quilted doublet and wounded him in such a manner that, entering obliquely, it did not kill him. Amazed at such an unusual shot, the Spaniards wished to see just what their highly burnished coats of mail, upon which they had depended so much, could withstand. On arriving at the pueblo, they set up in the plaza one of the baskets the Indians make of reeds, resembling vintage-baskets, and having chosen the best coat of mail that they had, they put it over the basket, which was very firmly woven. Taking off the chains of one of the Apalache Indians, they gave him a bow and arrow and ordered him to shoot at the coat of mail, which was fifty paces away.

The Indian, having shaken his arms with his fists closed in order to call up his strength, shot the arrow, which passed through the coat of mail and the basket so clean and with such force that if a man had been on the other side it would have passed through him also. Seeing the little or no protection that one coat of mail gave against an arrow, the Spaniards wished to see what two would do. Thus they ordered another, very fine one to be put on over the one on the basket, and giving the Indian another arrow, they told him to shoot it as he had the first one, to see if he were man enough to shoot through both of them.

The Indian, again shaking his arms as if he were gathering new strength, for the defense against him was now doubled, discharged the arrow. He struck the coats of mail and the basket through the center, and the arrow passed through the four thicknesses of steel and lodged there, halfway through. When the Indian saw that it had not come out clean on the other side, he showed great annoyance and said to the Spaniards: "Let me shoot another, and if it does not pass clear through both sides as the first one did, hang me here and now. The second arrow did not leave the bow as I wished it to and therefore did not pass through the coats of mail like the first one."

The Spaniards were unwilling to grant the Indian's request because they did not want their coats of mail further mistreated, and thenceforth they were undeceived with regard to the little defense that their much-esteemed coats of mail afforded against arrows. Thus the owners themselves made fun of them, calling them linen from Flanders, and in place of them they made loose quilted jackets, three or four finger-breadths in thickness, with long skirts that would cover the breasts and haunches of the horses. These jackets made from blankets would resist the arrows better than any other defensive armament; and the thick and unpolished coats of mail, which were not highly valued, with some other protection they put under them, were a better defense against arrows than the very elegant and highly burnished ones. Thus the cheaper ones came to be more valued and the expensive ones laid aside.

Other very notable shots that were made in the course of this discovery we shall mention below in the places where they occurred, and certainly they are amazing. But after all, considering that these Indians are born and bred in the midst of bows and arrows and brought up and nourished on what they kill with them, and are so expert in their use, there is no reason for our marveling at it so much.

XIX

PEDRO CALDERON CROSSES THE GREAT SWAMP AND REACHES THAT OF APALACHE

Taking up again the thread of our story we said that the Indians who came out of the woods to harass the Spaniards in their camp contented themselves with having killed Gonzalo Silvestre's horse and with having lost the Indian whom he killed, who must have been one of their principal men, for when they saw him killed they retired immediately and did not come back.

On the day after this occurrence the Castilians arrived at the crossing of the great swamp where they passed that night, and early on the following day they crossed it, with no opposition from the enemy and no trouble, except that which the swamp itself gave, which was quite enough. They continued their march through the whole province of Acuera, making each day's journey as long as possible. In order to save the infantry the labor of going [always] on foot, the cavalrymen dismounted and gave them the horses to ride from time to time. They did not take them up behind the saddles, in order not to fatigue the horses, saving them for time of need. With this diligence and care they marched until they came to the pueblo of Ocali, with no more opposition from the enemy than if they were going through an uninhabited country. The Indians abandoned the pueblo and went to the woods. The Spaniards took the food that they needed and arrived at the river. They crossed it in rafts that they made, without an Indian so much as shouting at them on either side.

Having crossed the Río de Ocali, they entered the pueblo of Ochile and traversed all the province of Vitachuco, and arrived at the pueblo where the proud Vitachuco and his people had died; the Castilians called it La Matanza. Passing the province of Vitachuco, they arrived at the Río de Osachile and crossed it in rafts, without an Indian appearing to say a word to them. From the river they went to the pueblo called Osachile, whose inhabitants abandoned it, as they had all the others that they [the Spaniards] had passed through.

The Spaniards, having taken supplies in Osachile, marched through the uninhabited country that lies before the swamp of Apalache. They reached the swamp after having marched almost 135 leagues in all the peace and quiet in the world. Except on the night when they [the Indians] killed Gonzalo Silvestre's horse, they gave them no trouble throughout this long road; we can find no reason to give for it, nor can one be found.

The Indians of the province of Apalache, being more bellicose than the former ones, were willing to supply the fault and negligence that the others showed in molesting and injuring the Spaniards, as we shall soon see. Our men having arrived at the dense forest that is on the edge of the swamp, they slept beyond it on an open plain, and when morning came they marched along the narrow road through the forest, which we said was half a league in length, entered the water, and came to the bridge with the small balustrade. They repaired three or four logs that they found fallen down, the infantry crossed over it, and those on horseback swam across the deepest part of the channel.

Captain Pedro Calderón, seeing that they had crossed the deepest and most dangerous part of the water, ordered, for the greater speed and safety of those who still had to cross, that ten horsemen, taking five crossbowmen and five rodeleros behind their saddles, go to occupy the narrow trail through the woods on the other bank. They proceeded to carry out these orders and went as quickly as possible through the water toward the opposite bank. At this moment many Indians emerged from various parts of the woods, where they had hitherto been in ambush behind the undergrowth and large trees. With a great shout and outcry they fell upon the ten horsemen who were carrying the infantrymen behind them, and shot many arrows at them. They killed the horse of Alvaro Fernández, a Portuguese from Yelves, and wounded five other horses that, as they assaulted them so suddenly, and as they were traveling so heavily laden and in water breast-deep, turned and fled, their masters being unable to hold them. The ten infantrymen who were riding behind were thrown off in water, almost all badly wounded, for when the horses turned around the Indians took them from behind, and could shoot arrows at them at their pleasure. Seeing them fallen in the water, the Indians rushed out fiercely to behead them, with a great shout to the other Indians to advise them of their victory so that they would come more swiftly and joyously to profit by it.

The sudden assault with which the Indians fell upon the Castilians, the foot soldiers falling into the water, the flight of the horses, and the many enemies who came up to combat them caused great confusion and alarm among them, and even fear of being routed and defeated, because the fighting was in the water where the swiftness of the horses could have no effect in succoring friends and attacking enemies.

On the other hand, the Indians, seeing how well their first assault had succeeded, took new spirit and courage, and came up with greater impetus to kill the infantry who had fallen into the water. The valiant Spaniards who were nearest came to their assistance, and the first to arrive were Antonio Carrillo, Pedro Morón, Francisco de Villalobos, and Diego de Oliva, who had crossed the bridge and stationed themselves in front of the Indians, preventing their going to kill the infantry. To the left of the Castilians there came up a large band of Indians who were gathering for the victory of which the first had shouted. More than twenty paces in front of all of them walked an Indian with a great plume on his head, with all the boldness and courage imaginable. He was coming to take a large tree that lay between the two forces, from which the Indians, if they gained it, could inflict much damage on the Spaniards and even keep them away from the crossing. As Gonzalo Silvestre, who was nearest the tree, saw this, he called loudly to Antón Galván, whom we mentioned above, and he, although he was wounded and was one of those who had fallen from the horses, had not lost his crossbow (like a good soldier). Putting a dart in it, he went after Gonzalo Silvestre, who went holding half of a packsaddle cover that he found in the water as a shield, and he persuaded him [Galván] not to fire at anyone except the Indian who was coming in front, who seemed to be their captain-general. This was true, though he said it as a surmise only. In this manner they reached the tree, and the Indian who was coming ahead, when he saw that the Spaniards had gained it because they had been nearer, shot three arrows at them in the winking of an eye. Gonzalo Silvestre received them on the shield that he was carrying, which resisted them because it was wet.

Antón Galván, who had waited until the enemy should come nearer so as not to miss his shot, seeing him in a good position, fired with such sure aim that he struck him in the center of the breast, and as the poor unfortunate wore no defense except his own skin, the dart went in all the way. The Indian, turning completely around but not falling from the shot, shouted to his men, saying: "These traitors have killed me." The Indians rushed to him, raised him up in their arms with a great murmuring and, passing him from one to another, carried him back by the same road that they had come.

XX

PEDRO CALDERON PROCEEDS ON HIS WAY. THE CONTINUOUS FIGHTING OF THE ENEMY WITH HIM

The fighting in other places was no less cruel and bloody, because to the right of the battle a large band of Indians came up against the Christians with much impetus and fury. A brave soldier from Almendralejo, named Andrés de Meneses, went out to oppose them, and with him went ten or twelve other Spaniards. The Indians charged on them so fiercely and bravely that they knocked Andrés de Meneses into the water with four arrow wounds that they gave him in the region of the genitals and thighs, for, as they saw that most of his body was covered by an oblong shield he carried, they shot at the unprotected part. They also wounded five of those who were with him.

The fight between Indians and Spaniards went on with this fury and cruelty wherever they could lay hands on one another. The Indians redoubled their efforts and courage to finish their conquest, as men who considered the victory theirs and were made arrogant by the good strokes that they had delivered. The Spaniards with their stout spirit urged themselves on to save their lives, as now they fought with no other purpose, and were getting the worst of the battle because their defense now consisted only of the fifty foot soldiers; for since the fighting was in the water, those who were on horseback were of no use to their own side nor of any damage to the enemy.

At this point the unhappy news spread among all the Indians that their captain-general was mortally wounded, whereupon they mitigated somewhat the fire and wrath with which they had fought hitherto. They began to retreat a little at a time, but always shooting arrows at their adversaries. The Castilians rallied and followed the Indians in the best order they could until they pushed them entirely out of the water and the swamp and put them on the trail through the dense woods that were on the opposite side of the swamp. They gained the site that we said the Spaniards had cleared for their camp when the governor passed there with his army.

The Indians had fortified that site and had their own camp there; they abandoned it to go to their captain-general. The Spaniards stayed there that night because it was a strong enclosed place where the enemy could not harm them unless it were by way of the trail; and since they guarded it, they were safe. They treated the wounded as well as they could, nearly all of them being wounded, and badly. They passed the night watching, the shouts and alarms of the Indians not allowing them to rest.

With the good shot that Antón Galván succeeded in making that day Our Lord succored these Spaniards; and certainly, if it had not been made, and on the person of the captain-general, it was to be feared that the Indians would have made great destruction among them or would have beheaded them all, since they were powerful, victorious, and very numerous, and the Spaniards few and most of them mounted. Inasmuch as the fight was in the water, the mounted men were not masters of themselves or of their horses in order to attack the enemy or defend themselves from him; therefore, the infantry fighting alone, they were all on the point of being lost. Thus many times in discussing afterward in the governor's presence the perils of that day, they always gave Antón Galván the honor of being the means of saving them from defeat and death.

As soon as it was light the Spaniards marched along the narrow road through the dense woods, driving the enemy before them until they emerged into another, more clear and open forest two leagues in extent. Here on either side of the road the heathen had built large palisades, or they were the same ones that they had made when Governor Hernando de Soto passed on this road, and had remained in place until this time. The enemy would come out from the palisades and shoot innumerable arrows, with the order and precaution of not attacking from both sides at the same time so as not to wound themselves with their own arms. In this manner they marched through the two leagues of forest where the Indians wounded more than twenty Castilians, and the latter could do no injury whatsoever to their enemies because they had enough to do in protecting themselves from the arrows.

Having passed through the woods, they came out on a level plain, where the Indians from fear of the horses did not dare attack the Spaniards or even wait for them. Thus they allowed them to march with less difficulty.

After marching five leagues, the Christians halted to make camp on that plain, because the wounded of that day and the previous one were fatigued with the continuous fighting they had undergone. As soon as it was dark the Indians came in large numbers and attacked at the same time from all sides, with much shouting and clamor. Those on horseback went out to oppose them, not keeping in regular order but each one going where he heard the Indians nearest to him. On seeing the horses, the Indians withdrew to a distance, always shooting arrows, with one of which they wounded badly a horse belonging to Luis de Moscoso. All through the night the heathen [did not] cease shouting at the Christians, saying to them: "Where are you going, luckless ones? Your captain and all his soldiers are already dead, and we have quartered them and hung them in the trees, and we shall do the same with you before you get there. What do you want? Why do you come to this land? Do you think that we who are in it are so despicable that you will make us abandon it and be your vassals and servants and slaves? Know that we are men, that we will kill all of you and the rest who are in Castilla." The Indians shouted these and other similar things, always discharging arrows, until daylight.

XXI

PEDRO CALDERÓN, WITH HIS PERSISTENT FIGHTING, ARRIVES WHERE THE GOVERNOR IS

With the day, our men continued their march and arrived at a stream that was deep and very difficult to cross, and the Indians had blocked it with strong palisades and ditches placed at intervals. Reconnoitering the crossing and what had been erected there, and with the experience of those who had passed it on the other occasion, the Spaniards ordered that those on horseback who were best armed dismount, and that thirty of them, taking shields, swords, and axes, go ahead to gain and break down the palisades and opposing defenses. Those more poorly armed were to mount the horses, as the latter were of no use at that pass, and go in the middle with the clothing and the serving-people. Twenty more of the well-armed men were to make up the rear guard so that, if the enemy should attack from behind, he would encounter a defense. In this order they entered the woods bordering the stream. Seeing the Castilians where they could not make use of their horses, which was what they most feared, the Indians charged with the greatest impetus, ferocity, and clamor to shoot arrows at them, attempting to kill all of them, as they were few and the crossing very difficult. The Christians, trying to defend themselves now that they could not attack because of the narrow place in which they were, reached the palisades, where the fighting was very bitter and obstinate, on the one side in order to force a passage and on the other to prevent it. They wounded one another cruelly. At last the Spaniards, some resisting the Indians with their swords and the others cutting with axes the ropes and fastenings made of reeds, which are like long vines and serve to fasten anything desired, gained the first palisade and the second, and all the rest. But it cost them many bad wounds, which most of them received, and in addition the Indians killed with an arrow wound in the breast a horse belonging to Alvaro Fernández, a Portuguese from Yelves, so that this fidalgo lost two good horses in this arroyo and in the swamp they had passed through. With these evils and injuries, the Spaniards passed over that bad crossing and marched with less trouble through the plains where there was no undergrowth, for wherever there was none the Indians withdrew from the Christians from fear of the horses. But wherever there were clumps of timber near the road there were always Indians in ambush who would come out suddenly to assault and shoot arrows at our men, shouting at them and repeating over and over these words: "Where are you going, thieves? We have already killed your captain and all his soldiers." They persisted so in this statement that the Castilians were almost ready to believe it because, being now so near the pueblo of Apalache that their shouts could be heard there, no one had come out to their assistance, nor had they seen men or horses or any other sign from which they could be sure that they were there. In this manner these 120 Spaniards marched, skirmishing and fighting all day with the Indians, and they arrived at Apalache at sunset. Although this day's journey had not been as long as the past ones, they had marched slowly because of the many wounded they had with them, ten or twelve of whom died afterward, among them Andrés de Meneses, who was a brave soldier.

Arrived in the presence of their captain-general, which they had so desired, and of their beloved companions, they were received with the gladness and rejoicing that may be imagined, as men who had been thought dead and passed from this life, according to what the Indians had told the governor and his men many times in order to grieve and depress them, saying that they had beheaded them on the road. And this story was very probable, because the governor had found himself in great danger and extremity, having more than eight hundred fighting men with him when he passed through those provinces and difficult passes, and it was very likely that those who were then on the way, numbering only 120, should have perished. Therefore they were received and welcomed generally and individually by their comrades as if they had come back from the dead, all giving thanks to God for having saved them from so many dangers.

The governor received his captain and soldiers like an affectionate father, very joyfully embracing and asking each one separately about his health and how he had fared on the way. He ordered the wounded to be treated and attended to carefully. Finally, he praised and thanked them with extravagant words for the hardships and dangers that both parties had passed through in going and returning, because when the occasion arose, this gentleman and good captain knew how to do this with much goodness, discretion, and prudence.

XXII

JUAN DE AÑASCO REACHES APALACHE, AND WHAT THE GOVERNOR PROVIDED FOR DISCOVERING A PORT ON THE COAST

It is to be noted that when Captain Pedro Calderón arrived at the pueblo of Apalache it had been six days since the accountant Juan de Añasco, who set out from the Bay of Espíritu Santo with the two brigantines for the Bay of Aute, had reached there, without anything noteworthy having happened to him at sea. He disembarked at Aute without opposition from the enemy because the governor, calculating more or less the time that he would spend on the voyage, two days before he reached the port sent a company of cavalry and another of infantry to safeguard the port and the road to the camp. They were relieved every four days, one group withdrawing from the bay when the others arrived. While they were in the port they put up flags on the highest trees so that they could be seen from the sea. Juan de Añasco saw them and went to the camp with the two companies, leaving the brigantines, which remained in the bay well guarded. Since these two captains, Juan de Añasco and Pedro Calderón, now found themselves together with the governor and the rest of the captains and soldiers, there was much satisfaction and rejoicing, for it seemed to them that in bearing their hardships together, however great these might be, they would become easy, because the company of friends is a comfort and relief in toil. In this mutual contentment the Spaniards passed the winter in the pueblo and province of Apalache, where some things occurred of which it will be well to give an account without observing the order in which they took place except to say that they happened in this camp.

A few days after the events just described, as the governor was never lazy but was contriving and planning in his own mind what seemed to him to be conducive to the discovery and conquest and later to the settlement of the country, he ordered a gentleman from Salamanca named Diego Maldonado (who was a captain of infantry and had served to the great satisfaction of the whole army in everything that had occurred up to that time) to turn his company over to another gentleman, named Juan de Guzmán, a native of Talabera de la Reyna and a great friend and comrade of his, and go to the Bay of Aute. Taking the two brigantines that the accountant Juan de Añasco had left there, he was to go along the coast toward the west for a distance of a hundred leagues and observe and reconnoiter with all care and diligence the ports, inlets, coves, bays, creeks, and rivers that he might find, and the shoals along the coast, and of all this he was to bring a satisfactory report. He [the governor] said that he thought it well to have all this information for future use, and he gave him two months' time to go and return.

Captain Diego Maldonado went to the Bay of Aute and from there he set sail on his mission, and having spent the two months in sailing along the coast, he came back at the end of them with a long report of what he had seen and discovered. Among other things he said that sixty leagues from the Bay of Aute he had discovered a very fine port called Achusi, sheltered from all winds and large enough for many ships, and with such a good depth up to the shore that it was possible to bring the ships up to land and disembark without building up breakwaters. He brought with him from this voyage two Indians who were natives of this same port and province of Achusi, one of them being a lord of vassals. He had seized them with a craftiness and cunning unworthy of a gentleman, for when he arrived at the port of Achusi the Indians received him peaceably, and with many kind expressions they invited him to come ashore and take whatever he needed as if he were in his own country. Diego Maldonado did not dare accept the invitation because he did not trust unknown friends. As the Indians sensed this, they began to traffic with the Spaniards freely to remove the fear and suspicion they might have of them. Thus they came to the brigantines in groups of three or four to visit Diego Maldonado and his companions, bringing them what they asked. The Indians being so friendly, the Spaniards now dared to sound and explore in their small boats all parts of the port, and as they had seen and purchased what they needed for continuing their voyage, they set sail and went away, taking the two Indians as prisoners; they happened to be the curaca and a relative of his. Confiding in the good friendship that heathen and faithful alike (though to them they were not so) had shown, and impelled by the story that the other Indians had told them of the brigantines and desiring to see what they had never seen before, they had dared to enter them and visit the captain and his soldiers. The latter, as they knew that one of them was the cacique, were glad to carry him off.

XXIII

THE GOVERNOR SENDS A REPORT OF HIS DISCOVERY TO LA HAVANA. THE STORY OF THE TEMERITY OF AN INDIAN

They were very pleased with the report that Captain Diego Maldonado brought of the whole coast and of the good port he had discovered in Achusi, because, according to the plans that the governor had made, it seemed to them that their conquest had begun and progressed auspiciously to accomplish the ends they desired for it, of settling and making an establishment in that kingdom; because the chief thing that the governor and his people wished for making a settlement was to discover a port such as had been found, where they might go to anchor the ships that would bring the people, horses, cattle, seeds, and other things necessary for new settlements. A few days after the arrival of Diego Maldonado, the governor ordered him to go to La Havana with the two brigantines of which he was in charge, and visit Doña Isabel de Bobadilla and tell her what they had done and seen up to that time, by sea and by land. He was to send the same report to all the other cities and villas of the island, and in the coming October (it was then the end of February of the year 1540) he was to return to the port of Achusi with the two brigantines and the caravel that Gómez Arias had taken, and with one or more other ships if he could find them to buy. He was to bring in them all the crossbows, harquebuses, lead, and powder available, and much footwear, such as shoes and sandals, and other things that the army needed. He gave him a written memorandum of these things with instructions of what he would have to do, because the governor expected to be in the port of Achusi at that time, after having made a large circle through the interior country and discovered the provinces that might lie in that region, in order to lay the foundations for a settlement. But it was well to settle at the port first, a step necessary for affairs at sea as well as on land. He also ordered him to tell Gómez Arias to come with him at the appointed time, for because of his great prudence in matters of government and his industry and long experience in those of war he wished to have him with him.

With this order and commission Captain Diego Maldonado left the Bay of Aute and went to La Havana, where because of the good news that he brought of the governor and of his army and of the successful progress made up to that time, and that which they expected to make in the future, he was very well received by Doña Isabel de Bobadilla and by all the city of La Havana. From there he at once sent the report to the other cities of the island, which celebrated the governor's success with great rejoicing. They made great preparations to send him at the appointed time the succor of men, horses, arms, and the other things needed for a settlement. The cities prepared all these things together, and the rich men in particular, each one endeavoring according to his ability to send or bring the most and the best that he could, to show the love that they had for their governor and captain-general and for the sake of the rewards that they expected. We shall leave them in the midst of these preparations and return to tell some incidents that were taking place in the province of Apalache, by which can be seen the ferocity of the Indians of that province, as well as their temerity, because certainly they showed by their actions that they knew how to dare and did not know fear, as will be seen in the following instance and in others that will be told, though not all of those that happened [will be mentioned], for in order to avoid prolixity, we shall omit most of them.

Thus it happened that one day in the month of January of the year 1540 the accountant Juan de Añasco and six other gentlemen were going along talking through the streets of Apalache, on horseback. Having traversed all of them, they were pleased to go out into the country surrounding the pueblo, without getting very far away from it, for the country was not safe because of the sudden attacks of the Indians who lay in ambush behind every shrub. Since they did not intend leaving the pueblo, it seemed to them that they could go without arms, at least defensive ones, and thus they went out wearing only their swords, except one of them named Estevan Pegado, a native of Yelves, who happened to be armed and wore a helmet on his head and carried a lance in his hand. Going along thus in conversation, they saw an Indian man and woman who were walking in a clearing in the woods near the pueblo gathering beans, which had been sown the year before. They must have been gathering them more to amuse themselves by seeing whether any Castilian would come out of the pueblo than for any need they might have for the beans, because as we have said the province was full of all kinds of foodstuff. When the Spaniards saw the Indians they went toward them to capture them. Seeing the horses, the woman stopped short, being unable to run. The husband took her up in his arms and ran with her to the woods that were close by, and having placed her in the first of the undergrowth, he gave her two or three pushes and told her to go into the inner part of the forest. Having done this, he could have gone with the woman and escaped, but he did not wish to do so. On the contrary he came back running to where he had left his bow and arrows, and recovering them, he went out to meet the Spaniards with as much determination and boldness as if they had been another lone Indian like himself. He made the attack in such a manner that he obliged the Spaniards to say to one another they would not kill him but would take him alive, for it seemed to them an unbecoming thing for seven mounted Spaniards to kill one lone Indian on foot, and they also thought that a spirit so gallant as the heathen showed did not justify their killing him, but on the contrary showing him all mercy and favor. All of them advancing with this determination, they reached the Indian, who, because the distance was short, had not yet been able to shoot an arrow, and rode him down and attempted to get him to surrender without allowing him to rise from the ground, first one and then another coming at him every time he tried to get up, and all shouting to him to surrender.

The more they pressed him the fiercer the Indian became, and fallen though he was, several times by putting the arrow in his bow and shooting it, and other times by pricking the bellies and thighs of the horses with it, he wounded all seven of them, although slightly, because he was not in a position to inflict more-serious wounds. Escaping from among the horses' feet, he stood up, took his bow in both hands, and gave Estevan Pegado, who was the one who had harassed him most with his lance, such a blow on the forehead with it that the blood flowed from above his eyebrows and covered his face, and he was half stunned. The Portuguese Spaniard, seeing himself so attacked and mistreated, was inflamed with anger and said: "In God's name, are we going to wait until this one Indian kills all seven of us?" So saying, he gave him a lance-thrust through the chest that came out on the other side and brought him down dead. Having performed this feat, they examined their horses and found them all wounded, though the wounds were slight. They returned to the camp, admiring the temerity and courage of the barbarian and shamed and abashed to tell that one Indian alone had withstood seven mounted men.

XXIV

TWO INDIANS OFFER TO GUIDE THE SPANIARDS WHERE THEY MAY FIND MUCH GOLD

Throughout the time that Governor Hernando de Soto was wintering in the camp and pueblo of Apalache, he always took care to inquire and learn what lands and provinces were beyond toward the west in the region that he had thought and planned to enter in the following summer, in order to see and discover that kingdom. With this desire he was always gathering information from the Indians who had been serving for some time as domestics in his army, and from those newly captured, importuning them to tell what they knew about that land or any part of it. Since the general and all his captains and soldiers were careful and diligent in doing this, it happened that, among the other Indians whom they took, those who were scouring the country captured a young Indian sixteen or seventeen years of age. Some of the Indians who were servants of the Spaniards and were attached to their masters knew him. They told them, so that they might tell the governor, that that youth had been a servant of some Indian merchants who were accustomed to enter with their merchandise, selling and buying, many leagues into the interior country, and that he had seen and knew what the governor was trying so hard to learn. It is not to be understood that the merchants went to seek gold or silver but to exchange some articles for others, which was the traffic of the Indians, because they did not make use of money. With this information they asked the youth what he knew. He replied that it was true that he knew about some provinces that he had visited with his masters, the merchants, and he would venture to guide the Spaniards twelve or thirteen days' journey, which was as much as he had seen. The governor turned the Indian over to a Spaniard, charging him to take particular care of him so that he would not escape from them, but the youth relieved them of this anxiety, for in a short time he became so friendly and familiar with the Spaniards that he appeared to have been born and bred among them.

A few days after the capture of this Indian they took another almost the same age, or a little older, and, as the first one knew him, he said to the governor: "Sir, this young man has seen the same lands and provinces as I, and others beyond, which he has traveled through with other, richer and more prosperous merchants than my masters."

The newly captured Indian confirmed what the first had said and very willingly offered to take and guide them through the provinces that he had traversed, which he said were many and large. Asked about the things that he had seen in them, and whether they had gold or silver or precious stones, which was what they most desired to know, and being shown gold jewelry and pieces of silver and fine stones set in rings that were found among some of the captains and principal soldiers, so that he might better understand the things that they were asking him about, he replied that in a province called Cofachiqui, which was the most distant one that he had visited, there was a great deal of metal like the yellow and the white, and that the chief traffic of the merchants, his masters, was to buy those metals and sell them in other provinces. He said that besides the metals they had a very large quantity of pearls, and to tell this he indicated a pearl in a setting he saw among the rings that they showed him. Our Spaniards were very pleased and rejoiced at this news, desiring to see themselves at once in Cofachiqui in order to be masters of so much gold and silver and so many precious pearls. But to return to the particular events that took place between the Indians and the Spaniards in Apalache: thus it was already at the beginning of March when it happened that twenty cavalry and fifty infantry left the camp and went one league from the chief pueblo to another in that jurisdiction to get maize, which abounded in all the little villages in that district, in such quantities that the Spaniards in all the time they were in Apalache never went a league and a half from the chief pueblo to provide themselves with Indian corn and the other grains and vegetables they ate. After they had gathered the maize that they were to carry, then, they concealed themselves in the pueblo itself, desiring to capture some Indians if they should come. They stationed a watchman on the highest part of a house that was very different from the others and seemed to be a temple. After some time had passed the watchman gave notice that there was an Indian in the plaza, which was very large, looking to see if there was anything there.

A gentleman named Diego de Soto, the governor's nephew, who was one of the best soldiers in the army and a very good horseman, rode out to capture the Indian, more to show his skill and courage than from any need he had for him. When he saw the rider the Indian ran with extreme swiftness to race with the horse to see whether he could escape by flight, for the natives of this great kingdom of La Florida are swift and famous runners, and pride themselves on it. But seeing that the horse was gaining on him, he got under a tree close by, which is a cover that foot soldiers, lacking pikes, are always accustomed to take as a protection against horses. Placing an arrow in his bow—for as we have already said, they always go armed with these weapons—he waited until the Spaniard should come within range. The latter, being unable to go under the tree, passed by on one side at a run and made a thrust at the enemy, the lance passing over the left arm, to see if he could reach him. Guarding himself from the blow of the lance, the Indian shot an arrow at the horse at the moment that he came abreast and struck him between the girth and the stirrup with such strength and skill that the horse stumbled on for fifteen or twenty paces and fell dead, not moving again. At this moment there came up at a canter another gentleman, named Diego Velázquez, the governor's groom, no less brave and skillful in horsemanship than the first one. He followed Diego de Soto to aid him if he should need it. Seeing, then, the shot that the Indian had made at his companion, he urged his horse and, not being able to go under the tree, he passed to one side, throwing another lance as Diego de Soto had done. The Indian did the same as in the first case, for as the horse came abreast he gave him an arrow wound behind the stirrup, and as before the horse stumbled along until he fell dead at his companion's feet. The two Spanish comrades rose hastily with their lances in their hands and assailed the Indian to avenge the death of their horses, but the latter, content with two good shots he had made in such a short time and with such good fortune, went running to the woods, ridiculing and jeering at them, and turning around to make wry faces and gestures. Keeping pace with them, not running as fast as he could, he said to them: "Let us all fight on foot and we shall see who are the better." With these words and others that he said in vituperation of the Castilians he got away safely, leaving them sorely grieved at such a loss as that of the horses, for since these Indians felt the advantage the Spaniards had over them on horseback, they endeavored and were more pleased to kill one horse than four Christians, and thus they carefully and diligently shot at the horse rather than at the rider.

XXV

CONCERNING SOME DANGEROUS FEATS OF ARMS THAT TOOK PLACE IN APALACHE, AND THE FERTILITY OF THAT PROVINCE

A few days after the misadventure of Diego de Soto and Diego Velázquez, another, no more fortunate [event] took place. This was that two Portuguese, one named Simón Rodríguez, from Villa de Maruán, and the other Roque de Yelves, a native of Yelves, went out beyond the pueblo on their horses to gather green fruit that grew in the woods near the pueblo. Having been able to gather that on the lower branches from their horses, they still wished to dismount and climb the trees to gather it from the higher branches, for it seemed to them that it was better. The Indians, who lost no opportunity that offered itself to them to kill or wound the Castilians, seeing the two Portuguese Spaniards up in the trees, advanced upon them. Roque de Yelves, who saw them before his companion did, gave the alarm and jumped down from the tree, running toward his horse. One of the Indians who was coming behind him shot at him with an arrow having a flint barb, and struck him between the shoulders, and a quarter of the arrow came out at his breast. He fell to the ground, unable to raise himself up. They did not allow Simón Rodríguez to come down from the tree but shot at him while he was in it as if he were some climbing wild beast. They brought him down dead, pierced from one side to the other with three arrows, and he had scarcely fallen when they cut off his head. I mean the whole scalp, all the way around (it is not known with what skillful trick they can take it off so easily), and they took it away as testimony of their exploit.[11] They left Roque de Yelves on the ground without scalping him because the relief of mounted Spaniards was coming so close, the distance being so short, that the Indians did not have time to take it. He told in a few words what had happened, and asking for confession, soon expired. At the noise and attack of

[11]This is one of the earliest accounts of scalping in the Southeastern ethnographic literature.

the Indians, the two horses of the Portuguese ran toward the camp. The Spaniards who were coming to their relief recovered them and found that one of them had a drop of blood on his thigh. They took him to a veterinarian to be treated, and having examined him, he said that the wound was only a scratch and did not require treatment. The next morning they found the horse dead.

Suspecting that it was an arrow wound, the Castilians opened the horse at the wound, and following the mark of it the length of the body, they found an arrow that had passed through the whole thigh, the stomach and the intestines, and had stopped in the hollow of the chest, lacking only four finger-breadths of flesh from coming out through the breast-leather. The Spaniards were amazed, it seeming to them that a ball from an harquebus could not have gone so far. These particulars are told, though they are of little importance, because they happened in this camp, because of their ferocity, which is notable, and because it is now time that we conclude [the account of] things that took place in the chief pueblo of Apalache by saying, in brief (because to tell all of them would be a very long task), that the natives of this province, during all the time that the Spaniards were wintering in their country, showed themselves to be very bellicose and solicitous, and used all care and diligence to attack the Castilians, losing no occasion or opportunity, however small it might be, when they could wound or kill those who strayed from the camp even for a very short distance.

Alonso de Carmona, in his *Peregrination*, notes particularly the ferocity of the Indians of the province of Apalache, of which he says the following, which is copied literally:

> These Indians of Apalache are of large stature and are very brave and spirited, because just as they saw and fought with the other [soldiers] of Pánphilo de Narváez and made them leave the country, in spite of all they could do, so we encountered them every day, and every day had skirmishes with them. As they could not gain any advantage over us because our governor was very brave, strong, and experienced in Indian warfare, they resorted to wandering through the woods in armed bands, and when the Spaniards went out for firewood, cutting it in the forest, the Indians came up at the sound of the axe and killed the Spaniards, took off the chains of the Indians whom they brought along to carry the wood on their shoulders, and scalped the Spaniards, for scalps were what they most prized to display at the end of the bow with which they fought. At the cries and the alarm they gave, we ran immediately and found the evil already done. In this manner they killed more than twenty of our soldiers, and this was on many different occasions. I remember that one day seven men

> left the camp on horseback on a foray to get feed and to kill some little dogs to eat, for in that country all of us made use of them and we considered ourselves lucky on the day when a part of one fell to our share, and even pheasants tasted no better to us. Going about seeking these things, they encountered five Indians who were waiting for them with their bows and arrows, and who drew a line on the ground and told them not to pass beyond it or they would all die. The Spaniards, refusing to notice such mockery, fell upon them, and the Indians unslung their bows from their arms and killed two horses and wounded two others. They also wounded a Spaniard badly, and the Spaniards killed one of the Indians. The others escaped by flight, for they are truly very swift and are not hindered by elaborate clothing; on the other hand going about without clothing is a great help to them.

Up to here is from Alonso de Carmona.

Besides their watchfulness against those who strayed [from the pueblo], they also exercised it against the whole army, harassing it with alarms and sudden attacks they made by day and by night, not wishing to give battle with the men drawn up in the form of squadrons, but with ambushes concealed in the underbrush and small clumps of timber that were thereabout, and where they were least expected. From these they would come out suddenly to do as much damage as they could. This is sufficient concerning the bravery and ferocity of the natives of the province of Apalache. We have also spoken of its fertility, which is great, for there is an abundance of Indian corn or maize and many other grains, of beans, calabashes (which in the language of El Perú they call *zapallu*), and other vegetables of various kinds, besides the fruits, which there are like those of Spain, such as all kinds of plums, three varieties of nuts, one of which is very oily, and acorns of live oaks and other oaks in such quantities that they remain on the ground at the foot of the trees from one year to the next, because, as these Indians have no tame cattle to eat them, they have no use for them and allow them to go to waste.

In conclusion, so that the abundance and fertility of the province of Apalache may be seen, we say that the whole Spanish army with the Indians whom they carried as servants, numbering in all more than fifteen hundred persons, and more than three hundred horses, in the five months and more that they wintered in this camp maintained themselves on the food that they collected at the beginning, and when they needed it they found it in the small pueblos in the vicinity in such quantities that they never went farther than a league and a half from the principal pueblo to bring it. In addition to this fertility in crops, the land is very well fitted for the breeding of all kinds of cattle because it has good forests and pasture-grounds with fine water, and swamps and lakes with many reeds and rushes for hogs, which do very well on them and, by eating them, do not need grain. This suffices for an account of what is in this province and of its good qualities, one of which is that it is capable of producing a great deal of silk because of the abundance of mulberries. It has also many and good fish.

END OF THE SECOND BOOK

Third Book of the History of La Florida, by the Inca

It tells of the departure of the Spaniards from Apalache; the good reception they gave them in four provinces; the hunger they suffered in some uninhabited regions; the infinite number of pearls and the other grandeur and riches that they found in a temple; the generosity of the Lady of Cofachiqui and of other Caciques, lords of vassals; a very bloody battle the Indians gave them after promising friendship; a mutiny certain Castilians attempted; the laws of the Indians against adulteresses; and another very fierce battle that took place at night. It contains thirty-nine chapters.

I

THE GOVERNOR LEAVES APALACHE, AND A BATTLE TAKES PLACE WITH SEVEN ON EACH SIDE

The governor and adelantado Hernando de Soto, having dispatched Captain Diego Maldonado, who went to La Havana for the purposes told above, and having ordered the provisions and other things necessary, prepared for leaving Apalache. The time now having come, he took his army from that camp at the end of March of the year 1540. He traveled three days' journey toward the north through the same province without meeting enemies who gave him trouble, though those of that country were very vexatious and warlike. On the last of the three days the Castilians lodged in a small pueblo, which was made into a peninsula by being almost entirely surrounded by a swamp more than a hundred paces wide, and having a great deal of mud, which came halfway up the thigh. They had wooden bridges at intervals by which one could leave the place in any direction. The pueblo was situated on a high point from which a large extent of country was visible, and many other small pueblos were seen, scattered about a beautiful valley. The army remained three days in this pueblo, which was the principal one of those in that valley, all of them being in the province of Apalache. On the second day it happened that there went out of the camp at noon five halberdiers of the general's guard and two other soldiers, natives of Badajoz. One of these was named Francisco de Aguilera and the other Andrés Moreno, whom they also called Angel Moreno because, being a merry and lively man, he was always putting into all his speech, without rhyme or reason, this word: "angels, angels."

These seven Spaniards left the principal pueblo without orders from the officials of our army, simply for recreation and to see what was in the other little pueblos. The five men of the guard carried their halberds. Andrés Moreno wore his sword and carried a lance in his hands, and Francisco de Aguilera had a sword and shield. They left the pueblo with these arms, not recalling the great vigilance and care that the Indians of that province always exercised in killing those who strayed away. They passed the swamp and a fringe of woods that was not more than twenty paces across. On the other side was open country with many maize fields.

These seven Spaniards had gone scarcely two hundred paces from the camp when the Indians fell upon them, for as we have seen they never ceased their stratagems against those who strayed. At the shout and outcry both sides gave while fighting, giving the alarm and asking for help, many Spaniards came out from the pueblo to defend their men and, so as not to lose time in searching for a crossing of the swamp, they passed over it at the nearest point, in water and mud waist- and breast-deep. But for all the haste they made they found the five halberdiers dead, each with his body pierced with ten or twelve arrows, and Andrés Moreno alive but with a barbed flint arrow, besides others in his body, that passed through him from breast to shoulders, and as soon as they took it out to treat him he died. Francisco de Aguilar, who was a stronger and more robust man than the others, and being such had defended himself better than the rest, was still alive though he had two arrow wounds, which passed through both thighs, and many blows over the head and the whole body, which they had given him with bows, because when he closed with the Indians they had used all their arrows, and seeing him alone, they grasped their bows with both hands and gave him such hard blows that they knocked his shield to pieces, only the handles being left. They gave him a glancing blow on the forehead that took off all the skin down to the eyebrows and left the skull exposed.

The seven Spaniards were left in this state and the Indians had taken cover before help arrived, because they had heard them coming. The Christians were unable to see the number of the enemy, and Francisco de Aguilar told them that they were more than fifty, and that because there were so many against so few, they had killed them so quickly. But afterward, from day to day, he continued to reveal things favorable to the Indians that had taken place in the fight, and more than twenty days after it, he being newly recovered from his wounds though still weak and convalescent, when other soldiers were joking with him about the blows that the Indians had given him and asking if he had counted them, if they hurt him much, if he would try to avenge them, if he thought he would challenge the enemy on condition that they come out one at a time so that they would not have the advantage of numbers over one man, and other such facetious things that soldiers are accustomed to joke about among themselves, Francisco de Aguilar replied, saying: "I didn't count the blows because they gave me no chance, nor were they delivered so slowly that they could be counted. Whether they hurt me a lot or a little you will know when they give you some like them, and that day will come, I promise you. Because we are speaking frankly and so that you can see what the Indians of this province are like, I wish to tell you seriously, without suppressing or adding anything to the facts (though what I shall say will be against myself), of a courtesy and bravery of spirit that they showed to me that day.

"You must know, then, that, as I told you at the time, more than fifty Indians came out to watch us, but as soon as they saw us and realized that we were only seven and that no horses were coming to support us, another seven Indians separated themselves from the squadron that they had formed, and the rest withdrew to a distance and did not attempt to fight. Only the seven attacked us, and as we did not carry crossbows or harquebuses with which we could hold them off, and as they were lighter and swifter than we, they walked in front of us, leaping about and making fun of us and shooting arrows at their pleasure as if we were captive wild beasts, without our being able to wound them. They killed my companions in this manner, and seeing me alone, to prevent my escaping them all seven set upon me and, holding their bows with both hands, they put me in the state in which you found me. Since they spared my life I forgive them the blows and have no thought of challenging them, for [my wrongs] do not demand that I make use of a challenge so that they can again put me in the state in which they left me before. I have been silent about all this for the sake of my honor and have said nothing about it until now, but this is what really happened, and God keep you from wandering about, so that the same thing may not happen to you." The companions and friends of Francisco de Aguilar were amazed at hearing him because they had never imagined that the Indians were capable of such a chivalrous action as to desire to fight on equal terms with the Castilians when they could attack them with the advantage [of numbers]. But all the Indians of this great kingdom presume so much upon their spirit, strength, and swiftness that, on not seeing horses, they would not admit that the Spaniards had any advantage, but assumed rather that they themselves had it, especially when the Christians were going about as lacking in defensive arms as the Indians themselves.[12]

[12]In the other chronicles these events took place in the province of Capachequi. Garcilaso fails to mention the arduous crossing of the river of Capachequi. Swanton, *Final Report*, 166–67.

II

THE SPANIARDS REACH ALTAPAHA, AND THE MANNER IN WHICH THEY WERE ENTERTAINED

With this misfortune of the loss of the six Spaniards, the governor left the peninsular pueblo of the province of Apalache, and having marched two more days, making five in all that they traveled to get out of this province, they entered the territory of another called Altapaha.[13] The adelantado desired to be the first to see it, in order to learn whether the natives of that province were as rough and warlike as those of Apalache, and also because it was a constantly observed custom of his that he must go himself to any new discovery of provinces because he was not satisfied with the reports of others, but wished to see with his own eyes. Therefore he chose forty cavalry and sixty infantry, [consisting of] twenty rodeleros, twenty harquebusiers, and twenty crossbowmen, for whenever they went on any expedition the infantry were always selected in this manner.

The governor marched with them for two days, and at dawn of the third day he entered the first pueblo of the province of Altapaha and found that the Indians had retired to the woods, taking their women, children, and possessions with them. The Castilians went through the whole pueblo and captured six Indians, two of whom were nobles and were captains who had remained in the pueblo to get the common people out of it. They took all six of them before the governor so that he might learn from them what was in the province.

Before the adelantado asked them a single question the principal Indians said: "What is it that you desire in our houses? Do you wish peace or war?" They said this without any sign that they felt uneasy at finding themselves captives in the hands of strangers; on the other hand they bore themselves in a lordly manner, as if they enjoyed full liberty and were talking with some of their Indian neighbors.

The general replied through his interpreter Juan Ortiz, saying that he desired war with no one, but peace and friendship with all; that they were going in search of certain provinces that were beyond and that they were in need of provisions for their march, because they must eat, and they would

[13]The events described by Garcilaso as taking place in the province of Altapaha actually refer to Ichisi. Altapaha, evidently the namesake of Altamaha, is yet another instance among many wherein Garcilaso confuses and transposes place-names.

make this exaction and no other on the road. This was what they desired, and nothing else.

The principal Indians said: "Well, it was not necessary for you to capture us for this purpose; we will give you here all the supplies that you need for your journey, and we will treat you better than they treated you in Apalache, for we know very well how you fared there." So saying, they ordered two of the four Indians who had been captured with them to go as quickly as possible to give the news to their curaca and principal lord, and tell him what they had seen and heard regarding the Castilians; on the road they were to notify all the Indians whom they should meet, telling them to pass the word along for all of them to come to serve the Christians who were in their country, because they were friends and did not come to harm them. On hearing the reasonable replies of the Indians, the governor, confiding in them and seeing that he could deal with them better by kindness than by force, ordered that they be released immediately and entertained and treated like friends.

The Indians left with the message, and the other four remained with the general. They asked if his lordship thought it well to go back to another better pueblo than the one where they were, saying that they would take him by an easier road than that by which he had come. The governor was glad to do what the Indians suggested because it would bring him nearer his army, and he ordered one of them to take word to the maese de campo to go directly to that pueblo and not go around by the route that he had come. When the Castilians arrived at the pueblo to which the Indians took them they were received with demonstrations of much affection, and as soon as he had news of the friendly compact made with the Spaniards the cacique came to kiss the governor's hands, and courteous and affable expressions were exchanged between the two. With the curaca came all his vassals and the women and children who had withdrawn to the fields, and they settled down in their pueblos.

Meanwhile the army arrived and encamped inside and outside of the pueblo. During all the time the Spaniards were in this province their relations with the Indians were entirely peaceful and friendly, which was no small satisfaction to our men after the many hostilities that those of Apalache had carried on against them.

After resting three days in the pueblo of Altapaha, the Castilians left it and marched for ten days along the bank of a river, upstream. They saw that that whole country appeared to be as fertile or more so than Apalache, and the people domestic and peaceful. They maintained the peace that they had made with them at the beginning in such a manner that the Indians received no molestation unless it was in regard to the food that they consumed, and the Spaniards took this very sparingly in order not to make the natives uneasy. They found extremely large mulberry trees in this province of Altapaha, and though they had been in the others also, they were as nothing compared with these.

At the end of the ten days' journey that our men traveled due north up the river, they passed out of the province of Altapaha, leaving the curaca and his Indians very satisfied with the friendship that they had contracted with them. They entered another province, called Achalaque,[14] which was poor and lacking in food. There were very few young Indians in it, almost all of its inhabitants being old; usually they were nearsighted, and many of them were blind. Inasmuch as the presence in a pueblo or a province of many old people is usually an indication that there will be many more young ones, the Spaniards wondered at not finding them in this country and even suspected that they might be in rebellion and concealed somewhere in order to perpetrate some mischief against the Christians; but on asking questions, they learned that there was nothing concealed, there was only what appeared in public. But they did not inquire into the reason why there were so many old people and so few young ones. The Spaniards traveled through this province of Achalaque making long daily marches, in order to leave it quickly both because it was poor in food and because they desired to reach that of Cofachiqui as soon as they could. There, because of the news that they had of there being much gold and silver in that province, they thought to load themselves down with rich treasure and return to Spain.

Whereupon they doubled their daily marches, and they could do it easily because the country was flat, without woods, mountains, or rivers to impede their swift pace. They crossed the province of Achalaque in five days' march and left its curaca and natives very peaceably inclined and friendly toward the Castilians. So that they would remember them, the governor

---

[14]In another possible instance of Garcilaso's tendency to transpose place-names, here he uses Achalaque for Altamaha. Achalaque is therefore duplicated, for it appears again as Chalaque in the territory beyond Cofitachequi. The name in the latter instance probably refers to speakers of the Cherokee language. It should be noted, however, that the name Chalaque (*Tciloki* in the Muskogean language) merely means "people of different speech" and was commonly used at a later time by Muskogees to refer to people who spoke languages such as Hitchiti. John R. Swanton, "Social Organization and Social Usages of the Indians of the Creek Confederacy," in *Forty-second Annual Report of the Bureau of American Ethnology* (Washington, D.C.: Government Printing Office, 1928), 157.

gave them, among other presents, two swine, male and female, for breeding. He had done the same for the cacique of Altapaha and the lords of the other provinces who had come out peacefully and made friends with the Spaniards. Though hitherto we have not mentioned that the adelantado had taken these animals to La Florida, it is true that he took more than three hundred head, male and female, which multiplied greatly and were exceedingly useful in the great necessities that our Castilians suffered in this discovery. If the Indians (abhorring more the memory of those who brought these animals than esteeming their usefulness) have not destroyed them, it is probable that, in consideration of the advantages that great kingdom has for breeding them, there are many of them there today, for besides those the governor gave to the friendly curacas, many others were lost along the roads, though they were well and carefully guarded. While on the march one of the companies of cavalry was assigned especially to herd and guard them.

III

CONCERNING THE PROVINCE OF COFA AND ITS CACIQUE, AND A PIECE OF ARTILLERY THAT THEY LEFT IN HIS KEEPING

The adelantado was always accustomed whenever he left one province and went on to another to send messengers on ahead to notify the cacique of his coming. He did this on the one hand to request peace and allay the fear that they might feel at seeing strange people in their country, and on the other to find out from the reply that the Indians gave him their favorable or hostile attitude toward them. When the Indians did not dare go from one province to another because of the enmity that existed between them, or when an uninhabited region intervened, then the governor himself made the discovery, as we have seen above, in the best way that he could. Observing this procedure, then, before he left the province of Achalaque he sent messengers to the curaca of the other province, called Cofa, which bordered upon it, letting him understand that he was coming to his country to recognize him as a friend and to treat him as a brother, as he had done with all the other lords of vassals who had received him peaceably.

Besides this message he ordered the Indians who carried it to take care to tell the cacique Cofa of the good treatment that the Spaniards had accorded to their curaca Achalaque and to all the natives of that province because they had received them in peace and had always maintained it.

The cacique Cofa and all his vassals showed much pleasure at the message, and thus with one accord and with much gladness and rejoicing they replied, saying that his lordship and all his army were very welcome to their house and state, where they were waiting with great desire to see and know them in order to serve them to the best of their ability. Therefore they begged that they hasten their journey.

The general and all his soldiers were satisfied with this favorable reply and hastened their march. On the fourth day after they had left the province of Achalaque they arrived at the first pueblo of the province of Cofa, where the cacique was awaiting them with all the rest of the people whom he had summoned to show the grandeur of his court, and with the common people whom he had ordered to be assembled to serve the Spaniards. When he knew that the Castilians were approaching his pueblo he went a third of a league beyond it to receive them, and kissing the governor's hands, he repeated the same words that he had sent to say to him in his reply. The governor embraced him, showing him much affection, and thus the Spaniards entered the pueblo, both foot soldiers and cavalry formed in squadrons.

The curaca lodged the governor in his own house and quartered the army in the pueblo, he himself designating the sections and districts for this and that company, accommodating them all in their order as if he were the maese de campo, which pleased the officials of the army very much because he showed himself to be a military man. Having assigned the lodgings, the cacique went with the governor's permission to another pueblo that was about two harquebus-shots distant from the first one.

This province of Cofa is fertile and abounds in the food that land affords, and it has all the other advantages of woodlands and open plains that we have described in the rest of the country for raising [cattle] and cultivating the soil. It is inhabited by numerous and very good people, gentle and affable, and there the governor and his men were entertained and rested in the first pueblo for five days, because the curaca would not consent to their leaving sooner, and the general agreed, in order to show his friendship.

We have not mentioned hitherto a piece of artillery the governor brought along with his army, and the reason has been that no occasion has arisen throughout the expedition to speak of it, until now. Thus it is that the adelantado, having seen that it served for nothing except a burden and annoyance, requiring men to care for it and pack mules to transport it, decided to leave it with the curaca Cofa to keep for him. So that he might see what he was leaving for him, the governor ordered the piece aimed from the house of the cacique himself at a large and very beautiful live-oak tree that was outside the pueblo, and he knocked it down entirely with two shots, at which the curaca and his Indians were amazed.

The governor told them that, as a proof of the love he had for them and in recompense for the good friendship and hospitality they had shown him, he wished to leave them that piece of which he thought a great deal, so that they might keep and guard it carefully until he should come back there or send to ask for it.

The cacique and all the principal Indians who were with him valued greatly the confidence he placed in them in leaving with them such an important object as a pledge. Thus having thanked him in the best terms that they could command (principally for the confidence and then for the piece of artillery), they ordered it to be guarded very carefully, and it may be believed that they have it still, regarding it with great veneration and esteem.

The army having rested five days, it left Cofa to go to another province named Cofaqui, which belonged to an elder brother of the cacique Cofa, richer and more powerful than he.[15] The curaca Cofa went out with the Indians, both warriors and servants, to accompany the governor one day's journey, and he would have gone with him all the way that he had to travel through his territory, but the general would not consent to it, desiring that he return to his house and not go farther. Seeing the governor's wish, the cacique kissed his hands with much affection and regret at parting from him and said that he begged his lordship to remember the love and good will that he felt for him, to make use of it in his service; that he was his very affectionate servant. The governor thanked him with very friendly words and thus they took leave of one another.

The curaca was careful to take leave of the maese de campo and of the other captains and the officials of the imperial hacienda, to all of whom he spoke as if he had known them for a long time. As soon as he had taken leave of the Spaniards, he summoned his captains and told them to go with all the Indian warriors and servants whom he had brought with him to serve and entertain the governor and all his army, and that they were to consider themselves fortunate in that the Castilians had received them into their friendship and service. He also ordered that one of the principal Indians go on ahead and notify his brother Cofaqui of the Spaniards' coming to his country,

[15]See note 5.

saying that he begged him to receive them peaceably and serve them as he had done, because they deserved it. The general sent another message to the curaca Cofaqui along with this one from the cacique Cofa, offering him peace and friendship. Having made these arrangements, the cacique returned to his house, and the adelantado proceeded with his discovery. After six more days of marching he left the province of Cofa, a country, as we have said, fertile, abundant, and inhabited by a docile and industrious people, more so than any other that the Spaniards had seen up to that time.

IV

IT DEALS WITH THE CURACA COFAQUI, AND OF THE GREAT HOSPITALITY THAT HE SHOWED THE SPANIARDS IN HIS COUNTRY

As soon as the curaca Cofaqui received the messages from his brother and from the governor, he ordered everything necessary made ready, both the nobles for displaying the grandeur of his house, and provisions and servants for the use and entertainment of the Spaniards. Before the governor should enter it [the province], he sent four of the chief nobles accompanied by many people to offer him welcome and congratulations on his arrival, and the obedience due him, and to tell him how they were awaiting him in all peace and friendship with the desire to serve and entertain him to the best of their ability and power.

The general was pleased with this embassy, as were all his men, for they did not desire forced friendship but that which was freely given. So they marched until they reached the limits of Cofaqui where they gave permission to the Indians who had come with them from the province of Cofa, both warriors and servants, to return to their houses. Those of Cofaqui brought others to replace them in carrying the baggage.

The governor arrived at the first pueblo of Cofaqui, where the cacique was. Knowing from his lookouts that the general was approaching, he went to receive him outside the pueblo, accompanied by many nobles handsomely equipped with bows and arrows and great plumes, with rich mantles of marten-skins and various other small skins as finely dressed as the best ones from Germany. Many friendly words passed between the governor and the curaca and also between the principal Indians and the gentlemen and captains of the army, they making themselves understood partly by words and partly by signs, and thus they entered the pueblo amid great festivity and rejoicing on the part of the Indians. The cacique assigned quarters to the Spaniards personally, and he himself went with the governor's permission to another pueblo that was close by to which he had moved his household in order to make room in that one for the Spaniards' lodgings. Early in the morning of the next day he came to visit the governor and, after talking at length about things concerning that province, the Indian said: "Sir, I desire to know your lordship's will; whether it is to remain here where we wish to serve you, or to pass on, so that in accordance with it there may be provided in time that which is conducive to your service." The governor said that he was going in search of other provinces that they had told him were beyond, one of which was called Cofachiqui, and that he could not make an establishment or remain anywhere until he had seen and traversed them all.

The curaca replied that that province bordered upon his own and that there was a large uninhabited region between them that could be passed over in seven days' march. He offered his lordship the Indian warriors and servants necessary for the journey to serve and accompany him as far as his lordship wished to take them. He offered as well all the provisions needed for the journey, begging him to request and order prepared that which he desired to take as if he were in his own country. All of that land was at his command and very desirous to serve him.

The governor thanked him for the offer and said that—inasmuch as he, as an experienced captain and as lord of that land, knew the road he would have to take and the supplies that would be needed—he asked him to provide them as if for his own use, saying that the Spaniards needed nothing except food, and that, in leaving everything to his will and judgment, he would see that they desired to give him as little trouble as possible.

This confidence that the governor placed in the cacique obliged the latter to do more than he would have done if he had asked specifically for what he needed, and he [the cacique] said as much. He ordered at once that the provisions be carefully and quickly assembled, and also the Indian carriers who were to transport them. This order was obeyed and carried out so promptly that in four days, while the Spaniards were resting in the pueblo of Cofaqui, four thousand Indian servants were assembled to carry the food and clothing of the Christians, and another four thousand warriors to accompany and guide the army.

The chief provisions that the Castilians procured, wherever they might be, was maize, which throughout the Indies of the New World is what wheat is in Spain. Along with the maize the Indians provided much dried fruit, which as we have told already the land produces by itself, without being cultivated, such as dried plums and raisins, two or three kinds of nuts, and acorns from the live oak and other oaks. There was no provision of meat because, as we have already said, they had no domesticated cattle, but only that which they killed while hunting in the woods.

Seeing such a gathering of people, though they were assembled to serve him, the governor and his men were cautious and kept watch night and day, more than ordinarily, so that the Indians, seeing them careful, would not dare attempt anything against them under cover of friendship. But the Indians themselves were heedless enough and had no thought of offending the Spaniards; rather with all their strength and will they busied themselves in serving and gratifying them, so that with their favor and protection they might avenge the injuries and damage that they had received from their enemies of Cofachiqui, as we shall soon see.

One day before the time appointed for the Spaniards' departure, the curaca being in the plaza of the pueblo with the general and other captains and principal gentlemen of the army, he ordered an Indian summoned whom he had named captain-general for all the affairs of war that might come up, and on the present occasion he was to go with the governor. When he appeared before him the curaca said to him: "You know well the war and perpetual enmity that our fathers and grandfathers and ancestors have always had and that we ourselves now have with the Indians of the province of Cofachiqui, where you are now going in the service of our governor and of these gentlemen; and also the many and notable offenses, evils and injuries that the natives of that country have continually committed and are now committing against us are well known. Therefore, since fortune offers us such a good opportunity as the present one to avenge ourselves, it will be a good thing to take advantage of it.

"As we have agreed, you, my captain-general, are to go in the company and in the service of the governor and of his invincible army, with whose favor and protection you are to do everything that you can think of against our enemies, in satisfaction for our injuries and wrongs. And because I know that there is no need to waste words in telling you what you must do, I confide in your spirit and good will, which I know will conform with my desires and with what is conducive to our honor in this case."

V

PATOFA PROMISES HIS CURACA TO TAKE VENGEANCE, AND A STRANGE THING THAT HAPPENED TO AN INDIAN GUIDE IS TOLD

The Indian *apu,* which in the language of El Perú signifies captain-general or he who is supreme in any office—whose own name was Patofa and who showed such nobility in his person and face that his appearance and aspect certified that the office of captain-general had been well bestowed upon him, and gave promise of all good conduct in peace and in war—rising to his feet and throwing off a mantle of cat-skins he wore like a cape, took a broadsword made of palm wood, which one of his servants carried behind him as a captain's insignia, and made many fine salutes with it before his cacique and governor, leaping from one side to the other with such dexterity and gracefulness and rhythm that a famous fencing-master could not have done better, so that our Spaniards wondered at it greatly. Having performed for a long time, he stopped, and with the broadsword in his hands went to his curaca and, making him a deep reverence after their custom, which differs little from ours, he said, according to the interpreters: "Our prince and lord, as your servant and the captain-general of your armies, I pledge my faith and word to your lordship to do in compliance with what you order me all that my strength and industry can accomplish, and I promise with the aid of these valiant Spaniards to avenge all the injuries, deaths, damages and losses that our ancestors and ourselves have received from the natives of Cofachiqui. And the vengeance will be such that with great satisfaction to your reputation and grandeur you can blot out from memory what now offends you therein, being unavenged. The surest sign that you can have of my having fulfilled that which you order me will be that, having done it satisfactorily, I shall dare to return to present myself before your honor. If fortune should run contrary to my hopes, your eyes will never see me again, nor will those of the Sun. I myself will inflict the punishment that my cowardice or my ill-luck may deserve, which will be death in case the enemy is unwilling to give it to me with his own hand." The curaca Cofaqui stood up and, embracing the general Patofa, said to him: "Your promises I consider as certain as if they were already fulfilled, and thus I reward them as services done, which I so desire to receive." So saying, he took off a cape of most handsome marten-skins that he wore and covered Patofa with it with his own hands, in payment for services not yet rendered. The marten-skins in the cape were so fine that the Spaniards estimated that in Spain its value would be 2,000 ducats.

The favor of a lord giving to a servant the cape or plume or any other article of personal adornment, especially if he took it off in the servant's presence to present it, was among all the Indians of this great kingdom of La Florida a thing of such great honor and esteem that no other reward could equal it, and it seems reasonable that this should be so among all nations.

Everything now being provided for the Spaniards' march, a strange thing happened on the night before their departure, at which they wondered. This was that, as we mentioned above, our men captured in the province of Apalache two young Indians who had offered to guide the Castilians. One of them, whom the Christians named Marcos, without having baptized him, had now guided them over all the road that he knew. The other, whom they had named Pedro, also without baptizing him, was the one who was to guide them from there on as far as the province of Cofachiqui, where he had said they would find much gold and silver and many valuable pearls. This youth went about with the Spaniards as familiarly as if he had been born among them. It happened that about midnight of the night before the departure he shouted loudly for help, saying that they were killing him. The whole army was aroused, believing that it was some treason of the Indians, and thus they sounded the alarm and very quickly got under arms, the cavalry and infantry drawn up in squadrons. But as they heard no enemies, they went out to see where the alarm had come from, and they found that the Indian Pedro had caused it with his shouts. He was trembling with fear, terrified and half dead. Being asked what he had seen or heard that caused him to call for help with such extraordinary cries, he said that the devil, with a horrible visage and accompanied by many servants, had come to him and told him not to guide the Spaniards where he had promised to guide them or he would kill him. As he said these words, he [the devil] had hissed at him and dragged him through the room, giving him many blows all over the body, flogging and pounding him so that he was unable to move. According to the way the devil was mistreating him, he knew he would have ended by killing him if two Spaniards had not been able to come so quickly to his assistance. As the big devil saw them come through the door of his room he had left him immediately and fled, and all his servants had gone after him. He knew from this that the demons fear the Christians, and therefore he wished to be a Christian. He begged them for the love of God to baptize him at once so that the devil would not come back to kill him; being baptized like the other

Christians, it was certain that he would not touch him because he had seen him flee from them.

The Indian Pedro, the Christian convert, said all this before the governor and the other Spaniards who were present, who wondered at having heard him and saw that it was not pretense, because the marks of lashes, the bruises, and the swelling that they found on his face and all over his body were testimonies of the blows that they had given him. The general ordered the priests, clerics, and friars to be summoned and told them to do what they considered best after inquiring into the case. Having heard the Indian, they baptized him immediately and remained with him all that night and the following day, confirming him in the faith and restoring his body, which he said was beaten and buffeted by the blows that had been given him. Because of his indisposition, the camp did not move that day, but the next, and for two days they carried him on horseback because he could not stand up.

From what we have said about the Indian Pedro it can be seen how easily these Indians and all those of the New World can be converted to the Catholic faith, and as a native personally acquainted with those of El Perú, I dare affirm that the example of this Indian alone, with what he had seen, would suffice for the conversion of all those in his province and for their requesting baptism, as he did. But our people, who had the intention of preaching the gospel after having won and pacified the land, at that time did nothing more than what has been told.

The army left the pueblo of Cofaqui, and the curaca accompanied it for two leagues, and would have gone farther if the governor had not begged him to return to his house. On taking leave, he showed the regret of a friend at parting with the governor and the Spaniards, and having kissed the hands of the chief men among them, he again charged his captain-general Patofa to take care to serve the adelantado and all his army. He replied that his actions would show how much he had taken all his commands to heart. Thereupon the cacique returned to his house, and the Spaniards continued their march toward the province of Cofachiqui, so desired by them.

VI

THE GOVERNOR AND HIS ARMY ARE VERY CONFUSED AT SEEING THEMSELVES LOST IN A WILDERNESS WITHOUT FOOD

The army of the Christians marched with the cavalry and infantry formed in squadrons. The captain-general Patofa, who as we have said had four thousand select warriors, also marched separately with his squadron, with vanguard and rear guard, and the servants and carriers in between. In this manner marched the two nations, so different from one another, though not in military organization, because it was a very fine thing to see the good order and arrangement that each of them maintained, competing with one another. The Indians were not willing to admit that the Spaniards had the advantage in anything pertaining to the art and science of war.

They also camped separately at night, for as soon as the four thousand Indian carriers delivered the provisions to our men they went to sleep with their own. The Indians as well as the Spaniards posted their sentries and kept watch and guard over one another as if they were declared enemies. The Christians in particular did this, because on seeing such order and regularity on the part of the heathen, they were cautious with regard to them, but the Indians proceeded openly enough and entirely without malice; on the other hand they showed their desire to please the Spaniards in everything. Their posting sentries and standing guard, and the other regulations that they observed, were done more to show themselves to be warriors than from suspicion of the Spaniards. They proceeded with this vigilance and care all the time that they were together. By the way that they were going, which proved to be the narrowest point of the province of Cofaqui, they left it in two daily journeys, and on the second night they slept at the beginning of the large uninhabited region that lies between the two provinces of Cofaqui and Cofachiqui.

They marched another six days through the deserted country and saw that the land was all pleasant, and the mountains and woods they found were not rough or dense, but they could pass through them easily. During these six days, among other smaller streams they crossed two large and swift rivers carrying much water, but because it was spread over a wide area they were able to ford them, making use of the horses with which they formed a wall from one side of the river to the other so that it would break the fury of the

On the Trail. This painting shows a portion of De Soto's entrada on the march. It was painted by Dan Feaser, National Park Service, Harpers Ferry Interpretive Design Center, and was commissioned by the National Park Service. The original 4' x 8' oil on wood mural completed in 1969 is on display at the visitors center, De Soto National Memorial, Bradenton, Florida. It is said to be the only piece of artwork in the United States that accurately portrays the arms and armor used by the De Soto expedition. The expedition generally followed Indian trails from one town to the next. (Courtesy of the U.S. Department of the Interior, National Park Service)

water. It was so rapid that the infantrymen, on going into it waist-deep, could not stand up; but with the help of the horses, by taking hold of them, all those on foot crossed without danger, Indians and Spaniards alike.

In the midst of the seventh day's march Indians and Spaniards found themselves in great confusion, because the road that they had been following up to that time, which appeared to be a very wide public highway, came to an end, and many narrow paths that led through the woods in every direction were lost after they had followed them for a short distance, and they were without a path. Thus after making many efforts, they found themselves closed up in that wilderness without knowing how to get out of it, and the woods were different from the former ones because they were taller and denser, and they could travel through them only with difficulty.

The Indians whom the governor brought with him as domestics, as well as those who came with the general Patofa, were lost, there not being among them all a single one who knew the road or could say what direction they must take in order to get out of that forest and wilderness more quickly. The governor summoned Captain Patofa and asked him why he had led them into those deserts under pretense of friendship, where no road could be found anywhere by which to get out of them, and how it was possible or believable that there was not one among the eight thousand Indians whom he brought with him who would know where they were or how they could get to the province of Cofachiqui, even though it meant cutting a way through the forest by hand. He said that it was not credible that, having had perpetual warfare with one another, they would not know the public and secret roads that passed from one province to the other.

Captain Patofa replied that neither he nor any of his Indians had ever been where they were at present and that the wars these two provinces had waged had never been in open battle between two forces, one taking an army to the territory of the other, but only at the fisheries on those two rivers and the other streams that they had left behind them and at the hunting grounds, between the parties that both sent out through those woods and uninhabited districts that they had passed. Meeting at these hunting grounds and fisheries, they killed and captured one another as enemies, and because those of Cofachiqui had been superior to his and had always gained many advantages over them in the fights that they had thus had, his Indians were intimidated and submissive, not daring to go any distance or leave their own boundaries. This was why they did not know where they were or how they could get out of that wilderness; and if his lordship suspected that he had led them into those deserts with cunning and deceit so that he might perish there with his army, he could undeceive himself, because neither his lord Cofaqui nor he, who prided themselves on being truthful men, having received them as friends, would have imagined, much less done, such a thing. In order to prove that what he said was true, he [the governor] might take any hostages that he wished, and if his own head was enough to satisfy him, he was very willing to give himself up immediately so that he could order it cut off, and not only his own but also those of all the Indians who came with him. They were all at his orders and disposal both because of the law of war, since he was their captain-general, and by the particular order his curaca and lord had given them, saying that they were to obey him in everything, even to the death.

Hearing the honest words of Patofa and seeing the passionate earnestness with which he was saying them, the governor told him, to prevent him from doing some desperate act, that he believed him and was satisfied of his friendship. He at once called the Indian Pedro, whom we said the devil had mistreated in Cofaqui. He had guided the Spaniards from the province of Apalache until that day with such thorough knowledge of the country that the night before he could tell everything they would find on the road on the following day. Like the rest of the Indians, this youth also lost the skill that he had shown up to that time and said that, as it had been four or five years since he had stopped going by way of that road, he had forgotten it in such manner that he found himself totally lost. He neither knew the road nor was he able to say definitely how they could get out to the province of Cofachiqui. Many of the Spaniards, seeing him silent and uncertain about the road, said that from fear of the devil who had mistreated and threatened him he was unwilling to guide them or to say how they must go to get out of that wilderness.

In this confusion and not knowing how to get out, our Spaniards traveled the rest of that day without any road, simply going where they found the forest more open and clear. Going on thus, lost, at sunset they reached a great river, larger than the two that they had crossed, which could not be forded on account of the large volume of water. The sight of it caused them even greater dismay because they had neither rafts nor canoes in which to cross it nor food to eat while they made them. This was what concerned them most, because the provisions that they had brought from Cofaqui had been apportioned for seven days, which they had said would be spent in passing through the uninhabited region, and although they had brought four thousand Indian carriers, their loads had been so light that they were not half of the usual ones, and an Indian can carry at most only half a *fanega* of

Indian corn or maize. Though they were thus laden, these Indians also carried their weapons like the rest who went as soldiers; for as all of them had left their country with the intention of revenging themselves on those of Cofachiqui, they went prepared with their arms. They carried them also in order not to return empty-handed through strange lands that belonged to the enemy. Therefore, because there were nearly ten thousand men and about 350 horses to eat maize, on the seventh day of their march they had nothing more to eat. And though on the day before an order had been issued to conserve the food and use it sparingly for fear that they would not find their way at once, it was already too late, for there was now no more to conserve. Thus our Spaniards found themselves without a guide, without a road, and without provisions, lost in a wilderness, cut off in front by a large river and behind by the extensive uninhabited region that they had passed through, and on all sides was the confusion of not knowing when or how they could get out of those brambles. Above all else was the lack of food, which was what caused the most uneasiness.

VII

FOUR CAPTAINS GO TO EXPLORE THE COUNTRY, AND A STRANGE PUNISHMENT THAT PATOFA IMPOSED UPON AN INDIAN

The governor having considered the difficulties and troubles in which his army found itself, it seemed to him best and even necessary for the camp not to move until a road had been found and a way out of that wilderness. Thus at dawn of the following day he ordered that four parties go out, two of cavalry and two of infantry. Two were to go upstream and the other two down, with orders and directions that two of them were to follow the riverbank without leaving it, and the other two were to follow the same route one league inland, to see whether by one way or the other they could come upon some road or discover inhabited country. He ordered each one of the captains to return within four or five days with [a report of] what he had found. These captains were the accountant Juan de Añasco, Andrés de Vasconcelos, Juan de Guzmán and Arias Tinoco.

General Patofa went with Captain Juan de Añasco, not wishing to remain in the camp, and they happened to be the ones who went along the riverbank, upstream. With them went the Indian Pedro, who was disgruntled at having lost his way, and it seemed to him that by going on that expedition he would succeed in his undertaking and put the Spaniards into the province of Cofachiqui, as he had promised to do. A thousand Indian warriors went with each one of the Spanish companies so that they could scatter through the woods and search for a road.

The governor stayed on the riverbank waiting for the news that his men should bring, and there he and his people suffered extreme scarcity of food, for they ate only the tendrils of wild vines that grew in the woods and along the streams. The four thousand Indian servants who remained with the governor went out early in the morning to hunt for food in the fields, and at night they came back with edible herbs and roots and with some birds and small animals that they had killed with their bows. Others brought fish they had caught, and they left nothing undone that they could possibly do to find food. All that they thus found they took without touching it or concealing any part of it to the Spaniards to whose company they were assigned, and such was the Indians' fidelity and respect toward them in this regard that although they were perishing of hunger they would not take anything until they had presented it to the Spaniards. The latter, overcome by such kindness, gave the Indians the greater part of what they thus brought, but all of it was nothing for so many people.

After being three days in that camp, the governor, seeing that such hunger could not be endured—and certainly its pangs could not be exaggerated—ordered that some of the swine they were bringing for breeding should be killed, and eight ounces of the meat given for the subsistence of each Spaniard, a succor that rather increased hunger than allayed it. The Spaniards also divided the meat with their Indians so that they might see that they did not wish to take advantage of them in any way, but to suffer their hardships along with them.

It was a source of extreme satisfaction to the soldiers to see the fine attitude the general showed toward his men in this affliction, to encourage them and help them endure their hunger, for he enjoyed no advantages of any kind, [acting] as if he were the least among them all. The soldiers conducted themselves in the same way toward their captain, concealing their pangs of hunger in order to mitigate the grief that he felt in the capacity of a good father at seeing his men in such want, and pretending that this was less than it really was. They showed in their faces the happiness and contentment of men who were enjoying all abundance and prosperity.

We neglected to tell above, in its place, of an exemplary punishment that

Patofa imposed upon one of his Indians. Because it is so strange, it ought not to be forgotten, and it will fit in well enough wherever it is included. Thus it was that, on the fifth day of their march through the uninhabited region, one of the Indian carriers (whom they called *tameme* in the language of the island of Española), without having received any injury, and impelled by cowardice or the desire to see his wife and children, or because the devil had told him about the hunger that they were going to suffer, or for some other reason that he alone knew, decided to run away. The Spaniard in whose charge he was missed him, and told General Patofa about it. The latter ordered four young Indian nobles to go back for that Indian as quickly as possible and not to stop until they overtook him and brought him back handcuffed. The Indians went so swiftly that in a short time they overtook him and came back to the camp, bringing him before their captain.

After censuring him in the presence of the soldiers for his cowardice and pusillanimity, his disrespect for his prince and curaca, his disobedience to his captain-general, and the treason and perfidy that he had shown toward his companions and his whole nation, the captain said to him: "Your crime and wrongdoing shall not go unpunished, so that others may not take a bad example from you." So saying, he ordered that they take him to a small stream that flowed near the camp, and in Patofa's presence they took off the few clothes that he was wearing, leaving only the trousers. Then at the captain's orders they brought a number of shoots from trees more than a fathom long, and he said to the Indian: "Lie down on your chest at this stream and drink all this water, and do not stop until you have drunk it up." He ordered four of the young men that whenever he raised his head from the water they were to beat him with the shoots until he drank again, and they were to stir up the water so it would be harder for him to drink. Put to this torture, the Indian drank until he could drink no more, but when he stopped they gave him cruel strokes with the shoots from head to foot, and they did not cease until he began to drink again. Seeing such a severe punishment and knowing that it would not stop short of killing him, some of his relatives went running to the governor and, throwing themselves at his feet, they begged him to take pity on their poor kinsman. The general sent a message to Captain Patofa asking that he please stop this punishment, though it was so justified, and not allow his anger to go further. Thereupon they left the Indian alone, now half dead, having drunk so much water without being thirsty.

VIII

OF A PARTICULAR ACCOUNT OF THE HUNGER THE SPANIARDS SUFFERED, AND OF HOW THEY FOUND FOOD

Returning to the hunger and necessity that the governor and his army suffered during those days, it seems fitting to tell of a particular case that occurred among some of the best soldiers who were in the camp, so that from it there may be seen and understood what they were all suffering, because if each special incident were told there would be no end and it would make our *History* very tedious. Thus on one of the days when they were suffering greatest hunger, four of the principal and most courageous soldiers—who, being such, were making light of and laughing (although falsely) about the hardships and necessities they were suffering—because they belonged to the same group, decided to see what provisions they had among them. They found that they had scarcely a handful of Indian corn. Before making a division they cooked it, in order to increase it somewhat, and it came to exactly eighteen grains apiece, without anyone being slighted. Three of them, who were Antonio Carrillo, Pedro Morón, and Francisco Pechudo, ate their share at once. The fourth, who was Gonzalo Silvestre, tied up his eighteen grains in a handkerchief and put them inside his shirt. A little later he met a Castilian soldier named Francisco de Troche, a native of Burgos, who said to him, "Have you got anything to eat?" Gonzalo Silvestre replied facetiously, "Yes, they just brought me some very good sweetmeats from Sevilla, recently made." Instead of becoming angry, Francisco de Troche laughed at the nonsense. At this point another soldier from Badajoz, named Pedro de Torres, came up and asked his question of those who were talking about sweetmeats, saying, "Have you two anything to eat?" (There was no other subject of conversation in those days.) Gonzalo Silvestre replied, "I have a very good and tender veal loaf just out of the oven; if you want some of it I will divide with you generously." They laughed at the second joke as they had at the first. Then Gonzalo Silvestre said to them: "Well, so that you may see that I have not lied to either of you, I will give you something that one of you can consider sweetmeats if you like them, and the other veal loaf if you care for it." So saying, he took out the handkerchief with the eighteen grains of maize and gave each of them six grains and took the other six for himself. All three ate it at once before some of their other comrades should come up, making the share of each one still smaller. Having eaten, they went to a stream that flowed close by and filled themselves up with water, since they could not do so with food. Thus that day passed without their eating any more, because there was nothing to eat. With these hardships and other similar ones, and not with eating sweetmeats and veal loaf, the New World was won, from which they bring to Spain every year 12 or 13 million in gold, silver, and precious stones. Therefore, I pride myself very much on being the son of a conquistador of El Perú, whose weapons and labors have won such honor and advantage for Spain.

Returning to the four captains who we said went to discover roads, they marched six days, suffering the same hunger and necessities that the governor and his army were experiencing. Three of the captains found nothing worth noting, only hunger and more hunger. The accountant Juan de Añasco alone had better luck, for after traveling continuously for three days upstream, without leaving it, at the end of that time he found a pueblo situated on the riverbank, on the same side as he was. He found few people in it but much food for such a small pueblo, for in one storehouse alone there were five hundred fanegas of meal made of parched maize, besides much more that was unground. Thereupon the Indians and Spaniards rejoiced, as may be imagined; and after having seen what was in the houses, they went up into the higher ones and discovered that, from there on up the river, the land was dotted with many pueblos, large and small, with many cultivated fields on all sides. For this our people gave thanks to God, and they and the Indians satisfied their hunger. After midnight they dispatched four mounted men to return as quickly as possible to notify the governor of what they had seen and discovered. The four Spaniards went back with the good news, and as proof of it they carried many ears of Indian corn and some horns of cattle [buffalo]. They were unable to learn where the Indians could have gotten these, because in all the places these Spaniards went in La Florida they never found cattle, and though it is true that in some places they found fresh beef, they never saw the cattle, nor were they able by cajolery or threats to get the Indians to tell them where they were.

During the night that they slept in the pueblo, General Patofa and his Indians sacked it and robbed the temple as secretly as they could, without the Spaniards knowing anything about their action. The temple served only as a burial place, where (as we shall tell below concerning other, more famous ones) they kept the finest and richest of their possessions. They killed all the Indians they could find, in and out of the pueblo, without sparing sex or age, and they took off the scalps of those whom they so killed, from the ears up, with wonderful dexterity and skill. They carried off these scalps so that their curaca and lord Cofaqui could see with his own eyes the revenge they had taken on their enemies for injuries received, because, as it was learned later, this pueblo belonged to the province of Cofachiqui, which had been so desired by the Spaniards and whose discovery had cost them so much hunger.

At noon the next day Juan de Añasco left the pueblo with all his Spaniards and Indians, not daring to wait there for the governor for fear that the people of that country would summon one another and gather together large numbers—for in view of the large population on the upper river they could assemble a great many—and attack and kill them all. They [the Spaniards] were not powerful enough to resist them, and thus it seemed safer to go back to meet the governor.

IX

THE ARMY REACHES THE PLACE WHERE THERE ARE SUPPLIES. PATOFA RETURNS TO HIS HOUSE, AND JUAN DE AÑASCO GOES TO EXPLORE THE COUNTRY

The four horsemen, whom we left on the way with the report and good news of having found food and an inhabited country, reached the place where the governor was, having returned in one day over the route that they had taken three days in going, which was more than twelve leagues. They reported to him what they had discovered.

As soon as day came the governor ordered his people to march where the four horsemen would guide them. The soldiers were so hungry and so anxious to go where they would find food that they traveled full speed, it being impossible to put them in order or have them march in squadrons as they usually did, but he who was best able to do so went ahead. They marched so swiftly that before noon of the next day all of them were in the pueblo.

The governor saw fit to remain there several days, both in order to allow the men to rest and recover from their past hardships and to wait for the three captains who had gone to explore the land in other directions. These latter—having followed for three days the route that each of them had taken, and all three of them having found almost the same sort of roads and paths that crossed the land in all directions, on which they found signs of Indians, but not having succeeded in finding one from whom to get information, nor having been able to discover a settlement—in order not to get farther away and because they had no other errand, they returned to the post at the end of the fifth day after they had left the governor. Not finding him there, they followed the trail that the army had left; and in two more days, having suffered the hunger and hardships that may be imagined of men who had eaten nothing but herbs and roots for more than eight days, and not very many of those, they reached the pueblo where the governor was. In his presence and in the company of all their comrades they rested and tried to recover themselves, telling one another about the hardships and hunger that they had experienced.

Alonso de Carmona in his account tells at great length about all the famine and necessity that we have described, which these Spaniards passed through in the uninhabited country, and he says that four hogs were killed to succor the people, and that they were very large ones, "on which (he says) we dined better than usual." He must have said this in irony, it being such a small thing for so many people.

The governor stayed seven days in this first pueblo of the province of Cofachiqui, where the whole army was assembled, so that the men could recover from their past fatigues. During this time Captain Patofa and his eight thousand Indians did all the harm and injury they could to their enemies, as secretly as possible. They scoured the country for four leagues in every direction, wherever they could do damage. They killed the Indians whom they could find, men and women, and took off their scalps to carry away as evidence of their exploits. They sacked the pueblos and temples whenever they could, but did not burn them, as they wished to do, so that the governor would not see or know about it. In short, they left nothing undone that they could think of to harm their enemies and avenge themselves. The cruelty would have continued if on the fifth day of this state of affairs the things that Patofa and his Indians had done and were doing had not come to the governor's attention. Considering that it was not just that one party should harm the other while under his favor or protection, and that it would not be a good thing to make enemies for the future because of the harm that another did without his consent, since he was proceeding with the intention of making peace with the Indians rather than of waging war against them, he decided to dismiss Patofa so that he might take all his men and return at once to his own country. This he did, and having thanked him for the friendliness and good companionship that he had shown him, and having given him pieces of cloth, silk, and linen, knives, scissors, mirrors, and other things from Spain that they value very much, for himself and for his curaca, he sent him away very well satisfied and happy at the kindness and favor that he had shown him. But he [Patofa] was much more so because he had complied fully with the charge that his lord had given him to take revenge against his enemies and aggressors.

After Patofa and his Indians left, the governor stayed in the same pueblo for two more days, resting; but now that he saw his people recovering he thought it well to go on and march along the riverbank, upstream, toward the settlements. The army went in this direction for three days without meeting a single live Indian, but coming upon many dead ones with their scalps gone. The Castilians saw here the butchery that Patofa had committed, for which reason the natives had withdrawn into the interior where they could not be reached. They found food in the pueblos, which was what they needed.

At the end of three days the army halted at a very beautiful site in a verdant country having many mulberries and other fruit trees, laden with fruit. The governor did not wish to go on until he knew what country that was, and having had all his men make camp, he summoned the accountant Juan de Añasco and ordered him to take thirty infantrymen and follow the same road that they had traveled up to that point (which, though narrow, passed on from there). He was to endeavor to capture an Indian that night, in order to find out what was in that country and what was the name of its lord, and the other things that it would be worthwhile for them to know. If he should be unable to take an Indian, he was to obtain a reliable account in some other way that would enable the army to go on without proceeding so blindly as they had done hitherto. After the governor had given him his orders he told him that, inasmuch as he had always been successful on all the special expeditions that he had made, he thus entrusted them to him rather than to another, and he was to endeavor to do as well on this one, which was so important to them.

Juan de Anasco and his thirty companions left the camp before dawn, on foot and as silently as possible, like people who are going on a foray. They followed the road indicated to them, and the farther they went the wider it became, turning into a public highway. Having marched along it thus for two leagues, they heard in the silence of the night a murmuring like that of a pueblo nearby, and going on a little farther to get out of a fringe of woods in front of them that cut off their view, they saw lights and heard dogs barking and children crying and men and women talking, so that they realized it was a pueblo. Our Spaniards therefore prepared to capture some Indian quietly on the outskirts, without being heard. Each one of them desired to be the first to lay hands on one, so as to enjoy the honor of having been more diligent. All of them were thus proceeding very cautiously when they found all their hopes dashed because the river, which hitherto had been to one side of them, cut across in front and passed between them and the pueblo. The Christians remained for some time on the banks of the river at a large beach and landing-place for canoes. After having supper and resting, it now being two o'clock in the morning, they went back to the camp, arriving there a little before dawn, and reported to the governor what they had seen and heard.

As soon as daylight came the governor left with a hundred infantry and a hundred cavalry and went to see the pueblo, and to reconnoiter and learn what was there favorable or unfavorable to their discovery. Reaching the canoe landing, Juan Ortiz and the Indian Pedro shouted to the Indians on the other side, telling them to come and hear what they had to say, and return with an embassy that they wished to send to the lord of that land. Seeing things so new to them as Spaniards and horses, the Indians hurried back to the pueblo and told what they had said to them.

X

THE LADY OF COFACHIQUI COMES OUT TO TALK WITH THE GOVERNOR, AND OFFERS FOOD AND PASSAGE FOR THE ARMY

Soon after the Indians gave the news in the pueblo, six of the principal Indians, who were understood to have been magistrates [*regidores*], came out. They were of good presence and about the same age, between forty and fifty years. They embarked in a large canoe, and other Indian servants came with them to propel and manage it.

When the six Indians came into the governor's presence they all made together three separate and deep reverences, the first to the Sun, all turning to the east; the second to the Moon, turning their faces to the west; and the third to the governor, facing the place where he was. He was seated in an easy chair that he always took wherever he went, in which he sat when he received the curacas and ambassadors, with the gravity and ceremony that befitted the importance of his charge and office. After paying their respects, the first words that the six principal Indians spoke were to say to the governor, "Sir, do you wish peace or war?" Because this was a general custom, it must be known that, in all the provinces that the governor discovered, as soon as he entered them they asked him this question with the first words that they spoke. The general replied that he desired peace and not war, and he asked of them only passage and provisions to enable him to go on to certain provinces that he was seeking. Since they knew that food was a thing that could not be dispensed with, they would forgive him for the inconvenience that they might have in giving it to him. He begged them also to provide him with rafts and canoes for crossing that river, and that they would treat him in a friendly manner while he was passing through their lands, for he would endeavor to give them as little trouble as possible.

The Indians replied that they accepted his offer of peace, and that as for food, they had very little because there had been a great pestilence throughout their province in the previous year, with a heavy mortality, from which only that pueblo had escaped. For that reason the inhabitants of the other pueblos in the state had fled to the woods and had planted no crops, and though the plague was over the Indians still had not all gathered in their houses and pueblos. They were vassals of a lady, a young marriageable woman who had recently inherited. They would go back to report what his lordship requested and would advise him at once of her reply. Meanwhile he might wait confidently because they knew that their lady, being a discreet woman of noble instincts, would do everything she could to serve the Christians. After making these statements, they returned to their pueblo with the governor's permission and advised their lady of what the captain of the Christians had requested for his journey.

The Indians could scarcely have delivered the message to their lady when the Castilians saw two large canoes being made ready, and an awning with many trappings and ornaments being raised over one of them. The lady of the pueblo embarked in this with eight noblewomen who attended her, and no other person embarked in that canoe. In the other the six principal Indians who had carried the message embarked, and with them came many oarsmen who rowed and steered the canoe, which towed the lady's canoe, in which there were no oarsmen nor any men whatever, but only the women. They crossed the river in this order and came to the place where the governor was. This is an action very similar, though inferior in grandeur and majesty, to that of Cleopatra when she went by the River Cydnus in Cilicia to receive Marc Antony, where destinies were changed in such manner that she who had been accused of the crime of lèse-majesté came out as judge of him who had condemned her; and the emperor and lord, as the slave of his servant—now become his mistress by the power of love because of the excellences, beauty and discretion of that most famous Egyptian; all of which is told at length by the master of that great Spaniard, Trajano, who was a worthy pupil of such a teacher. Because certain events of these two histories are so similar, we would like to plagiarize here from him as suits us, as others have done from the same author, who has something for everyone, if we did not fear that in doing it so openly his most elegant brocade would necessarily be discovered among our base sackcloth.

The Indian lady of the province of Cofachiqui, having come before the governor and made her obeisance, seated herself on a chair her people brought her, and she alone spoke to the governor without any of her Indians, men or women, saying a word. She referred again to the message that her vassals had given him and said that the pestilence of the year before had deprived her of the provisions she would have desired to have in order to be able to serve his lordship better, but that she would do all she could to assist him. So that he might see this by her actions, she immediately offered him one of two storehouses that she had in that pueblo, each of which contained six hundred fanegas of Indian corn, which she had collected to succor the vassals who had escaped from the plague. She begged that he be pleased to leave her the other for their own need, which was great; and if his lordship should need maize thereafter, she had collected two thousand fanegas in another pueblo near that one for these same necessities, and he could take as much as he liked from there. She would move out of her own house to provide lodgings for his lordship, and she would order that half of the pueblo be vacated for the captains and principal soldiers. For the rest of the people they would erect very good shelters of branches in which they would be comfortable. If he wished, they would move out of the whole pueblo and the Indians would go to another that was close by. Rafts and wooden canoes would be provided quickly to enable the army to cross that river, and they would all be ready on the following day so that his lordship might see how promptly and willingly they would serve him.

The governor replied to her friendly words and promises with many acknowledgments and was very gratified that during a time when her country was suffering want she offered him more than he asked. In return for that favor he said that he and his people would endeavor to get along with as little food as they could, in order not to give her so much inconvenience, and that the quarters and other things provided were very well ordered and planned.

Therefore in the name of the emperor of the Christians, his lord the king of Spain, he received all this in his service, to be acknowledged at the proper time and occasion, and on behalf of the entire army and of himself he received it as a particular favor and benefit, never to be forgotten.

Besides these things, they spoke of others concerning that province and the surrounding ones. The Indian replied to all the governor's questions to the great satisfaction of her listeners, so that the Spaniards marveled to hear such sensible and well-chosen words, which showed the discretion of a barbarian, born and bred far from all instruction and civilized life. But natural good sense, wherever it may be, flourishes by itself without teaching, in discretion and gentility; and on the contrary stupidity becomes duller the more it is instructed.

Our Spaniards noted particularly that the Indians of this province and of the two that they had left behind were of a gentler disposition, more affable and less fierce, than any of the others whom they had encountered in this discovery. For in the other provinces, while they offered peace and maintained it, they were always suspicious and their gestures and words showed that their friendship was more feigned than real. This was not true of the people of Cofachiqui or those of Cofaqui and Cofa, which they had left behind, who acted as if they had spent their lives among the Spaniards. They were not only obedient to them, but they endeavored in all their actions and words to disclose and show the true affection that they felt for them, and they were gratified that people who had never seen them before should treat them with such familiarity.

XI

THE ARMY CROSSES THE RÍO COFACHIQUI AND LODGES IN THE PUEBLO, AND THEY SEND JUAN DE AÑASCO AFTER A WIDOW

While talking with the governor about the things that we have said, the lady of Cofachiqui was taking off, a little at a time, a great rope of pearls as large as hazelnuts that was wound three times around her neck and hung down to her thighs. Having been gradually removing them during all the time that the conversation lasted, she told Juan Ortiz, the interpreter (holding them in her hands), to take them and give them to the captain-general.

Juan Ortiz said for her ladyship to give them to him herself, for he would thus esteem them more. The Indian replied that she did not venture to do so, as not to go against the modesty that women ought to observe. The governor asked Juan Ortiz what the lady was saying, and when he heard it he said to him: "Tell her that I shall esteem more the favor of her giving them to me with her own hands than I value the jewels themselves, and that her doing so does not go against her modesty, for the matter concerns peace and friendship, things so admissible and important between unknown peoples." The lady, having heard Juan Ortiz, stood up to give the pearls to the governor with her own hands. He did likewise to receive them, and taking from his finger a gold ring that he wore, set with a very handsome ruby, he gave it to the lady as a sign of the peace and friendship that was brought about between them. The Indian received it very courteously and put it on one of her fingers. After this incident she asked leave and returned to her pueblo, and left our Castilians very gratified and charmed, both with her discretion and with her great beauty, which she had in extreme perfection. They were so enthralled with her that neither then nor later did they think to ask her name, but contented themselves with calling her Señora, and in this they were justified because she was so in all respects. Since they did not know her name, I cannot give it here; there were many such oversights in this respect and others in the course of this discovery.

The governor remained on the riverbank to supervise the immediate crossing of the army. He sent to order the maese de campo to bring the men to the place where he was as quickly as possible. Meanwhile the Indians constructed large rafts and brought many canoes, and with their efforts and those of the Castilians they crossed the river in the course of the next day; though with misfortune and loss, for through the carelessness of some officials who were supervising the passage of the men four horses were drowned. Since they were so necessary and so important to the men, our Spaniards regretted it more than if their own brothers had died.

Alonso de Carmona says that seven horses were drowned, and that it was the fault of their masters who drove them into the water very precipitately without knowing where they ought to cross, and that when they reached a certain part of the river they sank and did not reappear. It might have been a strong whirlpool that sucked them in and swallowed them up. Having crossed the river, the army was quartered in the half of the pueblo that the Indians had given up to them, and for those who found no room there they made large new arbors, because there was plenty of very good timber with which to construct them. Among the arbors were many different kinds of fruit trees, particularly mulberries, which were larger and more luxuriant than any they had seen hitherto. We always take particular note of this tree because of its beauty and its usefulness for [producing] silk, which ought to make it valuable everywhere.

On the following day the governor took steps to inform himself concerning the nature and the various parts of that province called Cofachiqui. He found that it was fertile for anything that they might desire to plant, sow, and breed in it. He also learned that the mother of the lady of that province, being a widow, had retired to a place twelve leagues away. He made arrangements with the daughter to send for her, and she dispatched twelve principal Indians to request her to come to visit the governor and see a people never seen before, who brought some strange animals.

The widow was unwilling to come with the Indians; rather when she learned what her daughter had done with the Castilians she was much disturbed and grieved at the daughter's imprudence in having consented so quickly and easily to show herself to the Spaniards, a people whom she herself said had never been seen or heard of before. She quarreled bitterly with the ambassadors for having consented to it, and also did and said many other extreme things such as prudish widows are accustomed to do.

When the governor heard all this he ordered the accountant Juan de Añasco that, since he was adept at such things, he go by land down the river with thirty infantry to a place withdrawn from the vicinity of the other pueblos, where they had told him the *señora* widow was, and bring her back in an entirely peaceful and friendly manner, because he desired that all the land he discovered and left behind him should remain quiet and pacified and devoted to him without any opposition, so that there would be less to pacify when it should be settled.

Although it was now well into the day, Juan de Añasco set out at once on foot with his thirty companions, and besides some Indian servants, he took with him an Indian noble whom the lady of the pueblo gave him of her own accord as a guide. When they should approach the place where her mother was, he was to go on ahead and advise her that the Spaniards were coming to entreat her to come back willingly with them, and say that she and all her vassals begged her to do the same thing.

The widowed mother of the lady of Cofachiqui had brought up this young noble with her own hands, for which reason and because he was a near relative, and chiefly because the youth had grown up with an affable and most noble disposition, she loved him more than if he had been her own son. Therefore the daughter sent him on this embassy to her mother so that the message might vex her less because of her love for the messenger.

The Indian showed clearly in the aspect of his countenance and in his bearing his noble blood and generous spirit; where the one is the other must be also, for they are united like the fruit and the tree. He had a handsome face and a graceful body, and was twenty or twenty-one years old. He was very elegantly attired, as befitted an ambassador on such a mission, and wore on his head a large plume made of a pleasing combination of varicolored feathers that added to his gracefulness, and a mantle of fine deerskins in the place of a cape. In the summer, because of the heat, they do not use pelts; or if they do sometimes wear them, it is with the fur on the outside. He carried a most handsome bow in his hands, which besides being good and strong had been given a coating of something that looked like fine enamel, which these Indians of La Florida use on them, of whatever color they like, and it gives the bow or any other wood a glaze like crockery. On his shoulder he carried his quiver of arrows. The Indian went with all this ornate equipment, and he was so willing to accompany the Spaniards that his desire to serve and please them was plainly seen.

XII

THE INDIAN AMBASSADOR CUTS HIS THROAT, AND JUAN DE AÑASCO PROCEEDS ON HIS MARCH

Captain Juan de Añasco and his thirty gentlemen, having marched almost three leagues on their way in the manner that we have said, stopped to eat and to rest for a while in the shade of some large trees, because it was very hot. The Indian noble who was accompanying them as ambassador, having gone up to that time very happily and joyfully, entertaining the Spaniards all along the road by telling them what they asked him about the things of his country and of the surrounding ones, began to show sadness and fell to pondering with his hand on his cheek. He gave some long and profound sighs, which our men noticed well enough, though they did not ask him the reason for his sadness in order not to trouble him more than he was already.

Seated as he was in the midst of the Spaniards, the Indian took his quiver and, placing it in front of him, drew out very slowly, one by one, the arrows that were in it, which were admirable for the refinement and skill that had gone into their making. They were all made of reeds; some had heads made of the points of deer's antlers finished to extreme perfection, with four corners like the points of a diamond; others had fish bones for heads, marvelously fashioned for use as arrows. There were others with heads of palm wood and of other strange and durable timber that grows in that country. These arrowheads had two or three barbs as perfectly made in the wood as if they had been of iron or steel. In short, all the arrows were so exquisite, each one in itself, that they invited those nearby to take them up in their hands and enjoy examining them closely. Captain Juan de Añasco and each of his companions took up one to look at it, and all of them praised the skill and deftness of the maker. They noted particularly that they were feathered in triangular form so that they would leave the bow better. In short, each one had a new and different curiosity that embellished it separately.

What we have said about the arrows of this nobleman is not an exaggeration; rather, we have fallen short in a description of them, because all the Indians of La Florida, and especially the nobles, take the greatest pride in the beauty and elegance of their bows and arrows. Those they make for their adornment and carry every day, they fashion with the greatest possible nicety, each one striving to outdo the others with new inventions or greater elegance, so that it is a very gallant and honorable contest and rivalry that continually goes on among them. The many arrows that they make as munitions to expend in war are common and worthless, though in case of necessity they make use of all of them, not distinguishing between the fine and the ordinary, or the valuable and the worthless.

The Indian ambassador, who as we said was taking his arrows out of the quiver one at a time, drew out, almost among the last ones, one that had a flint head fashioned like the point and blade of a dagger, about six inches long. Seeing that the Castilians were inattentive and absorbed in looking at his arrows, he gashed his throat with it so that he was decapitated [*se degollo;* decapitated or slashed in the throat—DB] and immediately fell dead.

The Spaniards were amazed at such a strange event and grieved at not having been able to save him. Desiring to know the reason for that fatality and for his having killed himself in such sorrow after having been so happy and joyous a short time before, they called the Indian servants whom they had brought with them and asked whether they knew why he did it. With many tears and much sorrow at the death of their chief, because of the love that they all had for him, and because they knew how his sad death would grieve their mistresses, both mother and daughter, they said that so far as they could tell there could have been no other reason except that that noble had been seized with the idea that the embassy he was performing was against the pleasure and will of his elder lady. For it was well known that when they had sent her the first ambassadors she had been unwilling to come to see the Castilians, and now in guiding and conducting the same Spaniards to the place where she was, so that they might bring her, willingly or by force, he was not acting in accordance with her love for him or the upbringing that she had given him as mother and lady. Besides this he would have known that if he did not do what his young lady ordered him, which was to guide the Spaniards and carry the message (now that he had so thoughtlessly undertaken to do it), he would fall into disgrace with her and be dismissed from her service. The Indians affirmed that either of the two offenses, whether against the mother or the daughter, would have been more grievous to him than death itself. Seeing himself, then, in this dilemma, and being unable to get out of it without offending one of his ladies, he had wished to show both of them his desire to serve and please them, and in order not to do otherwise (having already fallen into one error and wishing to avoid a second) he had chosen death as preferable to angering either of them, and thus he had inflicted it with his own hands. The Indians said that they believed that this and nothing else had caused the death of that poor gentleman, and their conjecture seemed to the Spaniards not to be a bad one.

Juan de Añasco and his thirty companions, though grieved at the death of their guide, proceeded on their way and that afternoon marched three leagues along the road that they had followed up to that time, which was the public highway. In order to go on, they asked the Indians the next day whether they knew where and how far away the señora widow was. They answered that certainly they did not know, because the dead Indian held the secret of her dwelling, but that they would endeavor to guide them wherever they ordered them. The Castilians went on with their journey in all this confusion, and having marched almost four leagues, it now being nearly noon and the sun being extremely hot, they saw some Indians. They set an ambush and captured a man and three women, all who were there, from whom they attempted to learn the widow's whereabouts. The Indians replied readily that they had heard that she had withdrawn still farther away from where she had first been, but they did not know where, and that if they [the Spaniards] wished to take them along, they would ask about her on the way of the Indians whom they might meet along the road. It might be that she was near and it might be that she was far away. This is an expression from the common language of El Perú.

XIII

JUAN DE AÑASCO RETURNS TO THE ARMY WITHOUT THE WIDOW, AND THE FACTS CONCERNING THE GOLD AND SILVER OF COFACHIQUI

When they heard what the Indians said our Spaniards were doubtful as to what they ought to do, and after many different opinions had been advanced about it one of the companions said, more advisedly: "Gentlemen, it seems to me for many reasons that we are not proceeding very judiciously on this journey, for since this woman was unwilling to come with the principal Indians who took her the first message, but rather showed her displeasure at it, I do not know how she will receive ours. It is clear to us already that she is unwilling to go where the governor is, and it may be that, knowing that we are going to oblige her to do so by force, she would have men prepared to defend her and also to attack us. Whatever she intends to do, we are not in a position to oppose her or to defend ourselves and return safely because we have brought no horses, which are what put fear into the Indians. For the purposes of our discovery and conquest, I do not see that a widow in her solitary retreat is of such importance that we should have to risk the lives of all of us who are here to bring her out, without needing her, since we have her daughter, who is the ruler of the province, with whom to negotiate and arrange whatever may be necessary. Furthermore, we do not know the road nor what lies between us and that place, nor do we have a guide on whom we can depend; also the very unexpected suicide yesterday of the ambassador whom we were bringing warns us to be cautious, for it must have a bearing on some of the things that I have mentioned. Aside from these inconveniences (he said, turning to the captain), we see that you are fatigued both from the weight of the heavy armor that you are wearing and from the excessive heat of the sun, as well as because of your corpulence, for you are a very stout man. All these reasons not only persuade us but force us to go back peaceably."

What their companion said seemed reasonable to all the others, and by common consent they returned to the camp and reported to the governor everything that had happened to them on the road.

Three days later an Indian offered to guide the Castilians down the river and take them by water to the place where the mother of the lady of the pueblo was, and thus with the approval and consent of the daughter, Juan de

Añasco returned to his quest, and with him went twenty Spaniards in two canoes. On the first day of their navigation they found the four drowned horses lodged against a large fallen tree, and grieving for them anew, they proceeded on their voyage. Having done everything they could, they returned at the end of six days with news that the good old woman, having heard that the Christians had come after her on two occasions, had gone farther into the country and hidden herself in some high mountains where she was out of reach. Therefore the governor left her alone and took no further notice of her.

While the things that we have told were happening to Captain Juan de Añasco in the country, the governor and his people were not resting in the settlements, for they still held the hope that had been with them for so long that they would find much gold and silver and many precious pearls in this province of Cofachiqui. Desiring, then, to see themselves rich and free from this anxiety of mind, a few days after their arrival in the province they busied themselves in making inquiries about it. They summoned the two Indian youths who had told them in Apalache about the wealth of this province of Cofachiqui, and at the governor's order they spoke with the lady of the pueblo and asked her to order brought some of these metals that the merchants, whose servants they had been, were accustomed to buy in her country to take and sell in other places. These were the same ones that the Castilians were seeking.

The lady ordered to be brought at once [the metals] that were in her country of the colors that the Spaniards wanted, which were yellow and white, because they showed her gold rings and pieces of silver, and they had also asked her for pearls and stones such as those they had in the rings. At their lady's order, the Indians brought promptly a large quantity of copper of a very resplendent golden color, surpassing that of our brass,[16] so that the Indian servants of the merchants might very well have been deceived into thinking that that metal and the one the Castilians showed them were the same, because they did not know the difference between brass and gold.

In the place of silver, they brought some large slabs as thick as boards that were of an iron pyrite [rather, probably mica—VJK], and from the information they gave me I will not be able to describe them now as they really were,

---

[16]Native copper, cold-hammered into sheets and fashioned into a variety of decorative goods, was a premier wealth item among the Mississippian cultures. Here Garcilaso distinguishes between copper and brass (*azófar*), but hereinafter, when he says brass, the reader will infer copper.

except that at first sight they were white and shone like silver, and on taking them in the hands, though they were a vara in length and the same in width, they weighed almost nothing, and when handled they fell apart like a clod of dry earth.

As for precious stones, the lady said that in her country there were only pearls and that, if they wanted them, they might go to the upper part of the pueblo; and, pointing with her finger, she showed them a temple that was there (within sight) of the size of ordinary ones that we have here, and said: "That house is the burial place of the nobles of this pueblo, where you will find large and small pearls and many seed pearls. Take as many as you like, and if you still want more, one league from here is a pueblo that is the house and seat of my ancestors and the capital of our state; in it is another temple larger than this one, which is the burial place of my predecessors. There you will find so many seed pearls and pearls that, although you should load all your horses and as many of yourselves as may go there with them, you could not exhaust all that are in the temple. Take all of them, and if you still need more, we can get more every day from the pearl fisheries in my country."

With this good news and with the lady's munificence, our Spaniards consoled themselves somewhat for having been deceived in their hopes of the much gold and silver that they had thought to find in this province, though it is true that there were many Spaniards who persisted in saying that the copper or brass had quite a large admixture of gold. But since they had brought no nitric acid or metal filings, they could not make tests either to undeceive themselves entirely or to gain new and more definite hope.

XIV

THE SPANIARDS VISIT THE BURIAL PLACE OF THE NOBLES OF COFACHIQUI, AND THAT OF THE CURACAS

They waited to see the pearls and the seed pearls that were in the temple until the accountant and captain Juan de Añasco should come back from his second expedition; and meanwhile the governor ordered persons whom he could trust to guard the temple, and he himself made the rounds at night, so that no one would be impelled by greed at what he had heard to go out of turn and attempt to take away secretly the best of what was in the temple or burial place. As soon as the accountant came, the governor and the other officials of the imperial hacienda and thirty other gentlemen, including the captains and principal soldiers, went to see the pearls and the other things that were there.[17] They found that against all four walls of the house were wooden chests made in the same way as those of Spain, lacking only hinges and locks. The Castilians wondered that the Indians, having no tools like the workmen of Europe, could make them so well. In these chests, which were placed on benches half a vara high, they put the bodies of their dead, with no more preservatives from corruption than if they had placed them in underground sepulchers. The stench of the bodies while they were decaying did not trouble them because these temples served them only as charnel houses where they kept dead bodies, and they did not enter them to make sacrifices or to pray, for as we said at the beginning they live without such ceremonies. We shall say no more about this temple so as not to repeat ourselves [when we describe] that of the *señores curacas* (which we shall see and describe soon).

Besides the large coffers that served as sepulchers they had other smaller ones in which, and in some large baskets woven of reed—which the Indians of La Florida use with great artifice and subtlety for everything they desire to make of it, as they use wicker in Spain—there were great quantities of pearls and seed pearls and much clothing of both men and women, of the kind in which they dress, which is made of deerskins and other pelts. They dress these very skillfully with the hair on them, and use them for lining the clothing of princes and great lords. In our Spain they would be valued at large amounts.

The governor and his men rejoiced greatly at seeing so much wealth all together, because they were all of the opinion that there were more than a thousand arrobas of pearls and seed pearls. The officials of the real hacienda being provided with a steelyard [*Romana;* a Roman balance], in a short time they weighed twenty arrobas of pearls, while the governor left them to see

[17]John R. Swanton has given careful consideration to the ethnographic veracity of Garcilaso's lengthy and grandiose description of the temple at Talomeco, contained in this and the following chapters. Much is certainly exaggerated, as in the quantity of pearls discovered, the fifty thousand bows, the size of the structure and storehouses, and the size and character of the guardian images. Nonetheless many of the particulars are corroborated by independent accounts of other native Southeastern temples. Swanton concludes that "the description of this temple . . . represents an attempt to tell a straightforward story and contains material of value to the ethnologist and the archaeologist." Swanton, "Ethnological Value of the De Soto Narratives," 578–87.

what else was in the house. Returning to the officials, he told them that they would not be able to burden themselves with loads so useless and embarrassing to the army, and that his intention had been simply to take two arrobas of pearls and seed pearls, and no more, to send to La Havana as a sample of their quality and size; as for the quantity, he said that they would have to believe what they would write them about it. Therefore they were to put them back where they got them and take only the two arrobas. The officials begged him, saying that since they were already weighed out and could scarcely be missed from the amount that remained, he ought to allow them to take them, so that the evidence would be more abundant and rich. The governor agreed to it, and he himself, taking up the pearls by the double handfuls, gave one to each of the captains and soldiers who had come with him, telling them to make rosaries of them with which to say their prayers. And the pearls were fit to use for rosaries because they were the size of large chick-peas.

The Castilians left that burial house without doing any more damage than we have said, and were more desirous than ever of seeing the one that the lady had told them was that of her fathers and grandfathers. Two days later the general and the officials and other captains and chief soldiers went to it, thirty Spaniards in all. They marched a long league, all of which had the appearance of a garden, where there were many trees, fruit-bearing and others; and one could pass between them on horseback without any inconvenience because they were separated from one another as if they had been set out by hand.

The Spaniards traveled all that long league scattered through the country gathering fruit and noting the fertility of the soil. Thus they came to the pueblo called Talomeco, which was situated on an elevation overlooking the steep bank of the river. It had five hundred houses, all large and of better materials and workmanship than the ordinary ones. From its arrangement, it seemed to be the seat and court of a powerful ruler, having been constructed with more meticulousness and ornamentation than the other, ordinary pueblos. The houses of the ruler could be seen from a distance, because they were on the highest point and showed themselves to be his by their superiority to the others in size and construction.

In the middle of the pueblo, facing the lord's houses, was the temple or charnel house the Spaniards were coming to see. It contained things admirable for their grandeur, richness, rarity, and majesty, curiously made and arranged, which I would like much to be able to describe as my author desired them to be. Accept my willingness, and what I cannot say will remain for the contemplation of the judicious, whose discretion will supply what my pen is unable to write. For certainly (particularly at this point and at others as important that will be found in the *History*) our picture falls far short of their grandeur and of what would be required to describe them as they were. Thus ten and ten times (a phrase from the language of El Perú, meaning many times) I shall beg earnestly that it be believed that what has been said is an incomplete and fragmentary account, rather than an exaggerated one.

XV

AN ACCOUNT OF THE WONDERS FOUND IN THE TEMPLE AND BURIAL PLACE OF THE LORDS OF COFACHIQUI

The Castilians found the pueblo of Talomeco entirely deserted because the recent pestilence had been more severe and cruel there than in any other pueblo in the whole province, and the few Indians who escaped it had not yet been returned to their houses. Thus our men stopped only a short time in them until they came to the temple. It was large, being more than a hundred paces long and forty wide; the walls were high in keeping with the size of the room, and the roof was very high and steeply pitched, for since they did not have the invention of tiles it was necessary for them to build very steep roofs so that the rain would not come into the houses. The roof of this temple apparently was made of reeds and slender stalks of cane split in half lengthwise, from which these Indians make very nicely finished and well-woven mats similar to the Moorish mats. By placing four, five or six of these on top of each other, they make a roof that is beautiful within and without and very effective, keeping out both sun and rain. From this province on, the Indians for the most part do not use straw for roofing and covering their houses, but mats of cane.

On the roof of the temple there had been placed many shells of various marine animals arranged according to their size, from large to small ones. It is not known how they came to be so far inland, though perhaps they also are found in the rivers flowing through that country, which are so many and so large. The shells were placed with the inner side on top because of its greater luster. Among them there were also many periwinkles, extraordinarily large. There were spaces between the shells and the periwinkles, for they were all arranged in regular order. In those spaces were large skeins made of strings of pearls and seed pearls half a fathom long that were spread out on the roof, descending gradually, one string beginning where another left off. With the sun reflected on them they made a beautiful sight. The temple was covered with all these things on the outside.

To go inside, the Spaniards opened some large doors whose size was proportionate to the rest of the temple. Near the door were twelve giant figures carved from wood, such faithful imitations of life and with such a fierce and bold posture that the Castilians stayed to look at them for a long time without passing on, marveling to find in such a barbarous country works that, if they had been in the most famous temples of Rome in the most flourishing period of its power and empire, would have been esteemed and valued for their grandeur and perfection. The giants were placed as if to guard the door and oppose the entrance of those who might enter.

There were six on one side of the door and six on the other, one after the other, descending gradually in size from the largest to the smallest. The first were four varas high, the second somewhat less, and so on to the last.

They had various weapons in their hands made in proportion to the size of their bodies. The first two on each side, which were the largest, each held clubs the last quarter of which were embellished with diamond-shaped points and bands made of that copper [already mentioned]. They were so exactly like those clubs that are described as belonging to Hercules that it seemed that either might have been copied from the other. The giants held their clubs aloft with both hands, with such a fierce and bold aspect (as if threatening to strike anyone who entered the door) that it inspired terror.

The second on either side (this was the order in which they were all placed) had broadswords made of wood in the same form that they make them in Spain of iron and steel. The third had sticks, different from the clubs, that resembled the swingles used to beat flax, a fathom and a half long, the first two-thirds being thick and the last gradually becoming narrower and having a shovel-shaped end. The fourth in order had large battle-axes corresponding in size to the stature of the giants. One of them had a brass head, the blade being large and very well made and the other end having a four-sided point a handbreadth in length. The other axe had a head exactly like this, with its blade and point, but for greater variety and curiosity it was made of flint.

The fifth in order carried bows as long as their bodies, bent and with the arrows in place as if ready to shoot. The bows and arrows were fashioned with all the extreme care and perfection these Indians employ in their mak-

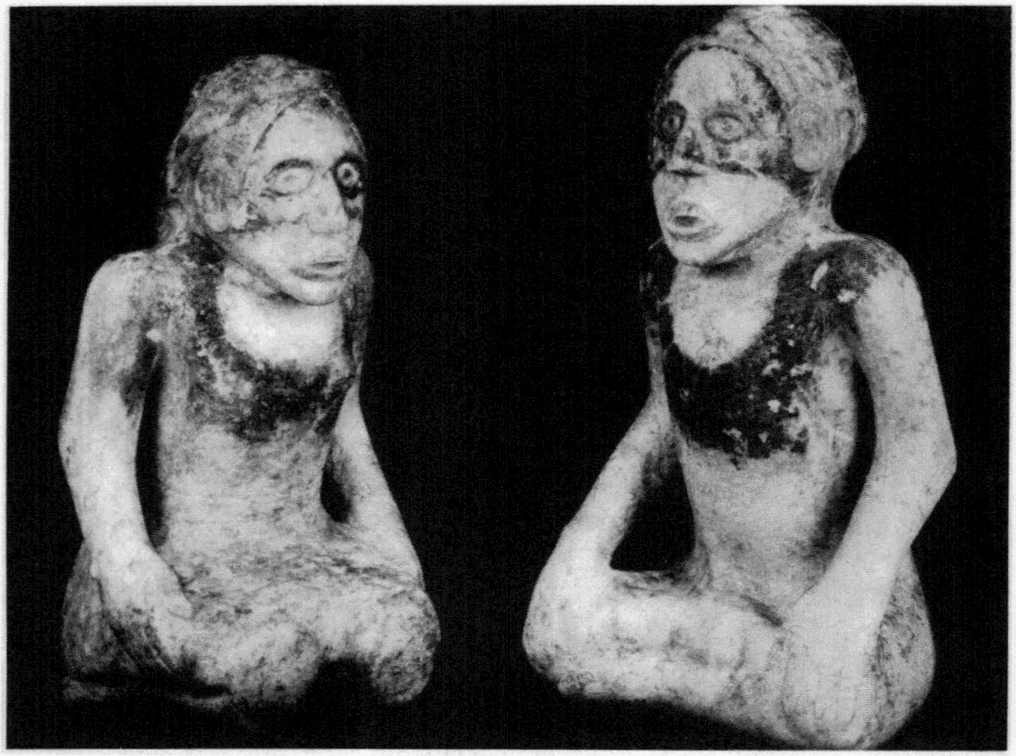

Mississippian Ancestor Figurines. When raiding the temple at Talomeco, according to the Garcilaso and Cañete accounts, De Soto's men saw human statues, perhaps similar to these examples of painted marble from a Mississippian mortuary temple site in northern Georgia. Made of either wood or stone, such kneeling or sitting figurines seem to represent the deified ancestors of the chief. (Courtesy of Etowah Mounds State Historic Site, operated by Georgia State Parks and Historic Sites Division)

ing. The head of one of the arrows was made of the tip of a deer antler carved into four points; the other arrow had a flint point for a head, the same shape and size as an ordinary dagger.

The sixth and last figures had very large and handsome pikes with copper heads. All of them, like the first ones, seemed to be threatening to wound with their weapons those who might want to enter the door. Some were ready to strike downward from above, like those with the clubs; others, as those with the broadswords and pikes, were ready to stab; others, as those with the axes, to hack; others, as the ones with the sticks, to give a diagonal stroke from left to right; and the archers threatened to shoot from a distance. Each of them was in the boldest and fiercest posture required by the weapon that he held in his hands, and this was what most amazed the Spaniards, seeing how natural and true to life they were in every respect.

The upper part of the temple above the walls was adorned like the roof outside with periwinkles and shells arranged in order, with skeins between them made of strings of pearls and seed pearls hanging from the roof, which kept to and followed its design. Among the strings of pearls, periwinkles, and shells on the roof were large plumes of multicolored feathers like those that they make for their own adornment. Besides the strings of pearls and seed pearls hanging from the roof, and the plumes thrust into it, there were many other plumes and strings of seed pearls and pearls hanging from thin threads of an indeterminate color, which, being invisible, made it appear that the pearl tassels and plumes were suspended in the air, some higher than others, giving the effect of falling from the roof. Such was the adornment of the upper part of the temple above the walls, and it was a pleasing thing to see.

XVI

A FURTHER DESCRIPTION OF THE RICHNESS OF THE BURIAL PLACE, AND THE DEPOSITORY OF ARMS THAT WAS IN IT

Lowering their eyes from the roof, our captains and soldiers saw that along the highest part of the four walls of the temple were two rows, one above the other, of statues of figures of men and women corresponding in size to the ordinary stature of the people of that country, who are as large as

Philistines. Each was set on its own base or pedestal, near one another, and they served no other purpose except to ornament the walls, so that the upper part of them would not be bare and uncovered. The figures of the men had various weapons in their hands, all those that we have named elsewhere. These were adorned with circles of pearls and seed pearls, each one made of four, five, or six loops, and for further embellishment they had at intervals borders of threads of exquisite colors, for these Indians make any thing they like extremely well. The statues of the women had nothing in their hands.

On the floor against the walls, on very well-made wooden benches, as was everything in the temple, were the chests that served as sepulchers, in which were the bodies of the curacas who had been lords of that province of Cofachiqui, and of their sons and brothers and nephews, the sons of their brothers. No others were buried in that temple.

The chests were well covered with their lids. Exactly one vara above each chest was a statue carved from wood, against the wall on its pedestal. This was a portrait taken while living of the deceased man or woman who was in the chest, at the age at which they died. The portraits served as a record and memorial of their ancestors. The statues of the men had weapons in their hands, but those of the children and women had nothing.

The space on the walls between the portraits of the dead and the statues on the upper part was covered with round and oblong shields, large and small, made of cane so strongly woven that they could turn a dart shot from a crossbow, though a harquebus-shot penetrated them more than did the dart. The oblong and round shields were interwoven with strings of pearls and seed pearls, and around the edges they had borders of colored threads that embellished them greatly.

On the floor of the temple, lengthwise, were placed on benches three rows of wooden chests, large and small, one on top of another. They were arranged in order so that the large ones came first, and on them other smaller ones, and then others still smaller; and in this manner four, five, or six chests were put one on top of another, rising from the largest to the smallest in the form of a pyramid. Between the various rows of chests were passages that went the length of the temple and crossed from one side to the other, by which one could walk all through the temple without any difficulty and see what was in each part of it.

All the large and small chests were full of pearls and seed pearls. The pearls were separated from one another according to size, the largest ones being in the first chests, those not quite so large in the second, and others still smaller in the third, and so on to the seed pearls, which were in the smallest chests on top. In all of these there were such quantities of seed pearls and pearls that with their own eyes the Spaniards confirmed the truth of the statement made by the lady of this temple and burial place, admitting that it was not a boast or an exaggeration, to the effect that although they all might load themselves, they being more than nine hundred men, and although they might load their horses, which numbered more than three hundred, they would be unable to take from the temple all the pearls and seed pearls that were in it. Such a quantity of pearls is no great cause for wonder, if it is considered that those Indians do not sell any of those that they find, but bring them all to their burial place, and that they have done so for many centuries. In making a comparison, it may be affirmed (since it is seen every year) that, if the gold and silver that has been brought and is being brought from El Perú to Spain had not been taken away from there, they could have covered many temples with roofs of silver and gold.

With the display and wealth of pearls that was in the temple there were also many and very large bundles of white deerskin and some tinted in various colors, and of this last each color was separate to itself. There were also large parcels of mantles of many colors, made of deerskin, and another large quantity of mantles of skins of all kinds of animals that are native to the country, large and small, dressed with the hair on them. There were many mantles made of the pelts of cats of different species and markings, and others of extremely fine marten-skins, all likewise dressed so perfectly that the best from Germany or Muscovy could not be better.

The temple was arranged with all these things in the manner and order that has been said, the roof, the walls, and the floor alike, each thing being placed with as much neatness and order as could be imagined of the most careful people in the world. It was all clean, without dust or cobwebs, from which it appeared that many people must have been engaged in the care and service of the temple, in cleaning and putting everything in its place.

Around the temple were eight rooms, separated from one another and placed regularly and in order. Apparently they were annexes of the temple for its embellishment and service. The governor and the other gentlemen wanted to see what was in them, and found that they were all full of arms arranged in the manner that we shall tell. The first room they happened to see was full of pikes, there being nothing else in it. All were very long and very well made, with heads of brass, which, because it was so highly colored, looked like gold. All were adorned with rings of pearls and seed pearls having three or four turns, placed at intervals along the pikes. Many were covered in the middle (where they would rest on the shoulder and where the head joined the haft) with strips of colored deerskin, and along both the upper and lower edges of this strip were borders of varicolored threads with three, four, five, or six rows of pearls or seed pearls that embellished them greatly.

In the second room there were only clubs such as those that we said the first giant figures held, which were at the door of the temple; except that those in the room, being arms that were among the lord's equipment, were decorated with rings of pearls and seed pearls and borders of colored thread placed at intervals so that the colors were blended with one another and all were intermingled with the pearls. The other pikes [clubs?] that the giants held had no ornamentation whatever.

In another room, which was the third, there was nothing but axes like those we said the giants had who were fourth in order at the door of the temple. They had copper heads with a blade on one side and a diamond-shaped point on the other, six inches and a hand's breadth long [respectively]. Many of them had flint heads fastened solidly to the handles with copper bands. These axes also had on their handles rings of pearls and seed pearls and borders of colored thread.

In another room, which was the fourth, there were broadswords made of various kinds of hardwoods such as those that the giants second in order had, all of them being decorated with pearls and seed pearls and borders on the handles and on the first third of the blades.

The fifth room contained only staffs such as those we said the giants of the third order had, but decorated with their rings of pearls and seed pearls and colored borders all along the handles to where the shovel-shaped end began. We shall tell the rest in the following chapter, so that this one may not be disproportionately longer than the others.

XVII

THE ARMY LEAVES COFACHIQUI IN TWO DIVISIONS

In the sixth room there was nothing except bows and arrows wrought in all the extreme perfection and care with which they make them. For arrowheads, they used points of wood, of the bones of land and sea animals, and of flint, as we told in connection with the Indian noble who killed himself. Besides these kinds of arrowheads made of copper, such as those they put on darts in Spain, there were others with harpoons, also made of copper, and in the form of small chisels, lances, and Moorish darts, which looked as if they had been made in Castilla. They noted also that the arrows with flint tips had different kinds of heads; some were in the form of a harpoon, others of small chisels, others were rounded like a punch, and others had two edges like the tip of a dagger. The Spaniards examined all these curiously and wondered how they could fashion such things out of a material as resistant as flint, though in view of what Mexican history says about the broadswords and other arms that the Indians of that land made of flint, a part of this wonderment of ours will be lost. The bows were handsomely made and enameled in various colors, which they do with a certain cement that gives them such a luster that one can see himself in them. In speaking of this temple, Juan Coles says the following: "And in one apartment there were more than fifty thousand bows with their cases or quivers full of arrows."

Not satisfied with this lustrous finish, they put on the bows many circles of pearls and seed pearls placed at intervals, these circles or rings beginning at the handles and going in order to the tips in such manner that the first circles were of large pearls and made seven or eight turns, the second were of smaller pearls and had fewer turns, and thus they went on decreasing to the last ones, which were near the tips and were of very small seed pearls. The arrows also had circles of seed pearls at intervals, but not of pearls, there being seed pearls only.

In the seventh room there were large numbers of round shields made of wood and of cowhide [buffalo-hide], both brought from distant countries. All were decorated with pearls and seed pearls and borders of colored threads.

In the eighth room there were a great many oblong shields, all made of cane very skillfully woven and so strong that the Spaniards had very few crossbows that could send a dart clear through them, as was experienced in other places outside of Cofachiqui. The oblong shields, like the round ones, were decorated with a network of seed pearls and pearls and with colored borders.

The eight rooms were filled with all these offensive and defensive arms, and each one of them contained so many of the particular kind of arms that were in it that the governor and his Castilians marveled especially at their number, besides the neatness and perfection with which they were made and arranged in their order.

The general and his captains, having seen and noted the grandeur and sumptuousness of the temple and its riches, the multitude of the arms, and the elaboration and order with which everything was made and arranged, asked the Indians what was the significance of such ostentation and pomp. They replied that the lords of that kingdom, especially those of that province and of others that they would see beyond, regarded the ornateness and magnificence of their burial places as the greatest [sign of] their dignity, and thus they endeavored to embellish them with all the arms and wealth they could, as they had seen in that temple. Because this one was the richest and most superb of all those that our Spaniards saw in La Florida, I have seen fit to write of it at such length, and particularly of the things that were in it, and also because he who gave me the account ordered me to do so. For, as he said, it was among the grandest and most wonderful of all the things that he had seen in the New World, in having traveled over most and the best part of México and El Perú, though it is true that when he passed through those two kingdoms they had already been sacked of their most valuable wealth, and their chief grandeurs had been destroyed.

The officials of the imperial hacienda discussed taking the fifth of the pearls and seed pearls and the rest of the wealth in the temple that belonged to his Majesty's hacienda and carrying it with them. The governor told them that taking it would serve only to load the army down with useless burdens, when they could not carry even the necessary ones of their arms and munitions. They were to leave it all as it was, for at present they were not parceling out the land, but discovering it, and when they should distribute and settle it then he who received it by lot would pay the fifth. Thus they did not touch anything that they had seen, and they went back to where the lady was, having wonders to tell of the magnificence of her burial place.

All that has been said of the pueblo of Cofachiqui, Alonso de Carmona tells in his *Relation,* though not at such length as our *History.* He speaks particularly, however, of the province and of the reception the lady gave the governor on crossing the river, and says that she and her ladies all wore long strings of large pearls around their necks and fastened to their wrists, and that the men wore them only around their necks. He says also that the pearls lost much of their beauty and fine luster by being taken out [of the shells] with fire, which made them black. He says that, in the pueblo of Talomeco where the burial place and rich temple was, they found four long houses full of bodies of those who died from the plague that had raged there; thus far Alonso de Carmona.

The adelantado spent another ten days after having seen the temple in informing himself of what was in the rest of the provinces that bordered upon that of Cofachiqui, and he heard that all of them were fertile and abounded in food and were inhabited by many people. Having learned these things, he ordered preparations made for continuing his discoveries, and, accompanied by his captains, he took leave of the Indian lady of Cofachiqui and of the principal men of the pueblo, thanking them heartily for the courtesy that they had shown him, and thus he left them friendly and well disposed toward the Spaniards.

The army left the pueblo in two divisions, because they did not have enough provisions to go all together. The general therefore ordered that Baltasar de Gallegos, Arias Tinoco, and Gonzalo Silvestre, with a hundred cavalry and two hundred infantry, go to a place twelve leagues from there where the lady had a storehouse containing six hundred fanegas of maize, which she had offered to give them. Taking as much maize as they could carry, they were to go to meet the governor, who would march by way of the public highway to the province of Chalaque, which was the one that bordered upon Cofachiqui on that side. With this order the three captains set out with the three hundred soldiers, and the governor with the rest of the army. After eight days' journey, which they made by way of the public highway, the latter reached the province of Chalaque, without anything worth mentioning having happened to them on the way.

The three captains had something to report, and this was that, having arrived at the storehouse, they took two hundred fanegas of Indian corn, being unable to carry more, and directed their march toward the public highway by which the governor was proceeding. On the fifth day of their march they reached the main highway, and by the signs that the army had left they saw that the general had passed and was going on ahead of them. Thereupon the two hundred foot soldiers rose up and demanded to march as rapidly as possible, in disobedience to their captains, until they overtook the general, because they said that they were carrying little food and did not know how many days they would take in reaching the governor, and thus it would be well to hasten while they could and overtake him as soon as possible before their provisions gave out and they died of hunger. The soldiers said this out of fear of what had happened to them in the wilderness before they reached the province of Cofachiqui.

XVIII

THE EXPERIENCES THAT THE THREE CAPTAINS HAD ON THEIR JOURNEY, AND HOW THE ARMY REACHED XUALA

The captains were troubled at the attempted mutiny of the infantry because they had three horses sick from a colic that had attacked them the day before, which prevented their traveling as rapidly as the foot soldiers desired. Thus they told them that one day more or less of marching was not sufficient reason for abandoning three horses, for they knew what an advantage and help they were against the enemy. The infantry replied, saying that the lives of three hundred Castilians were more important than the health of three horses, and that they did not know whether the march would last one day, or ten or twenty or a hundred, and that it was reasonable to have regard for the more important things and not for those of such little concern. So saying, being now mutinous, they began to march as rapidly as they could, without orders. The three captains stationed themselves in front of them, and one of them in the name of all said to them: "Gentlemen, observe that you are going to your captain-general, who as you know is a man so punctilious in affairs of war that he will be much grieved at learning of your disobedience, and of your nonobservance of commands and orders. It is probable, as I myself believe, that we shall overtake him today or tomorrow, or the next day at the latest, for it is not to be expected that he will make such haste when we are behind him. This being so, we shall have incurred much disgrace and dishonor, that without having suffered extreme necessity and simply through excessive fear of possible scarcity of food, we shall commit the weakness of abandoning three horses, which are so valuable. You know that they are the nerve and the strength of our army, and that because of them enemies fear us and friends do us honor. And inasmuch as when they kill one of them it is so regretted and mourned, how much more deplorable it will be for us to abandon and lose three horses through our own weakness and cowardice, without any necessity whatever except those we imagine. The most lamentable thing that I see in the whole matter is the loss of your reputations and ours, for the general and the other captains and soldiers will say with much justification that in the four days that we were away from them we did not know how to command or you how to obey. But when it shall be known how the thing happened, they will see that you were wholly to blame and that we were not obligated except to persuade you with reasonable arguments. Therefore, gentlemen, desist from doing such an ill-advised thing; it will be more honorable for us to die like good soldiers in the performance of our duty than to live in infamy for having fled from an imaginary danger."

The foot soldiers were placated at these words, and they shortened their daily marches, but not so much that they failed to travel five or six leagues [each day], which was as far as the sick horses could go.

On the day after the mutiny died down these soldiers were marching along at midday when suddenly a great tempest of strong contrary winds blew up, with much lightning and thunder, and quantities of large hailstones that fell upon them, so that if there had not happened to be some large walnut trees near the road and some other dense trees under which they took shelter, they would have perished, for the largest of the hailstones were the size of a hen egg and the smallest were the size of a nut. The rodeleros held their shields over their heads, but even so when the stones struck an unprotected part of their bodies they hurt them badly. It was God's will that the storm should last only a short time; if it had been longer the shelter they had taken would not have been enough to save their lives, and short as it had been they were so battered that they could not march that day or the next. On the third day they proceeded on their way and came to some small pueblos, whose inhabitants had not dared await the governor in their houses and had fled to the woods. Only the old men and women remained, almost all of them being blind. These pueblos were called Chalaques.

Three days' march after leaving the pueblos of Chalaques they reached the governor in a beautiful valley of a province called Xuala, where he had arrived two days before and had awaited the captains and the three hundred soldiers, being unwilling to pass on.

From the pueblo of Cofachiqui where the lady remained to the first valley of the province of Xuala, by the road these Castilians took, it was about fifty leagues, more or less, all of it through a level and pleasant country with small rivers flowing through it at a distance of three or four leagues from one another. They saw few mountains, and these had much grass for cattle and were easy to traverse on foot or on horseback. The whole fifty leagues generally, both that which they found inhabited and cultivated and that which was uncultivated and fit for tillage, had good soil.

The whole distance traveled from the province of Apalache to that of Xuala where we found the governor and his army was (if I have not miscounted) fifty-seven daily journeys. The march was generally northeast,

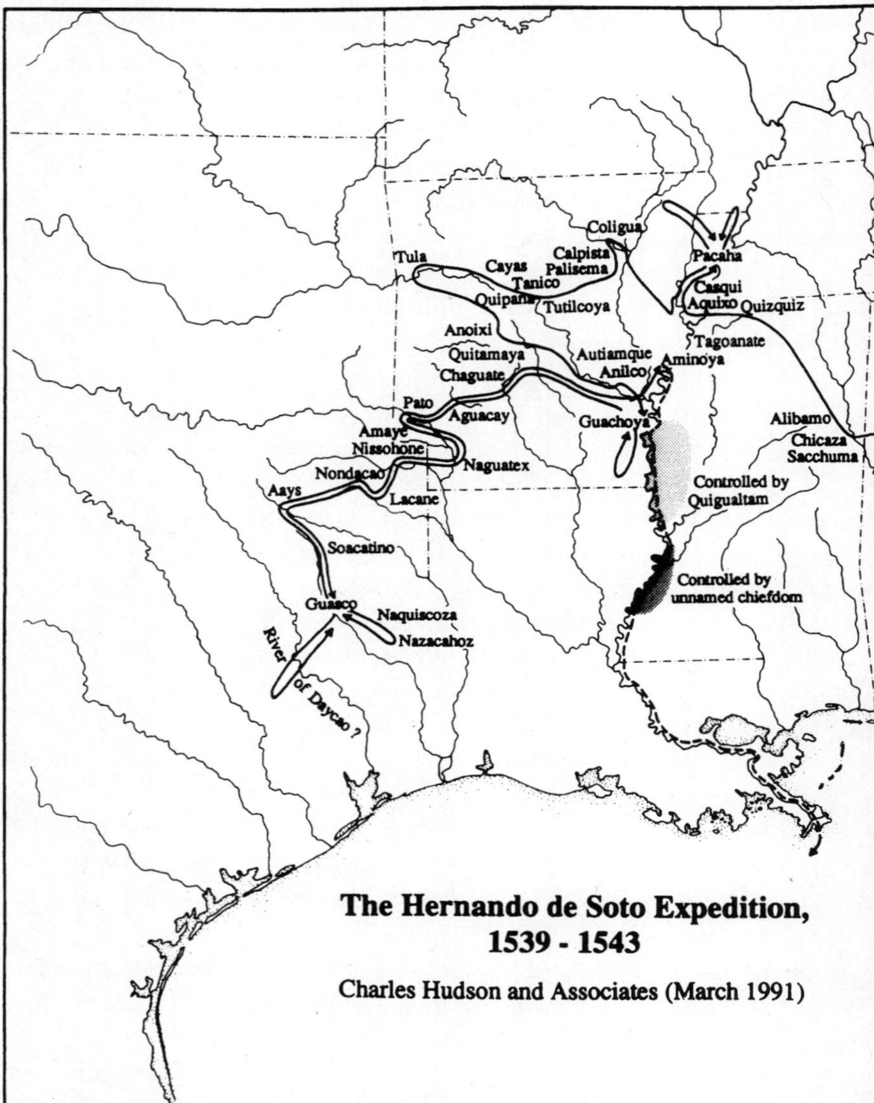

A Version of the Route of the De Soto Expedition, by Charles Hudson and Associates, 1991. This map exemplifies a new emphasis in De Soto scholarship. The chief motive for refining knowledge of the expedition's route is a desire to understand better the Native American chiefdoms at the time of first contact. Anthropologists and archaeologists attempt to match the chronicles to patterns of archaeological village sites. Seeking an

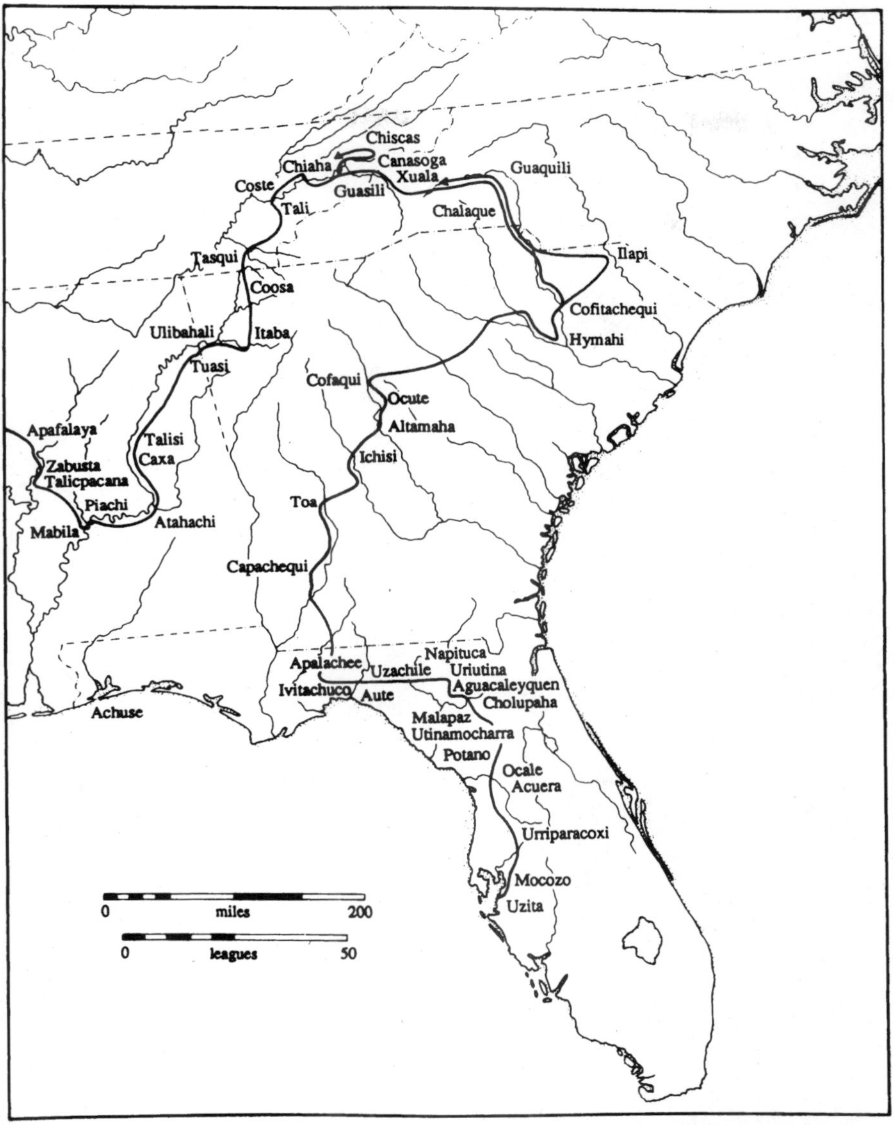

improved grasp of the route, along with a critical perception of the chronicles themselves, they hope to understand the native political geography of the Southeast. This research is a collaboration among cultural anthropologists, archaeologists, historians, geographers, and linguists. (Courtesy of Charles Hudson and Associates) and many days was toward the north. The large river that flowed through Cofachiqui, according to the mariners among the Spaniards, was the one which they called Santa Elena on the coast; they did not know this for certain, but according to the direction they had traveled, it seemed to them that it would be this one. This doubt and many others that our *History* leaves unsolved will be cleared up when God, our Lord, shall be pleased to have that land won for the increase of his holy Catholic faith.

We take four and a half leagues as an average of the fifty-seven daily journeys those Spaniards marched from Apalache to Xuala, though some may have been longer and others shorter. According to this calculation, they have marched a little less than 260 leagues to Xuala, and from the Bay of Espíritu Santo to Apalache we said that they traveled 150 leagues. Thus in all they covered a little less than four hundred leagues. [The Inca's calculations are somewhat low; they traveled a little *more* than four hundred.—DB]

In the pueblos under the jurisdiction and overlordship of Cofachiqui through which our Spaniards passed they found many Indians native to other provinces who were held in slavery. As a safeguard against their running away, they disabled them in one foot, cutting the nerves above the instep where the foot joins the leg, or just above the heel. They held them in this perpetual and inhuman bondage in the interior of the country away from the frontiers, making use of them to cultivate the soil and in other servile employments. These were the prisoners they captured in the ambushes that they set against one another at their fisheries and hunting grounds, and not in open war of one power against another with organized armies.[18]

We told above how the captain and accountant Juan de Añasco went twice after the mother of the lady of Cofachiqui, but we did not tell the chief reason why such persistent efforts were made to take her. This was that the Spaniards had learned that the widow had with her six or seven loads of large unpierced pearls, and that because they were unpierced, they were better than those they had seen in the burial places. Because these latter had been pierced with copper needles heated in the fire they had smoked a little and had lost much of their natural fineness and luster. Thus our men wished to see whether they were as large and good as the Indians claimed them to be.

---

[18]A similar procedure for disabling prisoners to be put to service in the fields was observed in the same general area by John Lawson over 150 years later. The description here of ambush warfare is generally applicable to the Southeastern tribes. John R. Swanton, *Indians of the Southeastern United States*, Bureau of American Ethnology Bulletin no. 137 (Washington, D.C.: Government Printing Office, 1946), 689–90.

XIX

WHERE IS RECOUNTED SOME OF THE MAGNANIMITY OF SPIRIT OF THE LADY OF COFACHIQUI

In the pueblo and province of Xuala (which, although it was a separate province from that of Cofachiqui, belonged to the same lady) the governor and his army rested for fifteen days, because in the pueblo and its environs they found much Indian corn and all the other grains and vegetables that we have said grow in La Florida. They needed to stop for this length of time in order to feed and rest the horses, which were lean and debilitated because of the little maize that they had to eat in the province of Cofachiqui. It was understood that this was the real cause of the three horses, which we mentioned above, having failed them, although at the time, to pass the matter over as lightly as possible in order to placate the mutineers, it was said that they had colic.

This pueblo was situated in the foothills of a mountain range on the bank of a river that, though not very large, had a very strong current. The territory of Cofachiqui extended to that river. In the pueblo of Xuala they served and entertained the governor and all his army most attentively, for as it was a part of the seigniory of the lady of Cofachiqui, and as she had sent orders to that effect, the Indians did everything in their power both to obey their lady and to please the Spaniards.

At the end of the fifteen days, the horses now being rested, they left Xuala. On the first day they marched through the cultivated fields and gardens that were there, which were many and good. They marched for another five days through a mountain range, uninhabited but a very good country. It had many oaks and some mulberries, and plenty of pasturage for cattle. There were ravines and streams with little water, though they flowed rapidly, and very green and delightful valleys. At the place they crossed it this range was twenty leagues wide.

But to return to the lady of Cofachiqui, whose seigniories we have not yet left: because it is fitting that her generosities be recorded, we say that, not content with having served and entertained the general and his captains and soldiers in her own house and court, nor satisfied with having provided the supplies that they would need for the march when her country was suffering such want as it did, nor with giving him Indian carriers to serve him throughout the fifty leagues of the province of Xuala, she ordered her vassals to carry from Xuala, where there was plenty of food, without any recompense whatever, all that the Spaniards might request for the twenty leagues of uninhabited country they would have to pass through before reaching Guaxule, and that they give them Indian servants and everything else necessary as if to her own person. Along with this she directed that four principal Indians go with the general, whose care would be to control and give orders to the servants so that the Spaniards might be better attended on their march. She made all these preparations for her own provinces.

But now it must be understood that neither did she overlook the others [i.e., other provinces], desiring that the Spaniards receive the same attentions in all of them. To this end she ordered the four principal Indians that, having entered the province of Guaxule, which bordered upon hers in that direction, they go on ahead and, acting as her ambassadors, charge the curaca of Guaxule that he serve the governor and all his army as she herself had done; otherwise she threatened him with war, with fire and bloodshed. The governor was ignorant of this embassy until the four principal Indians, after they had passed through the uninhabited country, asked his permission to go on ahead to carry it out. When the governor and his captains learned of this it caused them wonder and new gratification to see that that Indian lady had not been content with the service and entertainment she had given them in her own house and country with such affection and good will, but had also provided for it in other [provinces]. From this they came to understand more clearly the will and desire that this lady always had to serve the governor and his Castilians, for thus it was that though she did everything she could to please them, and they saw it, she always asked the general's pardon for being unable to do as much as she wished for them, which so afflicted and depressed her that the Spaniards themselves had to console her. By these manifestations of a generous spirit and others that she showed toward her vassals, according to what they themselves said publicly, she showed herself to be a woman truly worthy of the states she possessed and of other greater ones, and undeserving of being left in her heathenism. The Castilians did not offer her baptism because, as has been said already, they had the intention of preaching the faith after having made settlements and an establishment in that country, and marching continually as they did from one province to another, without stopping, they had little opportunity for preaching.

XX

WHAT HAPPENED TO THE ARMY UNTIL IT REACHED GUAXULE AND YCHIAHA

We have said already that the governor and his army had left Xuala and marched five days through the uninhabited district that lies between it and Guaxule. It must be told (going back in our story) that on the same day they left the pueblo of Xuala they missed three slaves who had fled the night before. Two were Negroes, the servants of Captain Andrés de Vasconcelos de Silva, and the other was a Moor from Barbary, the slave of Don Carlos Enríquez, a gentleman from Xerez de Badajoz, whom we mentioned above. It was understood that the flight of these slaves and their remaining among the Indians had been caused by the attraction of women more than by any other interest, and therefore they could not recover them though they made efforts to do so. The Indians of this great kingdom generally are much gratified (as we shall see more clearly further on) when anything pertaining to the Spaniards remains among them. The dereliction of the Negroes caused surprise because they were regarded as good Christians and friends of their master. The Berber did nothing new but rather confirmed the opinion that they had always had of him, as he was very bad in every respect.

Two days later it happened that, as the army was marching through this same wilderness, in the middle of the journey and of the day, when the sun was hottest, a foot soldier from Albuquerque named Juan Terrón, whose name fitted him well [Terrón means a lump or clod of earth], came up to another, mounted soldier who was his friend, and taking from his knapsack a small linen bag in which he was carrying more than six pounds of pearls, he said: "Take these pearls and carry them; I don't want them." He on horseback replied: "It is better for you to keep them, for you need them more than I do, and you can send them to La Havana where they will bring you three or four horses and mares, so that you will not have to walk. The governor says that he wishes to send messengers to that country soon with news of what we have discovered in this one." Angered because his friend would not accept the present that he made him, Juan Terrón said: "Well, if you don't want them, I swear that I won't take them with me either, so they will have to stay here." So saying, he unfastened the sack and grasping it by the bottom he flung out his arm like a person sowing, scattering all the pearls through the woods and grass, so as not to have to carry them on his shoulders, he being a strong and robust man who could carry almost as heavy a load as a pack mule. Having done this, he put the bag back in his knapsack as if it were more valuable than the pearls, to the amazement of his friend and all the rest who saw this reckless action. They had not imagined that he would do such a thing, for if they had suspected it, they would have stopped it in some way, because in Spain the pearls would have been worth more than 6,000 ducats, as they were all large, being the size of hazelnuts or large chick-peas. They had not been pierced, which made them more valuable, for their color was perfect, since they had not been smoked as had those they found already pierced. They recovered about thirty of them, searching among the grass and bushes, and seeing that they were so fine, they were regretful over the loss and made up a refrain they sang among themselves, which ran: "Pearls are not for Juan Terrón" [No son perlas para Juan Terrón]. He would never say where he got them, and as the men of his group often joked with him afterward about the loss and ridiculed him for the foolish thing that he had done, which corresponded with his rustic name, he said to them one day when he was very hard-pressed: "For the love of God, don't mention it to me again, because I assure you that every time I think of my foolishness it makes me want to go hang myself from a tree." Such are those whom prodigality enlists in its service, for after having made them throw away all their possessions through vanity, it provokes them to desperate actions. Liberality [on the other hand], being such an excellent virtue, gratifies very pleasantly those who embrace it and practice it.

Without anything else worth recording happening to them and having marched five daily journeys through the mountain range, the Castilians arrived at the province and pueblo of Guaxule, which was situated among many small streams that flowed through various parts of the pueblo. Their sources were in these mountains which the Spaniards had passed through and in others beyond.

The lord of the province, who also had the same name of Guaxule, came out half a league from the pueblo accompanied by five hundred nobles handsomely dressed in rich mantles made of various kinds of skins and wearing long plumes on their heads, in accordance with the common usage of that whole country. Thus ceremoniously he received the governor, showing by signs his regard for him and speaking to him most courteously and with a very lordly air. He took him to the pueblo, which had three hundred houses, and lodged him in his own. On receiving the message from the ambassadors of the lady of Cofachiqui, he had moved out of it to accommodate him and had prepared other things in order to serve him better. The house was on a high elevation like other similar ones we have described. All around it was a public walk along which six men could pass abreast.

The governor was in this pueblo four days, informing himself about the surrounding country, and from there he went in six daily journeys of five leagues each to another pueblo and province called Ychiaha, whose lord had the same name. The route he followed on this six days' march was downstream along the many rivers that flowed through Guaxule. All of them joined together within a short distance to form a large river of such volume that at Ychiaha, which was thirty leagues from Guaxule, it was larger than the Guadalquivir at Sevilla.

This pueblo Ychiaha was situated on the end of a large island more than five leagues long, which the river formed. The cacique went out to receive the governor and welcomed him cordially with all the demonstrations of affection and pleasure that he could show, and the Indians whom he brought with him did the same with the Spaniards, being very pleased to see them. Taking them across the river in many canoes and rafts they had ready for this purpose, they lodged them in their houses, as if they were their own brothers. All the other service and entertainment they accorded them were similar in measure, their desire being, as they expressed it, to take out their hearts and lay them before the Spaniards, so that they might see with their own eyes how much pleasure it gave them to know them. In Ychiaha the governor took the same steps that he had in the other pueblos and provinces to inform himself about what was in that country and its environs. The curaca told him, among other things that he said in response to his questions, that thirty leagues away there were mines of the yellow metal that he was seeking, and that in order to examine them his lordship might send two Spaniards, or more if he liked, to go and see them. He would furnish guides who would take and bring them back safely. On hearing this, two Spaniards offered to go with the Indians. One was named Juan de Villalobos, a native of Sevilla, and the other was Francisco de Silvera, a native of Galicia. They left at once, deciding to go on foot rather than on horseback, though they had horses so as to accomplish more in less time.

XXI

HOW THEY TOOK THE PEARLS OUT OF THEIR SHELLS, AND THE REPORT THE DISCOVERERS OF THE GOLD MINES BROUGHT

Early on the next day after the Spaniards left to visit the gold mines they so desired to find, the curaca came to visit the governor and made him a present of a handsome string of pearls. If they had not been pierced with fire they would have been a fine gift, because the string was two fathoms long and the pearls as large as hazelnuts, almost perfectly matched. The governor received them with many thanks, and in return he gave him pieces of velvet and cloth of various colors and other things from Spain, which the Indian valued highly. The governor asked him if those pearls were found in his country, and the cacique replied that they were, and that in the temple and burial place of their fathers and grandfathers, which was in that same pueblo, there were great quantities of them; if he wanted them, he would have all or as many as he desired brought to him. The adelantado told him that he appreciated his good will and that although he desired the pearls he would not injure the burial place of his ancestors, however much he might want them. The string that he had given him he had received only because it was a present from him, and he wished to know only how they took them from the shells where they grew.

The cacique told him that on the next day at eight o'clock in the morning his lordship would see how it was done, for that afternoon and the following night the Indians would fish for them. He immediately directed that forty canoes be sent out with orders that they fish for the shells with all diligence, and come back in the morning. When morning came, the curaca ordered much wood to be brought (before the canoes returned) and heaped up on a level space on the riverbank. It was set on fire and a large bed of coals made, and as soon as the canoes arrived he ordered it to be spread out and the shells that the Indians brought to be thrown upon it. These opened from the heat of the fire and they were enabled to hunt for the pearls inside them. From almost the first shells that they opened the Indians took out ten or twelve pearls as large as medium-sized chick-peas and brought them to the curaca and the governor, who were watching together to see how they took them out. They saw that they were very good and perfect except that the heat and smoke of the fire had already damaged their fine natural color.

Having seen them take out the pearls, the governor went to his lodgings to eat, and soon after he had eaten a soldier entered, a native of Guadalcanal named Pedro López. Showing a pearl that he carried in his hand, he said: "Sir, as I was eating some of the oysters that the Indians brought today, a few of which I took to my quarters and had cooked, I found this between my teeth, which almost broke them. As it seemed to me to be a fine one, I brought it to your lordship so that you might send it to my señora Doña Isabel de Bobadilla." The adelantado replied, saying: "I thank you for your good will and accept the present and the favor you do Doña Isabel so that she may thank you and repay you whenever the opportunity arises. But it will be better if you keep the pearl and take it to La Havana, so that you can get in exchange for it a couple of horses and two mares and anything else you may need. Because of the good will that you have shown toward us, I shall pay out of my own pocket the fifth [of the value of the pearl] that belongs to his Majesty's hacienda."

The Spaniards who were with the governor examined the pearl, and those among them who regarded themselves as lapidaries of sorts estimated that in Spain it would be worth 400 ducats, because it was the size of a large hazelnut with its husk entire, perfectly rounded and of a clear and lustrous color. Since it had not been opened with fire, as had the others, its color and beauty had not been injured. We give an account of these particulars, though so unimportant, because they show the wealth of that country.

On one of the days that the Spaniards were in this pueblo of Ychiaha a misfortune occurred that grieved all of them very much. This was that a gentleman who was a native of Badajoz, named Luis Bravo de Xerez, while walking across a plain near the river with a lance in his hand, saw a dog pass near him and threw the lance at it with the intention of killing it for food, because due to the general scarcity of meat throughout that country, the Castilians ate all the dogs they were able to get. The throw missed the dog, and the lance went skimming across the plain beyond until it fell over the bluff above the river, and it happened to strike in the temple a soldier who was fishing there with a cane pole, coming out on the other side of his head, from which he immediately fell dead. Luis Bravo, ignorant of having made this cruel throw, went to look for his lance and found it stuck through the temples of Juan Mateos, for this was the soldier's name. He was a native of Almendral. Among all the Spaniards who went on this discovery he alone had gray hair, wherefore everyone called him father and respected him as if he were the father of each of them. Thus there was general grief at the misfortune and miserable death that had overtaken him when he had gone out to enjoy himself. Death is as near and is equally certain for us, in all times and places.

The things mentioned took place in the camp while the two companions went out and returned from discovering the mines, spending ten days on their journey. They said that the mines were of very fine brass like that which they had seen formerly, but that because of the nature of the country, they were sure that gold and silver mines would be found if the veins and deposits were sought. In addition to this they said that the country they had seen was all very good for cultivation and pasturage. The Indians in the pueblos through which they had passed had received them very affectionately and joyfully, and had entertained and regaled them to such an extent that every night after they had feasted them they sent two handsome young women to entertain and sleep with them that night; but that they did not dare touch them, fearing that the Indians might shoot them with arrows the next day, because they suspected that they sent them [the women] to give an excuse for killing them if they should receive them. The Spaniards feared this, but perhaps their hosts did it by way of giving them special entertainment, seeing that they were young, because, if they had wished to kill them, they had no need to seek pretexts for doing so.

XXII

THE ARMY LEAVES YCHIAHA AND ENTERS ACOSTE AND COÇA, AND THE HOSPITALITY THAT WAS ACCORDED THEM IN THESE PROVINCES

Having received an account of the gold mines that they went to discover, the governor ordered preparations made for departing on the following day, which our Castilians did, leaving the curaca and his principal Indians very satisfied with the gifts the general and his captains gave them in return for their hospitality.

They marched that day down the island, which as we said was five leagues in length. At its point where the river came together again was founded another pueblo called Acoste; it belonged to another lord, quite different from the last one. He received the Castilians in a very different manner than the cacique of Ychiaha, for he showed no signs of friendship for them but on the contrary placed more than fifteen hundred Indian warriors under arms, decked out with plumes and having their weapons ready. They kept the latter in their hands, unwilling to put them down even though they had already received the Spaniards in their pueblo. They showed themselves to be so bold and anxious to fight that there was not a single Indian who in speaking with a Spaniard did not boast that he would scratch out his eyes, and they would have done so. If they asked them any questions, they replied so arrogantly, shaking and throwing their arms about with the fists closed (signs they make when they wish to fight), that their effrontery was insupportable, as were their words and manner, all of which provoked battle, so that often the Castilians lost patience and were ready to engage them. But the adelantado prevented it, telling them to endure everything that the Indians did simply in order not to break the record [of peace] that they had maintained up to that point since leaving the warlike province of Apalache. Thus they did as the governor commanded, but both sides passed that whole night with their squadrons formed, like declared enemies.

On the next day the Indians showed themselves to be friendlier, and the curaca and the chief men came with a new aspect to offer the governor all that they had in their country, and they gave him Indian corn for the march. He understood that a favorable message that the lord of Ychiaha had sent them regarding the Spaniards must have caused that civility. The general thanked them for the offer and paid for the maize, which satisfied them. On the same day the Spaniards left the pueblo and crossed the river in canoes and rafts, of which there were many, and gave thanks to God for having brought them out of that pueblo of Acoste without having broken the peace that they had kept up to that time.

Having left Acoste, they entered a large province called Coça. The Indians came out to receive them peaceably and treated them in a very friendly manner, giving them provisions and guides for their march from one pueblo to another.

The curaca and lord of this province had the same name as the province itself. At the place the Spaniards crossed it, it was more than a hundred leagues long, all fertile country and very populated, so that on some days of their march through it they passed ten or twelve pueblos, not counting those that were off the road on either side. It is true that the pueblos were small. The Indians came out of them to receive the Christians very gladly and joyfully, and entertained them in their houses. They gave them whatever they had very willingly, and all along the road those from one pueblo went to the next to serve them, and when the other pueblo had received them they returned to their own. In this manner they took the Spaniards throughout the hundred leagues, lodging them some nights in the settlements and others in the fields, as the day's march happened to end, each of which was about four leagues in length.

The lord of that province of Coça, who was at the other side of it, sent new messengers every day with the same message, repeated many times, welcoming the arrival of the governor, requesting that he travel very slowly through his country, resting and enjoying himself as much as he could, and saying that he himself was awaiting him in the chief pueblo of his province in order to serve his lordship and all his people with the affection and good will that they would see.

The Spaniards marched twenty-three or twenty-four days without anything of note happening to them, except the many repetitions of the welcome the Indians gave them, until they reached the chief pueblo, called Coça, from which the whole province took its name, and where its lord was. He advanced a long league to receive the governor, accompanied by more than a thousand nobles much adorned with mantles made of various kinds of skins. Many of them were of fine marten-skins that gave off a strong odor of musk. They wore long plumes on their heads, which are the decoration and adornment that the Indians of this great kingdom most value. These men were well disposed, as those of that country generally are; their plumes stood up half a fathom high and were of many and varied colors; and they were stationed in the field in order in the form of a squadron, with twenty men to a file. Thus they made a handsome and pleasing appearance.

With this military and lordly pomp and ceremony the Indians received the general and his captains and soldiers, making every possible demonstration of the satisfaction that they said they felt at seeing them in their country.[19] They lodged the governor in one of three houses that the curaca had in different parts of the pueblo, built in the same form as we have said other such houses were, situated on a height with the advantages that the lord's houses have over those of his vassals. The pueblo was established on the bank of a river and had five hundred large and good houses, which showed clearly that it was the head of a province so large and important as has been said. They had moved out of half the pueblo (in the vicinity of the governor's lodgings) where they quartered the captains and soldiers, and there was

[19]The formal approach of the chief of Coça to receive De Soto, accompanied by a fully dressed military escort, was undoubtedly part of a standard greeting protocol normally accorded to visiting chiefs. See George E. Lankford III, "Saying Hello to the Timucua," *Mid-America Folklore* 12 (1984):7–23.

Chief Coça Welcomes the Hernando de Soto Expedition. In this old engraving from a Dutch edition of the Elvas narrative, Chief Coça is shown arriving in the background, being carried on a litter and accompanied by military entourage and musicians. (From De Gedenkwaardige Voyagie van don Ferdinand de Soto, *Leyden: P. Van der Aa, 1706, courtesy of the W. S. Hoole Special Collections Library, The University of Alabama)*

room for all of them because the houses would accommodate many people. The Castilians stayed there eleven or twelve days, being served and entertained by the curaca and all his people as if they were much-beloved brothers, for certainly no expression suffices to tell the affection, care, and diligence with which they served them, so that the Spaniards themselves marveled at it.

XXIII

THE CACIQUE COÇA OFFERS HIS STATE TO THE GOVERNOR FOR AN ESTABLISHMENT AND SETTLEMENT, AND HOW THE ARMY LEAVES THAT PROVINCE

One day while the Spaniards were in this pueblo called Coça, its lord, who had eaten at the governor's table—having talked with him about many things pertaining to the conquest and settlement of the country and having replied to the entire satisfaction of the adelantado to everything that he had asked him on this subject—when it seemed to him time, arose, and making the general a deep and very respectful obeisance, after the custom of the Indians, and turning his eyes to the gentlemen who were on either side of the governor, speaking to them all, said: "Sir, the affection I have come to feel for your lordship and for all your people in these few days that I have known you leads me to beg that, if you are seeking good lands on which to settle, see fit to remain in mine and make an establishment in them. I believe that this is one of the best provinces that your lordship would have seen among all those that are in this kingdom, and moreover I assure your lordship that you have chanced to pass through and see the poorest and least desirable part of it. If your lordship should desire to examine it more closely, I will take you through other, better parts that will satisfy you entirely, and you can take whatever part of them seems best to you for settling and establishing your house and court. If you do not wish to grant me this favor at present, at least do not refuse to remain in this pueblo during the coming winter, which is near, where we will serve you, as your lordship will see by our actions. Then at your leisure your lordship can send your captains and soldiers to examine all parts of my country and bring you accurate reports of what I have said, for your lordship's better satisfaction."

The governor thanked him for his good will and told him that he was wholly unable to make an inland settlement until knowing what ports there were on the seacoasts to receive the ships and the people that would come to them from Spain or elsewhere with cattle and plants and the other things necessary for making settlements. At the proper time he would accept his offer and would always maintain friendship with him, and meanwhile he might rest assured that he would not delay in returning there and settling the country, and then he could do the things he asked for his gratification and satisfaction.

The cacique kissed his hands and said that he took these words of his lordship for pledges of his promise, and that he would keep them in his heart and memory until he should see their fulfillment, which he wished for extremely. This lord was twenty-six or twenty-seven years of age, of very elegant bearing, as are most of those in that country, and of good understanding. He spoke with discretion and gave good replies to all the questions that were asked him; he appeared to have been brought up in a most enlightened and polished court.

After the army had rested ten or twelve days in the pueblo of Coça, more to comply with the wishes of its curaca, who desired to have them in his country, than from their need for rest, the governor saw fit to continue his journey toward the sea, which he was seeking. Since leaving the province of Xuala he had marched toward the coast, making an arc through the country in order to come out at the port of Achusi, as he had agreed with Captain Diego Maldonado to do. The latter had remained to explore the coast and was to return at the beginning of the coming winter to the port of Achusi with reinforcements of men and arms, and cattle and provisions, as we said above. The governor's chief purpose was to go to this port to begin making his settlement.

The cacique Coça desired to accompany the general to the boundaries of his territory, and thus he set out with him, accompanied by many noble warriors, with many provisions and Indian carriers to transport them. They marched in the usual order for five days, at the end of which they reached a pueblo called Talise, which was the last one in the province of Coça and its frontier and defense. It was extremely strong, for in addition to its enclosure made of logs and earth, it was almost entirely surrounded by a large river that made it into a peninsula. This pueblo Talise was not wholly obedient to its lord Coça, because of its double-dealing with another lord, named Tascaluça, whose state bordered upon that of Coça, and he was not a safe neighbor or a true friend. Although the two were not openly at war, Tascaluça was a haughty and belligerent man, very cunning and deceitful, as we shall see below, and as such he had stirred up this pueblo to disobedience to its lord. The cacique Coça, having learned of this some time before, was glad to come with the governor both in order to serve him on the way and in the pueblo Talise itself, and to threaten its inhabitants and bring them to obedience with the Spaniards' assistance.

In the pueblo of Coça there had remained a Christian, if he were such, named Falco Herrado. He was not a Spaniard nor is it known from what province he came; he was a man of the lowest class and thus was not missed until the army reached Talise. Steps were taken to bring him back, without result, for he very shamelessly sent word by the Indians who went with the governor's messages that he wanted to stay with the Indians and not go with the Castilians, so that he might not have to see his captain every day, who had quarreled with him and spoken to him abusively; therefore they need not expect to see him again.

The curaca replied more civilly and courteously to the request that the governor made him to order his Indians to bring back that fugitive Christian, saying that, since all of them had not been willing to remain in his country, he would be much pleased to have only one of them stay there. He begged his lordship to pardon the man and not force him to return if he wished to stay of his own accord, for he would regard it as a favor. Seeing that he was some distance away and that the Indians would not compel him to return, the governor made no further demand for him.

We have forgotten to say that in this same pueblo of Coça there had remained a Negro named Robles, who was sick and unable to travel. He was a very good Christian and a good slave, and was entrusted to the cacique who very willingly and affectionately took upon himself the task of caring for and curing him. We have included an account of these details so that when God, our Lord, shall will that that country be conquered and won, an effort may be made to see whether some trace or memory remains of those who thus stayed among the natives of that great kingdom.

XXIV

CONCERNING THE FEARLESS CURACA TASCALUÇA, WHO WAS ALMOST A GIANT, AND HOW HE RECEIVED THE GOVERNOR

The governor was in the pueblo Talise ten days, making efforts to learn about all the remaining regions through which he must go on his journey and of what was in the surrounding provinces on either side of this pueblo. Meanwhile a son of Tascaluça arrived, a youth eighteen years old, of such good stature that he was head and shoulders taller than any of the Spaniards or Indians in the army. He was accompanied by many nobles and brought a message from his father in which the latter offered the governor his friendship, person, and state, to be made use of at his pleasure. The general received him in a very friendly manner and treated him with great respect, both because of his rank and of his elegance and fine bearing. After delivering his message and learning that the adelantado desired to go where his father Tascaluça was, he said: "Sir, in order to go there, though we are no more than twelve or thirteen leagues away, there are two roads. I beg your lordship to order two Spaniards to go by way of one and return by the other, so that they may see which one of them is better for your lordship to take. I will furnish guides who will take and bring them back safely." This was done, and one of the two who went to discover the roads was Juan de Villalobos, who had gone in search of the gold mines and had found them to be brass. He was always most anxious to see first, ahead of his companions, whatever was to be found in this discovery, and in his eagerness he offered to travel the road twice or even three times.

When the two companions came back with the report concerning the roads, the governor took leave of the good Coça and his people, who were very sad because the Castilians were leaving their country. The general went by way of the road that they told him was the most suitable and crossed the Río de Talise in rafts and canoes, it being so full of water that they could not ford it. They marched two days, and early on the third day they came in sight of the pueblo where the curaca Tascaluça was. It was not the chief pueblo of this state, but one of the other, ordinary ones.

Learning from his runners that the governor was approaching, Tascaluça went out from the pueblo to meet him. He was on a small high hill, an eminence from which much of the country could be seen in every direction.

He had with him only a hundred nobles, richly dressed in fine mantles of various kinds of furs with long plumes on their heads, according to their usual manner of dress. They were all on foot except Tascaluça, who was seated in a chair such as the lords of those lands use. They are of wood about a *tercia* [one-third of a vara, approximately eleven inches] in height, with a somewhat concave seat and without a backrest or arms, all made in one piece.[20] Near him was a standard-bearer carrying a large banner made of yellow deerskin with three blue bars dividing it from one side to the other. It was the same size and shape as the standards the companies of cavalry carry in Spain.

It was a new thing for the Spaniards to see military insignia, for up to that time they had not seen a standard or a banner or a guidon.

The build of Tascaluça was like that of his son, for he towered over all the others by more than half a vara and appeared to be a giant, or was one, and the rest of his body and his face were in proportion to his height. His countenance was handsome and habitually wore such a severe expression that his aspect showed well the ferocity and nobility of his spirit. His shoulders corresponded to his stature, his waist was a little more than two tercias around, his arms and legs were straight, well set and proportionate to his body. In short, he was the tallest Indian and of the finest figure that these Castilians saw in all their travels through La Florida.

Tascaluça was waiting for the governor in the manner that has been told, and though the gentlemen and captains of the army who marched ahead of him reached the place where he was, he made no move toward them nor any sign whatever of civility, as if he did not see them and they were not passing by him. Thus he remained until the governor came up, and when he saw him approaching he stood up and advanced fifteen or twenty paces to receive him.

The general dismounted and embraced him, and the two remained in the same place talking while the army was being quartered in the pueblo and outside of it, because there was not room for all the men in it. Then the two went together to the governor's house, which was near the house of Tascaluça, where he left the general and went with his Indians.

The Spaniards rested in that pueblo two days, and on the third they proceeded on their journey. As a sign of his great friendship for the governor,

---

[20]Wooden stools, though only rarely observed in the aboriginal Southeast, were an important emblem of chieftaincy throughout the circum-Caribbean area, particularly in the Greater Antilles.

Tascaluça wanted to accompany him, saying that he would do so in order to see that he would be well served in his country. The governor ordered that a saddle horse be made ready for him, as he had always done with the curacas, lords of vassals, who had traveled with him, though we have neglected to mention it until now. Among all the horses that were with the army not one was found that could bear and carry Tascaluça, because of his large body and not because he was fat, for as we said above his girth was less than a vara, nor was he corpulent with old age, because he was scarcely forty years old. Making further search for a horse that Tascaluça could ride, the Castilians found a hack belonging to the governor that was used as a pack horse because it was so strong; this horse could carry Tascaluça. He was so tall that when he mounted the horse his feet cleared the ground by only a handbreadth.

The governor was no little relieved that a horse had been found that Tascaluça could ride, and he was not disturbed because they mounted him on a pack horse. Thus they marched three daily journeys of four leagues each, at the end of which they reached the principal pueblo, called Tascaluça, from which the province and its lord took their names. The pueblo was strong, being situated on a peninsula the river formed; the stream was the same one that passed by Talise, and it became increasingly large and swift.

They spent the following day in crossing it, and because of the scarcity of rafts, it took almost the entire day. They camped half a league from the river in a beautiful valley.

At this camp two Spaniards were missing, one of them being Juan de Villalobos, whom we have mentioned twice. It was not known what became of them, though it was suspected that the Indians, finding them some distance from the camp, had killed them, because Villalobos, wherever he might be, was very fond of going about the country to see what he could find, a thing that costs the lives of all those who indulge in this bad habit in time of war.

The absence of the two Spaniards was a bad sign, and those who noted the novelty of the event feared that Tascaluça's friendship was not as true and loyal as he pretended it to be. To this unfavorable sign was added another, worse one, which was that when his Indians were questioned about the two missing Spaniards they replied very impudently, asking whether they had been appointed to guard them or what obligation they had to tell them about their Castilians. The governor was unwilling to insist further upon searching for them because he understood that they were dead, and that business would serve only to disturb and alienate the cacique and his vassals. It seemed better to him to leave the investigation and the punishment for a more favorable occasion.

At dawn on the following day the governor sent out two soldiers selected from among the best in the whole army. One was named Gonzalo Quadrado Xaramillo, an hidalgo who was a native of Zafra, an able and experienced man in all respects to whom could be entrusted implicitly any serious affair of peace or of war; the other was Diego Vázquez, a native of Villanueva de Barcarrota, also a man of good repute and entirely trustworthy. He sent them with orders to go to see what was in a pueblo called Mauvila, which was a league and half from that camp. There the curaca had many people ostensibly in order to better serve and entertain the governor and his Spaniards. He ordered them to wait for him in the pueblo, as he was marching after them immediately.

XXV

THE GOVERNOR ARRIVES AT MAUVILA AND FINDS INDICATIONS OF TREASON

As soon as the two soldiers left the camp, the governor ordered a hundred cavalry and a hundred infantry to prepare to go with him and with Tascaluça, both of them desiring to be in the vanguard that day. He left orders that the maese de campo follow immediately after him with the rest of the army. The latter was late in leaving, and his men marched scattered through the country hunting and enjoying themselves, quite overlooking the possibility of a battle because of the undisturbed peace that they had enjoyed throughout the summer, up to that time.

The governor, who was marching with more caution, reached the pueblo of Mauvila at eight o'clock in the morning. It contained few houses, scarcely more than eighty, but they were all very large and some had a capacity of fifteen hundred persons, others of a thousand, and the smaller ones of more than five hundred. We call a house any building of only one room, like a church, for the Indians do not build their houses by connecting several rooms together; but each one according to his ability builds a house with one room like a *sala,* and this has its apartments containing the necessary offices, which are few enough. These single rooms they call houses. Since those of this pueblo had been erected as a frontier and strong place and for displaying the power of the lord, they were very handsome. Most of them belonged to the cacique, and the others to the most important and richest men of his whole state.

The pueblo was situated on a very beautiful plain and had an enclosure three estados high, which was made of logs as thick as oxen. They were driven into the ground so close together that they touched one another. Other beams, longer and not so thick, were placed crosswise on the outside and inside and attached with split canes and strong cords. On top they were daubed with a great deal of mud and packed down with long straw, a mixture that filled all the cracks and open spaces between the logs and their fastenings in such a manner that it really looked like a wall finished with a mason's trowel. At intervals of fifty paces around this enclosure were towers capable of holding seven or eight men who could fight in them. The lower part of the enclosure, to the height of an estado, was full of loopholes for shooting arrows at those on the outside. The pueblo had only two gates, one on the east and the other on the west. In the middle was a spacious plaza around which were the largest and most important houses.[21]

The governor and the giant Tascaluça arrived at this plaza, and the latter, as soon as he had dismounted, summoned the interpreter Juan Ortiz and, pointing with his finger, said to him: "The governor will lodge in this large house, together with the gentlemen and nobles whom his lordship wishes to have with him, and his servants and equipage will be put in this other one that is near it. An arrow-shot outside of the pueblo my vassals have erected many good shelters made of branches for the rest of the people, in which they can be comfortably lodged, because the pueblo is small and we cannot all get into it." The general replied that as soon as the maese de campo arrived he would send [the men] into their quarters, and do everything else as he had arranged it. Thereupon Tascaluça entered one of the largest houses on the plaza where, as was learned afterward, he had the captains of his council of war. The governor and the cavalry and infantry who came with him stayed in the plaza, and they ordered the horses taken outside the pueblo until learning where they were to put them.

Gonzalo Quadrado Xaramillo, who, as we have said, had gone ahead to

---

[21]Stripped of its blatant exaggerations, Garcilaso's description of Mabila accords well with archaeologically known fortified native towns of the late prehistoric Southeast. The severest faults lie in the extraordinary size claimed for the houses, and in the size of the vertical members of the palisade. All archaeologically excavated examples of town palisades in the Southeast reveal evidence of closely spaced vertical posts of relatively small diameter.

see and reconnoiter the pueblo of Mauvila, as soon as the governor dismounted came up to him and said: "Sir, I have examined this pueblo carefully, and the things that I have seen and noted in it give me no assurance whatever of the friendship of this curaca and of his vassals; rather they arouse my suspicion that they have plotted some treason, for in these few houses that your lordship sees there are more than ten thousand chosen warriors. There is not a single old man or Indian servant among them, but all are warriors, nobles and young men. They are all supplied with a great many arms, and besides those which each one has for himself many of these houses are full of them [arms]. They are a common depository of arms. Furthermore, although these Indians have many women with them, all are young and none of them have children nor is there a single child in the whole pueblo, but they are free and unimpeded by any encumbrance. The country for a harquebus-shot surrounding the pueblo (as your lordship will have seen) they have cleaned and cleared of growth in such a curious manner that they have even pulled up the grass roots by hand, which seems to me to be a sign that they intend to give us battle and wish to have nothing in their way. There may be added to these bad signs the death of the two Spaniards who were missing at the last camp. For all these reasons it seems to me that your lordship ought to proceed cautiously with this Indian and not trust him. Though there was nothing else except the unfriendly countenances and still more unfavorable attitude that he and his people have hitherto shown us, and the arrogance and impudence with which they speak to us, it would be enough to warn us not to consider his friendship genuine, but false and deceitful."

The general's reply was to order that the word be passed from one to another among those who were there, warning them all to be secretly on their guard, and he particularly commanded Gonzalo Quadrado that as soon as the maese de campo arrived he was to notify him of what he had seen in the pueblo so that he might act for the best interests of all.

Alonso de Carmona in his manuscript volume gives a very long account of the journey that these Spaniards made, and he with them, from the province of Cofachiqui to that of Coça. He tells of the grandeurs of the province of Coça and of the generosity of its lord, and names many of the pueblos along that road, though not all that I have named. Concerning the stature of Tascaluça, he says that almost nothing was lacking to make a giant of him, and that he was very well favored. Juan Coles, in speaking of this huge fellow, says the following: "When we arrived at the province of this lord Tascaluça he came out to receive us peacefully. He was a large man, whose shin from the foot to the knee was as high as any other very tall men from the foot to the waist; he had eyes like an ox. He mounted a horse on the march, and the horse could not carry him. The adelantado dressed him in scarlet and gave him a very handsome cape of his own." Having told about the scarlet clothing, Alonso de Carmona adds these words:

> When the governor and Tascaluça entered Mauvila the Indians came out to receive them with dances and ceremonies to better dissemble their treason, the most important people taking part in them. When that entertainment ended another dance took place, performed by marvelously beautiful women, because as I have said those Indians are very well favored, and the women so much so that afterward, when we left that country and went to México, Governor Moscoso took an Indian from this province of Mauvila, who was a very handsome and graceful woman. She could compete in beauty with the most elegant from Spain who were in all México, and thus because of her extreme beauty, those ladies of México sent to beg the governor to send her because they wished to see her. He did so very gladly because it pleased him that they should envy her.

All these are words of Alonso de Carmona as he himself says them, and I am glad to include these and all that appear in the *History* in the names of these two soldiers, who were eyewitnesses, so that it may be seen how clearly they show that their accounts and ours correspond. A little further on Alonso de Carmona tells of the notice that we said that Gonzalo Quadrado Xaramillo (though he does not name him) gave to Governor Hernando de Soto. He adds that he told him how on that morning and on many others before the Indians had gone out to the fields to drill, and how every day before the skirmish and military exercise a captain harangued them.

The cacique Tascaluça (as has been said), as soon as he and the governor entered the pueblo, went into a house where his council of war was, waiting to conclude and decide upon the plan that they were to follow in killing the Spaniards, for that curaca had determined long since to kill them in the pueblo of Mauvila. For this purpose he had assembled the warriors that he had there, not only from among his vassals and subjects but also from the neighboring and outlying [provinces], so that all might enjoy the triumph and glory of having killed the Castilians and might have their part of the spoils that they carried. Those who were not his vassals had come on this condition.

When Tascaluça was among his captains, then, and the chief men of his army, he told them that they must determine quickly how they would carry out that purpose; whether they would immediately cut the throats of the Spaniards who were then in the pueblo and of the others after them, as they arrived, or whether they would wait until all of them had come. Because of their own strength and bravery they expected to be able to behead all of them together as easily as they could when they were separated into the three divisions of vanguard, center, and rear guard, into which the army was formed on the march. They must decide at once, because he only waited upon their resolution.

XXVI

THE MEMBERS OF TASCALUÇA'S COUNCIL DETERMINE TO KILL THE SPANIARDS. AN ACCOUNT OF THE BEGINNING OF THE BATTLE THAT TOOK PLACE

The captains of the council were divided regarding the proposals that Tascaluça presented to them. Some said that they ought not to wait until all the Castilians should be together, so that their enterprise would not be made more difficult, but that they ought to kill at once the ones who were there and then the rest as they should arrive. Others who were braver said that it seemed like a kind of cowardice and a sign of fear and even smelled of treason to wish to kill them when they were divided, but that inasmuch as they had the same advantage in bravery, dexterity, and lightness as in numbers, they should allow them to come together and behead all of them at one blow; that this would be more honorable and more befitting to Tascaluça's grandeur because it would be a greater exploit.

The first captains replied, saying that it was not a good thing to risk all the Spaniards joining together and putting themselves in a better defensive position, and killing some of the Indians. However few there might be, they would feel more the loss of a few friends than the satisfaction that the death of all their enemies would give them. It was enough to gain the end that they desired, which was to cut all their throats, and it could be accomplished better and more surely the more leisure they had for doing it.

This last counsel prevailed, for though the other was more in line with Tascaluça's arrogance and bravado, he was so desirous of seeing the Spaniards beheaded that any delay, however short it might be, seemed long to him. Thus it was agreed that for carrying out their decision they would seize any opportunity that was offered them, and that if there were none, they would do it arbitrarily, for it was not necessary to seek reasons for killing enemies.

While Tascaluça's council was discussing the death of the Spaniards, the governor's servants, who had gone on ahead and hurried their march and had been lodged in one of the large houses that faced the plaza, had prepared breakfast, or dinner, for they were all one, and summoned his lordship to eat, as it was now the hour. The general sent a message to Tascaluça by Juan Ortiz asking that he come to breakfast, for he had always eaten with the governor. Juan Ortiz delivered the message at the door of the house where the curaca was because the Indians would not let him come inside. Having delivered the message, they replied that their lord would come out soon.

After some time had passed Juan Ortiz again repeated his message at the door and received the same reply. Then after another interval he asked again, for the third time, that they tell Tascaluça to come out, for the governor was awaiting him with the food on the table. Then an Indian came out of the house, who must have been the captain-general, and spoke with extraordinary arrogance and haughtiness, saying: "Who are these thieves and vagabonds here calling to my lord Tascaluça to come out, come out, speaking with as little reverence as if they were talking to another like themselves? By the Sun and the Moon, one is not able to endure the boldness of these devils, and it is only just that they die for it today, being cut to pieces to put an end to their iniquity and tyranny!"

The captain had scarcely spoken these words when another Indian who came out after him placed a bow and arrows in his hands so that he could begin to fight. The Indian general, throwing back over his shoulders the folds of a very handsome mantle of marten-skins he wore fastened at his throat, took the bow and, placing an arrow in it, turned with it to shoot at a group of Spaniards who were in the street.

Captain Baltasar de Gallegos, who happened to be near, to one side of the door by which the Indian came out, seeing his treason and that of his cacique, and that the whole pueblo was implicated in it, raised a loud alarm and drew his sword. He gave the Indian a slash from the left shoulder downward that, as he wore no defensive armor nor even any clothing except the mantle, laid open his whole side, and with his entrails all protruding he immediately fell dead, without having a chance to shoot the arrow.

When this Indian went out of the house to speak those insulting words that he said against the Castilians, he had already given the Indians the word to fight, and thus there came out of all the houses in the pueblo, principally those that surrounded the plaza, six or seven thousand warriors. They fell with such impetus and courage upon the few Spaniards who were going carelessly through the principal street by which they had entered, that they very easily sent them flying, as they said, without allowing them to put their feet on the ground, until they drove them outside the gate more than two hundred paces into the fields. So fierce and bold was this inundation of Indians that it overwhelmed the Spaniards, though it is true that in all that time there was not a single Spaniard who turned his back on the enemy. On the other hand, they fought with all good spirit, valor, and strength, defending themselves and withdrawing because it was impossible for them to make a stand and resist the cruel and arrogant violence with which the Indians rushed out of the houses and of the pueblo.

Among the first Indians who left the house from which the Indian captain came was a young noble about eighteen years of age. Fastening his eyes upon Baltasar de Gallegos, he shot six or seven arrows at him with great fury and swiftness, and though he had more, seeing that he had not killed or wounded him with those, because the Spaniard was well protected with armor, he grasped his bow in both hands and closed with him, he being close by, and gave him three or four blows on the head with such velocity and force that he made the blood flow from under his helmet down his forehead. Baltasar de Gallegos, seeing himself so mistreated and to prevent his abusing him further, very hastily stabbed him twice in the breast, and with this his enemy fell dead.

It was surmised that this young Indian must have been the son of that captain who was the first to come out to the battle, and that it was with the desire of avenging his father's death that he had fought Baltasar de Gallegos with such courage and anxiety as he showed to kill him. But as a matter of fact all of them fought with the same eagerness to kill or wound the Spaniards.

The mounted soldiers, who, as we said, had their horses staked outside the walls of the pueblo, seeing the impetus and fury with which the Indians fell upon them, ran out of the pueblo to get their horses. Those who were most dexterous and made the greatest effort succeeded in mounting them. Others who underrated this avalanche of the enemy and its swiftness, being unable to mount their horses, contented themselves with loosing them by cutting the reins or halters so that they could run away before the Indians shot them. Others, still more unfortunate, who were unable either to mount their horses or even to cut the halters, left them tied where the enemy shot them with arrows, with extreme satisfaction and rejoicing. As the Indians were so numerous, half of them carried on the fight against the Castilians and half of them busied themselves in killing the horses that they found tied and in gathering up all the baggage and possessions belonging to the Christians that had already arrived and was piled against the wall of the pueblo and scattered around the plain, awaiting storage. The enemy got possession of all of this, without anything escaping them except the belongings of Captain Andrés de Vasconcelos, which had not yet arrived.

The Indians put all this in their houses and left the Spaniards despoiled of everything they were bringing. They had nothing left except their lives and what they wore on their persons, for which they fought with all the good spirit and strength that were necessary in such a crisis, though they were unused to arms because of the long peace that they had enjoyed from Apalache to that place, and had not expected to fight that day because of the false friendship that Tascaluça had shown them. But neither the one nor the other was enough to make them fail in their duty.

XXVII

WHERE ARE RECOUNTED THE EVENTS OF THE FIRST THIRD OF THE BATTLE OF MAUVILA

The few riders among those who left the pueblo who were able to mount their horses, with a few others who had arrived from the march, unexpectedly finding such a cruel battle, joined together and went to resist the impetus and fury with which the Indians were pursuing the Spaniards who were fighting on foot. These latter, however much they tried, could not prevent the Indians from driving them forward across the plain, until they saw the horses charging them. Then they held up a little and gave our men a chance to rally and form two divisions, one of infantry and one of cavalry. They fell upon the Indians with such courage and shame for the past affront that they did not stop until they had shut them [the Indians] up again in the pueblo. But when they attempted to enter, such a shower of arrows and stones rained upon them from the wall and its loopholes that they withdrew by common accord.

Seeing them retire, the Indians came out again with the same impetuosity as the first time, some through the gate and others jumping down from the wall. They engaged our men rashly, even grasping the cavalrymen's lances, and the Spaniards were forced, in spite of themselves, to retire more than two hundred paces from the wall.

As has been said, the Spaniards withdrew without turning their backs, fighting with all discipline and good order, because in this lay their salvation. They were few and lacked those who were behind in the rear guard, which had not yet come up.

Our men at once charged the enemy and drove them back toward the pueblo, but they made a strong attack from the wall, from which the Spaniards came to understand that it was better to fight them on the plain at a distance from the pueblo than near it. Thus from that time on, when they retired they purposely yielded more ground than the Indians forced them to lose, in order to draw them away from the pueblo so that by their retreat the cavalry would have more ground and room where they could charge them with lances. First one and then the other, attacking and withdrawing in this manner, as if in a tournament with reed spears—though it was a very cruel and bloody battle—and again standing their ground, Indians and Spaniards fought for three hours, savagely killing and wounding each other.

In these attacks and retreats that were thus made, there rode behind and among the Spaniards a Dominican friar named Fray Juan de Gallegos, the brother of Captain Baltasar de Gallegos. He was not attempting to fight, but he wished to give the horse to his brother, and with this desire he shouted to him to come out and mount the horse.

The captain, who had never ceased to be among the first, as he had happened to be at the beginning of the battle, made no effort to reply to his brother because he was unable to do so, nor would his reputation and honor permit him to leave the post that he occupied. In these advances and retreats the good friar made in his anxiety to help his brother with the horse, during an assault by the Indians one of them caught sight of him, and though he was some distance away he discharged an arrow at the moment when the friar happened to turn his horse to flee from them. It struck him in the back and wounded him, though slightly, because he wore his two cowls and all the other robes that those of his order usually wear, which are many, and over all this he had a large felt hat that was fastened around his neck with a cord and hung down over his shoulders. The arrow wound the Indian gave him with such good will was not mortal because of all these defenses. The friar took warning from it and went off some distance, fearing that they might shoot him again.

There were many wounds and deaths in this obstinate battle, but the one that caused the Spaniards the greatest regret and grief, both because of the misfortune through which it happened and because of the person upon whom it fell, was that of Don Carlos Enríquez, a gentleman from Xerez de Badajoz. He was married to a niece of the governor and, because of his great virtue and affability, he was esteemed and beloved by all; we have mentioned him on another occasion. From the beginning of the battle this gentleman had fought like a very valiant soldier during all the attacks and retreats, and his horse, having been wounded in the last retreat by an arrow that had gone into one side of his breast above the breast-leather, in order to draw it out he changed his lance from his right hand to his left, and grasping the arrow, pulled at it. With his body extended forward along the horse's neck he made an effort, turning his head slightly over his left shoulder so that his throat was uncovered at an unfortunate moment. Just then a stray arrow with a flint barb fell and happened to strike him in the small part of the throat that was unprotected and without armor, for all the rest of his body was well armored. It wounded him in such a manner that the poor gentleman at once fell down from his horse with his throat cut, though he did not die until the next day.

With such events incident to battles, Indians and Castilians fought with many deaths on both sides, although the mortality was greater among the Indians because they had no defensive arms. After fighting for more than three hours on the plain, the latter realized that they were getting the worst of the battle on an open field because of the damage that the horses were doing them, and they all decided to withdraw toward the pueblo, close the gates, and station themselves on the walls. This they did, calling to one another to assemble from every direction.

On seeing the Indians closed up, the governor ordered that all the mounted soldiers, because they were better armed than the infantry, dismount and attack the pueblo, taking shields to defend themselves and axes to break in the gates (most of them carried axes with them), and as brave Spaniards do what they could to win it.

Instantly a squadron of two hundred cavalry was formed, which attacked the gate, broke it down with axes, and entered through it with no little damage to themselves.

Other Spaniards who could not go in through the gate because it was narrow, so as not to wait in the fields and lose time in fighting, made vigorous strokes at the wall with their axes and knocked off the mixture of mud and straw that was on top of it, uncovering the transverse logs and the fastenings by which they were attached. Assisting one another they climbed up by them, got over the wall, and entered the pueblo to help their men.

The Indians, on seeing the Castilians inside the pueblo that they had considered impregnable, and that they were gaining it, fought with the spirit of desperate men, in the streets as well as from the roofs, from which they did much damage to the Christians. The latter, in order to defend themselves from those who were fighting from the flat roofs or terraces and to insure that they would not attack them from behind, and also in order that the Indians might not come back to gain the houses that they were taking, decided to set fire to them. They did so and, as they were made of straw, in a moment a great deal of flame and smoke arose, which added itself to [the confusion of] the blood, the many wounds, and the massacre that was taking place in such a small pueblo.

As soon as they closed themselves up in the pueblo, many of the Indians ran to the house that had been designated for the governor's service and chamber, which they had not attacked hitherto because it seemed to them that they had it safely [in their hands]. Thus they now went very boldly to enjoy the spoils that were in it. But they found the house well defended, because inside were three crossbowmen and five halberdiers of the governor's guard who were accustomed to accompany his equipage and servants, and one of the first Indians whom they captured in that country, who was now a friend and a faithful servant, and as such carried his bow and arrows to be ready when it should be necessary to fight against those of his own nation in the favor and service of the foreigner. There also happened to be in the house two priests, a cleric and a friar, and two of the governor's slaves. All these people stationed themselves to defend the house, the priests with their prayers and the seculars with arms, and they fought so courageously that the enemy could not gain the door. They then decided to go in through the roof and accordingly opened it in three or four places, but the crossbowmen and the Indian archer worked so effectively that all those who dared enter through the holes in the roof they shot down dead or badly wounded, as they appeared. These few Spaniards were conducting this spirited defense when the general and his captains and soldiers came up to the door of the house, fighting, and drove the enemy away from it. Thereupon those in the house were released and went out to the field, giving thanks to God for having saved them from such danger.

XXVIII

WHICH CONTINUES THROUGH THE SECOND THIRD OF THE BATTLE OF MAUVILA

When the things that we recounted in the last chapter took place Indians and Castilians had been fighting without ceasing for more than four hours, killing one another most cruelly. For it seemed that the more injury the Indians received, the more they persisted, and despairing of their lives, instead of surrendering they fought with greater eagerness to kill the Spaniards; and they, seeing the obstinacy, persistence, and rage of the Indians, wounded and killed them without any pity.

The governor, who had fought throughout the four hours on foot at the head of his men, went out of the pueblo and mounted a horse. So as to increase the fears of the enemy and the spirit and courage of his men, he went back into the pueblo, accompanied by Nuño Tovar who was also mounted, and both riders, calling the names of Our Lady and St. James the Apostle ["Santiago" (St. James) was a traditional battle cry of the Spanish] and shouting loudly to their men to make way, broke through the enemy squadron from one side to the other as it was fighting in the principal street and in the plaza. Then they turned back upon them, spearing them on either side, like the brave and skillful soldiers that they were.

During these attacks and withdrawals, at a time when the governor was standing in his stirrups to throw a lance at an Indian, another who was behind him shot an arrow above the hind bow of the saddle, which struck in the small unprotected space the general exposed between the saddlebow and the breastplate, and though he wore a coat of mail, the arrow broke through it and penetrated some six inches into the left hip. The good general, alike in order not to let it be known that he was wounded so that his men would not become alarmed because of this hurt, and because in the press of the fighting he had no opportunity to pull out the arrow, fought with it through all the rest of the battle, which was almost five hours, without being able to sit in the saddle, which was no small proof of the valor of this captain and of his skill in horsemanship.

They shot another arrow through Nuño Tovar's lance, which as it was slender it passed through the middle near the hand, and the haft of the lance was so fine that it was not split, but it appeared rather that the arrow was a gimlet that had bored delicately through it. Thus when the arrow was later cut away on either side the lance served as well as before. Though of little importance, this shot is described because such shots are seldom made, and also because it shows what we have said many times about the ferocity and skill that these Indians of La Florida have with bows and arrows.

These two gentlemen, although they fought all day and repeatedly broke through the squadrons that the Indians formed and reformed at every step, and were present at the most dangerous crises of this battle, received no other wounds than those that we have described, which was no small good fortune.

The fire that they had set to the houses increased momentarily and did the Indians much damage, for as they were numerous and could not all fight in the streets and plaza, because they could not all get into them, they fought from the terraces and flat roofs, and the fire trapped and burned them there or forced them in fleeing from it to fling themselves down from the terraces.

It did no less damage in the houses where it came in through the door, for as has been said, they were large rooms with only one door, and when the fire blocked it those who were inside could not get out and were burned and suffocated by the fire and smoke. Many women who were closed up in the houses perished in this way.

The fire was equally harmful in the streets, because sometimes the wind blew the flame and smoke over the Indians, blinding them and helping the Spaniards to drive them back without their being able to resist. Again it would turn in favor of the Indians against the Christians and enable them to regain the part of the street that they had lost. Thus the fire went favoring now one side and now the other, and increasing the mortality of the battle.

The fighting was sustained on both sides with the cruelty and fury that has been seen until four o'clock in the afternoon, the battle having been continuous for seven hours. At this hour the Indians, seeing how many of their men they had killed by fire and the sword and that for lack of fighters their strength was decreasing while that of the Castilians was increasing, summoned the women and ordered them to take up some of the many arms that were lying in the streets and set about taking vengeance for the death of their people; and if they could not avenge them, they could at least see to it that all of them should die before becoming the slaves of the Spaniards.

When they gave this command to the women many of them had already been fighting bravely for some time along with their husbands, but with this new order not one remained who did not go to the battle, taking up arms that they found lying on the ground, of which there was an abundance. Many of the swords, halberds, and lances that the Spaniards had lost came into their hands, and they turned them against their owners, wounding them with their own arms. They also took up bows and arrows and shot them with no less skill and ferocity than their husbands. They stationed themselves in front of the latter to fight, and resolutely exposed themselves to death with much more temerity than the men. They thrust themselves among the enemy's weapons with great fury and recklessness, showing well that the desperation and courage of women in what they have determined to do is greater and more heedless than that of men. The Spaniards, however, seeing that the Indian women were doing this more with the desire of dying than of conquering, and also out of regard for the fact that they were women, abstained from wounding and killing them.

While this long and stubborn battle lasted, the trumpets, fifes, and drums did not cease to sound the alarm very insistently, so that the Spaniards who had stayed behind in the rear guard would hurry to the assistance of their men.

The maese de campo and those who were coming with him marched scattered about the country hunting and enjoying themselves, ignorant of what was going on in Mauvila. But when they heard the noise of the military musical instruments and the shouts and outcries that sounded inside and outside the pueblo, and saw the clouds of smoke that rose up in front of them, suspecting what it might be, they passed the word back to the last ones and all of them marched at top speed, arriving during the last part of the battle.

Among them came Captain Diego de Soto, the governor's nephew and the brother-in-law of Don Carlos Enríquez, whose misfortune we have already told. When he learned what had happened to his brother-in-law, whom he loved devotedly, the grief that he felt at such a loss made him desire to avenge it. He leaped down from his horse and, taking up a shield, entered the pueblo sword in hand and went where the battle was raging most fiercely and cruelly, which was in the principal street, though it is true that in all the others there was no lack of blood, fire, and death, for the whole pueblo was filled with savage combat.

At four o'clock in the afternoon Diego de Soto entered the battle at that place, but it was to imitate the misfortune of his brother-in-law rather than to avenge his death. It was not a time for private vengeance but for the wrath of military fortune, which, apparently in abhorrence of having granted them so much peace in the land of such cruel enemies, now desired to give them all in one day the warfare that would have sufficed for a year, and perhaps it would not have been so disastrous to them as that of this day alone, as we shall see later. Few or no battles between Spaniards and Indians have taken place in the New World that would equal this one, both in the stubborn persistence of the fighting and in the length of time that it lasted, unless it were that of the presumptuous Pedro de Valdivia, of which we shall tell in the history of El Perú if God shall be pleased to grant us life.

As we were saying, then, Captain Diego de Soto came to the thick of the battle and had scarcely entered it when they shot him in the eye with an arrow, which came out at the back of his head. He fell to the ground at once and lay in agony without speaking until the next day, when he died, without their having been able to remove the arrow. This was the revenge that he took for his relative Don Carlos, to the greater grief and loss of the general and of the whole army, for these two gentlemen were most worthy nephews of such an uncle.

XXIX

IT TELLS OF THE END OF THE BATTLE OF MAUVILA, AND IN WHAT BAD CONDITION THE SPANIARDS WERE LEFT

The battle that took place in the country was no less bloody; it was for this purpose that the fields had been cleared of timber and cleaned even to uprooting the grass and herbs. Having enclosed themselves in the pueblo to make a defense, the Indians realized that because of their numbers they would hinder one another in fighting, and that because the space was limited[22] they could not profit by their lightness and agility. Thus many of them agreed to go out to the fields, letting themselves down from the walls, where they fought with all good spirit and courage and eagerness for victory. But they soon recognized that their plan was ill-advised, because if their lightness gave them an advantage over the Spanish infantry, those on horseback were their superiors and speared them in the field entirely at their pleasure, without their being able to defend themselves, for these Indians do not use pikes (although they have them), which are the defense against cavalry, be-

[22]The Varners' translation of this passage, in speaking of "the narrowness of the place," has sometimes led to the unwarranted supposition that the layout of Mabila was narrow or oblong. Varner and Varner, *The Florida of the Inca*, 371; Caleb Curren, *In Search of De Soto's Trail*, Bulletins of Discovery no. 1 (Camden: Alabama-Tombigbee Regional Commission, 1986), 11.

cause they had not permitted themselves to believe that the enemy would come up within reach of the pikes, but expected to assault and kill them with arrows a good distance before they should reach them. This is the chief reason they use the bow and arrows more than any other weapons. Thus a great many of them died on the field, ill-advised in their ferocity and vain presumption. The Spaniards of the rear guard came up, cavalry and infantry, and all attacked the Indians who were fighting in the field, and after engaging in battle for a long period of time and receiving many deaths and wounds—for though they arrived late they received a very good share of them, as we saw in the case of Diego de Soto and shall soon see in others—they routed and killed most of the Indians. Some escaped by flight.

At this time, which was now nearly sunset, the shouts and cries of those who were fighting in the pueblo still sounded. Many of those who were mounted entered to aid their men; others remained outside to be ready for whatever might be needed. Hitherto for lack of room none of the cavalry had fought inside the pueblo except the general and Nuño Tovar. Now, therefore, many mounted men entered and scattered through the streets, for there was work for them to do in all of them. Breaking through the Indians who were fighting there, they killed them.

Ten or twelve horsemen advanced along the principal street where the battle was fiercest and bloodiest, and where there was still a squadron of Indian men and women who were fighting most desperately, for now they attempted nothing else except to die fighting. The cavalry charged upon them, and taking them from behind they broke them more easily and passed through them so furiously that they knocked down many Spaniards in the wake of the Indians. They were fighting hand to hand with the enemy, all of whom they killed, for none wished to surrender or give up their arms, but to die with them, fighting like good soldiers.

This was the last encounter of the battle in which the Spaniards ended by conquering, just as the sun went down, having fought nine hours in both places without ceasing. This was the day of the blessed St. Luke the Evangelist in the year 1540, and on the same day, though many years later, this account of it was written.

At the same moment the battle ended, one of the Indians who had been fighting in the pueblo, dazed with his own struggle and courage, had not noticed what had happened to his people until, coming to himself, he saw them all dead. Since he saw himself alone and now unable to conquer, he attempted to save his life by fleeing, and with this desire he ran to the wall and jumped up on it with much agility, so as to escape across the fields. But seeing the Castilians on foot and on horses who were there and the massacre that had occurred and that he could not escape, he preferred death to giving himself up as prisoner, and quickly taking the cord from his bow, he fastened it to the branches of a tree that was growing on the wall in the spaces between the logs, which the Indians had left there as a point to reckon from in enclosing the pueblo. This tree was not the only one growing on the wall, for there were many others like it that they had left there purposely, which greatly beautified the wall.

Fastening one end of the cord, then, to a branch of the tree, and the other around his neck, he let himself fall down from the wall so quickly that, although some Spaniards desired to rescue him so that he would not die, they could not get there in time. Thus the Indian was hanged by his own hand, causing amazement by his action and by the certainty that he who would hang himself would be even more desirous of hanging the Castilians if he could. From this may be well surmised the recklessness and desperation with which all of them fought, for the one who was left alive killed himself.

The battle over, Governor Hernando de Soto, though he came out of it badly wounded, took care to order that the bodies of the dead Spaniards be recovered for burial on the next day and that the wounded be treated. There was such a lack of necessities for treating them that many died before they could be assisted, for it was found by actual count that there were 1,770 or more wounds that required treatment. These included only the ones that were dangerous and required the service of a surgeon, such as those that penetrated the body cavity, or a broken skull, or arrow wounds in the elbow, knee, or ankle, from which it was feared the wounded man might be left lame or maimed.

The number of such wounds found was that which we have stated. Of those which were through the calf from one side to the other, or through the thigh or the hips, or through the large or fleshy part of the arm, though made by lances, and of the knife wounds or stabs that did not endanger life, they took no account and did not have the surgeon treat them. The wounded themselves treated one another, though they might be captains or officials of the hacienda real. There was an almost countless number of such wounds, for there was scarcely a man who was not wounded, and most of them had five or six wounds, and many ten or twelve.

Having recounted (though badly) the events of the bloody battle of Mauvila and the victory that our men won there, from which they escaped with so many wounds as we have said, I must refer in what remains of this chapter to the consideration of those who may read it, so that they can

Warfare and Death: A Mississippian Motif. This native design, taken from an incised pottery beaker excavated in Alabama, illustrates a common artistic theme in Mississippian culture: skulls and forearm bones. The skulls bear conventional marks indicating that the victims had been scalped. (From the University of Alabama Museum of Natural History collections, Moundville Archaeological Park, Moundville, Alabama)

supply from their imaginations what I cannot tell fully here, the affliction and extreme necessity that these Spaniards suffered for everything needed to enable them to treat their wounds and save their lives. Even for people who were well and rested there was a great scarcity, as we shall soon see, and much more for men who had fought nine hours by the clock without stopping and had come out with so many and such severe wounds. I wish to avail myself of this means because, aside from my small ability, it is impossible that such momentous things can be written of adequately or described as they took place.

Therefore it must be considered first of all that, if they applied to the surgeon for treatment for such a multitude of wounds, there was only one in the whole army, and he was not as able and diligent as could have been desired; rather he was stupid and almost useless. Then if they asked for medicines, there were none, for the few that they were carrying, along with the olive oil they had reserved some days before for such needs, and the bandages and lint that they always had ready, and all the other linen such as sheets and shirts they could have used for making bandages and lint, and the rest of the clothing they were bringing, the Indians, as we said above, had taken into the pueblo, and the fire the Spaniards themselves set had consumed it. Then if they wished something to eat, there was nothing, because the fire had burned up the provisions that the Castilians had brought and those the Indians had in their houses, not one of which remained standing, all of them having been consumed.

Our Spaniards found themselves in these straits, without doctors or medicines, without bandages or lint, without food or clothing with which to cover themselves, without houses or even huts in which to take shelter against the cold and dew of the night. They had been deprived of all succor by the misfortunes of that day. Even if they had attempted to go in search of something for their relief, the darkness of the night would have prevented them, and not knowing where to find it, and seeing themselves all so wounded and weak from loss of blood that most of them could not stand on their feet. They had an abundance only of sighs and groans that the pain of their wounds and the poor treatment of them wrested from them.

In their hearts and aloud they called on God to protect and succor them in that affliction, and our Lord as a merciful Father aided them, by giving them an invincible spirit in that hardship, which the Spanish nation always had above all the nations of the earth to support it in its greatest necessities, and these availed themselves of it in the present one, as we shall see in the next chapter.

XXX

THE EFFORTS THE SPANIARDS MADE TO HELP THEMSELVES, AND TWO STRANGE EVENTS THAT TOOK PLACE DURING THE BATTLE

Our Spaniards finding themselves in the necessity, hardship, and affliction of which we have told, considering that they had no other recourse than their own spirit and courage, recovered it to such an extent that those who were least wounded went at once and with great diligence to the aid of the badly wounded. Some found a sheltered place in which to put them, making use for this purpose of the shelters and large huts that the Indians had built outside the pueblo for lodging the Spaniards. They made roofs from the arbors to fasten to the walls that were left standing. Others busied themselves in cutting open the dead Indians and taking the fat to use as ointment and oil in treating wounds. Others brought straw on which to lay the sick.

Others took the shirts off their dead comrades and took off their own to make bandages and lint from them. The ones that were made of linen were reserved for dressings only for those who were most dangerously wounded, not for all of them. The rest, whose wounds were not dangerous, had them dressed with coarser kinds of lint and bandages made of jackets and the linings of trousers and other such things that could be had.

Others worked at skinning the dead horses and in preparing and keeping the meat from them, to be given to the badly wounded in place of hens and young chickens, because there was nothing else to feed them.

With all the labor that they had to perform, others set themselves to stand guard and sentry duty so that, if the enemy should come, they would not find them unprepared, though very few of them were fit to take up arms.

In this manner they helped one another that night, all forcing themselves to endure with a good spirit the hardships that ill-fortune had inflicted upon them.

They remained four days treating the wounds that were considered dangerous, for as they had only one surgeon and as he was not very active, it was not possible to give them more attention. Thirteen Spaniards died during this time from their wounds. Forty-seven fell in battle, eighteen of whom were killed by arrow wounds in the eyes or mouth, for the Indians, knowing that their bodies were armed, shot at their faces.

Besides those who died before being treated and in the battle itself, another twenty-two Christians died afterward from poor treatment and poor doctors. Thus we can say that eighty-two Spaniards died in this battle of Mauvila.

To this loss was added that of forty-five horses that the Indians killed in the battle, which were no less lamented and mourned than their own comrades, because they saw that in them lay the greatest strength of their army.

Among all these losses, though they were so great, none was felt so much as that of Don Carlos Enríquez, for in all the toils and hardships, because of his great virtue and amiable disposition, he was a comfort and a solace to the governor, as good sons are to their fathers. To the captains and soldiers he was a help in their necessities and a protection in their shortcomings and faults, and brought peace and concord to their passions and private quarrels, setting himself to pacify and compose them. He did this not only among the captains and soldiers but also he served as their intercessor and patron with the general, to win his pardon and clemency for them in the derelictions they committed. The governor himself, whenever any trouble arose between important persons in the army, submitted it to Don Carlos so that he might compose and pacify it with his great affability and tact.

In these matters and other similar ones, besides fulfilling completely the duty of a good soldier, this true gentleman employed himself in favoring and assisting with deeds and words those who had need of him. Such acts ought to be held in esteem by those who pride themselves on the name of gentleman and hidalgo, for truly these titles sound false when unaccompanied by such works, because they are the very essence, origin, and principle from which true nobility springs, and upon which it sustains itself, and there can be no nobility where there is no virtue.

Among many other strange events that took place in this battle, we shall tell two that were the most notable. One was that in the first assault the Indians made upon the Castilians, when they fell upon them and drove them out of the pueblo with that unexpected and undreamed-of fury, sending them retreating across the fields, one Spaniard fled. He was a native of the village of Badajoz, a common man, very uncouth and rustic, whose name has been forgotten. At that time, only he turned his back and fled, and reaching a place out of danger (though to him it did not seem possible to do so), he fell headlong and then got up, but soon thereafter he fell dead, without a wound or any sign of a blow that they might have given him. All the Spaniards said that he had died of fright and of cowardice, because they found no other reason for it.

The other case was just the contrary. A Portuguese soldier named Men

Rodríguez, a nobleman from the city of Yelves of the company of Andrés Vasconcelos de Silva, a soldier who had served in Africa on the frontiers of the kingdom of Portugal, fought all day on horseback like the very valiant soldier that he was and performed memorable exploits in the battle. That night when the fighting was over, he dismounted and remained like a wooden statue, and without again speaking or eating or drinking or sleeping, after three days he passed from this life, without a wound or the sign of a blow that might have caused his death. It might have been that he was exhausted with much fighting. Thus in contrast to the other, it was said that this good fidalgo had died of valor and courage from having fought and labored excessively.

All that we have said in general and in particular about this great battle of Mauvila, both as to the time that it lasted, which was nine hours, and as to the events that took place in it, Alonso de Carmona tells in his *Relation.* He mentions the governor's wound and the arrow passing through Nuño Tovar's lance and says that they left it in the form of a cross. He tells of the unfortunate death of Don Carlos Enríquez and of that of Don Diego de Soto, his brother-in-law. Carmona adds that he himself put one knee upon his chest and the other on his forehead and endeavored with both hands to pull out the arrow, which pierced his eye, and says that he could not move it. He also tells of the hardships and fatigues they all suffered in common. Juan Coles tells the same things, though not at such length as Alonso de Carmona, and he refers especially to the number of serious wounds, which we mentioned. Both agree as to the number of Spaniards and horses that died in this battle, which was so much discussed that the memory of its events remained clear to them.

XXXI

THE NUMBER OF INDIANS WHO DIED IN THE BATTLE OF MAUVILA

The number of Indians, men and women, who perished in this conflict by the sword and by fire was thought to exceed eleven thousand persons, because more than 2,500 men were left lying round about the pueblo, and among them they found the young Tascaluça, son of the cacique. Inside the pueblo more than three thousand Indians died by the sword, and one could not walk through the streets for the dead bodies. The fire consumed more than 3,500 souls in the houses, for in one house alone a thousand persons were burned, the fire cutting them off from the door and suffocating and burning them inside without their being able to get out. It was pitiful to see how they were left, and most of them were women.

For four leagues round about in the woods, ravines, and streams, the Spaniards on going through the country found nothing but dead and wounded Indians, to the number of two thousand persons who had been unable to reach their houses. It was pitiful to hear them groaning in the woods, entirely helpless.

Concerning Tascaluça, who was responsible for all this calamity, it was not known what had become of him, because some Indians said that he had escaped by flight and others that he had been burned up. The latter seems more probable and was more in accordance with what he deserved, for as was learned later, from the first day that the Castilians knew that they would come to his country he had resolved to kill them there. With this determination he had sent his son to the pueblo of Talise to receive the governor (as was told above), in order that he and those who went with him under pretext of serving the governor and his army could act as spies and note the military organization that the Spaniards maintained by day and by night, so that in accordance with their watchfulness or carelessness he could plan the treason that he intended to carry out in order to kill them. It was also learned that when the Indians of the pueblo of Talise (who we said were disobedient to their curaca) complained to Tascaluça that their lord had ordered them to give the Spaniards a certain number of Indian men and women for whom the governor had asked, telling him of their resentment at their cacique who, without regard for the good of his own people, would give them up to foreigners and unknown persons to be taken away as slaves, Tascaluça had said to them: "Do not be troubled at giving up the Indian men and women whom your cacique orders you to send, for I shall return to you very soon not only your own but also those whom the Spaniards are bringing as captives and prisoners from other places. I shall give you even the Spaniards themselves to be your slaves and to serve you in cultivating and tilling your fields and gardens, digging and delving all the days of their lives."

The Indian women who remained in the hands of the Castilians after this battle of Mauvila also confirmed this statement of Tascaluça and declared openly the treason that he had plotted against the Christians, because they said that most of them were not natives of that pueblo nor of that province, but of various other neighboring ones, and that the Indians who had assembled for that battle at the summons and persuasion of Tascaluça he had attracted by the glowing promises that he had made them. Some he had promised to give scarlet capes, and others clothing of silk, satin, and velvet with which they could dress themselves for their dances and festivals. He had sworn with solemn oaths to give others horses, and that as a sign of their victory and triumph they should ride them before the Spaniards. Other women came away saying, "Well, he promised the Spaniards themselves for our servants and slaves," and each one stated the number of captives that had been offered to them to be taken to their houses.

Thus they confessed that many other promises had been made to them of linen, cloth, and other things from Spain. They also declared that many women who were married had come in obedience to their husbands, who had commanded them to do so. Others, who were single, said that they had come at the importunity of their relatives and brothers who had promised to bring them so that they might see some solemn festivals and great celebrations that they would observe and hold after the death and destruction of the Castilians, in rendering thanks to their great god the Sun for the victory that he would give them.

Many other women confessed that they had come at the request and petition of their gallants and sweethearts who wished to marry them, and who begged and persuaded them to come and see the valiant deeds and exploits they expected to perform against the Spaniards in their service and presence. These statements proved conclusively the length of time that this curaca had been plotting the treason that he perpetrated against our men. He and his vassals and allies were well punished for this, though at the cost of such injury to the Castilians as has been seen.

Their loss did not consist alone in the lack of the horses that were killed and in the comrades who were lost, but also in other things that concerned them more as a result of the uses to which they were dedicated. These were a little wheat flour, amounting to about three fanegas, and four arrobas of wine, for this was all they had when they reached Mauvila. For many days before they had kept this flour and wine very carefully and reverently for celebrating mass, and so that it might be carried more carefully and be better protected, the governor brought it in his own equipage. All this was burned, along with the chalices, altars, and ornaments they were carrying for divine worship. Thenceforth it was impossible for them to hear mass because they did not have the material of bread and wine for the consecration of the Eucharist, though the questions in theology were raised among the religious and secular priests [or, perhaps, "priests, religious, and seculars"—DB] as to whether or not they could consecrate bread made of maize. It was agreed by common consent that the most certain [decision] and above all that which the holy Roman church, our Mother and Lady, in her holy councils and sacred canons orders and teaches us, is that the bread shall be of wheat and the wine from the grape. Thus these Spanish Catholics concluded that they would not adopt doubtful remedies for fear of finding themselves thereby disobedient to their mother the Roman Catholic church, and also they omitted [celebrating mass] because even if they had the means for consecrating the Eucharist, they would lack chalices and altars for celebrating it.

XXXII

WHAT THE SPANIARDS DID AFTER THE BATTLE OF MAUVILA, AND A MUTINY THAT AROSE AMONG THEM

Since everything they were carrying for saying mass was burned in the battle of Mauvila, from that time on, by order of the priests, an altar was set up and adorned to be venerated on Sundays and feast days, whenever there was an opportunity to do so. A priest robed himself with ornaments that they made from deerskin, in imitation of the first garments that there were in the world, which were made of the skins of animals. Taking his stand at the altar he read the Confession and the Introit of the mass, and the Prayer [the Orison], the Epistle and the Gospel and all the rest to the end of the mass, without the consecration, and these Castilians called it the "dry mass." The one who celebrated it, or another of the priests, announced the text and upon it gave his discourse or sermon, and with this sort of ceremony that they conducted in the place of mass they consoled themselves in the affliction they felt at being unable to adore Jesus Christ our Lord and Redeemer in the sacramental elements. This lasted for three years, until they left La Florida for Christian lands.

Our Spaniards remained eight days in the rude huts that they erected within Mauvila, and when they were able to leave them they went to those the Indians had built for their lodgings, where they were better accommodated. They stayed there fifteen days longer treating the wounded, which included almost all of them. Those whose wounds were less serious went out to scour the country in search of food in the pueblos that were in the vicinity. There were many of these, though they were small, where they found enough food.

In all the pueblos in the surrounding four leagues the Spaniards found many wounded Indians who had escaped from the battle, but they did not find a single Indian, man or woman, who was caring for them. They understood that they came at night to bring them provisions and in the daytime went back to the woods. The Castilians gave aid to such wounded Indians and divided with them the food that they found, rather than mistreating them. Not a single Indian appeared in the open country, and after a diligent search by the mounted men they captured fifteen or twenty from whom to obtain information. Having asked them whether there was any body of Indians being assembled in any place to come against the Spaniards, they replied that inasmuch as the bravest, noblest, and richest men of that province had perished in the recent battle, no one remained in it who could take up arms. This seemed to be the truth because in all the time that our men were in that camp no Indians appeared by day or by night except to make sallies and raise alarms, which simply by disturbing them did them much harm and injury, such was their weakened condition after the battle.

In Mauvila the governor had word of the ships that Captains Gómez Arias and Diego Maldonado were bringing, exploring the coast and learning what was going on there. He received this report before the battle and afterward he verified it by the Indians who were captured, from whom he learned that the province of Achusi, which the Spaniards were going in search of, and the seacoast, were a little less than thirty leagues from Mauvila.

The governor was very pleased with this news, [which indicated] the conclusion and end of such a long peregrination, and the beginning and commencement of the new settlement that he intended to make in that province. His purpose, as we have said above, was to found a pueblo at the port of Achusi to receive and safeguard the ships that would come to it from all parts, and to found another pueblo twenty leagues inland from which to begin and to direct the conversion of the Indians to the faith of the holy Roman church, and to the service and augmentation of the Crown of Spain.

As a celebration of this good news and because he was assured that the roads were safe from Mauvila to Achusi, the governor set free the curaca whom Captain Diego Maldonado had brought as a prisoner from the port of Achusi. The adelantado had brought him with him, treating him well, and had not sent him back to his own country previously because of the long distance and the danger that the other Indians would kill or capture him on the road. Since the governor now knew that his country was close by and that he would be safe until reaching it, he gave him permission to go to his house, charging him strictly to preserve his friendship for the Spaniards, as he would very soon have them as guests in his country. The cacique took leave, gratified by the favor that the governor showed him, and said that he would be much pleased to see him in his country in order to return the favors that he owed his lordship.

All these desires that the adelantado had to settle the country and the method and plans that he had worked out for it in his own mind were destroyed and frustrated by discord, as it always ruins and throws down armies, republics, kings, and empires, where they allow it to enter. The door by which it found ours was that, since there were in this army some of the personages who had taken part in the conquest of El Perú and the imprisonment of Atahuallpa, and who saw the great riches there in gold and silver, and had told those who were going on this expedition about it, and since on the contrary there had not been seen in La Florida silver or gold, though the fertility and the other good qualities of the land were such as have been seen, they would not consent to settle or make an establishment in that kingdom.

To this disappointment was added the incredible ferocity of the battle of Mauvila, which had frightened and disturbed them extraordinarily, making them wish to leave the land and go away from it as soon as they could. For they said that it was impossible to rule such bellicose people or to subjugate such bold men. From what they had seen up to that time it seemed to them that neither by force nor by persuasion could they be brought under the authority and dominion of the Spaniards; that they would allow themselves to be killed first. There was no reason for going about expending their forces a little at a time in that country; rather they ought to go to others already won, and rich, such as El Perú and México, where they could enrich themselves without so much work. Therefore it would be well as soon as they should reach the coast to leave that bad country and go to New Spain.

A few of the persons whom we have mentioned whispered and discussed these things and other similar ones among themselves, but they could not keep them so secret that some of those who had come with the governor from Spain, and were his loyal friends and companions, did not hear them. These persons told him what was going on in his army, and how they were speaking resolutely of leaving the country as soon as they should reach a place where there were ships or any vessels at all.

XXXIII

THE GOVERNOR CONFIRMS THE MUTINY, AND CHANGES HIS PLANS

In such a serious matter the governor did not wish to give entire credit to those who had told him of it without first verifying it for himself. With this in mind he made the rounds at night as thoroughly as he could, in disguise, so as not to be recognized. Going about thus, one night he heard the treasurer, Juan Gaytán, and others who were in the hut with him saying that when they reached the port of Achusi where they expected to find the ships they intended to go to Mexico or El Perú, or to return to Spain, because they could not endure such a hard life to win and conquer such a poor and miserable country.

This hurt the governor exceedingly, for he understood from those words that his army was disintegrating and that his men, in finding a place to go, would all desert him as they did at the beginning of the discovery and conquest of El Perú in the case of the governor and marqués Don Francisco Pizarro, who finally was left with only thirteen men on the island of Gorgona. And he knew that, if those whom he then had should leave him, there would be no possibility of raising a new army, and he would be stripped of his grandeur, authority, and reputation, his money spent in vain, and the excessive hardships they had endured hitherto in the discovery of that country would be lost.

These things, considered by a man so zealous of his honor as was the governor, produced in him hasty and desperate resolutions. Though he dissembled his wrath at that time, reserving punishment for another occasion, he was unwilling to endure or to see and experience the bad actions that he feared from those whose spirits were weak and cowardly. Thus as rapidly as he could, without revealing anything of his anger, he gave orders that they would again go inland and withdraw from the coast, so as to deprive the ill-disposed of the occasion for disgracing themselves and stirring up all his men to rebellion.

This was the first beginning and the chief cause of this gentleman and all his army being lost. From that day, as a disillusioned man whose own people have betrayed his hopes and cut off the road to his ambition and destroyed the plan that he had made for settling and holding the land, he never again succeeded in doing anything profitable to him, nor was it thought that he attempted to do so. On the contrary, actuated only by indifference, he went about thereafter wasting his time and his life without any gain, always traveling from one place to another without order or purpose, like a man tired of life and desirous of ending it, until he died, as we shall see below. His contentment and hopes lost, and lost also to his successors and descendants the labors that he had undergone in that conquest and the wealth that he had consumed in it, he was the cause of all those who had gone with him to win that land being lost as well. He failed likewise to lay the foundations for a most glorious and beautiful kingdom for the Crown of Spain, and for the increase of the holy Catholic faith, which is what is to be most regretted.

Therefore it would have been very fitting for him, in such a serious business, to have asked and received counsel from the friends that he had, on whom he could depend, so as to act prudently and with their approval for the common good. This captain could have put down that mutiny by punishing its leaders, with which the others in the conspiracy, who were few in number, would have been frightened, and he would not have lost himself and injured all his men by being governed only by his own passionate feeling, which caused his own destruction. Though he was so discreet as we have seen, in his own cause and with his passions aroused he could not control and govern himself with the clear reasoning and unbiased judgment that serious matters demand. Thus he who refuses to ask and take advice invites disaster.

In fear of the mutiny, the governor wished to leave that camp quickly and go back into the interior through other provinces that they had not seen, so that his men would not suspect his purpose and guess his intentions, [as they might] if he should return by the road that they had followed previously. Thus with a dissembling spirit foreign to that which he had shown hitherto, he encouraged his soldiers, telling them to recover quickly in order to get out of that bad country where they had received so much injury, and he ordered a decree to be issued for the march to begin on a certain day in the future.

XXXIV

TWO LAWS THAT THE INDIANS OF LA FLORIDA OBSERVE AGAINST ADULTERESSES

Because we promised above to tell some of the customs, at least the most notable ones, that the Indians of La Florida have, before we leave Mauvila it will be well to say here that in the province of Coça, which we have left behind, and in that of Tascaluça where our Spaniards are at present, the Indians have and enforce a law for the punishment of the adulterous women who are found among them.[23] Thus it was that throughout all that great province of Coça it was the law that under penalty of death and of sinning gravely against their religion, any Indian who knew of an adulterous woman in his neighborhood, not as an actual witness of criminal acts, but because of suspicious signs, which signs were set forth in the law both as to their nature and their number, was obliged, after having verified his suspicion, to give notice of it to the lord of the province or in his absence to the judges of the pueblo. They would take secret testimony from three or four witnesses, and having found the woman guilty through circumstantial evidence, they would arrest her. On the first feast day that came among those that they observe in their heathenism, they would order by public proclamation that all the people in the pueblo come out after dinner to such and such a place in the country near the pueblo, and of the people who came out they formed a long or short lane, according to their number.

Two judges stationed themselves at one end of the lane and two more at the other. One of them ordered the adulteress before him, and summoning the husband, said to him: "This woman in accordance with our law is convicted [on the testimony] of witnesses to be bad and an adulteress; therefore do with her what that same law commands you." The husband immediately stripped off her clothes, leaving her as naked as when she was born, and with a flint knife (for in all the New World the Indians have not achieved the

[23]Regarding this, John R. Swanton states that "the severity with which adultery was punished by the Creeks and their neighbors struck Garcilaso's informants as forcibly as it did later explorers. . . . It is significant that, though the custom of killing adulteresses with arrows which he describes as a current usage among the Indians of Tuscaloosa had disappeared by the eighteenth century, James Adair's informants related it as a former custom well known to them." We might merely add that Garcilaso's soldier informants had ample opportunity to provoke such sanctions and thus to observe them firsthand. Swanton, "Ethnological Value of the De Soto Narratives," 576.

invention of scissors) he clipped off her hair (a most ignominious punishment, used generally among all the nations of this New World), and thus shorn and naked the husband left her in the hands of the judges and went away, carrying her clothing as a sign of divorce and repudiation.

The judges ordered the woman to go immediately, just as she was, through the lane formed by the people to the other judges and give them an account of her crime.

The woman went all the way down the lane and, standing before the judges, said to them: "I come sentenced by your associates to the punishment the law imposes upon adulterous women, because I have been such. They sent me to you so that you could order in this case whatever you regard as conducive to the public welfare." The judges replied to her: "Return to those who sent you here to us and tell them on our part that it is very fitting that the laws of our country, which our ancestors formed regarding chastity, be observed, complied with, and carried out against wrongdoers. Therefore we approve what they ordered you [to do] in accordance with the law, and we order you not to transgress it at any time."

The woman went back to the first judges with this reply, and this going and coming they ordered her to do in carrying the messages between the lane formed of people served no other purpose except to insult and shame her, forcing her to appear before all her people in disgrace and infamy, shorn, naked, and [convicted of] such a crime, for the punishment of such shame is a public one.

While the poor woman came and went between the two sets of judges, all the people of the pueblo, by way of insult and contempt, threw at her clods, pebbles, sticks, straw, handfuls of earth, old rags, fragments of hides, pieces of mats, and other such things, according to what each one of them happened to bring to throw at her in punishment of her crime. The law so commanded, making it understood that the woman had become a loathsome outcast.

Then the judges condemned her to perpetual exile from the pueblo and from the whole province, which was the penalty prescribed by law, and they turned her over to her relatives, admonishing them under the same penalty not to give her protection or assistance in re-entering any part of the state, openly or secretly. The relatives received her, and covering her with a mantle, they took her away where she would never again appear in the pueblo or in the province. The judges gave the husband permission to marry. The Indians of the province of Coça observed this law and custom.

In that of Tascaluça they observed another, more rigorous one in punishing adulterous women. It was that the Indian who should notice bad signs (such as to see a man entering or leaving another's house in a suspicious manner) that would lead him to suspect that the woman was an adulteress, after having verified his suspicion by seeing the man enter or leave three times, was obligated by their fallacious religion under penalty of a curse to tell the husband of his suspicion and of the woman's action. He had to produce two or three other witnesses who may have seen a part of what the accuser told or some other similar indication. The husband questioned each one of them separately, calling down terrible curses upon him if he should lie to him and great blessings if he should tell him the truth. On finding that the woman had incurred this suspicion by the bad signs that she had given, he took her into the country near the pueblo and fastened her to a tree, or if there were none to a post he planted in the ground, and shot at her with his bow and arrows until he killed her.

This done, he went to the lord of the pueblo or in his absence to the magistrate and said: "Sir, I left my wife dead in such and such a place, because certain of my neighbors said that she was an adulteress. Order them to be summoned, and if what they told me should be true, set me free, and if not impose the penalty upon me that our laws prescribe and order."

The penalty was that the woman's relatives shoot the surrendered with arrows until he died, and leave him unburied in the fields as he had done the woman, whom as an innocent person the law ordered to be buried with all pomp and ceremony. But if the judge found that the witnesses confirmed one another and that the signs and suspicions proved true, the husband was set free and given permission to marry. They ordered a proclamation issued to the effect that under penalty of death no person, whether relative, friend, or acquaintance of the dead woman, should dare bury her or even to pull a single arrow out of her body, but were to leave it to be eaten by the birds and the dogs as a punishment and example for her wrongdoing.

These two particular laws are observed in the province of Coça and Tascaluça, and throughout the kingdom in general adultery is punished very severely. Though I endeavored to learn what penalty they imposed upon the accomplice and the adulterous husband, he who gave me the account could not tell me anything except that he had heard no discussion of the men who were adulterers, but only of the women. It may have been because among all nations these laws are always more severe against women and favorable to the men, for as a woman of this bishopric whom I knew said, the men make them, being fearful of the offense, and not the women; if the women had the making of them, things would be arranged differently.

XXXV

THE SPANIARDS LEAVE MAUVILA AND ENTER CHICAÇA. THEY BUILD PIROGUES FOR CROSSING A LARGE RIVER

Taking up the thread of our *History,* then, after the Spaniards had spent twenty-three or twenty-four days in camp at Mauvila recovering from their wounds, and had regained some strength for continuing their discovery, they left the province of Tascaluça, and at the end of the three days' journey that they made through some pleasant though uninhabited country, they entered another, called Chicaça. The first pueblo of this province that our men reached was not the principal one, but one of the others in its jurisdiction. It was situated on the edge of a large and deep river having very high banks. The pueblo was on the side of the river from which the Spaniards approached.[24]

The Indians were unwilling to receive the governor peacefully but from the very beginning showed themselves to be hostile, replying to the messengers that he had sent them that they desired war with fire and sword. When our men came in sight of the pueblo they saw in front of it a squadron of more than fifteen hundred warriors, who came out to meet the Castilians as soon as they appeared. They skirmished with them, and having made some show of defense they withdrew to the river, abandoning the pueblo, from which they had taken their property, women, and children. They had decided not to fight a pitched battle with the Spaniards but to oppose their crossing the river, which—because it carried a great deal of water, was very deep, and had high and steep banks—they thought would obstruct their road and force them to take another route.

Therefore, as the Spaniards fell upon the Indians furiously, they threw themselves into the water and crossed the river, some of them in canoes, as they had many and very good ones, and some of them swimming, urged on by their fear.

---

[24]Garcilaso conflates and confuses the crossing of the River of Pafallaya (Elvas; Ranjel's Apafalaya) with the crossing of the River of Chicaça. Both crossings were contested.

They had the main body of their army on the other side of the river facing the pueblo, where there were eight thousand warriors, whose purpose was to defend the crossing of the river. Their encampment extended for two leagues along its banks, so that the Castilians could not cross in all that distance.

Besides this opposition that the Indians gave the Christians at the river, they harried them at night with the sudden attacks and alarms that they gave, bands of them crossing the river in their canoes at various points and then joining together, thus molesting our men greatly. In order to defend themselves the latter made use of a very clever stratagem. This was that in three landing places along the river in that space the Indians had occupied, where they came to disembark, they dug pits at night in which crossbowmen and harquebusiers could take shelter. When they saw the Indians they allowed them to land and leave their canoes, and then they fell upon them and did them much damage with their swords, because the enemy had nowhere to run. They mistreated them thus three times, whereupon the Indians, chastised for their boldness, did not dare cross the river again. They only waited with much care and alertness to oppose our men's crossing. The governor and his captains, seeing that it was impossible to cross the river where they were because of the strong opposition that the enemy was making, and that they would lose time in awaiting a moment of carelessness on their part, ordered that a hundred of the most diligent men who knew something of the art should build two large barks, which they also call pirogues. They are almost flat and will hold many people. In order that the Indians might not find out what they were doing, they went into a forest that was a league and a half up the river and a league back from the riverbank.

The hundred Spaniards assigned to this task worked so quickly that they finished the pirogues in the space of twelve days. In order to carry them to the river they made two carts of appropriate size, and by means of pack animals and horses that pulled them, and the Castilians themselves who pushed the carts and at difficult places carried the barks on their shoulders, they got them to the river one morning before dawn at a very spacious landing place that was there. There was also a good landing on the other side.

The governor was present when the barks were launched on the river because he had ordered that he be advised of it beforehand. He directed that ten cavalrymen and forty infantry who were expert marksmen embark in each of the boats as quickly as possible before the Indians should come to oppose their passage. The foot soldiers were to row, and the cavalrymen rode their horses into the boats so as not to be delayed in mounting when they reached the other side.

However silently the Spaniards attempted to launch the barks in the river and go aboard them, they could not avoid being heard by five hundred Indians who were patrolling the opposite bank of the river. They ran to the crossing and, seeing the barks and the Spaniards who were attempting to pass over, they raised a loud alarm, warning their men and asking for help, and then went to the landing to oppose their passage.

Fearing that still more enemies would come, the Spaniards embarked as hastily as possible. The governor wished to cross on the first trip, but his men prevented him because of the great danger there was on that first voyage, until the landing place should be cleared of enemies. Our men thus hastily applied themselves to the oars, and all of them reached the other bank wounded because the Indians shot arrows at them from the bluff entirely at their pleasure.

One of the barks struck the landing squarely and the other fell downstream from it, and because of the high bluffs along the river, the men could not land. Thus they were forced to row hard to get up to the landing.

Those in the first bark jumped ashore, and the first one to come out was Diego García, the son of the alcalde of Villanueva de Barcarrota, a brave soldier and very resolute in all feats of arms, wherefore all his companions called him Diego García de Paredes, not because he was related to him, though he was a nobleman, but because he resembled him in spirit, courage, and valor. The second mounted man who went ashore was Gonzalo Silvestre. These two fell upon the Indians and drove them more than two hundred paces back from the landing place, and came back at a run to their own side because of the great danger they were in, being two alone among so many of the enemy. Thus they attacked the Indians and fell back four times without receiving any help from their companions, because they got in one another's way and could not manage to get the horses ashore. The fifth time they attacked the enemy there were six mounted men, which put more fear into the Indians and prevented their coming so furiously to oppose the crossing. As soon as the infantry who were in the first boat came ashore, they went into a small pueblo that was on the very brink of the river, and did not dare leave it because they were few and all of them were wounded, as they had received most of the arrows. Those in the second pirogue, as they found the landing place free of the enemy, came ashore more easily and without any danger and ran to help their companions who were fighting on the plain.

The governor went across on the second trip with seventy or eighty other Spaniards, and as the Indians saw that their enemies were numerous and that they could not resist them, they retreated to some woods that were not far from the pueblo, and from there they went to the place where their people were encamped. The latter had heard the shout and alarm that their scouts had given and ran quickly to defend the crossing, but on meeting the scouts and learning from them that many Spaniards had already crossed the river, they went back to their army where they prepared to defend themselves.

The Christians went after them, intending to fight, but the Indians remained quiet, fortifying themselves with wooden palisades and with the same shelters that they had built for their lodgings. Some of them came out very boldly to skirmish, but they paid for their daring because they were killed with lances, as their swiftness could not equal that of the cavalry. That whole day was spent in this manner, and the following night the Indians left and did not reappear. Meanwhile the whole Spanish army had crossed the river.

XXXVI

OUR MEN ENCAMP IN CHICAÇA. THE INDIANS GIVE THEM A MOST CRUEL AND UNEXPECTED NOCTURNAL BATTLE

Our Spaniards overcame the difficulty of crossing the first river of the province of Chicaça with the labor and danger of which we have told, and as they found themselves free of the enemy, they dismantled the pirogues and kept the nails for making others whenever it might be necessary. Having done this, they went on with their discovery, and in four daily journeys they made through a level country, well populated, though the pueblos were scattered and had few houses, they reached the principal pueblo, called Chicaça, from which the whole province takes its name. It was situated on a level elevation extending from north to south between two streams having little water but much timber, consisting of walnuts, oaks, and live oaks, at the foot of which was the fruit of two or three years. The Indians let it go to waste because they had no cattle to eat it and they themselves did not use it, having other, better and more delicate fruits to eat.

The general and his captains reached the pueblo Chicaça at the beginning of December of the year 1540 and found it abandoned. Since it was now winter, it seemed to them that it would be well to winter there. Having decided to do so, they collected all the necessary provisions and brought from the outlying small pueblos much wood and straw from which to make houses, because those of the principal pueblo, though they numbered two hundred, were not enough.

Our men were in these lodgings almost two months, enjoying some degree of quiet and rest. They did nothing except ride through the country every day, and they took a few Indians, most of whom the governor sent with gifts and messages to the curaca, offering him peace and friendship. He replied, giving great hopes of his coming, making up excuses for his delay, and repeating his messages day after day to keep up the governor's expectations. In return for his gifts he sent him some fruit, fish, and venison.

Meanwhile his Indians did not cease disturbing our Spaniards with sudden assaults and alarms that they made two or three times every night. They did not stay to fight, for when the Christians came out against them they ran away. They did all this purposely as experienced warriors to keep the Spaniards awake with their unexpected attacks and make them careless with their show of cowardice, so that they would think that they would always do thus and would relax their military discipline, at which time they would fall upon them in earnest.

The Indians did not follow these cowardly tactics very long. On the other hand it seemed that, ashamed of having used them, they wished to contradict them and show that their past flights had been made purposely in order to reveal a greater spirit and courage in due time, which they did, as we shall soon see.

One night toward the end of January of the year 1541, having realized that the north wind, which was blowing furiously, was favorable to them, at one o'clock the Indians came in three squadrons, and as silently as possible, they advanced to within a hundred paces of the Spanish sentries.

The curaca, who was coming as captain of the middle squadron, which was the principal one, sent to find out where the other two were on either side, and having learned that they were in the same position as his own, he ordered the signal to be given. They did so with many drums, fifes, shells, and other rude instruments they brought along for making more noise. All the Indians together raised a great shout to strike terror and fright into the Spaniards. In order to set fire to the pueblo and to be able to see the enemy, they brought faggots made of a certain herb that grows in that country, which, when made into a rope or thin cord and lighted, smolders like the match-cord of a harquebus, and when waved through the air it bursts into flame that burned steadily like a wax taper with four wicks and gave as much light. They had twists made of the same herb on the points of their arrows so as to shoot them while burning and set fire to the houses from a distance.[25]

In this order and with these preparations the Indians came and attacked the pueblo, waving the torches and shooting many burning arrows into the houses. As the latter were made of straw, they caught fire immediately in the hard wind that was blowing.

The Spaniards, though attacked so suddenly and with such a fierce assault, did not fail to come out with all promptness to defend their lives. The governor, who in order to be prepared for such surprises always slept in his breeches and doublet, went out against the enemy on horseback ahead of all the rest of his gentlemen. Because of the enemy's swiftness, he had been unable to take up any defensive armor except a helmet and a jacket, which they considered as armor, made of quilted cotton three finger-breadths in thickness. Our men had found no better defense against arrows. The governor went out alone with these arms and his lance and shield against such a multitude of enemies, for he never learned to fear them. Ten or twelve other horsemen went after him, but not immediately.

The rest of the Spaniards, captains as well as soldiers, hurried with their accustomed courage to resist the ferocity and boldness of the Indians, but they could not fight with them because they brought in front of them in their favor and defense fire, flame, and smoke. The hard wind that was blowing turned all this against the Spaniards, hindering them seriously. But with all this our men came out of their quarters as well as they could to fight with the enemy, some crawling on all fours under the flames so that they would not overtake them, others running from house to house fleeing from the fire, and some of them thus reaching the open country, and others running to the infirmary to rescue the sufferers, for they had the sick by themselves in a separate house. Hearing the fire and the enemy, those who were able took refuge in flight, and those who were not burned to death before help reached them.

[25]The use of fire arrows by the Southeastern Indians is attested elsewhere in the ethnohistorical record for a later period.

The mounted men came out as well as they could, hastened by the fire and the enemy's fury, but since the attack was so sudden they had no time to arm and saddle the horses. Some they led out by the bridles, escaping with them so that the fire would not burn them; others they set loose, there being no other defense against the fire except flight. A few went out to help the governor, who had been fighting the enemy for a long time with the handful of men who had gone out at the beginning of the battle, and he was the first to kill an Indian that night because he always prided himself on being among the first in everything. The Indians of the two squadrons on either side entered the pueblo, and aided by the fire, which was in their favor, they did a great deal of damage. They killed many horses and Spaniards who had no time to escape.

XXXVII

THE BATTLE OF CHICAÇA PROCEEDS TO ITS END

From the eastern quarter of the pueblo where the fire and the impact of the enemy were greatest and most furious, forty or fifty Spaniards came out running at full speed (a shameful thing such as had not been seen up to that time in the whole expedition to La Florida). Nuño Tovar came after them with a naked sword in his hand, wearing a coat of mail all unclasped, for the enemy's haste had not given him time for more.

This gentleman went shouting loudly to his men, "Come back, soldiers, come back! Where are you going? There is no Córdoba or Sevilla to receive you. Remember that the safety of your lives lies in your stout spirit and strong arms, and not in flight." At this moment there came out to meet those who were fleeing thirty soldiers from the southern quarter of the pueblo, which the fire had not yet reached. Captain Juan de Guzmán from Talavera de la Reyna was lodged there, and the soldiers were from his company. Censuring those who were running away for their shameful action, they stopped them, and all of them together went around the pueblo because they could not pass through the fire that was between them and the enemy, and came out on the field on the east side to fight with them.

At the same time that these infantrymen came out, Captain Andrés de Vasconcelos, who was lodged in the same quarter, arrived, bringing twenty-four gentlemen fidalgos of his company, all Portuguese and chosen men, most of whom had been horsemen on the African frontiers. These gentlemen came out on the west side, and Nuño Tovar went with them on foot, just as he was. When they encountered the enemy, these two parties, one on one side and one on the other, closed with them and forced the center squadron, which was the principal one, to retire. There the battle was fiercest, and the governor and the few men who were with him had hitherto been fighting desperately and at great risk to their lives, because they were few and the enemy was numerous.

But when they saw help coming they fell upon them with new energy, and the general, with the desire to kill an Indian who had been distinguishing himself in the fight, closed with him, and having managed to wound him with his lance, in order to give the finishing stroke he bore down upon it and upon the right stirrup. With the weight and the force that he exerted, the saddle turned under him and he fell with it in the midst of the enemy. Seeing their captain-general in that danger, the Spaniards, both cavalry and infantry, ran to his rescue so promptly and fought so bravely that they prevented the Indians from killing him. His horse being saddled, he mounted and went back again to fight.

The governor had fallen because his servants, in the confusion of the sudden and furious assault by the Indians and perturbed by the threat of imminent death, had saddled the horse without fastening the girth. Thus the Spaniards who came to his aid found it doubled back over the saddle where they always put it when they unsaddle a horse, so that the governor had fought more than an hour with the girth unfastened when he fell, having availed himself of his great skill in horsemanship.

Seeing the force in which the Spaniards were gathering from all sides, and that many horses were coming out, the Indians abated the fury with which they had fought hitherto, but they still persisted in giving battle, sometimes attacking very spiritedly and again retreating in very good order, until at length they could no longer resist the force of the Spaniards and they called to one another to retire and abandon the fight. Turning their backs, they fled at full speed.

The governor and the mounted men followed at their heels, pursuing the enemy as far as they could by the light of the fire that was burning in the pueblo. After this sudden and furious battle, which lasted more than two hours, had ended, the general, who had followed in the pursuit, ordered the assembly sounded and went back to see the damage that the Indians had done. He found it to be greater than he expected, because forty Spaniards were killed and fifty horses. Alonso de Carmona says that eighty horses were killed and wounded, more than twenty of them having been burned to death or shot with arrows in the very stables where they were tied, because their masters, having found them very mettlesome as the result of the plentiful food that they had in that camp, in order to keep them more securely had made halters of heavy chains with which they fastened them. In their haste in the presence of the fire and the enemy, they had been unable to loosen them, and thus they abandoned the horses to the fire and to the enemy. Being tied, as they were, the latter shot them with arrows.

Besides the grief our Spaniards felt at the loss of their companions and the death of the horses, which were the strength of their army, they were saddened by a particular incident that happened that night. This was that among them there was just one Spanish woman, who was named Francisca de Hinestrosa, who was married to a good soldier called Hernando Bautista, and who was to give birth to a child within a few days. Since the enemy's attack came so suddenly, the husband went out to fight, and when the battle was over and he came back to see where his wife was he found her burned to a cinder, because she had been unable to run from the fire.

The contrary happened to a little soldier named Francisco Enríquez, who was worthless, though he bore a good name. He was a pusillanimous wretch, more of a buffoon than a soldier, at whom the Spaniards laughed a great deal. He was sick in the infirmary and for days they had carried him on their shoulders. But when he heard the fire and the enemy's onslaught he ran out of the infirmary and, after going only a few steps in the street, he met an Indian who wounded him in the groin, the arrow almost coming out on the other side, and left him stretched on the ground for dead, where he remained more than two hours.

After daylight they treated him, and in a short time he recovered from the wound, which had been thought mortal; and also from the illness, which had been very long and troublesome. Thus those who were accustomed to joke with him were making fun of him afterward and said: "You can thank that grievous misfortune that gave you, who aren't worth two pins, your health and life, and caused the death of so many gentlemen and principal soldiers as have died in these two last battles." Enríquez took it all and said other, worse things to them.

We have told above how the governor took swine to La Florida for breeding and had had them tended with much care for their feeding and increase. So as to keep them more safely at night in this camp of Chicaça, they had made a wooden pen inside the pueblo by setting stakes in the ground and making a covering of straw. Inasmuch as the fire on the night of the battle was so great, it overtook them also and burned all of them. Only the sucking pigs escaped, they being able to get out between the stakes of the pen. They were so fat with the abundance of food that they found in that country that the lard from the burned pigs ran out for more than two hundred paces. This loss was felt no less than the others, because our Castilians suffered for lack of meat and kept this to give to the sick.

Juan Coles and Alonso de Carmona agree with the account of this battle throughout, and both tell of the destruction of the swine by fire. They praise the governor's horsemanship highly and tell of his fall and of his having fought more than an hour without a saddle-girth. Alonso de Carmona adds that each Indian had three cords tied around his wrist, one for leading a Castilian, one for a horse, and the other for a pig, and that our men were highly incensed when they learned of it.

XXXVIII

REMARKABLE EVENTS THAT TOOK PLACE IN THE BATTLE OF CHICAÇA

As soon as they had buried the dead and tended the wounded, many Spaniards went out to the battlefield to see and examine the arrow wounds the Indians had given the horses that they killed. They opened them, as was their custom, both in order to see to what part the arrows had penetrated and in order to keep the meat for eating. They found that almost all of them had been pierced by arrows through the entrails and lungs or near the heart. They found in particular eleven or twelve horses shot through the center of the heart, and as we have said before, when these Indians could shoot them through the knees they would not shoot them elsewhere.

They also found four horses, each one of which had two arrows through the heart, that had happened to be shot at the same time, one from one side and one from the other. This is a marvelous thing and hard to believe, though it is certain that it happened, and because it was such an unusual thing, all the Spaniards who were walking through the field came up to see it.

They found another extraordinarily powerful shot. This took place when the horse of a trumpeter named Juan Díaz, a native of Granada, was killed by an arrow that had passed through the broadest part of the back and stuck out three finger-breadths on the opposite side. Since this shot had come from such a strong and powerful arm, because the horse was one of the broadest and heaviest in the whole army, the governor ordered that a record be made of it in writing and that a royal notary certify and attest to the shot. This was done, and immediately a notary came named Baltasar Hernández (whom I met afterward in El Perú), a native of Badajoz and an hidalgo, very upright and religious, which it is fitting and requisite that all should be who exercise this office, for to them is confided the property, life, and honor of the commonwealth. This hidalgo in blood and in virtue set down in writing and attested to what he saw with regard to that arrow, which was what we have said.

Three days after the battle our Castilians decided to move their camp to another place a league away from where they were, for it seemed to them a better site for the horses, and they did so very quickly and diligently. They brought wood and straw from the other neighboring pueblos and made ready as best they could a pueblo that Alonso de Carmona calls Chicacilla. He states that here they very hastily made saddles, lances, and shields, because he says that all these were destroyed in the fire, and that they were going about like Gypsies, some without jackets and some without breeches; all these are his own words.

In that pueblo they passed very laboriously what remained of the winter, which was extremely severe with cold and ice. The recent battle had left the Spaniards destitute of clothing with which to resist the cold, because nothing escaped the fire except what they happened to be wearing.

Four days after the battle the governor removed Luis de Moscoso from his office and gave it to Baltasar de Gallegos, because he learned from a secret investigation that the field officers had been negligent and careless in making the rounds and guarding the army, and that for this reason the enemy had come up without being heard and had done the damage they did. Besides the loss of the horses and the death of the men, the Spaniards admitted that they would have been defeated that night by the Indians if it had not been that the fidelity of certain individuals and common necessity had brought them to themselves and caused them to win the victory, which they already considered lost. They won it, however, at great cost to themselves and little damage to the Indians, because only five hundred of them died in that battle.

All that we have said about this sudden nocturnal battle of Chicaça, Alonso de Carmona tells at length in his *Relation*, having a great deal to say about the danger the Spaniards ran that night from the unexpected and furious assault that the Indians made, and he says that most of the Christians ran out in their shirts because the fire was so close behind them. In short, he says that they fled and were defeated, and that the persuasion of a friar caused them to turn back and miraculously win the victory that they had lost; and that the governor fought alone on horseback against the enemy for a long time until they came to his assistance, and that he had no saddle-girth. Juan Coles agrees with him in most of this and says particularly that the governor fought alone, like a good captain.

Besides what Alonso de Carmona says of this battle that confirms our account, he adds the following words:

> We were there three days, and at the end of them the Indians decided to come against us again and die or conquer. And certainly I do not doubt that, if determination could have accomplished it, they would have carried us all away in their claws, because of our lack of weapons and saddles. When they were a quarter of a league from the pueblo on their way to attack us, God was pleased to send a great downpour of water from the sky, which wet the cords of their bows, and they could do nothing, and so they went back. On going through the country the next morning, the Spaniards found their trail and captured an Indian who told and warned us of all that the Indians were going to do, and said that they had sworn by their gods to die in the attempt. Thus when the governor heard this he decided to leave there and go to Chicacilla. There we very hurriedly made shields, lances, and saddles, because in such times necessity makes everyone a master workman. We made bellows from two bearskins and we set up our forge with the two cannons that we had brought along, tempering our weapons and preparing as best we could.

All these are Carmona's words, copied literally.

Inasmuch as the enemy had realized and learned for certain the damage and ravages that they had made against the Castilians, regaining their spirit and boldness with the recent victory, they set about worrying them every night with sudden attacks and alarms, and not in a desultory manner, for they came in three or four squadrons from different directions, and with a great shouting and alarm they all attacked together at one time, so as to cause greater fear and confusion among the enemy.

So that they might not burn them in the camp as they had done in Chicaça, the Spaniards went outside the pueblo every night, formed in four squadrons on the four sides of it, with their guards stationed and everyone on watch. There was not an hour when they could sleep safely, for the Indians came two or three times every night, and there were many nights when they came four times. Besides the continual uneasiness they gave with these attacks, though most of them were light, they never failed to wound or kill some man or horse. The Indians also had many killed, but they did not take warning from this.

To make sure that the enemy would not come on the following night, the governor would send every morning to frighten them away four or five bands of fourteen or fifteen cavalry, which would scour the country around the pueblo. They did not leave a single Indian alive, whether they were spies or not, but speared them all and went back to their camp at sunset or later with the true report that for four leagues around the pueblo no Indian remained alive. But within four hours, or five at the latest, the Indian squadrons would again be facing those of the Castilians, a thing that excited the latter's wonder, that in such a brief time they could have assembled and come to harry them.

Though there were always deaths and wounds on both sides in these nightly skirmishes, nothing of particular note occurred to be told unless it was that one night, when a squadron of Indians went to attack the place where Captain Juan de Guzmán was with his company, he went out against them on horseback with five other riders, and the infantry also advanced. When the enemy waved their torches and made a light, because they were very near, our men—both foot soldiers and cavalry—could go against them together. Juan de Guzmán, who was a gentleman of great spirit, though slight of body, assailed the standard-bearer who was carrying a standard and was in the front line, throwing a lance at him. Avoiding the throw, the Indian seized the lance with his right hand and ran his hand along it until it touched that of Juan de Guzmán. Then he dropped the lance and seized him by the collar, and giving a hard jerk, dragged him from the saddle and jumped on him with both feet without letting go of the standard, which he carried in his left hand. It was all done so quickly that it was scarcely possible to see how it had happened.

When the soldiers saw their captain in such a predicament they assailed the Indian before he could do him further injury, and cut him to pieces, dispersed his squadron, and rescued Juan de Guzmán from that danger. But they did not escape without damage, because the Indians left two horses dead and wounded two others of the six that had gone against them. The Spaniards regretted the loss of the horses no less than that of their companions, and the Indians were more pleased at killing one horse than four horsemen, because they believed that it was only by means of the horses that their enemies had an advantage over them.

XXXIX

CONCERNING A PROTECTION THAT A SPANIARD INVENTED AGAINST THE COLD THEY SUFFERED IN CHICAÇA

Our Castilians remained in that camp until the end of March enduring these nocturnal battles, which being so numerous and so continuous caused them intolerable hardship and vexation. Besides the persecution and fatigues that the Indians gave them there, they suffered from the severe cold, which was most rigorous in that region. As they passed all the nights formed in squadrons and had such little clothing to wear—for the best equipped among them had only breeches and jackets of deerskin, and almost all were barefooted, without shoes or sandals—the cold that they suffered was unbelievable, and it was a miracle of God that they did not all perish.

In this necessity [for protection] against the cold, they made use of the invention of a man named Juan Vego, a homely enough rustic from Segura de la Sierra. In the island of Cuba at the beginning of this expedition there took place between him and Vasco Porcallo de Figueroa a friendly contest, though rather severe for the latter, which we do not include here because it was done in jest and facetiousness, except to say that Juan Vego, though crude and rough, was always friendly. He joked with everyone, jesting and talking nonsense with them, after the manner of the surroundings from which he had come. Vasco Porcallo de Figueroa, who also liked a jest, played a practical joke on him in satisfaction for which he gave him in La Havana, where this jesting took place, a sorrel horse. Afterward in La Florida, because the horse turned out to be so good, he several times offered him 7,000 or 8,000 pesos for him, for [use in] the first settlement that might be made, because the hopes our Castilians held at the beginning and in the midst of the discovery were as rich and magnificent as this. But Juan Vego would never consent to sell the horse, and he was right, for there was no settlement, but death and loss for all of them, as the *History* will tell.

This Juan Vego busied himself in making a grass mat (for the grass there is very good, being long, soft, and pliable) to protect himself from the cold at night. He made it four finger-breadths thick, and long and wide, putting half of it underneath for a mattress and the other half on top in the place of a blanket. As he found it to be very comfortable, he made many others for his companions, with their assistance, for everyone sets to work in a common necessity.

With these beds, which they took to the guardrooms and parade ground, where they were stationed in squadrons every night, they resisted that winter's cold, and they themselves admitted that they would have perished if it had not been for Juan Vego's help. The plentiful supply of maize and dried fruit that was available in the vicinity also aided them in resisting the severe weather, for although the Spaniards suffered from the rigors of cold and the molestation of the enemy, who did not allow them to sleep at night, they were not hungry but rather had an abundance of food.

END OF THE THIRD BOOK OF LA FLORIDA

Fourth Book of the History of La Florida, by the Inca

It deals with the combat of the Fort of Alibamo; the death of many Spaniards for the lack of salt; how they come to Chisca and cross the Río Grande; how Indians and Spaniards form a solemn procession to adore the cross, asking God for mercies; the cruel war and pillage between Capaha and Casquin; how the Spaniards discover a means of making salt; the ferocity of the Tulas in appearance and weapons; an agreeable winter the Castilians spent in Utiangue. It contains sixteen chapters.

I

THE SPANIARDS LEAVE THE CAMP OF CHICACILLA AND FIGHT AGAINST THE FORT OF ALIBAMO

The governor and his captains, seeing that the month of March was already past and that it was now time to go on with their discovery, consulted together with regard to leaving that camp and province of Chicaça. The rest of the men desired to do so in order to go out of that country where the Indians had committed so many hostilities against them and done them so much damage, always by night. In all the four months that the Spaniards were wintering there the Indians did not miss four nights in making their continuous attacks and raising alarms. Reaching this common decision, our men left that post at the beginning of April of the year 1541, and having marched on the first day four leagues through a level country dotted with many small pueblos having fifteen or twenty houses, they passed a quarter of a league beyond the inhabited region, it appearing to them that the Indians of Chicaça, who had been so troublesome to them in their own country, on seeing them beyond their pueblos, would stop pursuing them. But they had other, very different ideas, totally opposed to peace, as we shall soon see.

When the Spaniards halted to make camp in that field they sent cavalry to scour the country on every side and see what was all around the camp. They returned with the information that nearby was a fort built of wood, manned by very select warriors who apparently numbered about four thousand. The general, choosing fifty cavalry, went to reconnoiter the fort, and having seen it, he returned to his men and said: "Gentlemen, it is well that before night closes in we drive our enemies from the fort where they have fortified themselves. Not content with the molestation and trouble that they have given us so persistently in their own country, now that we are out of it they still wish to harass us, to show that they do not fear your arms, since they come to seek them outside their boundaries. Therefore it will be well for us to chastise them and for them not to remain where they are tonight, because if we leave them there they can come out successively in armed bands and shoot arrows at us all night, not allowing us to rest."

Everyone agreed with what the governor had said, and thus leaving a third of the infantry and cavalry to guard the camp, all the rest went with the governor to assail the fort, called Alibamo. It was square, with four equal curtains made of embedded logs, the curtain of each wall being four hundred paces long. Inside the square were two other curtains of wood, which crossed the fort from one wall to the other. The front curtain had three small doors, so low that a mounted man could not go through them. One door was in the middle of the curtain and the other two were at the sides near the corners. In line with these three doors there were three others in each curtain, so that if the Spaniards should take the first ones, the Indians could defend themselves at those of the second curtain, and of the third and the fourth. The doors of the last curtain opened on a river that passed behind the fort. Though narrow, this river was very deep and had such steep banks that one could go up and down them only with difficulty on foot and not at all on horseback. This was the intention of the Indians, to make a fort in which they could be sure that the Castilians would not attack them with the horses by entering through the doors or by crossing the river, but would fight on foot like themselves, for as we have said already on other occasions, they had no fear whatsoever of the infantry, as it seemed to them that they were equal or even superior to them. They had bridges over the river made of wood, but so shaky and ruinous that they could hardly pass over them. There were no doors at all on the sides of the fort.

Having seen and examined the fort well, the governor ordered that a hundred of the best-armed cavalry dismount and attack it, formed into three squadrons with three men to a file, and that the infantry, who were not so well supplied with defensive arms as the cavalry, should follow them, and all attempt to gain the doors. This disposition was made immediately. One door fell to Captain Juan de Guzmán, another to Captain Alonso Romo de Cardeñosa and the third to Gonzalo Silvestre, and they led their squadrons directly toward the doors to attack them.

The Indians, who hitherto had remained closed up in their fort, seeing that the Spaniards were preparing to attack, sent out a hundred men from each door to skirmish with them. They wore great plumes on their heads, and in order to appear more fierce they all came with their faces, bodies, arms, and legs painted in stripes with paints or clays of various colors, and they assailed the Spaniards with all the gallantry that can be imagined. With the first arrows they felled Diego de Castro, a native of Badajoz, and Pedro de Torres, a native of Burgos, both nobles and brave men; they were advancing in the first file on either side of Gonzalo Silvestre. They wounded Diego de Castro above the knee in the large muscle of the right leg with a flint barb, and they transfixed Pedro de Torres in the leg between the two shin-bones [*canillas*]. Francisco de Reynoso, a gentleman from Astorga, seeing his commander Gonzalo Silvestre advancing alone, passed from the second file where he was marching to the first, so as not to let him go by himself.

In the second squadron, which Captain Juan de Guzmán was leading, they downed with another arrow wound made by a flint barb another gentleman, named Luis Bravo de Xerez, who was at the captain's side, wounding him in the large muscle of the thigh. They removed from the side of Captain Alonso Romo de Cardeñosa, who was going to attack the third door, one of his two companions, who was named Francisco de Figueroa, very noble in blood and in virtue and a native of Zafra. He was also wounded in the large muscle of the thigh, likewise by a flint barb. These Indians being experienced warriors, they shot at the Spaniards from the thighs downward, these being the parts on which they wore no defensive armor; and they shot at them with flint barbs so as to be able to do more damage, because, if they did not wound them with the point, the edge would cut them in passing.

These three gentlemen died shortly after the battle, and all within an hour, because the wounds had been alike. Their deaths occasioned much grief because they were nobles, brave, and young, for none of them was as much as twenty-five years old. Besides the wounds of which we have told there were many others, because the Indians fought most valiantly, always shooting at their enemies' legs. Our men, on seeing this, all shouted together to close in at once on the enemy and not give them a chance to use up the arrows with which they were doing them so much damage. Thus they fell upon them so swiftly and furiously that they swept them back to the doors of the fort.

II

THE BATTLE OF THE FORT PROCEEDS TO ITS END

The governor had stationed himself with twenty horsemen on one side of the squadrons, and Captains Andrés de Vasconcelos and Juan de Añasco on the other side, with thirty more, and they all fell upon the Indians. One of them shot an arrow at the general, who was at the head of his men, and struck him such a severe blow on the helmet above the forehead that the arrow flew up more than a pike's length in the air above the helmet, and the governor confessed afterward that it had made him see stars. When the cavalry and the infantry attacked all together, the Indians retreated to the wall of the fort where, since the doors were so small and all the Indians could not take refuge inside, they suffered heavy losses. With the same fury with which they had assailed the Indians in the open, the Spaniards entered the doors, face to face with the enemy, and so nearly at the same time that it could not be ascertained which of the three captains had entered first.

Inside the fort there was a great butchery of the Indians, for as the Spaniards saw them closed up there and remembered the many and unceasing grievances they had suffered from them in their last camp, they bore down upon them mercilessly in their wrath and rage against them and killed great numbers very easily with stabs and thrusts, as they wore no defensive armor. Many Indians, being unable to escape through the doors leading to the river because they were so hotly pursued, trusting to their swiftness, jumped from the tops of the walls and fell into the hands of the cavalry who were patrolling the field, where they speared all of them. Many other Indians, who were able to get out through the doors to the river, crossed it by the wooden bridge, but because of the haste with which they pushed against one another in passing over, many of them fell into the river, and it was an amazing thing to see the great splashes they made in striking the water because they fell from such a height. Others, who could not reach the bridges because the enemy's fury did not give them time, threw themselves down from the bluffs and swam across the river. In this manner they abandoned the fort within a short time, and those who were able to cross the river, being now safe, formed themselves into a squadron. Our men remained on this side.

One of the Indians who had escaped, seeing himself out of danger and wishing to show his skill with his bow and arrows, went apart from his own men and shouted to the Castilians, making them understand by signs and a few words that [he wished] one of their crossbowmen to come out for a single combat, so that they might exchange shots to see which one of them was the better archer. One of our men, named Juan de Salinas, an hidalgo from Santander, came out very promptly from among the Spaniards (who had taken shelter under some trees that were in front of them, as a protection against arrows) and went down the river to place himself opposite the Indian. Though one of his companions called to him to wait, that he wanted to go with him and protect him with a shield, he refused, saying that since his enemy sought no advantages for himself he would not take any against him. He immediately put a bolt in his crossbow and aimed at the Indian to shoot at him; the latter did the same with his bow, having chosen one of the arrows from his quiver.

Both fired their shots at the same time. The man from Santander struck the Indian in the center of the breast, so that he fell, but before he reached the ground his people came to his assistance and carried him off in their arms, more dead than alive, for the bolt entered his breast all the way. The Indian struck the Spaniard in the neck, just behind the left ear (for in order to take aim at the enemy and also to turn the side of his body toward him, which presented a smaller target than the front, he had turned to one side to fire the crossbow), and the arrow went through the nape of his neck, standing out an equal distance on each side. Thus he went back to his companions, transfixed by the arrow and very satisfied with the shot that he had made at his enemy. The Indians (though they might have done so) would not shoot at Juan de Salinas because the challenge had been to have one-to-one combat. The adelantado, who was desirous of punishing those Indians for their impudence and audacity, calling to the mounted men and crossing the river by a good ford that was above the fort, drove them forward across a plain for more than a league, spearing them as they went, and they would not have stopped short of finishing them all if they had not been overtaken by darkness. Nevertheless more than two thousand Indians died in this conflict, and they paid well for their boldness, because now they could not boast about the Castilians who had died in their country nor of the great molestation that they had given them throughout the past winter. Having pursued them as far as they could, the Castilians went back to their camp and treated the wounded, who were numerous, for which reason they remained there four days, being unable to march.

III

MANY SPANIARDS DIE FOR LACK OF SALT, AND HOW THEY REACH CHISCA

Going back a little in our *History* from where we are, so that events may be told according to the time and place in which they occurred, and so that we shall not have to go back further to tell them, it must be said that as soon as our Spaniards left the great province of Coça and entered that of Tascaluça they were in need of salt. Having passed some days without it, they felt the lack of it greatly, and some whose constitutions required more than others died for the need of it in a most extraordinary manner. They were taken with a slight hectic fever, and by the third or fourth day no one could endure the stench of their bodies fifty paces away from them, it being more foul than that of dead dogs or cats. Thus they perished without any help for it, because they neither knew what it was nor what to do for them, as they had no physicians or medicines, and even if they had had them, it was understood that they would have been of no use because they were already corrupt when the fever came upon them, and their bellies were as green as grass from the breast down.

Thus some of them began to die, to the great horror and consternation of their companions. In their fear many of them made use of the remedy the Indians prepared to save and help themselves in that necessity. This was that they burned a certain herb they knew about and made lye with the ashes. They dipped what they ate in it as if it were a sauce and with this they saved themselves from rotting away and dying, like the Spaniards. Many of the latter in their arrogance and presumptuousness were unwilling to make use of this remedy because they regarded it as a filthy thing and unbecoming to their rank, and said that it was a mean thing to do as the Indians did, and such as these were the ones who died. When in their extremity they asked for this lye, it was now of no use to them, for the time was past when it could save them from the corruption. Once it had appeared nothing could stop it, and [the medicine] did not help those who asked for it too late. It is a deserved punishment of the arrogant not to find in time of need that which they disdained in prosperity. Thus more than sixty Spaniards died during the time when they had no salt, which was almost a year, and we shall tell in due time how they made salt and supplied their need.

It is to be noted also that when the governor reached Chicaça, because of the great variety of languages that he found as a result of the many provinces that he had passed through, almost every one of which had a language different from the others, ten, twelve, or fourteen interpreters were needed to talk with the caciques and Indians of those provinces. The statement would pass from Juan Ortiz to the last of the interpreters, all of whom stood up like a chorus to receive and pass on the words to the next one, according to the manner in which they understood one another. With such labor and trouble the adelantado asked and received information concerning the things that it was worthwhile for him to know about all that extensive country. This labor was unnecessary in the case of the individual Indians, men and women, whom our people took from any of the provinces as servants, because after two months of communication with the Spaniards they understood what their masters said to them in the Castilian language and they could make themselves understood in the most necessary and common matters in the same tongue. After six months of speaking with the Castilians they could serve as interpreters for them with other, new Indians. All those of this great kingdom of La Florida showed this facility in the language, and aptness in all other matters as well.

The army left the camp of Alibamo, which was the last one in the province of Chicaça, after the four days that they were forced to spend there on account of the wounded. After three more days' march through an uninhabited region, always going north in order to withdraw from the sea, they came within sight of a pueblo called Chisca.[26] It was near a large river, which because it was the greatest of all those that our Spaniards saw in La Florida they called the Río Grande, without giving it any other name. Juan Coles says in his *Relation* that in the Indian language this river was called Chucagua,[27] and below we shall describe its grandeur at more length, for it was a wonderful thing. The Indians of this province of Chisca, because of the continuous war that they have with those of Chicaça and because of the uninhabited region that lies between the two provinces, knew nothing of the Spaniards' coming to their country, and thus they were unprepared. As soon as our men saw the pueblo they attacked it without waiting for orders and captured many Indian men and women of all ages. They sacked everything they found in the pueblo, as if it had belonged to the Indians of the province of Chicaça where they had been treated so badly.

The curaca's house was to one side of the pueblo, situated on a small, high elevation erected artificially, and served as a fortress. There was no way of ascending to it except by two stairways. Many Indians gathered at this house, and others assembled in a very dense woodland that was between the pueblo and the Río Grande. The lord of that province was named Chisca, like the province itself. He was sick in his bed and was now an old man. Hearing the noise and uproar that were going on in the pueblo, he got up and went out of his apartment, and seeing the pillaging and capture of his

---

[26]In a transposition of names, Garcilaso has Chisca for the place called Quizquiz or Quizqui in the other chronicles. Chisca was the name of a province learned about but not visited by the main army while it was in the vicinity of Chiaha. Swanton, *Final Report*, 231.

[27]George Lankford has pointed out that the native term that Juan Coles here applies to the Mississippi River, Chucagua, is evidently an Algonquian term still in use much later during the French exploration of the Mississippi Valley. It survives in the name "Chicago."

vassals, he took up a battle-ax and went down as rapidly as he could, uttering fierce threats of killing all who might have entered his country without permission. With all his bravado the poor man had not the stature or strength to kill a cat, because in addition to being sick, he was a little old man so slight of body that among all the Indians these Spaniards saw in La Florida they saw no other of such forlorn appearance. But the spirit of the daring and exploits of his youth, which had been filled with warfare, and the lordship of such a large and fine province as his, gave him strength to make those threats and other, greater ones.

His wives and servants laid hold of him and begged him tearfully not to go down, reminding him of his illness. The Indians who came up from the pueblo told him that those who had come were men never seen before, nor heard of; that they were numerous and brought some very large and swift animals; that if he desired to fight with them, he must consider that his people were off their guard and not prepared; that in order to avenge his injury he should summon the people from the outlying districts and await a better opportunity; and that meanwhile he ought to make a fair show of complete friendliness and avail himself of such opportunities as might arise, exercising patience and endurance or wrath and vengeance as the case might be. He would not want to commit any unconsidered rashness to his own greater hurt and the injury of his vassals. With these and other similar arguments that his wives, servants, and vassals made to the curaca, they stopped him from fighting with the Christians, but he remained so angry he refused to listen to a message of peace and friendship the governor (knowing that he was in his house) sent to him. He said that he did not wish to hear a message from those who had offended him, but to give them war with fire and sword, and thus he declared it immediately so that they could look out for themselves, for he intended to cut all their throats forthwith.

IV

THE SPANIARDS RETURN THE BOOTY TO THE CURACA CHISCA AND ARE GLAD TO MAKE PEACE WITH HIM

The general and his captains and soldiers, who throughout the past winter had had enough and more than enough of fighting and had with them many sick and wounded, both men and horses, had no inclination for war, but wanted peace. Desirous of it and embarrassed by having pillaged the pueblo and angered the curaca, they sent him many other messages, all couched in the fairest, friendliest and most persuasive words that they could command, for besides the inconvenience that the Spaniards were suffering themselves, they saw that in less than three hours after their arrival in the pueblo almost four thousand warriors had joined the cacique, all with their weapons ready. Our men feared that inasmuch as those had come together in such a brief time, many others would come later. They noted also that the situation of the place, both in the pueblo and out of it, was very good and favorable for the Indians and very bad and inconvenient for the Castilians, for, because of the many streams and forests that were in all that region, they could not make use of the horses, which were needed to attack the Indians. And what was of more importance to them, as they had learned well by experience, was that they were gaining nothing from war and battles but rather were consuming themselves, because men and horses were being killed every day. For all these reasons they earnestly sought peace, desiring it greatly.

On the contrary, among the Indians (after they had assembled to discuss the messages from our men) there were many who desired war because they were offended by the capture of their women and children, their brothers and relatives, and by the property stolen. It seemed to them in the ferocity of their spirit that, in order to regain everything lost, there was no more direct way than that of arms, and any other would only cause delay. Desiring to engage in battle, they opposed peace, giving no other reason except that of their loss. There were likewise other Indians, who had lost nothing that they wished to recover, who opposed peace simply because they wished to show their courage and bravery and through the natural inclination that they generally have for war. These maintained that it was a matter of honor, saying that it would be a good thing to find out what sort of fighters these strange and unknown men were, and how much spirit and courage they had; and so that they and others after them would be warned away from their lands (in the future), it would be a very good thing to make them understand their own strength and bravery. There were other, more peaceable and discreet Indians who said that the peace and friendship the Spaniards offered ought to be accepted because they could recover their captive women and children and their lost property more surely by this means than by war and enmity, and make certain that other possible losses (such as seeing their pueblos burned and their fields laid waste when the crops were nearly mature) would not be incurred. There was no reason for making a trial of the bravery of those people, for their understanding told them clearly that men who had passed through so many hostile countries to reach there could not fail to be most valiant, and it was better to have peace and concord with them than war. Aside from the damage mentioned, the latter would cause the death of many of them and of their brothers, relatives, and friends, and would of itself give revenge to their enemies, the neighboring Indians. Therefore it would be better to accept their [the Spaniards'] friendship and see how they got on with it; if they were not satisfied, they could very easily take up arms again, with more advantages than they had at present, and carry out what they were now planning.

This advice outweighed the other, and the curaca agreed to it. Keeping his wrath for a better occasion, he replied to the governor's messengers, saying that they were to tell him first of all what it was the Castilians wanted. On their replying that they wanted nothing except that they [the Indians] move out of the pueblo so that they could lodge in it, and that they give them the food they needed, which would be little, so that they could continue on their way, as they could not stay long in their country, he [the curaca] replied that he was willing to concede them the peace and friendship they asked, and leave the pueblo, and give them the provisions, on condition that they immediately release his vassals and restore all the property they had taken, down to the last earthen pot (these were his words), and that they were not to ascend to his house or to see him. On these conditions he would be a friend to the Spaniards; otherwise he immediately challenged them to battle.

Our people accepted the conditions because they had no use for the Indians whom they had captured, as they had plenty of servants, and the property consisted of nothing except some trifles such as deerskins and some blankets, few and of poor quality. All of it was restored to them, not leaving out even a clay pot, as the curaca said. The Indians moved out of the pueblo and left the food they had in their houses for the Castilians. The latter remained in that pueblo called Chisca for six days in order to care for the sick. On the last day, with the cacique's permission, his anger having abated, the governor visited him and thanked him for his friendship and hospitality. The next day he left to continue his journey and discovery.

V

THE SPANIARDS LEAVE CHISCA AND BUILD BOATS FOR CROSSING THE RÍO GRANDE, AND ARRIVE IN CASQUIN

The army having left Chisca, it marched four short daily journeys of three leagues each, since the indispositions of the sick and wounded did not permit longer ones. On all four days they traveled upstream. At the end of that time they came to a passage where they could cross the Río Grande, not that they could ford it, but there was an open passage for reaching it, for previously all along its banks there had been extremely large and very dense woodlands, and the banks on either side were very high and steep and one could not go up or down them. The governor and his army were forced to stop at this pass for twenty days, for in order to cross the river it was necessary to make barks or pirogues like those they built in Chicaça, because immediately upon the arrival of our men at the river, more than six thousand Indian warriors showed themselves on the other side, well armed and with a large number of canoes in which to oppose their crossing.

On the day after the governor arrived at this camp four principal Indians came with a message from the lord of that same province where the Spaniards were, whose name is not set down here because it has been forgotten. Standing before the general, without having spoken a word or having made any other sign, they turned their faces to the east and made an obeisance to the Sun, with extreme reverence; then, turning to the west, they made another, not quite so deep, to the Moon; and then, facing the governor, they made him another, lesser one, so that all those present noted the three methods of veneration that they employed, according to their degree. Then they delivered their message, saying that their lord the curaca and all his nobles and the rest of the common people of his country had sent them in the name of all to welcome them and offer them their friendship, good will, and the service that his lordship might be pleased to receive from them. The adelantado spoke to them in a very friendly manner and sent them away very pleased with his affability.

All the time the Spaniards were in that camp, which was twenty days or more, these Indians served the army in a very friendly and peaceful manner, though the chief curaca never came to see the governor, but rather continued to excuse himself on the pretext of illness, from which it was understood that he had sent the embassy and performed the other services for fear they might lay waste the fields, which were very fruitful, with the crops nearly mature, and so that they might not burn the pueblos, more than from any love that he had for the Castilians or any desire to serve them. With the great diligence and industry with which the Spaniards applied themselves to building the boats (for all of them labored at it, without distinction between captains and soldiers, he being considered captain who worked hardest on them), at the end of fifteen days they launched two barks on the river, complete in every detail. They guarded them very carefully night and day so that the enemy might not burn them. The latter, throughout the time that the Spaniards were busy with their work, did not cease to molest them in their canoes. They had many and very good ones, and formed into squadrons, sometimes descending and sometimes ascending the river, on coming abreast they discharged many arrows. The Spaniards defended themselves and kept them back with harquebuses and crossbows, with which they did them much damage because they took care to fire so as not to lose a shot, and they dug pits on the riverbank where they concealed themselves, so that the Indians would come nearer. At the end of the twenty days that the Castilians spent in making the boats, they had four in the water, which would carry 150 infantry and thirty cavalry; and so that the Indians might see them well and understand that they could not damage them, they sailed and rowed them up and down the river. Realizing that they could not prevent their crossing, the heathen decided to break camp and go to their pueblos.

Without any opposition, the Spaniards crossed the river in their pirogues and in some canoes they had won from the enemy by their diligent efforts. Dismantling the boats in order to keep the nails, which were very necessary to them, they proceeded on their journey, and having made four daily marches through uninhabited country, on the fifth day they looked ahead from some high hills and saw a pueblo with four hundred houses, situated on the banks of a river larger than the Guadalquivir at Córdoba. All along the edges of that river and in its vicinity there were many fields of maize and Indian corn and great numbers of fruit trees, which showed the country to be very fertile. The Indians of the pueblo, who already had notice of the Castilians' coming, advanced all together without any personage being distinguished among them to greet the governor and offer him their persons, houses, and lands, and they told him that they made him lord of all these. Soon two principal Indians came on behalf of the curaca, accompanied by many others, and in the name of their lord and of the whole state they offered the general anew (as the first ones had done) their vassalage and service. The governor received them very kindly and spoke many friendly words to them, with which they returned very pleased.

This pueblo and its whole province and the curaca, its lord, had the same name, which was Casquin. The Spaniards rested there six days because of the plentiful supply of food that it had for the people and in order to attend to the sick and also to the horses. At the end of that time they went in two more days to the pueblo where the cacique Casquin resided, which was seven leagues up the river on the same side. All the land was very fertile and well populated, though the pueblos were small, with fifteen, twenty, thirty, or forty houses. The cacique, accompanied by many nobles, came out to receive the governor and offered him his friendship and service and his own house in which to lodge, this being on a high hill erected artificially, on one side of the pueblo, where there were twelve or thirteen large houses in which the curaca had all his family, consisting of wives and servants, who were numerous. The governor said that he accepted his friendship but not his house, so as not to inconvenience him. He was pleased to make camp in an orchard that the cacique himself designated when he saw that he did not desire his houses. There not being a single house in it, the Indians very soon erected large and fresh arbors, such as were necessary, for it was now May and very warm. Part of the army was quartered in the pueblo and part in the orchards, where all were very comfortable.

VI

A SOLEMN PROCESSION OF INDIANS AND SPANIARDS IS FORMED TO ADORE THE CROSS

The army had been quartered for three days in the pueblo called Casquin, much to the satisfaction of both Indians and Spaniards, and on the fourth day the curaca appeared before the governor accompanied by all the nobles of his state, whom he had convoked for that ceremony. He and all his people having made deep obeisances, he said to him: "Sir, as you have advantage over us in strength and in arms, so we believe that you enjoy it in that you have a better God than ours. These whom you see here, who are the nobles of my country (who because of their humble estate and little merit do not dare appear before you), and I with them, supplicate that you be pleased to ask your God for rain, because our crops are much in need of water." The general replied that although all those of his army, and he as well, were sinners they would pray to God, our Lord, as a merciful Father to grant them that blessing. He ordered immediately in the cacique's presence that the Genoese, Maestre Francisco, who was very expert in carpentry and in shipbuilding, make a cross from the tallest and thickest pine tree that could be found in the vicinity.

The one that was cut on advice of the Indians themselves, after being finished, that is, having the bark removed and being rounded to best advantage, as the carpenters say, could not be lifted from the ground by a hundred men. The master constructed the cross perfectly, in the proportion of five and three, without taking away anything from the height of the tree. It came out most handsomely because it was so tall. They set it up on a high artificially made hill that was on the riverbank and served the Indians as a lookout, and exceeded in height the other, small hills nearby. The work, which required two days, being finished, and the cross being erected, on the following day a solemn procession was formed in which the general and the captains and the most important men took part, and an armed squadron of infantry and cavalry kept watch, as was required for the safeguarding and security of the army.

The cacique went at the governor's side and many of his Indian nobles were interspersed among the Spaniards. In a separate group in advance of the general went the priests, clerics, and friars, chanting the litanies in chorus, and the soldiers responded. In this manner more than a thousand men, including the faithful and the heathen, marched a good distance until they came to the place where the cross was, and all knelt before it. Having said two or three prayers, they arose and went two by two with the priests leading and knelt on the ground to adore and kiss the cross. Following the ecclesiastics came the governor, and the cacique, who, without anyone telling him, did everything that he saw the general do, and kissed the cross. Behind them came the other Spaniards and the Indians, who did the same as the Christians.

On the other side of the river there were fifteen or twenty thousand souls of both sexes and all ages, who stood with their arms extended and their hands held up, watching what the Christians were doing. From time to time they raised their eyes to heaven, making signs with their hands and faces as if they were praying God to heed the Christians' petitions. Again they would give a low hoarse cry as of people mourning, and they told the children to cry, and they themselves did the same. All this ceremony and solemnity was observed on either side of the river in the adoration of the cross, which deeply moved the governor and many of his men, seeing that the sign of our redemption was venerated with such a demonstration of humility and tears in lands so far away and by people so far removed from the Christian doctrine. All having adored the cross in the manner that has been told, the procession returned in the same order in which it had come, the priests chanting the *Te Deum laudamus* to the end of the canticle. This concluded the ceremonies of that day, which had extended over a long four hours.

God, our Lord, in His mercy was pleased to show those heathen how He listens to His own who earnestly call upon Him, and at once on the following night, beginning at midnight, a very good rain commenced to fall, which lasted two more days, leaving the Indians very joyful and contented. The curaca and all his nobles formed a procession such as he had seen the Christians do to adore the cross, and went to render thanks to the governor for such favors as his God had bestowed upon them through his intercession. Finally, they told him in very well-chosen words that they were his slaves and that thenceforth they would boast of it and take pride in being so. The governor told them to give their thanks to God, who created heaven and earth and bestowed those mercies and other, greater ones.

These things have been told in such detail because they happened thus, and because it was the mandate and the care of the governor and the priests who went with him that the cross be adored with all possible solemnity, so that those heathen would see the veneration in which the Christians held it. Juan Coles recounts all this chapter concerning the adoration at great length in his *Relation,* and says that it rained fifteen days. After these matters were concluded, they now having been in that pueblo nine or ten days, the governor ordered the army to prepare to march on the next day to continue their discovery.

The cacique Casquin, who was about fifty years of age, begged the governor to permit him to go with him and to bring warriors and servants, the first to accompany the army and the second to carry the provisions, because they would have to go through uninhabited country, and to clear the roads and bring wood and grass for the horses when they were in camp. The governor thanked him for his kindness and told him to do whatever most pleased him, whereupon the curaca left well satisfied and ordered made ready, if they were not already so, a large number of warriors and servants.

VII

INDIANS AND SPANIARDS GO AGAINST CAPAHA. THE SITE OF HIS PUEBLO IS DESCRIBED

It must be said for the sake of a clearer explanation of our *History* that this cacique Casquin and his parents, grandparents, and ancestors for many centuries previously had war with the lord and lords of another province, called Capaha,[28] which bordered upon his own. These latter, because they were more-powerful lords of lands and vassals, had hemmed in Casquin, and were continuing to do so, having almost overcome him. He dared not take up arms for fear of angering Capaha and irritating him lest he [Capaha] do him [Casquin] the harm that he could do, being so powerful. He remained quiet, content only with guarding his boundaries, and not leaving them or giving occasion for being attacked, if it be enough not to give it to tyrants. Since Casquin now saw the good opportunity that was offered him to take revenge for all his past injuries with the aid of foreign strength and power, being astute and sagacious, he asked the governor for the permission that we have mentioned. With this, and with the intention of avenging himself, he took in addition to servants five thousand Indian warriors well armed and adorned with large plumes, for they never left their houses without these two things. He took also three thousand Indians laden with food, who carried their bows and arrows as well.

Casquin set out from his pueblo with all this ostentation, having asked permission to go ahead with his men under pretext of discovering the enemy, if they were there, and of supplying the camps with the necessary things before the Spanish army should arrive. He led his men out formed in squadrons and divided into three parts, vanguard, center, and rear guard, in good military order. The Spaniards left a quarter of a league behind the Indians, and they marched thus all that day. At night the Indians camped ahead of the Castilians and also posted their sentries as our men did, and the cavalry made the rounds between the two lines of sentries. They marched three days in this order, and at the end of that time they came to a swamp that was very difficult to cross, having deep miry places at the entrance and exit and clear water in the middle, but so deep that for the space of twenty paces it was necessary to swim (this swamp was the boundary between the two hostile

[28]Inverting the first two syllables, Garcilaso calls this province Capaha where the other chroniclers have Pacaha.

provinces of Casquin and Capaha). The men crossed over some poor wooden bridges that were there, and the horses swam across with much trouble because of the mud on either side of the swamp. They spent all the fourth day in passing over it, and half a league beyond Indians and Spaniards camped in some most beautiful pasture grounds in a very fine country. After crossing the swamp, they marched two days more, and early on the third they reached some high hills from which the principal pueblo of Capaha could be seen, which was the frontier and defense of the whole province against that of Casquin, and therefore it was fortified in the manner that we shall describe. The pueblo had five hundred large and good houses and was on a site somewhat higher and more elevated than its surroundings. They had made it almost an island with a ditch or moat ten or twelve fathoms deep and fifty paces wide,[29] or forty at the narrowest parts, all made by hand. It was full of water that it received from the Río Grande that we mentioned above, which flowed three leagues above the pueblo. The water came through an open canal, made laboriously, which went from the moat to the Río Grande for this purpose. The canal was three estados in depth and so wide that two of the large canoes could go up and down it abreast without the oars of one touching those of the other. The moat of water, of the width that we have said, surrounded three sides of the pueblo, the work not yet being complete. The fourth side was enclosed by a very strong palisade in the form of a wall made of thick logs set in the ground, touching one another, and other, transverse logs fastened and covered with packed mud and straw such as we have described above. This great moat and its canal contained so many fish that all the Spaniards and Indians who were with the governor took their fill of them, and it was still as if none had been taken out.

When his enemies, the Casquines, came in sight of the pueblo, the cacique Capaha was inside of it, but it seemed to him that because his people were unprepared and because he did not have as many as were needed he could not resist his adversaries, so he gave way to them. Before they arrived he got into one of the canoes that were in the moat and went through the canal to the Río Grande to take refuge on a fortified island he had there. The Indians of the pueblo who could get canoes followed their lord. Others who

---

[29] The use of moats in combination with wooden palisade fortifications is independently attested to in several archaeologically known Southeastern town sites. Etowah in northwest Georgia is a prominent example. See Lewis Larson, "Functional Considerations of Warfare in the Southeast During the Mississippi Period," *American Antiquity* 37 (1972):383–92.

Life in a Mississippian Village. Mississippian villagers of the interior Southeast at the time of the De Soto expedition depended upon corn agriculture, hunting, and fishing for their subsistence. They often lived in large, walled towns. The earth mounds in the background of this painting supported residences of chiefs and nobles and shrines dedicated to their ancestors. (Painting by H. Tom Hall © National Geographic Society)

could not obtain them fled to the woods that were close by. Others, who were slower and less fortunate, remained in the pueblo. The Casquines entered it, finding it undefended; not all at once, but cautiously, fearful that there might be an enemy ambush inside. Though they had the Spaniards' protection, still, as a people many times defeated, they feared those of Capaha and could not lose their dread of them. This delay gave opportunity for many people of the pueblo—men, women, and children—to escape by fleeing.

After the Casquines ascertained that there was no one in the pueblo to oppose them, they showed well the hatred and rancor that they felt against its inhabitants, for they killed the men on whom they could lay hands, numbering more than 150, and took off their scalps to carry to their own country as an indication of a great victory and of revenge for their wrongs, a sign used by all these Indians. They sacked the whole pueblo, particularly robbing the lord's houses with more satisfaction and enjoyment than any of the others, because they were his. They captured many boys, children, and women, and among them two very beautiful young women who were among the many wives of Capaha. They had been unable to embark with the cacique, their husband, because of the disturbance and great haste occasioned by the sudden and unexpected arrival of the enemy.

VIII

THE CASQUINES SACK THE PUEBLO AND BURIAL PLACE OF CAPAHA, AND GO IN SEARCH OF HIM

Not content with having pillaged the curaca's house and robbed the pueblo, and killed and taken as many prisoners as they could, the Casquines went to the temple, which was on a large plaza that the pueblo contained, which was the burial place of all the former lords of that province: the father, grandfathers, and ancestors of Capaha. Those temples and burial places, as has already been told elsewhere, are the most esteemed and venerated possessions that these Indians of La Florida have, and I believe that it is the same among all nations, not without good reason, because they are relics, not of saints, but of ancestors whom they represent to us as alive. The Casquines, summoning one another so that all could enjoy the triumph, went to this temple. Since they understood how much Capaha (being arrogant and haughty because he had not hitherto been attacked by them) would feel it that his enemies had the boldness to enter his temple and burial place contemptuously, they not only entered it, but committed all the ignominious and offensive affronts that they could, because they pillaged everything that the temple contained in the way of riches, ornaments, spoils, and trophies that had been gathered at the expense of their own ancestors.[30]

They knocked down on the ground all the wooden chests that served as sepulchers, and for their own satisfaction and revenge and to affront their enemies, they threw out on the ground the bones and dead bodies that were in the chests. Not content with throwing them on the ground, they stamped and kicked them in an excess of contempt and disdain. They took away many heads of the Indians of Casquin, which those of Capaha had placed on the points of lances at the doors of the temple as a sign of triumph and victory. In the place of them they put other heads, which they had cut off that day from the inhabitants of the pueblo. In short, nothing they could think of was left undone. They wanted to burn the temple and the curaca's houses and the whole pueblo, but did not dare do it for fear of angering the governor. The Casquines did all these things before the governor entered the pueblo. The latter, as soon as he learned that Capaha had gone to the island to fortify himself there, sent him messages of peace and friendship by some of his Indians who had been captured, but he would not accept them. On the other hand he summoned his people in order to revenge himself against his enemies.

When the governor learned of this he ordered that Indians and Spaniards make ready to go to attack the island. The curaca Casquin told his lordship to wait three or four days until a fleet of sixty canoes should arrive, which he would order to be brought from his country and which were needed to cross to the island. This fleet would have to come up by way of the Río Grande, which also passed through the lands of Casquin. He ordered his vassals to go as speedily as possible and come back with the canoes; that this was to be their revenge and the destruction of their enemies. Meanwhile the governor did not cease sending messages of peace and friendship to Capaha. But seeing that he disregarded them and knowing that the canoes were already on the way up the river, he ordered the whole army to come out to receive them

[30]Considering the pivotal importance of the chief's hereditary line to the well-being of a chiefdom, the defilement of Pacaha's ancestor shrine would have been a prominent goal of the Casqui raiders.

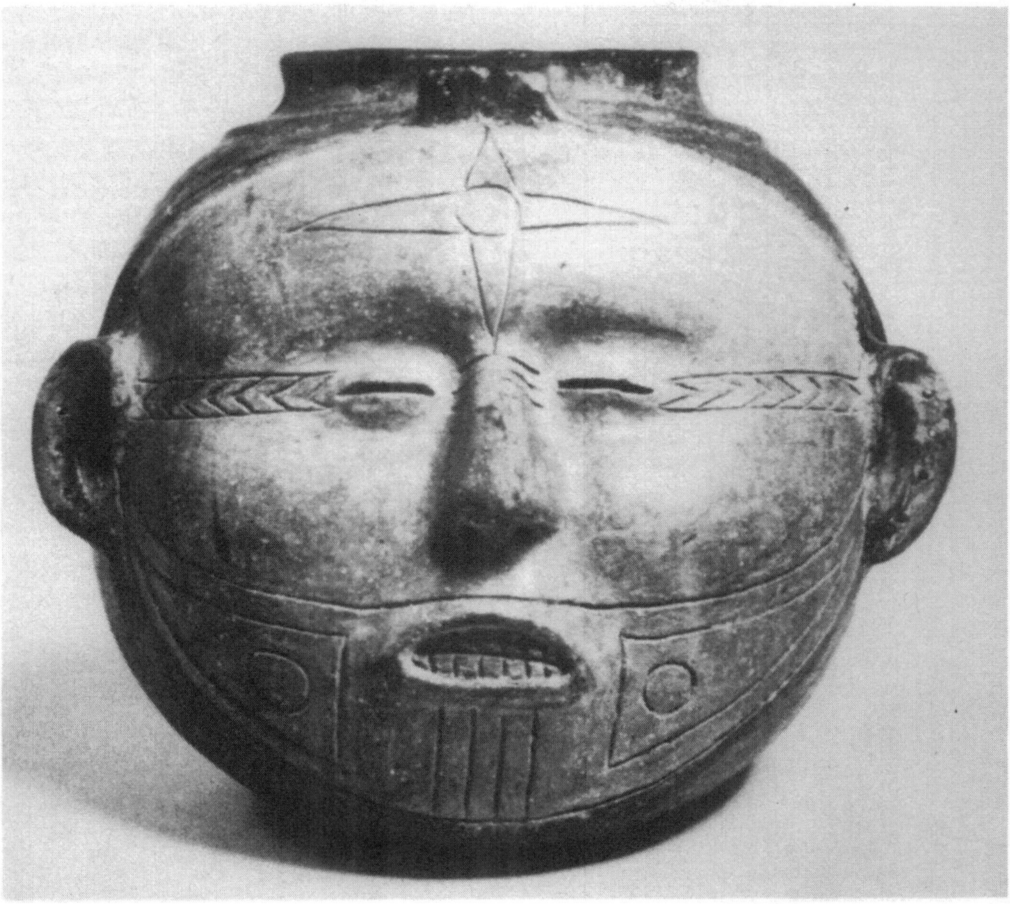

A Pottery Jar in the Form of a Human Head. This painted jar, perhaps portraying the severed head of a slain enemy, comes from the general area of the Mississippian chiefdom of Pacaha. At the time of De Soto's arrival, Pacaha was at war with the neighboring chiefdom of Casqui. The incised decorations on this piece probably represent facial tattooing. The notion of success in warfare is repeated in many forms of Mississippian art. (Courtesy of the National Museum of the American Indian, Flourney Collection/Smithsonian Institution)

and to go by water and by land to where the enemies were. The Castilians went out on the fifth day after they reached the pueblo of Capaha.

In order to damage their enemies' growing crops, the Casquin Indians marched out formed into a wing half a league across, laying waste and destroying everything they encountered. They found many of their Indians who were captives and who served as domestics on the estates and in the fields of those of Capaha. So that these slaves would not run away, they had crippled one of their feet,[31] as we have already told concerning others, and they held them in slavery in a cruel and perpetual imprisonment, more as a sign of victory than because of the advantage and service they could be to them. The Casquines set them free and sent them to their country. The governor and the cacique Casquin arrived with their armies at the Río Grande and found that Capaha was fortified on the island with palisades made of thick logs that were set in from one side to the other. Since there were many thickets of brambles and trees growing on the island, it was bad to enter and worse to travel through, and because of this roughness and of the many and very good warriors Capaha had there, he was certain that they would not take it. In the face of all these difficulties the governor ordered that two hundred Castilian infantry embark in twenty canoes, and three thousand Indians in the others, and that they all attack the island together and attempt to gain it, like good soldiers. The number of Indians and Spaniards mentioned went in this order in the sixty canoes. Upon landing, an accident took place that grieved all the Castilians generally. This was that one of them, named Francisco Sebastián, who was a native of Villanueva de Barcarrota and had been a soldier in Italy, a man of handsome body and face and of a very happy temperament, was drowned because he had been in such haste to jump ashore with a lance by thrusting the end in the ground. He was unable to make the shore, and as the canoe had moved backward, he fell into the water. Since he wore a coat of mail, he immediately sank to the bottom and did not reappear. Shortly before, while in the canoe, he had been (as on other occasions) very merry with his companions, telling them innumerable jokes and stories, and among others he had told the following: "Ill-fortune brought me into these desperate places. Would that God had sent me into a good country, such as Italy: There, after their manner of speaking, they addressed me as 'lordship,' as if I were a lord of vassals, while you here don't even pride yourselves on addressing me familiarly. There, being a generous and charitable people, they entertained me and helped me in my need as if I

[31]See note 18.

had been their son. I was treated thus in time of peace, and in war: if I happened to kill an enemy—Turk, Moor, or Frenchman—there were spoils to be had in the form of arms, clothing, or horses, which always brought me something. But here I have to fight with a naked man who leaps along ten or twelve paces ahead of me, shooting arrows at me as if at a wild beast, without my being able to overtake him. And if good luck comes to my aid and I overtake and kill him, I find nothing to take from him except a bow and a plume, as if they were of any use to me. My greatest complaint is that El Lucero of Italy, so called as a famous astrologer, told me to avoid going in the water, because I was to die by drowning, and it seems that luck brought me to a country where we never get out of the water." Francisco Sebastián said these things and other similar ones a little before he was drowned, much to the grief of his companions.

These latter landed to make the first attack upon the enemy, and with much spirit and courage they gained the first palisade, driving [the Indians] back to the second. They thereby struck such terror into the women and children and serving-people who were on the island that they very hastily embarked in their canoes, shouting, in order to flee up the river. The Indians who were stationed to defend the second palisade—seeing their cacique before them and knowing the danger their women and children and all of them ran of being slaves of their enemies, and that in this single battle, if they did not fight like men and win it, they would lose all the honor and glory their predecessors had left them—attacked furiously, like desperate men, ashamed of those who had retreated and run from the Casquines. They fought very courageously and wounded many Spaniards, preventing them and the Indians from advancing farther.

IX

THE CASQUINES FLEE FROM THE BATTLE, AND CAPAHA ASKS THE GOVERNOR FOR PEACE

Seeing that they had checked the impetus of their enemies, the Indians of Capaha, regaining their spirit and courage with this successful exploit, said to the Casquines: "Come on and take us, cowards, and carry us off as slaves, since you have dared enter our pueblo to injure our prince as you have done; remember well what you are doing and what you have done, so that when the strangers have gone we shall then see what kind of warriors you are."

These words alone were enough to make the Casquines, as a frightened people often defeated on other occasions, not only stop fighting but totally lose their courage, turn their backs, and run for the canoes, paying no attention to their cacique nor fearing the shouts and threats of the Spaniards and the governor ordering them not to desert the two hundred Christians who had come with them. Fleeing thus as if they were being pursued with spears, they took their canoes and attempted to take those the Castilians had carried, but they found two Christians in each one who had stayed to guard them and who defended them with their swords. The Indians wished to take them all so that the enemy would have no means of following them.

Thus the Casquines fled with such abjectness and meanness of spirit when shortly before they had been on the point of gaining the island with the protection and help of the Spaniards, without their adversaries daring to take up arms. Our infantry, seeing that they were few against so many enemies and that they had no horses, which were their greatest strength in resisting them, began to retire in good order to where they had left the canoes. Seeing that the Christians were alone and that they were retreating, the Indians of the island fell upon them very boldly to kill them. But the cacique Capaha, who was wise and prudent, wished to take advantage of this occasion to win the governor's favor and pardon for his rebelliousness and pertinacity in having refused to accept the peace and friendship that he had continuously offered him. It seemed to him also that he was obligated by the favor [on the governor's part] of his not having permitted the Casquines to do more damage in their pueblo and fields than they had done, which he regretted extremely.

With this intention he went out to his men and shouted to them loudly, ordering them not to harm the Christians, but to let them go freely. Because of this favor that Capaha did them our two hundred infantry escaped death, for if it had not been for his generosity and courtesy, they would all have died at that perilous time. The governor contented himself for the moment with having recovered his men alive through Capaha's magnanimity, which was esteemed and praised highly among all the Spaniards. Early on the morning of the following day four principal Indians came with an embassy from Capaha to the governor, asking his pardon for what had happened and offering his services and friendship in the future, and [requesting] that he not permit his enemies to do more damage in his country than they had done already. He begged his lordship to return to the pueblo and said that on the next day he would go personally to kiss his hands and offer the obedience that he owed him. This was the substance of the message, but the ambassadors delivered it in many words and with great solemnity, ceremony, and demonstrations of respect and veneration, which they accorded to the Sun and Moon, but not to the cacique Casquin. He was present, but [they acted] as if he were not there and as if they had not seen him.

The general replied, saying that Capaha might come whenever he wished, that he would always be well received, that he was glad to accept his friendship, and that they would do no more damage in his country, not even to the leaf of a tree. What had been done was caused by the fact that he had been unwilling to receive the peace and friendship that had been offered him so many times, and he begged him to speak no more of things already past. The governor sent the ambassadors back very well satisfied with this reply, having entertained them and made much of them with friendly words. Casquin was not at all pleased with the embassy from his enemy or with the governor's reply, for he hoped that Capaha would have persevered in his obstinacy, so that he could have taken revenge on him and destroyed him with the Castilians' help. As soon as he had received Capaha's embassy, the governor returned to the pueblo. On the road he ordered a decree issued to the effect that neither Indian nor Spaniard should dare take anything that might injure the people of the province. On arriving at the pueblo, he ordered that the Indians of Casquin, both warriors and servants, go immediately to their own country, some of them staying to serve their curaca, who wished to remain with the governor. At noon, while the army was on the march, an embassy came from Capaha to the general saying that he begged his lordship to send word concerning his health and to be certain and assured that on the following day he would come to kiss his hands. At sunset, when they had already reached the pueblo, another messenger came with the same message, and these two embassies were delivered with the same solemnity and ceremonies as the first, with the veneration of the Sun, the Moon, and the governor. The general replied very courteously and ordered the messengers to be entertained so that they would understand that he considered them friends. At eight o'clock the next morning Capaha came, accompanied by a hundred nobles adorned with very handsome plumes and mantles made of all kinds of skins.

Before he saw the governor he went to see his temple and burial place; it might have been because it was on the way to the general's lodgings or because he felt that affront more than all the others they had committed against him. As he went inside and saw the destruction done, he concealed his feelings and lifted up from the ground with his own hands the bones and dead bodies of his ancestors, which the Casquines had thrown out, and having kissed them he returned them to the wooden chests that served as sepulchers. This done as well as possible, he went to his house where the governor was lodged. The latter came out of his apartment to receive him and embraced him with much affability. The curaca made his offer of vassalage and they spoke of many particulars that the governor asked him concerning his country and the surrounding provinces. The cacique replied to the general's satisfaction and to that of the captains who were present, and he showed himself to be very intelligent. Capaha was twenty-six or twenty-seven years of age.

The latter, seeing that the governor ceased his questions and that he did not have to reply to him, and on the other hand being able no longer to dissimulate his wrath against the cacique Casquin because of the offenses he had committed against him, and of whom—though he had gone out with the governor to receive him and had been present throughout their conversation—he had taken no notice, as if he had not been there; seeing, then, that the field was clear, he turned to him and said: "You must be satisfied, Casquin, at having seen what you never imagined or hoped from your own courage, which is revenge for your insults and affronts; you can thank the outside help of the Spaniards for it. They will leave, and we shall remain here in our country as before. Pray to the Sun and the Moon, our gods, that they send us good weather."

X

THE GOVERNOR TWICE UPHOLDS CASQUIN, AND RECONCILES THE TWO CURACAS

Before Casquin could reply, the governor asked the interpreters what it was that Capaha had said, and having been informed, he said to him that the Spaniards had not come to his lands to leave them more inflamed with their wars and enmities than they were before, but to put them in peace and concord, and that he himself was to blame for the injury that the Casquines had done him because he had not waited in his pueblo when the Castilians were coming to it, or had not sent him a messenger on the road. If he had done so, his enemies would not have entered his pueblo or his territory, and inasmuch as his own negligence had caused the past damage, he begged him to lay aside his anger and forget the passions the two of them had felt hitherto, and thenceforth to be friends and good neighbors. He begged and charged them to do this as a friend of both of them; if necessary he ordered it under penalty of his own enmity toward him who did not obey.

Capaha replied to the governor that, because his lordship had so commanded and in order to serve him, he would take pleasure in being a friend to Casquin, and thus they embraced like two brothers, but the expressions on their faces and their looks at one another were not those of true friendship. With as much of it as they could feign, however, the two curacas talked with the general about many things, both pertaining to Spain and to the provinces the Spaniards had seen in La Florida. The conversation lasted until they were told that it was time for dinner, so they passed to another apartment where the table had been laid for all three, because the governor always honored the caciques by having them eat with him. The adelantado seated himself at the head of the table, and Casquin, who from the first day that he had eaten with him had been seated at his right hand, took the same place. When Capaha saw him he said, without showing annoyance: "You know very well, Casquin, that that place is mine, for many reasons, the principal ones being that my rank is higher, my seigniory more ancient, and my state greater than yours. Because of any of these three reasons you ought not to take that seat, for you know that by virtue of each of them it belongs to me."

The governor, who had been acting as Casquin's patron, sensing that something unusual was happening, wished to know what Capaha had said to him. When he learned what it was, he said: "Granting that all this you have said is true, it is fitting that Casquin's age and his gray hairs should be respected and that you, who are young, should honor the elder by giving him the most important place, because it is a natural obligation that the young have to respect the old, and in so doing they honor themselves." Capaha replied, saying: "Sir, if I had Casquin as a guest in my house, I would give him the first place at my table, gray hairs or no, and would do him all the other honor that I could, but when eating at another's table it does not seem to me right to yield my privileges, because they belong to my ancestors, and my vassals, especially the nobles, would be displeased with me. If your lordship wishes me to eat at your table, I must be given the place at your right hand, for it belongs to me. Otherwise I shall go eat with my soldiers, which would be more honorable to me and more pleasing to them than to see me disgrace myself and the position my fathers left me." Casquin, who on the one hand desired to placate Capaha's past wrath, and on the other saw that all he had said and asserted on his own behalf was true, got up from the chair and said to the governor: "Sir, Capaha is right and his demands are justified.

I beg your lordship to order him to be given his seat and place, which is this one, and I shall seat myself on the other side. I am much honored to be seated at any part of your lordship's table." So saying, he passed to the left side and sat down to eat without any ill-feeling, whereas Capaha was pacified and took his seat, and ate with the governor with an untroubled countenance.

These things are written in such detail, though they may seem unimportant, to show that the ambition for honor, more than any other impulse, is very strong in all men, however barbarous and far removed they may be from all good instruction and doctrine. Thus the governor and the gentlemen who were with him wondered to see what had passed between the two curacas, because they had not understood that the Indians drew such fine distinctions of honor or that they would be so punctilious therein.

As soon as the governor and the two caciques had eaten, they brought before them the two wives of Capaha whom, we said, the Casquines had captured when they entered the pueblo, and they presented them to Capaha, having freed all the other people who had been captured with them the day before. Capaha received them with many thanks for the generosity shown him, and after having accepted them, he said to the governor that he begged his lordship to make use of them, that he offered and presented them to him very willingly. The governor told him that he did not need them because he already had many servants. The curaca replied that, if he did not want them for his own service, he might pass them on to any captain or soldier to whom he wished to grant a favor, because they were not to return to his house or remain in his country. It was understood that Capaha abhorred them and put them away from him because of the suspicion that, since they had been captives in the power of his enemies, it would be impossible that they should not have been contaminated.

So as not to displease the curaca, the governor told him that he would accept them because they were a gift from him. They were extremely beautiful, but for all this, and though the curaca was young, the suspicion alone was enough to make him detest them and put them from him. From this action it may be seen how that crime is abominated among these Indians, and the exile and punishment of these women seems to confirm what we said above about their laws against adultery.

XI

THE SPANIARDS SEND TO SEARCH FOR SALT AND GOLD MINES, AND THEY PASS ON TO QUIGUATE

Seeing the great necessity for salt that his people were experiencing, for they were dying for lack of it, the adelantado made thorough inquiries of the curacas and their Indians in that province of Capaha in order to learn where they could get some. In the course of this questioning he found eight Indians in the hands of the Spaniards who had been captured the day they entered that pueblo, and were not natives of it, but strangers and merchants who had traversed many provinces with their goods; and among other things, they were accustomed to bring salt to sell. Being brought before the governor, they told him that in some mountains forty leagues away there was a great deal of very good salt, and to the repeated questions they asked them, they replied that there was also in that country much of the yellow metal they asked for.

The Castilians rejoiced greatly at this news, and two soldiers offered to go with the Indians to confirm it. These were natives of Galicia, one named Hernando de Silvera and the other Pedro Moreno, diligent men to whom anything could be entrusted. They were directed to note the nature of the country through which they passed and bring a report as to whether it were fertile and well populated. To barter for and purchase the salt and the gold, they took pearls and deerskins and some vegetables called *frisoles* that Capaha ordered to be given to them. They also took Indians to accompany them and two of the merchants to act as guides. Thus prepared, the Spaniards set out, and at the end of the eleven days that they spent on their journey they returned with six loads of rock-salt crystals, not made artificially, but found in this state. They also brought back a load of very fine and resplendent brass [copper], and concerning the quality of the lands they had seen, they said that they were not good, for they were sterile and thinly populated. Because they needed it so badly, the Spaniards consoled themselves with the salt for their disappointment and misunderstanding regarding the gold.

With the unfavorable reports that his two soldiers had given him concerning the lands that they had seen, the governor decided to go back to the pueblo of Casquin in order to make another journey to the west from there to see what lands there might be in that direction, because from Mauvila to that point they had always marched toward the north, in order to get away from the sea. Having so decided, the Castilians left Capaha in his pueblo and went back with Casquin to his, where they rested five days. At the end of that time they left it and marched four days' journey down the river through a fertile and well-populated country. Then they arrived in a province called Quiguate, whose lord and inhabitants came out peacefully to receive the governor, and entertained him. On the next day the cacique asked his lordship to go on to the chief pueblo of his province where he was better prepared to serve him than in that one.

The Spaniards traveled five more daily journeys, always down the river, through a country that, as we said of the last one, was well populated and had an abundance of food. At the end of the fifth day they reached the principal pueblo, called Quiguate, from which the whole province took its name. It was divided into three equal districts, in one of which was the lord's house, situated on a high elevation made by hand. The Spaniards lodged in two of the districts, and the Indians were assembled in the third, there being plenty of lodgings for everyone. Two days after they arrived all the Indians and the curaca ran away without any cause at all. Two days later they returned, asking pardon for their bad behavior. The cacique excused himself by saying that a certain urgent necessity had forced him to leave without his lordship's permission, thinking to return on that same day, and that it had not been possible for him to do so. It might have been that after his flight the curaca feared the Spaniards would burn his pueblo and fields on their departure, and that this fear caused him to return. Apparently he had left with bad intentions because in his absence his Indians had been rebellious, doing such damage as they could by stealth and wounding two or three Castilians. The governor overlooked all this so as not to break with them.

On one of the nights the Spaniards spent in this camp it happened that the assistant to the sergeant major, who was named Pablo Fernández, a native of Valverde, went to the governor at midnight and told him that the treasurer Juan Gaytán, having been summoned to make the rounds on horseback in the second night watch, had refused to do so on the grounds that he was his Majesty's treasurer. The governor was very angry because this gentleman was one of those who had complained about the conquest in Mauvila and had planned to leave the country as soon as they should arrive where there were ships, and return to Spain or go to México. This, as we have said already, was the cause of obstructing and disarranging the purposes and well-laid plans that the governor had in mind for conquering and settling the country.

Thus since the present disobedience recalled his past anger, the governor got out of bed and, stationing himself in the patio of the curaca's house, which was on a high place, he said in such a loud voice that, although it was midnight, the whole pueblo heard him: "What is this, soldiers and captains? Do the mutinies that were plotted in Mauvila for returning to Spain or going to México still persist, so that under pretext of being officials of the real hacienda you refuse to stand the watches that fall to you? Why do you want to return to Spain? Did you leave some inheritances there to go back and enjoy? Why do you wish to go to México? To show the weakness and cowardice of your spirits, when you could be lords of such a great kingdom where you have discovered and traversed so many and such beautiful provinces, you have thought it better (in abandoning them through your pusillanimity and cowardice) to go and lodge in a strange house and eat at another's table, when you could have your own in which to entertain and do good to many others? How much honor do you think they will do you when this becomes known? Be ashamed of yourselves, and understand that, officials of the real hacienda or not, we all have to serve his Majesty, and that no one shall presume to absent himself, whatever privileges he may have, or I shall behead him, whoever he may be. Understand further that while I live no one shall leave this country, but that we must conquer and settle it, or all die in the attempt. Therefore do your duty and give up your vain presumptions, because this is not the time for them."

The governor showed with these words, spoken in great anger and heaviness of heart, the reason for the perpetual discontent that he had felt all the way from Mauvila and that he felt continuously until his death. Those to whom they were addressed did as they were ordered from there on without raising any questions, because they understood that the governor was not a man to be trifled with, particularly when he had declared himself as decisively as he had done.

XII

THE ARMY REACHES COLIMA, FINDS A METHOD OF MAKING SALT, AND PASSES TO THE PROVINCE OF TULA

The Spaniards spent six days in the pueblo called Quiguate. On the seventh they left it, and in five daily journeys they made, always downstream along the banks of the Río de Casquin, they reached the principal pueblo of another province, called Colima. Its lord came out peacefully and received the governor and his army very cordially and with signs of affection, which greatly pleased the Castilians because they had heard that the Indians of that province were accustomed to use [the juice of a poison] herb on their arrows. Our men were very fearful of this, because they said that if poison were added to the usual ferocity and boldness with which the Indians shot their arrows, what recourse could they have? But finding that they did not use [the poison], they received the friendship of the Colimas with greater satisfaction, though it did not last long, for within two days they rose up, without any reason for it, and the curaca and his vassals went to the woods.

After remaining one day in the pueblo of Colima following the flight of the Indians, collecting provisions on the march, our men continued their journey. They marched over some fertile cultivated fields and through some open woodlands, easy to traverse, and at the end of four days' march they came to the bank of a river, where the army encamped. After making their camp, certain soldiers went down to walk by the river, and passing along its shore, they happened to see a blue sand at the water's edge. One of them took up some of it, tasted it, and found that it was brackish. He told his companions, and they said that they thought saltpeter could be made of it for making powder for the harquebuses. With this in mind they set to work handily to take up the blue sand without an admixture of the white. Having collected a quantity of it, they put it in water, rubbed it together between their hands, strained off the water, and put it to boil. As they made a large fire under it, it was converted into salt of a somewhat yellow color, but effective and with a very good taste.

Rejoicing at this new discovery, and because of their great need for salt, the Spaniards spent eight days in that camp and made a large quantity of it. There were some who in their craving for salt, seeing that there was now an abundance of it, ate it by itself in mouthfuls, as if it were sugar. To those who scolded them they said, "Let us get our fill of salt, because we have had a great craving for it." Nine or ten of them ate their fill of it in such a manner that in a few days they died of dropsy. Thus some died from lack of salt and some from too much.

Supplied with salt and happy over their discovery for making it whenever they should need it, the Spaniards left that camp and province, which they named La Sal. They marched two days to get out of its territory, and entered that of another province, called Tula, through which they marched for four days in an uninhabited region. At noon on the last day the army halted on a fine plain where it encamped. Though the guides told the governor that the principal pueblo of that province was half a league from there, he did not want the men to go on because they had marched for six days without stopping, but desired to enter it the next day after they had rested in that camp. He himself wished to see the pueblo on that same evening, however, so he chose sixty infantry and a hundred cavalry to go with him to reconnoiter it. It was situated on a plain between two streams, and its inhabitants were unprepared, having had no notice of the Castilians' coming. But as soon as they saw them they sounded the alarm and came out to fight with all the good spirit and courage that could be imagined. What our men wondered at most, however, was seeing that many women came out among the men with their weapons and that they fought as fiercely as the men themselves.

The Spaniards fell upon the Indians and broke through them, and they entered the pueblo fighting with one another. There the Christians had enough to do because they found rash enemies who fought without fear of death, and even though they lacked weapons and strength, they were unwilling to give themselves up, but wished to be killed. The women did the same and showed themselves to be even more desperate. During the struggle a gentleman from the kingdom of León, named Francisco de Reynoso Cabeza de Vaca, entered a house and ascended to an upper room that served as a granary, where he found five Indian women huddled in a corner. By signs he told them to be quiet and that he did not wish to do them harm. Seeing him alone, they all assailed him at once, and like mastiffs attacking a bull they seized him by the arms, legs, and neck, and one grasped him around the body. By a great effort Reynoso freed his body and arms so as to defend himself with his fists. He bore heavily upon one foot, and it broke through the floor of the room, which was of flimsy framework. The foot and leg sank through to the thigh, and he was left sitting on the floor. Thereupon, the Indian women completely subdued him with bites and fisticuffs, and were on the point of killing him. Francisco de Reynoso, though he found himself in such dire straits, for the sake of his honor, because of the struggle being with women, did not wish to call to his people for help.

At this juncture a soldier happened to enter the lower room of the house where they were throttling Cabeza de Vaca. Hearing the noise that was going on above, he raised his eyes and saw the suspended leg. Thinking that it must belong to some Indian because it was bare, without stocking or shoe, he raised his sword to slash it with a stroke, but at that moment he suspected whom it might be because of the great clamor he heard overhead. He hurriedly summoned two other companions, and all three went up to the apartment. On seeing how the Indian women were holding Francisco de Reynoso, they attacked them and killed them all, because none of them would let go of Reynoso or cease cuffing and biting him, even though they were killed for it. Thus his comrades saved Francisco de Reynoso from death, which was very near. In the year 1591 in which I am making a final fair copy of this *History,* I learned in the month of February that this gentleman was still living in his native country.

Another incident, equally unfortunate, happened that day to Juan Páez, a native of Usagre, who was captain of crossbowmen. Though he had no skill in horsemanship, but rather was awkward and heavy, he wished to fight on horseback, and going out in the last stages of the battle, he encountered an Indian who, though he was retreating, was still fighting. Juan Páez attacked him, and without aptitude, skill, or dexterity, for he did not have them, he threw a lance at him. The Indian jumped aside and warded off the lance with a piece of a pike more than a fathom long, which he carried as a weapon. Grasping it with both hands, he gave Juan Páez a blow on the mouth that broke all his teeth, leaving him choking, and made his escape safely.

XIII

CONCERNING THE STRANGE FEROCITY OF SPIRIT OF THE TULAS, AND THE ARMED ENCOUNTERS THE SPANIARDS HAD WITH THEM

Because it was already late, the general ordered the assembly sounded, and leaving many Indians dead and carrying back some of his own badly wounded men, he returned to the camp, not at all satisfied with that day's expedition. On the other hand he was amazed at the obstinacy and temerity with which those Indians fought, and at the fact that the women had the same spirit and ferocity.

On the following day the general entered the pueblo with his army, and finding it abandoned he encamped there. That afternoon bands of cavalry went out to scour the country in all directions to see whether there were any parties of the enemy there. They encountered some who were serving as lookouts, and captured them, but it was impossible to take any of them to the camp alive in order to obtain information from them, because when they laid hold of them to take them away, they immediately fell down on the ground and said, "Either kill me or leave me here." They would not answer a word to all the questions that were asked them, and if they tried to drag them along and raise them up they simply allowed themselves to be dragged. Thus the Castilians were forced to kill them all.

In the pueblo (because we are noting its peculiarities) our men found many cowhides tanned and dressed with the hair on them, which served as blankets on the beds. They found many other rawhides, not yet tanned. They also found beef, but they saw no cattle in the country, nor could they learn from where they had brought the hides. The Indians of this province of Tula are different from all the other Indians whom our Spaniards had encountered hitherto, for we have said that the others are handsome and graceful in person. These, however, both men and women, have ugly faces, and though they are well-proportioned, they deform themselves by deliberate distortion of themselves. Their heads are incredibly long and tapering on top, being made thus artificially by binding them up from birth to the age of nine or ten years. They prick their faces with flint needles, especially the lips, inside and out, and color them black, thereby making themselves extremely and abominably ugly. The hideous aspect of their faces corresponds to their bad dispositions, as we shall see more particularly below.

On the fourth night that the Spaniards spent in the pueblo of Tula the Indians came in great numbers just before dawn, and they arrived so silently that when the sentries heard them they were already surrounded. They attacked the camp on three sides, and though the Spaniards were not sleeping, the Indians who assaulted the crossbowmen's quarters came so suddenly and with such ferocity, impetus, and swiftness that they gave them no opportunity to prepare their crossbows or to make any other resistance. They could only run with their weapons in their hands toward the quarters of Juan de Guzmán, which were nearest to those of the crossbowmen. The Indians pillaged the few things that our marksmen had and fought desperately with the soldiers of Juan de Guzmán who came out to resist them, being inspired with new courage in that, in their opinion, they had snatched the victory out of their hands.

In the two other places where the enemy attacked the fighting was no less fierce, because everywhere there were deaths and wounds and great outcries and much confusion because of the darkness of the night, which kept them from seeing whether they were wounding friends or enemies. Therefore the Spaniards passed the word along for all of them to call out the name of Our Lady and the apostle St. James as they went, so that the Christians would thus recognize one another and would not harm their own men. The Indians

A Spanish Crossbowman. The De Soto expedition was one of the last to use crossbows, which were rapidly replaced by firearms in the later sixteenth century. The crossbow was a deadly weapon. Its advantage over the longbow was that it could be used effectively by relatively unskilled and unpracticed soldiers. Its disadvantage was that it took some time to reload. An Indian could fire several arrows in the time it took a crossbowman to reload. (From Albert F. Calvert, Spanish Arms and Armour, *London: John Lane, 1907)*

Lance and Spear Heads. The wooden lances tipped with metal heads, came in a number of sizes and with a number of different shapes of iron or brass tips. Lance tips have been found in archaeological excavations of native village sites in the Southeast and the Southwest. "The Pike I would have if it might be, of Spanish Ash, and between 20 and 22 feet long"—Sutcliffe, Practice of Arms *(1593). (From Albert F. Calvert,* Spanish Arms and Armour, *London: John Lane, 1907)*

did likewise, all of them having in their mouths the name of their province, Tula. In the place of bows and arrows with which they are always accustomed to fight, that night many of them carried clubs made of pieces of pikes two or three varas long, a new thing for the Spaniards. The reason for it was that the Indian who had broken Captain Juan Páez's teeth two days before had told his people of the lucky stroke he had made with his club. It appearing to them that good fortune lay in the kind of weapon and not in its skillful use (because the Indians generally are great believers in omens), that night they brought many clubs and gave mighty blows with them to many of the soldiers, particularly to a certain Juan de Baeza, who was one of the halberdiers of the general's guard. That night he happened to find himself with a sword and a shield between two Indians with their clubs. One of them broke his shield to pieces with the first stroke, and the other gave him another blow on the shoulders so hard that it knocked him down, and he would have finished killing him if his companions had not come to his rescue. In this manner many other valiant exploits took place, which, because they were blows with sticks, the soldiers laughed about afterward, comparing their experiences. It was a very good thing for them that they were sticks and not arrows, which would have done more damage.

The mounted men, who were the strength of the Spaniards and what the Indians feared most, broke through their squadrons and scattered their ranks, but they did not fail for this reason to fight with great courage and desire to kill the Castilians or to die in the attempt. Thus they fought very obstinately for more than an hour, and it was not enough for the horsemen to go in and out among them many times and kill large numbers of them (for since the country was level and clear they could spear them at pleasure) to make them stop fighting and leave, until daylight came. Then they withdrew by common consent into the woods along one of the streams that passed at the side of the pueblo, as a refuge and defense against the Castilians.

The Spaniards were greatly relieved when the Indians withdrew and stopped fighting, because they saw them battling desperately with great eagerness to kill the Christians, going in among their weapons as if they were insensible [to pain] in order to kill or wound them. The battle ended at sunrise, and the Spaniards, without pursuing the enemy, assembled in the pueblo to tend the wounded, who were numerous, though only four were killed.

XIV

THE ENGAGEMENT OF A TULA INDIAN WITH THREE SPANIARDS ON FOOT AND ONE ON HORSEBACK

Because historical truth obliges us to tell the exploits of the Indians as well as the deeds done by the Spaniards, and not to slight the ones or the others, neglecting to tell of the valor of one nation and recounting only that of the other, but on the other hand telling everything as it happened, in its proper time and place, it will be fitting for us to relate a strange and singular thing that a Tula Indian did shortly after the battle we have described. We beg that the reader may not be vexed because we recount it in such detail, for the event took place thus and its particulars should be noted.

It happened that some Spaniards who were considered to be among the bravest were walking two by two scattered over the field where the battle had taken place, examining the dead, as was their custom, and noting the serious wounds given by good strokes; they always did this when an important and hotly contested battle had taken place. One soldier, named Gaspar Caro, a native of Medellín, fought that night on horseback, and however it may have happened, either by the enemy knocking him down or his falling from the horse, finally he lost it [the horse], and the horse ran away from the battle out into the fields. In order to recover it, Gaspar Caro asked a friend for his horse and went in search of his own. Having found it, he returned driving it in front of him, and thus he came to where four soldiers were walking looking at the dead and wounded. One of them, named Francisco de Salazar, a native of Castilla la Vieja, mounted the horse to show off his horsemanship, on which he prided himself.

At this point Juan de Carranza of Sevilla, one of the three soldiers who were on foot, shouted, "Indians, Indians!" The reason was that he saw an Indian raise himself up out of some bushes close by and drop back into hiding. Believing that there were many of them there, the two mounted men, without looking farther, ran one in one direction and the other in another to intercept the Indians who might come out. Juan de Carranza, who had seen the Indian, went running toward the bushes where he was hidden, and one of his two companions hurried after him. The other, having seen only one Indian, followed them slowly.

As he saw that he could not escape because the horses and foot soldiers were cutting him off on all sides, the barbarian ran out of the bushes to meet

Juan de Carranza. He carried in his hands a battle-ax that had fallen to his lot from the spoils and booty that the Indians had taken that morning from the crossbowmen. The ax belonged to Captain Juan Páez, and being the weapon of a captain of crossbowmen the blades were well sharpened and it had a haft more than half a fathom long, very smooth and well polished. Holding it in both hands, the Indian struck Juan de Carranza a blow on the shield that knocked half of it on the ground and wounded him badly in the arm. The Spaniard was so stunned by the pain of the wound and the force of the blow that he had not the strength to attack the enemy. The latter turned upon the other Spaniard, who was near Carranza, and gave him another blow equal to the first one, which cut his shield in two and also wounded him badly in the arm, leaving him, like his companion, incapacitated for fighting. This soldier's name was Diego de Godoy, and he was a native of Medellín.

Francisco de Salazar, who was the one who mounted Gaspar Caro's horse, seeing the two Spaniards in such straits, attacked the Indian furiously. To avoid being trampled by the horse, the latter ran under an oak tree that was close by. Being unable to ride his horse under the tree, Francisco de Salazar came up to it and, good horseman that he was, made some very sad thrusts at the Indian as he was unable to reach him. The Indian came out from under the tree, being unable to swing the ax well because the branches of the tree hindered him, and stationed himself on the rider's left. Raising the ax in both hands, he struck the horse over the shoulder near the withers, and the curve of the blade opened him all the way to the knee, leaving the horse unable to move.

At this moment another Spaniard came up, who was on foot. He had not hurried more because it seemed to him that two Spaniards on foot and one on horseback would be enough for one lone Indian. This was Gonzalo Silvestre, a native of Herrera de Alcántara. When the Indian saw him coming, he went out to meet him with all ferocity and boldness, having gained new spirit and courage with the three such effective blows that he had delivered. Grasping the ax in both hands, he made a stroke that would have been like the first two if Gonzalo Silvestre had not been more cautious than the others, being able to avoid the blow, as he did. The ax glanced off the shield and did not break through it, and because of the great force of the blow, it did not stop until it reached the ground. The Spaniard then made a diagonal downward stroke at the Indian with his sword, which reached him and wounded him on the forehead, all down the face, in the breast, and in the left hand, cutting it off at the wrist. The heathen, seeing himself with only one hand and unable to use the ax with both hands as he desired, put the haft on the stump of the cut arm and made a desperate leap to wound the Spaniard by a stroke in the face. Warding off the ax with his shield, the latter thrust his sword from beneath it and gave him a diagonal stroke at the waist, which because of negligible protection from armor or clothing that the Indian wore or even from the bones of that part of the body, and also because of the Spaniard's strong arm, [cut] him entirely in two, so swiftly and with such a clean stroke of the sword that after it had passed, the Indian remained standing and said to the Spaniard, "Peace be with you!" Uttering these words, he fell dead, his body in two halves.

Just then Gaspar Caro arrived, it being his horse that Francisco de Salazar had brought to the fight. Seeing the state in which his horse was, he took him without saying a word, keeping his anger to be shown elsewhere, and brought him before the governor, saying to him: "So that your lordship may see the worthlessness of some of the soldiers that you have in your army, though they claim to be brave men, and so that you may see also the ferocity and boldness of the natives of this province of Tula, I inform you that one of them with three blows of an ax has incapacitated for fighting two Spanish foot soldiers and one on horseback, and would have ended by killing them if Gonzalo Silvestre had not come in time to their aid. With the first thrust that he gave the enemy he laid open his face and chest and cut off his hand, and with the second he cut him in half at the waist."

The governor and those who were with him wondered to hear of the Indian's valor and skill, and of the Spaniard's strong arm. So that Gaspar Caro, in his anger at the misfortune that had befallen his horse, would cease to regard the three Spaniards as luckless cowards, the general, wishing to uphold their honor—for assuredly they were brave men and fit for any valiant exploit—told him to moderate his anger and consider that these things were the chances of fortune, which nowhere shows itself to be more variable than in the events of war, today favoring one and tomorrow another. He told him to have the horse tended to at once, for it seemed to him that it would not die, since the wound was not a deep one; and that because of the wonder that he had excited by his account, he wished to go and see for himself what had happened, as in such extraordinary events it was well for many persons to be able to give testimony regarding them. So saying, he went accompanied by many persons to see the dead Indian and the brave exploits that he had performed. The governor learned the particulars that we have told from the wounded Spaniards themselves, and he and all those who heard them wondered anew.

XV

THE SPANIARDS LEAVE TULA AND ENTER UTIANGUE, WHERE THEY LODGE FOR THE WINTER

The Spaniards remained in the pueblo called Tula for twenty days, treating the many wounded who came out of the recent battle. During this time they made many forays throughout the province, which was well populated, and captured many Indians, both men and women, of all ages, but it was impossible either by cajolery or threats for them to make any of them consent to go with the Castilians. When they attempted to take them by force they fell on the ground without saying a word, making it clear that they could either kill them or leave them, whichever they wished to do. These Indians showed themselves to be so obstinate and ungovernable, as we have said, that it was necessary to kill the men who were capable of fighting. The women, boys, and children they let go, since they could not carry them off.

Only one Indian woman from this province remained in the service of a Spaniard, a native of León named Juan Serrano. She was so ill-tempered, bold, and haughty that if her master or any of the men belonging to his company said anything to her about what she was to do regarding the food or any other matter of service, she would throw the pot, or firebrands, or anything that came to hand in his face. She wanted them either to let her do what she liked or to kill her, because, as she said, she did not have to obey or to do what they ordered her. Thus they let her alone and endured her ill-temper, and even so she ran away, at which her master rejoiced, seeing himself free of that intractable woman. Because of the ferocity and inhumanity that characterize the Indians of this province, they are feared by all their neighbors; they are disturbed simply by hearing the name of Tula, and they frighten the children with it to make them hush when they cry. As a proof of this we shall come down from the ferocity of the elders to describe a children's game.

It happened that when the Spaniards left this province of Tula, they took with them only a boy nine or ten years old who belonged to a gentleman from Badajoz named Cristóbal Mosquera, whom I knew afterward in El Perú. In the pueblos that the Christians discovered later, where the Indians came out peacefully, the boys gathered for their games and childish diversions, which almost always took the form of battles against one another, they being divided either according to names or by districts. Often they became so inflamed in their fighting that many of them came out badly injured. The Castilians ordered the Tula boy to join one side and fight against the other, and he went out very pleased that they should order him to take part in the battle. Those on his side immediately named him captain, and with his soldiers he fell upon his adversaries with a great shout and outcry, calling the name of Tula, and this alone was enough to put the enemy to flight.

Then the Spaniards ordered the Tula boy to go over to the defeated side and fight the conquerors. He did so and overcame them with the same word, so that he always came out victorious. The Indians said that his elders did the same thing, because they were extremely cruel to their enemies and never took them alive. Their neighbors said that they deformed their heads, some of them being half a vara long, and painted their faces and mouths, inside and out, to make themselves uglier than they were already, so that their faces would be as forbidding as their bad dispositions and fierce natures, for they were most inhuman in every way.

After spending twenty days in the pueblo of Tula, more from necessity for healing the wounded than from any pleasure they might have had in remaining in the country of such a bad people, they left the pueblo and in two days' march passed out of its jurisdiction and entered another province, called Utiangue. Our people had the intention of wintering there if they could find the necessary conveniences, for winter was now approaching.

They marched through it for four days and noted that the land was good in itself and fertile, but thinly populated, having few people. These were very hostile, because they followed the road continuously, harrying the Spaniards with alarms and sudden attacks they gave them every half-league. They were in bands of one hundred, and when more assembled there were not as many as two hundred. They did the Christians little damage because, after having loosed one or two showers of arrows from a distance, with much shouting, they turned and fled, and the horsemen overtook them easily and speared them entirely at will because the country was level. But the Indians were not frightened away, for whenever they could get twenty men together they immediately came back to do the same thing, and in order to emerge more unexpectedly and cause greater surprise, they threw themselves down on the ground and covered themselves with grass so that they could not be seen, but they paid well for their audacity.

With these engagements, more injurious to the Indians than to the Castilians, the army marched these four days, and at the end of them they reached the principal pueblo of the province, which had the same name of

Utiangue, from which its whole territory was named. They lodged there without any opposition because the inhabitants had abandoned it. The Indians of this province are better favored than those of Tula and do not paint their faces or deform their heads. They showed themselves to be warlike, because they were never willing to accept the peace and friendship that the governor sent many times to offer them by the Indians of that province themselves, whom they succeeded in capturing.

The general and his captains, having seen the pueblo, which was large and had good houses containing plenty of food, and was situated on a fine plain with two streams on either side of it that had plenty of grass for the horses, and seeing that it was enclosed with a wall, decided to winter there because it was already the middle of October of the year 1541. They did not know whether, if they should go on, they would find such good accommodations as they then had. Having made this decision, they repaired the wall of the pueblo, which was made of wood and had fallen down in some places, and they collected diligently a good deal of maize, though it is true that there was so much in the pueblo that the supply was almost sufficient for the whole winter.

They stored up much firewood and a great deal of dried fruit, such as nuts, raisins, dried plums, and other kinds of fruits and seeds unknown in Spain. In the country they found large numbers of rabbits like those of Spain, and though these were in all parts of that great kingdom, in none of the provinces were there so many as in the environs of this pueblo Utiangue. There were also many deer and roe deer, of which both the Spaniards and their Indian servants killed a great many, going out to hunt for pleasure and entertainment, though they went prepared to fight in case they should encounter enemies. Often the deer hunt was converted into a battle with plenty of arrow-shots and spear-thrusts, but it was always with more damage to the Indians than to the Spaniards. It snowed hard during that winter in this province, when there was an interval of a month and a half in which they could not go out into the country because of the deep snow. With their plentiful supply of wood and provisions, however, they had the best winter of all that they spent in La Florida. They themselves admitted that they could not have spent it more comfortably, or as much so, in their fathers' houses in Spain.

XVI

CONCERNING THE GOOD WINTER THAT WAS SPENT IN UTIANGUE, AND A PLOT AGAINST THE SPANIARDS

Because of what we have said in the last chapter about the contentment and comfort in which our people passed the winter in the pueblo Utiangue, it is much to be regretted that these Spaniards neglected to conquer and settle a land so fertile and abundant in the things necessary for human life as they discovered, because of not having found gold or silver there. They did not consider that, if it had not been found, it was because these Indians do not seek these metals or value them. I have heard from trustworthy persons that the Indians of the coast of La Florida have happened to find bags of silver from the ships that have been wrecked there by storms, and that they will take away the bag as a thing that is useful to them, and leave the silver, for they do not value it or know what it is. For this reason, and because it is true that the Indians of the New World generally, though they have gold and silver, do not use it for buying and selling, it is not to be assumed that there is none in La Florida. If a search should be made, mines of gold and silver would be found, just as new ones are discovered every day in México and El Perú. And even though they should not be found, lands as broad and extensive as we have seen, and shall see, and provinces as fertile and abundant, would be sufficient to lay the foundations of an empire, because of what the land itself contains as well as because of the fruits, vegetables, grains, and cattle that could be introduced from Spain and México. Better lands could not be desired for planting and breeding, and with their wealth of pearls and the quantity of silk that could be produced immediately, they could trade with the whole world and become rich in gold and silver. Spain herself does not obtain these metals from her own mines, though she has them, but brings them from a distance, from what she has discovered and conquered in these parts since the year 1492. For all these reasons it is not right that this enterprise should be neglected, if only in order to establish the faith of the Holy Mother, the Roman church, in this great kingdom and remove from the power of our enemy so great a number of souls as he has blinded with idolatry. May our Lord provide for this event in accordance with His will, and cause the Spaniards to be animated to win and subjugate [the land]. Returning to our *History*, we said that the Castilians remained to winter in the pueblo of Utiangue in entire comfort and ease, lodged in a good pueblo and supplied with food for themselves and their horses.

The chief curaca of the province, seeing that the Spaniards had settled down, attempted by double-dealing, under cover of professed friendship, to drive them out of it. To this end he sent messengers to the governor with false messages, giving him hope that he would come out very soon to offer his services. These messengers acted as spies and came only at night in order to see how the Spaniards conducted themselves in their camp; whether they kept watch and were cautious or whether they slept carelessly and heedlessly, in what manner and where they kept their weapons, and how their horses were, so as to note all this and plan the attack in accordance with what they had seen. There was carelessness and lack of caution on the part of our men with respect to the Indian messengers, because when the Indian told the Spanish sentry that he came with a message from the curaca, instead of telling him to come back in the daytime, he would take him to the governor immediately, no matter what the hour of the night, and leave him with him to deliver his message. After giving the message, the Indian walked all through the pueblo, looking at the horses and the weapons, the sleeping and the watching of the Castilians, and he gave a long report of all this to his cacique.

When the governor learned about these things from his spies, he ordered the messengers not to come at night, but in the daytime. But they persisted in their evil intent, always coming at night and at all hours. The general complained repeatedly to his men about this effrontery, saying: "Is there no soldier who could give one of these nocturnal messengers one good sword-thrust and frighten them so that they will not come at night? I have ordered them not to come except in the daytime, and it does no good." These words aroused a soldier named Bartolomé de Argote, a nobleman who had been brought up in the house of the marqués of Astorga, and first cousin of the other Bartolomé de Argote who was one of the thirty horsemen who went with Juan de Añasco from Apalache to the Bay of Espíritu Santo. Being a sentry one night at one of the gates of the pueblo, he killed one of the spies who attempted to pass with his false message, contrary to his order. The governor was very pleased with this act and praised and approved it. Thenceforth the soldier had a place among the valiant, though up to that time they had not considered him as such nor thought him capable of such an action, but he did what no one else in the whole army had been able to do. The messages ceased with the death of the messenger, and also the plots of the

Indians, for they saw that the Castilians were aware of them and on the watch and that they could not succeed.

The general and his men busied themselves with guarding their pueblo and riding through the whole vicinity every day so as always to be informed of what the Indians might be plotting against them. The winter passed with these precautions, and with much rest and comfort even though they were at war with the natives, for they never did them any serious damage. After the worst of the snows were over, a captain went out with some men to make a foray and capture some Indians, as they needed them for servants. He returned at the end of eight days with a few Indian captives. The governor therefore ordered that another captain go out with more men. He did the same as the first one, and having spent another eight days on his foray, at the end of them he came back, bringing only a few prisoners.

Since the general saw the little skill that his two captains had shown, he decided to make an expedition himself, and choosing a hundred cavalry and 150 infantry, he marched twenty leagues with them until he reached the confines of another province, called Naguatex.[32] It was a fertile and abundant land, full of very handsome and well-disposed people.

In the first pueblo of this province, where its lord resided, though this was not the principal pueblo of his state, the governor made a surprise attack at dawn, and as he found the Indians unprepared, he captured many people, men and women of all ages. He returned with them to his camp, having spent fourteen days on the journey. He found that his people had been very uneasy at his delay for four or five days past. But they all rejoiced at his presence and shared his plunder, [the Indians] being divided among the captains and soldiers who were in need of serving-people.

END OF THE FOURTH BOOK

[32]In the following pages Garcilaso, as judged against our more reliable chroniclers, garbles the story to a somewhat greater degree than is usual for him. Firstly, Naguatex is here utterly misplaced. This province was encountered not on the army's first expedition west of the Mississippi but on the second, during 1542, and after De Soto's death.

First Part of the Fifth Book of the History of La Florida, by the Inca

Where an account is given of a Spaniard who remained among the Indians; the efforts that were made to recover him; a long journey of the Castilians, in which they traversed eight provinces; the enmity and cruel war between Guachoyas and Anilcos; the lamentable death of Governor Hernando de Soto, and two burials his men gave him. It contains eight chapters.

I

THE SPANIARDS ENTER NAGUATEX, AND ONE OF THEM REMAINS THERE

Throughout the time that the Spaniards were wintering in the pueblo and camp of Utiangue, which was more than five months, nothing of importance occurred except what has been told. Since it was then the beginning of April of the year 1542, it seemed to the governor that it was time to proceed with his discovery.

With this determination he left Utiangue and took the road for the principal pueblo of the province of Naguatex,[33] which had the same name, by which the whole province was also called. It was different from the one where we have said that the governor made his recent foray from Utiangue to Naguatex. By the way the Castilians went, it is twenty-two or twenty-three leagues through a fertile and well-populated country. Our men marched this distance in seven days without anything of importance happening to them on the road, except that in some narrow passes by streams or woods the Indians came out to make surprise attacks, but ran away when they met resistance.

At the end of the seven days they reached the pueblo Naguatex and found that its inhabitants had abandoned it. They lodged there and remained fifteen or sixteen days. They scoured the country in every direction and took the food they needed with little or no resistance from the Indians.

After the Spaniards had been in the pueblo for six days, its lord sent an embassy to the governor saying that he begged his lordship to pardon him for not having awaited him in his pueblo to serve him as would have been fitting, and that because of shame for his past bad behavior, he dared not come immediately, but that within a few days he would come out to kiss his hands and acknowledge him as lord; and that until he should arrive he would order his vassals to serve him in everything that he might order them. This message was delivered with great ceremony, such as we have described in the case of others. The adelantado replied that whenever he should come he would be well received, and that he would be pleased to know him and have him for a friend, as were most of the curacas through whose lands he had passed. The ambassador returned very well satisfied with the governor's words.

[33] See note 32.

On the next day, early in the morning, another messenger came, bringing with him four principal Indians and more than five hundred Indian servants. He said to the general that his lord was sending those four men, who were his very close relatives, so that, pending his own arrival, they might serve him and carry out his commands; and that he sent the most important men of his household and state as hostages for his coming so that he would be assured of it.

The governor replied in friendly terms, welcoming the arrival of the Indians, and ordered that no more Indians be captured in forays, as they had been doing hitherto. The cacique never came to see the governor, however, from which it was understood that he had sent the embassy and the principal Indians and the servants out of fear that they would lay waste the fields and burn the pueblos, and to prevent their capturing more people than they had already. The principal Indians and all the rest served the Castilians with every desire to please them.

The governor, having informed himself about what was in that province and its environs, both from the report of the Indians and from that of the Spaniards who went to explore the country, left the pueblo of Naguatex with his army, accompanied by the four principal Indians and by many other servants whom the cacique sent with provisions, which they carried until the Castilians entered another province.

After the Spaniards had marched two leagues, they missed a gentleman named Diego de Guzmán, who was a native of Sevilla. He had gone on this conquest as a noble and a rich man, taking much costly and elegant clothing, excellent arms, and three horses that he brought to La Florida. He comported himself in every way like a gentleman except that he gambled passionately.

As soon as they missed him, the governor ordered that the army halt and that the four principal Indians be held in custody until learning what had become of the Spaniard because they feared the Indians had killed him.

A close inquiry was made among the Spaniards, and it was learned that they had seen him in the camp the day before, and that four days previously he had gambled away everything he had, even to his clothing and arms and a very good black horse that he had remaining. Going still further in the passion and blindness of his play, he had lost an Indian serving-woman who, unhappily for him, had fallen to his lot from those whom we said the governor had captured in the foray he made on a pueblo of this same province of Naguatex. Diego de Guzmán had also taken part in this expedition.

It was learned also that he had paid all his losses very promptly except for the Indian woman. He told the winner to wait four or five days and he would send her to his lodgings, but he had not done so. The Indian woman was missing as well. It was suspected from these indications that he had gone to the Indians, so as not to have to give her up and through shame at having played away his arms and horse, which is considered among soldiers to be a most despicable action.

This suspicion was verified immediately, because it was learned that the Indian was the daughter of the curaca and lord of that province of Naguatex, a girl of eighteen and extremely beautiful. These things may have so blinded him that he thoughtlessly renounced his own people and went among strangers.

The governor ordered the four principal Indians to have that Spaniard who was missing in their country brought at once; otherwise he would understand that they had killed him treacherously, and by way of revenge he would order them and all the Indians whom they brought with them quartered.

In fear of death these chiefs sent messengers who were to go as quickly as possible to all the places where they thought they might get news of Diego de Guzmán, and they charged them to return with the same swiftness before the Spaniards should harm them because of their delay.

The messengers went and came back on the same day with the report that Diego de Guzmán was with the cacique, who kept him and entertained and honored him as much as possible, and that the Spaniard said he did not want to come back to his own people.

Because we said that these Spaniards gambled, and have not told what they played, it should be said that after the cards they had with them were burned in the bloody battle of Mauvila, along with all the other things that they lost there, they made cards of parchment and painted them remarkably well, for whenever the necessity arose they were forced to make whatever they needed. They did this as if they had been masters of that art all their lives. Because they could not or did not wish to make as many as were needed, they made enough to be used among the players by turns for a limited time, from which (or from some other similar occasion) we can say that there may have arisen that saying current among gamblers when they are playing: "Let us hurry, gentlemen, they are coming for the cards." Since those that our men made were of leather, they lasted a long time.

II

THE EFFORTS THAT WERE MADE TO RECOVER DIEGO DE GUZMÁN, HIS RESPONSE, AND THAT OF THE CURACA

The governor, on hearing the news that the messengers brought, told the four principal Indians that they had deceived him in saying that the Spaniard was alive, because he was convinced that they had killed him. Then one of them, not with the aspect of a prisoner but with the seriousness and authority these Indians seem to wish to show when they are most oppressed, said: "Sir, we are not men who would lie to your lordship, and so that you may see more clearly that the messengers have told the truth, your lordship can release one of us who will go and come back with evidence of what has been done with the Spaniard that will satisfy your lordship. The three of us who shall remain give our word and promise that he will return with the Christian or bring definite notice of his decision; and so that your lordship may make certain that he is not dead, you can order that a letter be written to him asking that he either come or reply to it to show with his own hand that he is alive, since we do not know how to write. In case our companion should not return with this proof, the three of us who remain will pay with our lives for his failure to comply with his promise and ours. It will be enough and more than enough, without your lordship killing our Indians, that three men like ourselves shall die for the treason of one Spaniard who denied his own people without our having forced him or known of his going." All these were the Indian's own words, for we added nothing to them but simply changed them from his language to Spanish or Castilian.

The general and his captains agreed to what the principal Indian had said and promised in the name of all four, and they ordered that he himself go for Diego de Guzmán and that Baltasar de Gallegos, who was his friend and countryman, write to him, shaming him for his bad action if he should persevere in it, exhorting him to return and do his duty as an hidalgo, and saying that his arms and horse would be restored to him and that they would give him others when should he need them.

The principal Indian left with the letter and with a verbal message the governor gave him for the cacique, begging him to be pleased to send the Spaniard and not to detain him. Otherwise he threatened to destroy his land with fire and blood, burning his pueblos, laying waste his fields, and killing the Indians—both the principal men and the others that were with him, and all the rest of his vassals that he could capture.

The Indian went, bearing these threats, on the second day of Diego de Guzmán's absence and returned on the third with the same letter that he had carried, and in it was the name of Diego de Guzmán, written with charcoal. He wrote it to show that he was alive, and did not reply another word. The Indian said that the Christian did not wish or intend to return to his own people.

The curaca replied to the governor that his lordship was to understand and be assured that he had not used any force to induce Diego de Guzmán to remain in his country, nor would he do so to make him leave, inasmuch as he did not wish to return. On the contrary, he would entertain and honor him to the best of his ability, as a son-in-law who had restored a much-beloved daughter to him, and he would treat all the Spaniards or Castilians who might wish to stay with him in the same manner. And if (because he was doing his duty in this matter) his lordship wished to destroy his country and kill his relatives and vassals, he would not be doing right or justice as he ought to do; and as a final reply he said that, being a powerful man, he [the governor] must do as he pleased, but that he himself would do only what he had said.

The adelantado having spent three days in attending to this affair, and seeing that the Spaniard did not want to come back and that the cacique was in the right and was making a just demand, decided to go on with his journey. He released the principal Indians and the servants, all of whom served him very affectionately until he left their boundaries and entered another's territory.

This poor gentleman committed this weakness through the blindness of play and love for the woman, and so as not to give her up to him who had won her, he was willing to give himself up to his enemies to do as they liked with him, rather than be without her. From this, in short, can be seen what reckless play leads to, and we could say a great deal about what we have seen with our own eyes as regards this passion, if it belonged to our profession to do so. This, however, is left for those whose business it is to reprimand vices.

Returning to Diego de Guzmán, we say that if, retaining the reputation and prestige that he had among the Indians of Naguatex, he would later have preached the Catholic faith to them, as was his duty as a Christian and a gentleman, we could not only excuse his wrongdoing but could praise him highly, for we could believe that his teaching would have borne much fruit because of the esteem the Indians generally have for those who remain with them. But since we never found out any more about him, we can tell nothing except what happened at the time.

Alonso de Carmona refers in his *Relation* to what we have said about Diego de Guzmán, though not at such length as we do, and he calls him Francisco de Guzmán.

After the loss of Diego de Guzmán, the Spaniards marched for five days through the province of Naguatex, and at the end of that time they came to another province, called Guancane.[34] Its natives were different from the others, for they had been affable and friendly to the Spaniards, while these showed themselves to be hostile and never desired their friendship, but on the other hand showed their hatred and eagerness to fight with them in every way that they could, offering them battle many times. The Spaniards refused, however, for they now had few horses left, the Indians having killed more than half of them, and they wished to keep those that remained. As we have said many times, they were their greatest strength, for the Indians had no fear of the infantry.

The Spaniards spent eight days in traversing this province of Guancane, and they did not rest there a single day, so as not to have to fight with the Indians, who were so desirous of doing so.

Throughout this province there were so many wooden crosses set on the tops of the houses that there was scarcely a house that did not have one. It was supposed that the reason was that these Indians had heard of the good works and miracles that Alvar Núñez Cabeza de Vaca and Andrés Dorantes and their companions had performed in the name of Jesus Christ our Lord, in the provinces of La Florida that they traversed during the years the Indians held them as slaves, as Alvar Núñez himself has written in his *Comentarios* [also known as *Naufragios*]. Although it is true that Alvar Núñez and his companions did not reach this province of Guancane nor many others that lie between it and the lands through which they traveled, yet the fame of those wonders wrought by God through the medium of those men

---

[34]A province named Guancane is not mentioned by the other chroniclers. John R. Swanton guessed that Garcilaso's informants may have corrupted the name from Rangel's Aguacay, but thought it perhaps more likely to correspond with Elvas's Lacane. Either way these latter provinces, like Naguatex, would be transplanted if the equation were granted. They properly belong in the account of the later westward expedition of the army in 1542 under the leadership of Moscoso. The story of Guzmán's defection after losing at cards is placed by Elvas in Chaguate, also visited during Moscoso's 1542 expedition. Swanton, *Final Report*, 278–79.

came to it, passing from person to person and from country to country. Inasmuch as those Indians understood and had heard it said that all the benefits those Christians had conferred in curing the sick was by making the sign of the cross over them, and that they carried it in their hands as an emblem, it gave rise to their observance of placing it over their houses, in the belief that it would also save them from all evil and danger, as it had cured the sick. This shows the facility those Indians in general had, and which those now have, for receiving the Catholic faith if there were someone to cultivate it, chiefly by setting a good example for them to observe, more than in any other manner.

III

THE GOVERNOR LEAVES GUANCANE, PASSES THROUGH SEVEN OTHER SMALL PROVINCES, AND REACHES THAT OF ANILCO

The governor left the province of Guancane with the intention of returning to the Río Grande, which he had left behind him, not by the same route that he had followed since crossing it but by another, different one, making a large circle so as to discover other new lands and provinces on the way back besides those that he had seen, and he intended to inspect them as he passed.

His motive for so doing was the desire to make a settlement before all the strength of his army was spent, for he saw that of both men and horses diminishing from day to day. Past battles and illnesses had destroyed more than half of both of them, or at least of the horses, and he regretted extremely that there should be lost without benefit to him or anyone else so much labor as they had undertaken and were undertaking in that discovery, and that such extensive and fertile lands should remain unpopulated by the Spaniards, especially those who were with him. For he did not fail to perceive that if he should not succeed, or should die without making a beginning in settling the country, it would be many years before there would be assembled again so many and such good men, and as many horses and arms as he had introduced for the conquest.

Therefore, repenting of his past anger, which had been the cause of not making a settlement in the province and port of Achusi, as he had determined to do, he now wished to remedy it as best he could. Because he was at a distance from the sea and would have to lose time if he should go in search of [a place] to settle on the coast, he proposed (as soon as he arrived at the Río Grande) to establish a pueblo on the best and most convenient site that he should find on its banks. He would immediately build two brigantines and send them down the river with trustworthy men whom he regarded as most friendly to him, who were to go out by way of the North Sea and give notice in México, Tierra Firme, the islands of Cuba and La Española, and in Spain of the large and extensive provinces he had discovered in La Florida, so that Castilian Spaniards could come from all parts with cattle and seeds of the plants that were not found there, to settle, cultivate, and enjoy them. All this could be done very easily, as we shall see later, but death put an end to these ambitious and excellent plans, as it has done to other greater and better ones that have been made in this world.

We said that the governor left Guancane and went toward the west in search of the Río Grande, and thus it is that although in this instance and in others of this, our *History*, we have told the route that the army took when it left one province to go to another, it has not been with a specification of the latitude and longitude of each province nor with a definite statement of the direction that our people took, because as I have already said elsewhere, though I endeavored to ascertain it, it was not possible for me to do so. The one who gave me the account, since he was not a cosmographer or a mariner, did not know it, and the army carried no instruments for determining the latitude, nor was there anyone who would attempt to do so or interest himself in it because they were all so disappointed at not finding gold or silver that they thought of nothing else. Thus I may be pardoned for this fault, along with many others that my work contains, for which I am happy not to have to ask indulgence.

The governor, having left Guancane, traversed seven provinces, making as long daily marches as possible, without stopping a day in any of them, so as to reach the Río Grande quickly and carry out the plans that he had made for beginning to settle the land and for forming an establishment in it during that summer. For this reason the names of these provinces were not remembered, except that four of them had fertile lands where our men found plenty of food. They had much timber, rivers that were not very large, and small streams flowing between them. The other three provinces were sparsely populated and their lands were not as fertile or as pleasant as the others, though it was suspected that the guides, who were from that same country, had taken them through the worst part of it. Some of the natives of these seven provinces came out peacefully to receive the governor, and others were hostile, but nothing of consequence or worth relating happened with any of them, except that they managed to keep the peace with those who were friendly and to avoid fighting and warfare with those who were hostile, for our people were now proceeding with all care to escape hostilities. Thus they passed through the seven provinces, which must have been a distance of at least 120 leagues.

At the end of this hasty march they reached the boundaries of a large province that was named Anilco, and they traveled twenty leagues through it to the chief pueblo, which had the same name. It was situated on the banks of a river larger than our Guadalquivir, and had four hundred large and good houses with a handsome plaza in the midst of them. The curaca's houses were on a high man-made hill that overlooked the whole pueblo.

The cacique, whose name was also Anilco, was under arms and had a squadron of fifteen hundred warriors, all chosen men, drawn up in front of the pueblo to meet our army. Seeing the Indians so prepared, the Spaniards halted to wait for the last ones to come up, and all placed themselves in order to fight with them.

While the Spaniards were waiting, the Indians put their women, children, and the property in their houses in safety, some taking them to the other side of the river in rafts and canoes, others placing them in the woods and thickets that were on the banks of the same river.

Having formed themselves into a squadron, the Castilians marched toward the Indians, but the latter dared not wait for them, and without firing a shot, they withdrew to the pueblo and thence to the river. Almost all of them crossed to the other side, some in canoes, some on rafts, and others swimming. They had not intended to fight with the Spaniards but to hold them back and prevent their entering the pueblo so quickly, in order to have time to place what was in it in safety.

Seeing the Indians fleeing, our men fell upon them and caught a few who were embarking. In the pueblo they found many women of all ages, and children and boys who had been unable to flee.

The governor immediately and hastily sent messages to the cacique Anilco, offering him peace and friendship and asking for his; he had also sent such messages before entering the pueblo. But the curaca was so strange that he would not reply to the first ones or to the second, nor did he speak a word to the messengers, but made signs to them with his hand as if he were mute, indicating that they were to leave his presence.

The Spaniards lodged in the pueblo, where they remained four days obtaining canoes and building large rafts. When they had a supply of them they crossed the river without opposition from the enemy. They marched four days through some uninhabited country that was very heavily forested [or very mountainous (*grandes montañas*)], and at the end of that time they entered another province, called Guachoya. We shall recount the notable things that happened there in the next chapter, God willing.

IV

THE SPANIARDS ENTER GUACHOYA. IT IS TOLD HOW THE INDIANS HAVE PERPETUAL WARFARE WITH ONE ANOTHER

After passing through the uninhabited region, the first pueblo that the Spaniards saw in the province of Guachoya was the principal one, which had the same name. It was on the banks of the Río Grande, which our people were seeking. It was situated on two high hills close together, and had three hundred houses. Half of them were on one hill and half on the other. The level space between the two hills served as a plaza, and the cacique's house was on the higher one of the two.

There was great hatred and enmity between these two provinces of Guachoya and Anilco, and they waged a cruel war. Therefore the Guachoyas could not receive notice of the Spaniards' coming to their pueblo and thus they found them unprepared. But the cacique and his vassals got under arms as best they could to defend the pueblo. Seeing their adversaries' strength and that they could not resist it, they gathered at the Río Grande and crossed it in very handsome canoes they always had ready for such necessities, being a people with many enemies; taking with them their women, children, and all their possessions that they could carry, and they abandoned the pueblo.

The Castilians entered it, finding there plenty of food in the form of maize and other grains and fruits that the land produces in abundance. They were very pleasantly lodged there.

Because, as we have seen, nearly all the provinces the Spaniards traversed were at war with one another, it will be well to tell here the kind of warfare that they waged. It must be known, then, that this was not a war of one power against another with armies drawn up and general engagements, except on very rare occasions. Nor was it a war of greed and ambition on the part of some lords to take away the states of others.

The warfare that they waged consisted of ambushes and stratagems, making surprise attacks on the fisheries, hunting grounds, cultivated fields, and roads, wherever they could find their adversaries off guard. Those whom they captured in such assaults were held as slaves, some in perpetual captivity with one foot disabled, as we have seen in some of the provinces, and others as prisoners for ransom, to be exchanged for others.

The enmity among them extended only to inflicting injury on their persons, with death or wounds or imprisonment, without attempting to take away one another's states, and if the war sometimes became general, it would lead to burning the pueblos and laying waste the fields. But as soon as the victors had done as much damage as they wished, they went back to their own country without attempting to take possession of that of others. It appears from this that the war and hostility that exist between them arise more from gallantry and the desire to show the valor and courage of their spirits, and to indulge in military pursuits, than from the desire for the property and territory of others.

The prisoners who are taken on both sides are ransomed easily, being exchanged for one another so that they can go back to their ambushes again. This kind of warfare has now become second nature to them and is the cause of their going about, wherever they may be, with their weapons constantly in readiness, because they are nowhere safe from their enemies. Having such constant practice in this continuous warfare gives them their bellicose nature and their skill with weapons, particularly with bows and arrows, which, since they are missile weapons that are effective at long range, they use more than any others, whether they are hunting men or animals.[35]

The cacique did not carry on this warfare with only one of his neighbors, but with all those whose boundaries touched his, there being two, three, four, or more, all of whom were at war among themselves.

This certainly is a laudable exercise in the military arts, so that none shall be careless and each one can show his personal bravery. In general, this is the nature of the hostility among the Indians of the great kingdom of La Florida. This in itself would be an important reason why that land could be won easily, because "the whole kingdom divided, etc."

After the Spaniards had been in the pueblo Guachoya three days, its lord, who had the same name—having learned what had taken place between the

---

[35] The preceding paragraphs constitute Garcilaso's second and more-comprehensive general discussion of native warfare in La Florida. The shorter account occurs in Book 3, in the Inca's discussion of warfare in Cofitachequi. See note 18.

Spaniards and the Indians of the province of Anilco and how that curaca had refused to receive the governor peacefully but on the other hand had disdained his friendship and messages and refused to answer them—did not wish to lose the occasion that he had in his hands for revenging himself on his enemies of Anilco. Being a clever man and full of cunning, he immediately sent a ceremonious embassy to the governor with four Indians who were leading nobles, and many other servants, who came laden with a great deal of fruit and fish. He sent word by them that he begged his lordship to pardon his inadvertence in not having awaited him and having received him in his pueblo, and asked permission to come and kiss his hands. If he should grant it, he would come within four days to greet him personally, and he offered him thenceforth his vassalage and service.

The governor was pleased with the embassy and replied to the messengers that they might tell their curaca that he was gratified by his good will and esteemed his friendship greatly; that he might come without any apprehensions, for he would be well received.

The messengers returned satisfied with this reply, and during the three days that the cacique delayed his arrival, he sent seven or eight messages every day. All contained the same terms, asking that his lordship send word of his health, and whether he could serve him in any way, and other trifling messages of no importance. Guachoya, being a cautious and astute man, sent these messages to see whether he could discover anything new by means of them, or how the adelantado took them.

Having seen that he received them in a friendly manner, he was reassured, and on the last of the four days he arrived, before dinner, as he had announced on the day before. He brought a hundred nobles with him, all very highly adorned after their custom with long plumes and handsome mantles of marten-skins and other very valuable pelts. They all carried the finest of their bows and arrows, which they make for gala occasions.

V

HOW GUACHOYA VISITS THE GENERAL, AND BOTH GO BACK AGAINST ANILCO

The governor, who was lodged in Guachoya's house, on learning that he was approaching, went as far as the door to receive him. He spoke very affectionately to the cacique and all his people, at which they were very flattered and well satisfied. Then they entered a large sala that was in the house, and the general spoke with the curaca through the many interpreters, who [were] placed like the members of a chorus [*como a tenoras*]. He informed himself about the things in his country and in the neighboring provinces that were favorable and unfavorable to the conquest.

While this was going on, the cacique Guachoya gave a loud sneeze. The nobles who had come with him—who were standing around the walls of the sala among the Spaniards who were present—bowing their heads, opening and closing their arms, and making other gestures of great veneration and respect, all saluted him together with various words that had the same meaning, saying, "May the Sun keep you, be with you, enlighten you, aggrandize you, protect you, favor you, defend you, prosper you, save you," and other such expressions, each one as the words came to him. For some time the murmur of these words continued among them. The governor wondered at it and said to the gentlemen and captains who were with him: "Do you not see how the whole world is alike?"

The Spaniards were much impressed by this incident, seeing that the same or even more elaborate formalities were observed among such a barbarous people when someone sneezed than were customary among people who considered themselves highly civilized. Thus it may be believed that this manner of salutation is natural among all peoples and was not caused by a pestilence, according to the common saying usually heard, though there is no lack of those who will affirm it.

The cacique ate with the governor, and his Indians stood all around the table, being unwilling to go and eat until their lord had finished though the Spaniards told them to do so. Our people also noted this incident. Later they gave them dinner in another apartment, for they had prepared food for all of them.

They cleared one of the rooms in his own house to give the curaca lodgings, and he stayed there with a few servants. The Indian nobles went at sunset to the other side of the river and came back in the morning, and they did this throughout the time that the Castilians were in that pueblo.

Meanwhile the curaca Guachoya persuaded the governor to return to the province of Anilco, offering to go with his men to serve his lordship, and to facilitate the crossing of the Río de Anilco he ordered eighty large canoes, besides other small ones, to be taken seven leagues down the Río Grande to the mouth of the Río de Anilco, which entered the Río Grande. They would ascend it to the pueblo of Anilco. The whole route that the canoes would have to go by both rivers would be about twenty leagues of navigation. While the canoes were descending the Río Grande and ascending the Anilco they would go by land, so that they could all arrive together at the pueblo of Anilco at the same time.

The governor was easily persuaded to make this expedition because he wished to see what was in that province that would be of benefit and assistance to his plan of building the brigantines. He also desired to win the devotion of the curaca Anilco by peaceful and friendly methods, so that he could make his settlement and establishment in those two provinces without the hardships and labors of a war. It seemed to him that they had an abundance of food, and that he could await there the completion of the two brigantines that he intended to send down the river.

The governor's purpose in returning to the pueblo of Anilco was what we have seen, but that of the curaca Guachoya was very different, because he intended to avenge himself on his enemy Anilco with foreign help.

During the wars and continual strife that went on between them, the latter [Anilco] had always kept him in a very ignominious and oppressed condition, and now on this occasion he was endeavoring to take satisfaction for all his past injuries.

Therefore he urged the governor with all possible dissimulation to return to the pueblo of Anilco and ordered with much solicitude and diligence that everything necessary for the journey be made ready.

As soon as all was prepared and they had brought the canoes, the governor ordered that Captain Juan de Guzmán and his company go in them to direct and give orders to four thousand Indian warriors who were embarking in them, in addition to the oarsmen. The latter also carried their bows and arrows. They allowed them a period of three full days for their navigation, which seemed time enough for both parties to arrive and join one another at the pueblo of Anilco.

Captain Juan de Guzmán set out with these orders down the Río Grande, and at the same hour the governor left by land with his Spaniards, and Guachoya with two thousand warriors, in addition to another great concourse of Indians who carried the provisions. Without anything of note happening to either party, they all arrived at the same time in sight of the pueblo of Anilco. Though the cacique was absent, its inhabitants sounded the alarm and stationed themselves to defend the crossing of the river with all possible spirit and courage. But they could not resist the fury of the enemy, who were both Indians and Spaniards, so they turned back and abandoned the pueblo.

The Guachoyas entered it as a pueblo of such hated enemies, and being an affronted people who desired vengeance, they sacked and robbed the temple and burial place of the lords of that state, where, besides the bodies of his dead, the cacique kept his best and richest and most valued possessions, and the spoils and trophies of the greatest victories that he had won over the Guachoyas. These consisted of numerous heads of the most important Indians that they had killed, placed on the points of lances at the doors of the temple, and many standards, and a large number of weapons that the Guachoyas had lost in the battles they had with the Anilcos.

They took the heads of their Indians down from the lances and put in their places others belonging to the Anilcos. They took away their military insignia and their arms with great satisfaction and joy at recovering them. They threw out on the ground the dead bodies that were in the wooden chests and trampled and kicked them with all the contempt they could show in revenge for their injuries.[36]

VI

THE CRUELTIES OF THE GUACHOYAS CONTINUE, AND HOW THE GOVERNOR PLANS TO ASK FOR HELP

The Guachoyas' rage still not being appeased with what they had done to the property and the dead of Anilco, nor satisfied with the restoration of their standards and arms, their wrath carried them on to other, worse things. They refused to capture alive any person that they found in the pueblo, regardless of sex or age, but killed them all, and they inflicted the greatest cruelties on those most deserving of mercy, such as old women, already in extreme senility, and infants. The stripped the old women of the little clothing they were wearing and killed them with arrows, shooting at the pudenda in preference to other parts of their bodies. The infants, no matter how small, they grasped by one foot, raised them up, and five or six marksmen or whatever number happened to be present would shoot at them in the air, before they fell to the ground.

With these cruelties and such others as they could commit without the Spaniards seeing them, the Guachoyas showed the hatred and rancor that

---

[36]See note 30.

they felt, as an affronted people, toward the Anilcos. When some of the Castilians saw these things, the Indians, having been unable to conceal [their hatred] as well as they desired, immediately notified the governor of them. He was very angered at their having so injured those of Anilco, since his intention had not been to do them harm or damage, but to win their friendship.

So that the Guachoyas' cruelty should not go further, he ordered the assembly to be sounded at once, and he rebuked the cacique for what his Indians had done. In order to make sure that no further damage would be done, he ordered a decree issued to the effect that on penalty of death no one should dare to set fire to the houses or harm the Indians, and to prevent the Guachoyas from ignoring the decree, he directed the interpreters to announce it in their own language. Because he feared that they would still do as much damage as they could, eluding the Spaniards, he left the pueblo of Anilco as rapidly as possible and went to the river, having ordered the Castilians to send the Indians on ahead of them so that they would not stay to burn the pueblo and kill the people who had hidden themselves in it.

These measures remedied the evil somewhat and prevented its being as great as it might have been. The general embarked with all his men, both Spaniards and Indians, and crossed the river to return to Guachoya.

But they had not traveled a quarter of a league when they saw smoke in the pueblo and many of the houses bursting into flames. The reason was that the Guachoyas, unable to resist burning the pueblo, now that they had been forbidden to set fire to it openly, had attempted to burn it in the best way they could. Thus they left burning sticks under the eaves of the houses, and as they were made of straw and had become dry as tinder during the summer, they needed little wind to burst into flames.

The governor wished to return to the pueblo to prevent its being entirely consumed, but at that moment he saw many of its Indian inhabitants running as quickly as they could to extinguish the fire, and thereupon he left it and continued on his way to the pueblo of Guachoya, concealing his anger in order not to lose the friends he had for the sake of those he could not gain.

Having arrived in the pueblo and settled down there with his army, he left all other affairs to the field officers and devoted himself to the business of building the brigantines. He thought about and worked on them day and night. He ordered the necessary timber to be cut, there being an abundance of it in that province. He collected all the ropes and cords that could be found in the pueblo and its vicinity for rigging. He ordered the Indians to bring him all the resin and gum from pine, plum, and other trees that they could find in that country. He directed that many more nails be made and that those which had been used in constructing the other pirogues and barks be prepared for use.

In his own mind he had already chosen the captains and soldiers whom he regarded as his most loyal friends, upon whom he could depend, to go back in the brigantines when he should send them to request the assistance for which he intended to ask.

When the time should come to send the brigantines, he had determined to cross to the other side of the Río Grande to a large province called Quigualtanqui. He had learned from certain scouts whom he had sent out, both cavalry and infantry, that it had an abundance of food and was well populated. Its principal pueblo was near the pueblo of Guachoya, with the river between them, and it contained more than five hundred houses. Its lord and cacique, who was also called Quigualtanqui, had replied unfavorably to the messages that the governor had sent him requesting peace and offering his friendship, having uttered very disrespectfully many insults and vituperations and made fierce threats and menaces, saying that he would kill them all in one battle, as they would see very soon, and put a stop to the evil lives they were leading, lost in foreign lands, robbing and killing like highwaymen and vagabonds, and he uttered other offensive words. He had sworn by the Sun and the Moon not to make friends with them as the other curacas had done through whose lands they had passed, but he would kill them and hang them from the trees.

At this point Alonso de Carmona says the following:

> Shortly before the governor died he ordered all the canoes in that pueblo to be collected. They joined the best ones together two by two and put horses in them, and they put men in the rest and crossed to the other side of the river. There they found very large settlements, though the people had risen up and fled, and thus they returned, without doing anything. The chief men of that country having seen this, they sent a messenger to the governor warning him not to dare to send Spaniards to their lands again, because none of them would come back alive, and saying that he could thank his good reputation and the good treatment that he had given the Indians of the province where he then was, that his people had not gone out to kill all the Spaniards who had passed to his territory. If he had any intentions with regard to his country, he would meet him with equal numbers and let him understand the lack of civility and prudence he had shown in having sent scouting parties into his territory; he was not to do so again, or he swore by his gods to kill him and all his people or die in the attempt.

All these are Alonso de Carmona's words, which we have copied literally, since they are almost the same as those we have spoken concerning Quigualtanqui.

The governor had always replied very reasonably and amiably to these insults, requesting peace and friendship, and though it is true that because of the general's great courtesy Quigualtanqui had exchanged his ill words for good ones, giving signs of peace and concord, it was always understood that he was false and deceitful and only wished to take the Spaniards off guard. The governor knew through his spies that he was plotting treason and evil and summoning his people and those from the neighboring provinces against the Christians, to kill them treacherously under guise of friendship. The general knew all this and bided his time to punish it when the occasion arose. He still had 150 horses and five hundred Spaniards, with whom, after he had dispatched the brigantines, he intended to cross the Río Grande and establish himself in the principal pueblo of Quigualtanqui, spending the present summer and coming winter there, until he should receive the aid that he intended to ask for. It could be sent to him very easily from the whole coast and city of México, and from the islands of Cuba and Santo Domingo, ascending by way of the Río Grande, which was large enough for all the ships that might wish to ascend it, as we shall see below.

VII

WHEREIN THE GOVERNOR'S DEATH IS RECOUNTED, AND THE SUCCESSOR WHOM HE NAMED

This heroic gentleman was absorbed day and night in the cares and endeavors that we have described, desiring like a good father that the many hardships he and his men had suffered in that discovery and the great expenditures he had made for it might not be lost without producing any result.

Then on the twentieth day of June of the year 1542 he felt a slight fever, which was slow on the first day and extremely severe on the third. The governor, seeing its excessive increase, understood that his illness was mortal. Thus he immediately prepared for death, and as a Catholic Christian made his will, almost in cipher, because there was not a sufficient supply of paper. With grief and repentance for having offended God, he confessed his sins.

He named as his successor in the office of governor and captain-general of the kingdom and provinces of La Florida, Luis de Moscoso de Alvarado, whom he had removed from the office of maese de campo in the province of Chicaça. In this *auto* he ordered summoned to his presence the gentlemen, captains, and most important soldiers, and in the name of his Imperial Majesty he ordered them, and in his own name he begged and charged them, that in view of the rank, virtue, and merits of Luis de Moscoso they accept him as their governor and captain-general until his Majesty should send new orders, and he received their solemn oaths that they would do so.

This done, he summoned the nobles in the army by twos and threes, and after them he ordered that all the other men enter in groups of twenty, and he took leave of all of them with much sadness on his part and many tears on theirs. He charged them with the conversion of those natives to the Catholic faith, and with the increase of the Crown of Spain, saying that death had stopped him in the attainment of those desires. He requested very affectionately that they maintain peace and love among themselves.

He spent five days in these affairs while the severe fever continued, always increasing, until the seventh day, when it deprived him of this present life. He died like a Catholic Christian, asking mercy of the Most Holy Trinity and invoking on his behalf and favor the blood of Jesus Christ our Lord, the intercession of the Virgin and all the Celestial Court, and the faith of the Roman church.

With these words, repeated many times, this magnanimous and unconquered gentleman gave up his soul to God. He was worthy of great estates and seigniories and did not deserve that his history should be written by an Indian. He died at the age of forty-two.

As we said at the beginning, the adelantado Hernando de Soto was a native of Villanueva de Barcarrota, an hidalgo through all four lines. His Caesarean Majesty, having been informed of this fact, had sent him the habit of Santiago, but he did not enjoy this favor because when the *cédula* reached the island of Cuba the governor had already entered upon the discovery and conquest of La Florida.

He was of more than medium stature, of good presence, and appeared well both on foot and on horseback. His face was animated and of dark complexion, and he was skillful in riding both *a la jineta* and *a la brida* [the two different schools of horsemanship then followed], but more so in the first. He was extremely patient in hardships and necessities, to such an extent that the greatest comfort his soldiers had in the midst of them was the sight of their captain-general's patience and endurance.

He was successful in the private exploits that he undertook personally, though in the principal one he was not so, for he expired at the critical moment.

He was the first Spaniard who saw and spoke with Atahuallpa, the tyrant king and the last of those of El Perú, as we shall tell in the history of the discovery and conquest of that empire itself if God, our Lord, is pleased to extend our life, which is now becoming very feeble and weary.

He was severe in punishing military derelictions; the rest he pardoned readily. He honored greatly the soldiers who were virtuous and brave. He was extremely courageous in his own person, to such a degree that wherever he chose to enter a general engagement, fighting, he left behind him place and room for ten of his men to pass, and thus all of them admitted that any ten lances in his army were not equal to his alone.

One notable circumstance concerning this brave captain in warfare, which ought to be remembered, is that when the enemy attacked his camp by day he was always the first or the second to come out armed, and never the third; and in the attacks they made by night he was never the second, but always the first. It seemed that, after having prepared to go out with his arms, he himself ordered the signal given. In time of war he was constantly as prompt and vigilant as this. In short, he was one of the best lancers who have passed to the New World. There were few as good and none better unless it was Gonzalo Pizarro, who by common consent was always given the honor of the first place.

He spent more than 100,000 ducats in this discovery, which he gained in the first conquest of El Perú from the apportionments of Casamarca, from the rich spoil that the Spaniards had there. He also spent his life and perished in the attempt, as we have seen.

VIII

TWO BURIALS THAT THEY GAVE THE ADELANTADO HERNANDO DE SOTO

The most lamentable death of the governor and captain-general Hernando de Soto inspired great grief and sadness in all his men because of having lost him and because of the bereavement those who regarded him as father suffered, and because they were unable to give him the sepulcher his body deserved or to accord him the honor of funeral rites such as they would have desired to give such a beloved captain and lord.

Their sadness and grief were doubled by the knowledge that they were forced to bury him in silence and secret rather than in public, so that the Indians would not know where he rested. They feared that they would commit such indignities and affronts on his body as they had done in the case of other Spaniards, whom they had disinterred, cut in pieces, and hung in the trees, each joint on a separate limb. It was probable that they would commit even greater affronts and insults on the governor's body, he being the principal leader of the Spaniards, in order to offend them more. Our people said that, inasmuch as he had not received such insults in life, there was no reason why he should receive them in death through their negligence.

Therefore they decided to bury him at night with sentries posted so that the Indians would not know where he was. They chose for a sepulcher one of the many large and broad pits that were on a plain near the pueblo. The Indians had taken earth from these for their buildings. In one of them they interred the famous adelantado Hernando de Soto, with many tears on the part of the priests and gentlemen who attended his sad obsequies.

On the following day, for the purpose of concealing the place where the body was and dissembling their own sadness, they spread the news among the Indians that the governor's health was improved, and to carry out this fiction they mounted their horses and made signs of great celebration and rejoicing, running them across the plain and going at a gallop among the pits and across the grave itself, things much at variance with and contradictory to the feelings in their hearts. While desiring to place him whom they loved and esteemed so much in the mausoleum or obelisk of Julius Caesar, they themselves trod upon him, to their own greater grief, but they did it to prevent the Indians from committing other, greater indignities upon him. So that the marks of the grave would be entirely destroyed, they had not been content to have the horses tread upon it, but before these celebrations they had ordered a great deal of water to be sprinkled over the plain and the pits under pretext of preventing the horses from raising a dust when they ran over them.

The Spaniards took all these steps to deceive the Indians and conceal their own grief and sorrow, but inasmuch as it is difficult to feign pleasure and dissimulate grief so that he who feels them may not be discerned at a distance, our people could not do so to such an extent that the Indians did not suspect both the death of the governor and the place where they had put him. Walking over the plain and among the pits they went slowly and examined everything attentively. They talked among themselves and nodded their heads and winked their eyes in the direction of the place where the body was.

Since the Spaniards saw and noted these gestures, which increased their first fears and suspicions, they agreed to take the body away from that place and put it in another sepulcher that would be more difficult for the Indians to find if they should look for it. For they said that should the heathen suspect that the governor lay there they would dig up that whole plain to its center and would not stop until they had found him. Therefore it seemed to them that it would be a good thing to give him the Río Grande for a sepulcher, and before doing so, they wished to see how deep the river was and whether it was sufficient to conceal the body.

The accountant Juan de Añasco and Captains Juan de Guzmán, Arias Tinoco, Alonso Romo de Cardeñosa, and Diego Arias, the alférez general of the army, undertook to examine the river. Taking with them a Biscayan named Ioanes de Abbadia, a seaman and a good engineer, they sounded it one afternoon, concealing their purpose as well as possible by making signs as if they were fishing and enjoying themselves on the river so that the Indians would not suspect them. They found that in midchannel it was nineteen fathoms deep and a quarter of a league in breadth. Seeing this, the Spaniards decided to inter the governor there, and inasmuch as there was no stone in the whole region with which to weight the body so that it would go to the bottom, they cut down a very thick oak tree and hollowed out on one side a space equal to the height of a man, into which they could put the body. On the following night they disinterred it as silently as possible and put it into the cut section of the oak tree with planks nailed over the body on the other side, and thus it was as if in a coffin. With many tears and much grief on the part of the priests and gentlemen who attended this second interment, they cast it into the middle of the river's current, commending his soul to God, and they saw it sink immediately to the bottom.

Such were the sad and doleful rites that our Spaniards performed over the body of the adelantado Hernando de Soto, their captain-general and governor of the kingdoms and provinces of La Florida. They were unworthy of such a heroic man, though upon examination they are found to be similar in almost all respects to those which the Goths, the Spaniards' predecessors, accorded 1,131 years before to their king Alaric in the province of Calabria in Italy, in the river Busento near the city of Cosenza.

I say similar in almost every respect because these Spaniards are descendants of those Goths, and both sepulchers were rivers, and the deceased were the leaders and commanders of their people and much beloved by them. Both were most valiant men who performed great exploits in foreign kingdoms, having left their own lands seeking a place to settle and make establishments.

Even the intentions of the two peoples were the same, being to inter their captains where their bodies could not be found, though their enemies might seek them. They differ only in that the rites performed by these arose from piety and fear that the Indians would mistreat the body of their captain-general, and those of the others were born out of presumption and vainglory that they wished to show to the world for the honor and majesty of their king. So that this similarity may be better seen it will be well to give an account here of the burial the Goths gave their king Alaric for the benefit of those who do not know of it.

That famous prince—having performed innumerable exploits throughout the world with his men, and having sacked the imperial city of Rome, the first sack that it had experienced in the course of its empire and monarchy, 1,162 years after its foundation and 412 after the virginal delivery of Our Lady—wished to go to Sicily. Having been in Reggio and attempted the crossing, he went back to Cosenza, forced to do so by a very rough sea, where he died within a few days. His Goths, who loved him devotedly, celebrated his funeral rites with many and excessive honors and grandeurs. Among others they invented one that was most impressive and admirable, which was that they ordered the many captives who were with them to divert and turn the river Busento from its bed, and in the middle of its channel they erected an elaborate sepulcher. In it they placed the body of their king, with an infinity of treasure (these are the words of Colenucio, and aside from him all the ancient and modern historians, Spaniards and others, who write of those times say the same thing), and having closed the sepulcher, they ordered that the river be turned back into its old channel. They killed all the captives who had labored in this work so that they would never tell where King Alaric rested.

It seems to me that this history belongs here because of its great similarity to ours, and in order to note that the nobility of these our Spaniards and that which exists today throughout Spain undoubtedly comes from those Goths, because no other nation has entered after them except the Arabs from Barbary when they conquered it in the time of the king Don Rodrigo. But the few remnants of these same Goths who survived drove them little by little out of all Spain and settled it as it is today. Even the descent of the kings of Castilla comes directly from those Gothic kings, whose notable antiquity and majesty gives them an advantage over all the kings of the earth.

All that we have said about the will, death, and funeral rites of the adelantado Hernando de Soto, Alonso de Carmona and Juan Coles tell in exactly the same way in their accounts. Both add that when the Indians did not see the governor they asked for him, and that the Christians replied to them that God had sent to summon him to order him to do great things as soon as he should return; and that they put off the Indians with these words, which all of them said.

Second Part of the Fifth Book of the History of La Florida, by the Inca

It tells how the Spaniards decided to abandon La Florida; a long journey that they made in order to get out of it; the insupportable hardships that they endured in going and returning on that journey, until they came back to the Río Grande; seven brigantines they built in order to leave by way of it; the league of ten caciques against the Castilians; the secret notice that they had of it; the offers of General Anilco and his good qualities; a remarkable flood on the Río Grande; the activity in building the brigantines; a challenge from the General Anilco to the Cacique Guachoya and the reason for it; the punishment that was given to the ambassadors of the league. It contains fifteen chapters.

I

THE SPANIARDS DECIDE TO ABANDON LA FLORIDA AND TO LEAVE IT

On the death of the governor and captain-general Hernando de Soto, the attempts and well-laid plans that he had made for settling and forming an establishment in that land not only were not carried forward, but on the other hand his captains and soldiers abandoned and turned against them, as usually occurs wherever the principal leader of an enterprise is absent. Since all the captains and soldiers of the army had been discontented at the failure to find in La Florida the things that they were seeking, though it had the other advantages that we have named, and inasmuch as they had desired to leave it and only their respect for the governor had restrained them, (he being dead) it was decided by common agreement of the most influential among them that as quickly as possible they would leave that kingdom. This was a thing that they afterward lamented all the days of their lives, as a determination that is made and carried out without prudence or advice is usually regretted. The accountant Juan de Añasco—who as a minister of his king's hacienda and a nobleman in his own right, and one of those who had labored hardest in the discovery, was obligated to uphold this very well-founded judgment of his captain-general and to carry on his enterprise and conquest if only in order not to lose their past labors, for it was of such honor and advantage to all of them and of such grandeur, majesty, and profit to the Crown of Spain as we have seen—not only did not oppose the other captains and gentlemen who were in favor of leaving that great kingdom, but he even offered to guide them himself and bring them quickly into the limits and jurisdiction of México. He prided himself on being a cosmographer and presumed upon his skill to put them promptly in safety, not considering the broad provinces and the large rivers, the rough woodlands lacking in food, and the difficult swamps that they had passed; on the other hand he disregarded all of them; because when our ambition and desire become disordered, we often make light of hardship and disregard the difficulties of its pretensions, so as to allow ourselves to perish in them later.

They were inspired and encouraged in this determination by the memory of certain false information that the Indians had given them in the past winter and the preceding summer, to the effect that to the west not far from where they were going there were other Castilians who were traversing and conquering those provinces.[37]

The Spaniards revived these past rumors in their memories and, accepting them as true, they said that these must be people who had gone out from México to conquer new kingdoms, and that according to what the Indians said, they ought not to be far from one another. It would be a good thing to go in search of them, and having found them, they could assist them in conquering and making settlements, as if they themselves had found nothing to conquer nor had anywhere to settle.

With this common determination, so ill-made, our Spaniards left Guachoya on the fourth or fifth of July, directing their march toward the west with the intention of turning neither to the right nor to the left, for it seemed to them that by following that direction they must necessarily come out in the territory of México. They did not consider that according to their own cosmography they were in a much higher latitude than the lands of New Spain.

Being thus desirous of entering them, they marched more than a hundred leagues, making as long daily journeys as possible, through different lands and provinces than those that they had seen hitherto, but not so abundant in food nor so well populated as the others. We cannot tell the names of these provinces because, as they now had no intention of settling, they did not attempt to learn the names nor to inform themselves of the nature of the country, but intended to pass through it as rapidly as they could. Therefore they did not record the names nor could they give them to me.

II

CONCERNING SOME INDIAN SUPERSTITIONS OF BOTH LA FLORIDA AND EL PERÚ, AND HOW THE SPANIARDS ARRIVED IN AUCHE

Going back in our story somewhat from where we are, it must be said that when the Spaniards left the pueblo of Guachoya, there went with them

[37]In 1541 the expedition of Coronado had reached as far eastward as Quivira, believed to lie along the Saline River of central Kansas. It is possible that news of this expedition had reached western Arkansas, where De Soto's army was at the time.

of his own accord an Indian sixteen or seventeen years old, with a graceful body and handsome face, as the natives of that province usually have. After they had marched three or four days, Governor Luis de Moscoso's servants noticed him, the Indian having approached them. As this was unusual and they saw that he was of a different rank, fearing that he might be a spy, they told the general about it. He sent to summon him and he asked him through the interpreters and Juan Ortiz to tell the reason why he had left his parents, relatives, friends, and acquaintances to go with the Spaniards, since he knew nothing about them. The Indian replied: "Sir, I am poor and an orphan. The death of my parents left me alone at a very early age, and a principal Indian of my pueblo, a near relative of the curaca Guachoya, taking pity on me, carried me to his house and brought me up among his sons. At the time your lordship left, this man was sick and his life despaired of.

"As soon as they saw him thus, his relatives, wife, and children chose and named me to be buried alive with my master upon his death, for they said that my lord had been very fond of me, and that because of this love it was fitting that I should go with him and serve him in the other life. And although it is true that, because he reared me, I was obligated to him and loved him devotedly, my love is not such as to make me take pleasure in being buried alive with him.

"In order to escape this death, finding no better remedy, I determined to come with your lordship's people, since I prefer being your slave to seeing myself buried alive. This, and nothing else, is the cause of my coming."

The general and those who were with him wondered at hearing the Indian and understood that the custom and abuse of burying alive the servants and wives with the body of the deceased chief was also followed and observed in that country, as in the rest of the New World hitherto discovered.[38]

Throughout the empire of the Incas who reigned in El Perú it was long the custom to inter with and near the kings and great lords their most loved wives and favorite servants, because in their heathenism they believed in the immortality of the soul and thought that after this life there was another one like it, not spiritual. It contained pain and punishment, however, for him who had been bad, and glory, reward, and recompense for the good. Thus they call heaven Hanampacha, which means the higher world, and the inferno Ucupacha, meaning lower world. They call the devil Zupay, saying that

[38]The execution of retainers to accompany a deceased noble to the afterlife is well attested in this same region much later among the Natchez, as described by the French in the early eighteenth century.

the wicked go with him. We shall discuss this at more length in the history of the Incas.

Returning to our Castilians, whom we left eager to travel a long distance—and they were later to regret having traveled so far—we said that after marching through the provinces we could not name, because we do not know what their names were, and through which they marched for more than a hundred leagues, at the end of this distance they came to a province called Auche.[39] Its lord came out to receive them very cordially and entertained them with many signs of affection. He said that it gave him much satisfaction to see them in his country, but as we shall see later all this was false and assumed.

The Spaniards rested in that pueblo of Auche for two days, it being the principal one of the province. On informing themselves about the things that would be helpful on their journey, they learned that two days' march from the pueblo there was a great uninhabited region that was four days' journey in extent. The cacique Auche gave them Indians laden with maize for six days, and an old Indian to guide them through the uninhabited country until he brought them out to the settlements. Making a great show of friendship, he ordered him in the Spaniards' presence to take them by the best and shortest road that he knew.

Thus prepared, our people left Auche, and in two days' march they reached the uninhabited country, through which they traveled four more days over a wide road that seemed to be a public highway. But at the end of the two days' journey it gradually became narrower until it disappeared entirely. They marched six more days without a road, wherever the Indian wanted to take them, he telling them that he was leading them by shortcuts off the road so as to reach the inhabited country more quickly.

At the end of eight days' wandering through those deserts, woodlands, and thickets, seeing that they were not getting out of them, the Spaniards noticed what had not hitherto come to their attention, namely, that the Indian had led them in a circle, sometimes guiding them toward the north, again to the west, other times to the south, and still others to the east. They had not noted this before because of their eagerness to pass on and because of the confidence they had that their guide would not deceive them. They considered also that it had been three days since they had eaten maize or any other

[39]Auche is not mentioned by the other chroniclers. John R. Swanton believed that it was probably intended for Biedma's Hais, known to later writers as Ha-ish, but the phonetic resemblance is slight. Swanton, *Final Report*, 279.

food except herbs and roots, and that their difficulties were increasing hourly and their hopes of getting out of those deserts were becoming less, because they had neither food nor road.

III

THE SPANIARDS KILL THE GUIDE. A PARTICULAR EXPLOIT OF AN INDIAN IS TOLD

Governor Luis de Moscoso ordered the Indian who had guided him summoned before him, and he asked him through the interpreters why he did not bring them out of that wilderness at the end of eight days, that they had wandered about through it lost; for upon leaving his pueblo, he had offered to pass through it in four days and come out in inhabited country. The Indian would not reply directly, but spoke some nonsense that he thought would excuse him for what he had done. The governor, being angered by this and at seeing his army in such want through the Indian's malice, ordered that he be tied to a tree and that the mastiffs they had with them be let loose upon him. One of them shook and dragged him badly.

The Indian, seeing himself so ill treated and overcome by the fear that they would kill him, begged them to take the dog away, saying that he would tell the truth about everything that had happened in that affair. When they took away the dog he said: "Gentlemen, my curaca and natural lord ordered me upon your departure to do what I have done with you, for he confided in me, saying that, since he did not have sufficient forces to cut all your throats in one battle, as he would like to do, he had determined to kill you by strategy and cunning, putting you into these wild forests and deserts where you would perish of hunger. He chose me, as one of his most faithful servants, to carry out this scheme, leading you off the road to where you would never be able to get back to the inhabited country. If I should succeed with the enterprise he promised to grant me many favors; if not, he would kill me cruelly.

"I, being a servant, did what my lord commanded me, as I believe that any one of you would do if yours should so order you. I was forced to do it out of respect and obedience to my superior and not through any will or desire of my own to kill you. I certainly have not wished nor do I wish to do so, because you have given me no reason for it. Rightly considered, the greater part of this blame you put upon me is yours, because you have allowed yourselves to be led thus, with so much carelessness on your own part that you have not even asked me a word about the road. If you had asked me some of the questions that you are now asking on the first day that it was lost, I would have told you all this in time to have remedied the present evil. Even yet it is not too late, and if you will spare my life (since I acted according to orders and could do nothing else), I will remedy the error we have all made. I will undertake to bring us out of this desert and put us into an inhabited country before the next three days have passed. By traveling straight toward the west, without turning to one side or the other, we shall soon come out of this uninhabited region. If I do not lead you out of it within that time, then kill me, for I offer myself for punishment."

General Luis de Moscoso and his captains became so indignant on learning of the curaca's bad intentions and the deceit the Indian had practiced upon them, that they would neither listen to the good reasons he gave for being pardoned for his fault nor grant his petition to spare his life, nor accept or believe his promises. On the other hand they all said together that he who had done them such harm hitherto would do worse in the future, and they ordered the dogs let loose. Being very hungry, in a short time they tore him to pieces and ate him.

This was the revenge our Castilians took on the poor Indian who had led them off the road, as if it were any satisfaction for past hardships or remedy for present evils. After they had done it, they saw that they were not revenged but worse off than before, as they had no one at all to guide them because they had given the other Indians, who had brought the maize, permission to return to their own country as soon as the food was used up, and thus they found themselves entirely lost.

The Spaniards being in these straits and confused and repentant of having killed the Indian—who, if they had left him alive, might perhaps have brought them out to the settlements, as he had promised—seeing that they had no other recourse, took the one that the Indian had told them, giving him credit after his death for what they refused to believe while he was alive. This was that they should march toward the west without turning to one side or to the other.

They did so and traveled three days suffering extreme hunger and necessity, because for three days previously they had eaten nothing except herbs and roots. It was of much advantage to them in this hardship that the forests in that uninhabited country were open and not dense as they are in other parts of the Indies, where they are like a wall. If these had been so, they would have perished of hunger before they got out of them.

Under these difficulties they continued their journey, always toward the west, and at the end of the three days they sighted inhabited country from the tops of some hills through which they were going. This gave them the relief that can be imagined, though on reaching the settlements, they found that the Indians had gone to the woods and that the land was poor and sterile. The pueblos were not like the others they had seen, but the houses were scattered through the fields in groups of four or five, badly built and worse arranged, looking more like huts of melon growers than dwellings. But for all this they satisfied their hunger with a quantity of fresh beef they found in them. They also found fresh cowhides, though they never saw the cattle alive nor would the Indians ever say where they got them.

On the second day of their march through that sterile and poorly inhabited province, which our people called the province of the Vaqueros[40] because of the meat and hides of cattle that they found in it, an Indian desired to show his spirit and valor with a strange and mad act that he performed. It happened that after the Spaniards had finished that day's march they encamped on a plain, and everything being quiet, they saw a lone Indian emerge from some woods not far from the camp and come toward them. He wore a handsome plume on his head and had his bow in his hands and a quiver of arrows on his back that inclined a little toward the right shoulder, as they all usually carry them.

The Castilians who were near the place where the Indian happened to come out of the woods, seeing that he was alone and so peaceable, did not give an alarm, but thinking that he was bringing a message from the cacique to the governor, they allowed him to come on. When he found himself fewer than fifty paces from a group of Spaniards on foot who were talking together, he very hastily and courageously placed an arrow in his bow and, aiming at the group, who were watching him, he shot it with extreme force. Seeing that he was shooting at them, the Christians hastily scattered to one side and the other and some fell down on the ground, thus escaping the shot. But the arrow passed beyond them and struck in the midst of five or six Indian women who were under a tree preparing their masters' dinner. It hit one of them in the back and passed clear through her, and struck the one who was

[40]In the judgment of John R. Swanton, this "province of the Vaqueros" most closely matches the Soacatino of Elvas or the Xuacatino of Biedma. Swanton, *Final Report*, 279.

facing her in the chest and also passed through her, though the arrow did not come clear, and the Indians immediately fell dead.

Having made this bold shot, the Indian turned and fled to the woods, running so swiftly and lightly that it was clear that he had depended upon this [speed] to come and do what he did.

The Spaniards sounded the call to arms and shouted to the Indian, being unable to follow him. Captain Baltasar de Gallegos, who happened to be on horseback, responded to the alarm, and seeing the fleeing Indian and hearing the Spaniards shout, "Kill him, kill him!" suspected what he must have done and ran after him. Just as the Indian reached shelter he overtook and killed him before the poor unfortunate could enjoy the fruits of his rash bravery, as is the case with most such feats that are performed in war.

IV

TWO INDIANS LET IT BE UNDERSTOOD THAT THEY CHALLENGE THE SPANIARDS TO SINGLE COMBAT

Three days after this affair, in this same province, which they called that of the Vaqueros, there happened another, no less remarkable one. This was that one day at ten o'clock in the morning, as the general and his captains and soldiers stopped marching to rest after their past labors on two long daily marches that they had just made, they saw coming across a beautiful plain two Indian nobles. They were decked out in long plumes with their bows in their hands and their arrows in quivers on their backs. When they came within two hundred paces of the camp, they began walking around a walnut tree that was there, and they did not walk together, shoulder to shoulder, but went one behind the other, so that each one could protect his companion from behind. They walked thus almost all day, paying no attention to the Negroes and Indians—men, women, and children—who passed near them carrying water and wood. The Spaniards understood from this that they were not doing it for the benefit of the servants, but for themselves, and they told the governor about it. He at once ordered that a decree be issued forbidding any soldier to harm them, but ordering that they be left alone as insane persons.

The Indians continued to walk around until evening, without doing anything else, as if they were waiting for the Spaniards who wished to do so to come out two by two for combat with them. When it was almost sunset a company of horse that had gone out that morning to ride over the country came back. Their camp was near the place where the Indians were walking, and when they saw them they asked what Indians they were. Learning about them and what had been ordered concerning them, namely, that they be left alone as madmen, they all obeyed except one, who chose to disobey in order to show his courage. Asking why in the name of heaven anyone else should be madder than they were, and saying that he would chastise their madness, he ran at them. This soldier was from Segovia and was named Juan Páez.

Seeing a single Castilian attacking them, the Indian who happened to be nearest advanced to meet him, in order to show that he had asked for a single combat. The other Indian stepped back and got under the walnut tree, showing further that their intention was to fight one against one, and that his companion did not wish help against a single Castilian, though he was on horseback.

Juan Páez attacked the Indian furiously in order to knock him down. The heathen, who was waiting for him with an arrow ready in his bow, seeing him come within range, shot it and struck him in the left arm at the place where it bled, through the sleeve of his coat of mail. Breaking through the sleeve on both sides, the arrow remained sticking through the arm. Because of his wound and the blow, which was very strong, Juan Páez could not move his arm. The reins fell from his hand, and the horse, who felt them fall, stopped galloping. It is very usual for horses to do this when they feel the reins fall, and it is likewise a rule of horsemanship to drop them suddenly when the horse runs away and will not stop.

Juan Páez's companions, who had not yet dismounted, seeing him in such danger, all ran up hastily to help him before the enemy should kill him. Seeing so many horses coming against them, the Indians fled toward some woods close by, but before they could reach them the Spaniards killed them with lances, not observing the rule of war that, inasmuch as the Indians had not desired to go two against one Spaniard, it was not fair for so many mounted Spaniards to go against two Indians on foot.

With these incidents, which, though they are unusual, we have told because no other, more important ones occurred, the Castilians traveled through the province they named that of the Vaqueros for more than thirty leagues. At the end of them that poor settlement ceased, and they saw that there were large mountain ranges and forests to the west and learned that they were uninhabited.

The governor and his captains, warned by the experiences of hunger and hardship they had passed through in the deserts that were behind them, wished to go no farther than was necessary to find a road that would bring them out into an inhabited country, and they endeavored to take precautions against the inconveniences that they would encounter. Therefore they ordered that three mounted companies, each with twenty-four horses, should all go toward the west by three routes to find out what there was in that direction.

They ordered them to go as far as possible into the interior country and bring a report not only of what they should see, but also they were to attempt to find out what was beyond. They gave them Indian interpreters from among those domestics who spoke the best Spanish [*los más ladinos*].

The seventy-two horsemen left camp with these orders, and within fifteen days they all came back with nearly the same report. They said that each of the bands had entered more than thirty leagues and had found a very sterile country with few people, and the farther they went the worse it became. This was what they had seen, and they brought even worse news of what was beyond, because many Indians whom they had captured and others who had received them peacefully had told them that it was true that there were Indians beyond, but they did not inhabit settled pueblos, nor have houses in which to live, nor cultivate their lands. They were a nomadic people who wandered in bands, gathering such fruits, herbs, and roots as the land afforded them of itself, and they supported themselves by hunting and fishing, moving from one place to another according to the advantages the seasons gave them in their fisheries and hunting grounds. All three parties brought this report, differing little from one another.

In addition to the account given, Alonso de Carmona adds at this point that the Indians told them that beyond that province where they were (to the west) were large settlements in a very level country with a great deal of sand. The cattle whose skins they had seen were bred there, and there were large numbers of them.

V

THE SPANIARDS GO BACK IN SEARCH OF THE RÍO GRANDE, AND THE HARDSHIPS THAT THEY EXPERIENCED ON THE ROAD

Governor Luis de Moscoso and his captains, having heard this fine report about the road by which they had promised themselves to come out in the territory of México, and having discussed the matter and considered the difficulties of their journey, decided not to go farther in order not to perish of hunger while lost in those deserts, of which they did not know the extent, but to go back in search of the same Río Grande that they had left. It now seemed to them that to get out of the kingdom of La Florida there was no more certain route than going down the river and coming out into the North Sea.

Having so determined, they endeavored to inform themselves about the road that they could take on their return that would avoid the bad country and the uninhabited regions they had passed through when they came. They learned that by returning by a circular route to the right of the one by which they had come, the road they would travel would be shorter, but they would have to traverse many other uninhabited districts and deserts. If they chose to return by a route to the left, however, also making a semicircle, though their road would be longer they would always be going through an inhabited country where they would find food and Indians to guide them.

On learning this, they made haste to leave those bad lands of the Vaqueros, and they marched in an arc toward the south, always obtaining information of the road ahead in order not to get into some desert that they could not get out of. Though the Castilians traveled taking care not to injure the Indians, so as not to incite them to make war upon them, and though they made long daily marches so as to leave their provinces quickly, the natives did not allow them to pass in peace. On the contrary they fell upon them with sudden attacks and alarms at all hours of the day and night. In order to surprise them more successfully, they hid themselves in the woods near the road, and where there were none they threw themselves down on the ground and covered themselves with grass, and when our men passed by unsuspectingly, seeing no one, they raised up and shot them with arrows mercilessly, but when the Spaniards turned upon them they ran away.

These attacks were so numerous and so continuous that the enemy had scarcely been driven away from the vanguard when others appeared in the rear, and often at three or four places at the same time. They always left damage behind them with deaths and wounds of men and horses. The Spaniards received more harm in this province of the Vaqueros, without coming to blows with the enemy, than in any other of the many through which they traveled, particularly on the last day of their march through it. The road happened to be rough, through woods and over streams and passes very convenient for highwaymen such as those Indians were. Going and coming there in safety, they did not cease their attacks that whole day, in which they killed and wounded many Castilians, Indian servants, and horses.

In the last attack, which occurred at the crossing of a stream where there were many trees, they wounded a soldier from Galicia named Sanjurge, whom we mentioned at the beginning of this *History.* Because he was an unusual man it will be fitting for us to tell some things about him in particular, for they all belong to our story and are extraordinary. I submit what I shall say about them and about anything else that I may say here or elsewhere to the correction and rule of the holy mother Roman church, whose most Catholic son I am, through the mercy of God, though unworthy of such a mother.

As Sanjurge was going through the middle of the stream, an Indian shot an arrow at him from among the undergrowth with such force that it penetrated the armor on his leg and went through the right thigh, and after going through the tree and pad of the saddle, two or three inches of the arrow passed on and wounded the horse. The horse ran out of the stream to a plain, kicking and curvetting to get rid of the arrow and of his master if he could.

The Spaniards who were near went to his assistance, and seeing that Sanjurge was pinned to the saddle and that the camp was near the place where they were, they took him and the horse, thus transfixed, to his quarters. There they lifted him up from the saddle and cut the arrow between it and the thigh, and then very carefully removed the saddle. They saw that the horse's wound was not deep, but they wondered that the arrow, being one of the ordinary kind that the Indians make for munitions, without a head, had penetrated so far. It was made of reed with the point of the same material cut obliquely and hardened in the fire.

They left Sanjurge lying on the plain to be assisted by his own efforts. Among his many other abilities, one was to cure wounds with oil, dirty wool, and words they call a charm. During this discovery he had made many cures that had excited great admiration as he appeared to have a particular gift from God for making them. After the oil, the dirty wool and everything else that the Castilians had were burned in the battle of Mauvila, however, he had stopped making these cures. Though he himself had been wounded on two other occasions—once with an arrow that entered his instep and came out at the heel, from which he was more than four months in recovering, and the other time by another arrow that entered the knee joint, where the head, which was made of deer horn, broke off, and he had undergone martyrdoms to get it out—with all this he had been unwilling to treat either himself or any other wounded man, believing that he could not make a cure without oil and dirty wool.

Seeing now, therefore, his own necessity, he was unwilling to call the surgeon because of a grudge he had against him caused by the roughness and cruelty with which he had treated his wounded knee. On that occasion, angered by his heavy-handedness, he had told him in a very insulting manner that if he should be wounded again he would not call him, even though he might know he was dying, and the surgeon had retorted for his part that although he might know how to save his life he would not treat him, and that he need not summon him if he should ever need him.

Since they felt this bitter anger against one another, Sanjurge would not summon the surgeon, nor would the surgeon show him the kindness of going to tend him, though he knew he was wounded. Thus he saw that he must help himself by what he knew, and in place of the oil he took lard, and instead of dirty wool he used thread raveled from an old Indian blanket. It had been a long time since any of the Castilians had had a shirt or anything made of linen. The treatment he gave himself was so effective that within the four days that the army remained in the camp, because of the many wounded among them, he was cured, and on the fifth day when our men marched, Sanjurge mounted his horse, and so that the Spaniards might see that he was well he ran from one side of the army to the other, shouting in a loud voice: "Kill me, Christians, for I have been a traitor to you and a bad comrade. Because I have not attempted to cure, believing that the virtue of my treatments lay in the oil and dirty wool, I have allowed more than a hundred and fifty of you to die."

With the events that we have told, the Castilians left the province of the Vaqueros and made long daily marches for twenty days through other lands whose names they did not know. They directed their journey in an arc toward the south, and as it seemed to them that they were going too far down from the province of Guachoya, to which they wished to return, they turned toward the east, taking care always to ascend somewhat to the north. Traveling in this manner, they came to and crossed the road that they had followed on going out, but they did not recognize it because of the little notice they had taken, in going, of the lands they left behind them.

When they reached that place it was already the middle of September, and having marched three months after leaving the pueblo of Guachoya, during all that time and on all that long road, though they had no pitched battles, they were never free from the sudden attacks and ambushes that the Indians gave them at all hours of the day and night. They never failed to do them damage, principally in the case of those who strayed away from the camp. Waylaying them like highwaymen, on seeing them apart from their companions, the Indians immediately shot them with arrows. In this manner they killed from time to time more than forty Spaniards on this journey alone. At night they entered the camp on all fours and, wriggling along the ground like snakes, without the sentries hearing them, they shot the horses and the sentries themselves, hitting them in the back as a punishment for their not having seen or heard them. They killed two sentries in this manner in one night. The Indians kept our Castilians very fatigued by these continuous persecutions.

One day during this journey it happened that, as some of the Spaniards lacked servants, they asked the governor's permission for eighteen of them to form an ambush and take ten or twelve of the Indians who, following the Spaniard's departure, were accustomed to come to their camp seeking whatever might remain there, as if they would have left anything of value.

With the general's permission a dozen cavalry and as many infantry remained hidden among some thick trees, in the highest of which they stationed a watchman who would tell them when the Indians appeared. In four attempts they very easily took fourteen Indians, without their making any resistance. When the Spaniards started to leave with their prizes, they having been divided among them, the Genoese, Maese Francisco, at whose request permission [to do this] had been asked, came out, and not being content with the two Indians that they had given him, he said that he needed another and that he would not go until he had taken one.

His companions told him to be satisfied for that time with those he had and that they would promise to go with him another day if he wished to take more. Persisting in his intention, Maestre Francisco said that although he stayed alone he would not leave there until he had taken the Indian he needed. Though each of his companions offered him the one that had fallen to his lot, in order to please him, for they knew that they would soon need him in building the brigantines, he would not accept them, saying that he would not be so rude as to take away from another what had been given to him for his own, and that he desired an Indian to be taken in his own name. With this obstinacy he forced his companions to remain in the ambush against the will of all of them, for it seemed that they foresaw the bad outcome. A little later the lookout called that there was an Indian in the place.

Being anxious to leave, the Castilians did not wait for more Indians to come, and thus one of them came out running on his horse. He was named Juan Páez, a native of Segovia, whom we mentioned above. Not warned by past experience, he fell upon the Indian. The latter got under a tree so that the horse would not trample him, put an arrow in his bow, and waited for the Castilian.

Passing to one side, the rider made an ineffectual crosswise thrust with his lance. As the horse came opposite him, the Indian shot the arrow at him and struck him near the left knee, causing him to go stumbling on for more than twenty paces and then fall dead. Another horseman had followed Juan Páez, this being Francisco de Bolaños, who was his comrade and from his own country. He attacked the Indian, and being unable to go under the tree he threw a lance at him from the side over his left arm, but it was of no effect.

The Indian, who intended to make better use of his arrows than the Castilians did of their lances, shot one at the horse and struck him in the same place as the first one, in such manner that he went running in the tracks of the other and fell dead at his feet. These were the two best shots, and if he had not had a reverse at the third that broke his succession of good luck, we would have another exploit to tell about like the one that happened in the province of Apalache.

VI

THE INSUPPORTABLE HARDSHIPS THAT THE SPANIARDS SUFFERED BEFORE THEY REACHED THE RÍO GRANDE

A gentleman from Badajoz named Juan de Vega, a member of one of the very noble families that are in that city (whom I knew in El Perú and afterward in Spain), believing that two mounted Castilians could cope with one Indian on foot, had remained behind, though he had followed them. Seeing them now fallen to the ground and their horses dead, he ran full speed to kill the Indian. On the other hand the two soldiers, raising themselves from the ground, ran at him with their lances in their hands. The Indian, seeing himself attacked from both sides, went running from under the tree to meet the horseman, giving more attention to him alone than to the two who had been made infantry and foot soldiers. It seemed to him that, if he could kill the horse as he had the other two, he would be free of all three of them and able to take to his heels before they could attack him, because of the usual advantage the Indians had over the Spaniards in running. He would have succeeded in carrying out his intention if Juan de Vega had not come so well prepared. His horse wore a breast-leather half a vara wide made of three thicknesses of cowhide, for the careful Spaniards made such breast-leathers from the skins of cows, lions, bear, and deer that they could obtain, for protecting their horses. The Indian had come out from under the tree with all the courage that a man in such danger could show, and shot an arrow at Juan de Vega's horse. It struck the breast-leather, passed through the three thicknesses of the skins, and wounded the horse, four finger-breadths of the arrow penetrating his breast. It went in so true that if he had not worn the breast-leather it would have gone to the heart, but the fortune of war willed otherwise.

Juan de Vega thrust his lance at the Indian and killed him, but his death did not console our men's sorrow at having lost two horses on that sad occasion, at a time when they needed them so much and had so few left. When they went to see the Indian their grief and anger were doubled, because his person was not like that of the other Floridos, who usually are of fine and robust figure. This one was small, lean, and weak, so that his appearance promised no courage whatever, but his good spirit and bravery made him so redoubtable that he amazed his enemies and left them cause for grief. Cursing their bad luck and Maestro Francisco who had been the cause of it, they started on their way and overtook the army. There all again bewailed the loss of the horses, for in them they had their greatest strength and hope in whatever hardship might present itself.

With so many and such continuous molestations as the Indians gave the Spaniards, the latter traveled toward the province of Guachoya and the Río Grande until the end of October of the year 1542, at which time a very severe winter set in, with much rain, cold, and hard wind. Since they wished to reach their intended destination, they did not fail to march every day, no matter how bad the weather, and they reached their camping places soaked with water and covered with mud. There they never found food without going after it, and most of the time they got it by force of arms and in exchange for their lives and blood.

Because of these hardships and the bad weather, they felt the fatigues of the march more than ever before. As the season advanced, the waters rose, much snow fell, the rivers were flooded, and it was increasingly difficult to cross them, for even the small streams could not be forded. Almost every day it was necessary to make rafts for crossing them, and at some passages of the rivers they were detained five, six, seven, and eight days by the perpetual opposition of the enemy and by the poor facilities for making the rafts. Thus their labor was augmented and lengthened.

On many nights, besides what they had endured in the course of the day, their hardships were so excessive that, because of the great amounts of water and mud, they could not find the ground in order to rest on it, and the mounted men slept or passed the night on their horses, not dismounting at all. The manner in which the foot soldiers passed it is left to the imagination of the reader, for they were at least knee-deep or thigh-deep in water.

Furthermore, as the clothing they were wearing was made of deerskin and other similar skins, and consisted of only one garment tied at the waist, which served as shirt, doublet, coat, and cape, and as it was always wet with the constant rain or snow and with crossing the many rivers, so that it was a rare thing for them to be dry, and as they went about barelegged, without stockings, shoes, or sandals, and inasmuch as to these personal deprivations and the inclemencies of the weather were added poor food, lack of sleep, and their great weariness on such a long and toilsome journey, many of the Spaniards and Indian servants whom they had with them became sick.

The sickness did not end with the people but passed to the horses, and increased more and more among all of them, both men and beasts beginning to die in large numbers. Every day two or three Spaniards expired, and one day there were seven. The horses and the Indian servants were in the same situation. The latter were mourned by their masters no less than their own companions, for they had served them like sons and they missed them very much. Almost none of these Indians escaped. There was one Spaniard who had four, and all of them died. In their haste to pass on they scarcely had time to bury the dead; many remained unburied, and those whom they interred were half buried because they could do no more. Most of them died on their feet on the march and there was no one to carry them; the horses were also sick, and they did not use the well ones for carrying the sick men because they needed them to go out against the enemy who came up to make continuous surprise attacks and assaults.

With all these miseries and afflictions our men endured, they did not neglect to keep watch night and day, posting their sentries and changing guard in due military form, so that the enemy would not find them unprepared. This added to their illness and afflictions, as has been said.

At this point Alonso de Carmona, having told at length of the miseries and hardships of this journey, says that they found a sow they had lost on the outward journey and that she had a litter of thirteen pigs, now well-grown, all of which were marked on the ears, each with a different sign. Perhaps the Indians had divided them among themselves and marked them with their own signs, from which it can be inferred that those Indians have conserved these animals.

With the inclemencies of the heavens and the persecutions of the air, water, and earth, and the hardships of hunger, sickness, and deaths of men and horses, and with care and diligence, though feeble enough, in watching and guarding against their enemies, and with the continual molestation of alarms, sudden attacks, and warfare the latter gave them, our Castilians marched throughout the months of September and October and up to the end of November, when they reached the Río Grande, so desired and longed-for by them, since they had come to seek it through such adversities and with so much anxiety of heart. On the contrary, not long before they had so hated and abhorred it that they had undergone the same hardships in fleeing and withdrawing from it. At the sight of the river they congratulated one another, it seeming to them that, upon reaching it, their miseries and labors were over.

On this last journey that our people made after the death of Governor Hernando de Soto they traveled, going and returning, and counting the expedition that the scouts made, more than 350 leagues, during which a hundred Spaniards and eighty horses died at the hands of the enemy and from sickness. This is what their bad counsel profited them, and though they arrived at the Río Grande the deaths did not cease. Fifty more Christians died in the camp, as we shall soon see.

VII

THE INDIANS ABANDON TWO PUEBLOS, WHERE THE SPANIARDS ESTABLISH THEMSELVES FOR THE WINTER

Our people looked upon the Río Grande with extreme contentment and gratitude in their hearts, for it seemed to them that in it all the labors of their journey would come to an end. They found on the banks of the river in the place at which they happened to reach it two pueblos, near one another, each having two hundred houses. A moat of water taken from the river itself surrounded them both and formed an island.

Governor Luis de Moscoso and his captains thought it would be well to lodge in them for the winter if it should be possible to gain the pueblos either by peaceful means or by war. Though that province was not Guachoya, which they had been seeking, it seemed enough for them to have reached the Río Grande, since for what they wished to do, which was to leave that kingdom by way of it, this was the most essential thing.

Having so determined, although they did not come to fight, they formed a squadron that still numbered more than 320 infantry and seventy cavalry, and attacked one of the pueblos, whose inhabitants abandoned it without making any defense. Leaving some men in it, our forces attacked the other pueblo and gained it with equal facility.

It was understood that the reason these Indians had not defended themselves was that they had thought the Spaniards were coming in such force as they had on the other two occasions that they had marched along the banks of that river. Though they themselves had not reached this province, their reputations must have come to it along with the news of other things that they had done in the provinces of Capaha and Guachoyá. This report must have so terrified them that they would not now defend their pueblos.

On entering them, the Spaniards found such quantities of Indian corn and other grains and vegetables and dried fruit, such as nuts, raisins, dried plums, acorns, and other fruits unknown in Spain, that in truth, though our people, with the intention of wintering in those pueblos, had spent the entire past summer in collecting provisions, they would not have gathered so many.

Alonso de Carmona says that when they measured the maize they found in these two pueblos there were eighteen thousand fanegas by actual count, which excited great wonder among them at seeing that there was so large a supply of maize in such a small settlement, to say nothing of the other grains. All this, and the fact that the Indians had abandoned the pueblos so easily, these Christians attributed to the particular mercy that God had been pleased to show them in their necessity. For it is true that if they had not found those pueblos so good and so well provisioned, certainly after the way in which they had been mistreated, being weak and sick, they would all have perished within a few days. They themselves admitted this, they now being in such a state that they could do nothing for the preservation of their lives and health. Even with the supplies and comforts that we have mentioned, more than fifty Castilians died after they had reached the pueblos, and as many Indian servants, because they were now so spent that they could not regain their strength. Among those who died was Captain Andrés de Vasconcelos de Silva, a native of Yelves, who bore two names representing the noblest blood to be found in the kingdom of Portugal.

There died also Nuño Tovar, a native of Xerez de Badajoz, a gentleman no less valiant than noble, though unfortunate because of such a severe superior having fallen to his lot. Because of an error of love that had forced him to marry without his [superior's] permission, he had always been out of favor and treated contemptuously, entirely contrary to what he deserved.

The faithful interpreter Juan Ortiz, a native of Sevilla, also died. Throughout the discovery he had served no less with his strength and courage than with his tongue, because he was a very good soldier and useful on all occasions. In short, there died many very noble gentlemen, and many very excellent, brave, and spirited soldiers. Those who died on this last journey numbered more than 150 persons. It occasioned great grief and sorrow that through the imprudence and bad management of the captains so many and such good men had perished to no purpose whatsoever.

Having gained the pueblos, the Spaniards agreed for their further convenience and safety to join the two together, so as not to be divided in whatever might arise in the future. They did so immediately, tearing down one of the pueblos and taking all the food, wood, and grass that was in it to the other, with which they enlarged and fortified it as best they could, and established themselves in it. Our people spent twenty days making these arrangements, because they were weak and debilitated and could not work as much as they liked, and as was necessary.

With the shelter of good houses and the comfort of plenty of food, the sick, who included almost all of them, began to convalesce, and the natives of that province were so good that though they were not friendly toward the Spaniards they did not annoy them or give them any trouble, nor attempt to attack them in the country, nor give sudden alarms and assaults by night. All this they attributed to a particular providence of the mercy of God.

That pueblo and its province were called Aminoya. It was sixteen leagues up the river from the pueblo of Guachoya, which our people had been seeking. When they had recovered their health and strength somewhat, seeing that the last days of January of the year 1543 had now come, they gave orders for cutting the timber for making the brigantines in which they intended to go by way of the river down to the North Sea. There was a great abundance of timber throughout the vicinity. They worked diligently to obtain the other things that were needed, such as rigging, tow, resin from trees for tar, blankets for sails, oars, and nails. Everyone applied himself to this work very busily and willingly.

Alonso de Carmona says in his account that upon entering this pueblo of Aminoya he and Captain Espíndola, who was captain of the governor's guard, were going [together] and that they found an old woman who had been unable to flee when the others left. She asked them why they were coming to that pueblo, and on their replying that they intended to winter there, she asked where they expected to stay and put their horses, because every fourteen years that Río Grande overflowed its bed and covered the whole country, and the natives took refuge in the upper parts of the houses; and she said that year was the fourteenth. Whereupon they laughed and forgot about it. All these are words of Alonso de Carmona himself, as he wrote them in this his *Peregrination*, which is the name he gives to the little that he wrote, not intended for printing.

VIII

TWO CURACAS COME IN PEACE. THE SPANIARDS SET ABOUT BUILDING SEVEN BRIGANTINES

At this time, and even before, there had already been circulated throughout the vicinity the news that the Castilians had returned from their journey and were lodged in the province and pueblo of Aminoya. The curaca and lord of the province of Anilco, whom we mentioned above, being informed of this and fearing that the Spaniards would do the damage in his country that they had done before, and in order that his enemies of Guachoya, under their protection, might not come to avenge themselves on him and commit the abominations that they had committed on their past expedition, desired to repair the error that he had made at that time in his rebelliousness and obstinacy, which had been so disastrous.

Not daring to trust his own person to the Spaniards, however, he ordered an Indian to be summoned who was a very near relative of his and who was and had been for many years his captain-general and governor throughout his state, and said to him: "Go in my name to the Spanish general and tell him that I send you to represent my own person, since ill-health prevents me from coming myself to serve them. Say that I beg them as earnestly as I can to receive me into their friendship and service; that I promise and give them my word to be their loyal and obedient servant in every way that I can serve them in my house and state.

"Say this to them on my behalf, and on your own and that of the other Indians who go with you, do as readily as possible everything that they may order you, so that the Castilians will believe my protestations and your intention of pleasing them in every way that may be conducive to their service."

The captain-general Anilco—since we do not know his own name, we give him that of his curaca—left on this embassy accompanied by twenty-four nobles, finely decked out with plumes and furred mantles, and as many other Indians who went laden with fruit, fish, and venison, and two hundred Indians to serve the whole army. He arrived in the presence of Governor Luis de Moscoso and delivered his message with a most respectful and friendly bearing, repeating the same words that the cacique had said to him. Following this, he offered his own person, indicating the good spirit and willingness that they all had to serve him. At the close of his friendly offers he said: "Sir, I do not desire your lordship to believe my words, but the deeds that you shall see us perform in your service."

The governor received him very affably and accorded him all the honors that he would have given the cacique himself. He said that his friendly words and spirit and his good will were very gratifying to him, and sent many compliments to the curaca, saying that he esteemed and valued his friendship. He was very attentive to the rest of the Indian nobles, thereby gratifying them very much. Anilco sent the governor's message to his lord, and he himself remained to serve the Spaniards.

Two days later the cacique Guachoya came to kiss the governor's hands, and to confirm their past friendship he brought a large present of the fruits, fish, and game that were in his country. The general also received this very affably and with many thanks. But Guachoya was not pleased to see Captain Anilco with the Spaniards, and still less that all of them accorded him such honors as they did, because as we have seen already, they were implacable enemies. He concealed his displeasure as well as he could, however, to show it in due time.

These two caciques Guachoya and Anilco performed services for the Castilians during all the time they were in that province called Aminoya, and every eight days they went to their houses and returned with new presents and offerings. Though they themselves left, their Indians remained to serve the Spaniards. Inasmuch as the latter, for the purpose of leaving that kingdom, had put their hopes in the brigantines that they were to build, they busied themselves very diligently in preparing the things necessary for them. The chief direction of the work was given to *Maestre* Francisco, the Genoese, an expert shipbuilder. Having calculated the size that the brigantines would have to be in order to hold all the people who must embark in them, he found that they would need seven. They provided the necessary materials for this number of brigantines, and in order to prevent the winter rains from hindering their work, they built four very large shelters that served as dockyards, where they all labored equally, without any distinction, each one performing to this end the task for which he was best fitted. Some sawed the timber to make boards, others dressed it with adzes, others beat iron into nails, others made charcoal, others fashioned the oars, and others twisted the ropes. The soldier or captain who labored hardest at these things was honored most.

Our people were engaged in these activities throughout the months of February, March, and April, without the Indians of that province disturbing them or hindering their work, which was no small favor that they did them.

In all this time, and afterward, General Anilco showed himself most friendly to the Spaniards, for he acted very promptly to provide everything that they asked him for that was needed for the brigantines. He brought many blankets, new and old, which were what the Spaniards had feared could not be provided, as there were very few in all of that kingdom, but the friendliness of this good Indian and his great industry facilitated what our people had expected to find most difficult.

They kept the new blankets for sails and from the old ones they made string to use for oakum in caulking the ships. The Indians of La Florida make these blankets of a certain herb similar to mallows, which has a fiber like linen. They make thread from it and color it beautifully in any shade they wish.

Anilco also brought quantities of thick and thin ropes for rigging, sheets, and cables. In all these things and others that this good Indian provided, what was most appreciated and most gratifying was the good will and generosity with which he gave them, because he always brought more than they requested and came so promptly at the times set for providing this thing or that, that he never allowed them to pass. He went about among the Spaniards like one of them, helping them in their work and saying for them to ask for whatever they needed, as he wished to serve them and show his affection for them.

For these reasons the general and his captains and soldiers accorded him the same honor that they would have given to Governor Hernando de Soto if he had been alive, and Anilco deserved it, as much because of his virtue as because of the fine aspect of his face and person, which were those of a very noble man.

IX

TEN CURACAS FORM A LEAGUE AGAINST THE SPANIARDS, AND THE APU ANILCO WARNS THEM OF IT

Though the curaca Guachoya supplied and provided the things that were needed for the ships, it was done so tardily and so grudgingly that it was easily seen how different his attitude was from that of Anilco. At the same time it was noted what displeasure and anger he felt at seeing the esteem and honor that the Spaniards felt for Captain Anilco—he being poor and the vassal of another—which was much greater than that which they accorded him, who was rich and the lord of vassals. It seemed to him that this should be reversed, and honor given to each one in accordance with his estate and not his virtue. This gave rise to great envy that irritated him constantly, giving him no rest, until one day, unable to endure his passion, he showed it very openly, as we shall see below.

It will be appropriate to tell here what the Indians of the neighborhood were doing while the Castilians were building their caravels. Thus it must be known that opposite the pueblo of Guachoya on the other side of the Río Grande (as we said above), there was a very large province called Quigualtanqui, abounding in food and well populated. Its lord was young and warlike and was beloved and obeyed throughout his state and feared in the others because of his great power.

This cacique, seeing that the Spaniards were building ships so as to leave by way of the river, and considering that inasmuch as they had seen so many and such good provinces as they had discovered in that kingdom, and would carry news of the wealth and good qualities of the country (being a covetous people who were seeking a place to settle), they would return in greater numbers to conquer and gain it for themselves, taking it away from its natural rulers. It seemed to him that it would be a good thing to prevent this by giving orders that the Spaniards should not leave that country, but should all die there, so that they could not spread the news in other places of what they had seen in that kingdom. With this evil purpose he ordered the nobles and chief men of his country summoned and told them of his intention and asked their opinion.

The Indians concluded that what their curaca and lord wished to do against the Castilians was a very good thing, and that their opinion and advice was that the cacique's plan be carried out as promptly as possible, and that they would serve him to the death.

With this common determination on the part of his people, Quigualtanqui, in order further to assure his success, sent ambassadors to the other caciques and lords of the region advising them of the determined stand he had taken against the Spaniards, and saying that, since the danger he feared and wished to guard against was common to all of them, he begged and exhorted them that, abandoning their hostilities and the past anger that had always existed among them, they unite all together and with one accord to forestall and prevent the evil that might befall them if foreigners should come to take away their lands, women, and children, making them slaves and tributaries.

Each one of the curacas and lords of the vicinity received Quigualtanqui's ambassadors very cordially and gladly, and gave formal approval to his opinion and advice. They praised his discretion and prudence highly, both because they believed he was right in what he said and in order not to slight and anger him by opposing him. All of them feared him because he was more powerful than they.

In this manner ten curacas on both sides of the river formed an alliance, and it was agreed among all of them that each one in his own country would make ready very secretly and diligently as many men as he could, and collect canoes and other equipment needed for the war that they intended to wage against the Spaniards on land and water. They agreed to pretend to be peaceful and friendly toward them so as to make them careless and take them unawares. Each one would send his ambassador separately, and they would not go all together, so that the Spaniards would not suspect the existence of the league and be on guard against them.

This conspiracy among the curacas being arranged, Quigualtanqui, as the principal mover of it, immediately sent his messengers to Governor Luis de Moscoso, offering him friendship and the service that he might be pleased to accept from him. The rest of the caciques did the same thing. The general replied to them, thanking them for their kind offer and saying that the Spaniards would be very glad to have peace and friendship with them. And in fact they were pleased with the embassy, not understanding the treason that lay beneath it. They were the more content because for a long time they had been tired of fighting.

Neither the cacique Anilco nor his captain-general, whom we also call Anilco, were willing to enter this league, though they were invited to do so. On the other hand it troubled them to learn that the rest of the caciques were plotting to kill the Castilians, for they loved them and wished them well. With this regard for them and in order to keep the faith and word that they had given them in loyal friendship, the apu Anilco on behalf of his cacique and himself told the governor what the Indians of the vicinity were plotting against them. Having given this information, he said that he offered his lordship anew the services and friendship of his cacique and of himself, and that they would serve him with the same love and loyalty as hitherto, and he promised to keep him informed of what went on among the conspirators.

The governor thanked General Anilco very sincerely for what he had told him, and sent similar messages to his curaca, esteeming his friendship and loyalty greatly.

It is to be noted that, though the cacique Anilco did the Spaniards the friendly services of which we have told, he was never willing to come to see the general and always excused himself with the plea of ill-health. But the truth is that he himself confessed to his own people that he was regretful and ashamed at not having accepted the peace and friendship that the Castilians had offered him when they first came to his country, and he said that this embarrassment prevented his appearing in their presence.

It was impossible to tell for certain whether or not the curaca Guachoya, who also professed friendship for our people, was in the league, but it was suspected that, since he did not give warning of it, he consented to it and would enter in due time. To this suspicion and bad sign was added another, worse one, which was the hatred and rancor he showed toward Captain Anilco, and his great irritation that the governor and the Spaniards should honor and esteem him as much as they did. They did this in their gratitude for the great assistance that he gave them in building the brigantines, and because he had put them under new obligations by his loyalty in warning them of the uprising in that country. But Guachoya, disregarding the Spaniards' obligations and instigated on the other hand by his old enmity and present envy, was constantly with the governor belittling and discrediting Anilco, saying secretly everything bad about him that he could. The general and his captains were of the opinion that he did this purposely and cunningly so that they would not believe Anilco if he had told them or should tell them anything about the league, for, since Anilco had refused to enter it, Guachoya suspected him of being against them all and feared that he would reveal the plot that the rest of the curacas had formed. Thus he went about dissimulating and scheming for his own ends.

X

GUACHOYA SPEAKS ILL OF ANILCO IN THE GOVERNOR'S PRESENCE, AND ANILCO REPLIES TO HIM, CHALLENGING HIM TO SINGLE COMBAT

Guachoya went about for some days suppressing his grievances, past and present, so as not to show them in public. But being unable to contain them, losing patience and all ordinary courtesy, he said to the governor publicly in the presence of many captains and soldiers who were with him, and before Anilco himself, many words that, according to the interpreters, ran thus:

"Sir, for a long time I have been much grieved at seeing the excessive honors that your lordship and these gentlemen, captains, and soldiers have accorded this man, for it seems to me that honor should be given to each according to his rank, and according to his quality and possessions. In him is found little or nothing of either of these, because he is poor, the son and grandson of poor parents and grandparents. His lineage is the same, as he has no higher rank than that of a servant and vassal of another lord such as I, and I also have servants and vassals who equal and surpass him in quality and wealth.

"I have said this to your lordship so that you may see upon whom you bestow your favor and trust, and henceforth may not give such credence to his words, which redound to the discredit of others. His being poor and having no lineage to respect can deceive your lordship easily unless you are warned against him."

This was the substance of what the cacique Guachoya said, but his expression and many other superfluous and injurious words that he spoke showed clearly his hatred and envy of Captain Anilco.

While Guachoya was speaking, Anilco made no sign of interrupting him that the Spaniards could see. On the other hand, he let him say as much as he liked without speaking a word or making a movement. When he saw that he had finished, he arose and said to the governor that he begged his lordship to do him the favor of permitting that, since Guachoya, in the presence of his lordship and of so many captains and soldiers, without respect for them, had insulted his honor, he might be allowed to defend it in their presence with truth and justice. He would be glad for Guachoya to protest any statement that was not such, so that the truth of that matter might be ascertained and made clear, and so that the little or no justification that Guachoya had for so maligning him might be made apparent. Inasmuch as his lordship was governor and captain-general and supreme judge of them all in peace and war, he would not deny his petition, as it was just and a matter concerning his honor, which he prized so highly.

Luis de Moscoso told him to speak as he saw fit, but that it must be without insulting or slandering Guachoya because he would not permit it. He ordered the Indian interpreters to state what Anilco should say without omitting anything in order to see whether he said anything discourteous to Guachoya.

Having made a most profound obeisance to the governor, Anilco said that he would speak the truth without abusing anyone, and he begged his lordship to pardon him if he should be long-winded. So saying, he sat down again and, turning toward Guachoya, he addressed the following discourse to him, a little at a time, so that the interpreters could tell what he was saying as he proceeded.

"Guachoya, without any reason whatever, you have seen fit to belittle and abuse me before the governor and his gentlemen, when you should honor me because of what I have done for you and your state, as you know and as I shall tell later. I have the governor's permission to reply to you and defend my honor. Do not contradict my true statements, because I shall prove them by your own vassals and servants to your greater shame and confusion.

"That which may not be true, or any unjustified boasting that I may do out of vanity and pride, I shall be pleased to have you contradict, because I desire that the governor and his whole army may know the truth or falsity of what you have said and see how unjustly you have said it. Therefore, do not stop me until I have finished.

"In saying that I am poor and that my parents and grandparents were also, you speak truly. They were not rich, but neither were they so poor as you have said. They always had possessions of their own on which to live, and through good fortune I have won in war from your spoils and those of other lords as great as you quite as much as I need to maintain my household and family in a manner befitting my rank. Thus I can be counted among the wealthy whom you so esteem.

"As for your saying that I am of humble ancestry, you well know that you are not speaking the truth. Though my father and grandfather were not lords of vassals, my great-grandfather and all his ancestors were, and this nobility has been transmitted to my person without having been defiled in any way, so that in the matter of rank and lineage I am equal to you and to any lord of vassals in the whole vicinity.[41]

"You say that I am the vassal of another, and that is true, for we cannot all be lords, because the eldest son of a lord inherits his estate and the other brothers remain as subjects. But it is also true that neither my lord Anilco nor his father or grandfather have treated me or my family as vassals, but as near relatives, being descendants of the second son of their house and their own flesh and blood. Being such, we have never served him in minor and servile offices, but in the most important ones in his household. In my own case you know that I had scarcely reached the age of twenty when he chose me for his captain-general, and a little later he named me his lieutenant and governor for his whole state and seigniory. Thus for twenty years, in peace and war, I have been the second person of my lord Anilco. You know that since I became his captain-general I have won all the battles that I have fought against his enemies.

"I triumphed signally in a battle against your father and later over all the captains that he sent against me. And now recently, since you inherited your estate six years ago, you joined all your forces and went in search of me for the sole purpose of revenging yourself on me. I went out to meet you, joined battle, and overcame you, capturing at that time you and two of your brothers, and all the nobles and rich men of your country.

"If I had so desired, I could then have deprived you of your state and taken it for myself, for there was no one in it to oppose me, and the common people among your vassals would perhaps have been pleased rather than hostile if I had done so. But I not only did not seize your state, nor even consider doing so, but I entertained and served you in prison as if you had

[41]This passage speaks of native nobility inherited through the male line, in a manner comprehensible to the European observers. Though it is impossible to emphatically rule this out, it is much more likely that nobility was inherited primarily through females, as in other Southeastern chiefdoms, in which case these Spaniards lacked the subtleties of communication necessary to understand this manner of inheritance in their efforts at translation.

been my lord rather than my prisoner, and I did the same with your brothers, vassals, and servants, down to the least of them. In the capitulations under which you and your people were released, I interceded for you, and it was due to my efforts that you left the prison, for without placing much confidence in the assurances [*palabras*] and promises that you made then, I was your guarantor and security for them. Thus when you broke them, as you did this past summer, I had the intention of returning you to prison, as I shall do when the Spaniards have gone. With their protection, they not understanding your evil purpose, you went to violate the temple and burial place of my lord Anilco and his ancestors, and to burn his houses and chief pueblo. You shall be called to account for it, I promise you.

"You say also that it is not fitting to accord the honor and esteem that is due a lord of vassals to him who is not so. You are right when he deserves to be a lord, but you know also that many subjects deserve to be lords, and that many lords are not even fit to be vassals and servants of others. If you had not inherited the rank of which you are so proud, you would never have been man enough to win it, and I who was born without it could have assumed it by taking it away from you if I had so desired. Inasmuch as it is not the part of men, but of women, to quarrel with words, let us resort to arms and prove which of the two deserves to be lord of vassals by reason of his virtue and strength.

"You and I will enter a canoe alone. They [the waters] go down the Río Grande to reach your country, and by another river that enters it seven leagues from here they go to mine; he who overcomes the other on the way will take the canoe to his own house. If you kill me, you will have avenged your injuries like a man, for you will fall heir to the advantages that my good fortune has given me, and to the honor and favor that these Castilians have done and are doing me, and also you will have satisfied the unreasonable envy and ill will that you hold against me. If I kill you, I shall prove to you that the merits of men do not consist in being very rich, nor in having many vassals, but in deserving them through their own virtue and courage.

"I make this reply to the words that you speak so unreasonably against my honor and ancestry, without my having offended you in any way unless you take offense at my having served my lord Anilco loyally and successfully. See whether there is anything in which you can contradict me, for I submit to proof so that these Spaniards may know that what I have said is true. If you are man enough to accept my challenge for us to go in the canoe, say whatever you like to me, and I will take satisfaction there for everything you have said against me."

XI

THE SPANIARDS WOUND AN INDIAN SPY, AND THE COMPLAINT THAT THE CURACAS MADE ABOUT IT

The cacique Guachoya made no reply to all that the captain-general Anilco said to him, but he showed by the expression on his face that he was ashamed and put out of countenance at having started the discussion (for very often it happens that he who attempts to affront another is himself offended). Thus the governor and those who were with him inferred that what Anilco had said was true, and thenceforth they regarded him even more highly.

General Luis de Moscoso, having considered that the enmity of the caciques would result in damage and prejudice to him if he allowed it to go on—because, in making war on one another, they would not continue to supply the things needed for building the brigantines—told them that, since they were both his friends, it was not reasonable for them to continue to be hostile to one another, because the Castilians would not know to which one to go in making friendly advances. Thus he begged them to forget the enmity that had existed between them and be friends.

The curacas replied that it gave them pleasure to obey his lordship and promised him to say no more about the matter. The governor, however, not confiding in the friendly promises that Guachoya had made, feared that he might set an ambush on the road when Anilco should go to his house, in order to take revenge on him. Thus four days after the events we have described, when Anilco wished to leave, he ordered thirty cavalry to escort him until he reached safety. Although Anilco refused it and showed so little fear of his adversary that he said he did not need the cavalry, he took them on that occasion out of obedience to the governor, but many other times he came and went to his house with only ten or twelve Indians to accompany him so as to let the Spaniards understand that he had little or no fear of his enemies.

While these things were going on in the Castilians' camp, the curaca Quigualtanqui and his fellow conspirators did not cease their evil machinations, but in pursuit of them they sent many messengers, by day and by night, with presents and false messages. After having delivered them, they would walk all through the Spanish camp, feigning friendliness, observing attentively how the Christians kept watch at night, how they kept their arms, and where the horses were, so as to make use in their treachery of any carelessness that our people might show. They paid no attention to the fact that the governor had ordered them repeatedly not to come at night. They came even more freely, because it seemed to them that, being friends, as they pretended to be, they were privileged to do all these things.

Gonzalo Silvestre, whom we have mentioned on other occasions, was exasperated by these actions of the Indians. Like the rest of the Spaniards, he had been ill and often at the point of death, but finding himself now convalescent and being on guard and sentry duty one night at one of the gates of the pueblo, standing the second watch, just at midnight by the light of a clear moon that was shining, he saw two Indians approach with long plumes on their heads and their bows and arrows in their hands. Having crossed the moat of water by a fallen tree that served as a bridge, they went directly to the gate. Gonzalo Silvestre said to the companion who was watching with him, who was named Juan Garrido, a native of the land of Burgos: "Here come two Indians, and I intend to stab in the face the first one who enters the gate, so that they will not come so shamelessly at night after the governor has forbidden it."

The Castilian replied: "Leave him to me, for I am somewhat stronger and you are weak and debilitated." Gonzalo Silvestre said: "Any attack that is made on them will be enough to frighten them." So saying, he prepared to receive the Indians, who were approaching. Seeing the gate, which was a small postern, standing open, they entered it without asking permission or speaking a word, as if they were going into their own house. The Spaniard's anger was doubled at seeing their boldness and fearlessness, and he stabbed the first one who entered in the forehead, from which he fell to the ground. He had scarcely fallen when he jumped up and, recovering his bow and arrows, he turned his back and ran, unable to fight any more. Gonzalo Silvestre did not wish to kill him, though he could have done so, because it seemed to him that what had been done was enough to frighten the Indians. The Indian companion of the wounded man, hearing the blow, began to run without waiting to see what had happened to his comrade. Gaining the tree across the moat, he passed over it and came to the place where he had left his canoe in the Río Grande. Without waiting for his friend, he jumped into it and crossed the river, giving the alarm to his people.

The wounded Indian, with the blood that was flowing in his eyes or in the fear he must have felt that they were pursuing him to finish killing him, jumped into the water of the moat and swam across it, shouting as he went to his companion, who had already reached safety. The Indians on the other side of the river, hearing the shouts of the wounded man, went to his aid, shielding him and carrying him away with them.

On the next day at sunrise four principal Indians came to see the governor to complain in the name of Quigualtanqui and all the neighboring caciques that he should have violated the peace and friendship that had been formed among them with such an affront and insult to all of them generally, because they said that the wounded Indian was one of their chief men, closely related to them by marriage. Therefore they begged his lordship, for the satisfaction of them all, to order the soldier or captain who had done it to be executed publicly, for the Indian was mortally wounded.

At noon four other Indian chiefs came with the same demand, and said that the Indian was dying. At sunset four others came with the same complaint, saying that the Indian was now dead, and that they asked satisfaction for his death through that of the Spaniard who had killed him so unjustly.

XII

THE ACTIVITY OF THE SPANIARDS IN BUILDING THE BRIGANTINES, AND A MOST REMARKABLE FLOOD ON THE RÍO GRANDE

General Luis de Moscoso replied on all three occasions that he had not ordered the Indian to be wounded, because he desired to maintain the peace and friendship that he had made with Quigualtanqui and the other curacas; but that a soldier who was very proud of his profession and punctilious in observing military regulations had done so as a matter of duty. If he should attempt to punish him in order to give satisfaction to the caciques, the other soldiers and captains would not consent to it, because in strict justice and according to military rules the soldier had not been to blame in having performed his duty well. The wounded or dead Indian who had entered without speaking to the sentries, and the caciques who had sent him at that hour after being warned not to send messages at night, were to blame. Though there was now no remedy for what was past, in the future the caciques must do as they had been told to avoid conflicts that would break the peace and destroy the friendship that existed among them.

The ambassadors left with this reply, highly incensed, and gave it to the caciques, inciting them to greater wrath and anger at the audacity and disdain of the Spaniards. Therefore all of them agreed that they would disregard the offense received in order to avenge it at the proper time and would further hasten the execution of the plot they had formed against them.

Nor was there lacking a captain among our men who upheld the Indians' quarrel, saying that it was a mistake not to punish the murder of a principal Indian, thereby giving the friendly caciques occasion to rebel against them. There would have been fine quarrels among the Spaniards over this opinion if the cooler and less passionate heads had not prevented them, for it had arisen from a certain secret grudge that existed among some of them.

It was already the beginning of March when the things that we have told took place, and to the Castilians in their eagerness to leave that country the days seemed like years. They never ceased to hasten their work on the brigantines, and most of those who labored at the forges and in the carpenters' shops were very noble gentlemen, who had never thought to perform such offices. They were the ones who proved most skillful in them because their better natural abilities and the great need of more skilled workmen had made experts of those who had never learned these trades.

We sometimes call these ships under construction brigantines and again caravels, after the usual custom of those Spaniards, who called them thus, but in reality they were neither the one nor the other. They were simply some large barks made in accordance with the few, poor and scanty resources that our people had for building them.

The captain-general Anilco was the moving spirit of this work because of the magnificent provision that he made of everything they requested for the brigantines. He supplied it so abundantly and so promptly that the Christians themselves admitted that, if it had not been for the favor and assistance of this good Indian, it would have been impossible for them to leave that country.

Other Spaniards who did not know how to work in iron or wood, they used for other things equally necessary, such as seeking food for all of them. These made special efforts to kill fish in the Río Grande, because it was Lent and they needed them. They made large and small hooks for the fishing, some of them managing to do it so skillfully and delicately that they seemed to have been engaged in this all their lives. They threw them into the water during the first night watch, baited and attached to long packthreads, and when they examined them in the morning they found extremely large fish caught on them.

There was one fish thus caught on a hook whose head alone weighed forty pounds, of sixteen ounces to each [pound]. With the industry of the fishermen, who on most days caught an excess of fish, and with the abundance of maize, vegetables, and dried fruit that the Spaniards found in the two pueblos called Aminoya, they had plenty of food during all the time they were in that province, and they even had enough left over to take away later in the brigantines.

While the work on the caravels was proceeding, Quigualtanqui and the other curacas of the neighborhood were not idle. Each one of them separately mustered all the warriors he could in his own country so that they would be able to assemble between them thirty or forty thousand fighting men to make a surprise attack on the Spaniards. They hoped to kill them all or at least to burn all the supplies and equipment that they had prepared for the boats, so that they could not leave their country at that time. It seemed to them that later, by waging continuous warfare against them, they could wear them out gradually without any difficulty, because they saw already that there were few horses, which were their principal strength, and the men were now so few that they had been informed that two-thirds of those who had entered La Florida were gone. And they knew that their captain-general Hernando de Soto, who was worth all of them, was now dead. This information increased their desire to carry out their evil intentions, and they awaited only the day they had set for their treason.

This day must already have been near, because some of the Indians who were accustomed to bring the presents and false messages from the curacas, on meeting alone some Indian women who were servants of Captains Arias Tinoco and Alonso Romo de Cardeñosa, said to them: "Be patient, sisters, and rejoice at the news that we are giving you. Very soon we shall rescue you from the captivity in which these thieving vagabonds are holding you, because you must know that we have planned to cut their throats and put their heads on every lance for the honor of our temples and burial places, and their bodies will be quartered and hung in the trees, for this is no more than they deserve." The Indian women immediately told their masters what these Indians had said to them.

Besides these signs, on clear nights the noise that the Indians made in various places was heard on the other side of the river, and many fires were visible, separated from one another. It was understood clearly that these were war parties that were assembling to carry out their treason.

For the time being God, our Lord, prevented this by a most excessive flood on the Río Grande. On those same days, which were about the eighth or tenth of March, a powerful flood of water began to come down. At first it began to cover some sand beaches that were between the channel of the river and its banks; soon it was rising slowly over them until they were completely submerged. Then it began to overflow into the fields very rapidly and copiously, and as the land was flat, without any hills, there was no impediment to prevent its inundation.

On the eighteenth of March 1543, which that year fell on Palm Sunday, as appears from the calculations [made] before the ten-day rectification of the calendar year [a reference to the Gregorian calendar]—while the Spaniards were marching in the procession they formed, in spite of all their labors, to celebrate the entrance of our Redeemer into Jerusalem, in accordance with the observances of the holy Roman church, our Mother and Lady—the river rose so furiously and with such a rush that it entered the gates of the pueblo of Aminoya, and two days thereafter one could not go through the streets except in canoes.

It was forty days before this rise reached its greatest height, which was on the twentieth of April. It was a most wonderful thing to see what had been woods and fields made into a sea, because the river extended over more than twenty leagues of country on either side of its banks, and all this expanse was navigated in canoes. Nothing could be seen except the new growth at the top of the tallest trees. Telling of the flood on the river, Alonso de Carmona says at this point: "And we remembered the good old woman who prophesied this flood to us." These are his own words.

XIII

THEY SEND A SPANISH CAPTAIN TO THE CURACA ANILCO FOR ASSISTANCE IN FINISHING THE BRIGANTINES

Because of such inundations this Río Grande and others that we have named in our *History* occasion with their floods, the Indians endeavor to settle on high places where there are hills, and where there are none they make them artificially, principally for the houses of their lords, both out of respect for their rank and so that they may not be inundated. They build the private houses three or four estados up from the ground mounted on thick beams that serve as pillars. These are joined together by other, crosswise beams that form the ground floor. Above this wooden foundation they erect the dwelling with its balconies on all four sides where they put their food and other valuables, and there they take refuge during the great floods.[42] These do not occur every year, but depend upon the amount of snow in the previous winter, and rain in the following summer in the regions where the rivers have their sources. Thus the flood of that year 1543 was very great because of the large amounts of snow that we said had fallen during the previous winter, if it were not, as the old woman said, that the floods came every fourteen years. This can be ascertained when the land is conquered, as I expect it to be.

During the overflow of the river it was necessary to send out a squadron of twenty soldiers who went in four canoes, joined together two by two, for if they had gone singly, they might have been upset against the submerged trees that they might run against. The soldiers were to go to the pueblo of Anilco, which was twenty leagues from Aminoya, to ask for old blankets from which to make tow for caulking the brigantines, and for ropes for rigging, and for resin from trees for pitch. Although they had collected supplies of all these things they did not have enough to finish the work.

The twenty soldiers chose Gonzalo Silvestre to go with them as commander, both because he was a very good soldier and captain and because a few days before he had done a great service and favor for the curaca Anilco. This was that on the expedition that Governor Hernando de Soto made against the pueblo of Anilco in the preceding year, as we have said above, where the Indians of Guachoya committed such cruelties and burned the pueblo, Gonzalo Silvestre had captured a boy twelve or thirteen years old who happened to be the son of the cacique Anilco himself. He had taken him with him over the whole route that the Spaniards had traveled to the country that we call that of the Vaqueros, and had brought him back to the province of Aminoya where they then were. Of the five Indian servants whom he had taken with him on that journey, this boy alone remained, having escaped the recent illness. When the Spaniards returned to the Río Grande the curaca Anilco had made inquiries about his son, and learning that he was alive, being a friend of the Spaniards, he asked for him. Because of the many favors that the cacique had done them, Gonzalo Silvestre had given him up very willingly, though the boy, like a boy, had refused to go

[42]This singular passage describing houses built on stilt pilings in the Mississippi Valley has been used to interpret certain archaeologically discovered post hole patterns in the same area and belonging to the Late Mississippian period. John M. Connaway, *The Wilsford Site (22-Co-516), Coahoma County, Mississippi: A Late Mississippi Period Settlement in the Northern Yazoo Basin of Mississippi.* Archaeological Report no. 14 (Jackson: Mississippi Department of Archives and History, 1984).

with his people when he was turned over to them, because he was now attached to the Spaniards.

Because of this service that Gonzalo Silvestre had done the curaca Anilco, the governor chose him [for this task], as it seemed to him that, having placed the curaca under obligations to him by the restitution of his son, he could obtain more favors from him than anyone else in the army.

Silvestre set out with the twenty men of his party, and they took some of Anilco's own Indians for guides and oarsmen. On reaching the pueblo, he found that it had become an island and that the inundation of the river had spread five or six leagues farther, so that at that place it had gone twenty-five leagues beyond its bed.

As soon as the cacique Anilco knew that the Castilians were in his pueblo and who their commander was and what he had come to ask, he ordered his captain-general Anilco to be summoned and said to him: "Captain, show the desire and willingness that we have to serve the Spaniards by ordering that they be entertained and feasted more than I myself would be, and by giving them the supplies that they request for the brigantines as readily as if they were for ourselves, because of the love that we have for all of them and the particular obligation under which this captain has placed us by the restoration of my son. Note that I confide this to your person rather than to my own because I know that you will attend to it better than I, as you do everything I entrust to you."

Having given this order, he had Gonzalo Silvestre summoned, and directed that none of his men come with him, because he said that, since he had not received them as friends the first time they had come to his country, he was so chagrinned and ashamed that he would feel all his life the regret and sorrow of that disgrace and reproach that he had brought upon himself, and that, because of this dereliction, he did not dare appear before the Spaniards.

He came out of his house to receive Gonzalo Silvestre and embraced him very affectionately, and took him to his apartment, being unwilling for him to leave it during all the time that the Castilians were in his pueblo. He enjoyed greatly talking with him and learning of the things that had happened to the Spaniards in that great kingdom, and which and how many provinces they had traveled through, and what battles they had fought, and many other things that they had experienced in that discovery. They entertained themselves in this manner during the days that Gonzalo Silvestre remained there, and the cacique's son, whom he had brought back to him, served as interpreter.

Among these conversations and others that they were accustomed to have, on one of the last days that Gonzalo Silvestre was with him the cacique said to him: "Well, Captain, neither Guachoya nor any of his people had ever had enough courage or boldness to set foot in any part of my state and seigniory, but he dared with the Castilians' protection to come to my pueblo and enter my own house, and pillage it shamelessly, with total lack of the respect that he ought to have had for me. He committed other insolences and cruelties upon the children and aged in such revenge as he had never hoped to take for his injuries. Not content with what he did to the living, he went on to insult the dead by taking the bodies of my parents and grandparents from their sepulchers and throwing them on the ground, dragging, trampling, and kicking the bones that I so revere. Finally, he dared to set fire to my pueblo and house, against the governor's will and that of all his Spaniards, for I am well informed about everything that happened then. I have no more to say about it except that you will leave this country, and we shall remain in it, and perhaps some day I shall even accounts for that lost game."

These are the very words that the cacique said to Gonzalo Silvestre, and he spoke them with all the feeling of outrage and anger that he could express. Thus it was understood why this curaca had shown and was showing such friendship for the Castilians; first because they had not been inclined to favor Guachoya against him, and second because, in order to avenge their insults, he desired that the Spaniards leave that country promptly. Therefore he had given and would give them so liberally the supplies that they requested for the brigantines, and thus he made every exertion and effort possible to grant their last petition, and soon gave them a supply of the blankets, ropes, and resin that they asked for in larger quantities than they had requested, or expected, for the Spaniards had been fearful when they came that through lack of the things they needed the cacique would be unable to give them enough.

Along with these supplies he gave them twenty canoes, and Indian warriors and servants and a captain to serve them and carry the baggage. On taking leave, he embraced Gonzalo Silvestre, and told him to make his excuses to the governor for not having gone in person to kiss his hands; and he said that, with regard to the league of Quigualtanqui and his confederates, he would advise him in time of what they were plotting against the Castilians. Gonzalo Silvestre returned to the governor with this message and gave him an account of what had happened to him on that journey.

XIV

EVENTS THAT TOOK PLACE DURING THE RISING AND RECEDING OF THE RÍO GRANDE, AND THE WARNING THAT ANILCO GAVE OF THE LEAGUE

During all the time that the flood in the Río Grande lasted, which was forty days, the Spaniards did not cease to carry on the work on the brigantines, though the water hindered them. But they went up into the large houses that we said they had built high above the ground, which they called dockyards, and there they labored with such dexterity and industry in all the crafts that they made even the charcoal for the forges inside those houses, in the wooden garrets overhead. They made it from branches that they cut from trees that stood up out of the water, as there was then no other wood, or firewood, all of it being under water. Those who aided most notably in these labors, not only as assistants, but as if they had been master workmen in iron work, carpentry, and caulking, were two gentlemen who were brothers, named Francisco Osorio and García Osorio, very close relatives of the house of Astorga. In Spain, Francisco Osorio was a lord of vassals.

Though they were of such high rank, they applied themselves to all this necessary labor with the same promptness, skill, and dexterity that they had always shown when it was necessary to fight, and their good example inspired all the other Spaniards, nobles or otherwise, to do the same, for work always inspires imitation more readily than giving orders.

As the inundation caused by the floodwaters of the Río Grande was so excessive, all the warriors whom the caciques of the league had raised against the Castilians were dispersed, because it was necessary and imperative for all of them to go to their pueblos and houses to arrange and put in a safe place everything that was in them. Thus for the time being our Lord prevented these Indians from carrying out their evil purpose, of killing the Spaniards or burning their boats. Though their men were dispersed, the curacas did not abandon their evil purpose, and to conceal it they continually sent messages of pretended friendship. The governor replied to them with all the dissimulation possible, leading them to believe that he was ignorant of their treachery. But with all this he did not cease to be cautious and watchful in all necessary matters, so that his enemies would not harm him.

At the end of April the river began to recede as slowly as it had risen, and even on the twentieth of May the Castilians could not walk through the pueblo except in their bare feet and bare-legged, because of the water and mud in the streets.

This going barefoot was one of the hardships that our Spaniards felt most of all among those that they endured on this discovery. For after the battle of Mauvila, where their extra clothing and footwear were burned, they were forced to go without shoes. Though it is true that they made some, they were of untanned leather and of deerskins, with soles of the same that became a shapeless mass as soon as they were wet. Though they might have used the abilities they showed in other, more important and difficult things in making hemp sandals such as the Spaniards in México and El Perú and other places make, they could not do so on this expedition to La Florida because they found no hemp or other material of which to make them. The same thing happened to them with regard to clothing, for as they found no blankets made of wool or cotton, they dressed in deerskin, and a single short garment served them as shirt, doublet, and coat. Since they had to march and cross rivers and work in the rain, having no woolen clothing to protect themselves from it, they were forced to go about almost continuously wet, and as we have seen they were often perishing of hunger, eating herbs and roots because they had nothing else. From the little that we have told in our *History* and shall tell before it is ended, any discerning person can infer the innumerable, and never sufficiently described or even half-told labors that the Spaniards endured in the discovery, conquest, and settlement of the New World, so profitless to themselves and their sons, for as one of the latter I can testify well to it.

At the end of May the river was back in its bed, having gathered up its waters, which had been so widely dispersed and extended over those lowlands. As soon as the country could be traversed, the caciques again called to the field the warriors whom they had made ready and went out with the determination of executing their enterprise and evil plans promptly. When the good captain-general Anilco learned of it he went to visit the governor, as was his custom, and on his own behalf and that of his cacique he secretly gave him a very detailed account of everything that Quigualtanqui and his allies had planned to the detriment of the Spaniards. He said that on a certain future day each curaca would send his ambassadors separately, and they would do this so that their league and treason would not be suspected, as it might be if they should all come together. As further proof that he was speaking the truth and knew the caciques' secret plans, he told what each ambassador would say on his mission and the gift and present he would bring in sign of friendship. Some would come in the morning, others at noon, and others in the evening, and these embassies would continue for four days. This was the time that the allied caciques had set and designated for assembling the last of the warriors and attacking the Spaniards. Their intention was to kill all of them, and if they could not accomplish this purpose, at least they would burn the boats so that they could not leave their country. They planned to exterminate them later at their leisure with the continuous warfare that they would wage against them.

General Anilco, after having told everything pertaining to the treason of the curacas, said: "Sir, my cacique and lord Anilco offers your lordship eight thousand warriors, chosen men and feared by all their neighbors, with whom your lordship can resist and attack your enemies, and I offer to come with them personally and [if need be] die in your service.

"My lord says also that, if your lordship desires to withdraw to his country, he offers it immediately for everything that may be conducive to your service, and he begs your lordship very affectionately to accept his friendship and his state and seigniory, and to make use of all of it as if it were your own. Your lordship may be assured that, if you go to the state of my lord Anilco, you will be safe from attacks by your enemies. Meanwhile your lordship can order that which seems best to you."

XV

THE PUNISHMENT THAT WAS GIVEN TO THE AMBASSADORS OF THE LEAGUE AND THE ACTIVITIES OF THE SPANIARDS UNTIL THEY EMBARKED

The governor, having heard the warning that the captain-general Anilco gave of the caciques' treachery, and the offers that he made him on behalf of his cacique and himself, thanked him earnestly for both and told him with very affectionate words that he would not accept the assistance of fighting men, in order that his curaca Anilco might not incur the hatred and enmity of the other curacas and Indians of the vicinity in the future because of having favored the Castilians so openly. Furthermore, because he was intending to leave so soon and go down the river, it was not necessary to make war against the enemy. For the same reasons he would not accept the good company of his person as captain-general, though he knew of his great bravery, and how important his support and assistance would be to the Spaniards if they had to overcome their enemies by fighting. Inasmuch as he must go, he did not wish to leave him hated by and at enmity with his neighbors, or that they should know anything about his having warned them against the league. For the same reason, and because for the time being it was not convenient for him to make an establishment in that kingdom, he refused to withdraw to his country. But although he could not take advantage of the offers that he and his cacique made him, at least he accepted the good intentions of both of them, to remember them and the obligation that their words and deeds had placed upon him and the whole Spanish nation. He would endeavor to repay it if the occasion should ever be offered him, and a report and memorial of it would be duly given to his lord the king of Castilla, who was emperor and chief of all the Christian kings, lords, and princes. He should know what they had done for his vassals and servants the Castilians, and he would order a memorandum to be made of it in writing for the gratification of his Majesty or the kings his descendants. He left his pledge and promise to them and their sons and successors as repayment for the benefits they had conferred upon them. With these words the governor took leave of Captain Anilco and was ready for what might come in the future, having consulted about it with his captains and principal soldiers.

Four days after the warning, which was at the beginning of June of the year 1543, the ambassadors of the caciques of the league arrived, in the same order and manner that Anilco had said, some in the morning, others at noon, and others in the evening. They brought the same verbal messages and the same gifts that Anilco had mentioned as a sign of their treason.

This being seen by the governor, he ordered that they be seized and each one put in a place by himself to be questioned about their league and conspiracy. When this was done the Indians did not deny it, but confessed very openly all the preparations they had made to kill the Spaniards and burn their boats.

So that the punishment that had to be inflicted upon the Indian ambassadors would not fall upon so many of them as would be the case if they should wait for all of them to arrive, the general ordered that it be carried out promptly upon those whom they had taken that day. They would give the word to the rest that their treachery was found out, and they would not send more ambassadors.

Their confessions having been taken, on the same day that they came they visited upon them the punishment for their caciques' wrongdoings. The reward for their embassy was to cut off the right hands of thirty of them.

They came up so patiently to receive the punishment that was given them that one severed hand was scarcely removed from the block when another was placed there to be cut off. This aroused the pity and compassion of those who saw it.

The punishment of the ambassadors broke up the league of their curacas, because they said that since the Castilians knew of their hostile plans they would be on guard and prepared so as not to be harmed. Thus each cacique returned to his own country, vexed at not having carried out his evil intentions. They kept these [intentions] in mind to show them again on some future occasion, and because they knew they were more powerful on the water than on land, they planned among themselves that each one would make ready as many men and canoes as he could to pursue the Spaniards when they should go down the river, where they were planning to kill them all.

Having seen that the great league and conspiracy that the curacas had formed against them was an actuality, the governor and his captains thought it would be well to leave their lands as soon as they could, before the enemy should form another, worse one. In this determination they hastened the work of completing the brigantines even more than before, though up to that time they had not been lazy.

Our Spaniards built seven little caravels, and since they did not have enough nails to cover them entirely, they covered one space at the stern and another at the prow on which they could place the ship-stores. They laid some loose planks across the center to make a deck, and by raising one of them up they could draw out the water that they might have taken in.

With the same industry that they had shown in building the boats, they collected the supplies they thought would be needed, asking the friendly caciques Anilco and Guachoya for stores of Indian corn and other grains and dried fruits that were in their country.

They butchered the hogs, which they had hitherto kept for breeding in spite of all their past hardships, and they still reserved eighteen of them, because they had not lost hopes of making a settlement near the sea if they should find a good situation. They gave three, two females and one male for breeding, to each of the friendly caciques. The meat of those that they killed was salted for the journey, and they used the lard in place of oil for softening the resin obtained from trees, so as to make it thin and liquid enough to run, it being used to pitch the brigantines.

They provided canoes to carry the horses that they had remaining, these being a few more than thirty. The canoes were fastened together by twos, so that the horses could be carried with their fore feet in one and their hind feet in the other. Besides the canoes for the horses, each brigantine carried one at the stern to serve as a ship's boat.

Alonso de Carmona says here that they killed twenty of the fifty horses that remained, these being the ones that were lame and most useless, and that in order to kill them they tied them one night to separate stakes and opened their veins, allowing them to bleed to death. This was done with much sadness on the part of their masters and to the grief of all of them because of the good service the horses had performed. The meat was parboiled and put in the sun to preserve it, and thus they kept it as ship-stores for their voyage. The things that we have told being finished, they launched the brigantines into the water on the day of the great precursor St. John the Baptist, and in the five days until the eve of [the day of] the princes of the church—St. Peter and St. Paul—they busied themselves in embarking the ship-stores and the horses, and in dressing the brigantines and the canoes with boards and skins of animals as a defense against arrows. Two days before they embarked, they took leave of the cacique Guachoya and the captain-general Anilco so that they could go to their own countries; they begged them to be true friends, and they promised that they would be. Then on the same day of the Apostles they embarked, having ordered to go as captains of the seven brigantines those whom we shall name in the following book and chapter.

Sixth Book of the History of La Florida, by the Inca

It contains the election of the Captains for the voyage; the multitude of canoes that opposed the Spaniards; the order and manner of their fighting, which lasted eleven days without ceasing; the death of forty-eight Castilians because of the rashness of one of them; the return of the Indians to their homes; the arrival of the Spaniards at the Sea; an encounter they had with the people of the coast; the events of their fifty-five days of navigation until they reached Pánuco; the many quarrels that they had there among themselves, and the reason for them; the good reception that the imperial City of México gave them; and how they were scattered through various parts of the World. It contains twenty-two chapters.

I

THEY CHOOSE CAPTAINS FOR THEIR CARAVELS, AND THE SPANIARDS EMBARK ON THEIR VOYAGE

Luis de Moscoso de Alvarado embarked on the caravel that served as flagship, being governor and captain-general of them all, as he was on land. Juan de Alvarado and Cristóbal Mosquera, the governor's brothers, were captains of the vice-admiral. They called these two brigantines or caravels by the names of flagship and vice-admiral; the others they called simply the third, fourth, fifth, sixth, and seventh. The accountant Juan de Añasco and the factor Biedma were captains of the third caravel. Captain Juan de Guzmán and the treasurer Juan Gaytán were captains of the fourth brigantine; Captains Arias Tinoco and Alonso Romo de Cardeñosa, of the fifth. Pedro Calderón and Francisco Osorio were captains of the sixth brigantine. Juan de Vega, a native of Badajoz who has been mentioned on other occasions, and García Osorio embarked in the seventh and last caravel as its captains. All these gentlemen were of noble blood and famous for their exploits, and had conducted themselves accordingly in the incidents of this journey and discovery. Two captains were named for each brigantine so that, when one might go ashore for some purpose, the other could remain in the caravel to manage it.

Under the command and direction of the captains just named, there embarked with them 350 Spaniards, rather less than more, nearly a thousand having entered that land. As many as twenty-five or thirty Indians, men and women, embarked with them, having been brought in their service from distant countries. They alone had escaped from the sickness and death that they had experienced during the past winter. All the rest of the more than eight hundred had died, and these thirty embarked and went with the Spaniards because they did not wish to stay with Guachoya or Anilco, because of the love they had for their masters. They said they preferred dying with them to living in foreign lands, and the Spaniards did not force them to remain, for it seemed very ungrateful and not in accordance with the love the Indians showed for them, as well as a great cruelty to abandon them so far from their homes.

On the same day of the Apostles—a day of such solemnity and gladness for all Christendom, though sad and lamentable for these Castilians because of the momentous thing that they did on it, which was to abandon and give up for lost all the fruits of the many labors that they had undergone in that land, and the reward and recompense for the great exploits that they had performed—they set sail, at sunset. They navigated by sail and oar all that night and the following day and night without any molestation from the enemy.

Each brigantine had seven oars to a side, with which all those who were in the boat rowed by turns for their assigned time, without excepting anyone unless it were the captains. The distance by the river that our Spaniards navigated during the two nights and the day was understood to coincide with the district and limits of the province of Guachoya, which as we mentioned above extended down the river. Inasmuch as Guachoya had shown himself to be a friend of the Spaniards, the Indians had not wished to attack them while they were traveling within his territory. Or perhaps it was due to some superstition and observance connected with the crescent or waning moon, which was near its conjunction, such as the Germans had, as Julius Caesar writes in his *Commentaries.* The exact reason they did not pursue them those first two nights and day is not known.

But on the second day there arrived at dawn a most handsome fleet of more than a thousand canoes, which the curacas of the league had assembled against the Spaniards. Because those of this Río Grande were the largest and finest that our people saw in the whole of La Florida, it will be well to give here a particular description of them, since from now on we shall have battles on the water to describe, rather than those on land.

II

DIFFERENT KINDS OF RAFTS THAT THE INDIANS MADE FOR CROSSING RIVERS

In the language of the Indians of the island of Española and its vicinity a *canoa*[43] is the same thing as a bark or small caravel without a deck. They call them all by the same name unless it is in the Río Grande of Cartagena, where, because they are larger, they call them pirogues. The Indians of every part of the New World, particularly in the islands and maritime countries, make them large or small according to the materials they have at hand. They

[43]From the Arawakan word *canoa,* borrowed by the Spaniards, comes the English "canoe."

seek the thickest trees they can find, shape them like a trough, and make them all in one piece, because their invention does not extend to making a boat with planks nailed to its ribs, one above the other. Neither do they have iron, nor know how to make nails; much less do they have forges, or understand caulking, or seeking pitch or tow, or making sails, rigging, cables, anchors, and the many other things that are necessary for the construction of ships. They only make use of what nature (in the things their own ingenuity does not attain) points out to them with her finger. Thus for crossing rivers and navigating the sea, the little that they do navigate it, where they do not find timber as large as is required for canoes (that is, throughout El Perú and its coast), they make rafts of a light wood similar to that of fig trees, which the Indians say grows in the provinces near Quito. They take it from there by order of the Incas to all the large rivers of El Perú, and they make the rafts of five logs joined together. The log in the center is longer than the others, the first two on either side are somewhat shorter, and the second two shorter still, for they can go through the water better thus than with the front [of the raft] entirely even. I crossed on some of them that were still in use from the time of the Incas.

They also make them of a thick bundle of reeds as large as the body of a horse, the bundle being tied very firmly and tapered to a sharp point projecting upward in front like the prow of a bark, so that it will cut the water. In the back it has a breadth of two tercias. On the upper part of the bundle of reeds they make a flat space or small platform where they put the cargo or the man who is to cross over the river. They charge him very strictly that he is by no means to move from the position in which they place him on the raft, secured by its fastenings, nor to raise his head from where it is placed face down on the raft, nor even to open his eyes to look at anything.

Once when I was crossing a large and swift river in this manner (it is on such rivers that the Indians caution their passengers as told above, rather than on the small and gently flowing streams, with which they do not concern themselves), because of the excessive warnings that the Indian boatman gave me not to open my eyes—for I being a boy he tried to make me fear that the earth would sink in or the heavens fall—I had an irresistible desire to look and see whether I could catch sight of some enchantment or something from the other life, and thus when I felt that we were in the middle of the river I raised my head a little and looked up at the water. And indeed it seemed to me that we were falling down from the sky, which was because of giddiness caused by the exceedingly swift current of the river and because of the fury with which the raft was cutting through the water, going with the current. It forced me to close my eyes and confess that the Indians are right in ordering that they shall not be opened. Only one Indian goes on each of these reed rafts. In order to navigate it, he bestrides the extreme end of the stern and, throwing himself on his chest on the raft, he paddles with both hands and feet and guides the raft along with the current until he puts it across the river. In other places they make rafts of matted calabashes fastened together until they form a flat surface a vara and a half square, more or less. In front they fasten a sort of breast-strap like that on a horse's saddle through which the Indian boatman puts his head and begins to swim, carrying the raft and its cargo above him until he crosses the river, bay, creek, or arm of the sea. If necessary he has one or two Indians go behind to help him, who swim and push the raft.

In other places where the rivers do not permit navigation because of their strong and furious currents, and where there are no places to embark and disembark because of the many rocks and cliffs and the absence of beaches, they run a thick cable from one side of the river to the other and fasten it to large trees or strong projecting rocks. A large basket with a wooden handle the size of one's arm runs back and forth on this cable. It has a capacity of three or four persons and carries two ropes, one on either side. They pull the basket with these to draw it from one side of the river to the other. As the cable is long and has a large curve or drop in the center, it is necessary to release the basket a little at a time, lowering it to the middle of the cable, and then to pull it up by main strength along the other half from the other side. There are Indians for this purpose, whose business it is to take travelers across, and those who go in the basket help lower and raise it by catching hold of the cable. I remember having crossed by this means two or three times, as a boy less than ten years old, and on the roads the Indians carried me on their backs. The Indians take their cattle across by this method, with much labor, for they hobble them and put them into the basket. They do the same with the smaller animals from Spain, such as sheep, goats, and hogs, but the large animals, such as horses, mules, asses, and cows, because of their strength and weight, are not carried in the baskets. They take them over other crossings such as bridges or fords. This method of crossing by the cable and basket is only for people on foot, and it is not found on the main highways, but on the private ones that the Indians have between their pueblos.

These are the methods of crossing rivers that the Indians have in El Perú, in addition to the bridges that they make of willows and reeds or rushes, as we shall tell in the appropriate place, if God is pleased to give us life.

But throughout the land of La Florida that our Spaniards traversed, because of the great abundance of large trees there suitable for canoes, the Indians do not use any other means of crossing the rivers except these, though as we have seen the Spaniards made rafts at certain places.

III

THE SIZE OF THE CANOES AND THE OSTENTATION AND ORDER THE INDIANS OBSERVED WITH THEM

Returning, then, to the subject of our *History*, we said that among the many canoes that were found to be following the Spaniards at dawn on the second day of their navigation, some extraordinarily large ones were seen that caused amazement. Those that were flagships and others similar to them were so large that they had as many as twenty-five oars per side, and in addition to the oarsmen, they carried twenty-five or thirty warriors, stationed in their order from bow to stern. Thus there were many canoes with a capacity of seventy-five or eighty men, who went in them placed in such manner that they could all fight without getting in one another's way. The oarsmen also took their bows and arrows in the canoes for munitions. These [canoes], even though so large, are made in a single piece, and it is to be noted that there are such fine trees in that country.

From these largest ones that we have mentioned, the size of the canoes diminished down to the small ones that had fourteen oars to a side, there being none in this fleet smaller than these. The oars usually are a fathom long, rather more than less, and the blades of the oars are three handbreadths long and a tercia in width. They are made all in one piece and are so smooth and highly polished that even horsemen's lances could not be more so. When one of these canoes goes with all hands rowing hard it is so swift that a horse running full speed hardly has the advantage of it.

For rowing evenly and in time, those Indians have made up various songs with different tunes, quick or slow, according to their speed or slowness in rowing. The themes of these songs are the exploits their ancestors or other foreign captains have performed in war, with whose memory and recollection they are incited to battle and to triumph and victory therein.

There is another remarkable and unusual peculiarity to tell concerning the canoes that were flagships of this fleet and those which belonged to the rich and powerful men. This is that each one individually was painted inside and out, even to the oars, with a single color, as for example blue, or yellow, white, red, green, rose, violet, black, or some other color, if there are any more than those mentioned. This was in accordance with the blazon or the fancy of the captain or curaca or rich and powerful man to whom the canoe belonged. Not only the canoes, but also the oarsmen and their oars, and the soldiers, down to the plumes and the skeins of thread that they wore wound about their foreheads as a headdress, and even their bows and arrows, were all tinted with this one color, without the admixture of any other. Even bands of horsemen who intended to take part in a tournament with reed spears could not have come out more meticulously arrayed than these Indians came in their canoes. As they came in such numbers and with so many different colors, and maintained such good order and arrangement, and as the river was very wide and they could spread out in every direction without disturbing their order, they presented a most beautiful sight to the eye.

In this grand and imposing manner the Indians followed the Spaniards on the second day until noon, without molesting them in any way, so that they could thus see and enjoy better the sight of their handsome and powerful fleet. They followed behind them rowing to the sound of their songs, and among other things that they said (according to the interpretation of the Indians whom the Spaniards had with them) was to praise and aggrandize their own strength and bravery and to condemn the weakness and cowardice of the Castilians. They said that now the cowards were fleeing from their arms and forces, and that the thieves feared their justice, and that it would do them no good to flee from the country, for all of them would soon die in the water; and that, if they would soon be food for birds and dogs on land, in the river they would make them food for the fishes and marine animals, and thus their iniquities and the vexation that they were giving the whole world would be ended. They came saying these and other similar things, and they rowed to the sound of them. At the end of every song they raised a great shout and outcry.

IV

THE MANNER IN WHICH THE INDIANS FOUGHT THE SPANIARDS WHILE DESCENDING THE RIVER

The Indians, having examined the Spaniards' fleet, small in number but great in quality and force, followed it until noon without molesting it in any way; after that hour the canoes divided into three equal parts, forming a vanguard, a center, and a rear guard. Among those in advance in the first party went the canoes of the curaca Quigualtanqui, captain-general of the leagues of the caciques on water and on land. It was not known for certain whether he himself came in one of them, but in the songs they sang and in the other shouts they gave the Indians called out his name very distinctly.

The canoes, divided into three groups, all followed the right bank of the river, going downstream. Those in the vanguard, forming a long and narrow squadron, advanced upon the Castilians' caravels, not for the purpose of attacking them, but in order to pass in front of them, leaving them to their left, so as to be able to discharge arrows at them more advantageously. Thus they crossed the river obliquely from one bank to the other and sent a shower of arrows upon the caravels, in such quantities that the boats were covered with them from top to bottom, and many Spaniards were wounded, the oblong and round shields they carried proving to afford them little protection.

The first canoes, having passed and reached the left bank of the river, immediately went ahead to the right to resume their former position. Meanwhile the canoes of the second division engaged the brigantines in the same order that the first ones had done, and having discharged their arrows and reached the left bank, they immediately returned to the right and took up their position ahead of the first canoes.

The canoes of the second squadron had scarcely finished passing by the brigantines when those of the third attacked in the same manner and order as the others. After discharging another shower of arrows, they went back to the right bank and placed themselves in front of the second squadron.

As the caravels did not cease navigating (though the Indians were molesting them), they now reached the place where the first canoes were. The latter, seeing them in a good position, attacked them a second time, repeating their first performance; then the second and third divisions did the same thing, always returning to their position at the right bank after discharging their arrows.

In this manner, as if in a very well-executed tournament with reed spears, advancing to discharge their arrows and then falling back to their positions, the Indians pursued the Castilians that whole day, not allowing them to rest a moment. At night they did the same, though not as continuously as during the day, for they contented themselves with making only two assaults, one during the first watch and the other just before dawn.

When the Indians first attacked them, the Spaniards, notwithstanding that they had the canoes that were carrying the horses fastened behind [their boats], stationed men in them to defend them, believing that the fighting would be hand to hand. Seeing, however, that they could do no good because the enemy would not come within reach of their swords but wounded them with arrows from a distance, and seeing that the Christians who were in the canoes were being badly injured because of their exposed position, they took them back into the brigantines, leaving the horses with the poor defense of the large shields and the shelters they had made for them with the skins of animals.

This same battle and strife the Indians had with the Spaniards on the first day and night proceeded continuously for ten days and nights with no change or innovation whatever. We shall not write of them in detail in order to avoid tediousness, and also because nothing extraordinary took place other than the things described in connection with the first day. It must be told only that during this time they killed almost all the horses with arrows, no more than eight remaining, which happened to be better protected.

Though all of them were wounded, not one escaping, the Spaniards defended themselves from the Indians with their oblong and round shields, and fired upon them with some crossbows they carried. They had used up all the harquebuses in making nails for the brigantines, because aside from the fact that their need of iron forced them to do so, they had been of little use throughout this expedition and discovery because of the little practice and experience that our harquebusiers then had. To this were added the poor facilities they had for making powder after the battle of Mauvila, because the supply they had brought was burned there. For these reasons the Indians not only had not feared the harquebuses but were contemptuous and made fun of them. Therefore our people did not bring them.

V

WHAT HAPPENED ON THE ELEVENTH DAY OF THE SPANIARDS' NAVIGATION

After the ten days of continuous warfare and fighting that the Indians had with the Spaniards, they desisted from it and withdrew their canoes a little more than half a league from the brigantines. Our people passed on, proceeding with their voyage, and saw near the riverbank a small pueblo of some eighty houses. As it appeared that the Indians had now left them and that they ought already to be near the sea, because they believed that they had traveled more than two hundred leagues during those days, as they had always navigated with both sails and oars (though contending with the enemy) and the river made no turns that would have detained them, they thus desired to provide themselves with food for the sea voyage. Word was sent to all the brigantines that all those who wished to go to the pueblo for maize should go with the commander who had been chosen.

A hundred soldiers went ashore and took the eight horses that remained so that they might rest and recover themselves and be ready for fighting if the necessity arose.

The Indians of the pueblo, seeing that the Spaniards were coming to it, abandoned it and raised the alarm, calling for help with many shouts and outcries and fleeing through the fields. Our men reached the houses after a hasty march. They were about two harquebus-shots from the river, and they found in them much maize, an abundance of several kinds of dried fruit, a large quantity of white deerskins and also some tinted in all colors, and many mantles made of different kinds of skins very well dressed. Among the latter they found a strip of extremely fine marten-skins eight varas long and four tercias wide. It was folded crosswise, making it double-faced and about the width of silk. It was decorated all over at intervals with strings of pearls and seed pearls, each one a separate tuft made like a tassel and placed in a regular design. It was believed to be a standard or some insignia used in their festivals, celebrations, and dances, because it was not suitable for personal adornment nor for a bed or a dwelling. Gonzalo Silvestre took this piece, he being the commander of those who went ashore, and with it and all the maize, fruit, and deerskins that they could carry on their backs they hurriedly returned to the brigantines, from which the trumpets had been summoning them very insistently. At the shout raised by the Indians of the pueblo, calling for help, both those in the canoes and those in the fields had come running to their assistance, and as there were few of them ashore, many had come from the canoes to join them and strengthen their forces and spirits for the battle.

Thus the enemy came up with great impetus and ferocity, by water and by land, to defend the pueblo and attack the Spaniards. The latter embarked in their canoes as hastily as they had gone ashore, and in their hurry to reach the brigantines they were forced to abandon the horses, because the swiftness and fury of the Indians made it impossible to embark them without all of them being cut off and killed. They were in such danger that, if the Indians on the river or on the shore had advanced a hundred paces more, none of them would have been able to embark in the brigantines, but God succored them and saved them from death that day.

Seeing that the Spaniards had reached safety, the enemy turned their fury against the horses they had left on land. Taking off their headstalls and halters so that they would not prevent their running, and the saddles so that they would not protect them from arrows, they turned them into the fields and then, as if they were deer, they shot arrows at them until they saw that they were down, with extreme joy and satisfaction.

Thus on this day the last of the horses perished that had entered La Florida for its discovery and conquest. They had numbered 350, and on none of the expeditions that have been made to the New World up to the present have so many and such good horses been seen together.

On seeing their horses killed when they were unable to help them, the Castilians felt the greatest grief and wept for them as if they had been their children. But seeing themselves saved from a similar fate, they gave thanks to God and proceeded on their voyage. This happened on the twelfth day of their navigation.

VI

THE INDIANS ALMOST CAPTURE A CARAVEL, AND THE MAD ACTION OF A RECKLESS SPANIARD

The Indians, having found out that however they might pursue the Spaniards they did not accomplish what they desired, which was to kill all of them, but on the contrary caused them to navigate in better order and concert, without separating from one another, made use of a stratagem of war. This was that they drew off from the brigantines or caravels in the hope that they would become careless and separate from each other, thus giving an opportunity of destroying them when they were divided. With this scheme they stayed upstream, letting it be understood that they were leaving the caravels alone; the latter were then sailing with a favorable wind. Proceeding thus with their voyage, one of them separated from the others, without any reason whatsoever, and fell out of the order in which all of them were sailing, remaining less than a hundred paces behind.

The Indians, seeing that their strategy and cunning were not without result, did not want to lose the occasion that was offered them, and thus they advanced swiftly upon the caravel from all directions and came alongside to subdue and capture it by main force.

The other six that were going on ahead, on noting the carelessness of their companion, lowered their sails and rowed back as fast as possible to its aid. Though the distance was short, since it was against the current of the river they ascended with much difficulty and labor, and when they reached the brigantine they found the Castilians who were in it so hard-pressed by this deluge of Indians that had fallen upon them that they were defending themselves with their swords. They could not get to all the places where they were needed, by which the enemies were entering the caravel. Some of them were already in it and many others had hold of it, but upon the arrival of our men they withdrew to a distance, taking with them the canoe that was fastened to the caravel's stern, containing five of the pigs they had reserved for breeding if they should make a settlement somewhere. This is what happened on the thirteenth day of the Spaniards' navigation. Attributing it to the mercy of God that they had not lost the caravel, they gathered themselves together and cautioned one another anew that all of them be careful not to fall behind or get out of order, so as not to incur another such attack and danger. Thus they navigated two more days, and the Indians always came less than a quarter of a league behind them, waiting for our people to commit some other imprudence in order to take advantage of it.

Our Spaniards navigated very cautiously and vigilantly, seeing how alert the Indians were not to lose an occasion for attacking them. But all the care they took was not enough, because on the sixteenth day of their voyage a misfortune and loss took place that caused much grief and sadness. It was even more lamentable in that the cause was foolish and absurd and not occasioned by any danger that forced or impelled them to risk the lives of forty-eight of the best and bravest men in the fleet, who were lost [on this occasion]. But there is no authority that can prevent the foolish actions of a reckless person, because a madman can destroy more than what a hundred sensible ones can build up. So that the misfortune of our people may be better understood, permit me to tell it fully as it happened, and to tell who was the cause of so much trouble and damage.

Among the Spaniards in this fleet there was one named Esteban Añez, a rustic who was a native of Villanueva de Barcarrota. He had brought to La Florida a horse that though of crude proportions was strong and stout, for which reason, or more probably because no arrows struck him in a vital spot, he had served until the end of the expedition and was one of the few that the Castilians embarked in the brigantines for the voyage of which we are telling.

Inasmuch as Esteban Añez, then, had always traveled on horseback and had taken part in many of their past dangers, though he had done nothing notable in the course of them, he had won and maintained a reputation for bravery. With this, helped along by his rustic and ordinary nature, he had become presumptuous and foolish. As proof of his madness he left his caravel and got into the canoe that it carried at the stern, saying that he was going to talk to the governor, who was ahead. Five other Spaniards went with him, whom he had deceived by telling that all six of them were to perform an exploit that would be the most famous and notable of all those that had taken place on the whole discovery. They were easily persuaded because they were all young, and among them was a gentleman twenty years old, a natural son of Don Carlos Enríquez, who died in the battle of Mauvila. He had the same name as his father and was of as graceful person and handsome face as it was possible for a human being to be. Even at this early age he had shown himself both in skill with arms and in the virtues of his life and habits to be a worthy son of such a father. Ambitious to win the honor that Esteban Añez promised them, this gentleman and four others entered the canoe, and under pretext of going to talk with the governor they left the caravel. When they were at a distance from it they charged toward the Indians, shouting loudly: "Toward them, for they are fleeing!"

The governor and the other captains of the caravels, on seeing the foolish thing that these six Spaniards were doing, hastily ordered the trumpeters to sound the assembly and shouted and made signs to them to watch out for the danger into which they were going, telling them to return to their caravel. But the more our men shouted to him the more Esteban Añez persisted in his rash madness and refused to come back. On the other hand he signaled for all the caravels to follow him.

Seeing this madman's disobedience, the governor ordered that thirty or forty Spaniards go after him in the canoes that the brigantines carried at their sterns, with the determination to order him hanged as soon as they should bring him back. But it would have been better to have left him to the Indians for punishment, who would have cured his madness, as they did, and not to send many others to their deaths to be lost for one who was lost already.

VII

THE INDIANS KILL FORTY-EIGHT SPANIARDS BECAUSE OF THE IMPRUDENCE OF ONE OF THEM

In response to the governor's commands, forty-six Spaniards quickly jumped into their canoes to bring back Esteban Añez. One of them was Captain Juan de Guzmán, who was very fond of going in a canoe and managing it himself. Although all the soldiers in his caravel begged him to stay, he would not consent to do so but was angered by their importunities, especially by those of Gonzalo Silvestre, who, as his best friend, was the one who most opposed his going and offered to go in his place. He replied angrily, saying: "You have always opposed and now oppose my liking for traveling by canoe, prophesying some misfortune for me in doing so. Well, for that [reason] only I must go, and you are to stay, for I do not wish you to go with me." So saying, he jumped into the canoe, and another gentleman from Badajoz, named Juan de Vega, the first cousin of the Juan de Vega who was captain of one of the caravels, and a great friend of Juan de Guzmán, followed him.

The Indians had constantly followed the caravels with their canoes formed into a squadron, there being so many of them that they covered the river from one bank to the other, and for a quarter of a league back the water could not be seen. Seeing the first canoe of Esteban Añez, which was going toward them, and the three that followed behind it, they did not go on from where they were, but on the contrary they all rowed backward very smoothly and in good order so as to separate the Spanish canoes from their brigantines. The latter having lowered their sails, they struggled with their oars very laboriously, as they were going against the current, to reach their canoes in order to assist them.

Esteban Añez, blind in his recklessness, on seeing the Indians rowing backward, instead of becoming cautious was made even more daring and pushed on in his canoe to overtake the enemy. He shouted louder than ever, saying : "They are fleeing, they are fleeing, toward them, for they are fleeing!" He thus obliged the other three canoes that were coming after him to hurry more in order to detain or assist him if they could.

Seeing the Castilians near them, the enemy parted their squadron in the form of a new moon, always rowing backward, to induce and make way for the Christians to enter and get between them. When they saw that they were now so far in that they could not withdraw again even if they wished to do so, the canoes on the right wing closed in and attacked the four of the Christians with such impetus and fury that, taking them broadside, they capsized them and threw everyone in them into the water. As such a multitude of canoes was passing over them all the Spaniards were drowned, and if one happened to appear swimming they killed him with arrows and blows on the head with the oars.

In this manner, forty-eight of the Spaniards who had gone in the four canoes perished miserably that day without being able to make any defense; of the fifty-two who went, only four escaped. One was Pedro Morón, a mestizo and a native of the island of Cuba, whom we mentioned above, and an expert swimmer and very skillful in rowing and managing a canoe, as a person who was born and bred in them. Though he had fallen into the water, his skill and strength enabled him to recover his canoe and escape in it, taking with him three others, among them a most valiant soldier named Alvaro Nieto (of whom we said at the beginning of the expedition that he was on the point of killing the interpreter Juan Ortiz by mistake, having gone for him to the pueblo of Mucoço with Captain Baltasar de Gallegos). Finding himself in his present danger, like the good soldier that he was he fought alone in his canoe (after a manner of speaking) against the whole Indian fleet, in imitation of the famous Horatio at the bridge and of the valiant centurion Sceva in Dirachio, and detained the enemy while Pedro Morón managed the canoe, to bring it to safety. But the strength and valor of the one and the diligence and skill of the others would have availed them nothing if they had not found near them the caravel of the brave Captain Juan de Guzmán. Inasmuch as its captain had gone to the skirmish, this boat had made greater efforts in rowing than the rest in order to assist him if they could, because of his soldiers' affection for him. Thus it went in advance of all the others and was able to rescue and save the lives of the two valiant companions Pedro Morón and Alvaro Nieto, who had many wounds, though they were not mortal, and they saved two other Spaniards with them.

That caravel also picked up poor Juan Terrón, concerning whom was told above the story of his contempt for the fine pearls he was carrying. He managed to reach the caravel by swimming, but he expired by the side of it before he could get aboard in the arms of those who had given him their hands to lift him up. He had more than fifty arrows driven into his head, face, neck, shoulders, and back.

Juan Coles says that almost sixty men took part in this disastrous exploit and died therein along with Captain Juan de Guzmán, and that he himself was in one of the three canoes. He says that it was forty-odd feet in length and more than four feet across, and he says that he escaped with two arrow wounds that passed through the coat of mail he was wearing. All these are his own words.

This was the sad and costly result, for him and his companions, of the vain arrogance and presumption of Esteban Añez, who considered himself a brave man. It caused the useless and unfortunate death of forty-eight Spaniards who were better than he, most of them being nobles and in fact braver men than he was, and being such they had offered to succor a madman.

The governor gathered up his caravels as best he could and, placing them in order, resumed his voyage, much grieved over the loss of his men.

All the most notable events that we have told about the navigation of these seven brigantines Alonso de Carmona mentions in his *Peregrination.* He speaks particularly of the danger that we mentioned of one of the brigantines being lost; and adds that the Indians had gained everything up to the deck at the stern, and that on driving them away from the brigantine with the reinforcements, they stabbed thirty of them to death, and that the rest jumped into the water and were picked up by the canoes. He tells how they abandoned the horses because of their haste in embarking. He recounts the death of Captain Juan de Guzmán and that of Juan Terrón, saying that it occurred aboard the caravel, though he does not name him. He says, finally, that [the Indians] followed them until they reached the sea.

I am glad to present these two eyewitnesses whenever they give me occasion to do so in their accounts, because they took part in this same expedition. Each one tells in his account little more than what I have said and shall say about them, because they wrote very briefly concerning only the most notable things that they experienced and could remember, and thus in all the many instances that I do not mention them it is because they have not a word to say.

VIII

THE INDIANS RETURN TO THEIR HOMES AND THE SPANIARDS NAVIGATE UNTIL THEY COME IN SIGHT OF THE SEA

After this good stroke that they delivered to their own advantage, which was on the sixteenth day of the Spaniards' navigation, the Indians followed them all that day and the next night, constantly shouting and clamoring at them as if triumphing over them because of their victorious exploit. On the seventeenth day, when the sun rose, they worshiped it with a solemn salutation consisting of a great shouting and outcry and the music of trumpets, drums, fifes, shells, and other noise-making instruments. Having given thanks to the Sun as their god for the victory that they had won over their enemies, they withdrew and returned to their own country, as it seemed to them that they had gone very far away from it. It was believed that they had followed and pursued our Spaniards four hundred leagues down the river with the continuous fighting and assaults that they gave them day and night. In their songs and at other times and in their shouts and outcries, they always called the name of their captain-general Quigualtanqui and never of any other cacique, as if they were saying that that great prince was the only one who was waging all that war. Therefore when the Spaniards afterward reached México and made a report to Don Antonio de Mendoza, who was then viceroy of that kingdom, and to his son Don Francisco de Mendoza, who was afterward generalissimo of the Spanish galleys, giving them an account of the events of this unhappy discovery, and particularly when they told of the perils through which they had passed on this Río Grande and the terrible persecution that his people had given them in the name of that famous Indian, Don Francisco de Mendoza always said to them jokingly, though sententiously, during these conversations and elsewhere, whenever he happened to meet any captain or soldier of importance: "Truly, gentlemen, Quigualtanqui must have been quite a man." This saying recalled anew this Indian's exploits and perpetuated his name.

When they saw that the Indians had left them, our Spaniards understood that they were already near the sea and that this was the reason the Indians had withdrawn and returned to their homes. At that place the river was now so wide that, from its center, land could not be seen on either side. Only some very tall rushes were visible, which resembled forests of large trees and in fact were so.

At that place the river was more than fifteen leagues wide, as well as could be judged from the sight of it, and for all this our men did not dare approach its banks or leave the center of the channel for fear of striking some marshes or sandbanks where they might be lost. They did not know whether they were now in the sea or whether they were still sailing on the river.

They navigated in this uncertainty for three days with sail and oar, having a favorable wind, these being the seventeenth, eighteenth, and nineteenth days of their navigation. At dawn on the twentieth day they saw clearly that they were at sea. On their left as they went they saw extremely large amounts of driftwood, which the river carried to the sea with its floods. It was heaped up in such a manner that it looked like a large island.

Half a league beyond the driftwood was an uninhabited island, which our people judged would be the one that large rivers ordinarily form when they enter the sea, and this proved that they were now in it. Since they did not know what place it was or how far it might be from there to a Christian country, they decided to inspect their brigantines or caravels before entering the sea. Thus they busied themselves with unloading them, and put their cargoes on the driftwood island, in order to careen them if it were necessary or to examine the seams to see whether they needed repairs. They also butchered nine or ten hogs that were still alive. They spent three days doing these things, though it is true that they spent them more in resting from their past hardships and gaining vigor and strength for the future than in working on the caravels, because there was very little to do to them. Our Castilians' greatest need was for sleep, for because of the continuous vigil that the Indians had forced them to keep day and night they were overcome with drowsiness, and thus they slept during those three days like dead men.

It is impossible to say exactly the number of leagues that our Spaniards navigated down the river in the nineteen full days and one additional night that their voyage to the sea lasted, to the place where they then were, because their continuous fighting with the Indians left them no time for calculating the number of leagues that they navigated. But when they found themselves free of the enemy they at once discussed it among themselves, and later in México in the presence of persons who had experience in navigating the sea and rivers. There were many opinions and assertions, because some said that in a day and a night they traveled twenty leagues, others thirty, others forty, and others more or less. But most of them finally agreed to assign twenty-five leagues to each day and night, because they always navigated with both sails and oars, and the wind never failed them nor did the river have turns that would have detained them.

According to this calculation, our Spaniards found that they had navigated from the place where they embarked to the sea a little less than five hundred leagues. In making this calculation everyone can use his own judgment and assign the number of leagues that he may see fit, noting beforehand that besides the help they had from the wind our men did what they could with the oars in order to pass on and leave the land of enemies who were so anxious to kill them.

Juan Coles says that they went seven hundred leagues, and he must have had the opinion of those who assigned thirty-five leagues of navigation to each twenty-four hours.

IX

THE NUMBER OF LEAGUES THAT THE SPANIARDS PENETRATED INTO THE INTERIOR

There will be some who will be amazed to see that our Spaniards advanced so far into the interior country as has been said, and perhaps they will doubt it. We say to them not to wonder at it, for they went much farther, because they arrived at the very sources of this Río Grande. Where they embarked afterward in the province of Aminoya, near that of Guachoya, it was nineteen fathoms deep and a quarter of a league wide, as was said when they sounded it in order to cast into it the body of the governor and adelantado Hernando de Soto. Those who claim to understand something of cosmography say that it was three hundred leagues from where they embarked to the source of the river, and others say many more. I accept the smaller number, so that it would give the river a course of eight hundred leagues to the sea, and these Spaniards went all that distance into the interior of the country.[44]

---

[44]In interpreting this comment, it will be noted that the Spaniards evidently deduced that the Tennessee River, encountered in the area of Chiaha, was an upper course of the Río Grande, i.e., the Mississippi. Biedma, for example, calls the Tennessee River at Chiaha the "River of Espíritu Santo," which since the days of Pineda's coastal exploration had been considered the primary drainage along the northern Gulf Coast. The chronicles of the later Tristán de Luna expedition call it the same thing. See also the configuration of the Tennessee River on the so-called De Soto Map in Swanton, *Final Report,* 343.

When God is pleased for that land to be won, they will find out by going by way of this river how far our people went from the sea. For the present I cannot verify this account further than I have done already, and it has been a great deal [of effort] even to bring to light this little after so many years have passed and [from the accounts of] people whose purpose was not to go through the land marking out its confines, though they were discovering it, but to seek gold and silver. Therefore I may be admitted here the excuse that I have given elsewhere for other deficiencies in this *History* with regard to cosmography. I should have liked to write it very fully to give a better and more complete notice of that country, because my principal intent in this labor of mine, which has not been small, has been none other than to give an account to my lord the king and to the commonwealth of Spain of what the Spaniards themselves have discovered so nearby, so that they would not allow their predecessors' labors to be lost but would be encouraged and animated to win and settle a kingdom so large and so fertile.[45] First of all [they should do this] for the augmentation of the Catholic faith, for there is a large field that can be sown among people who, because of the few heathen abuses and ceremonies that they would have to abandon, are disposed to receive it with facility. The Spaniards are obligated to this preaching more than are the other Catholic nations, since God in His mercy elected them to preach his gospel in the New World and they are already its rulers. It would be a great affront and insult if other peoples should win them ahead of us, even though it were for this same purpose of preaching.

Furthermore, almost all the nations who are our neighbors being, as they are, infected with the abominable heresies of these unhappy times, it is greatly to be feared that they may sow it among those peoples who are so simple, managing to make an establishment among them, as they have already attempted to do.

Jesus Christ, our Lord, and His spouse the Roman church, our Mother and Lady, having given us the seed of the truth and the faculty and power for disseminating it, as has been done for 110 years in these parts and as is being done in the most and the better part of the New World, it would be a count and charge against the Spanish nation if now, through its carelessness and because it has fallen asleep, the enemy should sow discord in this great kingdom of La Florida, so important a part of the New World, which is hers.

[45]By the time this was written, apparently unknown to Garcilaso, Pedro Menéndez de Avilés had long since founded permanent colonial outposts in La Florida, including St. Augustine. In Book I, Chapter IV, Garcilaso excuses himself for his imperfect knowledge of the exploits of that individual.

Aside from what is due religion, the Spaniards of today ought, especially for their own honor and profit, to make an effort to conquer this empire, where there are such broad, extensive, and fertile lands, so well adapted for human life as we have seen. It is not possible that the gold and silver mines that are so desired would not be found if they were sought for systematically, for since they have not been lacking in any province of the New World, neither would they be absent here. While they were being discovered, it would be possible to enjoy the wealth of pearls, so plentiful, large, and fine as we have told; and to produce silk, facilities for which we have noted in the large number of mulberry trees; and to raise and prepare for use all kinds of cattle, there could not be desired more-abundant pasturage or more-fertile lands than this country contains.

For all of this we pray that the Lord may animate these Spaniards so that they will not be careless regarding this region nor relax their good intentions, since in all the rest of the New World they are discovering and conquering every day new kingdoms and provinces more difficult to win than those of La Florida. For entering and conquering it, navigation from Spain is easy. The same ship can make two voyages a year. Horses can be had throughout the whole country of México, where they are plentiful and very good. For assistance, if it should be needed, they could apply to the islands of Cuba and Santo Domingo and those near them, and to New Spain and Tierra Firme, and with the facilities afforded by the Río Grande, which would accommodate any fleet, they could ascend by way of it easily whenever they liked. For my own part I say that if the Lord had given me the wealth in accordance with my will and desire, I would spend it joyfully, along with my life, in this heroic enterprise. But this must wait for some more fortunate person, for he who does it will be such, and then the errors of my *History,* for which I have so often asked pardon, will be corrected. With this let us return to it, for in my concern and desire to see it finished I have not shirked the labor that is intolerable to me, nor spared my poor health, which is now very feeble, nor let anything else stand in my way, so that Spain, to which I owe so much, may not be without this account if I should die before publishing it.

X

CONCERNING A BATTLE THAT THE SPANIARDS FOUGHT WITH THE INDIANS OF THE COAST

As we said, the Spaniards spent three days in repairing their caravels and in recovering their own strength, their chief need being for sleep, as they were very fatigued. On the last day, after noon, they saw seven canoes emerge from among some rushes and come toward them. In the first one came an Indian as large as a Philistine and as black as an Ethiopian, very different in color and appearance from those that they had left in the interior.

The reason why the coast Indians are so black is because they constantly go about in the salt water fishing, for because of the sterility of the country they depend upon fishing for their subsistence. The heat of the sun also helps to make them black, as it is more intense on the coast than in the interior. Standing in the bow of his canoe, the Indian said to the Castilians in a gruff and haughty voice: "Thieves, vagabonds, idlers without honor or shame, who go along this shore disturbing its natives, you are to leave this place immediately by one of those two mouths of this river, if you do not want me to kill all of you and burn your boats. See that I do not find you here tonight, or not a man of you will escape with his life."

They could understand what the Indian said by the gestures that he made with his arms and his body, pointing to the two mouths of the Río Grande that the island formed, which we said was ahead of them, and by many words that the Spaniards' Indian servants explained. Having said this, he went back into the rushes without waiting for a reply.

Here Juan Coles adds the following words that the Indian spoke, besides those already given: "If we had large canoes like yours (he meant the ships), we would follow you to your country and take it, for we also are men like you."

The Spaniards, having considered the Indian's words and the arrogance that he had shown in them and in his appearance, and seeing that canoes appeared from time to time among the rushes and then went back, as if they were in ambush, agreed that it would be a good thing to make the Indians understand that they were not afraid of them, so that they would not be encouraged to come and shoot arrows at them and set fire to the caravels. They could do this better at night than in the daytime, being a people who were well acquainted with the sea and the land thereabouts and who could attack and run away safely, while the Castilians were ignorant of it.

Having so decided, a hundred men entered the five canoes that remained for the service of the brigantines, and, taking Gonzalo Silvestre and Alvaro Nieto as commanders, they went in search of the Indians. They found large numbers of them behind some rushes, ready with more than sixty small canoes that they had brought together against our men.

The latter, although they saw so many Indians and canoes, were not dismayed, but on the contrary they engaged them with all good spirit and courage. By good fortune they capsized three canoes in the first encounter, wounded many Indians, and killed ten or twelve, because they carried twenty-two crossbowmen and three archers. One of these was a Spaniard who had lived in England from infancy to the age of twenty years, and the other was a native Englishman. Being skillful with the weapons of that kingdom and expert in the use of bows and arrows, they had been unwilling to use any other arms except these throughout the discovery, and thus they were carrying them on this occasion. The other archer was an Indian who had been the servant of Captain Juan de Guzmán, having been captured soon after he entered La Florida. He had become so fond of his master and of the Spaniards that he always fought with his bow and arrows as one of them against his own people.

With the skill and dexterity of the marksmen and with the courage of the whole party, they scattered the enemy canoes and made them run away. But our men did not come out of the battle so well that most of them were not wounded, the two captains among them. One Spaniard was wounded by a weapon that the Castilians in the Indies call a long arrow [*tiradera*], which we shall call more accurately a dart [*bohordo*] because it is shot with a strip [*amiento*] of wood or a cord.[46] The Spaniards had not seen this weapon in all the places they had been in La Florida until that day. In El Perú the Indians use it a great deal. It is a weapon a fathom long made of a firm rush, though spongy in the center, of which they also make arrows. They make heads for them of deer horn, fashioned in all perfection with four points or harpoons of palm or other wood that they have, as strong and heavy as iron. So that the part of the arrow or dart made of the rush will not be split by the barb when it hits its mark, they make a knot where the head or harpoon joins it, and another one at the other end, which the crossbowmen call *batalla* on

---

[46]This weapon was a spear thrower, or atlatl, primarily used by coastal natives of the Southeast during the early historic era.

their darts, where it receives the cord of the bow or the stock with which they shoot it. The stock is of wood two tercias long, and they shoot the dart with it with extreme force, so that it has been known to pass through a man armed in a coat of mail. The Spaniards in El Perú feared this weapon more than any other the Indians had, for their arrows were not so terrible as those of La Florida.

The dart or long arrow with which they wounded our Spaniard of whom we were speaking had three barbs in the place of one, similar to the three largest fingers of the hand. The barb in the center was a handbreadth longer than the two on the sides, and thus it went through the thigh from one side to the other. The two side barbs were lodged in the middle of the thigh, and in order to get them out, it was necessary to cut away a great deal of flesh from the poor Spaniard's leg, because they were harpoons and not smooth points. The butchery was such that he expired before they dressed his wound, the poor fellow not knowing whether to complain more of the enemy who had wounded him or of the friends who had hastened his death.

XI

THE SPANIARDS SET SAIL, AND THE INCIDENTS OF THE FIRST TWENTY-THREE DAYS OF THEIR NAVIGATION

Since we have not yet left the Río Grande, whose canoes we have described at length in the past chapters, it will be well to tell here of the dexterity and skill that the natives of the whole country of La Florida show in righting a canoe when it is turned bottom up in naval battles or in their fishing or in some other manner; we neglected to note this in the proper place. In such cases, since they are most expert swimmers, they take it between twelve or thirteen Indians, more or less, according to the size of the canoe, and again set it right side up. As it comes up full of water, all the Indians together tilt the canoe to one side, the water thus beginning to run out in that direction, and then they quickly tilt it to the opposite side, thus throwing the water out, so that after two such movements not a drop of water remains in the canoe, and the Indians again get into it. They do all this so quickly and easily that the canoe has scarcely capsized when they have it righted again. Our men admired this skill greatly, for however they tried they never managed to imitate it.

While the hundred Spaniards went in the canoes to fight the Indians, those who remained loaded the caravels with the things that they had taken out of them. They could do so without the aid of the canoes because the brigantines were tied up to the driftwood that we said formed an island, which made no other movement except to rise and fall with the motion of the sea.

The Spaniards who had gone to the fight came back to their people victorious, having driven the enemy out of the rushes, but fearing that they might return at night and set fire to them or do some other damage, they all embarked in the caravels and went to the uninhabited island at the mouth of the Río Grande. They anchored and went ashore, and walked over all of it, but found nothing remarkable there.

That night they slept in the anchored caravels, and at daylight they decided to set sail and go toward the west in the direction of the coast of México, always keeping the mainland of La Florida to their right, not drawing away from it. When they hoisted the anchors one of the cables broke; as it had been repaired in many places, very little was needed to break it. The anchor was lost, as they had not thrown out a buoy, and since it was so necessary to them, they did not wish to go without it. The best swimmers among them went into the water, but all their efforts to find it were of no avail until three o'clock in the afternoon, when they found it at the end of nine or ten hours of diving.

At that hour they set sail. They did not dare go out into the gulf because they did not know where they were or in what direction to sail in order to cross to the islands of Santo Domingo or Cuba, as they had no sailing chart or compass or astrolabe with which to take the altitude of the sun, nor a forestaff for finding that of the north star. They only knew that by constantly following the coast toward the west they must eventually reach the coast and territory of México. With this purpose they navigated all that evening and the following night, and until nearly sunset of the second day. In all that distance they found fresh water from the Río Grande, and our people were amazed that it should be found so far out at sea.

At this point Alonso de Carmona says the following, which is copied literally:

> Thus we navigated, following the coast more or less closely, for the Indians had burned our instruments of navigation, or we ourselves had done so, when we set fire to Maubila. Captain Juan de Añasco was a very careful man and he had recovered the astrolabe and kept it. As it was of metal it had not been

> much damaged. He made a sailing chart on a piece of deerskin and fashioned a forestaff from a ruler, and we set course by it. The mariners and others with them who knew that he was not a seaman and had never been at sea in his life until he embarked for this journey ridiculed him, and when he learned how they were jeering at him he threw all the instruments except the astrolabe into the sea. Another brigantine that was coming behind picked them up because the chart and the forestaff were fastened together. Thus we traveled, or rather navigated, seven or eight days, when we took shelter from a storm in a cove.

Thus far Alonso de Carmona.

Our Castilians navigated fifteen days more with good weather for their voyage, without anything of note happening except that during these fifteen days they went ashore five times to get water. They had no large vessels in which to carry it, only small jars and pitchers that were soon emptied. This was one of the chief causes, along with the lack of navigating instruments, for their not having dared to cross to the islands or to separate themselves from the mainland, because they needed water every three days.

When they found no river or spring from which to take it they dug in the ground ten or twelve paces from the sea and found at a depth of less than a vara a plentiful supply of fresh water. Thus they were never without water throughout their voyage.

At the end of the fifteen days of navigation they reached a place where there were four or five islets not far from the mainland, where they found innumerable waterfowl. These bred there and had their nests on the ground, and they were so numerous and so close together that our men could not find a place to set foot. When they returned to the brigantines they were loaded down with eggs and with fledglings, which were so fat that they could not eat them. Both they and the eggs tasted very much like fish.

On the following day they anchored to take water on a very pleasant beach that was clear of rushes, there being on it only many large trees separated from one another, which formed a beautiful open forest without shrubs or any kind of undergrowth.

Some of the Spaniards went ashore to gather shellfish on the beach, and they found there some slabs of black bitumen almost like pitch, which the sea washed up among its refuse. It might have come from some fountain of that liquid that entered the sea or had its origin in it. The slabs weighed eight, ten, twelve, or fourteen pounds, and there were large numbers of them.

The Castilians, seeing this assistance that good fortune offered them in their necessity—because the caravels were already leaking, and they feared that they would continue to do so increasingly until they foundered, and as they did not know how much more navigation was before them or have any other hope of reaching Christian lands except by means of the brigantines—decided to repair them, since they had the means and a good beach where they could bring them ashore.

With this purpose they spent eight days at that place, and every day they unloaded a brigantine and pulled it ashore by main strength, pitched it, and launched it in the water again in the evening. To soften the bitumen, which was dry, they used the fat from the little bacon that they were bringing to eat, thinking it better to use it on the boats than for their own subsistence, for they knew that they would be the means of saving their lives.

XII

THE NAVIGATION CONTINUES TO ITS FIFTY-THIRD DAY, AND A STORM THAT OVERTOOK THEM

In the eight days that our people occupied in careening their boats, on three different occasions eight Indians came up to them, advancing peacefully, and gave them ears of maize or Indian corn of which they brought a large quantity, and the Spaniards gave them in return some of the deerskins that they had with them. Notwithstanding all these friendly exchanges between them, the Spaniards did not ask them what land that was, or the name of the province, for they had no other desire except to reach the territory of México; thus it is impossible for us to know what region that might have been. All three times the Indians came with their bows and arrows and showed themselves to be very friendly, and they were always the same ones.

After the eight days that they spent in pitching the caravels, our Castilians left that pleasant shore and beach and continued on their voyage, always taking care to go from one point of land to another, so that a north wind, such as those that blow very furiously at times on that coast, would not carry them to the high seas. They also did this because, as we have seen, they had to take water every three days.

Where they found a good place they busied themselves in fishing, for after they had repaired the caravels and used up their bacon they had nothing else to eat except maize. Forced by necessity, some of them fished in the water with their hooks, and others went ashore to hunt for shellfish, and they always brought back a good supply. Also they were obliged to rest from their hard labor at the oars by fishing, because whenever the sea would permit, all those who were in the caravels, except the captains, took turns at them. They spent twelve or thirteen days from time to time in fishing, for wherever they found a good supply they stayed two or three days.

In this manner these Spaniards sailed many leagues (but we cannot say how many), with great eagerness to sight the Río de Palmas, which in view of the distance they had sailed it seemed to them could not be far away. Those who prided themselves on being cosmographers and expert mariners held out and affirmed this hope, but as a matter of fact the wisest among them did not know in what sea or what region they were navigating, except that it seemed undeniably true to them that by continuing their voyage from one cape to another they would reach the lands of México, unless the sea should devour them. This certainty was what gave them strength to suffer and endure the excessive hardships that they experienced.

Fifty-three days had passed since our Spaniards had left the Río Grande and entered the sea. They spent thirty of them in navigation and twenty-three in repairing the brigantines and in resting while they fished. On the last day the north wind rose after noon with the ferocity and force with which it blows on that coast, more than in any other place, and it blew them out to sea, which was what they had always feared.

Five of the caravels that were proceeding together, the governor's being among them, had seen the storm coming, and before it arrived they drew near the shore, and thus they navigated with their oars touching it, looking for a shelter where they could protect themselves from the bad weather. The other two caravels, which were those of the treasurer Juan Gaytán who had remained the sole captain of it after the death of the good Juan de Guzmán, and of Captains Juan de Alvarado and Cristóbal Mosquera, which had not observed the weather as closely as the other five, were some distance from the shore. Because of this carelessness they passed that whole night [in] a fierce storm, the force of the wind increasing hourly, so that they went with the Creed on their lips. The treasurer's caravel was in greater danger than the other, because a gust of wind displaced the mainmast and it came out of a wooden mortar in the keel in which it was encased, and they put it back in only with much labor and difficulty. Thus the two caravels struggled all night, forcing their way against the storm, so as not to get out of sight of land. At dawn (our people thought the wind would fall when daylight came) it blew even more furiously and strongly, and kept them on the point of drowning without its force abating, until noon. At this hour the two caravels saw that the other five were ascending a creek or river and had now reached a safe place, free from that storm in which they were found. Thereupon they persisted anew in trying to go against the wind to see whether they could reach the place where the others were. But in spite of their efforts they could not do it because the wind blew directly against them and was extremely strong, so that all their attempts to reach the river failed. On the other hand their persistence placed them in greater danger, for the caravels were often on the point of capsizing, but still with all this they struggled against the storm until three o'clock in the afternoon. Seeing that their labors were not only useless but that their peril was increasing, they agreed that it would be less dangerous to allow themselves to run forward along the coast where they might find some help.

Having so decided, they steered the boats toward the west and sailed with a side wind, it not having abated for them at all.

Our Spaniards went without any clothing except trousers, because so much water from the waves fell on the caravels that it kept them half drowned. Some worked to trim the sails, and others to bail out the water, for, as the brigantines had no decks, all that the waves washed in remained, and our men walked in it thigh-deep.

XIII

A SEVERE STORM THAT THE TWO CARAVELS PASSED THROUGH, AND HOW THEY WERE CAST ASHORE

The two caravels ran through the storm for twenty-five or twenty-six hours, as we have said, without its abating in the least; on the contrary it seemed to those who were in it to be increasing hourly. All this time our Spaniards were battling the waves and the wind without sleeping or eating a mouthful, for the fear of death, which was so close to them, drove away hunger and sleep. Nearly at sunset they sighted land ahead, which was found to be of two kinds.

That which was seen ahead and extending to the right of the direction in which our people were going was a white coast that appeared to be of sand, because with the hard wind that was blowing they saw many hillocks of it moving easily and rapidly from one place to another. The coast that extended to their left appeared to be as black as pitch. At this moment a youth named Francisco, twenty years old, who was in the caravel of Captains Juan de Alvarado and Francisco Mosquera, said to them: "Sirs, I know this coast, for I have navigated along it twice while serving as cabin boy on a ship, though I do not know the land, nor whose it is. That black coast that appears on our left is a land of flint and a rough coast that extends a long way until it reaches La Vera Cruz. There is no port on the whole of it nor any haven where we can take shelter; there are only broken cliffs and flint promontories where, if we are cast ashore, we shall all die, pounded to pieces between the waves and the rocks.

"The other land that is ahead extending to the right is a sandy coast and therefore appears white. It is all clear and smooth and thus it will be well for us to endeavor to reach this white coast before night comes on, because if the wind separates us from it and casts us on the black coast we have no hope left of escaping alive."

Captains Juan de Alvarado and Francisco Mosquera ordered that notice be given immediately to Captain Juan Gaytán's caravel of the information given by the youth Francisco, so as to warn them against the impending danger, but the waves were so high that they would not permit those of the two caravels talking to or even seeing each other. They made themselves understood as well as they could by signs, however, and by shouts given at intervals now and again as the caravels happened to come in sight over the waves so that they could see and talk with one another. They agreed by common consent to run ashore on the white coast. Only the treasurer Juan Gaytán, acting in his capacity as treasurer rather than as captain, opposed it, saying that it was not well to lose the caravel, which was valuable. At his words, the soldiers rose up and said all together: "What more do you have in it than any one of us? On the contrary you have less, or nothing at all, for presuming on your position as the emperor's treasurer you would not cut the wood or dress it, or make charcoal for the forges, or help there to beat the iron into nails, or work at the caulking, or at anything else of importance. You evaded all the labor that we endured under pretext of your royal office. This being so, what will you lose if the caravel is lost? Will it be better to lose the fifty men that are in it?" And there was not lacking someone who said, "It is a pity that he who gave you this stab in the neck did not cut it all the way across!"

Having spoken thus very freely, in order to prevent any reply being made or the captain presuming to give orders at that juncture, the chief soldiers busied themselves in trimming the sails, and a Portuguese named Domingos de Acosta grasped the rudder or helm, and they all turned the prow of the boat toward the shore. They made ready with their swords and shields for whatever they might find there, and tacking from side to side so as not to fall upon the black coast, they made the white coast with much danger and labor a little before the sun went down.

Because we mentioned the sword-wound of the treasurer Juan Gaytán, it will be well, though it has nothing to do with our *History*, to tell here how the incident happened. For this purpose it must be known that our Juan Gaytán was the nephew of the captain Juan Gaytán who, because of the marvelous exploits he performed in all parts with his sword and cape, won renown for his excellence in the proverb, "The sword and cape of Juan Gaytán." This one, his nephew, took part in the war in Tunis when our lord the emperor took it from the Turk Barbarossa in the year 1535 and gave it to the Moor Muley Hacen, who was his friend. In a quarrel over the division of the spoils Juan Gaytán had taken in that sack, he exchanged thrusts with another Spanish soldier whose sword must not have been inferior to that of his uncle. This man gave him a deep wound in the neck from which he nearly died. Finally he recovered, but he was left with a scar two finger-breadths deep. One of those who came up to pacify the quarrel reproached the one who had wounded him, saying that he had done ill in so mistreating the nephew of Captain Juan Gaytán; that he ought to have respected him because of his uncle's reputation. The soldier, unrepentant for his action, replied: "It is too bad that he was not the nephew of the king of France; I would have taken even more pleasure in having wounded or killed him, because it would have meant so much more honor and fame for me." The treasurer Juan Gaytán himself told this as a witty saying of the person who had wounded him.

XIV

WHAT THE CAPTAINS AND SOLDIERS OF THE TWO CARAVELS ORDERED

Returning to our story, it happened that Captain Juan Gaytán, feeling that the caravel had touched bottom, either because of his anger at the opposition the soldiers had made to him, or because he thought he knew from experience that in such situations it was less dangerous to enter the water by way of the stern rather than any other part of the boat, threw himself from it into the water. On coming up, his back struck against the rudder, and as he wore no clothes, he was badly hurt and wounded. All the rest of the soldiers stayed aboard the caravel. The first time it struck the shore, since the waves were so large, it was left more than ten paces beyond the water when they receded back to the sea. But when the waves returned to the combat they turned it on its side.

Those who were on it at once jumped into the water, as they wore no clothing to prevent their moving about in it. Some went on one side and others on the other to right the caravel and turn it so that the force of the waves would not sink it. Others busied themselves in unloading the maize and taking out the cargo. Others carried this ashore. With such activity they had it entirely unloaded within a very short time, and as it was now light they easily got it ashore, aided by the blows of the waves against it. They lifted it almost entirely from the ground and shored it so as to be able to launch it again if it should be necessary.

The same thing that happened to the caravel of the treasurer Juan Gaytán occurred also in that of Captains Juan de Alvarado and Cristóbal Mosquera, which was grounded at a distance of about two harquebus-shots from the other one. Its company unloaded it with the same rapidity and diligence and brought it ashore. The captains and soldiers, finding themselves free of the storm and the perils of the sea, immediately sent to visit one another to find out what had happened during their shipwreck. The messengers started out at the same moment, as if by agreement, and they met in the middle of the road. Exchanging their messages, questions, and replies, they both returned to their companions with a good report of everything. At this both parties rejoiced greatly and gave thanks to God for having saved them from so much hardship and danger. But not knowing what had happened to the governor and the rest of their companions gave them new cause for anxiety and care, for it is characteristic of human nature that we have scarcely emerged from one misery when we find ourselves in another.

To discuss what they ought to do in that necessity, the three captains and the chief soldiers of both caravels met at once, and all of them agreed that it would be well for some diligent soldier to go immediately that night to find out about the governor and the caravels that they had seen ascending that creek or river, and tell him what had happened to the two brigantines. But considering the excessive labors that they had undergone during the storm, and that for more than twenty-eight hours since it began they had not eaten or slept, and that since coming out of the sea they still had not rested even half an hour, they did not dare name anyone to go. For it seemed to them a great cruelty to choose him for further labor, and no less reckless to send him when he [would be] in such manifest danger of perishing on the way, because on that same night he would have to travel thirteen or fourteen leagues that apparently lay between them and the place where they had seen the caravels going inland. He would have to go through an unknown country, ignorant of whether there were other rivers or creeks on the road or whether it was safe from enemies, because, as has been said, they did not know in what region they were.

The confusion of our captains and soldiers and the difficulties of the proposed hardships and dangers were overcome by the generous and courageous spirit of Gonzalo Quadrado Xaramillo, whom we mentioned particularly on the day of the great battle of Mauvila. Standing before his companions, he said: "Notwithstanding our past hardships and those in prospect at present, along with imminent risk to my life, I offer to make this journey out of the love that I have for the general, because I am his countryman, and in order to bring you out of your present perplexity. I propose to travel all night and not to stop until I reach the governor in the morning, or die in the attempt. If there is anyone who wishes to do so, he may go with me, otherwise I say that I shall go alone."

The captains and soldiers were very gratified to see his good spirit, which was matched by that of another valiant Castilian, named Francisco Muñoz, a native of Burgos. Stepping out from among his companions and placing himself at the side of Gonzalo Quadrado Xaramillo he said that he would accompany him on that journey, whether he lived or died. Immediately, without any delay, they gave them some small knapsacks containing a little maize and bacon, both poorly cooked, because they had not even had time to cook it well. With this fine preparation and equipped with their swords and shields, and barefoot, as we have said all of them were, these two courageous soldiers set out at one o'clock that night. They marched all night with the seashore for their guide, because they knew of no other road. We shall leave them there to tell what their companions were doing meanwhile.

As soon as the two soldiers had been sent off, the others returned to their caravels and slept in them with sentries posted because they did not know whether they were in the land of enemies or of friends. As soon as it was light, they assembled again and chose three corporals, each of whom was to go with twenty men in a different direction to explore and see what land that might be. They were called corporals and not captains because of the few men they had with them. One of them was named Antonio de Porras, who went forward along the coast to the south; another, who was named Alonso Calvete, went north along the same coast; and Gonzalo Silvestre went inland toward the west. All carried orders that they were not to go very far so that those who stayed behind could help them if they should need it. Each of them went with a great desire of bringing good news.

XV

WHAT HAPPENED TO THE THREE EXPLORING CAPTAINS

The captains who went in either direction along the coast, each having marched more than a league over it, returned to their people. One party brought half of a white earthen plate, of the very fine sort that is made in Talavera, and the others brought a broken crock of gilded and painted earthenware such as is made in Malasa [Málaga?]. They said that they had not found anything else, and that these were very good signs and indications of their being in a Spanish country, for both pieces of earthenware were from Spain and were a proof of their statement. All our people rejoiced greatly at this and were extremely happy, holding these signs to be certain and propitious, according to their desires.

Gonzalo Silvestre and his party, who went into the interior, were more fortunate. Having advanced a little more than a quarter of a league from the sea and crossed over a little hill, they saw a lagoon of fresh water that extended for more than a league. On it were four or five canoes of Indians who were fishing, and so that the Indians would not see them and raise an alarm the Spaniards got behind some trees and marched through them a quarter of a league parallel with the lagoon, spread out in a line as if they were hunting hares. They advanced in this manner, looking carefully and attentively on all sides. They saw two Indians ahead (about the distance of two harquebus-shots from where they were going) who were gathering fruit under a large tree called a *guayavo* in the language of the island of Española and *savintu* in my language of El Perú.

When the Spaniards saw them they passed the word along to drop down on the ground so as not to be seen, and gave orders to surround them, some on one side and some on the other. They were to go like lizards, crawling along the ground, and encircle the Indians so they could not get away, and those who stayed behind were not to raise up from the ground until the ones ahead had got on the other side of the Indians.

With these orders they all went with their chests to the ground, and the ones ahead went on all fours almost three harquebus-shots to come in ahead of the Indians. Each one of the Spaniards was put on his honor not to let the quarry get past him. When they had them surrounded all raised up at the same time and charged at them, but for all their trouble one of the Indians got away, jumped into the water, and escaped by swimming.

The Indian who remained a captive shouted loudly, repeating many times the word *brezos*. The Spaniards, in their haste to return to their people before the Indians should come to take away their prisoner, paid no attention to what the Indian was saying, but were concerned only with leaving that place quickly. They hastily picked up the two baskets of guayavas that the Indians had gathered, and a little maize that they found in a hut, and a turkey such as are found in México—which they do not have in El Perú—and a cock and two hens like those of Spain, and a small quantity of conserve made from the prickly leaves of a tree called maguey, which are like the spikes of a thistle. The Indians of New Spain make many things from this tree, such as wine, vinegar, and syrup made from a sweet liquor that the leaves yield when taken from the stalk at a certain time of the year. The tender spikes when cooked and put in the sun are good to eat and similar in appearance to preserved pumpkin, though they do not equal its flavor. Of these same spikes, which are like those of a thistle, when they mature on the tree, the Indians make a fiber that is very strong and good. The maguey stalk, only one of which grows on each plant after the manner of the giant fennel of Spain, and which has a spongy wood like it though the outside is hard, they use to roof their houses where better wood is lacking.

The Castilians took with them everything we have said they found in the hut, and they took the captured Indian well bound so that he would not escape them. They questioned him by signs and with Spanish words, asking him what land this was and what his name was. The Indian understood from the gestures they made to him, as if he were mute, that they were questioning him, but he did not understand from their words what they were asking him. Not knowing how to reply, he repeated the word *brezos,* and many times; pronouncing it badly, he said "*bredos.*"

As he did not answer to the purpose, the Spaniards said to him: "Go to the devil, you dog, what would we want with *bledos* [amaranth]?" The Indian was trying to say that he was the vassal of a Spaniard named Cristóbal de Brezos, and as in his disturbed state he could not manage to say Cristóbal, and sometimes said brezos and again bredos, the Castilians could not understand him. Thus they carried him off hurriedly, before he should be taken away from them, in order to ask him later at more leisure the things they wished to find out.

In connection with the Spaniards' questionings and the Indian's unintelligible replies (because they did not understand one another), we had inserted here the derivation of the name *Perú,* which those Indians do not have in their language. It came from another such incident as this, and inasmuch as the printing of this book has been delayed longer than I had ever imagined, I took it away from here and put it in its proper place [a reference to Garcilaso's *Commentarios Reales*]. There it will be found in full along with many other names included by way of illustration, because, by Divine favor, in this year 1602 we are now in the last quarter of it and expect to finish it speedily.

XVI

THE SPANIARDS LEARN THAT THEY ARE IN THE TERRITORY OF MÉXICO

Gonzalo Silvestre and the twenty men of his party, along with the Indian whom they had captured, traveled swiftly. They asked questions that were poorly understood by the Indian, and his replies were worse interpreted by the Spaniards. Thus they marched until they reached the coast, where the rest of their companions were holding a great celebration and rejoicing over the pieces of the plate and crock that the other explorers had brought back. But as soon as they saw the turkey and the hens and the fruit and the rest of the loot that Gonzalo Silvestre and his men carried they could not restrain themselves from making signs of extreme joy, jumping and leaping like crazy men. For the greater satisfaction of all of them it happened that the surgeon who had treated them had been in México and knew something about the Méxican language. He spoke to the Indian in it, saying, "What are these?" and indicating some scissors that he had in his hand.

Having recognized that these people were Spaniards, the Indian had now come to himself somewhat and replied in Spanish, "Tiselas" [*tiseras*, or in modern Spanish, *tijeras*: scissors]. This word, though badly pronounced proved conclusively to our men that they were in the territory of México, and in their joy at learning it they insisted on embracing and congratulating Gonzalo Silvestre and the members of his party, and they raised them up on their shoulders and marched around with them, extolling and praising them without stint or restraint, as if every one of them had brought the seigniory of México and its whole empire.

This most solemn festival of rejoicing having passed, they questioned the Indian more quietly and to better purpose, asking what land that was and what river or creek the governor had entered with the five caravels.

The Indian said: "This land belongs to the city of Pánuco and your captain-general entered the Río de Pánuco, which flows into the sea twelve leagues from here. The city is twelve leagues farther up the river, and it is ten leagues from here by land. I am a vassal of a vecino of Pánuco named Cristóbal de Brezos, and about a league from here is an Indian lord of vassals who knows how to read and write, having been brought up from infancy by the priest who instructs us in the Christian doctrine. If you wish that I go summon him, I will go for him; I know he will come at once and will inform you about everything that you wish to know most."

The Spaniards were very pleased with the Indian's intelligent remarks and they entertained him and gave him presents from the things they had with them. They sent him immediately for the cacique and directed him to bring or send a supply of paper and ink for writing.

The Indian traveled with such haste and diligence that he came back with the curaca in less than four hours. The latter, learning that some Spanish ships had been stranded in his country, desired to visit them personally and carry them some present. Thus he brought eight Indians laden with chickens like those of Spain, and bread made of maize, and fruit and fish, as well as ink and paper, because he prided himself on being able to read and write and considered it a great accomplishment.

He presented everything he brought to the Spaniards and very affectionately offered them his person and his house. Our men thanked him for his visit and for the presents, and gave him in return some of the deerskins that they brought. They immediately dispatched an Indian to the governor with a letter in which they told him everything that had happened to them up to that time, and asked him for orders as to their future actions.

The cacique remained with the Spaniards all that day, questioning them about the events and adventures of their discovery, being very pleased to hear of them. He wondered at seeing them so black, spare, and worn in their persons and clothing, which showed clearly the hardships they had endured. When it was nearly night he returned to his house, and in the six days that the Spaniards stayed on that beach he visited them every day, always bringing them presents of the things that were in his country.

XVII

THE SPANIARDS ARE REUNITED IN PÁNUCO. BITTER QUARRELS ARISE AMONG THEM, AND THE REASONS FOR THESE

Gonzalo Quadrado Xaramillo and his companion Francisco Muñoz, whom we left marching along the coast, did not pause all night, and at dawn they reached the mouth of the Río de Pánuco, where they learned that the governor and his five caravels had entered safely and were going up the river. Encouraged by this good news, they did not want to stop and rest, but though they had marched twelve leagues that night without resting, they hastened their journey still more and traveled three leagues farther. At eight o'clock in the morning they reached the place where the governor and his men were, very sad and anxious in their fears that the two caravels they had left in the great storm at sea had been lost. It was still raging, nor did it cease for another five days thereafter.

But with the presence and the report of these two good companions, their grief and anxiety was changed to content and joy, and they gave thanks to God who had saved them from death. On the following day they received the letter that the Indian brought them, to which the governor replied that after they had rested as long as they wished they were to go to the city of Pánuco where he would await them, so they could all put their lives in order.

Eight days after the shipwreck all our Spaniards had assembled with the governor in Pánuco, and they numbered almost three hundred.[47] They were very well received by the vecinos and inhabitants of that city, who, though they were poor, showed them all the courtesy and good hospitality that they could. For among them were very noble gentlemen, and it aroused their pity to see them so disfigured, black, lean, wasted, barefoot, and unclothed. They wore no other garments except those of deerskin, cowhide, and the skins of bears and lions and other wild animals, so they looked more like wild beasts and brutish animals than human beings. The *corregidor* at once advised the viceroy Don Antonio de Mendoza, who resided in México, sixty leagues from Pánuco, how almost three hundred Spaniards had come out of

---

[47] The Gentleman of Elvas gives the number of survivors as 311. Ignacio Avellaneda considers the latter figure accurate, and he has accounted for 257 of these by name. Ignacio Avellaneda, *Los Sobrevivientes de La Florida: The Survivors of the De Soto Expedition* (Gainesville: University of Florida, P. K. Yonge Library of Florida History, 1990).

La Florida, of the thousand who had entered it with the adelantado Hernando de Soto. The viceroy sent to order the corregidor to entertain and treat them as his own person, and that when they were ready to travel he was to supply them with everything they needed and send them to México.

Following this message, he sent shirts and sandals and four pack mules laden with conserves and other delicacies and medicines for the sick, for our Spaniards, in the belief that they were ailing. But they were in perfect health though they lacked everything else necessary for human life.

At this point the accounts of Juan Coles and Alonso de Carmona say that the Cofradía de la Caridad [Brotherhood of Charity] of México sent these gifts by order of the viceroy.

It must be told now that when General Luis de Moscoso de Alvarado and his captains and soldiers found themselves reunited and had rested ten or twelve days in that city, the most prudent and informed among them observed attentively the mode of life of its inhabitants, which was then miserable enough, because they had no mines of gold or silver or any other wealth of which to avail themselves. They had only such scanty foods as the land afforded, and raised a few horses to sell to those who came from other places to buy them. Most of them dressed in ordinary cotton cloth, very few wearing clothing from Castilla, and the richest vecinos and principal lords of vassals had no wealth except what we have mentioned, though some were beginning to raise cattle in very small numbers. They busied themselves in planting mulberries for silk-culture and in setting out other fruit trees from Spain in order to enjoy their fruits in the future. The rest of their possessions and household equipment corresponded to the things that have been described. All the houses in which they lived were poor and humble, most of them being made of straw. In short, our Spaniards noted that everything they had seen in the pueblo represented no more than the beginnings of settling and cultivating miserably a country that was not as good as the one that they had left behind them and abandoned. They saw that in place of the cotton clothing that the vecinos of Pánuco wore, they could have dressed in very fine deerskins of many and varied colors, such as those they brought with them, and could have worn mantles of marten-skins and other very beautiful and elegant pelts, of which as we have said they have most handsome ones in La Florida. They would not have been forced to plant mulberries for growing silk, since they had found them in such quantities as has been seen, along with the other timber such as three varieties of walnuts, plums, live oaks, and oaks, and the abundance of grapevines that grow in the fields.

In thus comparing these things with the others, the memory of the many and fine provinces that they had discovered was emphasized. Those named alone amount to forty, not counting the others that have been forgotten and still others whose names it has been impossible to learn. They remembered the fertility and abundance of all of them, their advantages for producing crops of grain and vegetables that could be introduced from Spain, and their facilities in the form of pasture grounds, commons, woodlands, and rivers for the breeding and increase of the cattle that they might wish to put into them.

Finally, they carried the memory of the great wealth of pearls and seed pearls that they had despised, and the grandeurs that they had dreamed of for themselves, because each one of them had seen himself the lord of a great province. Comparing now, therefore, those abundances and seigniories with the present miseries and poverty, they told one another their imaginings and sad thoughts, and in their great heaviness of heart and pity for themselves, they said: "Could not we have lived in La Florida just as these Spaniards are living in Pánuco? Were not the lands that we left better than these where we are? If we wished to stop and settle, would we not be better off there than are our present hosts here? Perhaps they have more silver and gold mines than we found, and more riches than those we disdained? Is it not a fine thing that we have come to receive alms and hospitality from others who are poorer than we, when we could have entertained everyone from Spain? Is it just or becoming to our honor that, from the lords of vassals that we could have been, we have come to beg? Would it not have been better to die there than to live here?"

With these words and similar ones arising from their regret over the good things they had lost, they became enraged with one another, in such fury and anger that, desperate with grief at having abandoned La Florida where they might have won so much wealth, they fell to stabbing one another in their rage and desire to kill. Their greatest ire and wrath was directed against the officials of the real hacienda and against the captains and soldiers, nobles and others from Sevilla, because these had been the ones who, after Governor Hernando de Soto's death, had insisted most strongly that they leave La Florida and abandon it. They also had been most persistent in forcing Luis de Moscoso to make that long journey that they made to the province of the Vaqueros. On that road, as was seen at the time, they suffered so many inconveniences and hardships that a third of them and of the horses died. The lack [of horses] was the final cause of their all being lost, because it forced and impelled them to leave the country quickly. They could not stay or ask for the reinforcements that the adelantado Hernando de Soto had planned to request by dispatching the two brigantines that he had proposed to send down the Río Grande to give notice in México, in the islands of Cuba and Santo Domingo, and in Tierra Firme of what he had discovered in La Florida, so that they might send him assistance for settling the country. This aid could have been given them very easily because of the capaciousness of the Río Grande, by which any ship or fleet could enter and leave.

All these things being now clearly seen and considered by those who had held the contrary opinion and had wished to carry forward the proposals of Governor Hernando de Soto and to settle and establish themselves in La Florida, and seeing now from experience that they had been right in desiring to remain, and their present cause for indignation against the officials and those of their faction, their fury blazed up in such manner that, losing all respect for them, they went in pursuit of them with knives, so that some were killed and wounded. The captains and royal officials did not dare come out of their lodgings, and the soldiers were so enraged against one another that all the people of the city were unable to pacify them. These and other results arise from decisions made without prudence or counsel.

XVIII

HOW THE SPANIARDS WENT TO MÉXICO, AND THE WARM WELCOME THAT FAMOUS CITY GAVE THEM

The corregidor of Pánuco, seeing such discord among our Spaniards and that it was increasing day by day, being unable to stop it, sent a report to the viceroy Don Antonio de Mendoza. He ordered that they be sent immediately to México in bands of ten or twenty, directing that those who went in each group should be of the same party and not opposed, so that they would not kill one another on the way.

In accordance with this order and command, they set out from Pánuco twenty-five days after they had entered it.

Along the road both Castilians and Indians came out in great multitudes to see them, and they wondered at seeing Spaniards, on foot, dressed in the skins of animals and bare-legged, for the best provided among them had managed to get little more than the sandals that they gave them out of charity. They were astonished to see them so black and disfigured, and said that their appearance showed clearly the hardships, hunger, misery, and persecutions that they had suffered. Rumor, performing its office, had already spread great reports about these things throughout the kingdom, and therefore Indians and Spaniards entertained them very affectionately and attentively, and served and regaled them all along the road until, proceeding in bands as they did, they entered the most famous city of México, which because of its grandeurs and wonders today, has the name and preeminence of being the best city in the world. They were received and entertained there by the viceroy as well as by the other vecinos, gentlemen, and rich men of the city, who regarded them so highly that they insisted upon taking them in groups of five or six to their houses and entertained them as if they had been their own sons.

Juan Coles says at this point that a leading gentleman and vecino of México, named Xaramillo, took eighteen men to his house, all being from Extremadura, and that he dressed them in fine cloth [*paño veintiguatrexo*] from Segovia, and gave each one of them a bed with a mattress, sheets, blankets, and pillows, and a comb, brush, and all the rest needed by a soldier. He said that the whole city was moved by compassion at seeing them dressed in deerskin and cowhides, and that they accorded them this honor and charity because of the many hardships that they knew they had endured in La Florida. On the other hand they had been unwilling to do any favors for those who had gone with Captain Juan Vázquez Coronado, a vecino of México, to discover the Seven Cities, because they had returned to México without any necessity whatever, not being willing to make a settlement. These people had gone out a little before ours. All these statements are from the account of Juan Coles, a native of Zafra, and that of Alonso de Carmona agrees with it in every respect. He adds that among those whom Xaramillo took to his house was a relative of his; it must have been our Gonzalo Quadrado Xaramillo.

So that it may be seen how closely these two eyewitnesses conform with one another in many parts of their accounts, it seems fitting for me to include here the words of Alonso de Carmona, as I have included those of Juan Coles. They are as follows:

> I have said already that we left Pánuco in bands of fifteen or twenty soldiers, and thus we entered the great city of México. We did not enter in one day, but in four, because each party went in separately. They accorded us such charity in that city that I do not know how to tell of it here, for when a band of soldiers entered the city those citizens immediately came out to the plaza, and

> he who reached them first considered himself fortunate. Each one wanted to do more than the rest, and thus they took them to their houses and gave them their own beds, and then ordered enough stuff to be brought to dress them in fine black cloth from Segovia. They clothed them and gave them everything else they needed, which included shirts, doublets, caps, hats, knives, scissors, head cloths, and hoods, and even combs with which to comb their hair. After dressing them, they took them to mass on Sunday, and after eating with them, they said: "Brothers, the country is large, and you can make a place for yourselves, each one seeking his own fortune." A vecino from Extremadura was there whose name was Xaramillo. He went out to the plaza and found a band of twenty soldiers, and among them a relative of his, and he treated them all so well that no one could rival him. All the members of my group decided to go and kiss the hands of Viceroy Don Antonio de Mendoza, and though other vecinos invited us to their houses we did not wish to go with them. After we had kissed his hands, the viceroy ordered that food be served to us, and we were lodged in a large room. They gave each one a bed with mattress, sheets, pillows, and blankets, all of them new. He ordered that we should not leave until we were clothed, and after we were dressed we kissed his hands and left his house, thanking him for the favors and charity that he had granted us. We all went to El Perú, not so much because of its wealth as because of the disturbances that were taking place there when Gonzalo Pizarro began to make himself governor and ruler of the country.

With this Alonso de Carmona ends the account of his peregrination, and all these are his own words, copied literally.

The viceroy, being such a good prince, seated all of our men who came to eat at his table with much attention, making no difference between captain and soldier and between a gentleman and him who was not, because he said that, since all had been equal in exploits and hardships, they ought to be [equal] also in the little honor that he was able to show them. He not only honored them at his table and in his house, but he ordered proclaimed throughout the city that no other magistrate except himself was to take cognizance of the cases that might come up among our people. He did this, aside from wishing to honor and favor them, because he knew that an *alcalde ordinario* had arrested and put in the public prison two soldiers of La Florida who had stabbed each other because of the quarrels that had arisen among them all in Pánuco, and that flared up again in México with more smoke and fire of wrath and ill-feeling because they saw the esteem in which the gentlemen and principal men of wealth in that city held the things that they brought out of La Florida, such as the fine deerskins of all colors. For it is true that as soon as they saw them they made very elegant trousers and doublets from them.

They also valued highly the few pearls and some strings of seed pearls that they had brought, because they commanded a high price.

But when they saw the mantles of marten-skins and other pelts that our men brought, they esteemed them above all the rest. Although, because they had been used for mattresses and blankets, for lack of other bed-clothing, they were full of resin and pitch from the ships, and soiled with dust and mud that came from being walked on and dragged on the ground, they had them washed and cleaned, for they were extremely fine. They lined their best clothing with them and wore it to the plaza as very elegant and ornamental attire, and he who was unable to obtain a fur lining for his whole cape or cloak contented himself with a collar of marten-skins or other pelts, which he wore outside with the frill of his shirt as a valued and much prized adornment. All these things were the cause of greater desperation, regret, and anger to our people, seeing that such important and rich men thought so highly of that which they had despised. They remembered that they had inconsiderately abandoned lands that they had discovered at such cost to themselves, where these things and others as good existed in such abundance. They recalled the words that Governor Hernando de Soto had said to them in Quiguate about the mutiny that had been plotted in Mauvila with the intention of going to México, abandoning La Florida. Among other things he had said to them: "Why do you wish to go to México? To show the cowardice and weakness of your spirits, when you could be lords of so great a kingdom where you have discovered and traversed so many and such beautiful provinces, you have thought it better (in abandoning them through your pusillanimity and cowardice) to go and lodge in a strange house and eat at another's table, when you could have your own in which to entertain and do good to many others?" It seems that these words were a very accurate prophecy of the regret and sorrow that tormented them at present, for which reason they stabbed one another to death without regard for or memory of the companionship and brotherhood that had existed among them. In the course of these quarrels there occurred in México also, as well as in Pánuco, some deaths and many wounds.

The viceroy pacified them with all gentleness and suavity, seeing that they were beside themselves, and to console them he promised and gave his word to make the same conquest if they desired to go back to it. And it is true that having heard of the advantages of the kingdom of La Florida he desired to make the expedition, and thus he gave many of our captains and soldiers subsidies and gratuities, and offices and employments with which to maintain and occupy themselves while preparations were made for the expedition. Many accepted these, and many did not wish to do so, in order not to obligate themselves to return to a country they had abhorred, and also because they had fixed their eyes on El Perú, as appears from the following incident that took place about that time. It happened thus.

A soldier named Diego de Tapia—whom I knew afterward in El Perú, where he served his Majesty very well in the wars against Gonzalo Pizarro, Don Sebastián de Castilla, and Francisco Hernández Girón—while they were making him a suit, went about through the city of México dressed entirely in skins, just as he had come out of La Florida. As a wealthy citizen saw him in that garb and as he was of small stature and appeared to be one of the very destitute, he said to him: "Brother, I have an *estancia* for cattle raising near the city, where, if you wish to serve me, you may live a quiet and peaceful life, and I will give you good wages." Diego de Tapia, with an expression like a lion or a bear, in whose skin he was perchance dressed, replied: "I am going now to El Perú, where I expect to have more than twenty estancias. If you want to go with me and work for me, I will accommodate you with one of them, so that you can come back wealthy in a very short time." The citizen of México departed without saying another word, it seeming to him that, with a few more [words], he would not come out of the business very well.

XIX

THEY GIVE AN ACCOUNT TO THE VICEROY OF THE MOST NOTABLE THINGS THAT OCCURRED IN LA FLORIDA

Among the principal vecinos and gentlemen of México who entertained our men in their houses, it happened that the factor Gonzalo de Salazar, whom we mentioned at the beginning of this *History*, took Gonzalo Silvestre to his house. Talking with him about many things that took place during this discovery, they came to discuss the beginning of their navigation and what occurred on the first night after they left San Lúcar, and how the two generals found themselves in danger of being sunk. During this conversation the factor learned that Gonzalo Silvestre was the one who had ordered the two cannon-shots fired at his ship for having gone ahead of the fleet and placed itself to the windward of the flagship, as we described at length in the First Book of this *History*. For this reason from that time on he honored him even more, saying that he had acted like a good soldier, though he said also that it would have gratified him to see Governor Hernando de Soto in order to talk to him about what happened that night.

The factor learned later, from other soldiers, of the good fortune that Gonzalo Silvestre had had in the province of Tula in cutting an Indian in two at the waist with one stroke, and on seeing the sword, which was an old one of the sort that we now call *viejas*, he asked for it to place in his cabinet as a very choice ornament. When he learned that he had given the strip or banner of fine marten-skins decorated with pearls and seed pearls—which we said he got in the pueblo where they obtained food on their way down the Río Grande, where they abandoned the horses because the Indians hurried them so—to his host in Pánuco in return for the hospitality that he had accorded him, he was very regretful, saying that he would have given him 1,500 pesos for it, solely for the pleasure of having such a curiosity as this banner in his room, for the factor was truly most interested in such things.

On the other hand, the whole city of México in general and the viceroy and his son Don Francisco de Mendoza in particular enjoyed greatly hearing about the incidents of the discovery of La Florida, and thus they asked that they be told to them as they occurred. They were astonished when they heard of the many cruel torments that his master Hirrihigua had given to Juan Ortiz, of the generosity and admirable spirit of the good Mucoço, of the terrible pride and bravado of Vitachuco, and of the constancy and fortitude of his four captains and of the three young sons of lords of vassals whom they pulled out of the lake almost drowned. They noted the ferocity and indomitable spirit that the Indians of the province of Apalache showed, the flight of their crippled cacique, and the strange things that took place in the armed encounters in that province, as well as the very laborious journey that the thirty horsemen made in going from and returning to it.

They marveled at the great wealth of the temple of Cofachiqui, its grandeur and sumptuousness, and the abundance of various kinds of arms, with the multitude of pearls and seed pearls that the Spaniards found in it; and the hunger that they endured in the wilderness before arriving there. It pleased them to hear of the courtesy, discretion, and beauty of the lady of that province of Cofachiqui, and of the curaca Coça's kindness and generosity in offering his state as a site for a Spanish establishment. They were astonished to hear of the gigantic size of the cacique Tascaluça and his son, who was like his father, and of the bloody and obstinate battle of Mauvila, and of the surprise of Chicaça and the mortality of men and horses in these two battles and in that of the fort of Alibamo. They were interested in hearing about the laws against adultery. They were grieved by the want of salt that our people experienced, and the horrible deaths caused by lack of it; and by the very long and useless peregrination that they made because of the secret discord that arose among the Spaniards, which was the reason for their not making a settlement. They were very gratified by the adoration of the cross that was performed in the province of Casquin, and by the pleasant and comfortable winter that the Spaniards spent in Utiangue. They abhorred the monstrous deformity that those of Tula gave their heads and faces by artificial means, and the ferocity of their spirit and nature, corresponding to their appearance.

The death of Governor Hernando de Soto grieved them very much, and they mourned over the two burials that his people gave him. On the contrary, they were much gratified to hear of his exploits, his invincible spirit, his promptness in attacks and alarms, his patience in hardships, his courage and valor in fighting, and his discretion, wisdom, and prudence in peace and in war. When they told the viceroy of his death having cut short his plans for sending two brigantines down the Río Grande to ask assistance from his Excellency, and how (from what they had seen in their navigation to the sea) he could have given it very easily, he was very regretful and blamed greatly the general and captains who remained for not having proceeded with and carried forward the proposals of Governor Hernando de Soto, for they were of such advantage and honor to all of them. He swore with great oaths that he himself would have gone to the mouth of the Río Grande with reinforcements so that they would have been better and more promptly aided. And all the gentlemen and principal men of México said the same.

The viceroy was also pleased to hear of the beauty and fine appearance the natives of La Florida usually have; of the Indians' strength and courage, the ferocity and skill they show in shooting with their bows and arrows, the very wonderful and admirable shots that they make with them; the daring spirit that many of them exhibit individually, and that they all have in common; the perpetual warfare that they wage upon each other; the punctiliousness in affairs of honor they found in many of the caciques; the fidelity of the captain-general Anilco; the defiance that the cacique Guachoya made; the league of Quigualtanqui with the ten caciques who conspired with him; the punishment that they gave his ambassadors; the labors that our men underwent in building the seven brigantines; the great flood on the Río

Grande; the Spaniards' embarkation; the fine spectacle afforded by the multitude of canoes that appeared before them at dawn; and the cruel persecution that they gave them until they drove them entirely beyond their boundaries.

The viceroy also desired particularly to learn of the nature of the lands of La Florida. He was much pleased to hear that there was such an abundance of fruit trees like those of Spain in them, such as various kinds of plums and three varieties of walnuts, one with nuts so oily that the oil ran out when the kernel was pressed between the fingers; such quantities of acorns from oaks and live oaks; such an abundance of fine mulberries, and so many productive vines bearing very good grapes. Finally, the viceroy was very gratified to hear of the extensiveness of that kingdom, the advantages that it had for raising all kinds of cattle, and the fertility of the soil for crops of grain, fruit, and vegetables. All these things increased the viceroy's desire to make the conquest, but despite his efforts he was unable to induce the men who had come out of La Florida to remain in México in order to return there. On the contrary, within a few days after their arrival they were scattered in various places, as we shall soon see.

XX

OUR SPANIARDS ARE SCATTERED THROUGH VARIOUS PARTS OF THE WORLD. THE EFFORTS OF GÓMEZ ARIAS AND DIEGO MALDONADO TO OBTAIN NEWS OF HERNANDO DE SOTO

The accountant Juan de Añasco, the treasurer Juan Gaytán, and Captains Baltasar de Gallegos, Alonso Romo de Cardeñosa, Arias Tinoco, and Pedro Calderón, and others of less importance returned to Spain, choosing to go there poor rather than to remain in the Indies, because of their abhorrence of them, as well as because of the hardships they had suffered there and of what they had lost from their estates, they themselves having been the cause in most cases of the one and the other being wasted without any advantage whatever. Gómez Suárez de Figueroa returned to the house and estate of his father, Vasco Porcallo de Figueroa y de la Cerda.

Others who were more discreet entered religious orders, following the good example that Gonzalo Quadrado Xaramillo gave them, he being the first to take the habit. He chose to heighten his nobility and his past exploits by becoming a true soldier and nobleman of Jesus Christ our Lord, enlisting under the banner and standard of such a maese de campo and general as the seraphic father St. Francis, in whose Order and profession he died, having shown by his works that the true nobility and consummate courage that please and gratify God are acquired in religion. Because of this action, which as it had been performed by Gonzalo Quadrado, was much more observed and noted than if it had been done by anyone else, many of our Spaniards did the same, entering various religious orders so as to honor all their past lives by making such a good end.

Others, and these were fewest, remained in New Spain. Among them was Luis Moscoso de Alvarado, who married in México a rich and important woman who was a relative of his.

Most of them went to El Perú, where in all the events of the wars against Gonzalo Pizarro and Don Sebastián de Castilla and Francisco Hernández Girón, they conducted themselves in the service of the Crown of Spain like men who had passed through the hardships we have described. Even so it is true that we have not told a tenth part of what they actually endured.

In El Perú I knew many of these gentlemen and soldiers, who were very esteemed and acquired a great deal of property, but I do not know that any of them have managed to obtain repartimientos of Indians such as they could have had in La Florida.

In order to finish our *History,* which through the favor of the heavenly Creator we see now approaching its end, nothing more remains for us to tell except what Captains Diego Maldonado and Gómez Arias did after Governor Hernando de Soto sent them to La Havana with orders as to what they were to do in that summer and the following autumn, as was told in its place. Therefore it will be well to tell here what these two good gentlemen performed in compliance with their orders and their own obligation, so that their generous spirits and the loyalty they showed for their captain-general may not be forgotten, but recorded as an honor to them and an example to others.

Captain Diego Maldonado, as we said above, went with the two brigantines under his orders to La Havana to visit Doña Isabel de Bobadilla, the wife of Governor Hernando de Soto. He was to return with Gómez Arias, who had made the same voyage shortly before, and the two captains were to take between them two brigantines and the caravel and such other ships as they could buy in La Havana, laden with provisions, arms, and munitions. In the following autumn, which was in the year 1540, they were to take them to the port of Achusi which Diego de Maldonado himself had discovered.

Governor Hernando de Soto was to come out there, having made a large circle in exploring the interior country. This was not done, on account of the discord and secret mutiny that the governor discovered his men had plotted. For this reason he withdrew from the sea and went inland, where nearly all of them were lost.

Thus now it must be told that when Gómez Arias and Diego Maldonado had joined one another in La Havana and paid the visit to Doña Isabel de Bobadilla, and sent a report throughout all those islands of what they had discovered in La Florida, and what the governor was asking for to begin a settlement in that country, they purchased three ships and loaded them with food, arms, munitions, calves, goats, colts, mares, sheep, and [seeds of] grain, barley, and vegetables, in order to make a beginning of raising animals and plants. They also loaded the caravel and the two brigantines, and, if they had had two more ships, there would have been enough cargo for all of them, since the inhabitants of the islands of Cuba, Santo Domingo, and Jamaica, because of the good reports they had heard of La Florida and of their love for the governor, and for their own interests, had made an effort to assist him in every way they could. Diego Maldonado and Gómez Arias went to the port of Achusi with these things, to the place designated. Not finding the governor there, the two captains went out in command of the brigantines and coasted along the shore, one in either direction, to see whether the Spaniards might have come out at some other point to the east or west. Wherever they went they left signs on the trees and wrote letters, which they put into their hollow trunks, giving an account of what they had done and expected to do in the following summer. And when the severity of the winter would permit them to navigate no longer, they returned to La Havana with the sad news that they had none of the governor. But this did not keep them from returning in the summer of the year 1541 to the coast of La Florida and following it all the way to the lands of México and to Nombre de Dios, and along the eastern shore to the Tierra de Bacallaos, to see whether by some means or manner they could get news of Governor Hernando de Soto. Being unable to do so, they went back to La Havana in the winter.

Then in the next summer, of the year 1542, they went back to the same search, and having spent almost seven months in doing the same thing as before, they were forced by the weather to go back and winter in La Havana. At the beginning of the spring of the year 1543, though they had obtained no news whatsoever for the past three years, they set out again, persisting in their enterprise and search with the determination not to desist from it until they died or got news of the governor. For they could not believe that the land would have consumed them all, but that some of them must have come out somewhere. They traveled on this quest all that summer as in the preceding ones, suffering the hardships and inconveniences that may be imagined. To avoid prolixity, we shall not tell of them in detail.

XXI

THE PEREGRINATION OF GÓMEZ ARIAS AND DIEGO MALDONADO CONTINUES

Traveling thus with such anxiety and care, they arrived at La Vera Cruz in mid-October of the same year 1543, where they learned that their comrades had left La Florida, that less than three hundred of them had escaped, and that Governor Hernando de Soto had died there, along with all the rest who had perished out of nearly a thousand who had entered that kingdom. They learned in detail of all the misfortunes that had befallen the expedition. With this sad and lamentable news those two good and loyal gentlemen returned to La Havana and gave it to Doña Isabel de Bobadilla. As the grief and anxiety that she had felt continuously for three years at not having heard from her husband were now increased by this new sorrow of his death and the failure of the conquest, and by the waste and loss of his property, the fall of his estate, and the ruin of his house, she died soon after learning of it.

This tragedy, lamentable because of the loss of the many and excessive efforts made by the Spanish nation without profit or benefit to the country, was the end and outcome of the discovery of La Florida, which the adelantado Hernando de Soto made at such expense to his own fortune, and with so much equipment of arms and horses and so many noble gentlemen and valiant soldiers as we have told elsewhere. In none of the other conquests of all those that have been made in the New World up to the present has there been assembled such a fine and brilliant company of men, so well armed and disciplined, nor so many horses as were collected for this one. All of this was consumed and lost without any gain for two reasons. First, because of the discord that arose among them, for which reason they did not make a settlement at the beginning. Second, because of the governor's untimely death; if he had lived two years longer, he would have repaired the past damage by means of the reinforcements that he was going to request, and that could have been sent him by way of the Río Grande, as he had planned.

Thus it was possible that he could have laid the foundations of an empire that could compete today with New Spain and El Perú, because in the extent and fertility of the land and in its advantages for cultivation and cattle raising it is not inferior to any of the others. On the other hand it is believed that it has the advantage of them, for as to wealth we have already seen the incredible quantity of pearls and seed pearls that were found in only one province or temple, and the marten-skins and other rich furs that appertain solely to kings and great princes, aside from the other grandeurs to which we have referred at length.

There may be gold and silver mines, and I do not doubt that they would have been found if they had been sought for carefully. When they were won, neither México nor El Perú had the ones that they now have. Those of the Cerro de Potosí were discovered fourteen years after Governors Don Francisco Pizarro and Don Diego Almagro undertook their enterprise of the conquest of El Perú. The same thing could have been done in La Florida, and meanwhile they could have enjoyed the other wealth that we have seen is there, for gold and silver are not everywhere that people live.

Therefore I shall earnestly and repeatedly supplicate the king, our lord, and the Spanish nation not to permit that a land so good, which their people have traversed and of which they have taken possession, shall remain outside their empire and dominion, but that they make efforts to conquer and settle it in order to establish there the Catholic faith that they profess, as those of their own nation have done in the other kingdoms and provinces of the New World they have conquered and settled, so that Spain may enjoy this kingdom as well as the others, and so that it may not remain without the light of the evangelical doctrine, which is the chief thing that we should desire, and without the other benefits that can be conferred upon it, both in bettering its moral life and in improving it with the arts and sciences that flourish today in Spain. The natives of that country have great aptitude for these things, since without any teaching except that of their natural instincts they have done and said things so excellent as we have seen and heard. Often in the course of this *History* I have been apprehensive at finding them so civilized, magnificent, and excellent, fearing that it may be suspected that these things were inventions of my own and not virtues of the country. With regard to this, God, our Lord, is my witness that I not only have not added anything to the relation that was given me, but I confess to my own shame and confusion that I have not been able to describe these wonders as they really occurred, as they were recited to me by those who saw them. For this I ask pardon of that whole kingdom and of those who may read this book.

This should be sufficient to cause due credit to be given to him who without claims of interest or hope of rewards from kings or great lords or from anyone else, except that of having told the truth, undertook the labor of writing this *History,* wandering from country to country in ill-health and with excessive discomfort solely in order to give in it an account of what has been discovered in that great kingdom, so that our Catholic faith and the Crown of Spain may be augmented and extended. These are my first and second purposes, and holding to them will assure Divine favor for those who may go on this conquest, which may our Lord direct for the glory and honor of His name, so that the multitude of souls who live in that kingdom without the truth of His doctrine may be converted to it and may not perish. And may He accord me His favor and protection so that hereafter I may employ what remains of my life in writing the history of the Incas, the former kings of El Perú; their origins and beginnings, their idolatry and sacrifices, laws, and customs—in short, their whole commonwealth as it was before the Spaniards won that empire. All the greater part of this is now set in the loom. I shall tell of the Incas and all the rest mentioned what I have heard from my mother and her uncles and ancient relatives, and all the rest of the common people of the country, and from what I managed to see of those antiquities, which were not yet so entirely destroyed in my childhood that some shadows of them did not remain. I shall tell likewise of the discovery and conquest of El Perú what I heard from my father and his contemporaries, who won it, and from the same sources I shall recount the general uprising of the Indians against the Spaniards and the civil wars that took place over the partition between Pizarros and Almagros, for they gave this name to those factions that arose among them for the destruction and punishment of them all.

With regard to the rebellions that took place later in El Perú, I shall state briefly what I heard from those who participated in them on one side or the other, and what I myself saw. Though only a boy, I knew Gonzalo Pizarro and his maese de campo Francisco de Carvajal and all his captains, and Don Sebastián de Castilla, and Francisco Hernández Girón, and I am informed of the most important things that the viceroys have done since then in the government of that empire.

XXII

THE NUMBER OF CHRISTIANS, SECULARS AND RELIGIOUS, WHO HAVE DIED IN LA FLORIDA DOWN TO THE YEAR 1568

Having given lengthy accounts of the death of Governor Hernando de Soto and of other principal gentlemen, such as the great and noble captain Andrés de Vasconcelos, a Portuguese Spaniard, and the good Nuño Tovar, an Extremaduran, and of the many other noble and valiant soldiers who died on this expedition, as could have been seen in detail in the *History*, it seems to me that it would be unbecoming not to record the names of the priests, clergy, and religious men who died with them, both those who were then in La Florida and those who have gone afterward to preach the faith of the Holy Mother, the Roman church, which is the reason why they ought not to remain in oblivion. For captains and soldiers as well as priests and religious men died in the service of Christ, our Lord, since one and all went with the same zeal for preaching His holy gospel, the gentlemen to compel the heathen with their arms to subject themselves and come to hear and obey the Christian teachings, and the priests and religious men to oblige and impel them with their good lives and example to believe and imitate them in their Christianity and religion. Speaking first of the seculars, we said that the first Christian who died in this quest was Juan Ponce de León, the first discoverer of La Florida, a gentleman from León who in his childhood was a page of Pedro Núñez de Guzmán, the lord of Toral. All those who went with him died as well, for, as they came out wounded by the Indians, none of them escaped. I was unable to ascertain their number, except that it exceeded eighty men. Then Lucas Vázquez de Ayllón went, and he also died at the hands of the Floridos, along with more than 220 Christians whom he took with him. Following Lucas Vázquez de Ayllón, Pánphilo de Narváez went with four hundred Spaniards, no more than four of whom escaped. The rest died, some at the hands of the enemy, some drowned at sea, and those who escaped the sea simply died of hunger. Ten years after Pánphilo de Narváez, the adelantado Hernando de Soto went to La Florida, taking a thousand Spaniards from all the provinces of Spain. More than seven hundred of them perished. Thus those Christians who have died in that country, along with their commanders up to the year mentioned, exceed fourteen hundred. It remains now to tell of the priests and religious men who have died there.

Those for whom information is available are the ones who went with Hernando de Soto, and those who have gone there since. Of those who accompanied Juan Ponce de León, and the ones who went with Lucas Vázquez de Ayllón and Pánphilo de Narváez, there is no more mention in their histories than if they had never existed. Twelve priests went with Hernando de Soto, as we said at the beginning of this *History*, in Chapter 6. Eight of them were clergymen and four more were friars. Four of the eight clergymen died in the first year that they entered La Florida, and hence their names are not remembered. Dionisio de París, a Frenchman from the great city of Paris, and Diego de Bañuelos, a native of the city of Córdoba, both clerics, and Fray Francisco de la Rocha, a friar of the profession of the Most Holy Trinity and a native of Badajoz, died of illness in the lifetime of Governor Hernando de Soto. Since they had no physician or apothecary, if nature did not cure him who fell ill, there was no remedy through human skill. The other five, who were Rodrigo de Gallegos, a native of Sevilla, and Francisco del Pozo, a native of Córdoba, cleric priests, and Fray Juan de Torres from Sevilla, of the Order of the seraphic father St. Francis, and Fray Juan Gallegos of Sevilla, and Fray Luis de Soto, a native of Villanueva de Barcarrota, both of the Order of the divine St. Dominic, all of them of good life and example, died following the death of the adelantado Hernando de Soto, during those great hardships they experienced in going and returning on that long and ill-advised journey that they made in order to reach the lands of México, and in those which they suffered before embarking. Though because they were priests, their companions protected them in every way they could (where there was as great scarcity of comforts as there was an excess of hardships), they could not escape with their lives, and thus they all remained in that kingdom. These men, besides their piety and priesthood, were all nobles, and while they lived they performed their office in a manner well befitting religious men, confessing and inspiring to a good death those who were dying, and teaching and baptizing the Indians who remained in the service of the Spaniards. After the year 1549, five friars of the Order of St. Dominic went to La Florida. The emperor Charles V, king of Spain, sent them at his expense because they offered to go and preach the gospel to those heathen without taking soldiers with them, going alone in order not to alarm those barbarians. But the latter were still disturbed from the past expeditions, and would not listen to the religious' teachings. On the contrary, as soon as three of them set foot on the shore, they killed them with rage and cruelty. Among them died the good father Fray Luis Cáncer de Balbastro, who went as leader of his people, and had petitioned the emperor very insistently [to be allowed to make] that expedition, in the desire of augmenting the Catholic faith. Thus he died for it like a true son of the Order of Preachers. I did not learn from what country he was, nor the names of his companions; I should like very much to record here the one and the other. In the year 1566, three religious men of the holy Company of Jesus passed to La Florida with the same zeal as those mentioned above. He who went as superior was Maestro Pedro Martínez, a native of the famous kingdom of Aragón. It is renowned through the world in that, being so small in extent, it should have been so great in the valor and courage of its sons, who have performed the great exploits that are recounted in its histories and in others. He was a native of a village of Teruel. As soon as he went ashore the Indians killed him. Two companions whom he took with him, one a priest named Juan Rogel and the other a brother named Francisco de Villa Real, went back to La Havana, much grieved at being unable to carry out their desires of preaching and teaching the Christian doctrine to those heathen.

In the year 1568, eight religious men of the same Company went to La Florida, two priests and six brothers. He who went as superior was named Bautista de Segura, a native of Toledo, and the other priest was called Luis de Quirós, a native of Xerex de la Frontera. I did not learn the native countries of the six brothers, whose names were as follows: Juan Bautista Méndez, Gabriel de Solís, Antonio Zavallos, Cristóbal Redondo, Gabriel Gómez, and Pedro de Linares. They took with them an Indian lord of vassals who was a native of La Florida. We ought to tell how he came to be in Spain. It happened that the adelantado Pedro Menéndez went to La Florida three times from the year 1563 to that of 1568 to drive away from that coast certain French corsairs who were attempting to establish and settle themselves there.[48] On the second of those voyages he brought back seven Florido Indians who came willingly, wearing the same dress that we have described, in which they go about in their own country. They also brought the very fine bows and arrows they make for use on state occasions. When the Indians were passing through one of the villages of Córdoba, as they were taking them to Madrid so that his Majesty the king, Don Felipe II, could see them, the author who gave me the relation of this *History*, who lived there, knowing that Indians from La Florida were passing that way, came out to the camp to see them and asked them from what province they were. So that they might know that he had been in that kingdom, he asked them whether they were from Vitachuco, or Apalache, or Mauvila, or Chicaça, or some

[48]See note 45.

other where they had had great battles. Seeing that Spaniard was one of those who went with Governor Hernando de Soto, the Indians looked at him with hostile eyes and said to him: "Since you left those provinces in the ruinous state that you did, do you think that we are going to give you news of them?" They would not answer him further, and talking among themselves, they said (according to the interpreter who came with them) that each one of them would more willingly give him arrow-shots than the news he asked for. So saying (in order to show their desire to shoot the arrows and their skill in doing so), two of them discharged arrows into the air with such force that they were lost to view. In relating this to me, my author told me that he was afraid they were going to shoot them at him, in view of the mad and fearless nature of those Indians, especially in feats of arms and boldness. Those seven Indians were baptized here, and six of them died within a short time. The one who was left was a lord of vassals, and he asked permission to return to his own country, making great promises of what he would do as a good Christian in the conversion of his vassals to the Catholic faith, as well as the rest of the Indians of that whole kingdom. For this reason the religious men admitted him into their company, thinking that he would help them as he had promised. Thus they went to La Florida and entered many leagues into the interior country, crossing great swamps and marshes, and not wishing to take soldiers so as not to alarm the Indians with arms. When the cacique had them in his own country where he thought he could kill them at his pleasure, he told them to wait for him there, that he was going four or five leagues beyond to prepare the Indians of that province to hear the Christian teachings willingly and peacefully, and that he would return within eight days. The religious men waited for him fifteen days, and when they saw that he was not coming back they sent Father Luis de Quirós and one of the brothers to the pueblo where he had said he was going. Don Luis [the Indian] and many others of his people, seeing them in his presence, killed them with great rage and cruelty without saying a word to them, like an apostate traitor. Before the other religious ones should learn of their companions' deaths and go to some other, neighboring province for safety, they attacked them on the following day with great impetus and fury, as if they had been a squadron of armed soldiers. Hearing the noise of the Indians and seeing the weapons they carried in their hands, the religious men fell on their knees to receive the death that they were going to give them for preaching the faith of Christ, our Lord. The heathen gave it most cruelly, and thus they ended their present lives like good religious people, to enjoy eternal life. The Indians having killed them, they opened a chest they carried containing books of the holy Scriptures, breviaries, missals, and ornaments for saying mass. Each one of them took the ornament that struck his fancy and put it on to suit himself, mocking and making light of that majesty and richness and holding it to be a mean and vile thing. While the others were leaping and dancing about in the ornaments, three of the Indians took out a crucifix that was in the chest, and while they were looking at it they suddenly fell dead. All the rest of them fled, throwing the ornaments in which they had dressed themselves on the ground. The father maestro, Pedro de Ribadeneyra, also wrote of this incident. Thus these eighteen priests, ten belonging to the four Orders that we have named and eight being clergymen, and the six brothers of the holy Company, making twenty-four in all, are the ones who have died in La Florida up to the year 1568 in preaching the holy gospel. There are in addition the fourteen hundred secular Spaniards who went to that country in four expeditions, whose blood I hope in God is not crying out and pleading for revenge like that of Abel, but for mercy like that of Christ, our Lord, so that those heathen may attain the knowledge of His eternal Majesty, under the obedience of our mother the holy Roman church, and thus it is to be believed and hoped that a land that has been watered so many times with so much Christian blood may bear fruit in accordance with this watering of Catholic blood that has spilled upon it. Glory and honor be to God, our Lord, Father, Son, and Holy Spirit, Three Persons and the only true God. Amen.

THE END

He left them in Córdoba in the power and custody of a printer, and busied himself with other matters in the interest of his Order, abandoning his accounts, which were not yet in proper form for printing. I saw them and they were in very bad condition, half of them having been consumed by moths and mice. They covered more than a ream of paper. [The above statement appears at the end of the last page of the text of the 1605 edition but is not included in the text in the 1723 edition. Apparently it refers to the accounts collected by Fray Pedro Aguado, mentioned in the "Preface to the Reader" at the beginning of the present volume—CS.]

Appendix

GENEALOGY OF GARCÍ PÉREZ DE VARGAS BY HIS DESCENDANT GARCILASO DE LA VEGA, CALLED THE INCA

Translated and Edited by Frances G. Crowley

EDITORIAL NOTE

The manuscript of the *Genealogy of Garci Perez de Vargas by his descendant Garcilasso de la Vega, called the Inca,* original and autographed, Córdoba, 1596, contains approximately twenty-eight pages. It was published in Spanish by the Marquis del Saltillo under the title *The Inca Garcilasso and the Lassos in History*[1] in Madrid in 1929.

According to the Chronicles of King Ferdinand the Saint, Pérez de Vargas, with whom the genealogy begins, fought for Córdoba and Seville during the king's reign.[2]

For many years Garcilaso intended this to be Chapter 1 of *La Florida;* why is not clear. Perhaps because it showed how hidalgos such as De Soto had always fought for their kings; perhaps because some of De Soto's ancestry is articulated in this family tree. Perhaps because it was the best way of

[1] The Marquis del Saltillo, "El Inca Garcilasso y los Lassos en la historia," *Revista de historia y geneología española* (Madrid), 3, no. 16 (July–August 1929): 296–307.

[2] Raúl Porras Barrenechea, in "Report on the Genealogy of Garci Perez de Vargas," *Revista Archivo histórico del Cuzco* (Cuzco, 1959), 378–406.

Raúl Porras Barrenechea says that Garcilaso intended to dedicate his *Genealogy* to another Don Garcí Pérez de Vargas, a contemporary of Garcilaso and a descendant of the Pérez de Vargas with whom this account begins. A later decision induced him to change his dedicatory letter. He crossed out the previous dedication and substituted the one to Prince Theodosio of Portugal, which currently precedes the Princeps edition of *La Florida.* However, in the version we use he still dedicates the work to his contemporary, Garcí Pérez de Vargas.

In the actual manuscript the first pages are missing. To get the manuscript, this writer had to first call for the Porras Barrenechea article (cited at the head of this note) in order to identify the *Genealogy* manuscript as No. 18-109 in the Manuscript Room of the National Library, since there was some difficulty in locating it without the number.

getting the attention of the king, in order to emphasize Garcilaso's claim to being a Spaniard (on his father's side) and, therefore, deserving of royal favor. Why he eventually separated it from *La Florida* is also not very clear. Probably his publisher, Peter Crasbeeck, suggested that it be omitted, since its relation to *La Florida* is tenuous at best. However, in its four hundred-year history it has never been translated into English. We do so here because it has some parts that will be of interest to scholars of this period and because it is part of the provenance of *La Florida*.

The following translation is from the copy of Blas de Salazar, as found at the Biblioteca Nacional in Madrid.

Genealogy of Garcí Pérez de Vargas

[Preface?]

Although they are not small works to complete, for a major purpose I esteem these [pages] more than any other advantages Fortune could bring me were it prosperous and favorable, because I hope unto God that my works will bring me more honor and a better and more durable reputation than any other means of gaining wealth. For this reason, I am more Fortune's debtor than her creditor [the pronoun *her* may have a concealed antecedent that is not Fortune, but the lady who was executrix of some income Garcilaso had inherited], and, as such, I am grateful; and would be even more so, if happy to see me settled, she stopped persecuting me with these unpaid assignments, since I no longer ask her favors and mercies, having no good reason to do so. She pursues me, nonetheless. With this powerful lady it was not worth my while to pursue her, nor to try to escape her, because at all times she has been against me, even in the smallest things.

Because it is painful and not profitable to talk about her lack of favor and my disadvantage, it would be preferable to cease remembering them, as if they had never happened, and to resort to the sad consolation of the doctor who, for lack of a better remedy, dispenses to the patient a medicine that will make him forget his pain. To better forget mine, I will change from this subject to another about your [Don Garcí's] service [to your country], which makes up for all present and past adversities.

STORY OF THE DESCENDANCY OF THE FAMOUS PÉREZ DE VARGAS, WITH SOME PASSAGES WORTH REMEMBERING, DEDICATED TO DON GARCÍ PÉREZ DE VARGAS, HIS LEGITIMATE HEIR.

It seems impertinent of me to want to present you [Don Garcí Pérez de Vargas] with your genealogy and descendancy, of which you are so well aware. Although it is known as being that of [your great and famous ancestor] Pérez de Vargas, I nonetheless consider placing it here to show my fondness for you, so it may be seen how your grandparents and mine had the same first and second [generations] and that we honor [them also as] being of your lineage and family tree. Although this is well known in Extremadura, it is not so well known outside of there. For this reason, I shall beg you to allow me to draw your family tree for you, so your descendants may be placed in its shade, each in the proper place, so all of them, perceiving their natural and inevitable obligation, should try to imitate your ancestors and their own; especially [should they seek to imitate] Pérez de Vargas. So zealous was he in the service of his king and in the propagation of the Catholic faith, as to risk several times losing his life for it by fighting against the Moors who occupied Andalucía. The emulation of these and other virtues of his will make his successors proud of being worthy sons and descendants of this excellent man, whose deeds are amply described in the Chronicles of King Ferdinand, called the Saint, who conquered the cities of Córdoba and Seville and all of Andalucía. About 348 years after Seville was conquered, the following popular verses are still generally sung [there]:

> Hercules built me,
> Julius Caesar surrounded me
> with towers and large walls,
> The Holy King conquered me
> with Garcí Pérez de Vargas.

These verses are said to have been written on one of the doors of the city, from where the ravages of time consumed them, as they have done and will do to major works.

Recently Don Francisco Zapata de Cisneros, first count of Barajas, who was president of the Royal Council, while assistant in Seville, renewed them, not through his writings, but by that delightful work of the Alameda [a boulevard mall], which he carried out, because he was a great designer of the cities he governed, as can be seen by modern-day Córdoba and Seville.

In which Alameda he renewed and had dug up two stone columns of the many placed by Hercules in the foundation of that city [Seville]. He brought to life the histories of those times and lent reality to the fables of poets of years gone by about the columns of Hercules and of other written events. He placed in one of them, as is extant today, the statue of Hercules and in the other that of Julius Caesar, whom I admire, as founders of Seville. Three water fountains with quantities of orange trees and poplars greatly beautified that great city, rich in gold and silver and precious stones, a yearly tribute from Peru, my homeland. [Seville is] a city more enriched by outstanding and high minds than could be produced by a special favor of celestial influences [a conjunction of favorable stars].

The Alameda appears more distinguished, delightful, and agreeable to those who, like myself, knew the place before the work was done, as it was [before that] extremely smelly and abominable. It was called the lagoon, because it collected rainwater and all the refuse and dead animals of the city, and it had become a pestilential lake of water and mud contaminating the whole neighborhood, whereas now it is the cause of its greatest delight.

Returning to the outstanding virtues of your ancestor, the famous Garcí Pérez de Vargas, one must keep them perpetually in mind: (1) to imitate them in maintaining and preserving the honor of the gentleman who guarded the Men [the king?]; (2) to remember how, as the armies made the mistake of turning toward the king out of fear of the seven Moors, whom they saw on their way, [Garcí Pérez] sustained his honor by not giving away who [the king] was, although Lorenzo Suárez questioned him during the absence and presence of the king. He always said he did not know him well, but he actually did see him daily. With his eyes, he enjoined his squire to imitate him, lest he be discovered and should lose his honor as a good knight.

I consider this one of his major accomplishments, as his use of self-control to protect another person's honor, [honor being] something a gentleman must have, singled him out as a better knight than the others. I do not mention any further action, as I do not wish to take any honor away from those of others surrounding that king called the Saint. All that is needed to arouse respect is the mention of his name and the imitation of his virtues. Without this imitation it seems wrong to value fathers and grandfathers, as outstanding as they may be, because it would be more of a disgrace [a mere lip service] than an honor.

Chapter 4: [crossed out: "There continues the descendancy of Garcí Pérez de Vargas toward those who have their primogeniture."]

DESCENDANCY OF GARCÍ PÉREZ DE VARGAS

Pedro de Vargas, a gentleman of Toledo, descendant of the Goths, who remained in that city when Spain was lost, had as sons Garcí Pérez de Vargas and Diego Pérez de Vargas, nicknamed Machuca. He populated Xerez de la

Frontera from whom are descended the gentlemen of that name (whose name as that of many others does not need to be preceded by Don), famous for their arms and ability to play folk songs.

Garcí Pérez de Vargas had as a son Pedro Fernández de Vargas, who bore Lope Pérez de Vargas. His son was Alonso Fernández de Vargas, who lost the city of Burguillos by treason of a mayor.

[His son] Gonzalo Pérez de Vargas married María Sánchez de Badajoz, daughter of Mencia Vázquez de Goz and of Garcisánchez of Badajoz, among the most distinguished bearing this name in Extremadura.

[Although] it came from far away and from high estates, this name has been lost, because it has been joined with that of the Vargas and Figueroas, and the descendants have taken to calling themselves Sánchez de Vargas and Sánchez de Figueroa, for they had everything. It would have been right not to let go of the Badajoz name, as it was so ancient and noble. I have only seen it preserved until the arrival of that famous and constantly in love Garcí Sánchez de Badajoz, born in the very illustrious and generous city of Ecija (although his parents came to it from Extremadura). [The] Phoenix of Spanish poets, he was without equal, nor is there hope of another. So great were his works that I hold them in high esteem and veneration, the permitted ones in their written form, and the forbidden ones engraved in my memory as a sacred mandate, committed to it for so many years because they were most pleasant.

I have lived with this rich depository, eager to meet an outstanding poet-theologian who would express [to me] their real meaning, bearing for them the same affection I have, which in view of their spirituality could easily be done. I would like this divine transcription of that part of the Holy Scriptures forming the nine lessons for the dead returned to their pure spiritual meaning to prevent the loss of that most original and elegant, eminent and high-minded composition and Spanish verse. Considering this matter carefully, it would [not] be fair for the Spanish to imitate the Italians, the work being Spanish and so divine. Not unlike the Italians, who as soon as works are forbidden correct them and keep on printing them, lest the memory of the author be forgotten. The Spaniards should not allow his work to perish. They should not allow the others, unworthy of being disciples or servants of the one and only Garcí Sánchez de Badajoz, to take advantage of the fact that the work is forbidden and unprotected to plagiarize it to pieces, as they illustrate their own poems, incorporating his, as I saw it done by some poets who became rich and famous with the treasures of another.

Of this superior work, Christopher Castillejo, secretary of Emperor Ferdinand, as a man who understood it well, among many other stanzas written against those who abandon Spanish metric combinations to adopt Italian ones, says the following about Garcí Sánchez de Badajoz:

> Garcí Sánchez proved to be
> Somewhat angry, as he said:
> "It is not proper
> For a person born in Spain
> To make use of foreign lands."
> Because in my lessons alone,
> Having observed his stanzas well,
> You will see such consonance
> That Petrarch and his songs
> Remain behind him in elegance.

To increase and widen the extent of my hope, I express this wish here, that soon some Spaniard, for the above-mentioned reasons, may take him [Garcí Sánchez de Badajoz] up as his own, and fulfill my wish [to see a new printing of his poetry]. He will thus do a work that will please people of high intelligence, and that will benefit his nation. As much as I wish to do this work, I am not a poet. I have not attempted it on my own, nor have I been able to look for the poet-theologian I seek to find because of this work [the *Genealogy*] and the past one about León Hebreo. Although it is true that I agreed with the Reverend Father and teacher Juan de Pineda, born in Seville, who was an outstanding professor of writing in the Jesuit College in Córdoba, that during the summer vacations of [15]94, his Paternity, and I as his instrument, should reduce those divine lessons to their spiritual and holy meanings. It was impossible for me to carry out even my first essay. Urgent needs of my own, caused by difficulties in securing food supplies from my small property, forced me shortly before my vacation to let go of my studies and of this work I was eager to start, as I needed to provide for the necessities of life. If God would provide them, I would return to my [first] purpose. Until now my efforts [to discover the meanings of these poems] have not served me. They have only caused me great pain and sorrow for having lost in the carrying out of such a desired enterprise the opportunity, the time and the promise of [working with] such an eminent gentleman as Father and teacher Juan de Pineda. When I returned to Cordoba, after taking care of my needs, his vacations were over. In testimony of this loss, I certify that this clause was added and written during this sad absence and these wanderings of mine, even while I made a clean copy of this foreword, because to save time I take my first drafts, practically all I own, with me wherever I go.

Returning to our original task, Gonzalo Pérez de Vargas and María Sánchez de Badajoz had as their progeny Juan de Vargas, Hernando de Vargas, and García de Vargas.

Juan de Vargas married Leonor Suárez de Figueroa, daughter of the Master of Santiago Don Lorenzo Suárez de Figueroa, whose children were Juan de Vargas and Mencia de Vargas.

Juan de Vargas died childless. His sister Mencia de Vargas married, in Xerez of Badajoz, Vasco Fernández de Silva, descendant of the house of C[ifuentes], whose progeny were Arias Pérez de Vargas and Juan de Silva. Arias Pérez de Vargas married María Ponce de León whose successors were Franco de Vargas, Luis Ponce de León, and Arias de Silva.

Francisco de Vargas married Doña Mayor de Figueroa y de la Cerda, native of Córdoba, lady-in-waiting of the Catholic Queen Isabel. They gave birth to Don Juan de Vargas and Doña Mencia de Vargas.

Don Juan de Vargas married Doña Juana de Figueroa, daughter of Juan de Figueroa Sotomayor, granddaughter of Hernando Sotomayor, and great-granddaughter of Pedro Suárez de Figueroa and of Doña Blanca de Sotomayor; her son was Francisco de Vargas. Don Francisco de Vargas married Doña Juana de Bohorques, daughter of Pedro García de Bohorques and of his wife Doña Isabel de Alfaro. Their sons were Don Garcí Pérez de Vargas and Don Diego de Vargas, who was a religious and died early.

Don Garcí Pérez de Vargas married Doña Teresa de Arellano Portocarrero, daughter of Don Alonso Pacheco and of his wife Doña Angela de Arellano. The paternal grandparents of said Doña Teresa were Don Pedro Portocarrero and his wife Doña Juana Pacheco, sister of the marquis de Alcalá, and maternal grandparents were Don Hernandarias of Saavedra, count of Castellar and his wife Countess Teresa Ramírez de Arellano y Cuñiga, sister of the count of Aguilar, descendant of Don Carlos de Arellanos, lord of Cameros [double-beds].

Don Garcí Pérez de Vargas had two daughters, the elder being Juana de Vargas Bohorques and the second Doña Angela de Vargas y Arellano. She possesses today the rights of primogeniture [*mayorazgo*] of the town of Higuera de Vargas, rights derived from her famous antecedent Garcí Pérez de Vargas. She is head and oldest relative of all the Vargas [descendants] of Extremadura.

This is your [Mercy's] family tree, and the origin of the Vargas [branch] from Extremadura. Let me place here two of their branches to prove we are of your lineage.

[The heading of this unit, Chapter 5, reads: "Descendancy of Vargas men living in Mérida; first shoot of the lineage of Garcí Pérez de Vargas."]

Backtracking to pick up the first branch, it was stated that Gonzalo Pérez de Vargas married María Sánchez de Badajoz and had, as told, Hernando de Vargas as her son, to whom she bequeathed the primogeniture of Sierrabrava, which today belongs to his descendants who live in Mérida, the Spanish Rome of earlier times, according to the lovelorn Garcí Sánchez de Badajoz in his comparative complaints, which remained unfinished because of his sudden illness.

Hernando de Vargas married Beatrice of Tordoña who bore Alonso de Vargas. Alonso de Vargas married Doña Beatrice de Hinestrosa, daughter of Lope Alvarez de Hinestrosa Osorio, mayor "comendador" of León. They gave birth to Hernando de Vargas (whose descendants belong to the second branch) and Juan de Vargas and Doña Leonor de Vargas.

Fernando de Vargas married Doña Blanca de Sotomayor, daughter of Fernando de Sotomayor, whom we shall mention elsewhere; their sons were Alonso de Vargas, Juan de Vargas, Hernando de Sotomayor, Pero Suárez de Figueroa, and Gómez de Tordoña, who died in Peru in the so-called battle of Chupas, while he was field marshal of the imperial army, whose general was the lawyer Vaca de Castro who was governor of Peru during the battle against the mestizo Diego de Almagro.

The first born, Alonso de Vargas, had no male successors, only a daughter, Blanca de Vargas, who succeeded in the primogeniture of Sierrabrava, her first cousin being Doña Francisca de Vargas and Figueroa, who married Christopher de Xejas, mayor of Xerez de Badajoz, whose son was Alonso de Vargas of the war counsel and cavalry general in the Flemish wars, as well as a generalissimo in those of Aragón.

Doña Blanca de Vargas, who as only daughter inherited Sierrabrava, married Fernando de Vera, the eldest son, in Mérida. Their sons were Don Fernando, Don Alonso, and Don Antonio de Vargas. I knew the latter two gentlemen as captains in his Majesty's infantry.

Don Juan de Vera y Vargas married Doña Teresa de Figueroa in Badajoz. She was the daughter of Don Jerónimo de Figueroa and bore Don Fernando de Vera y Vargas.

Don Fernando de Vera y Vargas married Doña Juana de Cuñiga, daughter of the marquis de Mirabel.

This is the branch and the descendancy of the Vargas who live in Mérida, descendants of the second son of Gonzalo Pérez de Vargas and María Sánchez de Badajoz.

[Chapter 6, "The second branch of the Garcí Pérez de Vargas family Tree."]

To depict the second branch, in which I want to prove we are yours, let me track back to Alonso de Hinestrosa de Vargas, lord of Sierrabrava, and to Doña Beatrice de Hinestrosa, descendant of Garcí Pérez de Vargas by direct male lineage, as has been seen. In which attempt I shall pause with the descendancy of the Vargas [branch] to pen the descendancy of the Figueroas and the most distinguished house of Feria and of Sotomayor, of the not less outstanding house of Belalcaçar, which since God was so merciful will give us reason to publish it, not to take advantage of the name of relatives, as it is not decent for the poor, but to recognize them and serve them as natural lords, calling ourselves servants of their houses, not as mercenaries, but for being born in them. At least I always acted this way and was rewarded by men as generous as they were, and especially by two true ladies that I could never deserve in this world, the marquises de Priego, of the house of Feria and Aguilar, grandmother and granddaughter of glorious memory, both bearing the same first name, although with double last names, called Lady Catalina Fernández de Córdoba and Aguilar and Lady Catalina Fernández de Córdoba and Figueroa, examples of Christian religion, of princely greatness and magnanimity to confuse and shame those who will not emulate them.

For that descendancy it is necessary to know that Fernando Sánchez de Badajoz, owner of the pasture of the arches and other famous ones that are in that region, had as only daughter Mencia Sánchez of Badajoz, and he had her married to a second son of the house of Belalcaçar, named Juan de Sotomayor, whom her mother, after she became a widow, had marry Pedro Suárez de Figueroa, second son of Gómez Suárez de Figueroa, first count of Feria, and of Lady Elvira Lasso de la Vega, sister of Iñigo López de Mendoza, from whom the *duques* of the appanage [territory assigned to an infante] descended.

However, Suárez de Figueroa and Lady Blanca de Sotomayor had a son, Gómez Suárez de Figueroa, nicknamed "hoarse," a very respected name in Extremadura; they also had Hernando de Sotomayor, Garcilaso de la Vega, and Don Lorenzo Suárez de Figueroa who was ambassador to the most powerful Venetian signoria. They connected each of these to a primogeniture [mayorazgo], which their descendants still own—as shall be seen they were a great generation! Leaving aside the firstborn, whose descendancy is that of my father and his brothers, I shall move [be moving] from the last to the first to fulfill my obligation toward them; in view of the fact that, because I am an Indian from the Antarctic [South American] region, the majority do not know about me and are [not?] witnesses of what I may say in my favor. I say that Don Lorenzo Suárez de Figueroa, who was the fourth son, had a daughter, Lady Beatrice de Figueroa. She married Don Pedro de Fonseca and they had Don Juan de Fonseca and Don Lorenzo Suárez de Figueroa, and other gentlemen who live in Badajoz.

Garcilaso de la Vega [a captain in the Spanish army], who was the third son, had as sons Don Perolasso de la Vega and Garcilaso de la Vega [author of *La Florida*]. He was a model of gentlemen and poets, who as everybody knows and as he himself states, spent his life heroically wielding both the pen and the sword.

Don Pero Lasso de la Vega married Doña María de Mendoza in Toledo. They gave birth to Garcilasso de la Vega who was ambassador of his Catholic Majesty in Rome, and to Pedro González de Mendoza who was canon of the Holy Church in Toledo, and to Don Alvaro de Luna.

Garcilasso de la Vega married Lady Aldonza Niño; their sons were Don Perolasso de la Vega y Guzmán and Don Rodrigolasso de la Vega, Niño, who live today in Toledo.

Fernando de Soto, oldest second son of Pero Suárez de Figueroa and of Doña Blanca de Sotomayor, had Juan de Figueroa Sotomayor of whom we said that she married Fernando de Vargas, owner of Sierrabrava. Juan de Figueroa Sotomayor gave birth to Don Gerónimo and Doña Juana de Figueroa of whom we said she married Don Juan de Vargas, my lord and your grandfather, so that we are related through the Figueroas, the Sotomayors, and the Vargas. Don Gerónimo de Figueroa [crossed out: "and Lady Juana de Figueroa"] had as children Don Juan de Figueroa who lived without successors, and Don Diego de Figueroa Azavedo who today lives in Badajoz, and Lady Teresa de Figueroa of whom we said that she married Don Juan de Veras y Vargas in Mérida.

Gómez Suárez de Figueroa, the "hoarse," the first son of Pero Suárez de Figueroa and of Doña Blanca de Sotomayor, married Doña Isabel Mosquera Enríquez, had two daughters, the first named Blanca de Sotomayor, like her grandmother, and the second Doña Teresa de Figueroa, who married comendador Juan de Céspedes. They had many sons and daughters, one of them being Doña Leonor Lasso de la Vega, an exemplary nun who today lives in the convent of Santa Clara in Montilla, aunt of Doña Isabel de Figueroa who was abbess in the same convent, and of brother Juan de Céspedes who was living the previous three years in San Pablo de Sevilla, as well as of other gentlemen who dwell in that distinguished city, and other cities in Extremadura, bearing the name Céspedes, grandchildren of the above-mentioned Juan de Céspedes and Doña Teresa de Figueroa.

Doña Blanca de Sotomayor, first-born daughter of Gómez Suárez de

Figueroa the "hoarse," oldest sister of Doña Teresa de Figueroa, married Alonso de Hinestrosa de Vargas with whom we take a pause from our male descendancy of the Vargas, who had four sons and five daughters.

Gómez Suárez de Figueroa y Vargas was the oldest son. He married Doña Caterina de Alvarado. His first-born son [was] Alonso de Hinestrosa de Vargas y Figueroa; [there were] as well other sons and daughters, who, although some were married, all died without having successors.

Alonso de Hinestrosa de Vargas y Figueroa married Doña Isabel de Carvajal, his first cousin. Their daughter, Doña Catalina de Figueroa, married Alonso de Hinestrosa de Vargas her uncle, first cousin of her father, about whom more will be mentioned; they also had Doña Teresa de Vargas and Doña Blanca de Sotomayor who today are nuns in Badajoz. [About eight lines here are crossed through and not legible.]

The second son of Alonso de Hinestrosa de Vargas and of Doña Blanca de Sotomayor was Don Alonso de Vargas, cavalry captain of Emperor Charles V, king of Spain, one of the captains who accompanied the person of our lord King Philip as his faithful guards from Genova to Flanders when he was sworn in as ruler of those states. He spent thirty-eight years engaged in continuous war in three parts of the Old World without leaving it, fighting against the Moors, Turks, and heretics, and against the enemies of the Spanish Crown. He was called Francisco de Placencia until he became captain and, as we said, took the trip with Captain Diego de Aguilera. Having returned to his country with permission of his Majesty, he married Doña Luisa Ponce de León in Montilla, of the very noble blood and descendancy of the knights of Argote and Ponce de León, of whom there are many in the royal city of Córdoba. Don Alonso de Vargas died childless and for this reason he adopted me, although I was not worthy of being his.

[Erased: "Chapter 7; The descendancy of Alonso Hinestrosa de Vargas continues; Some instances of Indian and Spanish history are pointed out."]

The third son of Alonso Hinestrosa de Vargas and of Lady Blanca de Sotomayor was my father Garcilaso de la Vega. He spent thirty years of his life until it came to an end helping to conquer and populate the New World, especially the great kingdoms and provinces of Peru. There by word and deed he taught and instructed those gentiles in our holy Catholic faith, enlarged and magnified the Spanish Crown so greatly, richly, and powerfully that for that empire alone, which it owns among others, it is feared by the rest of the world. I was given birth by an Indian called Doña Isabel Chimpu Occlo. They are two proper names, the Christian, and the gentile by which Indians whether male or female, especially those of royal lineage, have been accustomed to add their previous name after the name by which they were baptized. This serves them well in representing and keeping alive the names and royal titles that were theirs in their old majesty. These names could only be given to men and women descendants of the male lineage, and they remain such to their survivors.

Doña Isabel Palla Chimpu Occlo was the daughter of Huallpa Tupac Inca Yupanqui and of Coya Mama Occlo, his legitimate wife. He was the brother of Huayna Capac Inca, who was the last natural king of the empire called Peru, as I said at length to his Catholic Majesty in the dedication of our [*Dialogues* of] León Hebreo and as shall be more amply told in the history of the origin of those Inca kings, about whom more shall be written [and was in *The Royal Commentaries*] if God gives me the health and I do not have the bad luck that usually prevents me from attacking my proposed goals.

The fourth of the above-mentioned brothers, Juan de Vargas, married Doña Mencia de Silva in Badajoz, had no children, and, although he arrived late after its discovery [Peru?], he had an early reversal according to the proverb, because after eight or nine years he spent in the service of his king, he entered the battle of Huarina on Diego Centeno's side as infantry captain, where he was shelled by four shots from a harquebus.

To these almost eighty years, during which my father and his two brothers served the Spanish Crown, I wish to add those few and useless ones that I served with the sword during my youth and the more useless present ones with the pen to boast and brag about the fact that I followed and imitated them in the service of my king, choosing as my reward (1) the fulfillment of our debt and obligation, although for all of it we possess no more than (2) the satisfaction of having spent them (3) as one should, and it is sufficient for us to have done our part. The contribution of great princes consists more in the benefits of the recipients than of the [their own] merits, nor do they depend on the liberality and magnificence of those who do them [these deeds], because it can be seen at every step that many who deserve well achieve nothing, and others without any merit, and by the hidden favor of their stars, more than by liberality or prodigality of the prince, receive them in abundance.

Of the five daughters of Alonso Hinestrosa de Vargas and of Doña Blanca de Sotomayor, the three youngest were nuns in the convent of Santa Clara in Cofra; the last one still lives and her name is Doña Blanca de Sotomayor, like her mother's.

The oldest daughter was Doña Beatrice de Figueroa, married to the famous captain Fernando de Guillada; they had as a son Alonso de Hinestrosa de Vargas, about whom we said that he married their niece, Doña Catalina de Figueroa. They currently live in Badajoz. They had likewise Juan de Sotomayor who was presbyter and Francisco de Guillada who was the firstborn, and Doña Blanca de Sotomayor. They all died early and did not marry.

Doña Isabel de Vargas was the second daughter, married in Badajoz to Alonso Rodríguez de Sanabria, descendant by direct male line from that Men Rodríguez de Sanabria whose good advice King Peter [Pedro] the Cruel did not want to take, for which he died by hands of the king Don Henry [Enrique] his brother through the infidelity of a French captain. Because this is an agreeable historical anecdote within the scope of our pursuit, it will be well for us to tell it for whose who do not know it.

King Henry was besieged by his brother Don Pedro in the castle of Monteil. The two brothers agreed to see each other alone, outside the castle. The mediator would be a famous French gentleman whose name was Mossem Beltrán de Chaclin, an aide of King Henry.

King Pedro informed Men Rodríguez de Sanabria, a most faithful servant who had been with him ever since his childhood and who was fond of him, that this agreement had been made. He [the servant] told him: "Sire, do not trust a Frenchman paid by your enemy, who will be more devoted to him than to your Royal person. If, the agreement having been made, you should not wish to go back on your word and should not want to retract it, take me with you, so I may be on your side. Since he is paid by the other, let us be two against two, because if anything happens during the meeting, you will have someone on your side to come to your rescue with loyalty and devotion."

As a brave and proud man, King Peter did not want to avail himself of such sound counsel; rather in confirmation of the first agreement, he and his opponent decided to meet alone, assisted by Mossem Beltrán for both parties.

During the meeting the two kings came to blows with hands and arms, and they say that King Peter, as the stronger and more robust, threw his brother to the ground; then the Frenchman entered the fray, saying, "I neither abandon a king, nor do I make a king, but I help my king." With these words, he confused the destinies of the contenders, making a winner out of the one who had fallen. Because King Henry did not know what to do at that moment, the Frenchman said: "Whoever is in such straits, let him not overlook his Girlfriend." He said this because King Henry always had with him his sword, called Girlfriend.

Then, taking hold of it with his hand, he killed his brother, King Peter. For which infidelity, among the recent nine men of fame, they paint Mossem

Beltrán's face turned backward. In other wars between France and England he [Mossem Beltrán] was extremely brave and, although he was a prisoner of the English, he was even braver in prison.

Men Rodríguez de Sanabria felt such pain and sorrow that his king had died for not believing him, that he donned sackcloth and tied it with a grass rope. He wore that habit the rest of his life, and his descendants incorporated in their coat of arms and the border of their shields the rope, which they wear as an emblem.

The said Doña Isabel de Vargas and Alonso Rodríguez de Sanabria had a son who was in the more than famous battle of Lepanto and who currently lives in Badajoz. They had also Doña Blanca de Vargas, currently abbess in Santa Clara de Cofra, and Diego de Sanabria who in arms, virtue, and human letters was a role model for the youth of his time. He and two of his sisters died in their early youth, nor were they married.

This is the briefest and clearest report that I have been able to glean from the wills and the marriage certificates of your predecessors with both branches derived from that tree and continuing down to the descendants still alive today, a daring endeavor for an Indian. I did not dare to pursue here other branches proceeding from this tree, such as the descendancy of the Vargas knights who live in Trujillo, because their line of succession is not as clear as this one. I ask them to forgive any trouble this may cause them, because much that I desired it, it was not possible. To remedy this, it must be noted that the tree has been planted and the garden opened. Anyone who wants to may come in and take a hold of any branch that is most pleasing and place it with any other and I shall be very happy.

[What follows was erased by Garcilaso and has not been included in the Saltillo version. The exclusion is of the greatest interest for this work, as it shows Garcilaso's intention to originally publish the genealogy with *La Florida*. The question that presents itself here is why the two works were eventually separated, and whether Pedro Crasbeeck influenced the separation. The part crossed out reads as follows: "And leaving apart such a great discussion, it will be reasonable for you to view the new building, badly traced and worked on more poorly, which I built of the history of Florida with my small strength and smaller ability to offer and dedicate it to you."

[This is followed by a paragraph from the dedication to Don Theodosio of Portugal in the *La Florida*, which reads as follows:]

"It is written in six Books, corresponding to the six years that were spent on the expedition. The Second Book and the Fifth are each divided into two parts; the Second so that it might not be so long as to weary the eye." The division in books follows the same scheme as that of the later preface. The fifth book has been divided into two parts to maintain reader interest. [He has then changed "because I am Indian and I am yours" to "I am Indian."]

[In the last paragraph Garcilaso asks for the Lord's blessing. The book has been written in "Córdoba from this poor rented house the fifth day of May 1596."]

Index

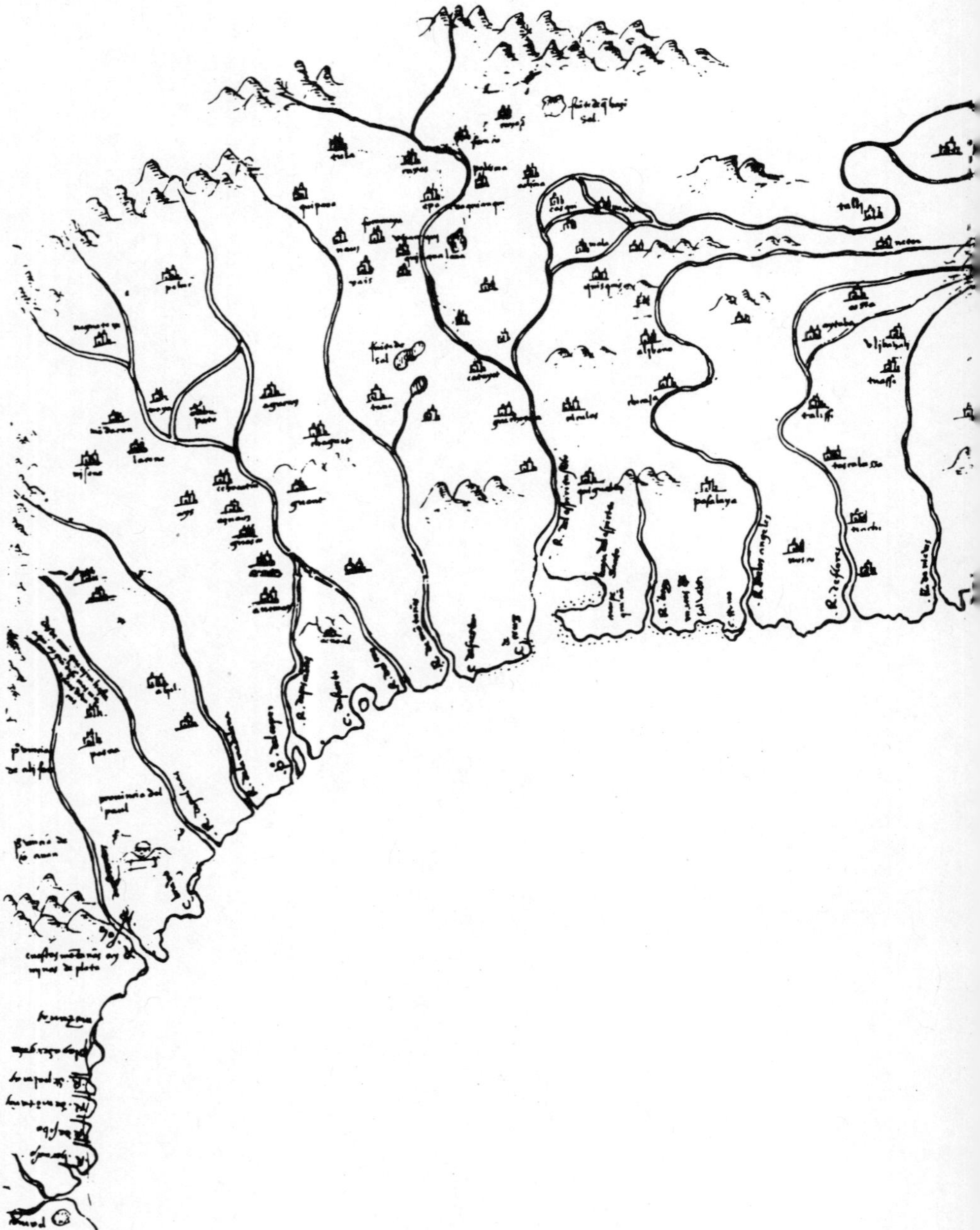

The "De Soto Map." This is a modern copy of a pen-and-ink-sketch map in the General Archive of the Indies in Seville. The original is unsigned and undated, but it is believed to have been drawn by the Spanish royal cartographer Alonso de Santa Cruz, among whose papers it was originally found. It is believed to date around 1544 and is the earliest known map giving any detail about the interior of North America. The source of the information was obviously one or more of the survivors of the De Soto expedition. The rendering of the coast comes from other contemporary sources, and the author has attempted, with limited success, to match the coastal river mouths and bays to the rivers crossed in the interior by De Soto's army. (Courtesy of the Smithsonian Institution)